Classic Interlinear Translations

THE WORKS

OF

P. VIRGILIUS MARO,

Including the Æneid, Bucolics and Georgics, with the
original text reduced to the natural
order of construction;

and an

INTERLINEAR TRANSLATION,

As nearly literal as the idiomatic difference of the
Latin and English languages will allow.

Adapted to the system of

CLASSICAL INSTRUCTION.

Combining the methods of

ASCHAM, MILTON, AND LOCKE.

By

LEVI HART AND V. R. OSBORN.

. . . . molle atque facetum
Virgilio annuerum gaudentes rure Camœnæ.—HORATIUS.

PHILADELPHIA:
DAVID McKAY COMPANY
WASHINGTON SQUARE.

Printed in the United States of America

ADVERTISEMENT.

In offering to the public a new version of VIRGIL, the translators unhesitatingly acknowledge their desire to promote the system of classical instruction formerly practised in the principal schools of England.

The same causes which, in the opinion of the wisest men of a former age, justified a departure from ancient modes of teaching, exist at the present day. It is not necessary to enumerate them; they are known and *felt* by all concerned in classical instruction, and *acknowledged* by many There is, indeed, *one* very powerful reason in favour of reform, which did not exist in the time of Erasmus and Cardinal Wolsey. Since their time, so *many subjects of study* have been introduced into our schools and colleges that the scholastic life of our youth is too brief to allow them time to become acquainted with all the branches which are required to constitute the education of a scholar, or to prepare him for the learned professions—and to leave him a sufficient space of time, required by the old systems, to obtain any competent knowledge of the Greek and Latin languages. Thus situated, he must either forego all acquaintance with these new and most important departments of knowledge, or he must lay aside all hope of obtaining what is called *a classical education*, so far as a competent familiarity with the Greek and Latin languages is concerned. He has not time for both. Two distinguishing features of the system which now, by common consent, is attributed to Locke, are—*dictation*, and *literal interlinear translation*. In tracing their history, it is not necessary to go back to the authorities of Cicero, the younger Pliny, and other distinguished ancients quoted or referred to by the advocates of these improvements; our object is to *disclaim*, in the first place, all pretensions of *our own* to originality;—and, in

A

the second, to render the honour which is due, to those great reformers of learning, to whom we are indebted for this most admirable system.

Cardinal Wolsey, Prime Minister to king Henry 8th, in a letter addressed to the masters of Ipswich School, written in the Latin language, dated Sept. 1st, 1528, enjoins them to lead their pupils to a knowledge of the learned languages by the easiest methods, chiefly by *oral dictation*, familiar illustrations, &c. &c.

Erasmus, "the most learned man of the age in which he lived," in his tract on "the education of youth," inculcates the same general principles. He was a contemporary of Wolsey, and contributed largely to the composition of Lilly's Latin Grammar—he laboured hard to strip learning of its terrors—denounced those teachers who *beat* learning into their pupils, instead of *auling* them to acquire it, as "illiterate butchers, who ruin many a hopeful lad." "In fact, the great object of Erasmus was, to combine pleasure with profit in the education of boys, and, according to some anecdotes given in his work, 'De Pueris Instituendis,' he goes so far as to recommend that they should play* and learn at the same time.†"

Roger Ascham, Latin Secretary to king Edward, queen Mary, and queen Elizabeth, wrote the "Schoolmaster," a work which is praised by Dr. Johnson, as containing more knowledge than any other book on the subject of education. In this work, Ascham proposes as "a plain and perfect way of teaching the learned languages, the plan of "Double Translation"—a method which he learnt from his tutor, Sir John Cheke, "the most eminent teacher of that age." Sir John pursued this method of instruction in the education of Edward the 6th, as Ascham did in that of Elizabeth. It was also warmly patronized by lord Burleigh, who earnestly recommends it, in a letter to his son at Cambridge. About an hundred years after the publication of the "Schoolmaster," by Ascham, Milton wrote his celebrated letter to Hartlib, in which he complains of the school system of his time as being "tedious, vexatious, and unprofitable." We do amiss," says Milton, "to spend seven or eight years merely in scraping together as much miserable Latin and Greek as might be learned *easily* and *delightfully in one year.*

* *Ludus play* is the term used by the Romans for "School," and the Greek σχολη, whence our own word is translated, signifies *ease* or *leisure.*
† An Essay on a system of classical instruction.

And that which casts our proficiency therein so much behind, is but time lost—partly in too oft idle vacancies, given both to schools and universities—partly in a preposterous exaction, given the empty wits of children to compose themes, verses, and orations, which are the acts of ripest judgement, and the final work of a head filled, by long reading and observing, with elegant maxims and copious invention. These are not matters to be wrung from poor striplings, like blood out of the nose, or the plucking of untimely fruit." After noticing the absurdities into which children are led by the former modes of teaching, he proceeds :—" Whereas if, after some preparatory grounds of speech by their certain forms got into memory, they were led to the praxis thereof, in some chosen short book *lessoned thoroughly,*" (i. e. *dictated*) "to them, they might then proceed to learn the substance of good things, and arts in due order, which would bring the whole language quickly into their power. This I take to be the most natural and most profitable way of learning languages, and whereby we may best hope to give account to God of youth spent herein." Of grammar, Milton says :—" First, they should begin with the chief and necessary rules of some good grammar, either that now used, or any better; and while this is doing, their speech is to be fashioned, to a distinct and clear pronunciation, as near as may be to the Italian, especially in the vowels. Next, to make them expert in the usefullest points of grammar ; and withal to season them, some *easy* and delightful book of education should be *read* to them.

Milton thus required only "the chief and necessary rules of grammar" to be taught, and " some easy and delightful book" to be *read*, (i. e. *dictated*) to children, till they had acquired a general knowledge of the *words* of the language. They are not to be turned to a dictionary to make out the sense of a passage, by ringing the changes upon two hundred meanings of twenty different words; but they are to be told the express term for each word by the teacher himself; who is also to explain all difficulties of grammatical construction, so that the teacher take all the trouble, and the child have nothing but pleasure in his book." Next to Milton, in the order of time, and perhaps the most zealous promoter of the reform we advocate, is John Locke, author of the " Essay on the Human Understanding." This great philosopher takes the same general view of the subject which Ascham and Milton had done before him. " When

I consider," says he, "what ado is made about a little Latin and Greek, how many years are spent in it, and what a noise and business it makes to no purpose, I can hardly forbear thinking, that the parents of children still live in fear of the schoolmaster's rod, which they look on as the only instrument of education; as a language or two to be its whole business. How else is it possible that a child should be chained to the oar, seven, eight, or ten of the best years of his life, to get a language or two, which, I think, might be had at a great deal cheaper rate of pains and time, and be learned *almost in playing.** Locke's first project is: "To trouble the child with no grammar at all, but to have Latin, as English has been, without the perplexity of rules, *talkea into him;* for if you will consider it, Latin is no more unknown to a child, when he comes into the world, than English; and yet he learns English without a master, rule, or grammar; and so might he Latin too, as Tully did, if he had somebody always to talk to him in this language. And when we so often see a French woman teach an English girl to speak and read French perfectly in a year or two, without any rule of grammar, or any thing else but prattling to her, I cannot but wonder, how gentlemen have overseen this way for their sons. If, therefore, a man could be got, who, himself speaking good Latin, would always be about your son, talk constantly to him, and suffer him to speak and read nothing else, this would be the true and genuine way, and that which I would propose, not only as the easiest and best, wherein a child might, without pains or chiding, get a language, which others are wont to be whipt for at school six or seven years together; but also as that, wherein at the same time, he might have his mind and manners formed, and be instructed in all other parts of knowledge of things, that fall under the senses, and require little more than memory. But if such a man cannot be got, who speaks good Latin; and, being able to instruct your son in those parts of knowledge, will undertake by this method: *the next best thing,* is to have him taught as near this way as may be, which is by taking some easy and pleasant book, such as Æsop's fables, *and writing the English translation (made as literal as can be) in one line, and the Latin words which answer each of them, just over it in another.* These let him read every day, over and over again, till he perfectly understands

* Essay on a System of Classical Instruction, p. 50, 51.

the Latin; and then go on to another fable, till he is also perfect in that, not omitting what he is already perfect in, but sometimes reviewing that to keep it in his memory.

Let it not be supposed from any thing in the foregoing quotations from Milton and Locke, that these great masters of language ever inculcated a disregard to the study of grammar, or that they thought any language could ever be acquired thoroughly without it. They both insist that it shall be taught to children, as they can *comprehend* it. They would not "charge the mind" of *a young child* "with the multiplied rules and intricacies of grammar," but first teach him to read and speak these languages correctly—at the same time teaching the rules of grammar just as fast, and no faster, than he can *understand their application.* Locke says:—"The formation of the verb first, and afterwards the declensions of the nouns and pronouns, *perfectly learned by heart,* facilitate his acquaintance with the genius and manner of the Latin tongue, which varies the signification of verbs and nouns, not as the modern languages do, by particles prefixed, but by changing the last syllable." "More than this of grammar, I think he need not have, till he can read himself, Sanctii Minerva," &c. As he advances in acquiring a knowledge of words, he must advance, *pari pasu,* in obtaining a thorough and critical knowledge of grammar. "When by this way of interlining Latin and English one with another, he has got a moderate knowledge of the Latin tongue, he may then be advanced a little farther, to the reading of some other easy Latin book, such as Justin, or Eutropius; and to make the reading and understanding of it the less tedious and difficult to him, let him help himself with the English translation. *Nor let the objection, that he will then know it only by rote, fright any one.* This, when well considered, is not of any moment *against,* but plainly *for,* this way of learning a language. For languages are only to be learned by rote; and a man who does not speak English and Latin perfectly by rote, so that having thought of the thing he would speak of, his tongue, of course without thought of rule or grammar, falls into the proper expression and idiom of that language, does not speak it well, nor is master of it. And I would fain have any one name to me that tongue, that any one can learn, or speak as he should do, by the rules of grammar. Languages were made, not by rules of art, but by accident, and the common use of the people. And he that speaks them well, has no other rule

but that; nor any thing to trust to but his memory, and the habit of speaking after the fashion learned from those, that are allowed to speak properly, which, in other words, is only to speak by rote." We could multiply our quotations to a much greater extent, but our limits will not allow it. Those of our readers who are desirous to extend their inquiries, are referred to "A compendious way of teaching Ancient and Modern Languages, by T. Phillips, Historiographer to his Majesty—London, 1750;" "American Journal of Education, vols. 1st and 2d;" and "An Essay on the System of Classical Instruction, &c.—London, printed for John Taylor, 1829." In recommendation of the *plan* we have adopted, we have brought together an *array* of the names of men, who, in all the high qualities and qualifications requisite to constitute them competent and impartial judges of the best mode of teaching languages, are not surpassed by any who have ever lived. If they differ in some of the minor details of their respective systems, let it be remembered that they wrote in times considerably remote, and that they perfectly agree in the more important points. "Ascham wrote at a time when the Latin language was not only the sole medium of communication between men of literature and science, but almost a necessary introduction to the common business of life; and, on this account, it was desirable that *Latin composition* should be more extensively studied in early youth. At the time Locke wrote, the use of the Latin language was far less general. Each of these writers dwells upon that part of his subject which was most worthy of consideration in his own age. Ascham gives directions more particularly for the *writing* of Latin: Locke, for the *reading* of Latin writers." Locke not only advocated the plan of interlinear translation, but actually translated Æsop's fables in this manner. The following title page is copied from the second edition of this work :—
" Æsop's fables, in English and Latin Interlineary, for the benefit of those who, not having a master, would learn either of these tongues. The second edition, with Sculptures—by John Locke, Gent. 1723." About the year 1816, Mr. Hamilton taught the *French language* on a plan resembling that of Locke, to which he gave his *own name*. Before this time, Messrs. Carre and Sanderson, two distinguished classical teachers of Philadelphia, published interlined translations of a part of Historia Sacra, and a part of Telemachus.
The same year, the Rev. Mr Osborn published "A Key

to the Latin and Greek Languages; or, the Method of Dictation, systematically arranged—containing an interlined translation of the first three books of the Æneid, and part of the Gospel of St. John.

In the winter of 1833, Mr. Joseph N. Lewis, bookseller, of Baltimore, applied to Mr. Osborn to revise the three books of the Æneid he had already published, and to complete a translation of the entire poem. Mr. Osborn, who is at the head of a large seminary in this city, could not, from want of time, accomplish the task himself, and engaged Mr. John L. Cary to execute it for him. After having completed the fourth book, Mr. Cary was obliged, from infirm health, to relinquish the undertaking—when Mr. Osborn applied to the writer of this prefatory note, to complete the work his friend Cary had left unfinished. He undertook, and has accomplished it, as well as he could, in the time allowed to him. To this he has added the Bucolics and Georgics.

It was our intention to have given a faithful account of the labours of *Hamilton*, and to have exposed the injury he had done to the cause of learning—first, by his departure from the system of Locke—and again by claiming more for *his own* system than *any* can ever possibly accomplish. But at the moment we write his name, we hear, for the first time, that he is *dead!*—and we yield to the sentiment, *de mortuis nil nisi bonum*. Not contented with the honour of reviving the system of Locke and his great associates, his unbounded ambition to give his own name to the improvements of others, led him astray. Yet he was a man of most ardent zeal, and untiring industry;—and although he deviated so far from Locke, he accomplished more than any man of the present age, to render the system of his illustrious predecessor known and appreciated—so that, while we cannot cease to lament what we consider his *heresies*, we shall ever consider him a *benefactor to the human race*. In our translation, taking Locke for our model, we have endeavoured to give the sense of Virgil simple and unadorned. The words of the original have been rendered into English corresponding in each part of speech, and conforming, as nearly as possible, to their various inflections and combinations. From this course we have never deviated, except when the idiomatic difference of the two languages has demanded it;—for, although the closest version would seem the most harmonious to the mere grammarian the outrage offered to the English idiom, by imposing thereupon the shackles of a foreign dialect, might sometimes grate harshly upon the ear of taste and feeling.* Respecting the *manner* of instructing, every teacher will adopt the plan which his own judgement indicates as best. Mr. Osborn's plan, as explained in his "Key," is to translate short sentences of the lesson—one of the class repeating after him—then, another;—and as many as will be necessary to give the whole class sufficient time to understand the sentence perfectly well. In this manner, he continues till they have completed the prescribed lesson—he then instructs them thoroughly in the declensions and conjugations, beginning with the noun substantive of the first declension, and continuing his explanation of a single word till the pupil can decline *any* word belonging to this declension, at the same time shewing him where it is found, with the required rule of concord or government. In this manner, his pupils are carried through the declension of nouns, till they have mastered them *all*. He then instructs them in the adjectives, in the same manner—then the pronouns, verbs, participles—after which, the indeclinable parts of speech, taking especial care never to leave any one part of speech till its forms are thoroughly understood. Having accomplished this, he requires his pupils to commit their grammar to memory, which they can do with great ease and satisfaction to themselves—inasmuch as they perfectly understand what they are about. The writer of this, who, during the last twenty years, has taught many hundred ladies and gentlemen on this plan, has adopted exactly the mode described above, except that, for several years past, he has required his pupils, in following his *dictation*, to speak all at once. When a class is first formed, there will always occur, for a short time, more or less discord;—but, when the members are worthy and desirous to learn, they will become accustomed, in two or three lessons, *to speak together*—so that he has often taught classes of thirty or forty members, who all recited together, in as perfectly harmonious concord, as he ever witnessed among a choir of singers, or a congregation reading prayers. This method is admirably adapted to teach children to *read* well, provided the *teacher* is a *good reader;* for, as *he* reads, his pupils will read after him. In this manner one teacher can instruct a very numerous class:

* Advertisement to Anacreon.

as many, indeed, as can conveniently hear his voice—provided they are well disposed.

In following out the plan above indicated, it will be found, that the dictation of the teacher can never be rendered *equally* beneficial to *each* of the members of a numerous class. Among the best, *some* will be more attentive than *others*, the members of the class will differ from each other in various degrees of preparatory education, in capacity memory, and quick apprehension—so that any specificd number of repetitions "will either be insufficient for one part of the class, or more than sufficient for another." There will be a loss of learning, or a loss of time, when the *dictation* of the teacher *alone* is relied on. Whereas, when every member of the class can resort to our interpretation, each can bestow just so much time as is necessary for a perfect understanding of the lesson. Besides, the book is always in good humour with its reader, and is never tired of answering inquiries, or correcting errors: so that it is accommodated to the tempers, as well as to the capacities of all; neither disgusting the quick scholar, by tedious repetition, nor discouraging the more backward, by impatient remonstrance. Not that it tends to induce negligence on the part of the learner: on the contrary, the greater the facility of learning correctly, the greater should be the accuracy required by the teacher at the time of examination. Neither does it preclude any exertion on the part of the teacher himself, which he may be desirous to bestow from his own resources.*" A competent teacher will always find sufficient occasion for his observations, according to the different capacities and dispositions of boys, which will come, with far more effect, when the lesson is in some degree familiar to all; and he will gain a vast deal of time for the communication of useful knowledge, by being thus relieved from the mechanical drudgery of working upon each boy's memory. We could readily have adduced the authority of many distinguished names, English, French, German, and from among the best scholars of our country, in support of this system of instruction—but the subject does not require it. We *have* brought forward the testimony of Milton and Locke—we can go no *higher*. He who, on a *subject like this*, will not yield his doubts to *their* opinions, would discredit "*Moses and the Prophets.*" The most distinguished

---

* Essay on a System of Classical Instruction.

of the foreign journals, the Edinburgh and Quarterly Reviews, with many others, only second to them in authority, nave powerfully advocated this system. "The American Journal of Education," the best periodical our country has ever produced, exclusively devoted to this subject, as long ago as December, 1826, describes this "method"'' as "pleas ant and expeditious, as well as *thorough*. There is no delay for idle formalities ; the learner is led at once to his object, in his very first efforts, *he is conscious of the efforts he is making*, and he goes on with a cheerful impulse, which accelerates his advances. He thus redeems a large portion of his time for other branches of study, and for useful accomplishments." In this age and country, we are not called upon to prove the value of education, or the importance of extending it to *females*. In many respects, it is quite as important that they should be well grounded in a competent knowledge of the learned languages, as the other sex. They *will* give the first impulse in all which is good and useful to the *next* generation—they *may* reform the present. Our country has already produced women, who, in classical acquirement, have equalled any who have lived in any other. Although, most fortunately for us, we have never had a "*queen Elizabeth*," or can we boast of "*the* venerable Elizabeth Carter," or "*the* beautiful Elizabeth Smith," so justly celebrated by their illustrious countrywoman, Hannah More, yet *our own* Hannah Adams and Martha Ramsay were, at least in classical learning, equal to the English Queen, or her great relative, lady Jane Grey (so infinitely her superior in moral qualities)—while in all the virtues which adorn the sex, they held equal rank with the other British ladies whose names we have recited. After many years experience in teaching languages to females, the writer of this can bear faithful (as he does most *grateful*) testimony to their capacity, docility, and industry. He has never known their *proficiency* equalled by the other sex : and, were he allowed to adorn this page with the *names* of his female pupils who have distinguished themselves as Latin scholars, with a simple statement of the *amount* of their acquirements, and the *time* they devoted to this study, he would thereby furnish an argument in favour of the system he advocates, quite as convincing as any he has used. The miserable prejudice which has withheld this better part of our race from an equal participation in these most delightful studies, is fast passing away. "The days are past, when the know.

ledge of tent-stitch, and the composition of a pudding, or cordial, was esteemed the chief glory of half the creation. The females of the present generation may boast, in the language of judicial astrology, *a most auspicious nativity.* Science allures them to her temple, and virtue commands them to dedicate to her altar, that influence which they derive from the courtesy of refined society. The genius of their country, as well as the spirit of the age, supplies another stimulant, *prompting them to become worthy of a name among the dignified and enlightened daughters of the greatest republic on earth.* *

L. HART.

Baltimore, March 10th, 1833.

* Journal of Education.

THE ÆNEID OF VIRGIL,

WITH AN

INTERLINEAR TRANSLATION;

AS NEARLY LITERAL AS THE IDIOMATIC DIFFER-
ENCE OF THE LATIN AND ENGLISH LAN-
GUAGES WILL ALLOW.

By LEVI HART & V. R. OSBORN.

Conditor Iliados cantabitur, atque Maronis
Altisoni dubiam facientia carmina palmam.
—JOVENALIS, SAT. 11.

incubuēre - syncopated form.

THE ÆNEID

OF

P. VIRGILIUS MARO.

BOOK FIRST.

_____

CANO, arma que virum qui, profugus fato, primus venit
I sing, arms and the hero who, driven by fate, first has come

ab oris Trojæ Italiam que Lavina littora: multum
from the coasts of Troy to Italy and the Lavinian shores: much

ille jactatus et terris et alto vi superum
he has been tossed both on land and on the sea by the power of the gods above,

ob memorem iram sævæ Junonis: et
on account of the lasting wrath of cruel Juno: and

passus quoque multa bello, dum conderet
he has suffered also many *things in* war, until he might build

urbem que inferret deos Latio: unde Latinum
a city and might bring in *his* gods to Latium; from whence *is* the Latin

genus que Albani patres atque mœnia altæ Romæ.
race and the Alban fathers and the walls of lofty Rome.

Musa memora mihi causas: quo numine læso ve quid
O Muse relate to me the causes; what deity *being* offended or why

Regina Deûm dolens impulerit virum insignem
the queen of the gods grieving may have compelled a man eminent

pietate volvere tot casus, adire tot labores.
for piety to endure so many calamities, to undergo so many hardships.

Tantæne iræ cœlestibus animis?
Are so great resentments *in* heavenly minds?

Antiqua urbs fuit Tyrii coloni tenuere
An ancient city has been *which* Tyrian husbandmen have inhabited

Carthago contra Italiam que ostia Tiberina
Carthage *by name,* over against Italy and the entrances of the Tiber

longè; dives opum que asperrima studiis belli:
but far off; abounding in wealth and most hard in the exercises of war

quam unam Juno fertur coluisse magis omnibus
which one *city* Juno is said to have revered more *than* all

terris Samo posthabita. Hìc illius arma hìc
lands Samos *being* less esteemed. Here *have been* her arms here

fuit currus: Dea jam tùm que tendit que fovet
has been *her* chariot: the goddess now *and* then both designs and cherishes

hoc esse regnum gentibus si qua
the hope that this is to be a metropolis for the nations if in any

fata   sinant.   Sed enim   audierat   progeniem
way the fates may permit.   But   truly   *she* had heard   that   a race

duci   a Trojano sanguine quæ olim   verteret
was descended from   Trojan   blood   which hereafter might overturn

Tyrias   arces: hinc populum latè   regem que superbum
the Tyrian towers: *that* hence a people extensively   a ruler   and   proud

bello   venturum   excidio Libyæ: sic   Parcas
in war is about to come   for the destruction of Libya: thus *that*   the destinies

volvere.   Saturnia   metuens id que   memor
had ordained.   The daughter of Saturn   fearing   that and   mindful

veteris   belli quod prima gesserat   ad Trojam pro
of the ancient   war which   first   she had carried on before Troy   for

caris Argis; necdum etiam causæ   irarum que sævi
her beloved Argos;   nor as yet   also the causes of *her* wrath   and *her* great

dolores exciderant animo;   judicium Paridis   manet
resentments had escaped from her mind;   the judgment   of Paris   remains

repostum   altà mente que injuria spretæ   formæ et
laid up   in *her* lofty mind   and the injury of her despised   form; and the

invisum genus et honores   rapti   Ganymedis: accensa
hated   race and the honors   of the ravished   Ganymede: incensed

super his   arcebat longè Latio   Troas   jactatos
about these *things*   she repelled far   from Latium the Trojans   tosssed

toto æquore, reliquias Danaum atque immitis Achillei; que
on all the sea,   the remains of the Greeks   and   of cruel   Achilles   and

errabant   per multos annos acti   fatis   circum omnia
they wandered   during many   years driven   by the fates   about   all

maria: condere Romanam gentem erat   tantæ   molis
seas: to found   the Roman   nation was *a work of* so great magnitude.

Vix   læti dabant vela   e conspectu Siculæ
Scarcely   *the Trojans* joyful   gave *their* sails   from sight of the   Sicilian

telluris in altum et ruebant spumas salis   ære;
land   upon the sea and ploughed   the foam of the sea with *their* brass beaks;

cùm Juno servans æternum vulnus sub pectore   hæc
when Juno   keeping an everlasting   wound in *her* breast *resolved* these

secum: mene victam   desistere incepto
things with herself: *does it become* me,   conquered,   to desist from *my* under-

nec posse   avertere regem Teucrorum   Italiâ,
taking, nor to be able   to drive away   the king of the Trojans   from Italy,

quippe vetor   fatis! Pallasne potuit exurere classem
because I am forbidden by the fates!   Has Pallas been able to burn   the fleet

Argivûm atque submergere ipsos ponto ob noxam unius
of the Greeks,   and   to drown   them in the sea   for the fault   of one,

et furias Ajacis   Oilei?   Ipsa jaculata e nubibus
even the frenzy of Ajax the son of Oileus?   She having darted from the clouds,

rapidum ignem Jovis, que disjecit   rates,   que evertit
the rapid lightning of Jupiter, both has scattered their ships, and   has up-

æquora ventis: turbine   corripuit illum expiran-
turned the seas with the winds: in a whirlwind   she has seized   him   breathing

tem flammas transfixo pectore, quæ infixit acuto
forth flames from *his* transfixed breast, and has thrust *him* upon a sharp

scopulo. Ast ego, quæ incedo, regina divûm, quæ et
rock. But I, who walk, the queen of the gods, and both

soror et conjux Jovis, (gero bella tot annos cum unâ
the sister and wife of Jove, carry on wars so many years with one

gente.) Et quisquam præterea adoret numen Junonis aut
nation. And can any one, hereafter adore the deity of Juno or

supplex imponat aris honorem?
suppliant put on her altars a sacrifice?

Dea volutans talia se secum flammato corde venit
The goddess revolving such *things* with herself in *her* inflamed mind comes

in Æoliam patriam nimborum, loca fœta furentibus
into Æolia the native country of storms, places pregnant with boisterous

Austris. Hìc rex Æolus vasto antro premit imperio ac
winds. Here king Æolus in a vast cave controls by authority and

frænat vinclis et carcere luctantes ventos que sonoras
restrains with chains and a prison the struggling winds and the roaring

tempestates. Illi indignantes fremunt circum claustra cum
tempests. They indignant roar around the barriers with

magno murmure montis. Æolus sedet celsâ arce
a great murmur of the mountain. Æolus sits on a lofty eminence

tenens sceptra; que mollit animos et temperat iras.
holding a sceptre; and calms *their* passions and moderates *their* wrath.

Quippe ni faciat rapidi ferant secum
For unless he may do thus they swift may bear away with themselves

maria ac terras que profundum cœlum que verrant per
the seas and the lands and the high heaven and sweep *them* through

auras. Sed omnipotens pater metuens hoc abdidit
the air. But the omnipotent father fearing this has confined *them*

atris speluncis; que insuper imposuit molem, et altos
in dark caves; and moreover hath put over *them* a huge mass and lofty

montes; que dedit regem qui jussus sciret et
mountains; and hath appointed a king who ordered might know *how* both

premere certo fœdere et dare laxas habenas: Ad quem
to restrain *them* by a sure rule and to give loose reins: To whom

Juno supplex tum usa est his vocibus: Æole (namque
Juno suppliant then has used these words: O Æolus (for the

pater Divûm atque rex hominum dedit tibi et mulcere
father of the gods and the king of men has given to thee both to calm

fluctus, et tollere vento:) Gens inimica mihi
the waves, and to raise *them* by the wind:) A nation hostile to me

navigat Tyrrhenum æquor, portans Illium que victos
sails upon the Tuscan sea, carrying Illium and *its* conquered

penates in Italiam. Incute ventis vim, que obrue
household gods into Italy. Strike into the winds force, and overwhelm

puppes submersas aut age diversas, et disjice corpora
their ships bilged or drive *them* apart, and scatter *their* bodies in

ponto. Sunt mihi bis septem nymphæ præstanti corpore;
the sea. There are to me twice seven nymphs of excellent body·

quarum Deiopiam quæ pulcherrima formâ jungam
of whom Deiopeia who is the most beautiful in form I will join to thee

stabili connubio, que dicabo propriam: ut exigat
in firm wedlock, and will appoint to be your own. that she may spend

omnes annos tecum pro talibus meritis, et faciat te
all her years with thee for such favours, and may make thee

parentem pulchrâ prole. Æolus contra hæc:
the father of a beautiful offspring. Æolus on the other hand answers these

O Regina, tuus labor explorare qui.1 optes: est
things. O queen, thy labour is to examine what you may desire: it is

fas mihi capessere jussa. Tu concilias mihi hoc
right for me to execute your commands. Thou gainest for me this

regni quodcunque, tu sceptra que
kingdom whatever there is, thou gainest for me, my sceptre and

Jovem: tu das accumbere epulis Divûm, que facis
Jove· thou givest to me to recline at banquets of the gods, and makest me

potentem nimborum que tempestatum. Ubi hæc
powerful over storms and tempests. When these things have

dicta impulit cavum montem in latus conversâ
been said he has struck the hollow mountain against the side with his turned

cuspide ac venti veluti facto agmine ruunt qua
spear and the winds as in a formed band burst forth where

porta, et perflant terras turbine. Incu-
an entrance has been given, and blow over the lands in a whirlwind. They have

buere mari que unâ que Eurus que Notus
hovered over the sea also at the same time both the east and the south wind

que Africus creber procellis, ruunt totum a
and the south-west wind thick with tempests, agitate the whole sea from its

imis sedibus; et volvunt vastos fluctus ad littora. Que
lowest foundations; and roll vast waves to the shores. Both

clamor virûm que stridor rudentum insequitur. Subitò
a cry of the men and a cracking of the cables succeeds. Suddenly

nubes eripiunt que cœlum que diem ex oculis Teucro-
the clouds snatch both the heaven and the day from the eyes of the Tro-

rum: atra nox incubat ponto. Poli intonuere, et æther
jans: dark night sits upon the sea. The Poles have thundered, and the sky

micat crebris ignibus: que omnia intentant præsentem
glitters with frequent lightnings: and all things threaten present

mortem viris. Extemplo membra Æneæ solvuntur fri-
death to the men. Immediately the limbs of Æneas are relaxed with

gore. Ingemit et tendens duplices palmas ad sidera, refert
fear. He groans and stretching both hands to the stars, relates

talia voce: O que ter que quater beati, queis
such things with his voice: O both thrice and four times happy they, to whom it

contigit oppetere ante ora patrum, sub altis
hath happened to die before the faces of their fathers, under the lofty

mœnibus Trojæ. O Tydide fortissime gentis Danaûm,
walls of Troy! O Tydeus' son the most brave of the nation of the Greeks,

mene nonpotuisse occumbere Illiacis campis que
why is it that I have not been able to fall on the Trojan plains and

effundere hanc animam tua dextra? ubi sævus Hector
to pour forth this soul by thy right hand? where stern Hector

jacet telo Æacidæ, ubi ingens Sarpedon: ubi
lies slain by the weapon of Achilles, where the great Sarpedon lies: where

Simois volvit sub undis correpta scuta virûm que galeas
Simois rolls under its waves, seized shields of men and helmets

et fortia corpora. Procella stridens Aquilone adversa
and brave bodies. A tempest roaring from the north opposite to him

jactanti talia ferit velum, que tollit fluctus ad sidera
throwing out such things strikes the sail, and raises the billows to the stars

Remi franguntur; tum prora avertit et dat latus
The oars are broken; then the prow inclines and gives the side to the

undis; præruptus mons aquæ insequitur cumulo. H.
waves; a broken mountain of water succeeds in a heap. These

pendent in summo fluctu; unda dehiscens aperit terram
hang on the highest wave: the water opening discloses the earth

his inter fluctus, æstus furit arenis. Notus torquet
to those between the waves, the tide mixes with the sand. The south wind hurls

tres abreptas in latentia saxa; quæ saxa in mediis flucti-
three others dragged away upon hidden rocks; which rocks in the midst of the

bus, Itali vocant Aras, immane dorsum summo
waves, the Italians call the Altars, a huge ridge on the highest part of

mari. Eurus urget tres ab alto in brevia et syrtes,
the sea. The east wind drives three from the deep on the flats and quick-sands,

miserabile visu; que illidit vadis atque cingit
lamentable to be seen; and dashes them on the shelves and surrounds them

aggere arenæ. Ingens pontus ante oculos ipsius ferit a
with a heap of sand. A great sea before the eyes of him strikes from

vertice in puppim unam quæ vehebat Lycios que fidum
the top against a ship one which conveyed the Lycians and the faithful

Orontem; magister excutitur que pronus volvitur in caput:
Orontes; the pilot is shaken off and downward is tumbled upon his head:

ast fluctus agens illam ter circum ibidem, torquet, et
but a wave driving that thrice around in the same place, whirls it, and

rapidus vortex vorat æquore. Apparent rari nantes in
a rapid eddy swallows it in the sea. They appear few swimming in the

vasto gurgite; arma virûm que tabulæ et Troïa gaza
vast deep; the arms of men and planks and Trojan treasure appear

per undas. Jam hiems vicit validam navem Ilionei
in the waters. Now a storm has overcome the strong ship of Ilioneus

jam fortis Achatæ, et quâ Abas vectus
now the ship of brave Achates, and the ship in which Abas has been carried

et quâ grandævus Alethes: omnes accipiunt
and the one in which the old Alethes has been carried, all receive

prospicio, 3 years, ..., look forward for

lateo 2, ui – to be hidden. sentio, sensi, sensum, percin...

lateri icis – liquor, wine

inimicum imbrem compagibus laterum laxis, que fathe hostile flood the closures of the sides being loose, and

tiscunt rimis.
gape with chinks.

fatisco 3 — — yawn, gape

Interea, Neptunus sensit pontum misceri magno
In the mean time, Neptune has perceived the sea to be disturbed with a great

murmure, que hyemem emissam, et stagna refusa
noise and a storm to be sent forth, and the deeps poured out from

imis vadis: graviter commotus, et prospiciens alto,
their lowest bottom: greatly irritated, and taking care for the sea, he

extulit placidum caput summa unda. Videt classem
has raised his calm head from the highest water. He sees the fleet of

Æneæ disjectam toto æquore, Troas oppressos fluctibus
Æneas scattered on all the sea, the Trojans overwhelmed by the waves

que ruina cœli. Nec doli et iræ Junonis latuere
and the ruin of heaven, Nor the wiles and wrath of Juno have been concealed

fratrem: vocat ad se Eurum que Zephyrum;
from her brother: he calls to himself the East wind and the West wind,

de hinc fatur talia; tantane fiducia vestris generis
then he speaks such things; has so great presumption of your race

tenuit vos? Jam audetis, venti, miscere cœlum que terram
possessessed you? Now dare you, O winds, to disorder heaven and the earth

sine meo numine, et tollere tantas moles? quos ego!
without my authority, and to raise so great heaps of waves? whom I

Sed præstat componere motos fluctus. Post
will punish: But it is better to compose the agitated billows. Afterwards

luetis mihi commissa pœnâ non simili. Maturate
ye shall expiate to me your offences by a punishment not similar. Hasten

fugam, que dicite hæc vestro regi: imperium pelagi
your flight, and declare these things to your king: that the empire of the sea

que sævum tridentem non datum illi sorte sed mihi: ille
and the mighty trident has not been given to him by lot but to me: he

tenet immania saxa, vestras domos, Eure: Æolus jactet
possesses huge rocks, your mansions, O Eurus: Æolus may boast

se in illâ aulâ, et regnet clauso carcere ventorum. Sic
himself in that palace, and reign in the inclosed prison of the winds. Thus

ait, et citius dicto placat tumida æquora, que fugat
he says, and quicker than the word he calms the swollen seas, and disperses

collectas nubes, que reducit solem. Simul Cymothoë
the collected clouds, and brings back the sun. At the same time Cymothoe

et Triton adnixus detrudunt naves acuto scopulo: ipse
and Triton pushing shove the ships from the pointed rock: he

levat tridenti, et aperit vastas syrtes, et temperat
assists them with his trident, and opens the vast quicksands, and calms

æquor; atque levibus rotis perlabitur summas
the sea and with the light wheels of his chariot glides over the highest

undas. Ac veluti cum sæpe seditio coorta est in magno
waves. And as when often a sedition has arisen among a great

se iactare 1 – to boast

adnitor nixus sum – press upon push

coorior 4 ortus sum – break out, arise

populo, que ignobile vulgus sævit   animis: jamque faces
multitude, and the ignoble vulgar rages in their minds: and now firebrands

et saxa volant; furor ministrat arma: si tum forte conspex-
and stones fly; rage affords arms: if then by chance they have

ere quem virum gravem pietate ac meritis, silent que
seen any man venerable for his piety and merits, they are still and

adstant arrectis auribus: ille regit   animos   dictis, et
stand with attentive ears: he rules their passions by his words, and

mulcet pectora. Sic cunctus fragor pelagi   cecidit, post-
calms their breasts. Thus all the noise of the sea has ended, after-

quam, genitor prospiciens æquora, que invectus aperto cælo
wards, the father surveying the seas, and borne in the open sky,

flectit equos, que volans secundo curru dat lora. Defessi
turns his horses, and flying in his favourable chariot, gives the reins. The weary

Æneadæ contendunt petere   cursu, littora   quæ
Trojans strive to gain in their course the shores which are

proxima, et vertuntur ad oras Libyæ.   Est locus in
the nearest, and are turned to the coasts of Libya. There is a place in

longo secessu: insula efficit portum, objectu   laterum,
a long recess: an island forms a harbour, by the interposition of its sides,

quibus omnis unda ab alto frangitur, que scindit sese in
by which every wave from the sea is broken, and divides itself into

reductas sinus.   Hinc atque hinc, vastæ rupes que gemini
retired bays. On this part and that, vast cliffs and two

scopuli   minantur   in cœlum, sub quorum ver-
rocks are raised up in a threatening manner to heaven, under whose sum-

tice æquora tuta late silent: tum scena   coruscis sylvis,
mit the seas secure all about are still: then a bower with waving woods

que atrum nemus horrenti umbra imminet desuper. Sub
and a dark grove with dismal shade hangs over from above. Under

adversa fronte antrum   pendentibus scopulis: intus
the opposite front is a cave among the hanging rocks: within

dulces aquæ, que sedilia vivo saxo, domus nympharum:
are fresh waters, and seats of living stone, the habitation of the nymphs:

hic non ulla vincula tenent fessas naves; non anchora alligat
here not any cables hold the weary ships; not any anchor moors

unco morsu. Æneas subit huc septem navibus
them by its crooked fluok. Æneas enters hither with seven ships

collectis ex omni numero: ac Troës, egressi magno
collected out of the whole number: and the Trojans, debarking with a great

amore telluris, potiuntur optata arena, et ponunt in littore
love of the land, enjoy the desired earth, and lay on the shore

artus tabentes sale. Ac primum Achates excudit
their limbs drenched with brine. And first, Achates has struck

scintillam silici, que, suscepit ignem foliis, atque de-
out a spark of fire from a flint, and received the fire in leaves, and has ap-

dit arida nutrimenta, circum, que rapuit flammam in
plied dry fuel around it, and has taken the flame among

corrumpo, rupi, ruptum, 3 break, destroy
torreo 2 ui, tostum, roast, toast
pasco 3 pavi, pastum, feed, nourish

fomite.   Tum fessi rerum expediunt cererem corruptam
the wood.   Then weary of affairs   they fetch out their grain damaged by

undis,   que Cerealia arma;   que parant et torrere
the waters, and the Cerealian instruments;   and prepare both to dry   on the

fregi, fractum flammis, et frangere saxo fruges, receptas
flames,   and to bruise with a stone their corn,   received from the wreck.

scendi,
scensum   Intereâ Æneas conscendit scopulum, et petit omnem
In the mean time Æneas   climbs   a rock,   and takes the whole

prospectum late   pelago, si   quà videat Antheâ jac-
prospect   all around upon the sea, if in any way he may see Antheus toss-

tatum vento,   que Phrygias biremes, aut Capyn, aut arma
ed by the wind, and the Phrygian   gallies   or Capys,   or the arms

Caïci in celsis puppibus. Prospicit nullam navem in con-
of Caicus on   the lofty decks.   He sees   no   ship   in

spectu;   tres cervos errantes littore: tota armenta
sight;   but he sees three stags   wandering on the shore: the whole   herd

sequuntur hos a tergo; et longum agmen pascitur   per
follow   these behind; and the long flock   feeds   through the

valles.   Constitit hìc, que corripuit manu arcum que
vallies.   He has stood here, and seized in his hand his bow   and

gero, gessi
gessum   celeres sagittas, quæ tela fidus Achates gerebat;   que
sterno, *swift   arrows,   which weapons the faithful Achates   carried;   and*
stravi, stratum

primum sternit   ductores ipsos ferentes capita alta
first   he strikes down the leaders themselves bearing their heads lofty with

misceo, mi   arboreis cornibus; et tum agens vulgus   telis inter
mistum *branching   horns;   and then   driving the herd with his weapons among*

frondea nemora, miscet omnem turbam. Nec absistit prius
the leafty   groves,   disorders the whole multitude.   Nor does he desist before

quam   victor   fundat   humi septem ingentia
that as a conqueror he may prostrate on the ground seven   huge bo-

corpora, et æquet numerum cum navibus.   Hinc petit
dies,   and equal   their number with his ships.   Hence he seeks the

portum, et partitur   in   omnes   socios.   Deinde heros
port,   and divides them among   all his companions   Then the hero

viri, visum dividit   vina quæ bonus Acestes onerârat cadis Trinacrio
distributes the wine which good   Acestes   had loaded in casks on the Sicilian

mulceo, mulsi littore, que dederat abeuntibus, et mulcet mœrentia pectora
mulsum 2 *shore   and had given to them departing, and soothes   their sad   minds*
mœreo 2

dictis: O socii (enim sumus neque ignari malo-
with these words: O companions, (for   we are   not   ignorant of misfor-

rum ante)   O   passi   graviora!   Deus dabit
tunes before now) O you having suffered more grievous things!   God will grant

his quoque finem.   Vos accêstis rabiem   Scyllæam
to these also   termination.   You have come to the madness of Scylla

que penitus sonàntes scopulos: et vos experti Cyclopea saxa:
and the deeply sounding   rocks: and you have tried the Cyclopean rocks:

revocate animos, que mittite mœstum timorem: forsan
resume your courage, and dismiss   sorrowful   fear: perhaps here

experior 4 pertus sum, try, test

memini esse def · remember be mindful
tendo 3 tetendi tensum, istretch haot, shoot
ostendo 3 ostendi, ostentum, show

olim juvabit   meminisse   et hæc.   Tendimus in
after it will delight us to have remembered also these *things.* We go   into

Latium per varios casus, per   tot   discrimina rerum, ubi
Latium through various perils, through so many   dangers   of affairs, where

fata ostendunt quietas sedes: illic   fas   regna
the fates   show   *to us* peaceful habitations: there *it is* justice that the realms

Trojæ resurgere. Durate et servate vosmet secundis re-
of Troy should rise again. Persevere and preserve yourselves for prosperous af-

bus. Refert talia   voce; que æger ingentibus curis,
fairs. He relates such *things* with his voice; and anxious with great   cares

simulat spem vultu;   premit altum dolorem   corde.
dissembles hope in his countenance; conceals deep   grief   in *his* heart.

Illi accingunt se   prædæ, que futuris dapibus, diripiunt
They   prepare themselves for the prey, and   future   viands; they tear the

tergora costis et nudant viscera: pars secant in frusta,
skins   from the ribs and make bare the entrails: a part   cut   into   pieces,

que figunt trementia verubus: alii locant ahena   littore,
and   fix *them* quivering on   spits: others place the caldrons on the shore,

que ministrant flammas. Tum revocant   vires victu; que
and   supply the   flames.   Then they recruit *their* strength with food; and

fusi per herbam, implentur veteris Bacchi, que pinguis
spread through the grass,   are filled / with old wine,   and   fat   veni-

ferinæ. Postquam, fames = f   exempta   epulis, que
son   After that, their hunger *has been* taken away by the feast, and

mensæ remotæ,   requirunt   amissos socios longo sermone,
the tables   removed, they inquire after *their* lost companions in a long discourse,

dubii   inter que spem que metum; seu   credant
doubtful between both hope and   fear; whether they may believe *them*

vivere, sive   pati extrema: nec, jam vocatos exaudire.
to be living, or *that they* had suffered death: nor, now invoked would hear.

Pius Æneas præcipuè gemit secum,   casum   nunc
Pious Æneas   especially laments with himself, the misfortune at one time

acris Orontei,   nunc   Amyci, et crudelia fata Lyci, que
of active Orontes, at another time Amicus, and the cruel fates of Lycus, and

fortem Gyan, que fortem Cloanthum. Et jam   erat
the brave Gyas, and the brave Cloanthus.   And now there was a con-

finis cum Jupiter, despiciens summo æthere velivolum
clusion, when Jove,   surveying from the highest heaven   the navigable

mare que terras jacentes, que littora, et latos populos, sic
sea   and the lands lying along, and the shores, and the wide nations, thus.

constitit vertice coeli, et defixit lumina regnis Libyæ.
has stood on the summit of heaven, and has fixed *his* eyes on the realms of Libya.

Atque Venus tristior et suffusa   nitentes oculos lacrymis,
But   Venus more sad and bedewed *as to her* shining   eyes   with tears,

alloquitur illum jactantem tales curas pectore: O   qui
addresses   him   revolving   such   cares in *his* mind: O *thou* who go

regis   res   que hominum que Deûm æternis imperiis, et
vernest the affairs both   of men   and of gods with eternal powers, an'

terres fulmine, quid tantum in te, meus
affrightest with thy thunder, what so great wickedness against thee has my

Æneas, quid Troes potuere committere quibus
Æneas, what have the Trojans been able to commit to whom

passis tot funera, cunctus orbis terrarum clauditur
having suffered so many deaths, the whole orb of the earth is shut

ob Italiam? Certe pollicitus Romanos olim,
account of Italy? Surely you have promised that the Romans hereafter,

annis volventibus, fore ductores hinc, à revocato sanguine
the years revolving, should be leaders hence, from the restored blood of

Teucri, qui mare, qui tenerent terras omni
Teucer, who might govern the sea, who might govern the countries with all

ditone: Genitor, quæ sententia vertit te? Equidem hoc
authority: O Father, what purpose has turned thee? Indeed with this

solabar occasum que tristes ruinas Trojæ, rependens fatis
I softened the fall and sad ruins of Troy, balancing by these fates

contraria fata. Nunc eadem fortuna insequitur viros actos
adverse fates. Now the same fortune pursues the men driven

tot casibus. Magne rex, quem finem laborum das?
by so many misfortunes. O great king, what end of hardships do you give?

Antenor elapsus mediis Achivis, potuit tutus
Antenor escaped from the midst of the Greeks, has been able safe to

penetrare Illyricos sinus, atque intima regna Liburnorum,
penetrate the Illyrian bays, and the inmost realms of the Liburnians,

et superare fontem Timavi; unde per novem ora
and to pass beyond the fountain of Timavus; whence through nine mouths it

it proruptum mare cum vasto murmure montis, et pre-
goes a swiftly flowing river with a vast murmur of the mountain, and over-

mit arva sonanti pelago. Ille, tamen locavit hìc
whelms the fields with a roaring sea. He, notwithstanding has placed here

urbem Patavi que sedes Teucrorum, et dedit nomen
the city of Padua and the habitations of the Trojans, and has given a name to

genti que fixit, Troïa arma; nunc compostus quiescit
the nation, and set up the Trojan arms; now composed he rests

placidâ pace. Nos, tua progenies, quibus annuis arcem
in calm peace. We, thy progeny, to whom thou promisest the court

cœli, navibus amissis (infandùm) prodimur, ob
of heaven, our ships being lost (Oh horrible) are abandoned, on account of

iram unius, atque disjungimur longè Italis oris / Hic
the wrath of one, and are separated far from the Italian coasts. Is this

honos pietatis? sic reponis nos in sceptra? Sator
the reward of piety? thus dost thou replace us into governments? The Father

hominum, atque Deorum subridens olli, vultu quo
of men, and Gods smiling upon her, with the aspect with which

serenat cœlum, que tempestates, libavit oscula
he clears up the sky, and the tempests, has touched lightly the lips of his

natæ; dehinc fatur talia: Cytherea, parce metu;
daughter: and then speaks such things: O Venus, abstain from fear

fata tuorum manent tibi immota; cernes urbem,
the fates of thy *people* remain to thee immovable; thou shalt see the city

et promissa mœnia Lavinî, que feres magnanimum
and the promised walls of Lavinium, and raise magnanimous

Æneam sublimem ad sidera cœli: neque sententia vertit me.
Æneas high to the stars of heaven: nor does any purpose turn me

Hic geret ingens bellum Italia, (enim fabor tibi, quando
He shall carry on great war in Italy, (for I will declare to thee, since

hæc cura remordet te, movebo arcana fatorum, volvens
this concern vexes thee, I will explain the secrets of the fates, tracing back-

longius,) que contundet feroces populos; que ponet mores
ward farther) and shall crush fierce nations; and appoint laws

et mœnia viris, dum tertia æstas viderit regnantem
and cities for his men, until the third summer, shall have seen *him* reigning

Latio, que terna hiberna transierint, Rutulis
in Latium, and three winter *seasons* shall have passed away, the Rutulians

subactis. At puer, Ascanius, cui nunc cognomen Iülo
being subdued. But the boy, Ascanius, to whom now the surname Iulus

additur (Ilus erat, dum Ilia res stetit regno) ex-
is added (Ilus he was, whilst the Trojan power has continued for a kingdom) shall

plebit imperio triginta magnos orbes, mensibus volvendis,
complete with his reign thirty great circles, the months rolling,

que transferet regnum ab sede Lavinî, et muniet, Albam
and transfer the kingdom from the seat of Lavinium, and shall fortify Alba

longam multâ vî. Hîc jam, regnabitur tercentum
longa with much strength. Here again, it shall be governed three hundred

totos annos sub Hectoreâ gente, donec Ilia, regina sacer-
whole years under the Hectorean race, until Ilia, a queen a priest-

dos, gravis Marte, dabit geminam prolem partu.
ess, teeming by Mars, shall bring forth a double progeny at a birth.

Inde, Romulus, lætus fulvo tegmine lupæ, nutricis,
Afterwards, Romulus, joyful in the tawny hide of a wolf, his nurse,

excipiet gentem, et condet Mavortia mœnia, que dicit
shall receive the nation, and shall build a Mavortian city, and shall call *the*

Romanos de suo nomine. Ego pono his nec
people Romans from his own name. I appoint for these neither the

metas nec tempora rerum; dedi imperium sine
bounds nor the duration of powers; I have given *to them* dominion without

fine: quin aspera Juno, quæ nunc metu fatigat mare, que
end: nay even severe Juno, who now from fear disturbs the sea, and

terras, que cœlum, referet consilia in melius, que fovebit
the lands, and heaven, shall change *her* counsels for the better, and will favor

mecum Romanos dominos rerum, que togatam gentem. Sic
with me, the Romans, the lords of affairs, and the gowned nation. Thus

placitum. Ætas veniet, lustris labentibus, cum domus
is my pleasure. An age shall come, the years gliding away, when the race

Assaraci premet servitio, Phthiam que claras Myce-
of Assaracus shall keep under with servitude, Phthia and the renowned Myce-

nas, ac dominabitur victis Argis. Cæsar nascetur Tro-
næ, and shall rule over the conquered Argos. Cæsar shall be born a Tro-

janus pulchrâ origine, qui terminet imperium Oceano,
jan of illustrious descent, who shall bound his empire by the ocean,

famam astris, Julius nomen dimissum à magno Iülo.
his fame by the stars, Julius called, a name derived from the great Iulus.

Tu olim securâ, accipies hunc cœlo, onustum spoliis
Thou hereafter safe, shall receive him to heaven, loaded with the spoils of

Orientis: hic quoque vocabitur votis. Tum aspera sæcula
the East: he also shall be invoked with vows. Then fierce people

mitescent, bellis positis. Cana fides, Vesta, et Quirinus
shall grow mild, wars being laid aside: Hoary faith, Vesta, and Quirinus,

cum fratre Remo, dabunt jura: diræ portæ belli claudentur,
with his brother Remus, shall give laws: the cruel gates of war shall be shut

ferro et arctis compagibus, impius Furor sedens intus
with iron and with tight closures, impious Fury sitting within

super sæva arma, et vinctus post tergum centum ahenis
upon direful arms, and bound behind his back with a hundred brazen

nodis, frement horridus cruento ore. Ait hæc,
chains, shall roar dreadful with his bloody mouth. He says these things,

et demittit ab alto genitum Maiâ, ut terræ, que ut
and sends down from heaven him born of Maia, that the lands, and that the

novæ arces Carthaginis pateant hospito Teucris;
new towers of Carthage may be opened for entertainment to the Trojans;

ne Dido, nescia fati arceret finibus. Ille volat
lest Dido, ignorant of fate might debar them from her territories. He flies

per magnum aëra remigio alarum ac citus astitit
through the spacious sky with the flying of his wings and quick has stood on

oris Libyæ; et jam facit jussa que Pœni
the coasts of Libya; and now he performs his commands and the Carthaginians

ponunt ferocia corda, Deo volente: imprimis Regina ac-
lay aside their ferocious hearts, the God willing: especially the Queen enter-

cipit quietum animum que benignam mentem in Teu-
tains a peaceable disposition and a kind mind towards the Tro-

cros. At pius Æneas volvens plurima per noctem,
jans. But pious Æneas revolving very many things through the night,

ut primum alma lux data est, constituit exire, que ex-
as first clear light has been given, has determined to go forth, and to ex-

plorare novos locos, quærere quas oras accesserit vento,
plore the new places, to seek to what coasts he may have come by the wind,

qui teneant, ne homines ne feræ, (nam videt in-
who may inhabit them, whether men or wild beasts, (for he sees uncul-

culta,) que referre sociis exacta. Occulit
tivated grounds, and to relate to his companions accurate things. He conceals

classem in convexo nemorum, sub cavatâ rupe clausam
his fleet in the convex space of the woods, under a hollow rock inclosed

circum arboribus atque horrentibus umbris: Ipse graditur
around with trees and with dismal shades: He walks forth

comitatus Achate uno, crispans manu bina hastilia lato
accompanied by Achates alone, brandishing in his hand two javelins of broad

ferro: cui mater obvia tulit sese mediâ
iron to whom his mother in the way has presented herself in the midst of the

sylvâ, gerens os que habitum virginis, et arma
woods, bearing the countenance and the garb of a virgin, and the arms of

Spartanæ virginis; vel qualis Threïssa Harpalyce, fatigat
a Spartan virgin; or like as the Thracian Harpalyce, wearies

equos que fugâ prævertitur volucrem Eurum: Namque
her horses and in speed outstrips the swift East wind: For

venatrix, suspenderat humeris habilem arcum de
as a huntress, she had hung from her shoulders a commodious bow according to

more, que dederat ventis diffundere comam, nuda
custom, and had permitted the winds to disturb her hair, naked to the

genu, collecta fluentes sinus, nodo. Ac prior
knee, girded as to the flowing folds of her garment, with a knot. And first

inquit, Heus, juvenes monstrate, si vidistis quam
she says, So ho, youths declare to me, if you have seen any one

mearum sororum forte hic, errantem, succinctam pharetrâ
of my sisters by chance here, wandering, girded with a quiver

et tegmine maculosæ lyncis, aut clamore, prementem
and with the skin of a spotted lynx, or with an outcry, urging

cursum spumantis apri. Sic Venus; at filius Veneris
the chase of a foaming boar. Thus Venus spoke; but the son of Venus

contra, orsus sic: nulla tuarum sororum
on the other hand, has begun to speak thus: no one of thy sisters has been

audita neque visa mihi. O virgo, quam memorem te?
heard nor seen by me. O virgin, whom may I name thee?

namque haud tibi mortalis vultus, nec vox sonat
for there is not to thee a human countenance, nor does thy voice sound

hominem. O dea certe!
like that of a human being. O a goddess surely!

An soror Phœbi, an una sanguinis Nympharum?
Art thou the sister of Phœbus, or one of the blood of the nymphs?

Quæcunque sis felix, que leves nostrum labo-
Whoever you are, may you be favourable to us, and ease our solicitude;

rem; et doceas sub quo cœlo, in quibus oris orbis
and inform us under what climate, on what regions of the globe

tandem jactemur: erramus ignari que hominum que lo-
at length we may be thrown: we wander ignorant both of the men and of the

corum, acti huc vento et vastis fluctibus. Multa hostia
places, driven hither by the wind and by the vast billows. So many a victim

cadet tibi ante aras nostrâ dextrâ. Tunc Venus:
shall fall for thee before thy altars by our right hand. Then Venus answered:

haud equidem dignor me tali honore. Mos est
not indeed do I think myself worthy of such honour. The custom is

Tyriis virginibus gestare pharetram, que vincire suras
for the Tyrian virgins to carry a quiver, and to bind the legs

altè purpureo cothurno. Vides Punica regna Tyrios,
high with a purple buskin. You see Carthaginian dominions, the Tyrians,

et urbem Agenoris; sed fines Libyci, genus intracta-
and the city of Agenor; but the territories *are* Lybian, a people fierce

bile bello. Dido regit imperium, profecta Tyriâ urbe,
in war. Dido rules the empire, having come from a Tyrian city,

fugiens germanum: injuria est longa, longæ ambages:
escaping *her* brother; the injury is long, long *are* the circumstances:

sed sequar summa fastigia rerum. Sichæus erat conjux
but I will trace chief points · of affairs. Sichæus was the husband

huic, ditissimus Phœnicum agri, et dilectus magno
to her, the richest of the Phœnicians in land, and beloved with the great affec

amore miseræ; cui pater dederat intactam, que
tion of the miserable *Dido*; to whom *her* father had given *her* undefiled, and

jugârat primis ominibus: sed Pygmalion germanus
had married *her* with the first omens: but Pygmalion · *her* brother

habebat regna Tyri, immanior scelere ante omnes alios:
possessed the dominions of Tyre, more cruel in wickedness before all others:

Inter quos medius furor venit. Ille impius, atque cæcus
Between whom a common hatred has come. He wicked, and blind

amore auri, clam superat ferro Sichæum, incau-
with the love of gold, privately overcomes with the sword Sichæus, unwary

tum ante aras, securus amorum germanæ; que diu
before the altars, regardless of the affections of *his* sister; and long

celavit factum; et malus simulans multa, lusit
has concealed the deed; and wicked, dissembling many *things*, has deluded

ægram amantem vanâ spe. Sed imago ipsa inhu-
the sick lover with a vain hope. But the apparition itself of her un-

mati conjugis venit in somnis, attollens pallida ora
buried husband has come to her in *her* sleep, · raising up *his* pale visage

miris modis: nudavit crudeles aras, que pectora tra-
in a wonderful form; he has laid open the cruel altars, and his breast thrust

jecta ferro, que retexit omne cœcum scelus
through with a sword, and has revealed · all the secret wickedness of the

domûs. Tum suadet celerare fugam que excedere
family. Then he counsels *her* to hasten *her* flight and to depart from her

patriâ; que recludit veteres thesauros tellure, auxilium
native country; and reveals *to her* ancient treasures *in* the earth, *as* an aid

viæ, ignotum pondus argenti et auri. Dido commota
of *her* journey, an unknown mass of silver and gold. Dido roused

his parabat fugam que socios. Conveniunt quibus
by these *things*, prepared *her* flight and companions. *All* assemble to whom

erat crudele odium aut acer metus tyranni: corripiunt
there was a mortal hatred or a sharp fear of the tyrant: they seize

naves quæ fortè paratæ, que onerant auro. Opes
ships which by chance *were* ready, and load *them* with gold. The riches

avari Pygmalionis portantur pelago: femina
of the covetous Pygmalion are carried away on the sea: a woman *was* the

dux facti. Devenêre locos, ubi nunc cernes ingentia
leader of the deed. They have come to places, where now you will see the huge

mœnia, que surgentem arcem novæ Carthaginis: que
walls, and the rising tower of new Carthage; and have

mercati solum Byrsam de nomine facti, quantum
purchased ground called Byrsa from the name of the deed, as much as they

possent circumdare taurino tergo. Sed qui tandem vos?
might be able to enclose with a bull's hide. But who at length are you?

aut a quibus oris venistis? ve quò tenetis iter? Ille
or from what coasts have you come? or whither do you direct your way? He

suspirans que trahens vocem ab imo pectore,
sighing and drawing his voice from the bottom of his breast, answered

talibus quærenti: O Dea, si repetens ab primâ ori-
with such words to her asking: O goddess, if rehearsing from the first begin-

gine pergam, et vacet audire annales nostro-
ning I shall pursue, and there may be leisure to thee to hear the annals of our

rum laborum, (Vesper componet diem, Olympo clauso
misfortunes; the evening star will close the day, heaven being shut up

ante.) Tempestas sua forte appulit
before my story will be finished. A tempest by its own adventure has driven

Libycis oris nos vectos per diversa æquora antiquâ
to the Libyan coasts us conveyed across divers seas from ancient

Trojâ, (si forte nomen Trojæ iit per vestras aures.) Sum
Troy, (if by chance the name of Troy has come to your ears.) I am

pius Æneas, qui veho mecum classe Penates raptos
pious Æneas, who carry with me in my fleet the household gods snatched

ex hoste, notus fama super æthera. Quæro Italiam patri-
from the enemy, known by fame above the skies. I seek Italy my native

am, et genus ab summo Jove. Conscendi Phrygium
country and my descent is from highest Jove. I have ascended the Phrygian

æquor bis denis navibus, Dea matre monstrante viam,
sea with twice ten ships, my goddess mother showing to me the way,

secutus fata data: septem convulsæ undis que
having followed the decrees given to me: seven shattered by the billows and

Euro vix supersunt. Ipse ignotus, egens, peragro
by the east wind scarcely remain. I myself unknown, poor, wander over

deserta Libyæ; pulsus Europâ atque Asiâ. Venus nec
the deserts of Africa; banished from Europe and Asia. Venus not even

passa querentem plura, sic interfata est medio
suffering him complaining to say more, thus interrupted him in the midst of

dolore: quisquis es, carpis vitales auras, credo haud
his grief: whoever thou art, thou enjoyest the vital breath, I believe not

invisus cœlestibus, qui adveneris Tyriam urbem. Perge
odious to the heavenly gods, who mayst have come to a Tyrian city. Proceed

modò, atque prefer te hinc ad limina reginæ: namque nun-
now, and convey thee hence to the house of the queen: for I de-

tio tibi socios reduces que classem has been
clare to thee that thy companions are returned again, and the fleet has been

relatam, et actam in tutum, Aquilonibus versis; ni
brought back, and driven into a safe place, the north winds being changed; unless

parentes vani docuere augurium frustra. Aspice bis
my parents vain have taught me divination to no purpose. See these twice

senos cycnos lætantes agmine, quos ales Jovis lapsa
six swans rejoicing in a flock, which the bird of Jove gliding from

ætheriâ plagâ, turbabat aperto cœlo; nunc videntur aut
the etherial region, chased in the open air; now they seem either to

capere terras longo ordine, aut despectare jam captas:
choose the earth in a long train, or to look down upon it now chosen:

ut illi reduces ludunt stridentibus alis et cinxere
as they returned safe sport with clapping wings, and have flown around the

polum cœtu, que dedere cantus; haud aliter que
heaven in a flock, and have given forth their songs; not otherwise both

tuæ puppes, que pubes tuorum aut tenet portum, aut
thy ships, and the youth of thy friends either possess the harbour, or

subit ostia pleno velo. Perge modò, et dirige
are entering the mouth with full sail. Proceed now, and direct thy

gressum quâ via ducit te. Dixit, et avertens
step whither the way conducts thee. She has said, and turning away, has

refulsit rosea cervice, que ambrosiæ comæ spiravere
shone bright with her rosy neck, and her ambrosial hair has breathed

divinum odorem vertice: vestis defluxit ad imos
divine fragrance from her head: her robe hath flowed to the bottom of

pedes, et incessu patuit vera Dea. Ille ubi
her feet, and by her gait she has been manifested a real goddess. He, when he

agnovit matrem, secutus est fugientem tali voce: quid
has recognized his mother, has pursued her fleeing with such speech: why

tu quoquê, crudelis toties, ludis natum falsis imaginibus?
dost thou too cruel so often, mock thy son with deceitful images?

cur non datur jungere dextram dextræ, ac audire
why is it not permitted to me to join my right hand to thy right hand, and to hear

et reddere veras voces? incusat talibus que tendit
and to return real words? he complains with such words and directs his

gressum ad mœnia. At Venus sepsit gradientes obscuro
step to the town. But Venus has covered them going with obscure

aëre, et Dea circumfudit multo amictu nebulæ,
air, and the goddess has encompassed them with a thick covering of mist,

ne quis posset cernere eos, neu quis con-
that not any one might be able to see them, nor any might be able to

tingere, vel moliri moram, aut poscere causas veniendi.
touch them or cause a delay, or demand the reasons of their coming.

Ipsa abit sublimis Paphum, que læta revisit suas sedes; ubi
She departs majestic to Paphos, and joyful revisits her own seats; where

templum illi, que centum aræ calent Sabæo thure, que
a temple is to her, and an hundred altars are hot with Sabean incense, and

halant recentibus sertis. Interea corripuere
exhale with fresh garlands. In the mean while they have hastened their

praesaepe, in n. hive.

viam, quà semita monstrat: jamque ascendebant collem, qui
way, whither the path   directs: and now they ascended the hill, which

plurimus imminet urbi, que desuper aspectat adversas arces.
very large hangs over the city, and from above   faces   the opposite towers.

Æneas miratur molém,   quondam magalia:
Æneas   admires   the pile _of buildings, where_ formerly   cottages _stood;_

miratur portas que strepitum et strata viarum.
ne admires the gates and the bustle and the causeways.   The Tyrians

Tyrii
ardentes instant: pars ducere muros, que moliri arcem,
earnest   urge _the work;_ a part to extend the walls, and   erect   a tower

et subvolvere saxa manibus;   pars optare locum tecto,
and   roll up   stones with their hands; a part to prepare a place for a building,

et concludere sulco.   Legunt   jura que magistra-
and enclose _it_ with a trench. They choose _sites_ for _their_ courts and   offices

tus, que sanctum senatum. Hic alii effodiunt portus: hic alii
and the sacred senate house. Here some   dig   harbors; there others are

locant alta fundamenta theatris;   que excidunt rupibus
laying the deep foundations for theatres; and   cut out   from the rocks

immanes columnas, alta   decora   futuris scenis.   Qualis
huge   columns, the lofty decorations for future scenes.   Such

labor exercet apes nova æstate per florea rura, sub
toil   employs bees _in_ the new summer through the flowery fields, under

sole cum educunt adultos foetus   gentis, aut cum
the sun when they lead forth the full grown young of _their_ race, or when

stipant liquentia mella, et distendunt cellas dulci
they lay up   their liquid honey, and   fill   the combs with sweet

nectare, aut accipiunt onera venientum,   aut facto
nectar,   or   receive   the burdens of _those_ coming,   or in a formed

agmine arcent à praesepibus fucos ignavum pecus: opus
band   drive away from _their_ hives   the drones an idle   flock: the work

fervet, fragrantia mella redolent thymo. O fortunati, ait
goes on busily, the fragrant honey casts a smell of thyme. O happy _ye,_ says

Æneas, quorum moenia jam surgunt! et suspicit fastigia
Æneas,   whose   walls now   arise! and _he_ surveys the heights of the

urbis. Infert se per medios,   septus nebulâ,
city.   He conveys himself through the midst _of them,_ covered with a cloud,

mirabile dictu! que miscet viris neque cernitur ulli.
wonderful to be told! and mingles with the men nor   is seen by any.

Lucus fuit in mediâ urbe, lætissimus umbrâ; quo
A grove has been in the midst of the city, most pleasant _for its_ shade; _in_ which

loco Poeni   jactati   undis   et turbine primùm
place the Carthagenians driven   by the waves and by the wind   first

effodere caput   acris equi, signum quod regia Juno
dug up   the head of a courageous horse, an omen which royal   Juno

monstrârat; nam sic   gentem fore egregiam
had shown;   for   thus _she signified_ that the nation would be   eminent

bello, et facilem victu per secula.   Hic Sidonia   Dido
in war, and easy to conquer through ages.   Here Sidonian   Dido

Poeni orum n. Carthaginians, Africans

còndebat Junoni ingens templum, opulentum donis et
built   to Juno a huge temple,   enriched   with gifts and with

numine   Divæ: cui   ærea   limina surgebant
the presence of the goddess: to which the brazen thresholds   rose

gradibus, que trabes nexæ   ære,   cardo stridebat
in steps,   and the beams were bound with brass, the hinge creaked with

ahenis foribus. In hoc luco nova res oblata primùm leniit
brazen doors. In this grove a new thing presented first has allayed

timorem: hic Æneas primùm ausus sperare salutem et
their fear: here Æneas first has dared to hope for safety and

meliùs confidère afflictis rebus: namque dum lustrat singula
better to trust to his afflicted affairs: for   while he surveys each

sub ingenti templo opperiens reginam; dum miratur
thing in the great temple waiting for the queen;   while he admires

quæ sit   fortuna urbi, que manus artificum que laborem
what may be the fortune to the city, and the hands of the artists and the labour

operùm inter se; videt Iliacas pugnas ex ordine, que bella
of the works mutually; he sees the Trojan battles in order, and the wars

jam vulgata famâ per totum orbém;   Atridas que
now published by fame through the whole world; he sees the sons of Atreus and

Priamum, et Achillem sævum ambobus. Constitit et lacry-
Priamus,   and Achilles unmerciful to both.   He has stood and weep-

mans inquit: Achate, quis locus jam, quæ regio in terris
ing   says: O Achates; what place now, what country on the earth

non plena nostri laboris? en Priamus, etiam hic sua præ-
is not full of our disaster! Behold Priamus, even here his own re-

mia sunt laudi: lacrymæ rerum sunt, et mortalia tangunt
wards are for praise: tears of misfortunes are here, and mortal affairs move

mentem. Solve metus: hæc fama feret tibi aliquam sa-
the mind. Dismiss your fears: this fame will bring to thee · some re-

lutem. Sic ait atque pascit animum inani picturâ, ge-
lief.   Thus he says; and he feeds his mind with an empty picture, lament-

mens multa,   que humectat vultum largo flumine.
ing many things, and   wets his face with a large flood of tears.

Namque videbat, uti Graii bellantes circum Pergama fuge-
For he saw, that the Greeks fighting around Troy would

rent hâc, Trojana juventus premèret;   hâc
flee on this part: whilst the Trojan youth would chase them, on that part

Phryges;   cristatus Achilles instaret   curru.
the Trojan would flee; while crested Achilles would pursue them in his chariot.

Nec procul hinc lacrymans agnoscit tentoria Rhesi
Not far off hence weeping he recognizes the tents of Rhesus from their

niveis   velis; quæ prodita primo somno cruentus
snow white vails; which betrayed in the first night the bloody son of

Tydides vastabat multâ cæde, que avertit   ardentes
Tydeus plundered with great slaughter, and has driven away his mettlesome

equos in   castra, priusquam gustassent   pabula
steeds into the Grecian camp, before they had tasted the pasture of

Trojæ, que bibissent Xanthum. (Aliâ parte) Troilus
Troy, and had drank of Xanthus. *In another part of the temple* Troilus

fugiens, armis amissis, infelix puer atque impar congressus
fleeing, *his* arms being lost, unhappy youth and unequal encountering

Achilli! fertur equis, que resupinus hæret inani
Achilles! is dragged by *his* horses, and supine hangs from the empty

curru, tenens lora tamen: que cervix que comæ huic
chariot, holding the reins notwithstanding: both the neck and the hair to him

trahuntur per terram, et pulvis inscribitur versâ hastâ
are drawn along the ground, and the dust is scrawled by the inverted spear

Intereâ Iliades, (passis crinibus, ibant ad
In the meantime the Trojan women, with dishevelled hair, went t

templum Palladis non æquæ, que ferebant peplum sup-
the temple of Pallas not impartial *to them,* and carried the robe hum-

pliciter tristes, et tunsæ pectora palmis. Diva
bly sad, and beaten *as to* their breasts with their hands. The goddess

aversa tenebat oculos fixos solo. Achilles ter raptaverat
unfavourable kept *her* eyes fixed on the ground. Achilles thrice had dragged

Hectora circum Iliacos mûros, que vendebat exanimum
Hector around the Trojan walls, and was selling the breathless

corpus auro. Tum vero dat ingentem gemitum ab imo
body for gold. Then indeed *he* gives a great groan from the bottom

pectore, (ut conspexit spolia, ut currus, que ut
of *his* breast, as *he* has seen the spoils, as *he has seen* the chariot, and as

corpus ipsum amici, que Priamum tendentem inermes
the body itself of *his* friend, and Priam stretching out *his* feeble

manus. Agnovit se quoque permixtum Achivis principibus,
hands. He has recognized himself also mingled with the Grecian commanders

que Eoas acies, et arma nigri Memnonis.
and the eastern armies, and the arms of swarthy Memnon.

Penthesilea furens ducit agmina Amazonidum lunatis
Penthesilea furious leads on *her* bands of Amazons with horned

peltis, que ardet in mediis millibus, subnectens aurea
shields, and rages in the midst of thousands, buckling *her* golden

cingula exertæ mammæ, bellatrix, que virgo audet con-
girdle under *her* bare breast, warlike, and a virgin dares to fight

currere viris. Dum hæc miranda videntur Dardanio
with men. While these wonderful *things* are seen by Trojan

Æneæ, dum stupet, que hæret defixus in uno ob-
Æneas, whilst he is astonished, and continues fixed with one intent pos

tutu; regina Dido pulcherrima formâ, incessit ad
ture of the eyes; queen Dido most beautiful in appearance, has come to the

templum, magnâ catervâ juvenum stipante. Qualis Dian
temple, a great multitude of youth attending. Like as Dian

in ripis Eurotæ, aut per juga Cynthi exercet choros,
on the banks of Eurotas or on the top of Cynthus leads the dances,

quam mille Oreades secutæ, glomerantur hinc
whom a thousand mountain nymphs having followed, are gathered on this part

atque hinc: illa fert pharetram humero que gradiens, super-
and that: she carries *her* quiver on *her* shoulder, and walking, appears

eminet omnes Deas: gaudia pertentant tacitum pectus
above all the goddesses: joys pass through the silent breast of

Latonæ. Talis erat Dido, læta ferebat se talem per medios,
Latona. Such was Dido, joyful she carried herself such in the midst,

instans operi, que futuris regnis. Tum resedit
intent upon the work, and *her* future dominions. Then she has sat down

foribus divæ mediâ testudine templi, septa
at the gates of the goddess in the midst of the arch of the temple, surrounded

armis que subnixa alté solio. Dabat jura que leges
with arms and raised up high on a throne. She dispensed justice and laws

viris, que æquabat laborem operum justis partibus
to the men, and equalized the labour of the works in proportionate parts,

aut trahebat sorte: cum Æneas subitô videt Anthea que
or drew *it* by lot: when Æneas suddenly sees Antheus and

Sergestum, que fortem Cloanthum que alios Teucrorum ac-
Sergestus, and the brave Cloanthus and others of the Trojans ad-

cedere magno concursu; quos ater turbo dispulerat æquore,
vance with a great concourse; whom a black storm had scattered on the sea,

que avexerat oras penitus alias. Ipse simul obstu-
and had carried to shores entirely different. He at the same time has been

puit, simul Achates perculsus que lætitiâ que
astonished, and at the same time Achates *has been* smitten both with joy and

metu; avidi ardebant conjùngere dextras; sed incognita
fear; eager they passionately desired to join their right hands; but the strange

res turbat animos. Dissimulant et amicti cavâ nube,
affair disturbs their minds. They dissemble and covered with a hollow cloud,

speculantur quæ fortuna viris; quo litore linquant
watch what *may* be the fortune to the men; on what coast they may

classem, quid veniant; nam lecti cunctis navibus
leave *their* fleet, why they may come; for chosen from all the ships

ibant orantes veniam, et petebant templum clamore.
they came soliciting favour, and were making to the temple with a clamour.

Postquam introgressi et copia data fandi coram,
After that *they have* entered and liberty *has been* given of speaking openly,

Ilioneus maximus, sic cœpit placidô pectore; O regina!
Ilioneus the greatest, thus has begun with a calm mind; O queen!

cui Jupiter dedit condere novam urbem, que frœnare
to whom Jupiter has given to build a new city, and to curb

superbas gentes justitiâ: miseri Tröes vecti omnia
proud nations with justice: *we* miserable Trojans carried *through* all

maria ventis oramus te, prohibe infandos ignes à navibus
seas by the winds intreat thee, avert the horrible flames from *our* ships

parce pio generi, et propiùs aspice nostras res. Nos
spare a pious race, and more favourably regard our affairs. We

non venimus aut populare Libycos Penates ferro,
have not come either to destroy the Libyan household gods with the sword.

aut vertere prædas raptas ad litora. Ea vis non
or   to turn the spoils seized to the shores. This violence is not   in our

animo, nec tanta superbia victis.   Est locus,
mind,   nor is so great insolence to the conquered.   There is a place, the

Graii dicunt Hesperiam cognomine: antiqua terra, potens
Greeks   call it   Hesperia   by name: an ancient land,   powerful

armis atque ubere   glebæ: Oenotrii viri   coluere;
in war   and in the fruitfulness of its soil: Oenotrian men   have inhabited it;

nunc fama   minores   dixisse   gentem Italiam, de
now   fame is that their posterity   have called the nation Italy,   from

nomine ducis.   Huc fuit cursus; cum subito nim-
the name of their leader.   Hither has been our course; when suddenly boister-

bosus Orion assurgens fluctu   tulit   in cœca vada
ous Orion   rising   from the ocean hath borne us upon the hidden shelves

que Austris   penitus procacibus dispulit   que per
and the south winds being altogether obstinate have dispersed us both over the

invia saxa, salo superante: pauci, adnavimus huc
impassable rocks, the sea overcoming us: we, a few, have swum   hither   to

vestris oris.   Quod genus hominum hoc? ve quæ patria, tam
your   coasts.   What race of   men   is this? or what country,   so

barbara, permittit hunc morem? prohibemur hospitio
savage,   allows   this custom? we are debarred from the refuge of

arenæ: cient bella que vetant   consistere primâ terrâ.
the shore: they raise wars and forbid that we should remain on the first land.

Si temnitis humanum genus et mortalia arma, at sperate
If you despise   the human   race and   mortal arms, but expect that

Deos memores fandi atque nefandi. Æneas erat rex nobis,
the gods are mindful of right and   wrong. Æneas   was king to us,

quo alter justior pietate nec fuit, nec major bello et
than whom another more just for his piety has not been, nor greater in war and

armis, quem virum, si fata servant, si vescitur æthe-
arms,   which man, if the fates may preserve, if he lives upon the ethe-

reâ aurâ, neque adhuc occubat crudelibus umbris: metus
real air,   nor   as yet is dead among the cruel   shades: fear is

non,   nec pœniteat te priorem certasse   officio.
not to us,   nor may it repent thee   first   to have vied with him in kindness.

Sunt urbes   Siculis regionibus, que arma que clarus
There are cities to us in the Sicilan regions,   and arms   and the renowned

Acestes à Trojano sanguine. Liceat   subdu-
Acestes is from Trojan   blood.   May it be lawful for us to draw on

cere classem quassatam ventis, et aptare trabes sylvis
shore our fleet   shattered by the winds, and to fit   planks from the woods

et stringere remos. Si datur tendere Italiam, sociis et
and to cut   oars.   If it is given to us to go to Italy, our companions and

rege recepto, ut læti   petamus Italiam que Latium; sin
king being recovered, that joyful we may make for Italy   and Latium;   but

salus absumpta et pontus Libyæ habet te, optime
if our safety may be destroyed and the sea of Libya possesse thee.   O best

pater Teucrûm, nec jam spes Iüli restat; at saitem peta-
father of the Trojans, nor now the hope of Iulus remains; but at least that we

mus freta Sicaniæ que paratas sedes, unde ad-
may go to the straits of Sicily and the prepared abodes, from whence we have

vecti huc, que regem Acesten. Ilioneus talibus;
been carried hither, and to king Acestes. Ilioneus entreated with such

simul cuncti Dardanidæ fremebant
words; at the same time all the Trojans express their approbation with

ore. Tum Dido demissa vultum profatur
their mouth. Then Dido downcast as to her countenance speaks

breviter: Teucri! solvite metum corde, secludite curas
briefly: O Trojans! banish fear from your heart, drive away your cares

Dura res et novitas regni cogunt me molir
My difficult circumstances and the infancy of my kingdom compel me to do

talia, et tueri latè fines. Quis nesciat genus
such things, and to protect far and wide my borders. Who knows not the race

Æneadûm? quis urbem Trojæ, que virtutes que
of the Trojans? who knows not the city of Troy, and their merits and

viros, et incendia tanti belli? Pœni non gestamus
the men and the flames of so great war? We Carthagenians do not carry

pectora adeò obtusa! nec Sol jungit equos tam aversus ab
hearts so unfeeling! nor has the sun joined his steeds so remote from

Tyriâ urbe. Seu vos optatis magnam Hesperiam que
the Tyrian city. Whether you choose the great Hesperia and

regem Acesten: dimittam tutos auxilio, que juvabo
king Acestes: I will dismiss you safe with assistance, and aid you with my

opibus. Et vultis considere pariter mecum his regnis?
wealth. And are you willing to settle equally with me in these dominions?

quam urbem condo, est vestra; subducite naves: Tros
The city, which city I build, is yours; bring ashore your ships: Trojan

que Tyrius agetur mihi nullo discrimine. Atque utinam
and Tyrian shall be treated by me with no difference. And O that

Æneas rex ipse compulsus eodem Noto afforet! Equidem
Æneas your king himself driven by the same wind might be present! Truly

dimittam certos per litora, et jubebo lustrare ex-
I will send trusty men along the shores, and I will order them to search the re-

trema Libyæ, si ejectus errat quibus sylvis aut urbibus.
motest parts of Libya, if cast out he wanders in any woods or cities.

Et fortis Achates et pater Æneas affecti animum
Both brave Achates and father Æneas encouraged as to their mind

his dictis, jamdudum ardebant erumpere nubem:
with these words, a long time desired to break the cloud:

Achates prior compellat Æneam: nate Deâ, quæ
Achates first addresses Æneas: O thou, born of a goddess, what

sententia nunc surgit animo? Vides omnia tuta,
purpose now arises in your mind? You see all things safe,

classem que socios receptos. Unus abest, quem ipsi
your fleet and companions recovered. One is absent, whom we ourselves

vidimus submersum in medio fluctu: cætera respondent
have seen sunk in the midst of the ocean: other *things* agree

dictis matris.
to the words of *your* mother.

Vix fatus erat ea, cum repente circumfusa nubes
Scarcely had he said those *things* when suddenly the circumambient cloud

scindit se, et purgat in apertum æthera. Æneas restitit
divides itself, and clears into open air. Æneas has stood

que refulsit in clarâ luce, similis Deo os oris
and has shone bright in clear light, like to a god *as to his* countenance

que humeros: namque genitrix ipsa afflârat nato
and shoulders: for his mother herself had breathed on her son

decoram cæsariem que purpureum lumen juventæ, et
graceful hair and the glowing light of youth, and

oculis lætos honores. Decus, quale manus addunt
on his eyes lively beauty. *Such* beauty, as the hands give

ebori, aut ubi argentum, ve Parius lapis circumdatur flavo
to ivory, or where silver, or Parian marble is inclosed with yellow

auro. Tum sic alloquitur reginam, que repentê improvisus
gold. Then thus he addresses the queen, and suddenly unexpected

cunctis ait: adsum coram Troïus Æneas, quem quæritis,
by all says: I am present openly, Trojan Æneas, whom you seek,

ereptus ab Libycis undis. O sola miserata infandos
snatched from the Libyan waves. O *thou* alone having pitied the unutterable

labores Trojæ! quæ urbe, domo socias nos reliquias
calamities of Troy! who, in *thy* city, *and* in *thy* house associatest us the remains

Danaûm, jam exhaustos omnibus casibus que terræ que
of the Greeks, now wasted by all the perils both of land and

maris egenos omnium. Dido! est non nostræ opis, per-
sea wanting all *things*. O Dido! it is not of our power, to re-

solvere dignas grates: nec Dardaniæ gentis,
turn *to thee* suitable thanks: neither *is it of the power* of the Trojan nation, what-

quicquid ubique est, quæ sparsa per magnum
soever of this race every where is, which *has been* scattered over the great

orbem. Dî (si qua numina respectant pios si quid jus-
world. The gods (if any deities regard the pious if any *thing* of jus-

titiæ usquam est) et mens conscia sibi recti) ferant tibi
tice any where is) and a mind conscious to itself of virtue may bring to thee

digna præmia. Quæ tam læta sæcula tulerunt te? qui
suitable rewards. What so prosperous ages have produced thee? what

tanti parentes genuere talem? dum fluvii current in freta,
so worthy parents have begotten *thee* such? while rivers shall run into the seas,

dum umbræ lustrabunt convexa montibus, dum
while clouds shall move round the convex *tops* of the mountains, while

polûs pascet sidera: semper tuum honos que nomen que
heaven shall sustain the stars: always thy honour and name and

laudes manebunt, quæcunque terræ vocant me. Fatus sic
praises shall continue. whatever lands call me. Having said thus

petit amicum Ilionea   dextrâ, que Serestum   lævâ:
he takes his friend Ilioneus with *his* right hand, and Serestus   with his left:

Pòst   alios que fortem Gyan que fortem Cloanthum. Si-
Afterwards others both the brave Gyas, and the brave Cloanthus.   Sido-

donia Dido obstupuit primò aspectu,   deinde tanto
nian, Dido has been astonished first at the appearance, then at so great

casu viri,   et sic locuta est   ore: nate
calamity of the man, and thus has spoken with *her* mouth: O thou born of

Dea,   quis casus insequitur te per   tanta pericula? quæ
a goddess, what fate   pursues   thee through so great adventures? what

vis applicat te   immanibus oris? Túne ille Æneas quem
power brings   thee to *these* barbarous coasts? *Art* thou that Æneas   whom

alma Venus genuit   Dardanio Anchisæ ad undam Phry-
fair   Venus has brought forth to Trojan   Anchises by the water of Phry-

gii Simoëntis? atque equidem memini Teucrum   venire
gian   Simois? and   indeed   I remember that Teucer   came to

Sidona, expulsum   patriis finibus, petentem nova regna
Sidon,   expelled from *his* native territories,   seeking   new dominions

auxilio Beli. Tum genitor Belus vastabat opimam Cyprum,
by the aid of Belus.   Then *my* father Belus destroyed rich   Cyprus.

et victor tenebat ditiône.   Casus Trojanæ urbis
and a conqueror ruled *it* by his authority)   The ruins of the Trojan city *have been*

cognitus mihi jam ex illo tempore, que tuum nomen,   que
known   to me   now from that   time,   and thy   name,   and the

Pelasgi reges. Hostis ipse ferebat Teucros   insigni
Grecian   kings.   The enemy himself extolled the Trojans with distinguished

laude, que volebat se ortum   à antiqua stirpe Teucro-
praise,   and was pleased that he had sprung from the ancient race of the Tro

rum. Quare agite O juvenes! succedite nostris tectis!
jans.   Wherefore come on O youths!   enter   our   houses

similis fortuna voluit   me quoque jactatam per multos la-
a like   fortune has chosen *that* I   also   tossed   through many dis

bores, demum consistere hâc terrâ. Non ignara   mali,
tresses,   at length should settle in this land.   *I* not ignorant of misfortune,

disco succurere miseris. Sic memorat,   simul ducit
know *how* to succor the distressed.   Thus *she* says,   at the same time *she* leads

Ænean in regia tecta: simul indicit honorem
Æneas   into the royal house: at the same time she appoints a sacrifice in the

templis Divûm. Intereâ nec minús mittit munera
temples of the gods.   In the mean time not   less *she* sends   presents *to his*

sociis   ad litora, viginti tauros, centum horrentia terga
companions to the shores,   twenty   bulls,   one hundred rough   bodies

magnorum suum, centum pingues agnos cum matribus, que
of great   swine, an hundred   fat   lambs   with the dams,   and

lætitiam Dei.   At interior   domus splendida
the joy of the god *Bacchus*.   But the inner *part* of the house   magnificent

instruitur regali. luxu, que parant convivia
is furnished with regal splendor,   and they prepare banquets   in the

[handwritten top margin: verso 1, handle, wield — with mente or pectore = revolve, meditate devise, consider. bilinguis is a — double tongued — fig, deceitful treacherous]

mediis tectis.   vestes   laboratæ arte que superbo
midst of the house. *Here are* garments wrought with art and rich

ostro: ingens argentum mensis, que fortia facta patrum
purple: massy plate *is* on the tables, and the brave deeds of *her* fathers

cœlata in auro, series rerum longissima ducta per
embossed in gold, a series of exploits of the longest extent continued through

tot viros ab origine antiquæ gentis. Æneas, (enim
so many men from the founder of the ancient race. Æneas, (for

patrius amor neque passus mentem consistere) præmitt t
paternal love *has* not suffered *his* mind to be at rest) sends befo e

Achaten rapidum ad naves, ut ferat hæc Ascanio,
Achates swift to the ships, *that* he may report these *things* to Ascanius,

que ducat ipsum ad mœnia. Omnis cura chari parentis
and conduct him to the city. All the care of the fond parent

stat in Ascanio. Præterea jubet ferre munera erepta
is placed in Ascanius. Besides he orders *him* to bring the presents rescued

Iliacis ruinis, pallam rigentem signis que auro, et
from the Trojan ruins, a robe stiff with figures and gold, and

velamen circumtextum croceo acantho: ornatus Argi-
a veil woven around with yellow brank-ursine: the ornaments of Gre-

væ Helenæ quos illa extulerat Mycenis: cum peteret
cian Helen which she has brought from Mycenæ: when she might be going

Pergama que inconcessos Hymenæos, mirabile donum
to Troy and to her unlawful nuptial rites, the wonderful gift of *her*

matris Ledæ. Præterea sceptrum quod Ilione
mother Leda. Besides *he orders them to bring* the sceptre which Ilione

maxima natarum Priami olim gesserat, et monile collo
the eldest of the daughters of Priam formerly had born, and a necklace for the neck

baccatum et coronam duplicem gemmis que auro.
set in pearls and a crown double with gems and gold.

Celerans hæc Achates tendebat iter ad naves. At Cy
Hastening these *things* Achates directed *his* way to the ships. But Vi

therea versat novas artes, nova consilia pectore: ut Cupido
nus resolves new plots *and* new designs in *her* breast: that Cupid

mutatus faciem et ora veniat pro dulci
changed *as to his* appearance and countenance may come instead of sweet

Ascanio, que donis incendat furentem reginam, atque
Ascanius, and with the gifts inflame the amorous queen, and

impliceat ignem ossibus. Quippe timet ambiguam domum
enwrap the fire in her bones. For she dreads the changeable race

que bilingues Tyrios: atrox Juno urit, et cura
and the double-tongued Tyrians: cruel Juno vexes *her*, and *her* anxiety

recursat sub noctem. Ergo affatur aligerum Amorem
returns in the night. Therefore she addresses winged love

his dictis: Nate meæ vires, mea magna potentia; nate
with these words: O son my strength, my great power; O son

qui solus temnis Typhoëa tela summi patris: confugio
who alone despisest the Typhæan thunderbolts of the supreme father: I fly

[handwritten bottom margin: celero 1 to speed, hasten. muto 1 to change position, to exchange something for something else]

ad te et supplex posco tua numina. nota
to thee and suppliant implore thy deity. *These things have been* known

tibi ut tuus frater Æneas jactetur pelago circum omnia
to thee that thy brother Æneas may be tossed on the sea about all

litora, odiis iniquæ Junonis: et sæpe doluisti nostro
shores, by the malice of partial Juno: and often thou hast grieved in my

dolore. Phœnissa Dido tenet hunc, que moratur blandis
grief. Phœnissian Dido entertains him, and detains *him* with pleasant

vocibus: et vereor quò Junonia hospitia vertant se:
words: and I fear whither the Junonian hospitality may turn itself: she will

haud cessabit tanto cardine rerum. Quocircà meditor
not be idle on so great a juncture of affairs. Wherefore I contrive

ante capere reginam dolis, et cingere flammâ ne-
before to ensnare the queen with wiles, and to beset *her* with a flame that she

mutet se quo numine, sed teneatur mecum
may not change herself by any divine impulse but *that* she may be held with me

magno amore Æneæ. Nunc accipe nostram mentem, quà
by the great love of Æneas. Now hear my advice, how

possis facere id, regius puer mea maxima cura, parat
you may be able to do that, the royal boy, my greatest care, prepares

ire ad Sidoniam urbem accitu chari genitoris, ferens
to go to the Sidonian city at the call of *his* beloved father, bearing

dona restantia pelago et flammis Trojæ. Ego recondam
presents remaining *from* the sea and the flames of Troy. I will hide

hunc sopitum somno super alta Cythera aut super Idalium
him lulled in sleep upon lofty Cythera or upon Idalium

sacratâ sede; ne quà possit scire dolos ve me-
in a sacred place; lest in any way he may be able to know the wiles or coming

dius occurrêre. Tu falle dolo illius faciem
between to interrupt *its success*. Thou counterfeit by delusion his face

unam noctem non ampliùs: et puer indue pueri notos
one night no longer: and a boy assume the boy's known

vultus: ut cùm Dido lætissima accipiet te gremio,
looks: that when Dido most joyful shall receive thee in *her* bosom,

inter regales mensas que laticem Lyæum, cùm dabit
amidst the royal tables and the liquor of Bacchus, when she shall give

amplexus atque figet dulcia oscula:
to thee her embraces and shall impress *upon thee* sweet kisses.

inspires occultum ignem que fallas veneno.
thou mayest inspire the secret flame and deceive *her* with the poison.

Amor paret dictis charæ genitricis et exuit
of love. The god of love obeys the commands of *his* dear mother and puts off

alas, et gaudens incedit gressu Iuli. At Venus irrigat
his wings, and rejoicing walks in the gait of Iulus, But Venus diffuses

placidam quietem per membra Ascanio, et Dea
gentle sleep through the limbs of Ascanius, and the goddess has

tollit fotum gremio in altos lucos Idaliæ, ubi mollis
removed him cherished in *her* bosom into the lofty groves of Idalia, where soft

amaracus aspirans complectitur illum floribus et dulci
majorum breathing encircles him with flowers and a pleasant

umbrâ. Jamque Cupido ibat parens dicto, et portabat
shade. And now Cupid went obeying the command, and carried

regia dona Tyriis, lætus Achate duce. Cùm ve-
the royal presents to the Tyrians, joyful in Achates his leader, When he has

nit regina jam composuit se superbis aulæis, que locavit
arrived, the queen now has set herself on rich tapestry, and has placed

mediam aureâ spondâ. Jam pater Æneas, que
herself in the middle on a golden couch. Now father Æneas, and

jam Trojana juventus conveniunt que discumbitur super
now the Trojan youth assemble and they sit down upon

ostro strato. Famuli dant lymphas manibus, que expe-
the purple couch. The servants give water for their hands, and serve

diunt cererem canistris, que ferunt mantilia villis tonsis.
bread in baskets, and bring towels the naps being shorn.

Intus quinquaginta famulæ, quibus cura struere
Within are fifty maid servants, to whom was the care to prepare

penum longo ordine, et adolere Penates flammis:
the provisions in long order, and to perfume the household gods with flames:

centum aliæ, que totidem ministri pares ætate, qui
there were an hundred others, and as many men servants equal in age, who

onerent mensas dapibus et ponant pocula. Et necnon
may load the tables with food and may place the cups. And

Tyrii frequentes convenêre per læta limina jussi
the Tyrians numerous have assembled in the joyful house commanded

discumbere pictis toris. Mirantur dona Æneæ,
to lie down on the embroidered couches. They admire the presents of Æneas,

mirantur Iülum que flagrantes vultus Dei, que simulata
they admire Iulus and the glowing looks of the god, and his dissembled

verba, que pallam et velamen pictum croceo acantho.
words, and the mantle and the veil adorned with the yellow acanthus

Præcipuè infelix Phœnissa devota futuræ pesti
Especially the unhappy Dido devoted to the future distraction of love

nequit expleri mentem, que ardescit tuendo, et pariter
is unable to be satisfied as to her mind, and is inflamed by beholding, and equally

movetur puero que donis. Ille, ubi pependit complexu
is affected with the boy and the presents. He, when he has hung on the embrace

que collo Æneæ, implevit magnum amorem falsi genitoris,
and neck of Æneas, has satisfied the great affection of his false father

petit reginam: Hæc hæret oculis, hæc
advances to the queen: She is fixed upon him with her eyes, she is fixed on him

toto pectore et interdum Dido fovet gremio, inscia
with her whole soul and sometimes Dido fondles him in her bosom, not knowing

quantus Deus insideat miseræ. At ille memor
how great a God lies in wait for her miserable. But he mindful of his

Acidaliæ matris, paulatim incipit abolere Sichæum et tentat
Acidalian mother, by degrees begins to abolish Sichæus and tries

vivo amore prævertere animos jampridem resides que
by a living love to prepossess *her* affections long since disengaged and

corda desueta. Postquam prima quies epulis que
her heart unused *to love.* After the first cessation *is* from the feast, and

mensæ remotæ, statuunt magnos crateras et coronant
the tables *have been* removed, they place the great goblets and crown

vina. Strepitus fit tectis, que volutant vocem per
the wine. A noise is made in the house, and they roll their voice through

ampla atria: incensi lychni dependent aureis laquearibus,
the spacious halls: the lighted lamps hang down from the golden ceilings

et funalia vincunt noctem flammis. Hìc regina poposcit
and torches expel the darkness with flames. Here the queen has called for

pateram gravem gemmis que auro, que implevit mero,
a goblet heavy with gems and gold, and has filled *it* with wine,

quam Belus et omnes a Belo soliti. Tum
which Belus and all from Belus *have been* accustomed to *fill.* Then

silentia facta tectis: Jupiter (nam loquuntur te
silence *has been* made in the house: O Jove (for they say that thou

dare jura hospitibus) velis hunc diem esse lætum
hast given laws to hosts) mayest thou be willing that this day may be fortunate

que Tyriis que profectis Trojâ, que nostror
both to the Tyrians and *to those* having departed from Troy, and that our

minores meminisse hujus. Bacchus dator lætitiæ ad·
posterity should remember this *day.* May Bacchus the giver of joy be pre

sit, et bona Juno: et vos O Tyrii, faventes, celebrate cœtum
sent, and good Juno: and you O Tyrians, favoring, celebrate *this* meeting

Dixit, et libavit honorem laticum in mensam
She has said, and has poured out in sacrifice an oblation of liquor upon the table

que libato prima attigit tenus summo
and being offered first she has gently *touched* *it* only *with* the extreme part of

ore. Tum dedit Bitiæ increpitans: ille impige,
her mouth. Then she has given *it* to Bitias reproaching *him:* he quick

hausit spumantem pateram, et proluit se pleno auro,
has drained the foaming bowl, and bathed himself from the full gold

pòst alii proceres. Crinitus Iopas personat auratâ
afterwards the other nobles. Long haired Iopas sounds on *his* gilded

citharâ quæ maximus Atlas docuit: hic canit errantem
harp what the greatest Atlas has taught: he sings the wandering

Lunam que labores Solis, unde genus hominum
moon and labors of the sun, from whence arise the race of men

et pecudes, unde imber et ignes, Arcturum que
and flocks, from whence rain and lightnings, *he sings* Arcturus and

pluvias Hyadas, que geminos Triones, quid hyberni soles
the rainy Hyades, and the two Triones, why winter suns

properent tantùm tingere se Oceano, vel quæ mora
should hasten so much to touch themselves in the ocean, or what hindrance

obstet tardis noctibus. Tyrii ingeminant plausum, que
may oppose the slow nights. The Tyrians redouble the applause, and

Troes sequuntur. Et necnon infelix Dido trahebat noctem
the Trojans follow *them.* And also unhappy Dido drew out the night

vario sermone, que bibebat longum amorem rogitans multa
in various talk, and drank long love inquiring many

super Hectore; nunc quibus armis filius Auroræ
things about Hector; one while in what arms the son of Aurora

venisset, nunc, quales equi Diomeḍis, nunc,
might have come, another while of what sort *were* the horses of Diomede, now,

quantus Achilles. Immò hospes, age, inquit, et à
how great *was* Achilles. Nay, O guest, come on, she says, and from

prima origine dic nobis insidias Danaûm que casus
the first origin relate to us the wiles of the Greeks and the misfortunes

tuorum que tuos errores: nam jam septima æstas
of thy *friends* and thine own wanderings: for now the seventh summer

portat te errantem omnibus terris et fluctibus.
carries thee roving *on* all lands and seas.

THE ÆNEID.

BOOK SECOND.

Omnes conticuere que intenti tenebant ora. Inde
All have been silent and attentive held *their* countenances. Then

pater Æneas, sic orsus ab alto toro: O regina, jubes,
father Æneas, thus has begun from *his* lofty couch: O queen, you command

renovare infandum dolorem: ut Danai eruerint
me, to renew unutterable grief: how the Greeks may have overturned

Trojanas opes et regnum lamentabile; quæque
the Trojan powers and *their* kingdom to be deplored; both which *things*

miserrima ipse vidi, et quorum fui magna pars
most pitiable I myself have seen, and of which I have been a great part.

Quis Myrmidonum, ve Dolopum, aut miles duri
Who of the Myrmydons, or of the Dolopes, or *what* soldier of stern

Ulyssei temperet â lachrymis fando talia? et jam hu-
Ulysses can refrain from tears in relating such *things?* and now hu-

mida nox præcipitat cœlo que cadentia sidera suadent
mid night hastens down from the sky and the setting stars advise

somnos. Sed si tantus amor cognoscere nostros casus
sleep. But if so great love *is to you* to know our misfortunes

et breviter audire supremum laborem Trojæ; quanquam
and briefly to hear the last struggle of Troy; although

animus horret meminisse que refugit luctu,   incipiam.
my mind   dreads   to remember   and declines through grief,   I will begin

Ductores Danaûm fracti   bello   que repulsi   fatis,
The leaders of the Greeks disheartened by the war and repulsed by the fates

tot   annis jam labentibus,   ædificant equum   instar
so many years now passing away,   construct   a horse   of the size of *a*

montis,   divinâ arte Palladis; que, intexunt costas   secta
mountain, by the divine art of Pallas;   and,   they line the ribs with sawn

biete. Simulant   votum pro   reditu: ea   fama
r.   They pretend *it to be* an offering for *their* return: that   story

vagatur.   Sortiti   delecta corpora virûm,   furtim
is spread abroad. Having chosen by lot select   bodies   of men,   secretly

includunt   huc cæco lateri: que penitùs complent in-
they shut *them* up here in the dark side: and   within   they fill   the spa-

gentes cavernas. que uterum armato milite. Tenedos est in
cious   caverns   and the belly with armed soldiery. Tenedos   is   in

conspectu, insula notissima famâ,   dives   opum, dum
sight,   an island most noted by fame, abounding in wealth, while

regna   Priami manebant; nunc tantùm sinus et statio ma-
the realms of Priam continued;   now   only   a bay and a station un-

lefida carinis: provecti huc condunt   se   in   deserto
safe   for ships: conveyed hither. they hide themselves on   the deserted

litore.   Nos rati   abiisse   et petiisse   Mycenas
shore.   We have imagined *them* to have gone and to have sought   Mycenæ

vento.   Ergo omnis Teucria solvit se   longo luctu:
with the wind. Therefore all   Troy   releases itself from long suffering:

Portæ panduntur: juvat   ire et videre Dorica castra,
The gates are thrown open; it delights *us* to go and view the Grecian camps,

que desertos locos que litus relictum. Hic manus
and the deserted places and the shore abandoned.   Here the bands of the

Dolopum, hic sævus Achilles tendebat; hic   locus
Dolopes   here stern   Achilles   encamped; here *was* the station for

classibus; hic acies solebant certare. Pars   stupet
their fleets; here armies were wont to engage. · A part is astonished

exitiale donum innuptæ Minervæ, et mirantur molem
at the fatal present of unmarried Minerva,   and   admire   the bulk of the

equi: que primus Thymœtes hortatur   duci   intra muros
horse: and first   Thymœtes   advises *that it* be drawn within the walls

et locari arce;   sive   dolo seu   jani
and be placed in the citadel; whether *he did this through* treachery or   now

fata Trojæ sic ferebant. At Capys et   quorum menti
the fates of Troy thus required.   But Capys and *others* to whose   mind

melior sententia, jubent aut præcipitare pelago insidias
was a better judgment,   advise either to precipitate in the sea the snares

que suspecta dona Danaûm, ve urere flammis subjec-
and the suspected   gifts of the Greeks, or to burn *them* by flames applied under-

tis, aut terebrare et tentare cavas latebras uteri. Incer-
neath, or   to pierce   and examine the hollow recesses of the womb. The in-

tum vulgus scinditur in contraria studia. Ibi Laocoon
constant populace is divided between different opinions. Then Laocoon

primus ante omnes, magnâ catervâ comitante, ardens
the first before all, a great crowd surrounding, eager

decurrit ab summâ arce: et procul O miseri
runs down from the top of the citadel: and from afar *cries out:* O wretched

cives, quæ tanta insania?   creditis hostes
citizens, what so great madness *is there to you?* do you believe the enemy

avectos? aut putatis ulla dona Danaûm carere
to have been carried away? or do you think *that* any gifts of the Greeks to be free

dolis? sic Ulysses notus? aut Achivi occul-
from deceit? *or* thus has Ulysses been known *to you?* either the Greeks are con-

tantur inclusi hoc ligno: aut hæc machina fabricata est in
cealed. shut up in this wood: or this machine has been framed against

nostros muros inspectura domos, que ventura urbi
our walls about to overlook *our* houses, and to come down upon *our* city

desuper; aut aliquis error latet: Teucri ne credite equo.
from above; or some guile lies hid: O Trojans trust not to the horse

Quicquid id est, timeo Danaos et ferentes dona. Sic
Whatever that is, I fear the the Greeks even offering presents. Thus

fatus, validis viribus contorsit ingentem hastam in
having said, with great powers he has hurled *his* huge spear against

latus feri, que in alvum curvam compagibus; illa
the side of the horse, and against *his* belly bending out in joints; that

stetit tremens, que utero recusso, cavæ cavernæ inso-
has stood trembling, and the inside being jarred, the hollow caverns have

nuere que dedêre gemitum. Et si fata Deûm, si
sounded and have sent forth a groan. And if the decrees of the gods, if *our*

mens non fuisset læva impulerat fœdare ferro
mind might not have been foolish he had persuaded *us* to tear open with the sword

Argolicas latebras; que Troja nunc stares que
these Grecian hiding places: and O Troy now thou mightest stand and thou

alta arx Priami maneres!
lofty tower of Priam mightest remain!

Intereà ecce Dardanidæ pastores magno clamore
In the mean time behold the Trojan shepherds with great clamor

trahebant ad regem juvenem, revinctum manus post
were dragging to the king a youth, bound as to *his* hands behind

terga: qui ultrò obtulerat se, ignotum, venien-
his back: who of *his* own accord had presented himself unknown, to *them* ad-

tibus, ut strueret hoc ipsum, que aperiret Trojam
vancing, that he might effect this very *design,* and open Troy to the

Achivis; fidens animi atque paratus in utrumque; seu
Greeks; daring of soul and prepared for either *event;* whether

versare dolos, seu occumbere certæ morti. Trojana
to manage frauds, or to yield to certain death. The Trojan

juventus circumfusa ruit undique, studio
youth. being scattered around *him* rush in from every quarter, through eager

visendi,　　que certant illudere capto.　Nunc　accipe
desire of seeing *him*, and they strive to insult the captive.　Now　understand

insidias Danaûm; et ab uno crimine disce omnes. Namque
the wiles of the Greeks; and from one　crime　learn　all.　For

ut constitit in medio conspectu, turbatus, inermis,.　atque
as he stood　in the midst of *our* view, alarmed, defenceless,　and

oculis　　circumspexit Phrygia agmina; inquit, heu, quæ
with *his* eyes looked round upon　the Trojan　bands;　he says,　alas,　what

tellus, quæ æquora nunc possunt accipere me! aut,　jam,
land,　what　seas　now　can　receive　me! or,　now,

quid denique restat mihi　misero,　　cui　　neque
what　finally　remains to me a wretched *man*, for whom *there is* neither

locus usquam apud Danaos; insuper Dardanidæ　ipsi
a place any where among the Greeks; and besides the Trojans themselves

infensi poscunt pœnas cum sanguine. Quo　　gemitu
incensed demand punishment with　blood.　By which lamentation *our*

animi　　　conversi, et omnis impetus compressus; horta-
minds　*have been* changed, and all　violence　restrained; we encour-

mur fari　　quo sanguine cretus;　memoret quid
age him to say from what　race he *may* be sprung; that he relate what *message*

ferat,　ve quæ fiducia sit　capto.　Ille　formidine
he may bring,　or what confidence may be to a captive.　He　*his* fear

tandem depositâ,　fatur hæc:　　Rex, equidem, inquit,
at length being laid aside,. speaks these *words:* O king,　indeed,　he says,

fatebor　tibi cuncta vera, quæcunque fuerint　neque
I will confess to you all *things* true,　whatsoever they may have been neither

negabo　me de Argolicâ gente; hoc primum:　　nec si
will I deny *that* I *am* of the Grecian　race;　this *is*　first:　nor if

improba fortuna finxit Sinonem miserum,　finget
base　　fortune hath made Sinon　wretched, shall she make　*him*

vanum que mendacem. Si fortè,　fando aliquid nomen
deceitful and　false.　If by chance, in speaking something the name

Palamedis Belidæ,　et gloria inclyta famâ pervenit ad
of Palamedes the son of Belus, and *his* glory renowned by fame has reached to

tuas aures: quem insontem Pelasgi sub falsâ　prodi-
your　ears:　whom innocent　the Greeks under　a false accusation of

tione　demisere　neci infando　indicio quia vetebat
treachery have condemned to death upon iniquitous evidence because he forbade

bella: nunc lugent　cassum lumine: pauper pater misit
the wars: now they mourn *him* bereaved of life:　*my* poor　father hath sent

me comitem illi　et propinquum consanguinitate huc　in
me a companion to him and　related *to him* by the ties of blood hither　in

arma ab primis annis. Dum　stabat incolumis regno, que
arms from *my* early years.　While he remained　safe in *his* kingdom, and *his*

regnum vigebat　consiliis,　et nos gessimus　que aliquod
kingdom flourished by *his* counsels, also we have borne both　　some

nomen que decus: postquam concessit　ab superis　oris
name　and　honor: *but* after he hath departed from the upper regions

invidiâ pellacis Ulyssei, loquor haud ignota, afflictus
by the hatred of lying Ulysses, I speak not *things* unknown, *I* afflicted

trahebam vitam tenebris que luctu et mecum indignabar
dragged out *my* life in darkness and sorrow and by myself I was indignant

casum insontis amici. Nec, demens, tacui; et
at the fate of *my* innocent friend. Nor, foolish, have I been silent, and

promisi me ultorem si qua fors tulisset
I have promised that *I would be* an avenger if any fortune should have afforded

si unquam remeâssem victor ad patrios Ar-
an opportunity, if ever I should have returned a victor to my native Ar-

gos, et movi aspera odia, verbis. Hinc prima
gos, and I have excited *his* cruel hatred, by my words. From hence *was* the first

labes mali mihi: hinc Ulysses semper terrere
source of misfortune to me: henceforth Ulysses *began* always to alarm *me*

novis criminibus: hinc spargere ambiguas voces in vul-
with new accusations: henceforth to spread ambiguous words among the com-

gum, et conscius quærere arma. | Nec enim requievit,
mon people, and conscious to seek arms. | Nor indeed has he stopped,

donec Calchante ministro.—Sed autem quid ego revolvo
until Calchas *being his* assistant.—But truly why do I go over again

ingrata? quidve moror? si habetis omnes Achivos
these unpleasant *things?* or why delay? if you hold all the Greeks

uno ordine que est sat audire id, sumite
in the same condition *of enemies,* and it is sufficient to hear that, inflict

pœnas jamdudum.
the punishment long since *deserved.*

Hoc Ithacus velit, et Atridæ mercentur magno.
This Ulysses may wish, and the sons of Atreus may purchase *it* at a great

Tum verò ardemus scitari, et quærere causas, ignari
price. Then indeed we are eager to inquire, and to ask the causes, ignorant

tantorum scelerum que Pelasgæ artis. Prósequitur pavitans
of so great crimes and Grecian artifice. *He* proceeds fearful

et fatur ficto pectore: Danaï sæpe cupiere moliri
and speaks from *his* false heart: The Greeks often have wished to effect *their*

fugam, Troja relicta et fessi discedere longo bello. Que
flight, Troy being left and wearied to depart from the long war. And

utinam fecissent! sæpe aspera hyems ponti
O that they might have done *so!* often the rough tempest of the ocean

interclusit ilios, et Auster terruit euntes. Præcipuè
has kept back them, and the south wind has terrified *them* departing. Chiefly

cum jam hic equus staret contextus acernis trabibus, nimb'
when now this horse might stand framed of maple planks, storms

sonuerunt toto æthere. Suspensi mittimus Eurypylum sci-
roared in all the sky. In suspense we send Eurypylus to in-

tatum oracula Phœbi que is reportat hæc tristia dicta
quire of the oracle of Apollo and he brings back these mournful words from

adytis: Danai placâstis ventos sanguine et virgine
the shrines: O Greeks you have appeased the winds with blood and a virgin

cæsâ, cùm primùm venistis   ad Iliacas oras: reditus
slain,   when   first   you have come to the Trojan shores: *your*   return

quærendi sanguine et   litandum Argolicâ animâ.   Quæ
may be sought by blood   and atonement made by a Grecian life.   Which

vox   ut venit ad aures   vulgi,   animi obstupuere,
answer when it came to the ears of the multitude, *their* minds were confounded.

que gelidus tremor cucurrit per   ima ossa;   cui·
and   a cold   shivering hath run through their inmost bones; *ignorant* for whom

fata   parent,   quem Apollo poscat.   Hic Ithacus
the fates may prepare *death* whom   Apollo may demand.   Here   Ulysses

protrahit vatem   Calchanta in medios   magno tumultu:
drags   the prophet   Chalchas into the midst *of them* with great   tumult

flagitat   quæ ea numina Divûm sint,   et multi jam
and demands *of him* what those responses of the gods may be, and many already

canebant mihi crudele scelus   artificis,   et taciti videbant
foretold   to me   the cruel plot of   the dissembler, and silent   saw

ventura.   Bis quinos dies ille silet, que tec-
the things about to come *on me.*   Twice five   days   he is silent, and   con-

tus recusat prodere quemquam suâ voce, aut opponere
cealed refuses to designate any one   by his voice,   or to expose   *him*

morti.   Tandem   vix   actus magnis clamoribus Ithaci,
to death.   At length with difficulty forced by the loud clamors of Ulysses,

rumpit   vocem compositò, et destinat me   aræ.   Omnes
he opens *his* mouth of purpose, and devotes   me to the altar.   All have

assensere; et tulere   quæ quisquis timebat sibi   conversa
assented;   and have suffered what every one   feared for himself *to be* turned

in exitium unius miseri.   Jamque infanda dies aderat;
to the destruction of one unhappy *being.* And now the fatal   day   had come;

sacra   parari mihi, et salsæ fruges, et   vittæ
the sacred rites *began to* be prepared for me, and the salted cakes, and the fillets

circum tempora. Eripui   me   leto, (fateor) et rupi
around *my* temples. I have delivered myself from death, (I confess) and broke

vincula: que obscurus delitui   per noctem   limoso
my chains: and   obscure I have lurked through the night in the muddy

tacu in   ulvâ, dum darent vela, si fortè   dedis-
fen among the weeds, until they should set sail, if by chance they might have sail-

sent. Nec jam   ulla spes mihi videndi antiquam   pa-
ed.   Nor   now *was there* any hope *to* me of seeing *my* ancient   coun-

triam, nec dulces natos que   exoptatum parentem: quos
try,   nor *my* dear children and *my* greatly desired parent: whom

illi fors reposcent ad pœnas   ob   nostra effugia,   et
they perhaps will demand for punishment on account of my   escape,   and

piabunt hanc culpam   morte   miserorum.
will expiate this   fault *of mine* by the death of *those* unhappy *beings*

Quod   oro   te per Superos   et numina conscia veri,
Wherefore I implore you by the powers above and the deities conscious of truth,

per, si est   qua intemerata, fides quæ adhuc restat   mor·
by, if there is any   inviolable,   faith which as yet remains to mor-

talibus usquam; miserere tantorum laborum; miserere animi
tals   any whǎre;   pity   so great   sufferings;   pity   a mind

ferentis non digna.
bearing   unworthy things.

His lachrymis damus   vitam, et   ultrò miserescimus.
To these tears   we grant *him his* life,   and willingly   pity *him.*

Priamus ipse primus jubet manicas atque arcta vincla le-
Priam   himself first   orders the handcuffs and   tight   cords to be un-

vari viro;   que fatur ita   amicis dictis: quisquis
loosed from the man; and   speaks thus *to him* with friendly words: whoever thou

es, hinc jam obliviscere Graios amissos.   Eris noster:
art, henceforth now   forget   the Greeks lost.   You shall be   ours

edissere hæc vera mihi roganti: quò   statuêre hanc
declare   these truths to me questioning: why have *they* built   thi

molem immanis equi? quis auctor?   ve quid petunt?
mass of an enormous horse? who *was* the author *of it?* or what do they intend?

quæ religio?   aut quæ machina belli?   Dixerat. Ille,
what religion *is there in it?* or what engine of war *is it?* He said.   He,

instructus dolis et Pelasgâ arte,   sustulit   ad   sidera
versed   in frauds and Grecian cunning, has raised towards the stars *his*

palmas, exutas vinclis: ait, æterni ignes,   testor vos   et
hands   freed from cords: he says, O eternal fires,   I call you to witness and

vestrum non violabile numen; vos aræ, que nefandi enses quos
your   inviolable   divinity; ye altars, and impious   swords which

fugi;   que vittæ Deûm quos hostia, gessi: fas
I have escaped; and *ye* fillets of the gods which a victim, I have borne: it is just

mihi resolvere sacrata   jura   Graiorum;   fas
for me to violate the sacred obligations of the Greeks; it is right *for me*

odisse, virosatque ferre sub auras omnia   si qua tegunt nec
to hate the men, and to bring into the air all *things* if any   lie hid   nor

teneor ullis legibus patriæ, modò tu,   Troja,   maneas
am I bound by any laws of *my* country, only mayest thou, O Troy,   adhere to

promissis, que servata,   serves   fidem; si feram
thy promises, and preserved, mayst thou keep   *thy* faith *to me*; if I may disclose

vera, si rependam magna   Omnis spes Danaûm et
truths, if I may repay *thee* great *things*.   Every hope of the Greeks and

fiducia belli cœpti, semper stetit   auxiliis Palladis.
confidence of the war commenced, always has depended on the aid of Pallas.

Sed enim ex quo   impius Tydides que Ulysses invéntor
But indeed from what *time* the impious Tydides   and Ulysses the contriver

scelerum aggressi   avellere fatale Palladium sacrato
of wickedness having attempted to drag away the fatal Palladium from *her* sacred

templo, custodibus summæ arcis cæsis   corripuere sacram
temple, the guards of *her* lofty   dome being slain have seized *her*   sacred

effiigiem; que ausí contingere virgineas vittas   Divæ
image;   and *have* dared to touch   the virgin   fillets of the goddess

cruentis manibus: ex illo   spes   Danaûm sublapsa
with bloody hands: from that *time* the hopes of the Greeks tottering *began*

fluere ac referri retrò: vires fractæ mens
to flag and to be carried backward: *their* powers *have been* broken *and* the mind

Deæ aversa. Nec Tritonia dedit ea signa dubiis
of the goddess *has been* averse. Nor Tritonia has given those signs by doubtful

monstris. Vix simulacrum positum castris; coruscæ
prodigies. Scarcely *has* the statue *been* set up in the camps; *when* sparkling

flammæ arsere arrectis luminibus, que salsus sudor
flames have flashed from *her* attentive eyes, and briny sweat

iit per artus, que ter emicuit solo mirabile
as flowed over *her* limbs, and thrice she has sprung from the ground wonderful

dictu, que ferens parman que trementem hastam. Extemplò
to relate, and bearing *her* shield and trembling spear. Forthwith

Calchas canit æquora tentanda fugâ: nec Pergama
Calchas declares that the seas must be attempted in flight: nor Troy

posse excindi Argolicis telis ni repetant omina Argis,
can be razed by Grecian arms unless they may repeat the omens at Argos,

que reducant numen quod advexere secum pelago
and bring back the goddess which they have conveyed with themselves on the sea

et curvis carinis; Et nunc quod petiere patrias
and in *their* curved ships. And now that they have sought *their* native

Mycenas vento, parant arma que Deos comites, que
Mycenas with the wind, they are providing arms and gods companions, and

pelago remenso, improvisi aderunt; ita Calchas
the sea being passed over again, unexpected they will be present; so Calchas

digerit omina. Moniti, statuêre hanc effigiem pro
interprets the omens. Warned, they have constructed this figure in

Palladio, pro numine læso, quæ piaret triste
place of the Palladium, for the goddess offended. which might expiate *their* horrid

nefas. Tamen Calchas jussit attollere hanc immensam molem
crime. But Calchas has ordered *them* to build this immense structure

textis roboribus, que educere cœlo; ne possit recipi
with compacted timbers, and to raise *it* to heaven that it may not be received

portis, aut duci in mœnia; neu tueri populum sub
in the gates, or be drawn within the walls; nor protect the people under

antiquâ religione. Nam si vestra manus violâs-
their ancient religion. For *he told them* if your hand should have

set dona Minervæ; tum magnum exitium futurum
violated the gifts of Minerva; then great destruction should be to the

imperio Priami que Phrygibus; (quod omen Dii priùs
empire of Priam and the Trojans; (which omen may the gods sooner

convertant in ipsum) sin ascendisset in vestram
turn on himself) but if *it* should have ascended into your

urbem, vestris manibus, Asiam, ultrò venturam magno
city, by your hands, *that* Asia, willingly would come with a great

bello ad Pelopeia mœnia et ea fata manere nostros nepotes.
war to the Pelopeian walls and those fates await our descendants.

Talibus insidiis, que arte perjuri Sinonis, res credita
By such wiles, and the artifice of perjured Sinon, the thing *is* believed

quos neque Tydides nec Larissæus Achilles,
and we whom neither Diomede nor Larissæan Achilles, *has subdued,*

quos decem anni non domuere mille carinæ non
whom ten years have not subdued *whom* a thousand ships *have* not

capti dolis que coactis lachrymis.
subdued, have been deceived by *his* frauds and forced tears.

Hic aliud majus que multò magis tremendum
Here another greater *prodigy* and much more to be dreaded

objicitur miseris, atque turbat improvida
is presented *to us* unhappy, and disorders *our* improvident

pectora. Laocoon, sorte ductus sacerdos Neptuno mac-
minds. Laocoon, by lot chosen a priest for Neptune, was sacri

tabat ingentem taurum ad solennes aras. Autem ecce!
ficing a huge bull at the appointed altars. But lo

gemini angues, à Tenedo per tranquilla alta,
two serpents, from Tenedos *coming* over the tranquil seas.

(horresco referens,) incumbunt pelago immensis orbibus,
(I shudder while relating,) press upon the sea with *their* immense folds,

que pariter, tendunt ad litora; quorum pectora arrecta
and together, stretch to the shore; whose breasts *are* elevated

inter fluctus, que sanguineæ jubæ exsuperant un-
among the waves, and *their* bloody crests rise above the bil-

das: cætera pars legit pontum ponè que sinuat
lows: the other part *of each* sweeps the sea behind and winds

immensa terga volumine. Sonitus fit sale spumante:
their huge backs in folds. A sound is made the sea. foaming:

jamque tenebant arva, que suffecti ardentes
and now they reached the fields, and spotted as to *their* glaring

oculos sanguine et igni lambebant sibila ora vi-
eyes with blood and fire they licked *their* hissing mouths with

brantibus linguis. Exsangues diffugimus visu; illi
quivering tongues. Pale *with fear* we fly at the sight; they

petunt Laocoonta, certo agmine: et primùm uterque serpens,
seek Laocoon, in a direct course: and at first each serpent,

amplexus, implicat parva corpora duorum natorum, et
embracing, twines around the little bodies of *his* two sons, and

depascitur miseros artus morsu. Pòst, corripiunt
feeds upon *their* wretched limbs with *their* fangs. Afterwards, they seize

ipsum subeuntem auxilio, ac ferentem tela, que
Laocoon himself coming to *their* assistance, and bringing arms, and

ligant ingentibus spiris; et jam bis amplexi
they bind *him* with *their* vast folds; and now twice embracing. *his*

medium, bis circùm dati collo squamea terga
middle, twice they are wound around *his* neck as to *their* scaly backs

superant capite et altis cervicibus. Ille
they elevate *themselves* above *him* with *their* heads and lofty necks. He at

simul tendit divellere nodos manibus, perfusus
the same time endeavours to force apart the folds with *his* hands, being stained

vittas sanie que atro veneno: simul tollit horrendos
as to *his* fillets with gore and black poison: at the same time he raises   horrid

clamores ad sidera;   mugitus quales taurus   cùm saucius,
screams to the stars; *such* bellowings as the bull *raises* when wounded,

fugit   aram, et excussit   cervice incertam securim.
he has escaped the altar, and has shaken off from *his* neck the erring axe.

At gemini dracones,   lapsu effugiunt ad summa delubra,
But the two serpents,   by gliding escape   to the lofty   temples,

que petunt arcem   sævæ   Tritonidis; que teguntur sub
and seek the shrine of stern Minerva;   and are concealed under

pedibus Deæ   que sub   orbe clypei. Tum, verò
the feet of the Goddess and under the orb of *her* shield.   Then, indeed,

novus pavor insinuat   cunctis, per tremefacta pectora, et
new fear insinuates *itself* into all, through *their* affrighted hearts, and

ferunt Laocoonta merentem, expendisse   scelus; qui
they declare Laocoon deserving *it*, to have suffered punishment;, who may

læserit   sacrum robur cuspide   et intorserit sceleratam
have injured the sacred wood with the point of *his* spear and hurled *his* impious

hastam tergo. Conclamant simulacrum ducendum ad
spear against *its* side. They cry out for the statue to be drawn to *its proper*

sedes que numina   Divæ   oranda. Dividimus muros,
seat   and the divinity of the Goddess to be implored. We break down the walls,

et pandimus moenia   urbis. Omnes accingunt
and lay open the fortifications of the city.   All   apply   *themselves*

operi: que subjiciunt pedibus lapsus rotarum,   et
to the work: and they place under *its* feet the rolling of wheels,   and

intendunt stupea vincula collo: fatalis machina, fœta armis,
fasten hempen cords to *its* neck: the fatal machine, pregnant with arms,

scandit muros: pueri que innuptæ puellæ circùm canunt
mounts the walls: boys and unmarried virgins around sing

sacra que gaudent contingere funem   manu. Illa subit,
sacred *hymns* and delight to touch the rope with *their* hand. That advances,

que minans illabitur mediæ   urbi.   O patria, O Ilium,
and menacing glides to the middle of the city.   O *my* country, O Ilium,

domus Divûm   que moenia Dardanidum inclyta bello!
habitation of the gods and *ye* walls of the Trojans renowned in war!

Quater   substitit in ipso limine portæ atque arma
Four times *it* has stopped on the very threshold of the gate and the arms

quater dedére sonitum utero. Tamen instamus imme-
four times have sent forth a sound from *its* womb. Yet we press on unmind-

mores que cæci furore, et sistimus infelix monstrum
ful and blinded with zeal, and we place the fatal monster

sacratâ arce. Tunc, etiam, Cassandra non unquam credita
in the sacred tower. Then, also, Cassandra not ever believed

Teucris, aperit ora   futuris fatis   jussu
by the Trojans, opens *her* mouth to *our* approaching fates by the command of the

Dei. Nos miseri, quibus ille dies esset ultimus, velamus
god.   We unhappy to whom that day would be *our* last.   deck

delubra Deûm festâ fronde per urbem. Intereâ
the temples of the gods with the festival bough throughout the city. Meanwhile

cœlum vertitur et nox ruit Oceano, involvens magnâ
the heaven is rolled round and night rushes from the ocean, involving in *her* vast

umbrâ que terram que polum que dolos Myrmidonum,
shade, both the earth and the sky and the wiles of the Greeks.

Teucri fusi per mœnia conticuere: sopor complectitur
The Trojans scattered through the city have been silent: sleep embraces

fessos artus. Et jam Argiva Phalanx ibat instructis
their weary limbs. And now the Grecian Phalanx went in *their* equippe

navibus à Tenedo, petens nota litora per amica silentia
ships from Tenedos, seeking the known shores by the friendly silence

tacitæ lunæ: cum regia puppis extulerat flammas; que
of the silent moon: when the royal ship had displayed the flames; and

Sinon defensus iniquis fatis Deûm, furtim laxat pinea
Sinon protracted by the hostile decrees of the gods, secretly unlocks the piny

claustra et Danaos inclusos utero: equus patefactus reddit
prisons and the Greeks shut up in the belly: -the horse opened returns

illos ad auras; Tisandrus que Sthenelus duces et dirus Ulys-
them to the air; Tisandrus and Sthenelus chiefs and direful Ulys-

ses lætii promunt se cavo robore, lapsi per
ses joyful bring forth themselves from the hollow wood, sliding down by

funem demissum, que Athamas, que Thoas que Neoptolemus
a rope let down; and Athamas, and Thoas and Neoptolemus

Pelides, que Machaon primus et Menelaus et Epeûs
grandson of Peleus, and Machaon first and Menelaus and Epeus

ipse fabricator doli.
himself the architect of the fraud.

Invadunt urbem sepultam somno que vino: vigiles
They attack the city buried in sleep and wine: the sentries

cæduntur; que accipiunt omnes socios portis patentibus
are killed; and they admit all *their* associates by the gates opened

atque jungunt conscia agmina Erat tempus quo prima
and join the conscious bands. *It* was the time in which the first

quies incipit ægris mortalibus, et serpit gratissima
rest begins to wearied mortals, and spreads over *them* most grateful

dono Divûm. Ecce Hector mœstissimus visus
by the favor of the gods. Lo Hector most mournful *has* seemed

adesse mihi ante oculos, in somnis, que effundere largos
to be present to me before *my* eyes, in *my* slumbers, and to shed many

fletus, raptatus bigis ut quondam que ater cruento pulvere,
tears, dragged by the chariot as formerly and black with gory dust,

que trajectus lora per tumentes pedes. Hei mihi,
and pierced as to thongs through *his* swelling feet. Alas me,

qualis erat! Quantum mutatus ab illo Hectore qui redit
such he was! How much changed from that Hector who returned

indutus exuvias Achillis, vel jaculatus Phrygios ignes
clothed in the spoils of Achilles, or *who* darted Phrygian flames into the

puppibus Danaûm¹ gerens squalentem barbam et crines
ships of the Greeks¹ wearing a squalid beard and *his* hair

concretos sanguine, que illâ vulnera quæ plurima accepit
clotted with blood, and those wounds which very many he has received

circum patrios muros: flens ipse videbar ultrò compellare
around *his* native walls: weeping I myself seemed willingly to address

virum, et expromere mœstas voces: O lux Dardaniæ!
the hero, and to utter *these* mournful words: O light of Troy!

O fidissima spes Teucrûm! quæ tantæ moræ tenuere?
O most trusty hope of the Trojans! what so great obstacles have delayed *you?*

Hector expectate, ab quibus oris venis? ut defessi
Hector earnestly longed for from what shores do *you* come? that wearied

aspicimus te post multa funera tuorum, post varios labores
we behold thee after many deaths of thy *friends*, after various toils

que hominum que urbis? quæ indigna causa fœdavit
both of men and of the city? what unworthy cause has deformed *thy*

serenos vultus? aut cur cerno hæc vulnera? Ille nihil:
serene looks? or why do I see these wounds? He *said* nothing:

nec moratur me querentem vana: sed graviter ducens
nor detains me inquiring vain things: but heavily drawing

gemitus de imo pectore, ait: nate Deâ heu! fuge, que
groans from the bottom of *his* breast, says. goddes-born, ah! fly, and

eripe te his flammis. Hostis habet muros; Troja
snatch thyself from these flames. The enemy possesses the walls; Troy

ruit ab alto culmine; sat datum patriæ que
tumbles down from *her* lofty top; enough *has been* given to *my* country and

Priamo: si Pergama possent defendi, dextrâ,
to Priam· if Troy might be able to be defended, *by any* right hand

fuissent defensa hâc. Troja commendat tibi sa
it would have been defended by this. Troy commends to thee *her* sa

cra que suos Penates, cape hos comites fatorum: quære
cred *things* and· her own gods, take these companions of *thy* fates: search

mœnia his quæ magna denique statues ponto
out a city for these which great finally you shall build the ocean being

pererrato. Sic ait, et effert manibus vittas, que
wandered over. Thus he says, and brings forth with *his* hands the fillets, and

potentem Vestam, que æternum ignem penetralibus adytis.
powerful Vesta, and the eternal fire *from* the inmost shrines.

Intereà mœnia miscentur vario luctu; et sonitus
In the mean time the city is confused with various mourning; and the sounds

clarescunt magis et magis, que horror armorum ingruit,
grow clear more and more, and the clashing of arms increases

quamquam domus parentis Anchisæ secreta que recessit
although the house of *my* parent Anchises was private and was retired

obtecta arboribus. Excutior somno, et ascensu supero
surrounded by trees. I am roused from sleep, and by climbing up I ascend

fastigia summi tecti, atque asto arrectis auribus. Veluti
the tops of the highest roof, and stand with listening ears. As

cúm flamma incidit in segetem, Austris furentibus;
when a flame hath fallen among the standing corn, the south winds raging;

aut rapidus torrens montano flumine sternit agros, sternit
or a rapid torrent with *its* mountain flood lays waste the fields lays waste

læta sata, que labores boum, que trahit sylvas
the abundant crops of corn, and the labors of the oxen, and draws *away* the woods

præcipites: pastor stupet inscius, accipens sonitum
precipitate: the shepherd is amazed ignorant *of the cause*, hearing the roaring

de alto vertice saxi. Tum verò fides manifesta, que
from the lofty summit of a rock. Then indeed the truth *is* manifest, and

insidiæ. Danaûm patescunt; jam ampla domus Deiphobi
the wiles of the Greeks are apparent; now the spacious house of Deiphobus

dedit ruinam, Vulcano superante: jam, Ucalegon
has formed a ruin, the fire overpowering *it:* now, Ucalegon

proximus ardet: lata Sigea freta relucent igni. Que
next blazes: the wide Sigean streights shine *with* the flame. And

clamor virum exoritur, que clangor tubarum. Amens capio
the shout of men arises, and the sound of trumpets. Frantic I seize

arma, nec sat rationis in armis: animi ardent
my arms, nor *was there* enough of reason in arms: *my* passions are ardent

glomerare manum bello, et concurrere in arcem cum
to collect a band for the war, and to rush into the citadel with

sociis, furor que ira præcipitant mentem que succurrit
my associates, fury and rage hurry on *my* mind and it occur

pulchrum mori in armis. Autem ecce
to me, that it is glorious to die in arms. But lo

Pantheus elapsus telis Achivûm, Pantheus
Pantheus escaping from the weapons of the Greeks, Pantheus

Otriades, sacerdos arcis que Phœbi, ipse • trahit
the son of Otreus, priest of the tower and of Apollo, himself draws along

sacra que victos Deos que parvum nepotem
the sacred utensils and *his* conquered gods and *his* little grandson with

manu; que amens tendit ad limina cursu: Pantheu, in quo
his hand; and frantic makes to *my* gates in *his* course: O Pantheus, in what

loco summa res? quam arcem prendimus? Vix fatus
state *are our* highest concern? what fortress do we seize? Scarcely had

eram ea cùm reddit talia gemitu: summa dies
I spoken those *words* when he returns such *things* with a groan: our last day

venit, et ineluctabile tempus Dardaniæ: fuimus Troes,
has come, and the unavoidable period of Troy: we have been Trojans,

Ilium fuit et ingens gloria Teucrorum; ferus Jupiter
Ilium *has* been and the great glory of the Trojans; cruel Jupiter,

transtulit omnia Argos; Danai dominantur in urbe
has transferred all *things* to Argos; the Greeks govern in the city

incensâ. Arduus equus astans in mediis mœnibus fundit
fired. The towering horse standing in the middle of the city pours forth

armatos, que victor Sinon insultans miscet incendia;
the armed *men,* and the conqueror Sinon insulting scatters the flames.

alii   adsunt   portis   bipatentibus,   millia   quot
others are present at the gates open on *both* sides, *so many* thousands   as

nunquam venêre magnis Mycenis.   Alii oppositi   obse-
never   have come from great Mycenæ.   Others opposed *to us* have be-

dêre angusta   viarum   telis: acies ferri   stat
sieged the narrow *passages* of the streets with arms: the edge of the sword stands

stricta   corrusco   mucrone, parata neci: primi vigiles
drawn with *its* glittering point,   prepared for slaughter: the first guards

portarum vix tentant prælia, et resistunt   cæco   marte
of the gates scarcely try   the fight, and resist   in the blind encounter.

Talibus dictis Otriadæ et numine Divûm,   feror   in
With such words of Pantheus and by the will of the gods, I am carried among

flammas et in arma, quò tristis Erinnys, quo   fremitus
flames   and among arms, whither the direful Fury,   whither the tumult

et clamor sublatus ad æthera vocat.   Ripheus et   Iphitus
and uproar   raised   to the skies calls *me.*   Ripheus and   Iphitus

maximus annis, que Hypanis que Dymas oblati   per
eldest   in years, and Hypanis and   Dymas brought together by *the*

    lunam addunt se   socios;   et agglomerant nostro
light of the moon join themselves as confederates and   adhere   to our

lateri; que juvenis Chorœbus Mygdonides,   fortè venerat
side;   and the youth Chorœbus son of Mygdon, *who* by chance had come

illis diebus ad Trojam incensus insano amore Cassandræ;
in those days to   Troy   inflamed with a violent passion for Cassandra;

que gener ferebat auxilium Priamo que Phrygibus: infelix
and son-in-law brought assistance to Priam and the Trojans: unfortunate

qui non audierat   precepta   furentis sponsæ. Quos con-
who had not regarded   the precepts of *his* prophetic spouse. Whom closely

fertos, ubi vidi   audere   in   prælia, super his   incipio:
united, when I saw to have courage for the flight, upon these *things* I begin

Juvenes, pectora fortissima frustrà; si certa cupido est vobis
O youths,   hearts   most valiant in vain; if a fixed resolution is to you

sequi audentem extrema;   videtis quæ fortuna sit
to follow *me* daring the most extreme *things:* you see what fortune may be to

rebus.   Omnes Dî quibus hoc imperium steterat   exces-
our affairs. All the gods by whom this   empire   has stood have de-

sere   adytis que aris relictis: succurritis urbi incensæ:
parted from *their* shrines and altars abandoned: you aid a city in flames:

moriamur, et ruamus in media arma.   Una salus
let us die,   and let us rush into the midst of arms. The only safety to the

victis   sperare nullam salutem. Sic furor additus animis
conquered *is* to hope for   no   safety. Thus phrenzy is added to the minds

juvenum. Inde ceu raptores lupi in atrâ nebulâ, quos
of the youth. Then as the ravenous wolves in a dark fog, whom the

improba rabies ventris exegit cœcos,   quosque catuli
fierce   hunger of the belly has driven blind *to danger, and* whom the whelps

relicti expectant siccis faucibus: vadimus per tela   per
left behind wait for with parched jaws: we march through arms,   through

hostes in mortem haud dubiam, que tenemus iter mediæ
enemies to death not uncertain, and we hold the way of the middle

urbis: atra nox circumvolat cava umbrâ. Quis
of the city: gloomy night hovers around us with its hollow shade. Who can

explicet cladem illius noctis, quis fando funera, aut
describe the slaughter of that night, who by relating can describe the deaths, or

possit æquare labores lachrymis? Antiqua urbs dominata
can equal our disasters with his tears? An ancient city having governed

per multos annos ruit: que plurima inertia corpora
for many years is demolished: and many feeble bodies

sternuntur passim per vias, que per domos et
are slain every where through the streets, and through their houses and

religiosa limina Deorum. Nec Teucri soli dant pœnas
the sacred temples of the gods. Nor do the Trojans alone suffer punishment

sanguine: quondam virtus redit in præcordia etiam
with their blood: at times courage returns into the hearts also to the

victis, que victores Danai cadunt: ubique crudelis
conquered, and the victorious Greeks fall: every where there is cruel

luctus, ubique pavor et plurima imago mortis.
sorrow, every where fear and very many a form of death.

Androgeos, magna caterva comitante primus offert se
Androgeos, a great crowd accompanying him, first offers himself

nobis inscius, credens agmina socia: atque ultro
to us ignorant of the affair, believing our troops to be friendly: and voluntarily

compellat amicis verbis: festinate viri: nam quæ segnities
addresses us with friendly words: haste men: for what sloth

tam sera moratur? alii rapiunt que ferunt incensa Pergama:
so late detains you? others ravage and bear away inflamed Troy:

vos nunc primum itis celsis navibus? dixit: et extemplo
do you now first come from the lofty ships? he has said: and quickly

sensit delapsus in medios hostes, enim neque satis
has perceived that he had fallen into the midst of enemies, for neither sufficiently

fida responsa dabantur. Obstupuit que retro repressit
friendly answers were given. He has been astonished and backward has checked

pedem cum voce. Veluti qui nitens humi pressit
his step with his voice. As one who walking on the ground hath pressed

anguem improvisum aspris sentibus, que trepidus repente
a snake unexpected from the rough thorns, and trembling suddenly

refugit attollentem iras et tumentem cœrula colla
hath escaped him raising his wrath and swelling as to his azure neck.

Haud secus, Androgeos tremefactus visu abibat. Irruimus
Just so, Androgeos affrighted at the sight departed. We rush on

et circumfundimur densis armis, que passim sternimus
and we are surrounded by thick arms, and every where we overthrow them

ignaros loci et captos formidine: fortuna aspirat primo
ignorant of the place and taken with fear: fortune favors our first

labori. Atque hìc Chorœbus exultans successu que animis
undertaking. And here Chorœbus exulting with success and courage

inquit, O   socii   quà fortuna prima monstrat iter   salutis,
says,   O companions where fortune first points out the way of safety.

quaque ostendit se dextra sequamur. Mutemus clypeos
and where she shows herself propitious let us follow.   Let us change shields

que aptemus nobis insignia Danaûm: quis requirat in hoste,
and   fit   to us the armor of the Greeks: who asks in an enemy,

an   dolus an virtus? ipsi dabunt arma. Sic fatus
whether there'be fraud or courage? they themselves shall furnish arms   Thus

deinde induitur comantem galeam Androgei que decorum
having said then he is clad with the waving helmet of Androgeos and the beautiful

insigne   clypei,   que accommodat lateri Argivum ensem.
impress of his shield,   and   fits to his side a Grecian   sword.

Ripheus   hoc, Dymas ipse   hoc, que omnis juventus
Ripheus   does this, Dymas himself does this, and   every   youth

læta facit: quisque armat se recentibus spoliis.
pleased does this· every one arms himself with recent spoils.

Vadimus immixti Danais haud nostro numine: que
We march on mingled with the Greeks not with our god: and

congressi conserimus multa prælia per cæcam noctem
encountering we wage   many fights during the dark night.

demittimus multos Danaum Orco. Alii diffugiunt ad
we send down many of the Greeks to the gods below. Others fly to the

naves et   cursu petunt fida littora: pars rursus scandunt
ships and in their flight seek the faithful shores: a part again   ascend

ingentem equum turpi formidine et conduntur in   nota
the vast horse from base fear and are concealed in the known

alvo. Heu! nihil fas quenquam   fidere   Divis,
belly.   Alas! it is not right that any one should trust in any thing, the gods

invitis.   Ecce Cassandra virgo   Priameia trahebatur
being against him. Lo Cassandra the virgin daughter of Priam was   dragged

crinibus passis à templo que adytis Minervæ, frustra
with hair dishevelled from the temple and shrines of Minerva, in vain

tendens ardentia lumina ad cœlum, lumina, nam vincula
raising her glaring eyes to heaven, her eyes, I say, for   cords

arcebant teneras palmas. Chorœbus furiata mente non
confined her tender hands.   Chorœbus with his enraged mind has not

tulit hanc speciem et moriturus, injecit sese in medium
endured this spectacle and about to die, has thrown himself into the midst

agmen. Cuncti consequimur et incurrimus   densis
of the band. We all   follow and   rush on them with close

armis. Hic primum   obruimur   telis nostrorum, ex
weapons. Here first we are overwhelmed by the darts of our friends, from the

alto culmine delubri, et   miserrima cædes oritur
elevated roof of the temple, and a most deplorable slaughter commences from

facie   armorum, et   errore Graiarum jubarum.
the appearance of our arms, and the mistake of the Grecian plumes.

Tum Danai undique collecti invadunt gemitu atque
Then the Greeks from all quarters assembled attack us through grief and

ıra   virginis ereptæ: Ajax acerrimus, et gemini
resentinent *of* the virgin rescued *from them:* Ajax most fierce,   and the two

Atridæ que omnis exercitus Dolopum.   Ceu adversi
sons of Atreus   and all the   army   of the Dolopes.   As the adverse

venti, que Zephyrus que Notus et Eurus lætus   Eois
winds, both the west   and the south and the east joyous with *his* eastern

equis, quondam confligunt turbine rupto;   sylvæ stridunt
steeds, at times contend a whirlwind having burst forth;   the woods roar

que spumeus Nereus sævit tridenti, atque ciet æquora
and foaming Nereus rages with *his* trident,   and stirs up the seas from *their*

imo fundo. Illi etiam apparent si fudimus   quos insidiis
lowest bottom. They also   appear   if we have routed any by stratagem

per umbram obscura nocte, que agitavimus   tota urbe:
through the shade in the dusky night, and have driven over the whole city:

primi agnoscunt clypeos que mentita tela atque signant
they first recognise the shields and the false weapons and mark

ora discordia sono.   Ilicet   obruimur   numero,
our words differing in sound *from theirs.* Instantly we are overpowered by number,

que primus Chorœbus procumbit dextra Penilei ad   aram
and   first   Chorœbus   falls by the   right hand of Penileus at the altar

armipotentis Divæ: et Ripheus cadit unus qui fuit justissimus
of the warlike goddess: and Ripheus falls   one   who was most just

et servantissimus æqui in   Teucris;   visum   aliter
and most observant of right among the Trojans; it has seemed otherwise to the

Dîs. Que Hypanis que Dymas, confixi a   sociis pereunt:
gods. Both Hypanis   and Dymas,   pierced by *their* friends   perish.

nec tua plurima pietas   Pantheu nec   infula Apollinıs
nor thy   very great pity   O Pantheus   nor the fillet of Apollo

texit   te labentem.
hath protected thee falling.

Cineres Illaci et extrema flamma meorum,   testor
Ye ashes of Troy and   last   flame   of my *people*, I call *you* to witness

vitavisse   nec tela nec ullas vices Danaûm in vestro
that I have shunned neither darts nor   any   attacks of the Greeks at   your

occasu: et si fata   fuissent   ut caderem,   meruisse
fall: and if the fates might have been that I should fall, *I* have deserved it *by*

manu. Iphitus et Pelias mecum   divellimur   inde:
this hand.   Iphitus and Pelias with myself are forced away from thence:

quorum Iphitus jam gravior   ævo,   et Pelias tardus,
of whom   Iphitus   now *was* more infirm with age and Pelias halting by a

vulnere Ulyssei. Protinus   vocati   clamore ad sedes
wound of Ulysses.   Forthwith *we have* been called by the outcry to the palace

Priami. Hic vero ingentem pugnam, ceu cætera   bella
of Priam. Here indeed *we see* a great   fight,   as if   other   battles

forent nusquam, nulli morerentur ın tota urbe: cernimus
might be   to where, *or as if* none might be dying in the whole city: we behold

Martem sic indomitum, que Danaos ruentes ad tecta, que
Mars   so   ungoverned,   and the Greeks rushing   to the palace, and

limen obsessum testudine   acta.   Scalæ hærent parietibus,
the gate   besieged   the testudo being formed.   Ladders are fixed to the walls

que nituntur   gradibus sub ipsos postes, que   protecti
and they strive to *ascend* by the steps to the very door-posts, and   protected

sinistris objiciunt   clypeos ad tela, prensant   fastigia
by *their* left hands they oppose *their* shields   to the darts, *and* grasp   the roofs

dextris.   Contra Dardanidæ convellunt turres   ac
with *their* right. On the other hand   the Trojans tear down the turrets and

tecta culmina domorum; quando cernunt ultima
the covered tops of *their* houses; when   they see their last   *extremit*

parant   defendere   se   his   telis jam in extrem
they prepare to defend themselves with those weapons now in   the las

morte: que   devolvunt auratas trabes alta   decora
catastrophe: and they tumble down the gilded rafters the lofty decorations *of thei*

veterum parentum: alii   obsidere   imas   fores
ancient   parents: others have possessed *themselves* of the lowest doors

strictis mucronibus: servant has denso agmine.   Animi
with drawn swords: they guard these in a close   band.   *Our* courage

instaurati succurrere   tectis   regis, que levare viros
has been renewed   to succor   the palaces of the king, and to relieve the men

auxilio, que addere vim   victis. Erat   limen que
with *our* aid, and to give   vigor to *the* conquered. There was an entrance and

cæcæ fores et pervius usus tectorum Priami inter   se,
private doors and a passable use of *the* palaces of Priam between each other,

que postes relicti a tergo: qua infelix Andromache   inco-
and gates   left from behind: by which unhappy   Andromache   unat-

mitata sæpius solebat ferre se ad   soceros   dum
tended   often   was wont to bring herself to *her* parents in law,   whilst

regna manebant et trahebat puerum Astyanacta ad   avo.
the kingdom remained and *she* drew   the boy   Astyanax   to *his* grand-

Evado ad fastigia summi culminis unde   miseri
sire. I ascend to the top of the highest roof from whence   the wretched

Teucri jactabant irrita   tela manu   Circum aggressi
Trojans were casting unavailing darts with *their* hand. *We* around assaulting

ferro   turrim stantem in præcipiti que eductam   sub
with the sword a turret standing on   a precipice and   built up   to

astra   summis   tectis, unde   omnis Troja, et naves
the stars with *its* highest roofs, from whence   all   Troy, and the ships

Danaûm   solitæ videri,   et Achaica castra, quà summa
of the Greeks were wont to be seen, and the Grecian camps, where the highest

tabulata dabant juncturas labantes, convellimus   altis
stories   gave   joints   giving way, we have torn it *from its* lofty

sedibus que impulimus   ea repente lapsa trahit ruinam
foundations and pushed *it forward*,   that suddenly falling draws destruction

cum sonitu et   latè   incidit supra agmina   Danaûm
with a sound and far and wide hath fallen upon the troops of the Greeks;

ast alii subeunt; nec saxa nec ullum genus telorum   cessat,
but others succeed;   nor rocks nor   any   kind of weapons   ceases.

interea.   Ante vestibulum ipsumque in primo limine,
in the mean time. Before the entrance itself and in the first gate,

Pyrrhus exsultat corruscus telis et ahena luce.   Qualis ubi
Pyrrhus exults glittering in arms and brazen light.   As when

coluber, pastus mala gramina,   in lucem;   quem
a snake, having fed on noxious herbs, comes forth to the light; whom

tumidum frigida bruma tegebat sub terra, nunc novus exuviis
swollen cold winter hid under the earth, now renewed his skin

positis que nitidus juventa convolvit lubrica terga, pectore
being cast and sleek with youth he rolls his slippery back, with breast

sublato arduus ad solem, et micat trisulcis linguis
raised up lofty towards the sun, and vibrates with a three-forked tongue

ore.   Unà ingens Periphas, et armiger Auto-
from his mouth. At the same time huge Periphas, and the armor-bearer Auto-

medon agitator equorum Achillis, una   omnis Scyria
medon the driver of the horses of Achilles, at the same time all the Scyrian

pubes succedunt tecto, et jactant flammas ad culmina. Ipse
youth come up to the palace, and toss flames to the roofs. He

inter primos, bipenni correptâ perumpit dura limina que
among the first, a battle axe being seized breaks down the hard gates, and

vellit æratos postes à cardine; jamque cavavit   firma
tears the brazen posts from the hinge and now has pierced through the firm

robora, trabe excisa et dedit ingentem fenestram   lato
wood, the bar being cut off and made a great gap with a wide

ore. Domus intus apparet et longa atria patescunt;
mouth. The palace within appears and the long galleries are open to view;

penetralia   Priami et veterum regum apparent, que
the private recesses of Priam and of the ancient kings appear, and

vident armatos   stantes in primo limine. At interior
they see the armed guards standing on the first threshold. But the interior part

domus miscetur gemitu que misero tumultu: que cavæ
of the house is confused with groans and a miserable tumult: and the arched

ædes ululant fœmineis plangoribus: clamor ferit aurea sidera.
chambers ring with female shrieks: the noise strikes the golden stars.

Tum pavidæ matres errant ingentibus   tectis   que
Then the trembling mothers wander through the spacious apartments and

amplexæ tenent postes, atque figunt oscula.   Pyrrhus
embracing hold fast the door posts, and fix their lips to them. Pyrrhus

instat   patria   vi; nec claustra neque custodes ipsi
presses on with his father's violence; nor bars nor the guards them-

valent suffere: janua labat crebo
selves are able to sustain his attacks; the gate gives way by the frequent strokes of

ariete, et postes emoti   cardine procumbunt. Via fit
the ram, and the gates removed from the hinge fall. A way is made

vi: rumpunt aditus, que Danai immissi trucidant
by violence: they force the passages, and the Greeks let in massacre

primos, et latè complent loca milite. Amnis cum
the first, and around fill the places with soldiery. A river when it hath

exiit spumeus aggeribus ruptis, que evicit   oppositas
rushed forth foaming *its* banks being broken, and hath overcome the opposing

moles   gurgite,   non fertur in arva sic furens
mounds with *its* whirling current, is not borne into the fields so furious

cumulo que trahit armenta cum stabulis per omnes campos.
with *its* flood and sweeps away the herds with *their* stalls over all the plains.

Ipse vidi Neoptolemum furentem cæde, que geminos
I myself have seen Neopotolemus raging with slaughter, and the two sons

Atridas in limine: vidi Hecubam que centum nurus,
of Atreus in the gate: I have seen Hecuba and *her* hundred daughters-in-law,

que Priamum per aras fœdantem sanguine ignes quos
and Priam by the altars defiling with *his* blood the fires which

ipse sacraverat. Illi quinquaginta thalami tanta
he himself had consecrated. Those fifty bed chambers the so great

spes nepotum, superbi postes Barbarico auro que
hope of descendants, *those* stately pillars decorated with foreign gold and

spoliis, procubuere: Danai tenent quâ ignis deficit. For-
spoils, have fallen: the Greeks occupy where the fire abates. Per-

sitan, et, requiras, quæ fuerint fata Priami. Ubi
haps, also, you may require, what may have been the fates of Priam. When

vidit casum captæ urbis que limina tectorum con-
he saw the destruction of the captured city and the gates of *his* palace broken

vulsa, et hostem medium, in penetralibus; senior
down, and the enemy *in* the midst, in *his* private apartments; the aged *king*

nequicquam circumdat, humeris trementibus ævo, arma
in vain puts on, *his* shoulders trembling with age, *his* arms

diu desueta et inutile ferrum cingitur ac moriturus,
for a long time disused and *his* useless sword is girt on and ready to die,

fertur in densos hostes. In mediis ædibus que sub
is borne among *his* thick enemies. In the middle of the courts and under

nudo axe ætheris, fuit ingens ara, que juxtâ veterrima
the naked axle of heaven, has been a great altar, and near a very ancient

laurus, incumbens aræ atque complexa Penates
laurel, overhanging the altar and embracing the household gods with *its*

umbrâ. Hic Hecuba et natæ nequicquam condensæ
shade. Here Hecuba and *her* daughters in vain are crowded

circum altaria ceu columbæ præcipites atrâ tempestate.
around the altars as pigeons *flying* in haste from a dark tempest.

et amplexæ tenebant simulacra Divûm. Autem ut vidit
and embracing held fast the statutes of the gods. But as soon as *she* has seen

Priamum ip um juvenilibus armis sumptis inquit miser-
Priam himself youthful arms being assumed, she says, O most

rime conjux, quæ tam dira mens impulit cingi
unhappy spouse, what so direful a purpose hath forced *you* to be arrayed

his telis? aut quo ruis? Tempus eget non tali auxilio,
in these arms? or whither do you rush? The time needs not such aid

nec istis defensoribus, non si meus Hector ipse nunc
nor those defenders, not if my Hector himself now

afforet.   Tandem concede huc; hæc arą tuebitur   omnes
might be present.   At length retire   hither: this altar shall protect   all

aut moriere   simul.   Sic effata   recepit   ad
or you will die at the same time *with* us.   Thus having said she has taken *him* to

sese, et locavit longævum   in sacratâ sede. Autem ecce
herself, and has placed the aged *monarch* on the sacred seat.   But   lo

Polites unus natorum Priami, elapsus de   cæde of Pyrrhi,
Polites   one   of the sons of Priam,   escaped   from the slaughter   Pyrrhus,

fugit longis porticibus, per tela,   per hostes,   et saucius
flies   in the long galleries,   through darts, through enemies,   and wounded

lustrat   vacua atria: Pyrrhus ardens insequitur illum
goes around the vacant courts: Pyrhus   raging   pursues   him with a

infesto vulnere, jam jamque, tenet   manu,   et premit
hostile   wound,   now even now, grasps *him* with *his* hand, and presses on

hastâ.   Tandem ut evasit, ante oculos et ora
him with a spear.   At length   as he has come before   the eyes and faces of *his*

parentum, concidit et fudit   vitam cum multo sanguine.
parents,   he has fallen and poured forth *his* life   with   much   blood.

Hic Priamus, quanquam jam tenetur in mediâ morte tamen
Here   Priam,   although   now he is placed in the midst of death   yet

non abstinuit, nec pepercit voci que iræ   at exclamat,
he has not   forborne,   nor   spared *his* voice and anger but he exclaims,

Dî   persolvant dignas grates et reddant tibi debita præmia
may the gods make you suitable   returns and   render to you due   rewards

pro scelere, pro talibus ausis, si   est qua pietas cælo
for *your* wickedness, for   such outrages, if *there* is any justice in heaven

quæ curat talia,   qui fecisti me coram cernere lethum
which regards such *things*, who hast made me openly   to see   the death of

nati, et fœdasti patrios vultus, funere. At Achilles   ille
my son, and hast defiled a father's looks, with a corpse.   But Achilles   himself

a quo mentiris te   satum fuit non talis in
from whom you falsely say that you *was* begotten has been not such towards

Priamo hoste; sed erubuit   jura   que fidem
Priam *his* enemy;   but he has blushed at the laws *of nations* and the faith of a

supplicis; que reddidit exsangue corpus Hectoreum sepulchro,
suppliant,   and has restored the lifeless body   of Hector for the sepulchre,

que remisit me in mea regna. Senior   fatus   sic que
and   has sent me back to my kingdoms.   The aged *king* has spoken thus,   and

conjecit imbelle telum sine ictu; quod protinus   repulsam
has thrown a feeble   dart   without force; which instantly *has been* repelled

rauco ære et pependit nequicquam summo   umbone
by the hoarse brass and has hung   without effect from the highest   boss

clypei.   Cui Pyrrhus: ergo referes   hæc
of *his* buckler. To whom Pyrrhus *answered:* therefore you shall carry back these

et ibis nuncius genitori Pelidæ: memento narrare
things and you shall go a messenger to *my* father Achilles: remember to tell him

mea tristia facta que   degenerem Neoptolemum   Nunc
of my horrid deeds and *his* degenerate   Neoptolemus.   Now

morere. Dicens hæc,   traxit   trementem ad ipsa
die.   Saying these *things*, he has drawn *him* trembling to the very

altaria, et lapsantem in multo sanguine nati; que   lævâ
altars,   and slipping   in much   blood *of his* son; and with *his* left

implicuit comam; que dextrâ   extulit   coruscum
hand he has twisted *his* hair;   and with *his* right hath drawn *his* glittering

ensem et abdidit   lateri tenus capulo. Hæc finis fatorum
sword and hath hid it in *his* side   up to the hilt. This *was* the end of the fates

Priami: hic exitus tulit illum   sorte,   videntem
of Priam: this death has carried him off by divine appointment,   beholding

Trojam incensam et   Pergama   prolapsa,   quondam
Troy   burnt   and the fortress of Troy   fallen *in ruins*,   once

superbum regnatorem tot   populis que terris Asiæ: jacet
the proud   ruler   over so many nations and countries of Asia: he lies

ingens truncus litore,   que caput avulsum humeris,   et
a huge   trunk   on the shore, and *his* head   torn   from *his* shoulders, and

corpus sine nomine.
a body   without a name.

At tum primùm sævus horror circumstetit me: obstu
But then first   direful horror gathered   around me: I was aston-

pui: imago   cari genitoris subiit   ut vidi regem
ished. the image of *my* dear father occurred *to my mind* when I saw the king

aquævum exhalantem   vitam crudeli vulnere: Creusa,
of equal age breathing out *his* life by a cruel   wound: Creusa,

deserta subiit   et domus direpta, et casus parvi
abandoned came to *my mind*, and *my* house plundered, and the danger of little

Iuli. Respicio et lustro quæ copia sit circum me. Omnes
Iulus. I look about and I survey what force may be around me.   All

defessi, deseruere et saltu misere   ægrea corpora
wearied, have left *me* and by a spring have thrown *their* fainting bodies

ad terram aut dedere ignibus.   Que, adeo, jam superaram
to the earth or given them to the flames. And, so, now I remained

unus, cum aspicio Tyndarida, servantem limina Vestæ, et
alone, when I behold Helen,   watching   the temple of Vesta, and

tacitam latentem in secretâ sede, clara incendia dant lucem
silent   lurking in a secret place, the bright flames give   light

erranti que ferenti   oculos passim per cuncta
to me wandering and moving *my* eyes every where over   all

Illa communis Erinnys Trojæ et patriæ, permetuens
things. She the common fury of Troy and *her* country, dreading the

Teucros infestos sibi ob Pergama eversa, et pœnas
Trojans hostile to her on account of Troy overthrown, and the punishments

Danaûm, et iras   deserti conjugis abdiderat se, atque
of the Greeks, and the wrath of *her* deserted husband had hid herself, and

invisa sedebat aris. Ignes exarsere animo;
detested was sitting by the altars. Flames have flashed in *my* mind; *my* resent-

ira subit ulcisci cadentem patriam et sumere sceleratas
ment rises to avenge *my* falling. country and to take   exemplary.

pœnas.   Hæc sicilet incolumis aspiciet Spartam que
punishments.   Shall she forsooth safe   behold   Sparta   and *her*

patrias Mycenas, que ibit regina, triumpho parto? que
native   Mycenæ,   and shall she go a queen, a triumph being obtained?   and

videbit que conjugium que domum patres que natos,
shall *she* see both *her* husband   and *her* home, *her* fathers and children,

comitata turbâ Iliadum   et Phrygiis ministris? Priamus
attended by a train of Trojan matrons and by Phrygian servants?   shall Priam

occiderit ferro?   Troja   arserit   igni? lius
have fallen by the sword? shall Troy have been consumed by fire? shall the shor

Dardanidum toties sudarit sanguine?
of the Trojans   so often have been wet with the blood?

Non ita: nam etsi est nullum memorabile nomen in fœmineâ
Not so: for although there is no   memorable   name in   female

pœnâ nec ista victoria habet laudem; tamen laudabor
punishment nor that victory   has   glory;   yet I shall be praised

extinxisse nefas   et sumpsisse pœnas
to have destroyed a monster of wickedness and to have taken punishment *of one*

merentis; que juvabit   explêsse   animum flammæ
deserving *it;*   and it shall delight *me* to have satisfied *my* desire of burning

ultricis, et satiasse cineres meorum. Jactabam
revenge,   and to have satiated the ashes of *my* friends.   I was throwing out

talia, et ferebar   furiatâ mente, cum alma
such *words*, and was hurried along by *my* enraged   mind,   when *my* kind

Parens non tam clara   oculis ante obtulit   se mihi
Parent   not so manifest to *my* eyes   before has presented herself to me

videndam et refulsit in purâ luce, confessa Deam, que
to be seen   and has shown forth in clear light,   manifesting the goddess, and

qualis et quanta   solet videri   cœlicolis,   que
such   and as great as *she* is accustomed to be seen by the immortals,   and

continuit   prehensum dextrâ,   que insuper addidit
she has restrained *me* caught by the right hand,   and besides she has added

hæc   roseo ore; nate, quis tantus dolor excitat
these *words* from *her* rosy mouth;   O son, what so great indignation excites

tuas indomitas iras? quid furis? aut quonam   cura tibi
your ungoverned wrath? why do you rage? or whither has *the* regard to thee

nostri recessit? Non   prius aspicies ubi liqueris
of us departed?   Will you not first   see   where you may have left *your*

parentem Anchisen fessum ætate? ne   conjux Creusa
father   Anchises   helpless from age? whether *your* wife   Creusa

superet que puer Ascanius? circum quos omnes Graia
may survive   and the boy Ascanius?   around   whom   all the Grecian

acies   errant,   undique, et   flammæ   jam
troops   are roaming,   on every side,   and *whom* the flames   already

tulerint   et inimicus ensis   hauserit   ni mea
may have carried off and the hostile   sword have devoured   unless my

cura resistat. Non facies Lacænæ Tyndaridis invisa tibi ve
care interpose.   Not the form of Lacedemonian Helen hateful to thee or

Paris culpatus: inclementia Divûm, Divûm evertit
Paris   blamed: *but* the cruelty of the Gods, of the Gods overthrows

has opes, que sternit Trojam à   culmine.   Aspice:
hese powers, and levels   Troy   from *her* summit.   ^   Behold.

namque eripiam omnem nubem quæ nunc obducta
   for   I will remove   every   cloud   which now spread before *you*

hebetat mortales visus tibi tuenti et humida caligat circum·
dims the mortal   sight to thee beholding and humid throws a mist around.

tu ne time qua jussa   parentis neu recusa parere
do you fear not any commands of *your* parent   nor   refuse to submit to *her*

præceptis.   Hìc ubi vides moles disjectas que saxa avulsa
instructions.   Here where you see vast ruins thrown down and rocks torn

saxis, que fumum undantem pulvere mixto,   Neptunus
from rocks, and smoke   waving with dust intermingled,   Neptune

quatit muros que fundamenta emota magno tridenti que
shakes the walls and   foundations removed by *his* mighty trident and over-

eruit totam urbem a sedibus. Hìc, sævissima Juno prima tenet
turns the whole city from *its* basis.   Here. most fierce Juno first occupies

Scæas portas que furens vocat socium agmen a navibus,
the Scæan gates   and furious, summons the social band from the ships,

accincta ferro. Respice jam   Tritonia Pallas insedit
armed with a sword. Observe now *where* Tritonian Pallas has placed *herself*

summas arces effulgens nimbo   et sævâ Gorgone.
on the highest   towers resplendent with the cloud and terrible Gorgon.

Pater   ipse sufficit animos que secundas vires Danais:
Father *Jupiter* himself supplies courage and successful strength to the Greeks:

ipse suscitat Deos in Dardana arma.
he excites the Gods against the Trojan arms.

Eripe fugam nate que impone finem labori. Nus-
Haste *thy* flight O son   and   put   an end to *thy* labor.   I will

quam abero, et sistam te tutum   patrio limine.
never be absent, and I will place you safe on *your* paternal   threshold.

Dixerat, et condidit se spissis umbris noctis.   Diræ
She had said, and has hid herself in the thick shades of night   Awful

facies apparent que magna numina Deûm inimica   Trojæ.
forms   appear   and the great powers of the gods hostile   to Troy.

Tum vero omne Ilium visum mihi considere in ignes, et
Then indeed all   Ilium appeared to me to sink down into the flames and

Neptunia Troja verti ex· imo.   Ac veluti cum
Neptunian Troy to be overturned from *its* foundation. And as when

agricolæ certatim instant eruere antiquam ornum in
the swains emulously strain to overthrow the ancient ash on

summis montibus accisam ferro que crebris bipennibus;
the lofty mountains   cut with the iron and with the frequent axes,

illa usque minatur,   et tremefacta comam,   nutat
that a long while threatens *ruin*. and   shaken as to *its* leaves,   nods

vertice concusso; donec, paulatim,   evicta vulneribus,
its top being agitated; until, by little and little overcome   by wounds.

congemuit supremùm, que avulsa   jugis   traxi*
it hath groaned   at last,   and   torn from the mountain's sides hath drawn

ruinam. Descendo, ac Deo ducente, expedior   inter-
ruin after it.   I descend,   and the God leading, I am extricated   amidst

flammam et hostes: tela   dant locum, que flammæ rece-
the flame and enemies: the weapons give   place, and the flames   re-

dunt. Ast ubi jam perventum ad limina   patriæ sedis,
cede.   But when now I have come   to the gates of my paternal seat,

que   antiquas domos, genitor quem primum optabam
and to my ancient habitations, my father whom first   I wished

tollere in altos montes que primum, petebam,   abnegat
to convey to the lofty mountains first,   I sought,   refuses

producere vitam que pati exilium, Trojâ excisâ. O vos, ait,
to prolong his life and to suffer exile, Troy being razed. O ye, he says,

quibus   sanguis integer   ævi, quē   vires   stant
to whom there is blood intire on account of age, and whose powers remain

solidæ   suo robore; vos agitate fugam. Si   cœlicolæ
unimpaired in their vigor; do you attempt flight.   If the inhabitants

voluissent me ducere   vitam, servassent has
of heaven had willed that I should lengthen out my life, they had preserved these

sedes mihi: satis que super   vidimus una excidia
seats for me: it is enough and more that we have seen one destruction of my

et superavimus captæ urbi. O affati
country and have survived the captured city. O ye, having addressed my

corpus, sic, sic, positum, descedite. Ipse inveniam mortem
body, thus, thus, laid out, depart.   I myself shall find death

manu: hostis miserebitur que petet exuvias: jactura
by this hand: the enemy will pity me and seek my spoils: the loss of

sepulchri est facilis. Jampridem invisus Divis, et inutilis,
burial is easy. Long since hated by the gods, useless,

demoror annos, ex quo   Pater Divûm atque Rex
I linger out my years, from what time the Father of the gods and King

hominum afflavit me   ventis fulminis et contigit
of men has blasted me with the winds of his thunder and has struck me with

igni. Memorans talia perstabat que manebat   fixus
lightning. Relating such things he persisted and remained resolute.

Contra, nos, effusi lacrymis que conjux Creusa que
On the other hand, we, dissolved in tears both my wife Creusa and

Ascanius que omnis domus   pater ne vellet
Ascanius and all the family conjure, that my father would not be willing

vertere cuncta secum que incumbere fato urgenti.
to ruin all things with himself and to meet the fate pressing on.

Ille abnegat et hæret   inceptc et in iisdem sedibus.
He refuses and adheres to his design and in the same seats.

Rursus feror in arma que miserrimus opto mortem.
Again I am borne away to arms and most wretched I wish for death.

Nam quod consilium aut quæ fortuna jam dabatur? genitor
For what design or what chance now, was given? O father

sperasti   ne me posse efferre pedem, te relicto? que
hast thou hoped that I   could   stir   a foot,   you being left? and

tantum   nefas excidit patrio ore? si placet   Superis
hath so great wickedness fallen from a father's mouth? if it pleases   the Powers

nihil relinqui tanta urbe; et hoc sedet   animo,
above that nothing be left of so great a city; and this remains fixed in *your* mind,

que juvat   addere que te   que tuos Trojæ   perituræ:
and it delights *you* to join both yourself and yours to Troy about to perish:

janua patet isti letho. Jamque Pyrrhus aderit   de
the gate lies open to that death.   Soon   Pyrrhus will be present from

Priami multo sanguine qui obtruncat natum ante   ora   o
Priam's copious blood   who   murders the son before the face of the

patris, et patrem ad aras.
father, and the father at the altars.

Erat   hoc, alma parens, quod eripis me per tela
Was *it for* this, O propitious mother, that you rescue me among darts

per ignes? ut cernam hostem in mediis   penetralibus,
among the flames? that I may see the enemy in the midst of *these*   recesses,

utque   que Ascanium,   que meum , patrem,   que,
and that, *I may see* both Ascanius,   and   my   father,   and,

Creusam juxtâ, mactatos alterum in sanguine alterius? arma
Creusa near,   slaughtered the one in the blood of the other? arms

viri, ferte arma: ultima lux vocat victos. Reddite me
O men, bring arms: the last light summons the vanquished. Return me

Danais, sinite   revisam prœlia instaurata: nunquam
to the Greeks, permit *that* I may revisit the fight   renewed: never *will we*

omnes moriemur inulti hodie. Hìc rursus accingot
all   die   unrevenged to day. Here again I am equipped

ferro: que insertabam sinistram,   clypeo aptans
with a sword: and I inserted *my* left hand, in *my* shield   fitting *it*

que ferebam me   extra tecta. Autem, ecce, conjux
and I brought myself without the palace. But,   lo, *my* wife

amplexa pedes, hærebat   in limine que tendebat parvum
embracing *my* feet,   clung to *me* on the threshold and reached' out   little

Iulum patri. Si abis periturus rape nos et tecum
Iulus to *his* father. If you will go about to perish take   us also with you

in omnia: sin   expertus ponis aliquem spem in armis
to all *danger:* but if having experienced you place any   hope   in   arms

sumptis tutare hanc domum primùm. Cui parvus Iulus;
assumed defend this   house   first.   To whom *is* little Iulus *left*;

cui   pater, et cui relinquor, quondam dicta tua conjux?
to whom your father, and to whom am I left, once called thy   wife?

Vociferans talia   replebat omne   tectum gemitu:
Exclaiming such *words* she filled all the building with groans:

cum subitum monstrum, que mirabile dictu, oritur.
when a sudden prodigy,   and wonderful to be told, arises.

Namque inter manus que ora   mœstorum parentum,
For   between the hands and faces of *his* mournful   parents,

ecce, levis apex   visus fundere lumen de summo
lo,   the light plume *was* seen to pour forth   light   from the   top

vertice Iuli que innoxia flamma lambere   comas molli
of the head of Iulus and the harmless flame to glide along *his* hair with a gentle

tactu et pasci circum   tempora.   Nos pavidi metu
touch and to feed around   *his*   temples.   We   fearful with dread *begin*

trepidare que excutere   flagrantem crinem, et restinguere
to tremble   and to shake off *his* flaming   hair,   and to extinguish

sanctos ignes fontibus. At pater Anchises lætus extulit
the sacred fires with water.   But father Anchises joyful has raised *his*

oculos ad sidera et tetendit   palmas cœlo cum   voce
eyes   to the stars and stretches *his* hands to heaven with *his*   voice

Omnipotens Jupiter, aspice nos   flecteris   ullis precibus:
O Omnipotent Jupiter,   behold us if thou art moved by any prayers

  hoc, tantum; et pater, si meremur   pietate, deinde
we ask this,   only; and O father, if we merit *any thing* by *our* piety, then

  da   auxilium atque firma hæc omina. Vix   senior
grant to *us thy* aid   and confirm these omens.   Scarcely has the aged

  fatus erat ea,   que lævum   intonuit
sire uttered those *words*, and the left part *of the heaven* has thundered *with*

subito fragore, et stella lapsa de cœlo, cucurrit per umbras
a sudden peal,   and a star falling from heaven, has run through the shades

ducens facem   cum multâ luce.   Cernimus illam
drawing a trail of flame with much light   We see   that

labentem super summa culmina tecti condere se claram,
gliding   over the highest   tops of the roof to hide itself bright, in the

Idæâ sylvâ que signantem vias: tum sulcus dat lucem
Idean woods and marking the way: then a trail gives light with a

longo limite, et loca circum latè fumant sulfure.
long path,   and the places around far and wide smoke with sulphur.

Hìc verò genitor victus tollit se ad auras, que
Here indeed *my* father conquered raises himself towards heaven,   and

affatur Deos et adorat sanctum sidus: jam, jam, est
addresses the Gods   and adores   the holy star: now, now, there is

nulla mora; sequor et quà ducitis, adsum.   Patrii
no delay;   I follow and whither you lead, am present.   O paternal

Dî servate   domum, servate   nepotem: vestrum est hoc
Gods protect *our* house, protect *my* grandson: yours   is this

augurium que Troja est in vestro numine.   Nate equidem
omen   and Troy is in your power.   O son   indeed

cedo nec recuso ire   comes tibi.   Ille dixerat: et jam
I yield nor refuse to go a companion to thee. He   had said: and now

ignis   auditur clarior per mœnia, que incendia volvunt
the conflagration is heard clearer through the city, and the flames   roll the

æstus propius. Age ergo care pater, imponere nostræ
fire nearer.   Come therefore dear father, be placed   on my

cervici: ipse subibo   humeris, nec iste labor gravabit me.
neck: I will bear *you upon my* shoulders, nor that load will oppress me.

Quocunque res   cadent, periculum   unum et commune,
However things shall happen, the danger *shall be* one   and the same

ambobus, salus erit una: parvus Iulus sit
to both,   safety shall be one *and the same to us:* let little   Iulus be a

comes   mihi et   conjux Creusa servet   vestigia longè.
companion to me and *my* wife   Creusa may keep *my* steps at a distance.

Vos, famuli, advertite vestris animis,   quæ dicam,
Ye,   servants,   turn   with your minds, *to those things* which I shall say,

Est tumulus   egressis   urbe, que vetustum tem-
There is a rising ground to you departing from the city, and   an old   tem-

plum desertæ Cereris, que juxta   antiqua cupressus ser-
ple   of deserted   Ceres,   and   near *there is* an ancient cypress   pre-

vata religione   patrum multos annos. In hanc unam
served by the devotion of *our* fathers for many   years.   To   this   one

sedem, veniemus ex diverso.   Genitor tu cape   sacra
seat,   we will come by different *ways.* O Father do thou take   the sacred

manu que   Patrios Penates.   Nefas   me
things in *your* hand   and *our* paternal   gods.   It is a wickedness that I

digressum è tanto bello et recenti cæde, attrectare; donec
having come from so great a war and recent slaughter, should touch *them*; until

abluero   me   vivo flumine. Fatus hæc
I shall have washed myself in the living stream. Having said these *things,*

insternor super latos humeros que subjecta colla,   veste
I am covered upon *my* broad shoulders   and   bended   neck, with a garment

que pelle   fulvi leonis, que succedo   oneri: parvus Iülus
and the skin of a tawny lion,   and   I succeed to the load: little   Iulus

implicuit se   dextræ que sequitur patrem passibus non
has linked himself to *my* right hand and   follows   *his* father with steps   not

æquis. Conjux subit ponè. Ferimur   per opaca locorum,
equal.   *My* wife follows behind. We are carried through gloomy   places,

et nunc omnes auræ   terrent, omnis sonus excitat   me
and now   every breath of wind terrifies,   every   sound   alarms   me

suspensum, et pariter timentem comiti   que oneri,   quem
in suspense,   and equally   fearing for *my* companion and *my* load,   whom

dudum non ulla tela, injecta, neque   Graii   glomerati
lately   not   any darts, thrown,   neither the Greeks   collected together

ex adverso agmine, movebant. Jamque   propinquabam
in   a hostile   band,   moved.   And now   I drew near

portis que videbar evasisse   omnem   viam; cum
to the gates and   seemed to have escaped   all *the danger of* the way;   when

creber sonitus pedum subito visus   adesse ad aures: que
a frequent sound   of feet suddenly seemed to be present to *my* ears: and *my*

genitor prospiciens per umbras exclamat, nate, nate,   fuge,
father   looking   through the shades   cries out,   O son, O son,   fly

propinquant: cerno ardèntes clypeos atque micantia   æra.
they approach: I see *their* glittering   shields   and   gleaming   brass.

Hì :   male-amicum numen nescio quod   eripuit mihi   tre-
Here *same* unfriendly   deity I know not   what *one* took from me   fear-

pido contusam mentem. Namque dum   cursu   sequor
ful *my* confused   mind.   For   whilst in *my* course   I seek for

avia   et excedo   notâ   regione viarum: heu!
unfrequented *places* and depart from the known direction of the ways: alas!

conjux Creusa substitit,   incertum ne   erepta
my wife   Creusa stayed behind, *it is* uncertain whether snatched   from *me*

misero fato, erravit-ne   viâ seu lassa resedit: nec
by distressing fate, or has wandered *from* the path or wearied sat down: nor

reddita est nostris oculis pòst. Nec respexi   ve reflexi
was she restored to our   eyes afterwards. Nor have I looked back or turned back

animum   amissam, priusquam venimus tumulum   que
my mind *that she* was lost,   before   we have come to the eminence   and

sacratam sedem antiquæ Cereris; hic, omnibus   demum
sacred   seat   of ancient   Ceres;   here,   all   at length

collectis   una defuit   et fefellit   comites,   que
being collected one was wanting and has disappointed *her* companions.   and

natum, que virum. Quem que hominum que   Deorum,
son,   and husband. Whom both   of men   and   of gods,

amens non incusavi? aut quid crudelius vidi   in   urbe
frantic   have I not blamed? or   what more cruel have I beheld in   the city

eversa? Commendo Ascanium que patrem Anchisen   que
destroyed? I commend   Ascanius   and *my* father   Anchises   and

Teucros   Penates   sociis et recondo   curvâ
the Trojan household gods to *my* associates and I conceal *them*   in a winding

valle. Ipse   repeto urbem et   cingor fulgentibus   armis.
valley. I myself seek again the city and am   arrayed   in shining   arms

     Stat renovare omnes casus que reverti per   omnem
My purpose is fixed to renew   all   perils and to return over   all

Trojam et rursus objectare caput periculis.   Principio repeto
Troy   and again   to expose *my* head   to dangers.   First I seek again

muros que obscura limina portæ,   quà   extuleram
the walls and   the dark   entrances of the gate, whence I had brought forth *my*

gressum: sequor retro vestigia observata per noctem   et
step: I follow back *my* footsteps   observed   in the darkness   and

lustro   lumine.
search *them* out by the light *of the flames.*

    Ubique   horror   simul   silentia   ipsa terrent
Every where *is* horror at the same time the   silence   itself   terrifies

animos. Inde refero   domum   .   si fortè
my mind.   Thence I bring   *myself* again home *that I might see* if by chanc

     tulisset   pedem.   Danai irruerant et
Creusa might have brought   her foot   *thither.*   The Greeks had rushed in and

tenebant omne tectum. Ilicet   edax   ignis volvitur
possessed the whole   house   Quickly the devouring fire is rolled by the

vento ad summa fastigia;   flammæ exsuperant;   æstus
wind   to the highest   roofs.   the flames   rise above;   the conflagration

furit ad auras   Procedo ad sedes Priami que reviso arcem.
rages   to the air   proceed to the mansions of Priam and revisit the citadel.

Et jam Phœnix et dirus Ulysses, lecti custodes,
And now, Phœnix and execrable Ulysses, chosen guards,

asservabant prædam vacuis porticibus asylo Junonis.
were watching the spoil in the vacant aisles in the temple of Juno.

Troia gaza erepta incensis adytis, que mensæ
Trojan treasures carried off from the burning temples, and the tables

Deorum, que solidi crateres auro, que captiva vestis
of the gods, and solid goblets of gold, and captive vestments

congeritur huc undique. Pueri et pavidæ matres stant
are piled up here all around. Boys and fearful matrons stand

circum longo ordine. Quin etiam ausus jactare vocem
around in a long train. But even I have dared to throw my voice

per umbram, implevi vias clamore: que mœstus
through the shade, I have filled the streets with my cry and mournful

ingeminans Creusam nequicquam, vocavi iterum que
repeating Creusa in vain, I have called her again and

iterum. Infelix simulacrum atque umbra Creusæ ipsius
again. The unhappy ghost, and the shade of Creusa herself

et imago major notâ, visa est ante oculos mihi
and an image larger than the known, appeared before my eyes to me

quærenti et furenti tectis urbis sine fine.
seeking her and raving in the houses of the city without end.

Obstupui que comæ steterunt et vox hæsit
I have been astonished and my hair has stood erect and my voice has adhered to

faucibus. Tum sic affari et demere curas
my jaws. Then she began thus to address me and to take away my cares

his dictis: O dulcis conjux quid, tantum, juvat
with these words: O dear spouse why, so much, doth it delight you

indulgere insano dolore? hæc eveniunt non sine numine
to indulge in immoderate grief? these things happen not without the will

Divûm: nec fas aut ille regnator superi Olympi sinit
of the gods: nor was it lawful or does he the ruler of high heaven permit

te asportare Creusam comitem. Longa exilia tibi, et
thee to carry away Creusa a companion. Long exile will be to thee, and

vastum æquor maris arandum. Venies ad Hesperiam
an immense surface of sea to be ploughed. You shall come to the Hesperian

terram ubi Lydius Tybris fluit leni agmine inter arva
land where Tuscan Tyber flows with its gentle stream between lands

opima virum. Lætæ res que regnum et regia
rich in heroes. Prosperous circumstances and a kingdom and a royal

conjux parta tibi illic: pelle lacrymas dilectæ Creusæ.
spouse is provided for thee there: banish your tears for beloved Creusa.

Ego Dardanis et nurus Divæ
a descendant from Dardanus and the daughter in-law of goddess

Veneris, non aspiciam superbas sedes Myrmidonum ve
Venus, shall not behold the proud seats of the Greeks or

Dolopum, aut ibo servitum Graiis matribus. Sed magna
of the Dolopes, or shall I go to serve the Grecian matrons. But the great

genitrix Deûm detinet me his oris. Jamque vale et
mother of the gods detains me on these coasts. And now farewell and

serva amorem communis nati. Ubi dedit hæc
keep your love of our common son. When she has spoken these

dicta, deseruit lachrymantem et volentem dicere multa
words, she left me weeping and wishing to say many things

que recessit in tenues auras. Ibi, ter conatus circuindare
and vanished into the thin air There, thrice I attempted to throw my

brachia collo; imago comprensa frustra ter effugit
arms around her neck; the image seized in vain three times escaped

manus, par levibus ventis que simillima volucri somno.
my hands, equal to the light winds and most like a fleeting dream.

Sic demum nocte consumptâ reviso socios. Atque hic
Thus at length the night being spent I revisit my companions. And here

admirans, invenio ingentem numerum novorum comitum
admiring, I find that a vast number of new companions

affluxisse que matres que viros, pubem collectam exilio,
to have flowed in both matrons and men, youth collected for exile,

miserabile vulgus! convenere undique parati
a miserable crowd! they have assembled from every quarter prepared

animis que opibus in quascunque terras velim
with minds and their effects to follow to whatsoever lands I may be willing

deducere pelago. Jamque Lucifer surgebat jugis
to conduct them on the sea. And now the morning star was rising on the tops

summæ Idæ que ducebat diem que Danai tenebant limina
of highest Ida and ushered in the day and the Greeks kept the entrance

portarum obsessa, nec ulla spes opis dabatur. Cessi et
of the gates besieged, nor any hope of assistance was given. I yielded and

petivi montem genitore sublato.
sought the mountain my parent being lifted up.

ÆNEID.

BOOK THIRD.

Postquam visum Superis evertere res Asiæ
After it has pleased the gods above to overthrow the power of Asia

que gentem Priami immeritam, que superbum Ilium cecidit,
and the nation of Priam undeserving, and stately Ilium has fallen,

et omnis Neptunia Troja fumat humo; agimur
and all Neptunian Troy smokes from the ground; we are driven

auguriis Divûm quærere diversa exilia et desertas terras,
by the omens of the gods to seek remote exiles and unoccupied lands.

que molimur classem sub ipsâ Antandro et montibus
and we build a fleet under the very Antandros and the mountains of

Phrygiæ Idæ que contrahimus viros, incerti quò, fata
Phrygian Ida and we draw together our men, uncertain where, the fates

ferant, ubi detur sistere. Vix prima æstas
may conduct us, where it may be granted to settle. Scarcely the first summer

inceperat, et pater Anchises jubebat dare vela fatis.
had begun, and father Anchises ordered us to hoist sails by the fates.

Tum lacrymans relinquo litora patriæ que portus, et
Then weeping I leave the shores of my country and the ports, and

campos ubi Troja fuit: feror exul in altum cum
the plains where Troy has been; I am carried an exile to the deep with my

sociis que nato Penatibus et magnis Dîs. Procul
companions and my son my household gods and the great gods. At a distance

Mavortia terra vastis campis colitur, Thraces arant, quon-
a martial land with vast plains is inhabited, the Thracians cultivate it, for-

dam regnata acri Lycurgo; antiquum hospitium Trojæ, que
merly governed by fierce Lycurgus; an ancient retreat of Troy and

Penates socii dum fortuna fuit. Feror huc
its gods were our companions while fortune has been to us. I am carried hither

et loco prima mœnia curvo littore ingressus fatis
and I place my first walls on the winding shore having entered with fates

iniquis; que fingo Æneadas nomen de meo
unkind; and I call the inhabitants Æneadæ a name derived from my

nomine. Ferebam sacra matri Dionææ que Divis
name. I was offering sacrifices to my mother Venus and the gods

auspicibus operum cœptorum: que mactabam nitentem
the patrons of our works begun: and was sacrificing a white

taurum in littore supero regi Cœlicolûm. Fortè
bull on the shore to the high king of the heavenly inhabitants. By chance

tumulus fuit juxtà quo summo cornea virgulta et
a rising ground was near on which summit were cornel twigs and

myrtus horrida densis hastilibus. Accessi que conatus
a myrtle awful with thick spears. I drew near and endeavoured

convellere viridem sylvam ab humo, ut tegerem aras
to tear the verdant wood from the ground, that I might cover the altars

frondentibus ramis: video horrendum monstrum et mirabile
with leafy boughs: I see a dreadful prodigy and wonderful

dictu. Nam çoæ arbos prima vellitur solo
to be told. For which tree first is pulled up from the ground, its

radicibus ruptis, guttæ atro sanguine liquuntur huic et
roots being broken off, drops of black blood ooze out to this tree, and

maculant terram tabo. Frigidus horror quatit membra
stain the earth with gore Cold trembling shakes the limbs

mihi, que sanguis gelidus formidine, coit. Rursus in-
for me, and my blood chilled through fear, collects together. Again I pro-

sequor et convellere lentum vimen alterius et penitus
ceed also to pluck up the limber shoot of another and thoroughly

ientare latentes causas et ater sanguis sequitur de coitice
o examine the hidden causes and black blood follows from the bark

alterius. Movens multa animo venerabar agrestes
of the other. Revolving many *things in my* mind I prayed to the rural

nymphas que patrem Gradivum, qui præsidet Geticis
nymphs and father Mars, who presides over the Thracian

arvis, secundarent visus ritè que levarent omen.
territories, *that* they would prosper the vision in due form and avert the omen.

Sed postquam aggredior tertia hastilia majore nixu, que
But after I attempt the third spears with greater effort and

genibus obluctor adversæ arenæ; eloquor an si-
with *my* knees I struggle against the opposite sand; shall I speak or shall I be

leam? lacrymabilis gemitus auditur imo tumulo,
silent? a mournful groan is heard from the bottom of the rising ground,

et vox reddita fertur ad aures: Ænea, quid laceras
and a voice returned *from it* is brought to *my* ears: O Æneas, why do you tear

miserum? parce jam sepulto, parce scelerare pias
_ wretched *being?* spare *me* now buried, forbear to pollute *your* pious

manus: Troja tulit me non externum tibi: hic cruor
hands: Troy has produced me not a stranger to you: this blood

manat haud stipite. Heu! fuge crudeles terras, fuge
flows not from the trunk. Ah! fly the cruel lands, fly

avarum litus; nam ego Polydorus; ferrea seges telorum
the avaricious shore; for I *am* Polydorus; an iron crop of darts

texit confixum hìc et ingrevit acutis jaculis. Tum,
has covered *me* pierced through here and grown with sharp javelins. Then,

verò pressus mentem ancipiti formidine obstupui
indeed weighed down as to *my* mind with doubtful fear I was astonished

que comæ steterunt et vox hæsit faucibus. Quondam
and *my* hair stood up and *my* voice clung to *my* jaws. Formerly

infelix Priamus furtim mandârat hunc Polydorum Threïcio
unhappy Priam secretly had sent this Polydorus to the Thracian

regi alendum cum magno pondere auri; cum jam diffi-
king to be brought up with a great weight of gold; when now he de-

deret armis Dardaniæ que videret urbem cingi obsidione.
spaired of the arms of Troy and saw the city to be beset with a siege.

Ille ut opes Teucrûm fractæ, et fortuna
He as soon as the powers of the Trojans *have been* broken down and *their* fortune

recessit, secutus Agamemnonias res que victricia arma,
has receded, following Agamemnon's cause and *his* victorious arms,

abrumpit omne fas, obtruncat Polydorum et potitur
breaks every sacred law, murders Polydorus and possesses *his*

auro vi. Sacra fames auri! quid non cogis mortalia
gold by force. O cursed desire of gold! what dost thou not force the mortal

pectora! postquam pavor reliquit ossa, refero monstra
hearts *to do!* after fear has left *my* bones, I relate *these* prodigies

Deûm ad delectos proceres populi que primum parentem
of the gods to chosen leaders of the people and first to *my* fathe.

et posco quæ sit sententia. Idem animus omnibus ex-
and require what may be *their* opinion. The same disposition *is* to all   to decedere sceleratâ terrâ, linquere pollutum hospitium et dare
part   from the execrable land, to quit *the place* of violated hospitality and to give

Austros classibus. Ergo instauramus funus   Polydoro
the winds to *our* fleet. Therefore we renew   the funeral rites to Polydorus

et ingens tellus aggeritur tumulo; aræ   stant
and a huge pile of earth is thrown up for the tomb: altars   are standing

manibus mœstæ cæruleis vittis que atrâ cupresso: et   Ilia-
to *his* Manes mournful with azure fillets and gloomy cypress: and the Trojan

des solutæ crinem   de   more   circum. Inferimus
matrons loose as to *their* hair according to custom *stand* around.   We offer

cymbia spumantia tepido lacte et pateras sacri sanguinis:
bowls   foaming   with warm milk and goblets of consecrated   blood:

que condimus animam sepulchro et supremùm ciemus magnâ
and   we hide   the soul in the grave and   lastly   we call with a loud

voce. Inde ubi   prima fides pelago que venti dant
voice. Thence when *there is* the first trust to the ocean and the winds grant

placata maria et Auster lenis crepitans vocat in   altum;
tranquil   seas and the south wind mild rustling invites us to   the deep:

socii deducunt naves et complent litora.   Provehimur
my companions launch the ships and cover   the shore. We are wafted from

portu, que terræ que urbes recedunt.
the port and the lands and the cities recede.

Gratissima tellus, sacra   matri Nereidum et Ægæo
A most pleasant land, sacred to the mother of the Nereids   and Ægean

Neptuno colitur   medio mari; quam errantèm circum
Neptune is inhabited in the midst of the sea: which   wandering   around

oras et litora pius Arcitenens revinxit celsâ Mycone
he coasts and shores the pious Archer   has bound with high Mycone

que Gyaro; que dedit immotam coli   et contemnere
and Gyaros: and has rendered *it* unmoved to be inhabited and to contemn

ventos. Huc feror: hæc placidissima   accipit
the winds. Hither I am brought: this most peaceful *land* receives   *us*

fessos   tuto portu. Egressi veneramur urbem Apollinis.
wearied in *its* safe port.   Landing we venerate   the city of Apollo.

Rex Anius, idem rex hominum que sacerdos Phœbi
The king Anius, the same king of men   and   priest *of Phœbus

redimitus   tempora vittis et sacrâ lauro occurrit, agnoscit
bound   as to *his* temples with fillets and sacred laurel meets   *us*, he knows

veterem amicum Anchisen. Jungimus dextras hospitio
his old   friend Anchises.   We join   right hands in amity

et subimus   tecta. Venerabar templa Dei structa
and we come under *his* roof.   I reverenced the temples of the god built

vetusto saxo: da Thymbræe propriam domum da mœnia
of ancient rock; grant O Thymbræus   a fixed   home grant walls to *us*

fessis et genus et mansuram urbem: serva altera
wearied and an offspring and an abiding   city: preserve other

Pergama Trojæ reliquias   Danaûm atque immitis Achillei.
forts of Troy the remnant of the Greeks   and of merciless Achilles.

Quem sequimur? ve quò jubes ire? ubi ponere
Whom do we follow? or whither do you order *us* to go? where to place

sedes?   pater da   augurium atque illabere nostris
our seats?   O father grant *us*   a sign   and   glide into   our

animis. Vix fatus eram ea: omnia   repentè
minds.   Scarcely had I spoken those *words:* all *things* suddenly

visa   tremere que limina que laurus   Dei: que
have seemed to tremble   both the gates and the laurel of the god: and

totus mons circum moveri et cortina mugire adytis
the whole mountain around to be moved and the oracle to bellow the sanctuary

reclusis. Submissi petimus terram, et vox fertur ad
being opened. Humble   we seek the ground, and a voice is conveyed to

aures: duri Dardanidæ eadem tellus, quæ prima tulit
our ears: ye hardy Trojans   the same land,   which first has produced

vos   a stirpe   parentum, accipiet vos reduces læto
you from the stock of *your* forefathers, shall receive you returned in *its* joyful

ubere: exquirite   antiquam matrem. Hìc domus Æneæ
soil: search out *your* ancient   mother.   Here the family of Æneas

dominabitur cunctis oris, et natorum nati, et qui
shall bear rule over all lands, and *his* children's children, and who

nascentur ab illis.   Hæc   Phœbus: que ingens
shall be born from them.   These *things said* Phœbus: and great

lætitia exorta mixto tumultu; et cuncti quærunt quæ
joy has arisen with mingled tumult; and all inquire what

ea mœnia, sint, quo Phœbus vocet errantes, que jubeat
those walls may be, whither Phœbus may call *us* wandering, and command

reverti. Tum genitor volvens monumenta veterum
us to return.   Then *my* father   revolving the memorials of the ancient

virorum ait, O proceres, audite et discite vestras spes.
men says, O nobles,   hear and learn   your   hopes.

Creta insula magni Jovis jacet medio ponto, ubi
Crete an island of great Jove lies in the middle of the sea, where *is*

Mons Idæus et cunabula nostræ gentis: habitant centum
Mount Ida and the nursery of our   race: they inhabit an hundred

magnas urbes, uberrima regna; unde Teucrus maximus
great cities, most fertile realms; whence Teucer   our first

pater, si ritè recordor   audita, primùm advectus est
ancestor, if rightly I remember *things* heard, first has been carried

in Rhœteas oras, que optavit locum   regno; Ilium et
to the Rhœtian coasts, and has selected a situation for *his* kingdom; Ilium and

Pergamæ arces nondum steterant; habitabant imis vallibus.
Pergamæan towers not yet had stood; they dwelt in the lowest vales.

Hinc   mater Cybele, cultrix, que Corybantia æra,
Hence *came* mother Cybele, the protectress, and the Corybantian brass,

que Idæum nemus: hinc fida silentia   sacris,
and the Idæan grove: hence the faithful silence in *her* sacred rites

et juncti leones subiere currum dominæ Ergo
and the coupled lions have come under the chariot of the goddess. Therefore

agite et quà jussa Divûm ducunt sequamur.
come and where the commands of the gods lead let us follow.

Placemus ventos et petamus Gnossia regna. Nec
Let us appease the winds and let us seek the Gnossian realms. Nor are they

longo cursu distant, modo Jupiter adsit, tertia lux
a long way distant; provided that Jupiter be with us, the third light

sistet classem in Cretæis oris.
shall place our fleet on the Cretan coasts.

Sic fatus mactavit meritos honores aris: taurum
Thus having said he offered suitable sacrifices upon the altars: a bull

Neptuno; taurum tibi pulcher Apollo; nigram pecudem
to Neptune; a bull to thee O beautiful Apollo; a black sheep

hyemi, albam felicibus Zephyris. Fama volat Idome-
to winter, a white one to the propitious Zephyrs. A rumor flies that Idome-

nea ducem pulsum cesisse paternis regnis, que
neus a leader banished has departed from his paternal kingdoms, an

littora Cretæ deserta, domos vacare
that the shores of Crete have been deserted, and the houses are free from the

hoste, que sedes astare relictas. Linquimus portus Orty-
enemy, and the regions remain abandoned. We leave the port of Orty-

giæ, que volamus pelago: que legimus Naxon Baccha-
gia, and fly on the sea: and we coast by Naxos where the Baccha

tam jugis que viridem Donysam, Olearon, que niveam
nals revel on its tops and green Donysa, Olearos, and snowy

Paron, que Cycladas sparsas per æquor et freta consita
Paros, and the Cyclades scattered through the sea and the straits sown

crebis terris. Nauticus clamor exoritur vario certamine.
with many lands. The naval clamor arises with various emulation.

Socii hortantur, petamus Cretam que proavos.
Our companions encourage each other, let us seek Cretam and our ancestors.

Ventus surgens à puppe prosequitur euntes: et tandem
The wind rising from the stern follows us proceeding: and at length

allabimur antiquis oris Curetum. Ergò avidus molior
we arrive at the ancient shores of the Curetes. Therefore eager I raise

muros optatæ urbis, que voco Pergamean: et hortor
the walls of the wished for city, and I call it the city of Pergamus: and I exhort

gentem lætam cognomine amare focos, que attollere
my people delighted with the name to love their homes, and to raise

arcem tectis. Jamque puppes ferè subductæ in
a tower on their houses. And now the ships have been mostly drawn upon

sicco littore: juventus operata connubiis que novis
the dry shore: the youth have been busily employed in nuptials and their new

arvis, dabam jura que domos: cum subito tabida que
fields, I was distributing laws and houses: when suddenly a wasting and

miseranda lues, tractu cœli corrupto, venit membris
pitiable disease, a space of the air corrupted, came upon their limbs

que   arboribus que satis, et annus   lethifer.
and *their*   trees   and crops, and the year   *becomes* destructive of life.

Linquebant dulces animos, aut trahebant   ægra corpora: tum
They left   *their* pleasant   lives,   or   dragged *their* sick   bodies: then

Sirius   exurere steriles agros.   Herbæ arebant,   et
the dog-star *began* to burn   the sterile fields.   The herbs   were dried,   and

ægra   seges negabat   victum.   Rursus pater hortatur ire
the diseased crop   denied *them* sustenance.   Again *my* father   advises   to go

ad oraculum Ortygiæ, que Phœbum mari   remenso,
to   the oracle   of Ortygia,   and   Apollo   the sea   being measured back

precari quem finem   ferat   fessis rebus;   unde
to inquire what   end   he may make to *our* afflicted affairs;   whence

jubeat tentare auxilium laborum;   quò vertere cursus.
he may order *us* to seek   relief of *our* sufferings; whither to turn *our* course.

Erat nox, et somnus habebat   animalia   terris.   Sacræ
It was night, and   sleep   possessed living creatures on the earth.   The sacred

effigies Divûm que Phrygii   Penates,   quos   extuleram
images   of the gods and the Trojan household deities, which   I had brought

mecum a Trojâ que ex mediis   ignibus   urbis,   visi
with me from   Troy   and from the middle of the flames of the city, have seemed

astare ante oculos   jacentis insomnis, manifesti   multo
to stand before the eyes *of me* lying   awake,   conspicuous   by much

lumine: quà plena Luna fundebat se   per   insertas fenes-
light: where the full moon   poured   herself through the inserted   win-

tras.   Tum sic   effari, et demere   curas   his
dows.   Then thus *they have seemed* to speak, and to diminish *my* cares with these

dictis;   quod Apollo dicturus   tibi   delato Ortygiam hìc
words;   that which Apollo is about to tell to thee   carried back to Ortygia   here

canit: et, en, ultro mittit nos ad tua limina.   Nos
he reveals: and, lo, willingly he sends us   to   thy dwelling.   We *have*

secuti   te que tua arma, Dardaniâ incensâ; nos, sub   te
accompanied thee and thy arms,   Troy   being burnt; we,   under   thee

permensi tumidum æquor classibus;   iidem   tollemus
have measured   the swollen   sea   in ships: *we* the same   will raise

venturos nepotes in astra que dabimus urbi   imperium
thy future   descendants to the stars and   will give to *thy* city   the empire

Tu   para magna mœnia   magnis,   neque
of the world.   Do thou prepare great   walls for a powerful *people*,   neither

linque longum laborem fugæ.   Sedes   mutandæ:
relinquish the long   labor of *thy* flight.   *Your* abodes   must be changed:

Delius Apollo non suasit   tibi hæc littora, aut   jussit
Delian   Apollo   has not advised for thee these   shores,   or   commanded

considere Cretæ.   Est locus   Graii dicunt   Hesperiam
to settle   at Crete.   There is a place the Greeks   call *it*   Hesperia

cognomine: antiqua terra, potens armis atque   ubere
by name: an ancient land,   powerful in arms and   the fertility

glebæ.   Œnotrii viri coluere: nunc   fama
of the soil.   Œnotrian men have inhabited *it*:   now *there is* a report *that their*

minorés dixisse gentem Italiam, de nomine ducis. Hæc
descendants have called the nation   Italy, from the name of the chief. These

sedes propriæ nobis: hinc   ortus Dardanus, que   pater
seats *are* destined   to us: from hence has sprung Dardanus,   and   father

Iasius; à quo principe nostrum genus.   Age, surge et
Iasus; from which prince   our   race *is derived*. Come, arise and

lætus refer longævo parenti hæc dicta haud   dubitandà.
joyful relate to *thy* aged   sire   these words by no means   to be doubted.

Require Coritum que Ausonias terras: Jupiter negat   tibi
Search out   Coritus   and the Ausonian lands: Jupiter   denies   to thee

Dictæa arva.   Attonitus talibus visis ac voce Deorum
the Cretan fields. I *have been* astonished at such visions and the voice of the gods

nec erat illud sopor; sed videbar mihi agnoscere   vultus
nor was that sleep; but I seemed to myself to distinguish *their* looks

coram que comas velatas,   que   præsentia ora: tum
openly   and *their* hair adorned with fillets, and *their* present   faces: then

gelidus sudor manabat   tota corpora, corripio   corpus
cold   sweat   ran down *from my* whole body,   I snatch   *my* body

    stratis, que tendo manus supinas ad cœlum cum   voce,
from the bed, and spread out *my* hands lifted up to heaven   with *my* voice,

et   libo   focis intemerata munera.   Honore
and I pour forth on the hearths the pure   offerings.   The offerings

perfecto, lætus facio Anchisen certum, que   pando
being completed, joyful I make Anchises   sure, and   disclose

rem   ordine.   Agnovit ambiguam prolem, que
the circumstance in order. He acknowledged the doubtful offspring,   and

geminos parentes, que se   deceptum   novo   errore
the double   founders, and that he has been deceived by the recent   mistake

veterum locorum. Tum memorat: nate, éxercite   Iliacis
of the ancient places.   Then   he relates: O son, exercised   by the Trojan

fatis, Cassandra sola canebat mihi tales casus. Nunc repeto
disasters, Cassandra alone foretold to me such events. Now I recollect

    porténdere hæc   debita nostro generi, et
that she foretold *that* these *places have been* destined for our   nation,   and

sæpe vocare Hesperiam, sæpe Itala regna. Sed quis
often   called it Hesperia, often the Italian realms. But who

crederet Teucros venturos ad littora Hesperiæ?
would believe that the Trojans were about to come to the shores   of Hesperia?

aut quem tum   vates   Cassandra moveret? Cedamus
or   whom then could the prophetess Cassandra   move?   Let us yield

Phœbo, et moniti, sequamur meliora. Sic ait; et
to Phœbus, and being advised, let us follow better *counsels*. Thus he says, and

cuncti, ovantes, paremus dictis. Deserimus hanc sedem
we all, rejoicing, obey *his* words. We quit   this   land

quoque, que paucis relictis damus vela, que currimus vastum
also,   and a few being left we make sail, and we run over the vast

æquor   cavâ trabe. Postquam rates tenuere altum, nec
sea *in our* hollow ships.   After   the ships have gained the deep, no.

ullæ terræ jam amplius apparent undique, cœlum   et
any lands now longer appear all around, the heavens *appear* and

undique pontus; tum cœruleus imber astitit supra   caput
all around the ocean; then a leaden colored cloud stood over the head

mihi, ferens noctem que hyemem; et unda inhorruit   te-
to me, bringing night and a storm; and the sea grew terrific with

nebris. Continuò venti volvunt mare, que magna   æquora
darkness. Forthwith the winds roll the sea, and vast wav

surgunt: jactamur, dispersi vasto gurgite.
arise: we are tossed, scattered on the vast abyss.

Nimbi involvêre diem, et humida nox abstulit   cœlum
Clouds have obscured the day, and humid night has taken the heave

ignes ingeminant abruptis nubibus. Excutimur
from our view: lightnings redouble from the broken clouds. We are driven

cursu, et erramus in cæcis undis. Palinurus   ipse
from *our* course, and we wander on the dark waves. Palinurus himself

negat discernere diem que noctem cœlo,   nec   memi-
denies to distinguish the day and the night in the heavens, nor to have

nisse   viæ in mediâ undâ. Adeo erramus pelago
remembered the course in the midst of the waves. Thus we wander on the sea

tres incertos soles cæcâ caligine, totidem   noctes   sine
three doubtful days in thick darkness, the same number of nights without

sidere. Tandem quarto die terra primùm visa attollere
a star. At length on the fourth day the earth first *has been* seen to raise

se, montes procul aperire, ac volvere fumum.   Vela
itself, the mountains from afar to open, and to roll smoke. The sails

cadunt: insurgimus remis;   haud mora, nautæ adnixi
drop: we rise on *our* oars: *there is* no delay, the sailors striving

torquent spumas, et verrunt cœrula.
turn   the foam, and sweep the azure *seas.*

Littora   Strophadum primùm accipiunt me servatum
The shores of the Strophades first receive me preserved

ex undis. Insulæ dictæ Strophades   Graio nomine
from the waves. *Those* islands called Strophades from a Grecian name

stant in magno Ionio: quas dira Celæno que aliæ
are situated in the great Ionian *sea.* which direful Celæno and other

Harpyiæ colunt: postquam domus Phineia   clausa,
Harpies inhabit: since the palace of Phineus *has been* closed *against*

que liquére   priores mensas metu. Haud monstrum
them, and they have left *their* former tables through fear. Not a monster

tristius illis, nec ulla sævior pestis, et ira Deorûm
more fell than they, nor any more cruel pest, and scourge of the gods

extulit sese   Stygiis undis. Vultus   volucrum
hath raised itself from the Stygian waves. The faces of *those* fowls

virginei, fœdissima proluvies ventris, que uncæ
are like virgins' *faces,* a most foul efflux of the belly, and hooked

manus et ora semper pallida fame. Delati huc ubi
hands and faces always pale from hunger Wafted hither when

intravimus portus: ecce videmus læta armenta boum
we have entered the harbor: lo we see fat herds of oxen

passim campis que pecus caprigenum per herbas,
all about on the plains and a flock of goats along the meadows,

nullo custode. Irruimus ferro, et vocamus
with no keeper. We rush on them with the sword, and invoke

Divos et Jovem ipsum in partem que prædam: tunc
the gods and Jupiter himself to a share and the booty: then

extruimus toros curvo littore, que epulamur opimis
we erect the couches on the winding shore, and we feast upon the rich

dapibus. At Harpyiæ subitæ adsunt horrifico lapsu
meats. But the Harpies sudden are present with a dreadful descent

de montibus, et quatiunt alas magnis clangoribus
from the mountains, and they shake their wings with mighty noises

que diripiunt dapes, que fœdant omnia immundo con-
and seize our meats, and defile all with their filthy touch:

tactu: tum dira vox inter tetrum odorem.
then a dreadful voice was to them amidst a horrid scent.

Rursùm instruimus mensas, que reponimus ignem aris,
Again we spread our tables, and we replace the fire on the altars,

in longo secessu sub cavatâ rupe, clausa circum arboribus
in a long retreat under a hollow rock, inclosed around with trees

atque horrentibus umbris. Rursùm ex diverso cœli,
and gloomy shades. Again from a different part of the sky,

que cæcis latebris, sonans turba circumvolat prædam
and dark retreats, the whizzing flock flies around the prey

uncis pedibus, polluit dapes ore. Tunc edico
with hooked feet, and spoils the meats with their mouth. Then I order

sociis capessant arma, et bellum gerendum
my companions that they may take arms, and that war be waged

cum dirâ gente. Faciunt haud secus ac
with the horrid brood. They do no otherwise than they have been

jussi, que disponunt enses tectos per herbam,
commanded, and they dispose their swords concealed among the grass,

et condunt latentia scuta. Ergo, ubi delapsæ
and they hide their secreted shields. Wherefore, when gliding down

dedere sonitum per curva littora; Misenus dat
they have made a noise through the bending shores; Misenus gives the

signum cavo ære, ab altâ speculâ; socii invadunt
signal from his hollow brass, from the lofty eminence; my friends attack them

et tentant nova prœlia fœdare ferro obscœnas volucres
and try new battles to mangle with the sword these filthy fowls

pelagi. Sed neque accipiunt ullam vim plumis,
of the sea. But neither do they receive any stroke on their feathers,

nec vulnera tergo: que lapsæ celeri fugâ sub sidera,
nor wounds on the back: and gliding with rapid flight under the stars,

relinquunt semesam prædam et fœda vestigia.
they leave the half-eaten prey and their foul tracks.

Celæno sola consedit in præcelsâ rupe infelix vates
Celæno alone alighted upon a very high rock an ill boding prophetess

que rupit hanc vocem pectore: Laomedontiadæ
and sends forth this voice from her breast: Ye sons of Laomedon

paratis-ne inferre bellum, etiam bellum pro cæde
do you prepare to make war, even war for the slaughter of our

boum, que juvencis stratis? et pellere insontes Harpyias
cattle, and bullocks slain? and to drive the innocent Harpies

patrio regno?
from their paternal kingdom?

Ergo accipite, atque figite hæc mea dicta in animis; ego
Wherefore attend to, and fix these my words in your minds; I

maxima Furiarum pando vobis quæ omnipotens pater
the chief of the Furies disclose to you what the almighty father revealed

Phœbo, Phœbus Apollo prædixit mihi. Petitis
to Phœbus, and which Phœbus Apollo hath foretold to me. You seek

Italiam, cursu; que ventis vocatis ibitis Italiam,
Italy in your course and the winds being invoked you shall go to Italy.

que licebit intrare portus. Sed non cingetis
and it shall be permitted you to enter the ports. But you shall not inclose

datam urbem mœnibus, antequam dira fames, que injuria
the given city with walls. before dreadful famine, and the injury

nostræ cædis, subigat vos absumere ambesas mensas
of our murder, may force you to consume your half eaten tables with your

malis. Dixit: et ablata pennis, refugit in sylvam. At
jaws. She said: and borne up on wings, has flown back to the wood. But

sanguis gelidus subitâ formidine, diriguit sociis:
the blood chilled by sudden fear, grew thick in my companions: their

animi cecidere, nec jam amplius jubent exposcere pacem
minds have sunk, nor now any more do they order to require peace

armis, sed votis que precibus, sive sint Deæ, seu diræ
by arms, but by vows and prayers, whether they may be goddesses, or direful

que obscœnæ volucres. At pater Anchises, palmis passis
and foul birds. But father Anchises, his hands being stretched

de littore, vocat magna Numina, que indicit meritos
out from the shore. invokes the great gods, and appoints proper

honores: Dî, prohibite minas; Dî, avertite talem casum,
offerings: ye gods prohibit the threats; ye gods, avert such a misfortune,

et placidi servate pios. Tum jubet diripere funem
and propitious preserve the pious. Then he orders to tear away the rope from

littore, que laxare rudentes excussos. Noti tendunt
the shore, and to let fly the sheets shaken out. The south winds stretch

vela: ferimur spumantibus undis, quâ que ventus
the sails: we are borne on the foaming waves, whithersoever both the wind

que gubernator vocabant cursum. Jam nemorosa Zacynthos
and the pilot invited our course. Now woody Zacynthos

apparet medio fluctu, que Dulichium que Same, et Ne-
appears in the midst of the waves, and Dulichium and Samos, and Ne-

ritos ardua saxis. Effugimus scopulos Ithacæ, regna.
ritos lofty with *its* rocks. We escape the rocks of Ithaca, the realms of

Laërtia et execramur terram altricem sævæ Ulyssis. Mox et
Laertes and execrate the land nourisher of cruel Ulysses. Soon also

nimbosa cacumina montis Leucatæ, et Apollo formidatus
the cloudy summit of the mountain of Leucates, and Apollo dreaded

nautis aperitur. Nos fessi petimus hunc, et succedimus
by sailors is discovered. We wearied seek this, and repair

parvæ urbi. Anchora jacitur de prorâ; puppes stant littore
to the little city. The anchor is cast from the prow; the ships stand on the shore

Ergo tandem potiti insperatâ tellure, que lustramu
Therefore at length possessed of the greatly desired land, we both sacrifice

Jovi, que incendimus aras votis: que celebramus
to Jupiter, and we kindle the altars with vows: and we render celebrated

Actia littora Iliacis ludis. Socii nudati exercent
the Actian shores with Trojan games. *My* companions naked practise *their*

patrias palæstras labente oleo; juvat evasisse tot
country's wrestlings with slippery oil; it delights *them* to have escaped so many

Argolicas urbes, que tenuisse fugam per medios
Grecian cities, and to have held *their* flight through the middle of *their*

hostes. Interea sol circumvolvitur magnum annum, et
enemies. Meanwhile the sun is rolled round the great year, and

glacialis hyems asperat undas Aquilonibus. Figo
icy winter roughens the waves with the north winds. I fix to the

adversis postibus clypeum cavo ære, gestamen
fronting door posts *of the temple* a buckler of hollow brass, the armor

magni Abantis, et signo rem carmine: Æneas
of great Abas, and I inscribe the transaction by *this* verse: Æneas

hæc arma victoribus Danais. Tum jubeo
suspended these arms *taken* from the victorious Greeks. Then I order *them*

linquere portus, et considere transtris. Socii feriunt
to leave the ports, and to sit on the benches. *My* associates strike

mare certatim, et verrunt æquora. Protinus abscondimus
the sea eagerly, and sweep the surface. Soon we lose sight

aërias arces Phæacum, que legimus litora
of the aerial towers of the Phæacians, and we coast along the shores

Epiri, que subimus Chaonio portu, et ascendimus celsam
of Epirus, and enter the Chaonian port, and we go up to the lofty

urbem Buthroti.
city of Buthrotus.

Hìc incredibilis fama rerum occupat aures, Helenum
Here an incredible report of things takes *our* ears, that Helenus

Priamiden regnare per Graias urbes, potitum
the son of Priam reigned over Grecian cities, possessed

conjugio que sceptris Pyrrhi Æacidæ, et
of the spouse and the sceptre of Pyrrus the grandson of Æacus, and

Andromachen iterum cessisse marito patrio
that Andromache again had fallen to a husband of *her own* country

Obstupui;   que   pectus   incensum   miro   amore
I was amazed;   and *my* breast has been inflamed with a wonderful   desire

compellare virum,   et cognoscere tantos   casus
to   address   the hero,   and   to know   so great   events

Progredior   portu, linquens classes   et   litora. Tûm
I advance from the port, leaving   the fleet and the shores.   Then

fortè Andromache libabat solemnes dapes et tristia
by chance Andromache   was offering the yearly feasts and mournful

dona cineri,   ante urbem, in luco, ad undam falsi
gifts to the ashes *of Hector*, before the city, in a grove, at the water of the false

Simoëntis, que vocabat manes ad Hectoreum tumulum,
Simois,   and was invoking the manes at the Hectorean   tomb,

quem inanem   sacraverat   viridi cespite, et geminas
which empty she had consecrated with green   turf,   and   two

aras   causam   lachrymis. Ut   amens conspexit me
altars the incentive *to her* tears.   As soon as amazed she has seen me

venientem, et   Troïa arma circum; exterrita   magnis
coming up,   and the Trojan arms around;   terrified at the mighty

monstris, diriguit in medio visu; calor reliquit   ossa;
prodigies, she fainted in the midst of the sight; heat   has left *her* bones:

labitur: et tandem vix fatur   longo tempore: Nate
she falls: and at length scarcely speaks after a long   interval: O born of a

Deâ, affers ne te   mihi, vera facies, verus nuncius?
goddess, do you bring yourself to me, a real form,   a true   messenger?

vivisne? aut si alma lux recessit,   ubi est Hector?
do you live?   or if cheerful light has gone from *you*, where is Hector?

Dixit, que effudit lachrymas et implevit omnem locum
She said, and poured forth   tears   and   filled   all   the place

clamore. Vix subjicio pauca   furenti, et
with *her* cry.   Scarcely do I answer a few *words* to *her* raving,   and

turbatus hisco raris vocibus: equidem vivo, que duco
affected I open *my* mouth in few words: indeed   I live,   and draw out

vitam per omnia extrema. Ne dubita, nam vides vera.
life   through all   perils.   Do not doubt, for   you see realities.

Heu! quis casus excipit te dejectam   tanto
Ah!   what misfortune hath befallen thee dejected *by the loss* of so great a

conjuge? aut quæ fortuna satis digna revisit?
husband?   or   what fortune sufficiently worthy hath returned *to you?*

Andromache   Hectoris,   servas connubia
O Andromache   *once* Hector's   *wife*, dost thou preserve the marriage o

Pyrrhi?   dejecit   vultum et locuta est demissâ
Pyrrhus? she has cast down *her* countenance and has spoken   in a low

voce: O virgo   Priameia una felix ante alias, jussa
voice: O virgin   daughter of Priam alone happy above others, doomed

mori ad hostilem tumulum sub   altis mœnibus Trojæ:
to die at an enemy's   tomb   under the lofty walls   of Troy;

quæ   non pertulit ullos sortitus, nec captiva tetigit
who   hath not borne   any   lots,   nor as a captive hath touched

cuoile victoris heri! nos vectæ per diversa æquora,
tre bed of a victorious lord! we conveyed over various seas, our

patriâ incensâ enixæ, servitio tulimus
country being burnt being brought forth, in servitude have endured the

fastus stirpis Achilleæ, que superbum juvenem;
haughtiness of the offspring of Achilles, and the proud youth;

qui deinde secutus Hermionen, Ledæam, que
who afterwards having followed Hermione, the daughter of Leda, and

Lacedæmoneos hymenæos transmisit me famulam Heleno
the Lacedemonian marriages hath delivered me a slave to Helenus

famulo que habendam. Ast Orestes inflammatus magno
a slave also to be possessed by him. But Orestes inflamed with ardent

amore conjugis ereptæ, et agitatus furiis scelerum,
love of his spouse torn from him and driven by the furies of his crimes,

excipit illum incautum que obtruncat ad patrias aras.
surprises him unprepared, and murders him at his native altars.

Morte Neoptolemi pars regnorum reddita cessit
By the death of Neoptolemus a part of his kingdoms restored has fallen to

Heleno; qui dixit campos cognomine Chaonios, que
Helenus; who has called the plains by the name Chaonian, and the

omnem Chaoniam à Trojano Chaone: que addidit Per-
whole country Chaonia from Trojan Chaon. and has built Per-

gama que hanc Iliacam arcem jugis. Sed qui venti,
gamus and this Trojan tower on the mountains. But what winds,

quæ fata dedere cursum tibi? aut quis Deus appulit
what fates have directed the course hither to you? or what god• has driven

te ignarum nostris oris? quid puer Ascanius? superat ne,
you ignorant to our coasts? what does the boy Ascanius? does he live,

et vescitur aurâ?
and live upon the air?

Quem Troja jam tibi—jam est ecqua cura puero
Whom Troy now to you—now is there any concern to the boy

amissæ parentis? et ecquid pater Æneas et avunculus
of his lost parent? and what does his father Æneas and his uncle

Hector excitat in antiquam virtutem que viriles animos?
Hector excite him to ancient valour and manly courage?

Lacrymans fundebat talia, que incassùm ciebat longos
Weeping she poured forth such words, and in vain excited long

fletus; cùm heros Helenus Priamides affert sese à
weeping; when the hero Helenus the son of Priam brings himself from

mœnibus, multis comitantibus que agnoscit suos que
the walls, many accompanying him and recognizes his friends and

lætus ducit ad limina; et fundit lachrymas multùm
pleased conducts them to the palace; and pours forth tears abundanly

inter singula verba. Procedo, et agnosco parvam Trojam
between each word. I move forward and I know little Troy

que Pergama simulata magnis, et arentem rivum
and Pergamus resembling the great, and the dry river called

cognomine Xanthi: que amplector limina   Scææ   portæ.
by the name of Xanthus: and I embrace   the threshold of the Scæan   gate.

Et necnon Teucri   simul fruuntur   sociâ urbe.   Rex
And also   the Trojans at the same time enjoy the friendly city.   The king

accipiebat illos in amplis   porticibus.   In medio   aulaï
received   them in the spacious   galleries.   In the middle of the court

libabant pocula Bacchi, dapibus impositis auro, que tenebant
they drank   cups   of wine,   the meats being served on gold, and   they held

pateras.
the goblets.

Jamque   dies, que alter dies, processit; et   auræ vocant
And now *one* day,   and another day, has passed by; and the gales   call

vela, que carbasus inflatur tumido   Austro.   Aggredior
the sails, and the canvass is inflated by the swelling south wind.   I accost

vatem   his dictis, ac quæso talia: Trojugena, Interpres
the prophet in these words, and I intreat such *things:* Trojan born, Interpreter

Divûm,   qui sentis numina Phœbi, qui   tripodas, qui
of the Gods, who knowest the will of Phœbus, who *knowest* the tripods,   who

lauros   Clari,   qui   sidera, et   linguas
knowest the laurels of the Clarian *God,* who *knowest* the stars, and   the notes

volucrum, et omina   præpetis pennæ, age fare,   namque
of the birds,   the omens   of the swift   wing,   come say,   for

prospera relligio dixit   omnem cursum mihi; et cuncti
propitious   auspices have directed the whole   course   to me; and   all

Divi   numine   suaserunt   petere Italiam et tentare
the Gods by *their* authority   have persuaded *me* to seek · Italy   and to explore

terras repôstas: Celæno Harpyia sola canit novum prodigium
lands   reserved: Celæno   the Harpy alone predicts a new   prodigy,

que nefas dictu, et denuntiat tristes iras que   obscœnam
and horrible to be told, and   foretells   vengeful wrath and   furious

famem.   Quæ pericula prima vito? ve sequens quid
hunger.   What   dangers   first   do I shun? or   following   what *counsel*

possum superare tantos labores? Hìc Helenus   juvencis
can I   surmount so great difficulties? Here   Helenus'   bullocks

primùm cæsis de   more, exorat pacem   Divûm, que
first   being slain according to custom, implores the favour of the Gods,   and

resolvit vittas   sacrati capitis, que ipse ducit me   manu
unbinds the fillets of *his* consecrated   head, and he himself leads   me by the hand

ad tua limina, Phœbe! suspensum multo numine: atque
to thy   temples, O Phœbus!   anxious at the mighty power   and the

sacerdos deinde canit hæc   ex divino ore: Nate   Deâ;
priest   then   declares these *things* from *his* divine mouth: Oh Goddess born;

nam fides manifesta te   ire per altum majoribus auspiciis:
for the evidence   is clear   that you go over the deep with greater   auspices:

rex Deûm   sic sortitur   fata, que volvit   vices:
the King of the Gods thus dispenses *his* decrees, and   rolls the series of events

is ordo   vertitur. Expediam tibi dictis pauca
that order (*or course of things*) is fixed.   I will unfold   to you in words   a few

è multis, quò tutior   lustres   hospitia æquora,
particulars- of many   that more safe you may survey thè intervening seas

et possis considere Ausonio portu: nam Parcæ prohibent
and be able   to settle in the Ausonian port: for the Fates   forbid *you*

scire cætera: que Saturnia Juno vetat Helenum   fari.
to know the rest: and Saturnian Juno prohibits Helenus   to speak.

Principio, longa via   invia   longis terris dividit Italiam
First,   a long voyage interrupted by extensive lands separates   Italy

procul,   quam tu, ignare jam rere   propinquam que
at a distance *from you*, which you, O ignorant now think *to be*   near   and

paras invadere vicinos portus.   Et remus lentandus   in
you prepare to enter   the near   ports.   And the oar   must be bent   in

Trinacriâ undâ et   æquor   Ausonii salis   lustrandum
the Sicilian   wave and the surface of the Ausonian   sea   must be sailed over

navibus que inferni lacus   que   insula
by *your* ships   and the infernal lakes *are to be passed over* and   the island

Ææ Circæ   antequam possis componere urbem
Ææan   Circe *is to be approached*   before   you can be able   to build   a city

tutâ terrâ. Dicam   tibi signa: tu teneto   condita
in a safe land.   I will declare to you the signs: do you retain *them*   laid up

mente.   Cum ingens sus inventa tibi solicito ad undam
in *your* mind.   When a great   sow discovered for you anxious   by   the waves

secreti fluminis sub   ilicibus   litoreis enixa
of a secret river   under the holm trees along the shore   having brought forth

fœtus triginta capitum jacebit   solo recubans   alba
a litter of thirty   heads   shall lie on the ground reclining *herself*   white

albi nati circum ubera; is erit locus   urbis   ea
and her white young   around *her* dugs; that shall be the scite of *your* city   that

certa requies   laborum.   Nec tu horresce futuros morsus
a certain rest *of your*   labours.   Nor do you dread   the future   eating

mensarum, fata invenient viam que Apollo   vocatus
of your   tables,   the fates shall find   a way and Apollo   invoked

aderit.   Autem effuge has terras que hanc oram   Itali
shall be present. But   shun   these countries and   this   coast of the Italian

litoris quæ proxima perfunditur æstu nostri æquoris: cuncta
shore   which nearest   is washed by the tide of our   sea: all

mœnia habitantur   malis Graiis. Hìc, et,   Narycii
those cities   are inhabited by the wicked Greeks.   Here, also, the Narycian

Locri posuerunt mœnia et Lyctius Idomeneus   obsedit
Locrians have placed *their* walls   and Cretan   Idomeneus   has occupied

Salentinos campos milite: hìc illa parva Petilia   subnixa
the Salentine   plains with soldiery· here *is* that   little   Petilia   defended

muro Philoctetæ Milibœi ducis. Quin ubi   classes
by the wall of Philoctetes the Melibœan Chief   But   when   *your* fleet

transmissæ trans æquora steterint et jam solves   vota
wafted   across   the seas shall have stood and now you shall pay *your* vows

aris   positis   litore; velare adopertus   comas
altars being placed on the shore; be thou veiled covered as to *your* hair   with a

purpureo amictu: ne qua hostilis facies occurrat inter
purple   veil: lest   any   hostile countenance may appear   amidst

sanctos ignes in honore Deorum, et turbet omina.
the sacred fires in   honor   of the Gods, and disturb the omens.   *Let your*

Socii   hunc morem   sacrorum,   ipse teneto hunc:
friends *observe* this   custom of the sacred rites, do *you* yourse.f observe   this;

casti nepotes   maneant in hac religione.
your pious descendants may persevere in these   rites.

Ast ubi ventus admoverit   te digressum, Siculæ oræ,
But when the wind shall have brought you   departed, to the Sicilian coast,

et claustra angusti Pelori rarescent, tellus læva et
and the straights of narrow Pelorus shall grow wider,   the land on the left   and

æquora læva   petantur   tibi longo circuitu: fuge
the seas on the left may be sought for you by a long   circuit: fly

dextrum litus et undas. Ferunt   hæc loca,   quondam
the right   shore and waves.   They report *that* these places,   formerly

convulsa vi et vastâ ruinâ,   dissiluisse: longinqua
orn away by violence and vast desolation, to have broke asunder: long

vetustas ævi valet mutare   tantùm cùm utraque tellus
duration of time is able to change *things* so much when   each   land

foret protinùs una, pontus venit medio vi, et
might be entirely   one,   the sea   rushed in between with violence,   and

undis abscidit Hesperium latus   Siculo, que
with *its* waves separated   the Italian   shore from the Sicilian, and   with a

angusto æstu interluit arva et urbes diductas   litore.
narrow   current flows between fields and cities   separated   by a shore.

Scylla obscidet dextrum latus   implacata Charybdis lævum:
Scylla   occupies   the right   side *and*   implacable   Charybdis   the left:

atque ter sorbet vastos fluctus abruptum in imo gurgite
and   thrice she swallows vast   waves   precipitately in the deep   gulf

barathri, que rursus erigit   alternos sub auras, et verberat
of *her* maw,   and   again   raises *them* alternate   to   the air, and   strikes

sidera   undâ. At spelunca cohibet in cæcis latebris
the stars with the waves. But a cavern   confines   in *its* dark   recesses

Scyllam exsertantem   ora, et trahentem naves in saxa.
Scylla   opening   *her* mouth, and   drawing   the ships among the rocks.

Prima facies   hominis et virgo   pulchro pectore
Her upper part *is* of a human being and a virgin *with* a handsome   breast

tenus pube: postrema   Pristis   immani corpore,
as far as the middle: *her* lowest *part* is a Pristis of an enormous   body

commissa Delphinûm caudas   utero luporum.
joined   a Dolphin's   tails   to the belly of wolves.

Præstat   cessantem lustrare metas Trinacrii
It is best *that you* delaying should sail around the borders   of Sicilian

Pachyni, et circumflectere longos cursus, quàm semel
Pachynus,   and   to wind about   long   circuits,   than   at once

vidisse informem Scyllam sub   vasto antro, et
that you should see mishapen   Scylla   in   *her*   vast   cavern and the

саxa resonantia   cœruleis canibus. Præterea si qua pru-
rocks resounding with her sea green   dogs.   Besides   if any know-

dentia est Heleno si qua fides   vati si Apollo implet
ledge   is to Helenus if any trust *is* to a prophet if Apollo fills   *his*

animum veris; Nate Deâ,   prædicam tibi illud unum
mind   with truths; Goddess born, I will foretell to you that   one

que unum præ omnibus   et repetens que iterum
thing and one above all *others*, and repeating *it* and again

que iterum   monebo.   Primum adora   prece
and again   I will admonish *you*. First   worship   with prayer

numen magnæ Junonis;, libens cane vota   Junoni, que
the divinity of great Juno;   willing offer vows to Juno,   and

supera potentem dominam supplicibus donis; sic denique
overcome the powerful queen with suppliant offerings: thus at length

mittêre   victor   Italos fines, Trinacriâ
you shall be sent   conqueror to the Italian territories, Trinacria

relictâ.   Ubi delatus huc accesseris   Cumeam
being left. When wafted hither you shall have arrived at the Cumean

urbem, que divinos lacus, et Averna sonantia   silvis,
city,   and the divine   lakes,   and Avernus roaring in the woods,

aspicies   insanam vatem,   quæ   canit fata sub
you shall see   the inspired prophetess, who reveals the fates under the

imâ   rupe que mandat   notas et nomina foliis.
bottom of the rock and commits *her* characters and words to the leaves.

Virgo digerit in numerum, atque relinqut seclusa antro,
The virgin arranges in measure,   and   leaves   laid up in *her* cave,

quæcunque carmina   descripsit in foliis: illa manent
whatsoever predictions she has inscribed on the leaves: they   remain

immota   locis, neque   cedunt ab   ordine. Verùm
unmoved *in their* places, nor do they recede from *their* order.   But

cùm tenuis ventus impulit eadem, cardine verso   et
when a gentle wind has moved the same, the hinge being turned and

janua turbavit teneras frondes, nunquam deinde   curat
the gate has deranged the tender leaves, never afterwards she cares

prendere   volitantia cavo saxo, nec revocare   situs,
to catch   *them* flying about in the hollow rock, nor to restore *their* situations,

aut jungere   carmina.   Abeunt inconsulti, que odere
or to connect the prophecies. They depart unadvised,   and have hated

sedem   Sibyllæ. Hìc nequa dispendia moræ   fuerint
the cave of the Sybil.   Here not any expense of delay shall have been

tibi   tanti   quamvis   socii incrêpitent, et
to you of so much *value* although *your* companions may chide,   and *your*

cursus   vocet vela in altum,   vi que possis implere
voyage may invite *your* sails into the deep, with force and *you* may be able to fill

secundos sinus, quin   adeas   vatem, que precibus
the prosperous sails,   but *that* you may go to the prophetess, and with *prayers*

poscas ipsa   canat oracula, que volens resolvat vocem
implore *that* she may declare the oracles, and willing unloose *her* voice

ıtque ora.   Illa expediet tibi populos Italiæ, que bella
and *her* mouth.   She will explain to you the people of Italy,   and the wars

ventura, et   quo modo que   fugias que feras quemque
about to come, and in what manner both you can escape and bear   every

laborem; que venerata dabit   secundos cursus.   Hæc sunt
hardship;   and reverenced will give *you* a prosperous voyage.   These   are

          quæ   liceat   te   moneri nostrâ
those things of which it may be permitted that you should be admonished by our

voce.   Age, vade, et   factis fer ingentem Trojam ad
voice. Come, proceed, and by *your* deeds   raise   mighty   Troy   to

æthera.   Quæ   postquam vates   sic effatus est
the skies.   Which *words*   after   the prophet   thus   has spoken

amico ore,   dehinc imperat   dona gravia auro   que
with friendly mouth,   then   he commands   presents heavy with gold   and

secto elephanto ferri   ad naves,   que stipat carinis
with cut   ivory   to be carried to the ships,   and he stows in the ships

ingens argentum que Dodonæos lebetas,   loricam
much   silver   and Dodonean   kettles,   a coat of mail

consertam hamis que trilicem auro, et conum   insignis
fastened   with rings and triple with gold, and the cone   of a handsome

galeæ que comantes cristas,   arma Neoptolemi: sua dona
helmet and   hairy   crests, the arms of Neoptolemus: his own gifts

sunt   parenti.   Addit equos, que addit duces: supplet
are to *my* father.   He adds horses, and he adds   guides: he supplies

remigium:
rowers:

    Simul   instruit   socios armis.   Intereà
At the same time he furnishes *my* adherents with arms.   In the mean while

Anchises jubebat aptare classem velis, ne qua   mora
Anchises   ordered *us* to equip   the fleet with sails, lest any   delay

fieret   vento ferenti.   Quem interpres Phœbi   com-
should be made to the wind favoring.   Whom the interpreter of Apollo   ad-

pellat multo honore: Anchisa dignate superbo   conjugio
dresses with great respect: O Anchises   honored with the exalted   marriage

Veneris, cura Deûm, bis erepte   ruinis Pergameis, ecce
of Venus, the care of the gods, twice saved from the ruins   of Troy,   lo!

tellus Ausoniæ tibi; arripe hanc   velis.   Et tamen
the land of Italy *is to* you;   take   this with *your* ships.   And yet

necesse est   præterlabare hanc pelago.   Illa pars Ausoniæ,
it is incumoent that you sail beyond this on the ocean.   That part of Ausonia

quam Apollo pandit procul.   Vade, ait, O felix   pietate
which   Apollo   reveals *is* remote.   Go, he says, O happy   in the piety

nati: quid provehor ultrâ, et   fando demoror surgentes
of *your* son: why am I carried farther, and by speaking delay   the rising

Austros? Nec minus Andromache, mœsta supremo digressu,
winds?   Likewise   Andromache,   sad   at our final   departure,

fert   vestes picturátas subtemine auri, et   Phrygiam
brings forth garments   wrought with a thread of gold, and   a Phrygian

chlamydem Ascanio: nec cedit   honori: que
military cloak   for Ascanius: nor does she fall short of *her* dignity: and

onerat   textilibus donis, ac fatur talia: Puer,   accipe
she loads *him* with woven   presents, and speaks such *words:*   O boy,   accept

hæc et   quæ sint monumenta tibi mearum manuum,   et
these also which may be   memorials · to you of my   hands,   and

testentur longum amorem Andromachæ, conjugis Hec-
may evidence the lasting   love   of Andromache,   the spouse   of Hec-

toreæ. Cape extrema dona tuorum.
tor.   Receive the last   gifts ' of thy *friends.*

O   sola imago mei Astyanactis super mihi!   Sic ille
O *thou the* only image of my   Astyanax remaining to me!   Just so he

ferebat oculos, sic manus, sic   ora;   et nunc
moved *his* eyes, just so *his* hands, just so *his* countenance; and now he might

pubesceret cum te,   æquali ævo.   Digrediens ego affabar
have bloomed with you, *being* of equal age.   Departing   I   addressed

hos lachrymis obortis: vivite felices   quibus jam   sua
them   tears   gushing *forth:* live *ye* happy *ones* for whom now   your

fortuna   peracta est: nos vocamur in alia   fata ex
fortune has been accomplished: we are called to different calamities   from

aliis.   Quies   parta vobis; nullum æquor   maris
different. Rest *has been* provided for you;   no   expanse   of sea

arandum: neque arva Ausoniæ semper cedentia   retrò
is to be ploughed: nor the lands of Ausonia always retreating   backward

quærenda: videtis effigium Xanthi que Trojam quam vestræ
are to be sought: you see the image of Xanthus and Troy   which   your

manus fecere, opto melioribus auspiciis, et quæ   fuerit
hands   have built, I hope for better   fortune, and which shall   be

minús obvia Graiis. Si quando intrâro   Tybrim que
less   exposed to the Greeks. If ever I shall have entered the Tyber   and

vicina arva Tybridis, que cernam mœnia data   meæ
the contiguous lands of the Tyber, and shall see   the walls destined   for my

genti: faciemus olim que cognatas urbes, que propinquos
nation: we will make hereafter both the kindred cities, and   the resembling

populos   Epiro,   Hesperiâ, quibus idem Dardanus
people   *yours* in Epirus, *and mine* in Italy, to whom the same Dardanus *was*

auctor, atque   idem casus, faciemus   utram Trojam
founder,   and *to whom was* the same fortune, we will make *I say* each   Troy

unam animis: ea cura maneat nostros nepotes. Provehimur
one in affections: that concern may await our   posterity.   We are carried

pelago juxta vicina Ceraunia: unde   iter que
on the sea near the neighboring Ceraunian *mountains:* whence *our* passage   and

cursus brevissimus Italiam undis.   Sol ruit intereà, et
course   *is* shortest   *to* Italy on the waves. The sun sets meanwhile, and

opaci montes umbrantur. Sternimur gremio   optatæ
the dusky mountains are shaded.   We are laid on the bosom of the wished for

telluris ad undam,   sortiti   remos; que passim
land   by the water, having distributed *our* oars by lot: and here and there

curamus   corpora in sicco litore: sopor irrigat   fessos
we refresh *our* bodies on the dry shore: sleep invigorates *our* weary

artus. Necdum nox acta horis subibat medium orbem:
limbs. • Nor yet night wafted by the hours reached the middle orb.

Palinurus haud segnis surgit   strato et explorat   omnes
Palinurus not inactive rises from *his* bed and examines all

ventos, atque captat aëra   auribus. Notat cuncta sidera
the winds, and takes the air with *his* ears. He observes all the stars

labentia tacito cœlo Arcturum   que pluvias Hyades que
gliding in the silent sky Arcturus and the rainy Hyades and

geminos Triones que circumspicit Oriona armatum auro.
the two bears and he looks around upon Orion armed with gold.

Postquam videt cuncta   constare sereno cœlo,   dat
After he sees all *things* to be settled in the clear sky, he gives

clarum signum è puppi; nos movemus   castra que
the clear signal from the stern; we move *our* camp and

tentamus viam, et pandimus alas velorum. Jamque
attempt *our* voyage, and spread open the wings of *our* sails. And now

Aurora rubescebat stellis fugatis;   cúm procul
the morn began to redden the stars being chased away; when far off

videmus obscuros colles que Italiam humilem. Achates
we see the obscure hills and Italy *lying* low. Achates

primus conclamat Italiam; socii   salutant Italiam læto
first shouts Italy; *my* companions salute Italy with joyful

clamore. Tum pater Anchises induit magnum cratera
clamor. Then father Anchises has adorned a large bowl

coronâ, que implevit mero, que stans in celsâ puppi
with a garland, and has filled *it* with wine, and standing on the lofty stern

vocavit Divos; Dii, potentes maris et terræ que
he has invoked the gods; O gods, presiding over the sea and the land and

tempestatum ferte facilem viam vento, et spirate
tempests grant to *us* an easy voyage by a *fair* wind, and blow

secundi. Optatæ auræ crebrescunt, que jam portus
propitious. The desired gales begin to increase, and now the port

patescit propior, que templum Minervæ apparet in arce.
opens nearer, and the temple of Minerva appears on a mount.

Socii legunt vela, et torquent proras ad litora.
My companions furl the sails, and turn about *their* prows to the shore.

Portus curvatur in arcum ab Eoo fluctu; objectæ cautes
The port is curved into a bow from the eastern sea; the opposite cliffs

spumant salsâ aspergine;   ipse latet: turriti scopuli
foam with briny spray; *the port* itself lies hid: turreted rocks

demittunt brachia gemino muro, que templum refugit
let down *their* arms with a double wall, and the temple recedes

à litore. Hic vidi in gramine primum omen, quatuor
from the shore. Here I saw on the mead the first omen, four

equos nivali candore tondentes campum latè.   Et pater
horses of snowy whiteness cropping the plain all around. And father

Anchises;   O hospita terra portas   bellum: equi
Anchises   *says;* O hospitable land thou bringest war: *these*   steeds

armantur bello: hæc armenta minantur bellum.   Sed tamen
are equipped for war; these   herds   threaten war.   But notwith

iidem   quadrupedes   sueti   olim
standing   the same   quadrupeds   have been accustomed in times past

succedere curru, et   jugo   ferre concordia fræna:
to come to the chariot, and in the yoke to bear the quiet   reins: *there*

est ait spes pacis.   Tum precamur sancta numina Palladis
is he says hope of peace.   Then we supplicate the sacred divinity   of Pallas

armisonæ,   quæ prima accepit ovantes: et ante   aras
sounding in arms, who   first   received *us* joyful: and before *her* altars

velamur   capita Phrygio amictu; que   præceptis
we are covered as to *our* heads with a Phrygian veil;   and by the admonitions

Heleni,   quæ dederat   maxima,   rité adolemus jussos
of Helenus, which he had given *us* most important, rightly we offer the prescribed

honores Argivæ Junoni.   Haud mora; continuò,   votis
sacrifices to Grecian   Juno. *There is* not   a delay; immediately, *our* vows

perfectis ordine, obvertimus cornua antennarum velata-
being performed in order, we turn about the ends of *our* yards   rigged with

rum, que linquimus domos Grajugenûm que suspecta arva.
sails,   and we leave the abodes   of the Greeks and the suspected lands.

Hinc   sinus   Herculei Tarenti cernitur, si fama est vera.
From hence the bay of Herculean Tarentum is seen,   if report is true.

Contrà   Diva Lacinia attollit se que   arces
On the other side the goddess Lacinia raises herself and   the towers

Caulonis, et navifragum Scyllacæum.
of Caulon,   and shipwrecking Scyllacæum.

Tum   procul è fluctu Trinacria Ætna cernitur: et
Then at a distance from the waves Trinacrian Ætna is seen: and

audimus longè ingentem gemitum pelagi, que saxa pulsata,
we hear   from afar the loud   roaring of the sea, and the rocks beaten

que voces fractas ad litora; que vada exultant
by the waves, and the sounds broken to the shores; and the shallows   boil

atque arenæ miscentur æstu.   Et pater Anchises:
and   the sands are mingled with the tide.   And father   Anchises *says.*

Nimirum hæc illa Charybdis: Helenus canebat   hos
Doubtless this *is* that   Charybdis: Helenus   foretold   these

scopulos, hæc horrenda saxa. O socii eripite,   que
shelves,   these horrible   rocks. O friends save *yourselves,*   and

pariter insurgite remis. Faciunt haud minùs ac   jussi:
equally   rise on *your* oars.   They do   not otherwise than commanded.

Palinurus primus contorsit rudentem proram ad lævas undas:
Palinurus   first   has turned the roaring prow   to the left waves.

cuncta cohors petivit lævam remis que   ventis.
all   the squadron sought the left with oars and   with the winds

Tollimur in cœlum curvato gurgite, et iidem   descen
We are raised to heaven on the vaulted wave, and *we* the same   de

dimus ad imos manes, undâ subductâ. **Scopuli**
scend to the lowest shades, the waves being drawn from *under us.* The rocks

ter dedere clamorem inter cava saxa; ter vidimus
thrice have made a roaring among the hollow rocks; thrice we have seen

spumam elisam et astra rorantia; Intereà ventus cùm
the foam dashed up and the stars bedewed; Meanwhile the wind with

sole reliquit fessos: que ignari viæ, allabimur oris
the sun has left *us* wearied: and ignorant of *our* course, we sail to the coasts

Cyclopum. Portus immotus ab accessu ventorum, et
of the Cyclops. The port *is* undisturbed by the approach of winds, and

ingens ipse; sed Ætna tonat juxtà horrificis ruinis: que
capacious itself; but Ætna thunders near by with frightful ruins: and

interdum prorumpit atrum nubem ad æthera, fumantem
sometimes sends forth a black cloud to the skies, smoking

turbine piceo et candente favillâ; que attollit
with a whirlwind as black as pitch and burning embers; and raises up

globos flammarum et lambit sidera. Interdum eructans
balls of fire and touches the stars. Sometimes belching forth

erigit scopulos que viscera montis avulsa, que glomerat
it raises up rocks and the entrails of the mountain torn *loose,* and whirls about

liquefacta saxa sub auras cum gemitu, que exæstuat imo
melted rocks into the air with a groan, and boils from *its* lowest

fundo. Est fama, corpus, Enceladi semiustum fulmine
bottom. *There* is a report, the body of Enceladus half consumed by lightning

urgeri hac mole, que ingentem Ætnam _ impositam
is pressed under this mass, and ponderous Ætna being placed

insuper, expirare flammam ruptis caminis; et quoties
upon *him,* casts up flames *from its* burst apertures; and as often

mutat fessum latus omnem Trinacriam intremere
as he changes *his* weary side that all Trinacria trembles with the

murmure, et subtexere cœlum fumo. Illam noctem
uproar, and hides the heaven with smoke. That night

tecti sylvis preferimus immania monstra: nec videmus
sheltered by the woods we suffer frightful prodigies: nor do we discern

quæ causa det sonitum. Nam neque erant ignes
what cause can produce the sound. For neither were *there* lights

astrorum, nec lucidus polus sidereâ æthrâ; sed
of the stars, nor a bright heaven in the starry firmament; but *there were*

nubila obscuro cœlo, et intempesta nox tenebat lunam in
mists in the dusky sky, and profound darkness kept the moon in

nimbo. Jamque postera dies surgebat primo Eoo que
a cloud. And now the next day arose at the first dawn, and

Aurora dimoverat humentem umbram polo: cùm subitè
Aurora had dispelled the humid shade from the sky: when suddenly

nova forma viri ignoti confecta supremâ macie,
a strange form of a man unknown *to us* wasted away with extreme leanness.

que miseranda cultu, procedit è sylvis, que supplex
and to be pitied for *his* dress, advances from the woods, and a suppliant

tendit manus ad litora. Respicimus. Dira illuvies,
stretches *his* hands to the shores. We look back. Horrible filth *was to him,*

que barba immissa, tegmen concertum spinis:
and a beard hanging down, *and his* covering was fastened together with thorns:

at cætera Graius, et quondam missus Trojam in
but as to the rest *he was* a Greek, and formerly sent to Troy in *his*

patriis armis. Isque ubi procul vidit Dardanios habitus
country's arms. And he when afar off he has seen the Trojan garments

et Troïa arma, paulùm hæsit territus aspectu que
and Trojan arms, a little he has hesitated affrighted at the sight and

continuit gradum: mox præceps tulit sese ad litora cum
has checked *his* steps: next swift he has brought himself to the shores with

fletu que precibus: Teucri testor per sidera, pe_
weeping and prayers: O Trojans, *he says,* I implore *you* by the stars, by

superos, atque hoc spirabile lumen cœli tollite me
the powers above, and this vital light of heaven take me *hence:*

abducite quascunque terras: hoc erit sat. Scio
transport *me* to whatsoever land *you please:* this shall be enough. I know

me unum è Danais classibus, et fateor petiisse
myself *to be* one from the Grecian fleet, and I confess *that I* have attacked

Illiacos Penates bello. Pro quo si, injuria nostri sceleris est
the Trojan abodes in war. For which if, the injury of my crime is

tanta, spargite me in fluctus, que immergite vasto ponto.
so great, scatter me upon the waves, and plunge *me* in the vast ocean.

Si pereo, juvabit periise manibus hominum.
If I perish, it will delight *me* to have perished by the hands of men.

Dixerat; et amplexus genua, que volutans genibus,
He had said; and embracing *our* knees, and throwing *himself* on *his* knees,

hærebat. Hortamur fari qui sit, quo sanguine
he clung to *us.* We exhort *him* to say who he may be, from what family

cretus; deinde fateri quæ fortuna agitet. Pater Anchises
sprung; then to confess what fortune may trouble him. Father Anchises

ipse moratus haud multa, dat dextram juveni, atque
himself delayed not much, gives *his* right hand to the youth, and

firmat animum præsenti pignore. Ille fatur hæc
confirms *his* mind *with the* ready pledge. He speaks these *words,*

formidine tandem depositâ: sum ex patriâ Ithacâ,
fear at length being laid aside: I am from the country Ithaca,

comes infelicis Ulyssei, nomen Achemenides: profectus
a companion of unfortunate Ulysses, *my* name *is* Achemenides: I went to

Trojam, genitore Adamasto paupere, que utinam fortuna
Troy, *my* parent Adamastus *being* poor, and O that fortune

mansisset! Hìc socii, immemores, deseruere
could have remained! Here *my* companions, forgetful, have left

me in vasto antro Cyclopis, dum trepidi linquunt crudelia
me in the vast cavern of the Cyclop, whilst trembling they quit *his* cruel

limina. Domus intus opaca, ingens sanie, que
abodes. *His* habitation within is dark vast *and full* of gore. and

cruentis dapibus: ipse   arduus, que pulsat alta sidera;
bloody   meats: he himself *is* tall,   and he touches the lofty   stars;

Dî avertite talem pestem   terris! Nec facilis visu,
ye gods avert such   a pest from the earth! Nor *is he* easy to be looked *upon*,

nec affabilis dictu ulli. Vescitur   visceribus
nor   easy   to be spoken to by any one. He feeds   on the entrails of the

miserorum, et atro sanguine. Egomet vidi, cum resupinus
wretched *victims*, and black   blood.   I myself have seen, when   lying on

in medio   antro, frangeret duo corpora de nostro
his back in the middle of *his* cavern, he would dash two   bodies   of   our

numero, prensa magnâ manu ad saxum, que   limina
number,   caught by *his* great   hand against a rock,   and   the threshhold

aspersa sanie natarent: vidi,   cum   manderet
sprinkled with blood would swim: I have seen *him* when   he would devour *their*

membra fluentia   atro tabo, et   tepidi artus tremerent
members   dripping with black gore, and *their* warm limbs   would tremble

sub dentibus. Haud impunè quidem: nec   Ulysses
under *his* teeth.   Not with impunity indeed: nor   Ulysses

passus talia,   ve Ithacus oblitus est sui   tanto
suffered such *things*, or Ithacus   has forgotten himself *in* so important

discrimine. Nam simul expletus dapibus, que sepultus vino
a crisis.   For   as soon as gorged with food, and   buried in wine

posuit inflexam cervicem que immensus jacuit per antrum,
he reclined *his* bent   neck   and   immense   lay along the cavern,

eructans saniem ac frusta   commixta   cruento
belching up gore   and pieces *of human bodies*   mingled   with bloody

mero per somnum; nos, precati magna numina,   que
wine   in *his* sleep;   we, having implored the great   gods,   and

sortiti   vices, unà   circum fundimur   un-
having drawn by lots *our* parts. at once we are scattered around *him*   from all

dique, et acuto telo terebramus ingens lumen, quod
quarters, and with a sharp weapon we dig out   *his* vast   eye,   which

latebat solum sub torvâ fronte, instar Argolici clypei aut
lay concealed alone under *his* stern forehead, as big as a Grecian shield   or

lampadis Phœbeæ: et tandem læti ulciscimur umbras
the lamp   of Phœbus: and at length joyful we avenge   the shades of *our*

sociorum. Sed fugite, O miseri, fugite, atque   rumpite
companions.   But   fly,   O *ye* wretched, fly,   and   break *your*

funem ab litore. Nam, qualis que quantus Polyphemus
cable   from the shore. For,   such   and so great   Polyphemus

claudit lanigeras pecudes, in cavo antro atque pressat
shuts   *his* fleecy   flocks,   in *his* hollow cavern   and   milks *their*

ubera; centum alii infandi cyclopes vulgò habitant ad hæc
dugs;   an hundred other horrible   cyclops commonly   dwell upon   these

litora, et errant   altis montibus. Cornua lunæ jam
shores,   and wander upon *these* lofty   mountains.   The horns of the moon now

complent se lumine tertia cùm traho vitam in
are filling   themselves with light the third time since I drag out *my* life   in

sylvis, inter deserta lustra que domos ferarum, que
the woods, among the deserted haunts and abodes of wild beasts, and

prospicio vastos Cyclopas ab rupe, que tremisco sonitum
I view the vast Cyclops from a rock, and I tremble at the sound

pedum que vocem. Rami dant infelicem victum,
of their feet and their voice. The boughs afford me scanty sustenance

baccas, que lapidosa corna et herbæ pascunt vulsis
berries, and stony cornels and the herbs feed me with their torn up

radicibus. Collustrans omnia primum conspexi hanc
roots. Surveying all things, first I have discovered this

classem venientem ad litora: addixi me huic,
fleet approaching to the shore: I have surrendered myself to it,

quæcunque fuisset: satis effugisse nefan-
whatsoever it might have been: it is enough for me to have escaped the execra-

dum gentem. Vos potiùs absumite hanc animam quocunque
ble race. You rather take away this life by any

leto. Vix fatus erat ea, cum videmus summo
death. Scarcely had he spoken those words, when we behold on the highest part

monte pastorem Polyphemum ipsum moventem se
of the mountain the shepherd Polyphemus himself moving himself

vastâ mole inter pecudes, et petentem nota litora:
with his vast bulk among his flocks, and seeking the well known shores

horrendum monstrum, informe, ingens, cui lumen ademp-
a horrid monster, deformed, huge, whose eye has been

tum. Trunca pinus regit manum, et firmat vestigia:
taken out. A cut pine guides his hand, and strengthens his steps: his

lanigeræ oves comitantur: ea sola voluptas, que solamen
fleecy sheep accompany him: this is his only pleasure, and solace of his

mali: fistula pendet collo. Postquam tetigit altos
misfortune: his pipe hangs from his neck. After he has touched the high

fluctus, et venit ad æquora, inde lavit fluidum cruorem
waves, and has come to the sea, then he has washed the flowing blood

luminis effossi infrendens dentibus gemitu: jamque graditur
of his eye dug out gnashing with his teeth with a groan: and now he stalks

per medium æquor, nec dum fluctus tinxit ardua latera
through the middle of the sea, nor yet the wave hath wet his lofty sides.

Nos trepidi celarare fugam procul inde, supplice
We fearful begin to hasten our flight far from thence, our suppliant

recepto sic merito, que taciti incidere funem: et
being received thus deserving, and silent we begin to cut the cable: and

proni verrimus æquora certantibus remis. Sensit,
bending forward we sweep the sea with struggling oars. He has perceived

et torsit vestigia ad sonitum vocis. Verùm ubi nullâ
this, and has turned his steps at the sound of a voice. But when no

potestas datur affectare dextrâ, nec potis æquare
power is given him to grasp us with his right hand, nor he is able to equal

Ionios fluctus sequendo; tollit immensum clamorem, que
the Ionian sea in pursuing us; he sets up a vast clamor, by which

pontus et omnes undæ intremuere, que tellus Italiæ penitùs
the sea, and all the waves have trembled, and the land of Italy entirely

exterrita, que Ætna immugiit curvis cavernis.   At
has been affrighted, and   Ætna has roared in its winding caverns.   But

genus Cyclopum excitum è sylvis et altis montibus ruit
the race of the Cyclops roused from the woods and lofty mountains rushes

ad portus, et complent litora. Cernimus Ætnæos   fratres
to the port, and   fill   the shores. We see   the Ætnian   brothers

nequicquam adstantes torvo lumine, ferentes alta   capita
in vain   standing with a stern eye,   bearing their high   heads

cœlo, horrendum concilium: quales cum æriæ quercus aut
to heaven, a horrid assembly: such as when the ærial oaks   or

coniferæ cyparissi constiterunt   celso vertice, alta
cone-bearing cypresses have stood together with their lofty top,   the stately

sylva Jovis, ve lucus Dianæ. Acer metus agit
wood of Jove, or the grove of Diana. Violent fear forces   my companions

præcipites excutere rudentes quocunque,   et
swift   to let out   the sheets what way soever they may be able,   and

intendere vela secundis ventis. Contrà,   jussa
to spread   the sails to the favorable winds. On the other hand,   the orders

Heleni monent Scyllam atque Charybdim;   ni teneant
of Helenus warn them of Scylla   and   Charybdis;   that they may not hold

cursus inter utramque viam, parvo discrimine   leti;
their course between   either   way, at a little distance   from death;

certum est dare lintea retrò. Autem ecce   Boreas
it is determined to spread the sails backward. But   lo!   the north wind

missus à angusta sede Pelori adest: prætervehor   ostia
sent   from the narrow seat of Pelorus is present: I am wafted by the mouths

Pantagiæ vivo saxo, que sinus Megaros, que   Tapsum
of Pantygia of living rock,   and the bay of Megara, and   Tapsus

jacentem. Achemenides comes   infelicis   Ulyssei
lying low.   Achemenides   the companion of unfortunate   Ulysses

monstrabat talia   relegens retrorsùm litora   errata.
pointed out   these things to us coasting   backward the shores wandered over.

Insula jacet prætenta Sicanio sinu contra   undosum
An island lies   situated before the Sicilian bay over against   boisterous

Plemmyrium: priores dixere nomen Ortygiam.   Est
Plemmyrium·   the ancients have called its name   Ortygia.   There is

fama Alpheum, amnem Elidis, egisse occultas vias   huc
a report that Alpheus, a river of Elis, has worked   secret channels hither

subter mare; qui nunc confunditur Siculis undis   tuo
beneath the sea; which now   is mingled with the Sicilian waves   by thy

ore, Arethusa. Jussi, veneramur magna numina   loci;
mouth, O Arethusa. Commanded. we worship the great divinities of the place;

et inde exsupero præpingue solum stagnantis Helori. Hinc
and thence I pass by the very fertile soil of stagnant Helorus.   Hence

radimus altas cautes et projecta saxa Pachini; et procul
we coast along the high cliffs and projecting rocks of Pachynus; and afar off

apparet Camarina nunquam concessa fatis moveri, que
appears Camarina never permitted by the fates to be moved, and

Geloi campi, que immanis Gela dicta cognomine fluvii.
the Geloian plains, and immense Gela called by the name of the river.

Inde arduus Agragas quondam generator magnanimûm
From thence lofty Agragas formerly the breeder of high mettled

equorum ostentat longè maxima mœnia. Que ventis
horses shows at a distance its most stately walls. And the winds

datis linquo te palmosa Selinus: et lego Lilybeia
being given I leave thee O palmy Selinus: and I coast along the Lilybeian

vada dura cæcis saxis. Hìnc portus et illætabilis ora
shallows dangerous with latent rocks. Hence the port and unjoyous coast

Drepani accipit me. Hic, actus tot tempestatibus pelagi,
of Drepanus receives me. Here, tossed by so many tempests of the ocean,

heu! amitto genitorem Anchisen, levamen omnis curæ que
alas! I lose my parent Anchises, the solace of every care and

casus: Hìc optime pater, deseris me fessum, heu!
misfortune: Here, O most excellent father, thou forsakest me wearied, ah!

erepte nequicquam tantis periculis. Nec vates Helenùs
rescued in vain from so great perils. Nor has the prophet Helenus

cum moneret me multa horrenda, prædixit hos luctus
when he might warn me of many dreadful things, predicted these afflictions

mihi; non dira Celæno. Hic extremus labor, hæc
to me; not the dreadful Celeno. This was my last calamity, this

meta longarum viarum. Deus appulit me vestris oris
the bound of my long voyages. A god has driven me to your coasts

digressum hinc. Sic pater Æneas, omnibus intentis,
having departed from hence. Thus father Æneas, all being attentive

unus renarrabat fata Divûm, que docebat cursus
alone related the purposes of the gods, and declared his wanderings

tandem conticuit, que fine facto hìc, quievit.
at length he has been silent, and an end being made here, he has rested.

ÆNEID.

BOOK FOURTH.

AT Regina jamdudum saucia gravi curâ, alit vulnus
But the queen long since wounded with painful care, cherishes the wound

venis, et carpitur cæco igni. Multa virtus viri,
in her veins, and is consumed by the unseen flame. The great virtue of the man,

que multos honos gentis recursat animo; vultus que
and the great honor of his race recur to her mind; his countenance and

verba hærent infixi pectore, nec cura dat placidam quietem
his words dwell fixed in her heart, nor does care allow peaceful rest

membris. Postera Aurora lustrabat terras Phœbeâ lampade,
to her limbs. Returning Aurora illumined the earth with the solar lamp,

que dimoverat humentem umbram polo; cum malesana
and had scattered the dewy shade from the sky; when the love-sick

sic alloquitur unanimem sororem: "Soror Anna, quæ
queen thus addresses her affectionate sister: "O sister Anna, what

insomnia terrent me suspensam! quis novus hospes hic
dreams terrify me disturbed! what wonderful guest is this who

successit nostris sedibus? quem ferens sese ore!
has come to our habitation? what dignity displaying itself in his counte-

quàm forti pectore et armis! Credo, equidem, nec
nance! how brave in heart and in arms! I believe him, indeed, nor

fides vana, esse genus Deorum. Timor arguit degeneres
is the belief vain, to be the offspring of the gods. Fear argues degenerate

animos. Heu! quibus fatis ille jactatus! quæ bella exhausta
souls. Alas! by what fates has he been driven! what wars undergone by

canebat! Si non sederet mihi fixum que immotum
him did he sing! If it might not remain to me fixed and steadfast

animo, ne vellem sociare me cui jugali
in my mind, that I should not be willing to unite myself to any one in the nuptial

vinclo, postquam primus amor fefellit deceptam morte:
bond, after my first love has disappointed me deceived by death;

si not fuisset pertæsum thalami que tædæ, forsan
if it had not been unpleasant to think of marriage and the nuptial torch, perhaps

potui succumbere huic uni culpæ. Anna, (enim fatebor)
I could yield to this one fault. Anna, (for I will confess)

post fata Sichæi miseri conjugis, et Penates
since the fate of Sichæus my unhappy husband, and since the household gods

sparsos fraternâ cæde, hic solus inflexit sensus,
were stained with fraternal blood, this stranger alone has moved my feelings,

que impulit labentem animum; agnosco vestigia veteris
and has interested my wavering mind; I know the symptoms of my former

flammæ. Sed optem   vel   ima tellus prius   dehiscat
flame.   But I would wish either *that* the deepest earth first may yawn open

mihi, vel omnipotens pater adigat me fulmine   ad umbras,
for me, or *that* the almighty father may hurl me by his thunder to the shades,

pallentes umbras Erebi que profundam noctem,   antequam
to the pale   shades of Erebus and   profound   night,   before

violo te, pudor,   aut resolvo tua jura.   Ille qui   primus
I violate thee, O modesty, or   break   thy laws.   He who   first

junxit me sibi   abstulit   meos amores; ille   habeat
united   me to himself has borne away   my affections; may he retain them

secum,   que   servet   sepulchro. Effata   sic,
with himself and may he preserve *them* in his grave. Having spoken   thus

implevit   sinum obortis lacrymis. Anna refert: "O magis
she has filled her bosom with flowing tears. Anna replies: "O more

dilecta sorori luce,   ne sola mœrens carpere perpetuâ
dear to thy sister than light, will you alone mourning waste away through entire

juventâ, nec nôris dulces natos, nec prœmia   Veneris?
youth,   nor know   dear children, nor the rewards   of Venus?

Credis   cinerem aut sepultos manes curare id?   Esto,
Do you believe that ashes or the buried dead   regard that? Be it so,

nulli mariti quondam flexere   ægram, non Libyê,   non
that no suitors   formerly have moved *you* mourning, not in Libya,   not

Tyro antè;   Iarbas despectus, que alii ductores,   quos
in Tyre before; *that* Iarbas has been slighted, and other princes,   whom

Africa terra dives triumphis alit, ne pugnabis   etiam
Africa   a land rich in triumphs maintains, will you contend   also

placito amore?   Nec venit in mentem quorum arvis
with a pleasing passion? Nor does it come into your mind upon whose territories

consederis?   Hinc Getulæ urbès genus insuperabile   bello,
you are settled? Here Getulian cities, a race unconquerable   in war,

et infræni Numidæ, et inhospita syrtis cingunt. Hinc
and the untamed Numidians, and inhospitable quicksands surround *you.*   Here

regio deserta   siti, que Barcœi furentes   latè
a region made desert *on account* of thirst, and the Barcæans raging far and wide

      Quid   dicam   bella surgentia Tyro,   que
surround you. Why should I mention the wars rising from Tyre,   and

minas germani? Equidem reor   Illiacas carinas tenuisse
the threats of your brother? Indeed I think that the Trojan ships   have held

cursum huc vento,   Dîs auspicibus et   Junone
their course hither with the wind,   the gods favouring and   Juno

secundâ.   Soror, quam urbem tu cernes hanc! quæ regna
being propitious. O sister, what a city shall you behold this! what kingdoms

surgere tali conjugio!   quantis rebus   Punica
to rise from such a marriage! by what great exploits   shall the Carthagenian

gloria attollet se, armis Teucrûm comitantibus! Tu modo
glory   exalt itself, the arms of the Trojans accompanying! Do you   only

posce veniam Deos,   que   sacris   litatis,   indulge
entreat the favour of the gods, and the sacred rites being performed,   indulge

hospitio,   que innecte causas morandi,   dum hiems
in hospitality, and   devise   causes for detaining *your guest*, while   winter

desævit pelago, et Orion aquosus, que rates quassatæ,   et
rages   on the sea, and Orion   is rainy,   and his ships *are* shattered,   and

cœlum non tractabile. His dictis inflammavit   animum
the weather not   endurable.   By these words she has inflamed   her mind

incensum amore, que dedit spem dubiæ menti,   que
excited   with love, and has given hope to her doubtful mind,   and

solvit   pudorem. Principio adeunt delubra, que exqui-
has banished her modesty.   First   they go to the temples, and   en-

runt pacem per aras;   mactant lectas   bidentes
treat   favour through the altars; they sacrifice chosen *victims*   two years old

de   more,   legiferæ Cereri, que Phœbo, que patri
according to custom, to the law giving Ceres,   and to Phœbus,   and to father

Lyæo; ante omnes Junoni, cui jugalia vincla   curæ.
Bacchus; above   all   to Juno, to whom the nuptial bonds *are objects* of care.

Pulcherrima Dido ipsa tenens pateram dextrâ,   fundit
The most beautiful Dido herself holding   the cup in her right hand,   pours *it*

inter   media   cornua candentis vaccæ, aut spatiatur ad
between in the middle of the horns of the white heifer,   or   walks   to

pingues aras ante ora   Deûm, que instaurat   diem
the rich   altars before the images of the gods, and renews   the day

donis,   que inhians reclusis pectoribus pecudum, consulit
with offerings, and examining the opened breasts   of the victims,   consults

spirantia exta. Heu! ignaræ mentes vatum! quid   vota,
their panting entrails. Alas! the ignorant minds of augurs! what   do vows,

quid delubra juvant furentem?   Intereâ   mollis
what do temples avail   a raging *lover?* In the meantime   the gentle

flamma est medullas, et tacitum vulnus vivit sub pectore.
flame   feeds upon her vitals, and the silent wound   lives in   her breast.

Infelix   Dido uritur,   que furens vagatur totâ   urbe;
The unhappy Dido burns *with love*, and frantic   roams *over* the whole city;

qualis cerva, sagittâ conjectâ,   quam pastor   agens
as   a deer, an arrow   being shot,   which a shepherd   pursuing

telis,   fixit   incautam   procul inter Crëssia
with weapons has wounded unsuspecting   at a distance among the Cressian

nemora, que liquit volatile ferrum nescius;   illa
groves,   and has left the winged steel   unconscious *of its success*;   she

fugâ   peragrat sylvas que Dictæos saltus; lethalis arundo
in her flight bounds over woods   and the Dictæan lawns;   the fatal   arrow

hæret lateri. Nunc ducit Ænean secum   per   media
sticks in her side   Now she conducts Æneas   with her through   the midst

mœnia,   que ostentat Sidonias opes, que urbem
of the fortifications, and shows him her Sidonian wealth, and the city *which she had*

paratam. Incipit effari, que resistit in mediâ   voce.
laid out.   She begins to speak, and stops short in the middle   of her speech.

Nunc labente   die, quærit eadem convivia; que   iterum
Now at the declining day, she longs for the same banquets;   and   again

aemens exposcit audire Iliacos labores, que iterum pendit
madly fond she begs to hear the Trojan disasters, and again hangs

ab ore narrantis.   Pòst ubi   digressi, que   luna
on the lips of him relating. Afterwards when *they had* retired, and the moon

vicissim   obscura premit lumen, que cadentia   sidera
in her turn *growing* dim suppresses her light, and the setting stars

suadent somnos, mæret ṣola vacuâ domo, que incubat
invite sleep, she mourns alone in the vacant hall, and presses

stratis relictis;   absens,   que audit que   videt
the couch left *by Æneas;* absent, *she in imagination* both hears and sees

illum absentem; aut detinet Ascanium gremio, capta
him absent, or holds Ascanius *to her* bosom, captivated *with his*

imagine genitoris, si possit fallere infandum
resemblance *of* his father, *as* if she could be able to beguile her unutterable

amorem. Turres cœptæ non assurgunt; juventus non
love. *Her* towers *which were* begun do not rise; *her* youth do not

exercet arma ve parant portus, aut tuta propugnacula bello;
exercise *their* arms or construct harbours, or protective bulwarks for war

opera interrupta pendent, que ingentes minæ murorum,
the works interrupted stop, and the great battlements of the walls,

que machina æquata cœlo.   Quam simul   ac
and the machinery equalling the sky *are discontinued.* Whom as soon as

Saturnia cara conjux Jovis persensit teneri   tali
Juno   the dear wife of Jupiter has perceived to be possessed *with* such

peste, nec famam   obstare furori, aggreditur
a passion *of love,* nor that her honour *was able* to oppose *its* fury, she addresses

Venerem talibus dictis. Que tu verò que tuus puer refertis
Venus   with such words.   Both thou indeed and thy boy acquire

egregiam laudem et ampla spolia, magnum et memorabile
distinguished praise and ample spoils, a great and memorable

nomen, si una femina est victa dolo duorum Divûm.
name, if one woman is overcome by the artifice of two deities.

Nec adeò fallit me te veritam nostra mœnia, habuisse
Nor entirely does it escape me that you fearful of our walls, have held

domos altæ Carthaginis suspectas; sed quis erit modus?
the buildings of lofty Carthage suspected; but what shall be the bound ?

aut quò   tanto certamine? Quin potiùs
or whither *are we hastening with* so great a contention? Why not rather

exercemus æternam pacem que pactos Hymenæos? habes
bring about a lasting peace and firm marriage? you possess

quod petîsti   totâ mente; amans Dido
that which you have sought *with your* whole mind; the affectionate Dido

ardet, que traxit furorem per ossa. Ergo regamus
burns *with love,* and has drawn *its* fury into her bones. Therefore let us govern

hunc populum communem, que paribus auspiciis; liceat
this people in common, and with equal favour; let it be lawful

    servire Phrygio marito, que permittere tuæ   dextræ
for her to yield to a Trojan husband. and to give up into your hand

Tyrios dotales. Olli Venus contrà sic ingressa est;
the Tyrians *as a* dowry. To her Venus on the other hand thus   replied:

(enim sensit   locutam simulatâ mente   quò
(for she has perceived *that Juno* spoke with a deceitful mind   that

averteret regnum Italiæ Lybĭcas oras.) Quis demens
she might transfer the empire of Italy to the Lybian coasts.) Who   mad

abnuat talia aut malit contendere tecum bello? Si modò
can reject such *terms* or choose *rather* to contend with thee in war? If   only

fortuna sequatur factum quod memoras. Sed feror
fortune   may follow the undertaking which you mention. But I am inclined

incerta fatis si Jupiter velit   unam urbem esse
to be doubtful by the fates whether Jupiter be willing *that* the same city should be

Tyriis, que profectis Trojâ, ve   probet
to the Tyrians, and *to those* who are come from Troy, or whether   he approve

populos misceri, aut fœdera jungi. Tu conjux;
that the people be mingled *together*, or alliances be joined. Thou *art* his wife;

fas tibi tentare animum precando. Perge, sequar.
it belongs to you to work upon his mind by entreating. Go on, I will follow.

Tum regia Juno sic excepit: Iste labor erit mecum; nunc
Then royal Juno thus answered: That labour shall be with me;   now

adverte, docebo paucis quâ ratione quod instat
attend, I will instruct *you* in a few *words* in what manner that which concerns *us*

possit confieri. Æneas que miserrima Dido, unâ
can be accomplished. Æneas and the most unhappy Dido,   together

parant ire venatum in nemus, ubi crastinus Titan extu-
are preparing to go to hunt in the grove, when to-morrow's sun shall have

lerit primos ortus, que retexerit orbem radiis.
brought forth the first dawn, and shall have enlightened the world with *his* rays.

Dum alæ trepidant, que cingunt saltus indagine, ego
Whilst the horsemen hurry, and surround the lawns with nets, I

desuper infundam his nigrantem nimbum, grandine
from above will pour upon them a blackening storm, with hail

commixtâ, que ciebo omne cœlum tonitru. Comites
intermingled, and I will shake all heaven with thunder. *Their* attendants

diffugient, et tegentur opacâ nocte; Dido et Trojanus dux
shall fly, and be covered with dark night; Dido and the Trojan leader

devenient eandem speluncam; adero et si tua voluntas
shall come to the same cavern; *I* will be present and if your consent

certa mihi, jungam stabili connubio, que dicabo
be sure to me, I will unite *them* in firm wedlock, and I will consecrate *her*

propriam. Hic erit Hymenæus. Cytherea, non adversata,
as his own. This shall be marriage. Venus, not opposed,

annuit petenti, atque risit dolis repertis. Interea
agreed *to her* requesting, and smiled at the fraud discovered. Meanwhile

Aurora surgens reliquit Oceanum. Delecta juventus it
Aurora rising has left the Ocean. The chosen youth proceed

portis, exorto jubare. Rara retia, plagæ, venabula
from the gates, with the rising day-star. The wide nets, the toils, hunting spears

ato   ferro, que Massili   equites et   odora   vis
with broad *pointed* steel, and the Massylian horsemen and   a quick-scented pack

canum ruunt.   Primi   Pœnorum   ad   limina
of dogs pour forth.   The chiefs of the Carthagenians before   the threshold

expectant reginam cunctantem thalamo;   que   sonipes
await   the queen   delaying   in her chamber;   and   her steed

stat insignis ostro   et auro, ac ferox mandit   spumantia
stands decorated with purple and gold,   and fierce champs   the foaming

fræna.   Tandem progreditur, magnâ catervâ   stipante,
bits.   At length   *she* advances,   a great   crowd   surrounding *her.*

circumdata Sidoniam chlamydem   picto   limbo;   cui
enveloped in   a Sidonian   mantle with an embroidered fringe;   whose

pharetra ex auro, crines nodantur in aurum,   aurea fibula
quiver *was* of   gold,   her hair   was tied   in a golden *knot*, a golden   clasp

subnectit purpuream vestem.   Et nec non Phrygii comites.
binds   *her* purple   robe.   And   also   the Trojan   bands,

et   lætus Iülus incedunt;   Æneas ipse pulcherrimus   ante
and the joyous Iulus   advance;   Æneas himself   the most beautiful   above

omnes alios, infert se   socium,   atque jungit   agmina:
all   others, adds himself as a companion, and   joins   the bands:

qualis ubi Apollo deserit hibernam Lyciam. que   fluenta
such as when Apollo   leaves   the wintry   Lycia   and   the streams of

Xanthi, ac invisit maternam Delum, que instaurat   choros;
Xanthus, and revisits his maternal Delos,   and ◦ renews   the dances;

que Cretes, que Dryopes, que picti Agathyrsi,   misti
and the Cretans, and the Dryopes,   and the painted   Agathyrsi,   mingled

circum altaria fremunt; ipse graditur   jugis   Cynthi, que
around   the altars   shout;   he himself moves *over* the heights of Cynthus, and

fingens fluentem crinem premit   molli   fronde,
adjusting   his flowing   hair   presses *it*   with a soft   wreath of leaves,

atque implicat   auro.   Tela   sonant   humeris.
and   entwines *it* with gold.   His arrows   rattle   on   his shoulders.

Æneas ibat haud segnior illo;   tantum decus enitet
Æneas   moved   not   inferior   to him;   so much   grace shines forth

egregio   ore.   Postquam ventum   in   altos
from his handsome countenance.   After   they were come among   the lofty

montes, atque invia   lustra, ecce! feræ   capræ
mountains,   and the pathless haunts,   lo!   the wild   goats

dejectæ vertice   saxi   decurrêre jugis; de   aliâ
driven   from the summit of the rock have run down the heights; from   the other

parte cervi transmittunt patentes campos   cursu,   atque
part   the deer   pass over   the open   plains   in their course,   and

fugâ glomerant pulverulenta agmina, que   relinquunt
in their flight   collect   their dusty   herds,   and   leave

montes.   At puer Ascanius gaudet   acri   equo   in
the mountains. But the boy Ascanius   exults with his sprightly steed   in

mediis vallibus, que jam præterit hos, jam illos cursu; que
the mid   valleys,   and   now   passes   by these, now those in his course; and

optat spumantem aprum   dari   votis   inter   inertia
desires that a foaming   boar might be given to his wishes among   the feeble

pecora, aut   fulvum leonem descendere   monte.
herds,   or that a tawny lion   would descend   from the mountain.

Interea   coelum incipit misceri   magno murmure;
In the mean time the air begins to be disturbed   by a great   roaring

nimbus insequitur grandine commistâ; et Tyrii   comites
rain   follows   with hail   intermingled; and the Tyrian   attendants

et Trojana juventus, que Dardanius nepos Veneris   passim
and the Trojan   youth,   and the Dardanian grandson of Venus every where

petiere diversa tecta per   agros metu: amnes ruunt de
have sought different shelters through the fields for fear; rivers pour   from

montibus.   Dido et Trojanus dux deveniunt ad   eandem
the mountains. Dido and the Trojan leader   come   to   the same

speluncam: et Tellus prima et Juno   pronuba   dant
cavern: and the earth first   and Juno the goddess of marriage give

signum; ignes   fulsere et æther   conscius
the signal; lightnings have flashed and the sky *brightened*   *as* conscious

connubiis; que Nymphæ ululârunt summo   vertice.
to the nuptials; and the nymphs have shrieked from the highest *mountain* top.

Ille dies primus fuit causa lethi,   que primus
That day   first has been the cause of death *to Dido,* and first   *the cause*

malorum; enim Dido neque movetur specie   ve
of her woes; for Dido neither is moved by the appearance *of her crime* or

famâ, nec jam meditatur furtivum amorem; vocat   conju-
by honour, nor now does she meditate a secret   love;   she calls *it*   mar

gium; hoc nomine prætexit culpam. Extemplò Fama it
riage; with this name   she screens her fault.   Immediately Fame goes

per magnas urbes Libyæ; Fama, malum   quo
through the great cities of Lybia; Fame, an evil *being* than whom *there is*

non ullum aliud velocius; viget mobilitate, que   acquirit
not   any   other more swift; she increases by motion, and   acquires

vires eundo; primò parva metu, mox attollit sese   in
strength by advancing; at first small through fear, soon she raises herself into

auras, que ingreditur solo,   et condit caput inter nubila.
the air, and   stalks on the ground, and hides her head among the clouds.

Parens Terra, irritata   irâ   Deorum, progenuit illam, ut
Mother   Earth, provoked by the anger of the Gods, brought forth her,   as

perhibent, extremam sororem Cœo que Encelado, celerem
they say,   the last   sister to Cœus and Enceladus,   quick

pedibus et pernicibus alis; monstrum horrendum, ingens,
on feet   and with swift wings; a monster,   hideous,   huge,

cui   tot   vigiles oculi subter, (mirabile dictu)
to whom *there are* as many watchful eyes beneath,   (wonderful to be told

tot linguæ, totidem ora sonant, subrigit tot aures, quot
as many tongues, as many mouths sound, she pricks up as many ears, as *there*

sunt plumæ corpore. Nocte volat   medio   cœli, que
are   feathers on her body. By night she flies through the midst of the air, and

per umbram terræ stridens, nec declinat lumina   dulci
through the shade of the earth buzzing, nor does she close her eyes in sweet

somno. Luce sedet custos, aut culmine summi tecti, aut
sleep.   By day she sits a spy, either on the roof of a very high building, or

altis turribus, et territat magnas urbes, tam tenax nuncia
upon lofty towers, and terrifies great cities, as constant a messenger

ficti   que pravi, quam veri. Hæc tum gaudens, replebat
of falsehood and error, as of truth. She then rejoicing, filled

populos multiplici sermone, et pariter canebat facta   atque
the people with various reports, and equally uttered facts an

infecta: Ænean cretum a Trojano sanguine, venisse, cui
untruths: That Æneas descended from Trojan blood, had come to which

viro pulchra Dido dignetur jungere se; nunc luxu   inter
man the beautiful Dido thought fit to wed herself; now in luxury among

se   fovere hiemem quàm longa, immemores
themselves they enjoyed the winter however long, unmindful of their

regnorum, que captos turpi cupidine.
kingdoms, and captivated by a base passion.

Fœda Dea passim diffundit hæc in ora virûm.
The cruel goddess every where scatters these reports in the mouths of men

Protinus detorquet cursus ad regem Iarbam; que   incendit
Forthwith she turns her course to king Iarbas; and inflames

animum dictis atque aggerat iras. Hic satus Ammone,
his mind with her words and aggravates his rage. He sprung from Ammon,

raptâ nymphâ Garamantide, posuit Jovi centum im-
by the ravished nymph Garamantis, placed to Jupiter an hundred spa-

mania templa. latis regnis, centum aras, que   sacraverat
cious temples in his wide realms, a hundred altars, and had consecrated

vigilem ignem, æternas excubias Divûm, que solum
the wakeful fire, the eternal watch of the gods, and a spot of ground

pingue cruore pecudum, et limina florentia   variis
rich with the blood of victims, and the gates blooming with various

sertis. Que is amens animi et accensus amaro rumore,
garlands. And he frantic in mind and inflamed by the bitter tidings,

dicitur supplex órasse Jovem multa supinis manibus,
is said suppliant to have prayed to Jupiter much with uplifted hands.

ante aras inter media numinâ Divûm: Omnipotens
before the altars amid the immediate statues of the gods: O omnipotent

Jupiter, cui Maurusia gens epulata pictis toris nunc libat
Jupiter, to whom the Moorish nation feasting on painted couches now pours out

Lenæum honorem, aspicis hæc? An, genitor,
wine as an offering, dost thou behold these things? Or, O father,

horremus te necquicquam, cum torques fulmina? que
do we dread thee to no purpose, when thou hurlest the thunderbolts? and

cæci ignes in nubibus terrificant, et inania murmura
do blind lightnings in the clouds terrify, and do vain thunderings

miscent animos. Femina, quæ errans in nostris finibus
disturb our minds. A woman, who wandering in our territories

posuit exiguam urbem pretio, cui dedimus litus
has settled a small city by purchase, to whom we have given land

arandum, que cui leges loci, repulit nostra
for tillage, and to whom *we gave* the laws of the country, has rejected our

connubia, ac recepit Æneam in regna dominum, et nunc
alliance, and has taken Æneas into her kingdom as her lord, and now

ille Paris cum semiviro comitatu, subnexus mentum que
this Paris with his effeminate train, bound as to his chin and

madentem crinem Mæoniâ mitrâ, potitur rapto; quippe
his moistened hair with a Lydian bonnet, possessed the ravished *prize*; truly

nos ferimus munera tuis templis, que fovemus inanem
we bear gifts to thy temples, and cherish a vain

famam
fame.

Omnipotens audiit orantem talibus dictis, que
The almighty *Jupiter* heard him praying with such words, and

tenentem aras, que torsit oculos ad regia mœnia et
grasping the altars, and turned his eyes to the royal towers and

amantes oblitos melioris famæ. Tunc sic alloquitur Mer-
to the lovers forgetful of their better fame. Then thus he addresses Mer

curium, ac mandat talia. Nate, age, vade voca Zephyros,
cury, and commands such *things*. O son, haste, go call the Zephyrs,

et labere pennis; que alloquere Dardanium ducem, qui
and glide on *thy* wings; and address the Trojan leader, who

nunc expectat Tyriâ Carthagine, que non respicit urbes
now loiters in Tyrian Carthage, and does not regard the cities

datas fatis, et defer mea dicta per celeres
allotted *him* by the fates, and carry my words *to him* through the swift

auras. Pulcherrima genetrix non promisit nobis illum
air. His beautiful mother has not promised to us that he *should be*

talem, que ideò bis vindicat armis Graiûm;
such *a man*, and thus twice does she rescue *him* from the arms of the Greeks;

sed fore qui regerit Italiam gravidam imperiis que
but that he should be *one* who should rule Italy pregnant with empires and

frementem bello, proderet genus a alto sanguine
fierce in war, *who* should evince his descent from the high blood

Teucri, ac mitteret totum orbem sub leges. Si nulla gloria
of Teucer, and should send the whole world under his laws If no glory

tantarum rerum accendit, nec ipse molitur laborem super
of such great things inflame *him*, nor he undertakes the labour for

suâ laude, ne pater invidet Ascanio Romanas arces?
his own fame, does he a father envy Ascanius the Roman towers?

Quid struit? aut quâ spe moratur in inimicâ
What does he purpose or in what expectation does he delay among a hostile

gente, nec respicit Ausoniam prolem et Lavinia arva?
nation, nor regards the Ausonian race and the Lavinian fields?

Naviget. Hæc est summa; hic esto nuncius nostri.
Let him sail. This is the substance; let this be the message of ours.

Dixerat; ille parabat parere imperio   magni patris;   et
He had said; he   prepared   to obey the command of his great father;   and

primùm nectit aurea talaria pedibus, quæ portant sublimem
first   he binds the golden sandals to his feet, which bear him   aloft.

alis,   sive super æquora, seu   terram, pariter   cum
on wings, whether above   seas,   or above land,   equal in speed   with

rapido flamine; tum capit virgam; hâc   evocat   pallentes
the rapid wind: then he takes his wand; with this he calls forth   the pale

animas Orco, mittit alias sub   tristia Tartara, dat   que
ghosts from Orcus, sends others under the gloomy Tartarus, gives   and

adimit somnos, et resignat lumina morte;   fretus   illâ
takes away sleep, and closes   eyes   in death;   relying upon this

agit   ventos, et tranat turbida nubila. Que   jam
he manages the winds, and skims along the turbid clouds.   And   now

volans cernit apicem et ardua latera duri Atlantis, qui fulcit
flying   he sees   the top and the lofty sides of rugged Atlas,   who props up

cœlum vertice; Atlantis cui piniferum caput assiduè cinctum
the sky with his summit; of Atlas whose pine-bearing head   always   encircled

atris   nubibus pulsatur et vento   et imbri; nix   infusa
with dark clouds   is beaten both by the wind and rain;   snow   spread over

tégit humeros; tum flumina præcipitant mento   senis,
covers his shoulders; also   rivers   roll   from the chin of the aged man,

et horrida barba riget glacie.   Hìc Cyllenius nitens paribus
and his rough beard stiffens with ice.   Here   Mercury poising upon   equal

alis primùm constitit; hinc præceps misit   se
wings first   has alighted; hence   headlong he has thrown   himself

toto   corpore ad undas, similis avi   quæ volat humilis
with his whole body   to the waves,   like to a bird   which flies   low

juxta   æquora circum litora, circum piscosos scopulos.
near the surface of the sea around the shores, around   the fishy   rocks

Proles Cyllenia,   veniens ab materno   avo,   haud
The son of Cyllenian Maia, coming   from his maternal grandsire,   just

aliter legebat arenosum litus Lybiæ inter   terras que cœlum,
so   chose   the sandy   shore of Lybia between the earth and   heaven,

que secabat ventos.   Ut primùm tetigit magalia
and   cut   the winds.   When   first he has touched the buildings of Carthage

alatis   plantis, conspicit Æneau fundantem arces   ac
with his winged feet   he beholds Æneas   founding   towers   and

novantem tecta; atque ensis erat illi stellatus fulvâ iaspide,
making new edifices;   and   a sword was to him gemmed with yellow   jasper,

que læna demissa ex humeris ardebat Tyrio murice;   quæ
and   a robe   flowing from his shoulders glowed with Tyrian purple;   which

munera dives Dido fecerat,   et   discreverat   telas
presents   wealthy Dido   had made him, and she had interwoven   the web

tenui auro.   Continuò invadit: Tu nunc locas funda
with fine gold.   Forthwith he accosts him: Do you now   place the founda-

menta altæ Carthaginis, que   uxorius   extruis pulchram
tions   of lofty Carthage,   and devoted to a wife do you raise   a beautiful

urbem? heu! oblite   regni que tuarum   rerum.
city?   alas! forgetful of your kingdom and of your own   concerns.

Regnator Deûm ipse, qui torquet cœlum et terras numine,
The ruler of the gods himself, who   turns   heaven and earth   by his will,

demittit me tibi   claro Olympo; ipse jubet me ferre
sends   me to you from the bright heaven;   he   orders me to bear to you

hæc mandata per celeres auras: Quid struis?   aut
these commands through the swift   air: What do you propose?   or

quâ   spe   teris   otia   Lybicis   terris?
with what expectation do you waste away your leisure in the Lybian   land? ?

Si nulla gloria tantarum rerum movet te, nec ipse   moliris
If no   glory   of such great things   moves thee, nor yourself   undertake

laborem super tuâ laude, respice surgentem Ascanium   et
labour   for thy own fame,   regard   the rising   Ascanius   and

spes Iüli hæredis, cui regnum Italiæ que   Romana
the hopes of Iulus thy heir, to whom the kingdom of Italy   and   the Roman

tellus debentur. Cyllenius locutus tali   ore,
land   are due.   Mercury having spoken with such   discourse,

reliquit mortales visus   medio sermone et   procul
relinquished his mortal appearance in the midst of his speech and   afar

evanuit   ex oculis in tenuem auram. At verò   Æneas
vanished from his eyes into   thin   air.   But indeed   Æneas

amens aspectu obmutuit   que comæ   arrectæ
confounded at the sight was speechless   and his hair   stood upright

horrore,   et vox hæsit faucibus.   Ardet
through horror, and his voice clung to his jaws.   He burns with impatience

abire fugâ, que relinquere dulces terras   attonitus
to go away by flight, and   to leave   the sweet lands,   thunder-struck

tanto   monitu que imperio Deorum. Heu! quid   agat?
at so great warning and command of the gods.   Alas!   what can he do?

quo   affatu nunc audeat ambire furentem reginam? Quæ
with what language   now can he dare to address the raving   queen?   What

prima exordia   sumat?   Atque dividit   celerem
first   introduction of the subject can he take? And   he turns   his rapid

animum nunc huc,   nunc illuc, que rapit in   varios
mind   now on this side, now on that,   and hurries it into   various

partes, que versat per omnia.
directions, and changes through   all.

Hæc sententia visa est potior   alternanti: vocat
This determination seemed preferable to him fluctuating: he calls

Mnesthea que Sergestum, que fortem Cloanthum, ut taciti
Mnestheus   and Sergestus,   and the brave   Cloanthus,   that silent

aptent   classem, que cogant socios   ad litora, parent
they may prepare   the fleet,   and collect their comrades at the shore, provide

arma, et dissimulent quæ sit   causa novandis   rebus;
arms, and dissemble   what may be the cause of their changed   affairs;

interea quando optima Dido   nesciat, et non
in the mean time while the most excellent Dido may not know, and   not

speret tantos amores rumpi, sese tentaturum aditus,
suspect such great love to be broken off, that he would try to find the avenues

et quæ mollissima tempora fandi; quis
to her heart, and what might be the most favourable times for speaking; what

dexter modus rebus. Omnes ociùs læti parent
might be a suitable plan for his affairs. All speedily joyful obey

imperio, ac facessunt jussa. At regina præsensit dolos
his command, and execute his orders. But the queen has perceived the frauds

(quis possit fallere amantem?) que prima excepit
(who may be able to deceive a lover?) and she first has conjectured

futuros motus, timens omnia tuta; eadem
their future motions, fearing all things when seeming safe; the same

impia fama detulit furenti, classem armari,
wicked fame has conveyed the news to her frantic, that the fleet was equipping

que cursum parari. Sævit inops animi, que incensa
and a voyage was preparing. She rages destitute of reason and furious

bacchatur per totam urbem: qualis Thyas excita commotis
roams wildly over the whole city; like a Bacchanal excited by the agitated

sacris ubi trieterica orgia stimulant, Baccho audito,
sacred rites when the triennial orgies arouse her, the name of Bacchus being heard

que nocturnus Cithæron vocat clamore. Tandem ultro
and the nightly Cithæron calls her with clamour. At length, spontaneously

compellat Æneam his vocibus: Perfide sperâsti etiam
she addresses Æneas with these words: O treacherous man hast thou hoped even

posse dissimulare tantum nefas, que tacitus decedere
to be able to dissemble such great wickedness, and silent to depart

meâ terrâ? nec noster amor, nec dextera quondam data,
from my land? nor can our love. nor thy right hand once given

nec Dido moritura crudeli funere tenet te?
in pledge of faith, nor Dido about to die by a cruel death detain thee?

Quin etiam moliris classem hiberno sidere, et properas ire
But even you prepare your fleet in the wintry season, and you hasten to go

per altum mediis aquilonibus. Crudelis! quid? si
through the deep in the midst of tempests. O cruel man! what? if

non peteres aliena arva que ignotas domos, et antiqua Troja
you did not seek foreign lands and unknown habitations, and if ancient Troy

mæneret, Troja peteretur classibus per undosum
might yet remain, would Troy be sought by your fleet through this boisterous

æquor? Fugis ne me? ego oro te per has lachrymas, que
sea? Do you fly from me? I beseech thee by these tears, and

tuam dextram (quando ipsa reliqui jam nihil aliud mihi
thy right hand (since I have left now nothing else to me

miseræ) per nostra connubia, per Hymenæos inceptos, si
miserable) by our wedlock, by our conjugal loves just begun, if

merui quid bene de te, aut quicquam meum fuit
I have deserved any thing well of thee, or if any quality of mine has been

dulce tibi; miserere labentis domus, et exue istam
pleasing to thee. pity a falling family, and put off that

mentem, si   quis locus adhuc precibus. Propter   te
determination, if *there is* any   room   yet for prayers.   On account of thee

Libycæ gentes, que tyranni   Nomadum odere,   Tyrii
the Lybian nations, and the kings of the Numidians have hated me, the Tyrians

infensi: propter eundem te pudor extinctus, et prior
are displeased *with me:* on account of thy same self my honour is lost and *my* former

fama quâ solâ adibam   sidera; cui   deseris   me
fame by which alone I was raised to the stars; to whom dost thou abandon me

moribundam, hospes? quoniam hoc nomen solum restat mihi
about to die,   my guest? since   this   name   alone remains to me

de   conjuge. Quid moror? an dum frater Pygmalion
of *that of* husband.   What do I wait for? is it until my brother   Pygmalion

destruat mea mœnia, aut Getulus Iarbas ducat me captam?
shall destroy my walls,   or the Getulian Iarbas shall lead me   a captive?

Si saltem qua soboles fuisset suscepta mihi de te   ante
If only any offspring had been begotten to me of thee   before

fugam, si quis parvulus Æneas luderet mihi aulâ   qui
thy flight, if any   little   Æneas might sport for me in my hall,   who

tantùm   referret   te ore,   equidem non viderer
only   might represent thee in countenance, indeed I should not seem

omnino capta aut deserta.   Dixerat. Ille   monitis
entirely bereft or abandoned. *She* had spoken. He   by the commands

Jovis tenebat lumina immota, et obnixus   premebat
of Jupiter held   his eyes unmoved, and struggling   suppressed

curam sub corde. Tandem refert pauca: Regina, ego
the anxiety in his breast. At length he replies a few *words:* O queen,   I

nunquam negabo te   premeritam plurima,   quæ
never   will deny that thou hast conferred very many *favours on me,* which

vales   enumerare fando; nec pigebit me meminisse
you may be able to enumerate by speaking; nor shall I be unwilling to remember

Elisæ, dum ipse memor mei, dum spiritus reget   hos
Elisa, whilst I am mindful of myself, whilst   a soul shall govern   these

artus. Loquar   pauca pro re: ego nec speravi abscondere
limbs. I will speak a few *words* on *this* subject: I have not hoped   to conceal

hanc fugam furto, ne finge; nec unquam   prætendi
this   flight by stealth, suppose it not; nor   ever   have I pretended

tædas   conjugis, aut veni in hæc fædera. Si fata
to the ceremonies of marriage, or have I come into those bonds.   If the fates

paterentur me ducere vitam meis   auspiciis, et componere
would permit me to conduct my life by my own directions, and   to quiet

curas   meâ sponte, primùm colerem Trojanam urbem, que
my cares by my own inclination, first I would cherish the Trojan city,   and

dulces reliquias meorum, alta tecta Priami manerent,
the dear remains of my *country,* the lofty buildings of Priam should remain,

et   manu possuissem   victis   Pergama recidiva.
and *with this* hand I would have placed on its ruins   Pergamus rebuilt.

Sed nunc Grynæus Apollo   magnam
But now   Grynæan Apollo *has commanded me to occupy*   great

Italiam, Lyciæ sortes jussere   capessere   Italiam
Italy,   the Lycian oracles have ordered *me* to occupy   Italy.

Hic amor, hæc est patria. Si arces Carthaginis,   que
This *is* my love, this is my country. If the towers of Carthage,   and

æspectus Lybicæ urbis detinet te Phœnissam, tandem quæ
the sight   of a Libyan city   detain thee   a Phœnician,   then   what

invidia est   Teucros considere Ausoniâ   terrâ?
displeasure is *there to you* for the Trojans to settle   in Ausonian   land?

fas   et nos quærere extera regna.   Quoties   nox
let it be right also for us to seek   foreign realms.   As often   as night

operit   terras humentibus umbris, quoties ignea   astra
o'erspreads the earth with its damp   shades,   as often as the bright   stars

surgunt, turbida imago patris Anchisæ admonet et   terret
arise,   the troubled ghost of my father Anchises   admonishes and   affrights

me in somnis; puer Ascanius   que injuria   cari
me in my dreams; the boy Ascanius *admonishes me* and the injury of *his* dear

capitis, quem fraudo   regno   Hesperiæ et fatalibus arvis.
person,   whom I defraud of the kingdom of Italy   and the destined   lands.

Nunc etiam interpres Divûm missus ab Jove   ipso
Now   even   the messenger of the gods sent from Jupiter   himself

testor utrumque caput) detulit   mandata   per
(I call to witness each   divinity) has brought *to me* his commands   through

celeres auras. Ipse vidi Deum, in manifesto   lumine.
the swift air.   I myself have seen the god, in   the clear   light,

intrantem muros, que hausi vocem his auribus.   Desine
entering   *your* walls, and I received his voice in these   ears.   Cease

incendere que me que te   tuis querelis; sequor   Italiam
to torment   both me and thyself with thy complaints; I pursue   Italy

non sponte.   Jamdudum   aversa tuetur dicentem
not of my own accord. For some time   *Dido* averse   views him speaking

talia, volvens oculos huc   illuc, que pererrat   totum
such *words*, rolling her eyes hither *and* thither, and   surveys   *his* whole

tacitis luminibus, et accensa profatur sic: Perfide
person with silent   looks,   and inflamed   speaks thus: O perfidious *man*

Diva   nec parens, nec Dardanus auctor   generis,   sed
a goddess *is* not thy parent, nor *is* Dardanus the founder of *thy* race,   but

horrens Caucasus genuit   te duris cautibus, que Hyrcanæ
frightful   Caucasus brought forth thee on its hard rocks,   and   Hyrcanian

tigres admôrunt ubera. Nam quid dissimulo? aut ad   quæ
tigers administered   suck *to thee.* For   why do I dissemble? or to   what

majora   reservo me? Num ingemuit nostro   fletu?
greater *injuries* do I reserve myself? Whether has he sighed at my   weeping?

num   flexit lumina? num victus dedit lachrymas? aut
whether has he turned his eyes? whether overcome has he shed tears?   or

miseratus est amantem? Quæ   anteferam   quibus?
has he pitied me   loving?   What *complaints* shall I put before   these:

jam jam nec maxima Juno, nec pater Saturnius   aspicit
even now neither greatest   Juno,   nor father Jupiter   regards

hæc æquis oculis. Tuta fides nusquam. Excepi
these *things* with just eyes.   Firm faith *is* no where.   I have received *him*

ejectum littore, egentem, et demens locavi in parte
cast   on the shore, needy,   and *I* foolish have placed *him* in   part

regni: reduxi classem amissam, socios a
of my kingdom: I have recovered his fleet *which was* lost, *and his* companions from

morte Heu! feror incensa furiis; nunc augur
death.   Alas! I am carried away inflamed with fury;   now   the prophetic

Apollo, nunc Lyciæ sortes, et nunc interpres Divûm missus
Apollo,   now the Lycian oracles, and now   the messenger of the Gods   sent

ab Jove ipso fert horrida jussa per auras. Scilicet is
from Jove himself bears the horrid commands through the air.   Indeed   this

est labor Superis, ea cura solicitat quietos! Neque teneo
is labour for the Gods, this care disturbs *them* peaceful!   Nor   do I detain

te, neque refello dicta. I, sequere Italiam ventis,
thee.   nor   do I dispute *your* words,   Go, pursue   Italy   with the winds

pete regna per undas; equidem spero hausurum
seek   realms through the waves;   indeed   I hope   that you will draw

supplicia mediis scopulis, si pia numina possunt
punishment *upon you* in the midst of rocks, if the just deities   can do

quid, et vocaturum sæpe Dido nomine; absens
any thing, and *that* you will call   often *on* Dido   by name: *though* absent

sequar atris ignibus, et cum frigida mors seduxerit
I will pursue *thee* with dark flames,   and when   cold   death shall have sepa-

artus animâ, umbra adero omnibus locis.
rated *these* limbs from the soul,   a shade I will be present *to you* in all   places.

Improbe dabis pœnas; audiam, et hæc fama
O wicked *man* you shall suffer punishment; *I* shall hear *it*, and this   report

veniet mihi sub imos Manes. His dictis abrumpit
shall come to me under the lowest shades.   With these words   she breaks off

medium sermonem, et ægra fugit auras, que avertit,
in the midst of her speech, and distressed she avoids the air,   and she turns away,

et aufert se ex oculis, linquens cunctantem multa
and throws herself from his eyes, leaving him   hesitating   much

metu, et parantem dicere multa. Famulæ suscipiunt
through fear, and preparing   to say   much.   Her maids   raise *her* up

que referunt collapsa membra marmoreo thalamo, que
and bear   her fainting   limbs   to *her* marble   chamber,   and

reponunt stratis. At pius Æneas quanquam cupit solando
lay *her* upon the couch. But pious Æneas   although   he desires by consoling

lenire dolentem, et avertere curas dictis, gemens
her to soothe her grieving, and to turn away her cares by words,   groaning

multa, que labefactus animum magno amore, tamen exse-
much,   and weakened as to his mind by great love,   yet   fol

quitur jussa Divûm, que revisit classem. Tum verô
lows   the commands of the Gods, and   revisits   his fleet.   Then   indeed

Teucri incumbunt, et deducunt celsas naves toto
the Trojans ply earnestly,   and   launch   the lofty ships   *along* the whole

litore; que ferunt sylvis frondentes remos, et robora
shore; and *they* bring from the woods leafy oars, and timber

infabricata, studio fugæ. Cernas migrantes, que
unfashioned, through desire of flight. You may see *them* moving, and

ruentes ex totâ urbe; ac veluti cum formicæ memores
rushing from the whole city; and as when the ants mindful

hyemis populant ingentem acervum farris, que reponunt
of winter plunder a great heap of corn, and lay it up

tecto, nigrum agmen it campis, que convectant
in their cell, the black troop moves *over* the plains, and they carry

prædam per herbas angusto calle; pars obnixa humeris
their booty through the grass in a narrow path; a part pushing with their shoulders

trudunt grandia frumenta; pars cogunt agmina, que
shove along the heavy grains of corn; part collect the bands, and

castigant moras; omnis semita fervet opere.
chastise the slow; the whole path stirs with the work.

Dido, quis sensus tunc tibi cernenti talia? ve quos
O Dido, what emotion then *was* to you beholding such *things* or what

gemitus dabas, cum prospiceres ex summâ arce litora
groans did you utter, when you might behold from the lofty tower the shores

latè fervere, que videres ante oculos totum æquor
far and wide to stir *with bustle*, and see before your eyes the whole sea

misceri tantis clamoribus. Improbe amor, quid non
confused with such great shouts. O cruel love, what do you not

cogis mortalia pectora. Iterum cogitur ire in lachrymas,
compel mortal hearts *to do.* Again she is compelled to go in tears.

iterum tentare precando, et supplex submittere animos
again to assail *him* with entreaty, and suppliant to yield her soul

amori, ne relinquat quid inexpertum moritura frustra.
to love, lest she might leave any thing untried, *and* be about to die rashly.

Anna vides properari toto litore circùm;
O Anna you see *them* to be hurrying over the whole shore around;

convenêre undique; carbasus jam vocat auras, et
they have assembled from all sides; the canvass now invites the air, and

læti nautæ imposuêre coronas puppibus. Si potui
the joyful sailors have placed garlands on the sterns *of the ships.* If I had been

sperare hunc tantum dolorem—et soror, potero
able to anticipate this so great grief—and O sister, I will be able

perferre: Anna, tamen exsequere hoc unum mihi miseræ;
to bear *it:* O Anna, yet perform this one *thing,* for me wretched;

nam ille perfidus colere te solam, etiam credere arcanos
for that perfidious *man was wont* to respect thee alone, even to entrust his secret

sensus tibi; sola, nôras molles aditus, et
feelings to thee; *thou* alone, hast known the gentle avenues *to his heart,* and

tempora viri. Soror, I, atque supplex affare
the *accessible* times of the man, O sister, go, and suppliant address

superbum hostem; ego non juravi Aulide cum Danais
this proud foe; I have not sworn at Aulis with the Greeks

exscindere Trojanam gentem, ve misi classem ad Pergama,
to extirpate   the Trojan   nation,   or sent   a fleet   to   Pergamus

nec revelli   cineres ve manes   patris Anchisæ.   Cur
nor have I disturbed the ashes   or the manes of his father Anchises.   Why

negat demittere mea dicta in duras aures? Quò   ruit?
does he refuse to admit   my words into his cruel ears? Whither does he rush?

det   hoc extremum munus miseræ amanti; exspectet
et him grant this   last   favour to a miserable lover: let him wait

facilem fugam que ferentes ventos. Jam non oro antiquum
for an easy flight   and favourable winds.   Now I do not plead our former

conjugium quod prodidit; nec ut   careat
wedlock   which he has betrayed; not that   he should deprive himself

pulchro Latio, que relinquat regnum; peto inane tempus,
of beautiful Latium, and   relinquish his kingdom;   I beg a trifling   time,

requiem que spatium furori, dum mea fortuna   doceat
a rest   and   a space for my fury, until my   fortune   may instruct me

victam dolere. Oro hanc extremam veniam   (miserere
overcome to mourn. I beg this   last   favour   (pity

sororis) quam cùm   dederit mihi, remittam, cumulatum
thy sister) which   when he shall have granted to me, I will dismiss him,   gratified

morte. Orabat talibus,   que miserrima soror fert
in my death. She entreated with such words, and her most wretched sister bears

que refert tales fletus;   sed ille movetur   nullis
and bears again such lamentations to Æneas; but he   is moved   by no

fletibus, aut tractabilis audit ullas voces.   Fata obstant:
lamentations, or   complying   does he hear any words.   The fates oppose.

que Deus obstruit placidas aures viri.   Ac veluti   cùm
and the God   stops the compassionate ears of the man, And   as   when

Alpini Boreæ, nunc hinc, nunc illinc, certant   inter
he Alpine north-winds, now on this side, now   on that,   strive   among

se flatibus eruere annosam quercum   valido
themselves with their blasts to overthrow an ancient   oak   of sturdy

robore; stridor it,   et frondes altè consternunt   terram
strength;   the sound goes forth, and the leaves deeply   strew   the ground

stipite concusso; ipsa hæret scopulis, et tendit   tantum
the trunk being shaken;   it   cleaves to the rocks, and shoots   as much

radice   ad Tartara, quantum vertice   ad   ætherias
with its roots towards Tartarus,   as   with its top towards   the etherial

auras. Haud secus heros tunditur hinc atque   hinc
air.   Just so   the hero is assailed on this side and   on that side

assiduis vocibus, et præsentit curas magno   pectore;
with constant intercessions, and   feels   cares in his great   breast;

mens manet immota; inanes lachrymæ volvuntur.   Tum
his mind remains unmoved;   vain   tears   roll.   Then

verò infelix Dido exterrita fatis orat mortem;   tæde:
indeed the unhappy Dido   affrighted at her fate prays for death; it wearies her

tueri convexa cœli. Quò magis peragat inceptum que
to see the arch of heaven. That more she may accomplish her design   and

relinquat lucem, cùm imponeret dona aris thure-
relinquish life, when she would lay offerings *upon* the altars burning

cremis, vidit (horrendum dictu) sacros latices nigrescere,
with incense, she saw (horrible to be told) the sacred liquors grow black,

que vina fusa vertere se in obscœnum cruorem. Effata
and the wine poured out change itself into loathsome blood. *She* told

hoc visum nulli, non sorori ipsi. Preterea, templum
this vision to no one, not to her sister herself. Besides, a shrine

antiqui conjugis de marmore fuit in tectis, quod colebat
of her former husband of marble was in the palace, which she reverenced

miro honore, revinctum niveis velleribus et festâ
with wonderful honour, bound with snowy fillets of wool and with festive

fronde. Hinc voces et verba viri vocantis
leaves. From this *shrine* voices and the words of her husband calling *her*

visa exaudiri, cùm obscura nox teneret terras; que
seemed to be heard, when dark night would possess the earth; and

sola bubo sæpe queri ferali carmine culminibus,
the solitary owl often *seemed* to complain with a dismal song on the house-tops,

et ducere longas voces in fletum; que preterea, multa
and to draw out *his* long notes in lamentation; and besides, many

predicta piorum vatum horrificant terribili monitu. Æneas
predictions of pious prophets terrify *her* by *their* terrible warning. *Æneas*

ipse ferus agit furentem in somnis; que semper videtur
himself cruel disturbs *her* raving in her sleep; and always she seems

sibi relinqui sola, semper ire longam viam incomitata,
to herself to be left alone, always to be going a long journey unattended,

et quærere Tyrios desertâ terrâ; veluti demens Pentheus
and to be seeking *her* Tyrians in a desert land; as frantic Pentheus

videt agmina Eumenidum, et geminum solem, et Thebas
sees troops of Furies, and a two-fold sun, and Thebes

ostendere se duplices; aut Orestes Agamemnonius agitatus
to show itself double; or *as* Orestes the son of Agamemnon distracted

scenis, cùm fugit matrem armatum facibus et atris
on the stage, when he flies from his mother armed with firebrands and black

serpentibus, que ultrices Diræ sedent in limine. Ergo
serpents and the avenging Furies sit in the threshold. Then

ubi evicta dolore concepit Furias, que decrevit mori,
when overcome with grief she has conceived the Furies, and has determined to die,

ipsa exigit secum tempus que modum; et agressa
she considers with herself the time and the manner; and addressing

mæstam sororem dictis, tegit consilium vultu,
her mournful sister with *these* words, *she* covers her design by her countenance,

ac serenat spem fronte; Germana, gratare sorori! inveni
and brightens hope in her face; O sister, congratulate thy sister! I have found

viam quæ reddat eum mihi, vel solvat me amantem eo.
a way which shall restore him to me, or release me loving from him

Juxtà finem Oceani què cadentem solem, est ultimus
Near the extremity of the ocean and the setting sun, is the as

locus Æthiopum, ubi maximus Atlas humero   torquet
spot   of Æthiopia, where the mighty Atlas on his shoulder   whirls

axem   aptum ardentibus stellis; hinc sacerdos Massyliæ
the heavens studded with glowing stars; from hence a priestess of the Massylian

gentis monstrata,   custos templi   Hesperidum,
nation appeared *to me*, the guardian of the temple   of the Hesperides,

quæque dabat epulas draconi, et servabat sacros   ramos
and who gave food to the dragon, and watched the sacred   boughs

in arbore, spargens humida mella que soporiferum papaver:
on the tree, sprinkling liquid honey and the soporiferous   poppy;

hæc promittit se   solvere carminibus mentes   quas
she promises *that* she *is able* to release by charms the minds   which

velit,   ast immittere duras curas aliis; sistere aquam
she may will, and to throw grievous cares upon others; to stop the water

fluviis, et vertere sidera retro;   que   ciet   nocturnas
in rivers, and to turn the stars backward; and she can call up the nocturnal

manes. Videbis terram mugire sub pedibus, et   ornos
ghosts. You shall see the earth bellow under her feet, and the wild ashes

descendere montibus.
come down   from the mountains.

Cara germana,   testor   Deos et te, que tuum dulce
O dear sister, I call to witness the Gods and thee, and thy   dear

caput,   invitam   accingier magicas artes.   Tu
life, *that* against my will I have recourse to these magic arts,   Do you

secreta erige pyram interiore tecto sub auras;   et
secretly erect a funeral pile in the inner palace under the air;   and

superimponas arma viri, quæ impius reliquit   fixa
place upon it   the arms of the man, which wicked he has left   fixed

thalamo,   que omnes exuvias, que jugalem lectum   quo
in my chamber, and all *his* clothes, and the nuptial couch   on which

perii.   Sacerdos jubet que monstrat abolere   cuncta
I was undone. The priestess commands and directs *me* to destroy   all

monumenta viri.   Effata   hæc   silet;
the memorials of the man. Having spoken these *words*   she is silent;

simul   pallor occupat   ora.   Anna   tamen
at the same time paleness seizes *her* countenance. Anna   nevertheless

non credit germanam prætexere funera   novis
does not believe *that her* sister conceals *her own* death   *under these* new

sacris; nec concipit tantos furores   mente,   aut
sacred rites; nor does she conceive such great fury *to be in her* mind,   or

timet graviora quam   morte Sichæi.
does she fear worse *things* than *those which happened* at the death of Sichæus.

Ergo parat   jussa. At Regina, ingenti pyrâ
Therefore she prepares *the things* ordered. But the queen, a great funeral pile

erectâ sub auras in penetrali sede, tœdis atque sectâ
being erected under the air in the inner court, of pine-wood and   cut

ilice, que intendit locum   sertis, et coronat   funereâ
oak,   both encircles the place with garlands, and crowns it   with funeral

fronde; super locat toro ejus exuvias, que ensem
leaves; above *she* places on the couch his clothes, and the sword

relictum, que effigiem, haud ignara futuri. Aræ
left by *him*, and *his* image, not ignorant of what was to come. Altars

stant circum; et sacerdos effusa crines tonat
stand around; and the priestess dishevelled *as to her* hair thunders

ore tercentum Deos, que Erebum, que Chaos,
with her voice on the three hundred Gods, and Erebus, and Chaos,

que tergeminam Hecaten, tria ora virginis Dianæ.
and three fold Hecate, the three appearances of the virgin Diana.

Sparserat et simulatos latices fontis Averni; et
She had sprinkled also counterfeited waters of the fountain of Avernus; an

pubentes herbæ messæ ahenis falcibus ad lunam quæruntur,
full-grown herbs cut with brazen sickles by moon-light are sought for,

cum lacte nigri veneni; et amor revulsus de fronte
with the juice of black poison; and the love-knot torn from the forehead

nascentis equi, et præreptus matri, quæritur.
of a new foaled colt, and snatched away *from the* mother, is sought for.

Ipsa moritura, exuta unum pedem vinclis, in recinctâ
She herself about to die, having stripped one foot *of its* sandal, in a loose

veste, juxta altaria, molâ que piis manibus testatur
robe, near the altars, *with the* salt cake and pious hands calls to witness

Deos, et sidera conscia fati; tum precatur numen, si
the Gods, and the stars conscious of fate; then she prays *to* the deity, if *there is*

quod que justum que memor habet curæ amantes non
any *deity* both just and mindful *who* has *any* care of lovers in an

æquo fœdere. Erat nox, et fessa corpora per terras
unequal union. *It* was night, and weary bodies through the earth

carpebant placidum soporem, que sylvæ et sæva aquora
enjoyed placid sleep, and the woods and the raging seas

quiêrant; cùm sidera volvuntur medio lapsu; cùm
were calm; when the stars are rolling in the midst *of their* course; when

omnis ager tacet; pecudes, que pictæ volucres, quæque
every field is still; beasts and variegated birds, which

latè tenent liquidos lacus, quæque tenent rura aspera
far and wide occupy the liquid lakes, and which occupy the fields rough

dumis, positæ sub silenti nocte lenibant curas somno;
with brambles, stretched under the silent night soothed their cares with sleep,

et corda oblita laborum. At non Phænissa
and their hearts *were* forgetful of their labours. But not so the Phœnician *Dido*

infelix animi; neque unquam solvitur in somnum, ve
unhappy in mind; nor ever is *she* relaxed in sleep, or

accipit noctem oculis aut pectore: curæ ingeminant
does she receive nightly *rest* to her eyes or breast: her cares redouble

que amor resurgens rursus sævit, que fluctuat magno æstu
and love rising afresh again rages, and fluctuates with a great tide

irarum. Sic adeò insistit, que ita volutat secum corde:
of passions. Thus then she persists, and thus *she* revolves with herself in her heart.

En quid ago? irrisa ne experiar rursus priores procos?
Lo what am I doing? scorned shall I try again my former suitors?

que supplex petam connubia Nomadum, quos ego jam
and suppliant shall I seek the alliance of the Numidians, whom I already.

toties dedignata sum maritos? Sequar igitur Illiacas classes
so often have disdained *as* husbands? Shall I follow then the Trojan fleet

atque ultima jussa Teucrorum? quia ne juvat antè
and the lowest commands of the Trojans? *is* it because it delighted *me* formerly

levatos auxilio, et gratia veteris
that they should be assisted by *my* aid, and does the thankfulness for my former

facti stat apud bene memores? Autem quis (fac
action remain with *them* well remembering? But who (grant *me*

velle) sinet, que accipiet invisam superbis ratibus.
to be willing) will allow, and receive me detested in their proud ships?

heu! perdita nescis, necdum sentis perjuria
alas! undone *Dido* dost thou not know, nor yet dost thou perceive the perjuries

gentis Laomedonteæ? Quid tum? sola fugâ comitabor
of the race of Laomedon? What then? alone in *my* flight shall I accompany

ovantes nautas? an insequar stipata Tyriis, que omni
the exulting sailors? or shall I follow *them* surrounded by *my* Tyrians, and all

manu meorum? et rursus agam pelago, et jubebo
the band of my *people?* and again shall I lead *them* to the sea, and command *them*

dare vela ventis, quos vix revelli Sidoniâ
to spread sails to the winds, whom with difficulty I have torn *from the* Sidonian

urbe? Quin morere, ut merita es, que averte dolorem
city? But die, as you have deserved, and avert thy grief

ferro. Germana, tu prima evicta meis lachrymis, tu
by the sword. O sister, thou first overcome by my tears, thou

oneras furentem his malis, et objicis hosti.
dost load me distracted with these woes, and exposest *me* to my enemy.

Non licuit sine crimine degere vitam expertem
Was it not lawful *for me* without crime to pass my life free

thalami, more feræ, nec tangere tales
from the marriage bed, *after the* manner of the wild beast, nor feel such

curas? Fides promissa cineri Sichæo non servata. Illa
cares? The faith promised to the ashes of Sichæus *is* not preserved. She

rumpebat tantos questus. Æneas jam certus eundi,
broke out into such great complaints. Æneas now determined on going

carpebat somnos in celsâ puppi, rebus jam ritè paratis.
was enjoying sleep in his lofty ship, things now rightly being prepared.

Forma Dei redeuntis eodem vultu obtulit se
The figure of the God returning with the same countenance presented itself

huic in somnis, que visa est rursus ita monere; similis
to him in *his* sleep, and seemed again thus to warn *him*; like to

Mercurio omnia, que vocem, que colorem, et flavos crines,
Mercury in all *things*, both in voice, and complexion, and yellow hair

et decora membra juventæ: Nate Deâ, potes ducere
and graceful limbs of youth: O Goddess-born, can you prolong

somnos sub hoc casu? nec cernis quæ pericula deinde
sleep   under this conjuncture? nor do *you* see what dangers   thence

circumstent te? demens   nec   audis   secundos
may surround thee? thoughtless *man!* nor do you hear the   favourable

Zephyros spirare?
breezes   blow?

Illa versat dolos que dirum nefas in pectore,   certa
She meditates wiles and dire wickedness in her breast,   determined

mori, que fluctuat vario   æstu irarum.   Non   fugis
o die, and fluctuates with a various tide of passions. *Why* do you not   fly

hinc præceps, dum potestas   præcipitare? Jam videbis
hence hastily,   whilst the power *is yours* to hasten away? Now you shall see

mare   turbari trabibus que sævas faces collucere; jam
the ocean to be disturbed with oars and fierce torches   to glare; now *you shall see*

litora fervere flammis, si Aurora attigerit te   morantem
the shores to glow with flames, if the morning shall reach thee   delaying

his terris. Eia, age, rumpe   moras: femina   semper
on these lands. Away, come, break off *your* delay: woman   always *is*

varium et mutabile. Sic fatus, immiscuit se   atræ
variable and changeable. Thus having said, he mingles himself   *with* dark

nocti. Tum verò Æneas, exterritus   subitis   umbris,
night.   Then indeed Æneas,   affrighted at *this* sudden   shadow,

corripit   corpus è somno, que fatigat socios: Viri,
raises suddenly *his* body from sleep,   and rouses his companions: O men,

vigilate præcipites, et considite   transtris;   citi solvite
awake   hastily,   and seat *yourselves* on the benches: quick loosen

vela; ecce! Deus missus ab alto æthere iterum   stimulat
the sails; lo! a God sent from the high sky   again   urges *me*

festinare fugam, que incidere tortos funes.   Sancte
to hasten *my* flight,   and to cut the twisted cables.   O sacred *power*

Deorum, sequimur te, quisquis es, que iterum   ovantes
of the Gods, we follow thee, whoever thou art, and   again   rejoicing

paremus imperio.   O adsis,   que placidus juves,
we obey thy command. O mayst thou be present, and friendly   assist *us,*

et feras dextra sidera cœlo.   Dixit, que   eripit
and give propitious stars in heaven. He has said, and   snatches

fulmineum ensem vaginâ, que ferit retinacula   stricto
his flashing   sword from its scabbard, and strikes the hawsers with the drawn

ferro. Idem ardor   simul   habet omnes; que rapiunt
steel.   The same ardour at the same time possesses all;   and *they* sieze

que ruunt; deseruere litora; æquor latet-sub   classibus;
and hurry *about*; they have left the shores: the sea is hid under   their fleet:

adnixi torquent spumas, et verrunt cærula.   Et   jam
labouring they dash the spray, and sweep over the azure *sea.* And   now

Aurora, linquens croceum cubile Tithoni, prima   spargebat
Aurora,   leaving the saffron bed of Tithonus, first   sprinkled

terras novo lumine: ut primùm Regina è   speculis
the earth with new light: when first the queen from   her watch-towers

vidit lucem albescere, et classem procedere æquatis velis,
has seen the light to dawn, and the fleet to proceed with balanced sails

que sensit litora et portus vacuos sine remige; que
and has perceived the shores and the ports empty without a rower; and

percussa decorum pectus manu ter que quater, que
striking her beautiful breast with her hand thrice and four times, and

abscissa flaventes comas; Pro Jupiter, ait, hic ibit, et
tearing her yellow hair; O Jupiter, she says, shall he go, and

advena illuserit nostris regnis? Non expedient
a stranger shall he have mocked our realms? Will they not bring forth

arma, que sequentur ex tota urbe? que alii diripien
arms, and pursue him from the whole city? and will not others tear

rates navalibus? ite, citi ferte flammas, date vela,
my ships from the docks? go, quick bring flames, spread sails

impellite remos. Quid loquor? aut ubi sum? quæ insania
ply oars. What am I saying? or where am I? what madness

mutat mentem? Infelix Dido! nunc impia facta tangunt
turns my mind? O unhappy Dido! now do thy wicked deeds touch

te? Tum decuit, cum dabas sceptra. En
thee? Then it had become thee, when thou didst give to him thy sceptre. Is this

dextra que fides quem aiunt portare secum patrios
the honour and the faith of him whom they report to carry with him his paternal

Penates! quem subiisse humeris, parentem
household Gods! whom they report to have borne on his shoulders, his father

confectum ætate! Non potui divellere abreptum corpus,
worn out with age! Have I not been able to tear his mangled body

et spargere undis? Non absumere socios,
and to scatter it to the waves? Have I not been able to destroy his companions,

non Ascanium ipsum ferro, que opponere
have I not been able to destroy Ascanius himself with the sword, and to place him

epulandum patriis mensis? Verùm fortuna pugnæ fuerat
to be eaten at his father's tables? But the fortune of battle had been

anceps: fuisset: moritura quem metui?
doubtful: it might have been. about to die whom have I feared? I might have

tulissem faces in castra, que implêssem foros flammis;
thrown firebrands into his camp, and I might have filled the hatches with flames;

exstinxêm que natum que patrem cum genere;
I might have extirpated both son and father with the race;

ipsa dedissem memet supra. Sol, qui lustras omnia opera
I might have cast myself upon them. O Sun, who surveyest all the works

terrarum flammis, tuque et Juno, conscia interpres
of the earth with thy beams, and thou also O Juno, the conscious witness

harum curarum, que Hecate ululata per urbes nocturnis
of these my cares, and O Hecate howling through the cities in the nightly

triviis, et ultrices Diræ, et Dî morientis Elisæ. accipite
crossways and ye avenging Furies, and Gods of the dying Elisa! receive

hæc, que advertite meritum numen malis, et audit
these my words, and turn a deserved regard to my woes, and hea

nostras preces.   Si   necesse est infandum caput   tangere
my   prayers.   If it is necessary for the wicked person   to touch

portus, et adnare terris, et sic fata   Jovis poscunt,   hic
harbours, and to reach lands, and thus the fates of Jupiter require,   if this

terminus hæret;   at vexatus bello et armis   audacis
determination shall remain; but harassed by war and the arms   of a bold

populi, extorris   finibus, avulsus complexu   Iüli,
people   banished from his own territories, torn from the embrace   of Iulus,

imploret   auxilium, que videat indigna   funera   suorum;
may he implore assistance, and   see the dishonourable deaths of his friends;

nec fruatur   regno aut optatâ luce,   cùm   tradideri
nor may he enjoy his kingdom or the desired light of life, when he shall have sub-

se sub leges   iniquæ pacis; sed   cadat
mitted himself to the conditions of a disadvantageous peace; but   may he fall

ante diem, que inhumatus mediâ arenâ.   Precor
before his time, and be unburied in the midst of the sandy shore.   I pray

hæc;   fundo hanc extremam vocem cum   sanguine.
for these things; I pour forth this   last   speech with   my blood.

Tum vos O Tyrii odiis exercete stirpem, et omne   ejus
Then ye Tyrians with hatred harass his offspring, and all   his

futurum genus, que mittite hæc munera nostro cineri; sunto
future   race,   and   send   these offerings to my ashes; let there be

nullus amor nec fœdera   populis. Exoriare   aliquis
no   friendship nor leagues between the nations. Arise   some

ultor ex nostris ossibus, qui sequare Dardanos   colonos
avenger from my   remains, who shall pursue these Trojan   colonists

face que ferro, nunc, olim quocunque tempore   vires
with fire and sword, now, hereafter and at whatever time   means

dabunt se. Imprecor   litora   contraria   litoribus,
shall afford themselves. I pray that our shores may be opposed to their shores,

undas   fluctibus, arma armis: que   nepotes
our waters to their waters, our arms to their arms: and may our descendants

ipsi pugnent.
themselves contend.

Ait hæc,   et versabat animum in omnes   partes,
She says these words, and turned   her mind in all   directions,

quærens quàm primùm abrumpere invisam lucem.   Tum
seeking   as soon as possible to throw off her hated life.   Then

breviter affata Barcen nutricem Sichæi, namque ater cinis
briefly she has addressed Barce the nurse of Sichæus, for   dark ashes

habelat suam   antiquâ patriâ: cara nutrix, siste huc
possessed her own nurse in her ancient country: O dear nurse, send hither

sororem Annam mihi; dic   properet spargere corpus
my sister Anna   to me; tell that she may hasten to sprinkle her body

fluviali lymphâ, et ducat pecudes secum,   et
with running water,   and bring the victims with her,   and

monstrata piacula; sic veniat; tuque ipsa   tege
the things shown her for expiation; thus let her come: and you yourself cover

tempora   piâ   vittâ.   Animus est preficere   ritè
your temples with the pious fillet.   My mind is to perform   the rightly

incepta sacra quæ   paravi   Stygio Jovi, que imponere
begun   sacrifices which I have prepared to Stygian Jove, and   to put

finem curis, que permittère flammæ rogum   Dardanii
an end to my cares, and to commit to the flame   the pile   of the Trojan

capitis. Sic ait.   Illa celerabat gradum anili   studio.
prince.   Thus she said. She quickened her step with an old woman's zeal.

At Dido trepida et effera immanibus cœptis,   volvens
But Dido trembling and distracted at her horrid designs.   rolling

sanguineam aciem, que interfusa   trementes   genas
her bloody   eyes,   and marked as to her trembling   cheeks

maculis, et pallida futurâ morte, irrumpit interiora
with spots, and pale at the.coming death,   bursts   through the inner

limina domus, et furibunda conscendit altos rogos,   que
gates   of the palace, and raving   ascends   the lofty pile,   and

recludit Dardanium ensem, munus non quæsitum in hos
unsheaths the Trojan sword, a gift not   designed for these

usus. Hìc, postquam conspexit Illiacas vestes,   que
uses. Here,   after   *she* has viewed the Trojan vestments   and

  notum   cubile, paulùm morata lachrymis et mente, que
the well known couch, a little while delaying through tears and meditation, and

incubuit   toro   que dixit novissima verba: Dulces
reclined   upon the couch and spoke   her last   words: Ye dear

exuviæ, dum fata que Deus sinebant, accipe hanc animam,
remains, whilst the fates and the God permitted, receive   this   soul

que exsolvite me his curis. Vixi, et   peregi
and   release   me from these cares. I have lived, and   I have finished

cursum quem fortuna dederat; et nunc mei magna imago
the course which fortune had given me; and now   my   great   shade

ibit sub terras. Statui praclaram urbem;   vidi
shall go under the earth. I have built a glorious   city;   I have seen

mœnia mea;   ulta   virum, recepi   pœnas à
walls   of my own; having avenged my husband. I have executed punishment on

inimico fratre; felix, heu! nimiùm felix, si   tantùm
an unfriendly brother; happy, ah!   too happy, if   only

Dardaniæ carinæ nunquam tetigissent nostra litora. Dixit; et
the Trojan   ships   never   had touched our   shores. She said; and

impressa os   toro,   ait, Moriemur inulta?   sed
pressing   her face to the couch, she says, shall I die unrevenged?   but

moriamur: sic, sic juvat ire sub umbras.   Crudelis
let me die: thus, thus it delights *me* to go under the shades.   Let the

  Dardanus hauriat oculis hunc ignem ab alto, et ferat
cruel Trojan   behold   this   flame from the deep, and bear

secum omina nostræ mortis.   Dixerat; atque   comites
with him the signs of my   death. She had spoken; and   her attendants

aspiciunt illam collapsam ferro inter media talia,   que
behold   her   fallen   upon the sword in the midst of such *words*, and

ensem spumantem, que ejus manus sparsas cruore. Clamor
the sword reeking, and her hands sprinkled with blood. The outcry

it ad alta atria, fama bacchatur per concussam urbem;
goes to the lofty halls; the report flies wildly through the agitated city;

tecta fremunt lamentis, que gemitu, et femineo ululatu;
the houses ring with lamentations, and groans, and with female shrieks;

æther resonat magnis plangoribus: non aliter quàm si omnis
the air resounds with great screams: not otherwise than if all

Carthago, aut antiqua Tyros ruat, hostibus immissis,
Carthage, or ancient Tyre should fall down, enemies being let in,

que furentes flammæ volvantur per que culmina hominum
and the furious flames should roll over both the buildings of men

que per Deorùm.
and over the *temples* of the Gods.

Soror audiit exanimis, que exterrita trepido cursu,
Her sister has heard *it* breathless, and affrighted with trembling haste,

fædans ora unguibus et pectora pugnis, ruit per
disfiguring her face with her nails and her breast with blows, rushes through

medios, ac clamat morientem nomine: Germana, fuit hoc
the midst, and calls her dying *sister* by name: O sister, was this

illud? petebas me fraude? iste rogus, ignes, que aræ
it? did you approach me by fraud? did this pile, *these* fires, and altars

parabant hoc mihi? Deserta quid primùm querar? moriens
prepare this for me? Deserted what first shall I complain? dying

ne sprevisti sororem comitem? vocâsses me ad eadem
hast thou despised thy sister as a companion? had you called me to the same

fata, idem dolor atque eadem hora tulisset ambas
fate, the same pain and the same hour had taken off both of us

ferro. Struxi etiam his manibus, que vocavi
by the sword. Have I raised *the pile* even with these hands, and have I in-

patrios Deos voce, ut crudelis abessem te
voked the paternal Gods wih my voice, that cruel I should be absent thou

sic positâ. Soror, extinxtî me que te, que
thus being placed *upon it*. O sister, thou hast destroyed me and thyself, and

populum que Sidonias patres, que tuam urbem. Date,
thy people and the Sidonian fathers, and thy city. Give,

abluam vulnera lymphis; et si quis extremus halitus
that I may wash her wounds with water; and if any last breath

errat supra, legam ore. Sic fata,
may linger above, I may catch *it with my* mouth. Thus having said,

evaserat altos gradus, que amplexa semianimem germa-
she had mounted the lofty steps. and embracing her expiring sister

nam sinu, fovebat cum gemitu, atque siccabat atros
in her bosom, cherished *her* with a groan, and dried up the black

cruores veste. Illa conata attollere graves oculos,
blood *with her* robe. She endeavouring to raise her heavy eyes,

rursus deficit; infixum vulnus stridet sub pectore. Ter
again sinks down: the deep-fixed wound hisses in her breast. Thrice

attollens que adnixa cubito levavit sese; ter revoluta
arousing and leaning on her elbow she has raised herself; thrice she has fallen

est toro; que errantibus oculis quæsivit lucem alto
back upon the couch; and with wandering eyes has sought the light of the high

cœlo, que ingemuit repertâ. Tum omnipotens Juno
heaven, and groaned having found it. Then omnipotent Juno

miserata longum dolorem que difficiles obitus, demisit Irim
pitying her long pain and uneasy death, has sent Iris

Olympo, quæ resolvent luctantem animam que nexos artus.
from heaven, who might separate her struggling soul and united limbs.

Nam quia peribat nec fato nec meritâ morte, sed
For since she perished neither by fate nor by a merited death, but

misera ante diem, que accensa subito furore, Proserpina
miserable before her time, and inflamed with sudden fury, Proserpine

nondum abstulerat illi flavum crinem vertice que
not yet had taken to herself the yellow hair from the crown of her head and

damnaverat caput Stygio Orco. Ergo roscida Iris devolat per
condemned her life to Stygian Orcus. Therefore dewy Iris flies through

cœlum croceis pennis, trahens mille varios colores
the sky on saffron wings, drawing a thousand various colours

adverso sole, et astitit supra caput: Ego jussa
from the opposite sun, and has stood above her head. I being commanded

fero hunc sacrum Diti, que solvo te isto corpore. Sic
bear away this hair sacred to Pluto, and I release thee from this body. Thus

ait, et secat crinem dextrâ; et unâ omnis calor
she says, and cuts her hair with her right hand; and at once all heat

dilapsus, atque vita recessit in ventos.
is dissipated, and life has vanished into the air.

ÆNEID.

BOOK FIFTH.

Interea Æneas certus jam tenebat medium iter
In the meantime Æneas resolved now held the intermediate way

classe, que secabat fluctus atros aquilone, respiciens
with his fleet, and cut the waves blackened by the north wind, looking back

mœnia, quæ jam collucent flammis infelicis Elisæ.
upon the walls, which yet glow with the flames of the wretched Dido.

Causa quæ accenderit tantum ignem latet: sed duri
The cause which had enkindled so great a fire is concealed but the cruel

dolores magno amore polluto, quidque furens femina possit
torments from great love violated, and what a raging woman can do

notum,   ducunt pectora Teucrorum per triste   augurium
being known,   lead   the hearts of the Trojans   to   sad   conjecture.

Ut rates tenuere   pelagus, nec ulla tellus jam   amplius
As the ships have reached the sea,   nor any   land   now   more

occurrit, undique cœlum, et undique maria;   cæruleus
appears,   on every side the sky,   and on every side the ocean;   an azure

imber astitit supra olli caput, ferens noctem que   hiemen,
cloud   stood   above   his   head,   bearing   night   and   tempest,

et unda inhorruit tenebris. Ipse gubernator   Palinurus
and the wave grew dreadful by darkness.   The   helmsman   Palinurus

ab   altâ puppi,   Heu! quianam tanti   nimbi
from the high   stern *exclaimed*, Alas!   why   have so great   clouds

cinxerunt æthera? ve quid   paras,   O pater   Neptune?
overspread   the heavens? or   what do you prepare,   O father   Neptune?

Deinde locutus sic,   jubet   colligere arma,   que
Then   having spoken thus, he commands to gather up the sails,   and

incumbere validis remis; que obliquat sinus in ventum,   ac
to press on   the strong oars;   and   turns   the sails to the wind,   and

fatur talia: magnanime Ænea,   non sperem   contingere
speaks these *words*: O high-minded Æneas, I could not   hope   to reach

Italiam hoc   cœlo, si Jupiter auctor spondeat   mihi.
Italy   with this weather, if   Jupiter our patron should promise *it*   to me.

Venti   mutati fremunt transversa,   et consurgunt   ab
The winds changed   rage   in opposite directions, and   rise   from

atro vespere; atque aër   cogitur in nubem. Nos nec
the gloomy west;   and the atmosphere is collected into a cloud.   We neither

sufficimus obniti contra   nec tantùm tendere: Quoniam
are able   to strive against *them*, nor   even   to advance: Since

Fortuna superat, sequamur; que vertamus iter   quò
Fortune   conquers, let us follow;   and let us change   our course   where

vocat: nec reor   fida   fraterna litora Erycis, que Sicanos
she calls: nor do I think the faithful fraternal shores   of Eryx,   and the Sicilian

portus   longè, si modò memor ritè   remetior   astra
harbours *are* far distant, *if*   only   mindful rightly I measure back   the stars

servata. Tum pius Æneas, Equidem cerno ventos   poscere
observed.   Then pious Æneas *said*, Indeed   I observe the winds   demand

sic jamdudum, et te frustra tendere contra. Flecte viam
thus   long since,   and you in vain   steer   against *them*. Guide *your* course

velis.   An   ulla tellus sit gratior mihi,   quòque
by the sails. Whether *can* any   land   be more grateful to me,   and where

magis optem demittere fessas naves, quam quæ   servat
I can more desire   to lay up my wearied ships,   than which   preserves

mihi Dardanium Acesten et gremio complectitur   ossa
to me   Trojan   Acestes and in its bosom   embraces   the bones

patris   Anchisæ? Ubi hæc   dicta,   petunt   portus,
of my father Anchises? When these *words* were spoken, they seek the harbours,

et secundi Zephyri intendunt vela: classis cita   fertur
and the favouring   breezes   swell   the sails: the fleet swift   is borne

gurgite; et tandem læti advertuntur notæ arenæ.
on the deep; and at length joyful they are turned to the well-known sand.

At Acestes excelso vertice montis procul miratus
But Acestes from the high summit of a mountain from afar admiring

adventum, que socias rates, occurrit, horridus in
their approach, and *knowing* the friendly ships, meets *them* roughly *adorned* with

jaculis, et pelle Libystidis ursæ: quem Troïa mater genuit
arrows, and the skin of a Lybian bear: whom a Trojan mother had borne

conceptum Criniso flumine. Ille non immemor veterum
conceived from Crinisus a river. He not unmindful of his ancient

parentum gratatur reduces, et lætus excipit agresti
parents congratulates *them* returned, and joyful receives *them* with rustic

gazâ, ac solatur fessos amicis opibus. Cum postera
abundance, and consoles *them* wearied with friendly assistance. When the next

clara dies fugârat stellas primo oriente, Æneas advocat
bright day had scattered the stars with the first dawn, Æneas calls together

socios in cœtum ab omni littore, que fatur ex
his associates to a meeting from all the shore, and addresses *them* from

aggere tumuli: Magni Dardanidæ, genus ab alto sanguine
the mound of a hill:: Ye mighty Trojans, *whose* race *is* from the exalted blood

Divûm, annuus orbis completur mensibus exactis ex
of Gods, a yearly circle is completed the months being accomplished, from

quo condidimus terrâ reliquias que ossa divini
which *time* we have buried in the earth the remains and bones of my divine

parentis, que sacravimus mœstas aras. Que jam dies
parent, and have consecrated mournful altars. And now the day

adest, ni fallor quem ego semper habebo acerbum
is present, unless I am mistaken, which I ever shall esteem mournful

semper honoratum: Dî sic voluistis. Si ego exsul
ever honoured: Ye Gods, thus have you decreed. If I an exile

agerem hunc in Getulis syrtibus, ve deprensus
should pass this *day* among the Getulian quicksands, or overtaken

Argolico mari et urbe Mycenæ, tamen exsequerer annua
on the Grecian sea and in the city of Mycenas, yet I will pay my annual

vota, que solennes pompas ordine, que struerem altaria
vows, and solemn funeral pomps in order, and I would spread the altars

suis donis. Nunc ultro adsumus ad cineres et
with their own gifts. Now unexpectedly we are present at the ashes and

ossa ipsius parentis, equidem reor, haud sine mente,
bones of this my father, indeed I suppose, not without the purpose,

sine numine Divûm, et delati intramus amicos portus.
without the will of the Gods, and borne on we enter friendly harbours.

Ergo agite, et cuncti celebremus lætum honorem:
Wherefore come on, and let *us* all celebrate this joyful observance.

poscamus ventos atque velit me urbe positâ
let us ask for winds and that he be willing that I, our city being founded

quotannis ferre hæc sacra templis dicatis sibi. Acestes
yearly offer these sacrifices in temples dedicated to him. Acestes

generatus Trojâ   dat vobis in naves bina capita   boüm
descended   from Troy gives to you for the ships two   heads   of oxen

    numero: adhibete   penates   et   patrios
according to the number: send for your household Gods and those of your country

epulis,   et quos hospes Acestes colit.   Præterea, si   nona
to the feast, and whom our host Acestes honours.   Besides,   if the ninth

aurora extulerit almum diem mortalibus, que   retexerit
morning shall introduce a fair day   to mortals,   and   shall unveil

orbem radiis,   ponam   Teucris prima certamina citæ
the globe with its rays, I will propose to the Trojans the first   trials of the swift

classis. Que qui valet cursu pedum, et qui incedit audax
fleet.   And who excels in the race on foot, and who advances daring

viribus, aut melior   jaculo, que levibus sagittis, seu
in strength, either more excellent with the dart, and light   arrows,   or

fidit   committere pugnam crudo   cæstu; cuncti adsint,
has confidence to engage in contest with the cruel gauntlet; let all be present,

que expectent præmia palmæ meritæ. Omnes   favete
and   await   the rewards of victory deserved.   All   favour us

ore,   et cingite tempora ramis. Fatus sic   velat
with prayer, and bind   your temples with boughs. Speaking thus   he veils

tempora   maternâ myrto. Elymus facit hoc,   Acestes
his temples with his mother's myrtle. Elymus does this.   Acestes

maturus ævi   hoc, puer Ascanius hoc; quos cætera pubes
mature   in age does this, the boy Ascanius this; whom the other youth

sequitur. Ille ibat medius è concilio cum multis millibus
imitate.   He went in the midst from the council with many   thousands

ad tumulum, magna catervâ comitante. Hic ritè   libans
to the tomb,   a great   band   accompanying. He in order   offering

fundit humi duo carchesia mero Baccho, duo   novo
pours out on the ground two bowls   of wine to Bacchus, two   of new

acte duo sacro   sanguine, que jacit purpureos   flores,
milk.   two of consecrated   blood,   and scatters purple   flowers,

ac fatur talia: Sancte parens, salve!   vos cineres
and speaks these words: O holy parent,   hail!   ye   ashes

nequicquam recepti, que animæ que umbræ paternæ iterum,
in vain   recovered, and thou soul and ye shades of my father,   again

salvete! non licuit tecum quærere Italos fines, que arva
hail!   it has not been allowed with you to seek the Italian confines, and fields

fatalia,   nec Ausonium Tybrim, quicunque est.
decreed by fate, nor Ausonian   Tiber,   whatsoever it is.

Dixerat hæc; cum anguis lubricus, ingens septem
He had spoken these words; when a snake shining,   huge in his seven

gyros, traxit septena volumina ab imis adytis,
folds,   he drew along his seven fold coils   from the inmost shrines

placidè amplexus tumulum, que lapsus per aras: cui
peacefully embracing   the tomb,   and gliding over the altars,   whose

terga cæruleæ notæ et squamam fulgor maculosus auro
back of azure mark and scales a brightness speck'd with gold

Incendebat, ceu arcus nubibus trahit mille varios
inflamed,   as   a bow   in the clouds draws a thousand   varied

colores adverso sole. Æneas obstupuit visu.
colours from the opposing sun. Æneas stood amaz'd   at the sight.

Tandem ille serpens longo agmine inter pateras et
At length the snake creeping in a long path   within the goblets and

levia pocula, que libavit dapes, que rursus innoxius
smooth bowls, both sipped the feast, and again   harmless

successit imo tumulo, et liquit altaria depasta.
entered   the bottom of the tomb; and left the altars he had fed on.

Magis hoc instaurat genitori honores inceptos, incertus
The more for this he renews to his father the honours begun,   doubtfu

ne putet esse genium loci, ne famulum
whether he should think it to be the genius of the place, or an attendant

parentis; cædit quinas bidentes de more, que tot
of his father; he kills five   sheep   according to custom, and as many

sues, totidem juvencos nigrantes terga; que fundebat
swine, as many bullocks   black as to their backs; and poured forth

vina è pateris, que vocabat animam magni Anchisæ, que
wine from goblets, and invoked the spirit of great Anchises, and

manes remissos acheronte. Necnon et socii læti ferunt
his remains released from hell. Likewise his associates joyful bear

dona, quæ copia est cuique; que onerant aras, que
gifts, which plenty is to each;   and they load the altars,   and

mactant juvencos. Alii locant ahena ordine, que
sacrifice bullocks.   Others place brazen vessels in order,   and

fusi per herbam subjiciunt prunas verubus, et torrent
scattered along the grass they place coals under the spits, and roast the

viscera. Dies expectata aderat, que equi Phaëthontis jam
entrails. The day expected had arrived, and the horses of Phaeton now

vehebant nonam auroram serenâ luce; que fama et
led up   the ninth morning with clear light; and fame   and

nomen clari Acestæ excierat finitimos. Complêrant
the name of renowned Acestes had excited the neighboring people. They fill'd

litora læto cœtu, visuri Æneadas, pars et parati
the shores with a joyful band, to see the Trojans, a part also prepared

certare. Principio munera locantur ante oculos,
to contend. In the first place the rewards are placed before their eyes,

que in medio circo: sacri tripodes, qùe virides coronæ
and in midst of the circle: sacred tripodes, and green coronets,

et palmæ, pretium victoribus; que arma, et vestes perfusæ
and palms, the reward to the conquerors; and arms, and dresses dyed

ostro, talenta argenti que auri: et tuba canit
with purple, talents of silver and gold; and the trumpet sounds

ludos commissos medio aggere. Quatuor carinæ
that the games are begun in the midst of the mound. Four ships

delectæ ex omni classe, pâres gravibus remis, ineunt
selected from all the fleet, equal with heavy oars,   enter

prima certamina. Mnestheus agit velocem   Pristin
on the first   contests.   Mnestheus commands the swift   Pristis

    acri remige, Mnestheus   mox   Italus a   quo
with a strong rower,   Mnestheus   presently *to be* an Italian from which

nomine genus Memmî: que Gyas   ingentem Chimæiam
name   the race of Memmius: and Gyas *commands* the great   Chimera

    ingenti mole, opus urbis; quam Dardana pubes
with its great   bulk, the work of the city; which   the Trojan   youth

impellunt triplici versu, remi consurgunt terno ordine: que
urge on   in triple rank, the oars   rise   in a triple order: and

Sergestus, a quo   Sergia domus tenet nomen, invehitur
Sergestus,   from whom the Sergian family derives its name,   is borne

    magna Centauro; que Cloanthus cœruleâ Scyllâ, unde
in the great   Centaur,   and   Cloanthus in the azure Scylla,   whence

tibi genus, O Romane Cluenti.
your descent, O Roman   Cluentius.

    Procul in pelago contra spumantia litora est saxum quod
    Far off   in the sea   against the resounding shores is   a rock   which

submersum olim tunditur   tumidis fluctibus, ubi hiberni
sunk   sometimes is beaten by the swelling waves,   when the wintry

    Cori condunt sidera: silet   tranquillo   que ex   undâ
west winds hide   the stars: it lies still in the tranquil *sea* and from the wave

immotâ attollitur campus, et   statio   gratissima
unmoved   it is raised *as* a plain, and is a resting place   most grateful

apricis mergis. Hìc pater Æneas constituit   viridem
to the basking cormorants. Here father Æneas   placed   a verdant

metam frondenti ilice, signum nautis, unde   scirent
goal   of budding oak,   a signal for the sailors, where   they may know

reverti, et ubi circumflectere longos cursus. Tum   legunt
to return, and where to bend around their long circuits. Then   they choose

    loca sorte: que ipsi ductores longè effulgent in puppibus,
their places by lot: and   the   leaders   far off   shine   in   their ships,

decori auro que ostro. Cætera juventus velatur populeâ
decorated with gold and purple. The other   youth are veiled with the poplar

fronde, que perfusa nudatos humeros oleo   nitescit.
leaf,   and overspreading their naked shoulders with oil   they shine.

Considunt transtris, que brachia intenta remis: intenti
They sit   on the benches, and their arms are extended to the oars: attentive

exspectant signum, que pavor pulsans, que arrecta cupido
they await   the signal, and fear beating high, and the increased desire

laudum, haurit exsultantia corda. Inde ubi clara   tuba
of praise, exhausts their throbbing hearts. Then when the shrill   trumpet

    dedit sonitum, omnes prosiluere suis finibus,   haud
had given forth a sound,   all   leaped   to their stations, *there is* no

mora; nauticus clamor ferit æthera; freta versa lacertis
delay: the sailor's   shout   strikes the skies; the seas upturned by their arms

adductis spumant. Pariter infindunt sulcos; que   totum
drawn back   foam.   Together they cleave the furrows; and   the whole

æquor convulsum remis que tridentibus rostris   dehiscit.
ocean   convulsed   with oars and   trident   beaks   yawns.

Currus non tam præcipites corripuere   campum
Chariots not so   swift   have scoured   the plain

        bijugo   certamine, que ruunt effusi   carcere.
in a double yoked chariot   race,   and rush forth let loose from the goal,

nec aurigæ sic concussere undantia lora jugis immissis
nor do charioteers thus   shake   the waving reins the yokes being loosened

que pendent proni in verbera. Tum omne nemus consonat
and   hang   bending over the lash. Then the whole grove resounds

    plausu   que fremitu virûm, que studiis   faventum
with the applause and   noise of the men, and the anxiety of those favouring

que litora inclusa volutant vocem; pulsati colles resultant
and the shores inclosed roll back their voice; the beaten hills re-echo

    clamore. Gyas effugit ante alios, que elabitur primis undis
with the cry. Gyas flies before others, and glides over the first waves

inter turbam que fremitum; quem Cloanthus,   melior
amidst the crowd and   the noise;   whom Cloanthus,   more skilled

remis, deinde consequitur, sed tarda pinus tenet pondere.
with oars, then   follows,   but his slow boat restrains by its weight.

Post hos Pristis que Centaurus tendunt superare priorem
After these the Pristis and Centaur   attempt to pass beyond the first

locum, æquo discrimine: et nunc Pristis abit, nunc ingens
place, in equal distance: and now the Pristis passes, now the huge

Centaurus præterit victam; que nunc ambæ   feruntur
Centaur   goes before her conquered; and now   both   are borne on

unà junctis frontibus, et sulcant salsa vada   longâ
together with united fronts,   and plough the salt shallows with their long

carinâ; que jam propinquabant scopulo, que tenebant metam;
keel;   and now they approached the rock, and reached   the goal;

cum Gyas princeps que victor in medio   gurgite,
when Gyas the chief and conqueror in the midst   of the sea

compellat voce Menœten rectorem navis: Quò
addresses with his voice Menœtes the steersman of the ship: Whether

tantùm abis dexter mihi? dirige cursum huc,   ama
so much do you go to the right of me? direct your course hither, incline to

litus, et sine palmula stringat lævas cautes: alii teneant
the shore, and let the oar   graze the left cliffs; let others hold

altum. Dixit: sed Menœtes timens cæca saxa,   detorquet
the deep. He said: but Menœtes fearing hidden rocks,   turns

proram ad undas pelagi. Quò abis diversus?   Gyas
his prow to the waves of the sea. Why do you go a different way? Gyas

iterum revocabat cum clamore, O Menœte, pete saxa; et
again called out with a shout, O Menœtes, seek the rocks; and

ecce respicit Cloanthum instantem tergo,   et
lo he looks back upon Cloanthus   pressing on his back,   and

tenentem propiora. Ille interior radit lævum iter inter
holding a nearer course. He within grazes the left path between

que navem Gyæ que sonantes scopulos, que   subitus
both   the ship of Gyas and the resounding   rocks,   and   suddenly

præterit priorem, et tenet tuta æquora,   metis
he goes before the former, and holds the safe water,   the boundaries

relictis.   Tum verò ingens dolor exarsit ossibus juveni;
being left behind.   Then indeed great   grief   inflamed the bones of the youth,

nec   genæ   caruere lacrymis; que oblitus sui   decoris.
nor did his cheeks want   tears;   and forgetful of his own   honour,

que salutis   sociûm,   deturbat segnem Menœten   ab
and the safety of his companions, he hurled the slothful Menœtes   from

altâ puppi præcipitem in mare. Ipse subit gubernaculo
the lofty stern   headlong   into the sea. He succeeds   to the helm

rector, ipse magister, que hortatur viros, que   torquet
as pilot, he as commander, and exhorts the men, and   turns

clavum ad litora. At ut Menœtes gravis tandem   vix
the helm to the shores. But as Menœtes   oppressed at last   scarcely

redditus est   imo fundo, jam senior, que fluens   in
had returned from the deep bottom, now old   and streaming   in

madidâ veste, petit summa scopuli, que resèdit   in
his wet   dress, he seeks the summit of the rock, and sits down   on

siccâ rupe. Teucri risere illum et labentem, et natantem,
the dry cliff. The Trojans ridicule him both   falling,   and   swimming,

et rident   revomentem salsos fluctus pectore. Hìc
and they laugh at him   throwing up the salt waves from his breast. Here

læta spes accensa est duobus extremis Sergesto,   que
joyous hope had inflamed the two   last   Sergestus,   and

Mnestheo, superare Gyan morantem. Sergestus ante capit
Mnestheus, to overcome Gyas delaying.   Sergestus   anticipates

locum, que propinquat scopulo; nec tamen ille   prior
the place, and approaches   the rock; not such as he was before

totâ carinâ præeunte; parte   prior; æmula   Pristis
his whole keel   going before; in part he was first; his rival   Pristis

premit partem rostro. At Mnestheus incedens   per
presses him in part with her bow. But Mnestheus walking   among

ipsos socios mediâ nave hortatur.   Hectorei
his   companions in the midst of his ship exhorts them. O my Hectorean

socii, quos delegi   comites supremâ   sorte
associates, whom I have selected as companions in the last   fortune

Trojæ, nunc, nunc insurgite remis; nunc promite illas
of Troy, now,   now   rise   on your oars; now draw forth those

vires, nunc animos quibus usi in Getulis syrtibus,
powers, now that courage which you exhibited in the Getulian quicksands.

que mari Ionio, que sequacibus undis Maleæ. Mnestheus
and the sea of Ionium, and the persecuting waves of Malea.   Mnestheus

jam non peto prima, que ne certo   vincere:
now do not. seek the first rewards, and neither do I strive   to conquer:

quanquam ô! sed superent, Neptune, quibus dedisti
yet   O! but let them conquer, O Neptune, to whom you have granted

noc: pudeat rediisse extremos. Cives, vincite
this: let it shame *us* to have returned last. My countrymen, conquer

et prohibete hoc nefas. Olli procumbunt summo
and forbid this disgrace. They press on with the greatest

certamine; ærea puppis tremit vastis ictibus, que solum
strife; the brazen keel trembles with vast blows, and the sea

subtrahitur. Tum creber anhelitus quatit artus que
is drawn from under them. Then frequent panting shakes their limbs and

arida ora: sudor fluit undique rivis. Ipse casus attuli
parched mouths: sweat flows on every side in streams. This chance brough

viris optatum honorem: namque dum Sergestus interior,
to the men the desired honour: for while Sergestus within,

furens animi suburget proram ad saxa que subit
raging in mind urges on the prow to the rocks and enters

iniquo spatio, infelix hæsit in procurrentibus saxis.
an incommodious space, unhappy he hangs on the projecting rocks.

Cautes concussæ et remi obnixi crepuere in acuto
The cliffs are shaken and the oars struggling crash upon the sharp

murice, que prora illisa pependit.
pointed rock, and the prow dashed against *it* is suspended.

Nautæ consurgunt, et morantur magno clamore, que
The sailors arise together, and give over with great clamour, and

expediunt ferratas sudes et contos acutâ cuspide, que
they apply iron-pointed stakes and poles with sharp points, and

legunt fractos remos in gurgite. At Mnestheus lætus, que
they gather the broken oars in the sea. But Mnestheus joyful, and

acrior ipso successu, petit prona maria, celeri agmine
more active by this success, seeks the open seas, with swift motion

remorum, que ventis vocatis, et decurrit aperto pelago.
of oars, and the winds being invoked, and runs on the open sea.

Qualis columba, cui domus et dulces nidi in latebroso
As a dove, whose home and sweet young *are* in a dark

pumice, subitò commota speluncâ, volans fertur in arva,
cleft, suddenly aroused from the cave, flying is borne to the fields,

que exterrita dat pennis ingentem plausum tecto;
and terrified gives with her wings a great beating against the nest;

mox lapsa quieto ære radit liquidum iter, que ne
presently gliding through the still air she grazes the liquid way, and does not

commovet celeres alas: sic Mnestheus, sic ipse Pristis
move her swift wings: thus Mnestheus, thus the Pristis

fugâ secat ultima æquora; sic ipse impetus fert illam
in her flight cuts the remotest waters; thus the impulse bears her

volantem. Et primùm deserit Sergestum luctantem in
flying. And first she deserts Sergestus struggling in

alto scopulo, que vadis brevibus, que frustra vocantem
the high rock, and quicksands *and* shallows, and in vain invoking

auxilia, et discentem currere fractis remis. Inde consequitur
aid, and learning to run with broken oars Then he pursues

Gyan, que ipsam Chimæram ingenti mole: cedit, quoniam
Gyas, and the Chimera with her great mass: she yields, since

est spoliata magistro, que jam Cloanthus solus superest in
she is deprived of a master, and now Cloanthus alone remains on

ipso fine; quem petit, et adnixus urget summis viribus.
the boundary; whom he seeks, and striving presses with his utmost strength.

Tum verò clamor ingeminat, que cuncti studiis instigant
Then indeed the noise redoubles, and all with anxiety encourage him

sequentem, que æther resonat fragoribus. Hi indignantur
pursuing, and the sky resounds with noise. These are angry

ai teneant proprium decus et honorem partum;
est they should not hold their appropriate glory and honour already obtained;

que volunt pacisci vitam pro laude. Sucessus alit hos:
and they wish to bargain life for praise. Success cherishes these:

possunt, quia videntur posse. Et fors cepissent
they are able, because they seem to be able. And perhaps they had taken

præmia æquatis rostris, ni Cloanthus tendens utrasque
the rewards with equal beaks, unless Cloanthus extending both

palmas ponto, que fudisset preces, que vocasset Divos
his hands over the sea, and had uttered prayers, and had invoked the Gods

in vota: Dî, quibus est imperium pelagi, quorum
in his vows: Ye Gods, to whom is the power of the sea, through whose

æquora curro, ego lætus constituam vobis ante aras
waters I run, I cheerfully will place to you before your altars

candentem taurum in hoc litore, reus voti, que porriciam
a white bull on this shore, obliged by my vow, and I will scatter

exta in salsos fluctus, et fundam liquentia vina. Dixit:
the entrails on the salt waves, and I will pour out the liquid wines. He said.

que omnis chorus Nereidum que Phorci, que
and all the band of Nereids and the train of Phorcus, and

Panopea virgo audiit eum sub imis fluctibus; et ipse
the Panopean maid heard him beneath the lowest waves; and the

pater Portunus magnâ manu impulit euntem. Illa
father Portunus with his powerful hand urged on the boat advancing. She

fugit ad terram citiùs Noto que volucri sagittâ, et
flies to the land swifter than the south wind and swift arrow, and

condidit se alto portu. Tum satus Anchisâ, cunctis
hid herself in the deep harbour. Then the son of Anchises, all

vocatis ex more, declarat Cloanthum victorem
being summoned according to custom declares Cloanthus conqueror

magnâ voce præconis, que advelat tempora viridi lauro:
with a loud voice of a herald, and veils his temples with a green laurel:

que dat optare ternos juvencos, que vina, et ferre
and permits him to choose three bullocks, and wine, and to bear

magnum talentum argenti, munera in naves. Addit
a great talent of silver, gifts for the ships. He adds

præcipuos honores ipsis ductoribus; victori auratam
distinguished honours to the leaders; to the conqueror a gilded

chlamydem, circum quam plurima Meliboea purpura
cloak, around which much Melibean purple

cucurrit duplici Mæandro; que regius puer intextus
ran in a double maze; and the royal boy Ganymede interwoven

jaculo que cursu fatigat veloces cervos in frondosâ
with the dart and in the chase fatigues the swift stags upon leafy

Idâ, acer, similis anhelanti, quem præpes armiger Jovis
Ida, eager, like to one panting, whom the swift armour-bearer of Jove

uncis pedibus rapuit sublimem ab Idâ: longævi custodes
with crooked claws seized on high from Ida: the aged guards

nequicquam tendunt palmas ad sidera; que latratus canum
in vain extend their hands to the stars; and the barking of dogs

sævit in auras.
rages to the skies.

At donat huic viro, qui deinde tenuit secumdum locum
But he presents to that man, who afterwards held the second place

virtute, habere loricam consertam levibus hamis, que
by his courage, to have a corslet set about with smooth rings, and

trilicem auro, quam ipse victor detraxerat Demoleo sub
triple. with gold, which the conqueror drew from Demoleus under

alto Ilio apud rapidum Simoënta, huic decus et tutamen in
lofty Ilium by the swift Simois, his ornament and protection in

armis. Phegeus que Sagaris famuli vix ferebant illam
war. Phegeus and Sagaris men-servants scarcely bore it

multiplicem, connixi humeris; at Demoleus, olim
many fold, struggling with their shoulders; but Demoleus, formerly

indutus cursu agebat palantes Troas. Facit geminos
clothed in it in the course drove the wandering Trojans. He presents two

lebetas ex ære tertia dona, que cymbia perfecta argento,
kettles of brass for the third gifts, and bowls wrought of silver

atque aspera signis, que jam adeo omnes donati, que
and rough with figures, and now thus all being rewarded, and

superbi opibus, ibant evincti tempora puniceis tæniis:
proud of their wealth, went bound as to their temples with crimson ribbands:

cum Sergestus agebat irrisam ratem sine honore, vix
when Sergestus brought up the despised boat without honour, scarcely

multâ arte revulsam e sævo scopulo, remis amissis,
with much art torn from the cruel rock, his oars being lost,

atque debilis uno ordine. Qualis sæpe serpens
and weak with one tier. As often a serpent

deprensus in aggere viæ, quem ærea rota transiit
overtaken on the height of the way, which a brazen wheel had passed

obliquum, aut viator gravis ictu liquit seminecem que
across, or a traveller heavy with a blow has left half dead and

lacerum saxo: nequicquam fugiens dat longos tortus
mutilated with a stone: in vain flying gives long wreaths

corpore; parte ferox, que ardens oculis, et arduus
with his body; in part fierce; and glowing with his eyes, and high

attollens sibila colla, pars clauda vulnere,   retenta
raising   his hissing neck,   a part lame with his wound,   holds *him* back

nexantem nodos, que plicantem   se   in sua membra: tarda
folding   his knots, and winding himself in his own limbs: the slow

navis movebat se tali remigio; tamen facit vela, et   subit
ship   moved itself with such rowing; yet he makes sail, and   enters

ostia plenis velis. Æneas lætus donat Sergestum promisso
the port with full sails. Æneas rejoiced presents Sergestus with his promised

munere, ob   navem servatam que socios   reductos.
reward, on account of the ship preserved and his associates   restored.

Serva   datur olli, haud ignara operum   Minervæ.
A female slave is given to him, not ignorant of the labours   of Minerva.

Cressa genus,   Pholœ, que gemini nati sub   ubere.
A Cretan in her race, *named* Pholœ, and her two children at   her breast.

Hoc certamine misso,   pius Æneas tendit in gramineum
This   contest being dismissed pious Æneas marched to   the grassy

campum, quem sylvæ curvis collibus undique cingebant;
plain,   which woods with winding   hills on each side surrounded;

que in mediâ valle erat circus theatri; quò   heros
and in the midst of the vale was the circuit of a theatre; whither   the hero

iulit   se   medium cum multis millibus que   resedit
withdrew himself in the midst with many thousands,; and   sat down

consessu extructo. Hìc pretiis invitat animos
in the assembly on a high seat. Here by rewards he invites the attention *of those*

qui fortè velint contendere rapido cursu, et ponit præmia.
who by chance may wish to contend in the swift race, and places the prizes.

Teucri   que Sicani misti conveniunt undique,   primi,
The Trojans and Sicilians intermingled assemble   on every side,   first,

Nisus et Euryalus: Euryalus insignis   formâ que   viridi
Nisus and Euryalus; Euryalus distinguished for beauty and   blooming

juventà; Nisus pio   amore pueri; quos regius Diores de
youth;   Nisus by the pious love of the boy; whom the royal Diores from

egregiâ stirpe Priami, deinde secutus. Salius,   simul
the renowned race of Priam, then   followed. Salius,   at once

et Patron .   hunc; alter quorum   Acarnan;   alter
and Patron *followed* him;   one of whom *was* an Acarnanian; the other

ab Arcadià, sanguine Tegeææ gentis. Tum duo Trinacrii
from Arcadia, of the blood of the Tegean nation. Then two   Sicilian

juvenes, Elymus que Panopes, assueti   sylvis,
youths,   Elymus and Panopes, accustomed   to the woods,

comites   senioris Acestæ; præterea multi, quos obscura
the companions of the elder Acestes; besides many whom   obscure

fama recondit.
fame hides.

In mediis quibus Æneas deinde locutus sic: Accipite
In the midst of whom Eneas afterwards spoke thus: Receive

haec   animis que advertite lætas mentes: nemo
these things in your mind and turn your joyful attention: No one

ex hoc numero abibit non donatus mihi   Dabo
of this   number shall depart not rewarded by me,   I will give to *each*

ferre bina Gnossia spicula lucida levato ferro   que
to bear off two Gnossian darts bright with polish'd iron   and

bipennem cœlatam argento. Hic unus honos   erit
an axe   wrought with silver. This one honour   shall be

omnibus. Primi tres accipient præmia, que   nectentur
to all.   The first three shall receive their rewards, and   bind

caput flavâ olivâ Primus victor habeto equum
their heads with the yellow olive. Let the first conqueror have   a horse

insignem phaleris: alter Amazoniam pharetram   que
distinguished for trappings; the other an Amazonian   quiver   and

pienam Threciis sagittis, quam balteus circum amplectitur
full   of Thracian arrows, which a belt around   embraces

lato auro, et fibula subnectit tereti   gemmâ: tertius
with broad gold, and a buckle fastens with a tapering jewel; let the third

abito contentus hâc Argolicâ galeâ. Ubi hæc dicta,
depart contented with this Grecian helmet. When these things were said,

capiunt locum que corripiunt spatia, signo repentè
they take the place, and seize the open space, the signal suddenly

audito, que effusi relinquunt limen, similes nimbo;
being heard, and let loose they leave the goal, like to a storm;

simul signant ultima. Nisus abit primus que   longè
at once they mark the last *limit*. Nisus starts first and   far off

emicat ante omnia corpora, ocyor et   ventis   et
he springs before all *their* bodies, swifter even than the winds and

alis fulminis. Salius insequitur proximus huic, sed
the wings of lightning. Salius follows   next   to him. but

proximus longo intervallo. Deinde spatio relicto post
next   with a long space between. Then   a space being left behind

Euryalus tertius que Elymus sequitur Euryalum   Sub
Euryalus the third and Elymus follows Euryalus   Next

quo ipso ecce Diores deinde volat; que jam terit calcem
to whom lo Diores afterwards flies; and now wears his heel

calce, incumbens humero; et si plura   spatia
with his heel, reclining on his shoulder; and if more   space

supersint transeat elapsus prior ve relinquat ambiguum.
had remained he had passed gliding before or had left *it*   doubtful.

Que jam adventabant ferè extremo spatio que fessi sub
And now they approached almost the last space and wearied near

ipsum finem cum infelix Nisus labitur levi sanguine,
to the very end when the unhappy Nisus falls in the slippery blood,

ut fortè juvencis cæsis fusus super   humum
as by chance bullocks being slain it had been shed upon the ground

que madefecerat virides herbas. Hic juvenis ovans, jam
and had moistened the green grass. Here the youth rejoicing now

victor haud tenuit vestigia titubata presso   solo
a conqueror did not restrain his footsteps tottering on the trodden ground;

sed concidit pronus in que ipso immundo fimo que sacro
but fell headlong upon both the filthy mire and consecrated

cruore. Ille tamen non oblitus Euryali, non amorum;
blood. He nevertheless *was* not forgetful of Euryalus, nor of his loves.

nam surgens per lubrica: opposuit sese Salio; autem ille
for rising through slimy dirt. he opposed himself to Salius; but he

jacuit, revolutus in spissâ arenâ. Euryalus emicat et
fell, rolling back on the thick sand Euryalus sprang up and

victor munere amici tenet prima que volat
conqueror by the favour of his friend holds the first space, and flies

plausu que secundo fremitu. Post Elymus subit, et
with applause and favouring shout. Afterwards Elymus comes up, and

Diores nunc tertia palma. Hìc Salius implet totum
Diores now the third victor. Here Salius fills the whole

concessum ingentis caveæ et prima ora patrum magnis
assembly of the extensive theatre and the front faces of the fathers with great

clamoribus; que poscit honorem ereptum dolo reddi
cries, and demands the honour snatch'd by fraud to be restored

sibi. Favor tutatur Euryalum que decoræ lacrymæ et
to him. Favour guards Euryalus and beautiful tears and

virtus veniens gratior in pulchro corpore. Diores
virtue coming more grateful in a beautiful body Diores

adjuvat et proclamat magnâ voce, qui subiit palmæ
assists and proclaims with a great voice, who succeeds to the palm

que venit ad ultima præmia frustra si primi honores
and approaches to the last rewards in vain if the first honours

redduntur Salio. Tum pater Æneas inquit, Pueri, vestra
are given to Salius. Then father Æneas said, Boys, your

mumera manent vobis certa, et nemo movet palmam
ewards remain to you sure, and no one removes the prize

ordine; liceat me miserari casus
from its order; it may be allowed to me to pity the misfortune

insontis amici. Sic fatus dat Salio immane tergum
of my innocent friend. Thus speaking he gives to Salius a huge skin

Getuli leonis onerosum villis atque aureis unguibus
of a Getulian lion loaded with hair and golden claws

Hìc Nisus inquit, si tanta præmia sunt victis,
Here Nisus says, if so great rewards are *bestowed on* the vanquished

et te miseret lapsorum, quæ digna munera dabis
and you pity the fallen, what appropriate rewards will you give

Niso? qui merui primam coronam laude, ni
to Nisus? *I* who have deserved the first prize by my desert, had not

inimica fortuna quæ Salium tulisset me. Et
the unhappy chance which *bore off* Salius borne off me. And

simul his dictis ostentabat faciem, et membra
at the same time with these words he showed his face, and limbs

turpia udo fimo. Optimus pater risit olli, et
filthy with moist dirt. The most indulgent father *Æneas* smiled on him, and

jussit clypeum efferi,   artes Didymaonis,   refixum
ordered   a shield   to be brought, the skilful work of Didymaon,   taken down

Danais   de sacro poste Neptuni. Donat   egregium
by the Greeks from the sacred pillar of Neptune He rewards   the worthy

juvencm hoc præstanti munere. Pòst   ubi   cursus
youth   with this excellent   present. Afterwards when   the races

confecti, et peregit   dona,   nunc si cui   est
were finished, and he had bestowed the rewards, now   if to any one   there is

virtus, que animus præsens in pectore,   adsit,   et
courage,   and resolution   present   in his breast, let him advance,   and

attollat brachia, palmis evinctis. Sic ait, et   proponit
raise   his arms, his hands being bound   Thus he said and   proposes

geminum honorem pugnæ; victori   juvencum velatum
a double   honour   to the battle, to the conqueror a bullock   adorned

auro que vittis: victo   ensem atque insignem galeam,
with gold   and fillets   to the conquered a sword   and   a splendid   helmet,

solatia.   Nec mora continuò Dares effert ora cum
as a consolation. There is no   delay forthwith   Dares presents his face with

vastis viribus, que tollit se   magno murmure virûm; qui
his great strength, and raises himself with great murmuring   of men,   who

solus   solitus   contendere contra Paridem; que idem   ad
alone was accustomed to contend   against   Paris;   and the same at

tumulum quo maximus Hector occubat, perculit   victorem
the tomb   where most heroic Hector   lies,   struck down   victorious

Buten immani corpore, qui ferebat se veniens   de-
Butes   of huge   body,   who boasted himself proceeding   from

Bebryciâ gente Amyci, et extendit moribundum in fulvâ
the Bebrycian race of Amycus, and stretched him   dying   on the yellow

arenâ. Talis Dares tollit altum caput in prima prœlia,
sand   Such was Dares who raised his   lofty   head   in the first   contest

que ostendit latos humeros, que protendens   jactat
and   showed his broad shoulders, and   extending   he throws about

brachia alterna, et verberat auras ictibus. Alius   quæritur
his arms alternately, and   beats   the air with blows. Another   is sought

huic, nec quisquam ex tanto agmine audet adire virum,
for him,   nor   did any one   from so great   a band   dare   approach the man,

que inducere cœstus manibus. Ergo alacris que putans
and   draw   the gauntlets on his hands Therefore joyful   and thinking

cunctos excedere   palmâ,   stetit ante pedes Æneæ; nec
that all   had withdrawn from the prize, he stood before the feet of Æneas; nor

moratus plura, tum   lævâ   tenet taurum cornu, atque
did he delay   more,   then with his left hand he holds the bull by the horn,   and

ita fatur: Nate Deâ si nemo audet credere se   pugnæ;
thus he speaks Son of a Goddess, if no one dares   to trust himself to the fight,

quæ finis standi?   quo   usque   decet   me   teneri?
what is the end of standing?   how   long   does it behoove me to be detained?

jube   ducere dona. Simul cuncti   Dardanidæ
command them to bring out the gifts   At once   all   the Trojans

fremebant   ore   que jubebant   promissa
murmured assent with their mouths and   ordered   the promised *rewards*

reddi   viro. Hìc gravis Acestes castigat   Entellum
to be paid to the man. Here grave Acestes rebukes   Entellu.

dictis,   ut consederat proximus   viridante toro herbæ:
in these words, as   he sat   nearest   on the green couch of the grass.

Entelle quondam fortissime heroüm, frustra,   tamne
O Entellus formerly   the most brave of heroes, in vain,   will you so

patiens sines tanta dona   tolli   nullo certamine?   ubi
patiently suffer so great prizes to be carried off with no opposition?   where

nunc nobis ille Deus Eryx nequicquam memoratus
now   to us *is* that God Eryx   in vain   commemorated *as your*

magister? ubi   fama per omnem Trinacriam, et   illa
master   where *is your* fame through all   Sicily,   and   those

spolia pendentia tuis tectis? Ille sub hæc.   Nec
spoils hanging from your roofs? He to these things *answers*. Neither

amor laudis, nec gloria cessit   pulsa metu: sed enim gelidus
love of praise, nor glory has left *me* banished by fear· but *my* cold

sanguis hebet tardante senectâ, que vires   effetæ
blood is chilled by debilitating age,   and my strength   worn out

frigent in corpore. Si illa juventa nunc foret mihi, quæ
is weakened in *my* body.   If that youth now could be to me, which

quondam fuerat, que quâ iste improbus   fidens exsultat,
formerly had been, and in which this wretched *boaster* trusting   exults,

equidem venissem haud inductus pretio que   pulchro
indeed   I had come not led on by the prize and   the beautifu

juvenco; nec moror dona. Deinde locutus sic projecit
bullock; nor do I wait for prizes. Then having spoken thus he cast

in medium geminos cæstus immani pondere, quibus acer
in the midst two gauntlets of vast weight, with which brave

Eryx   suetus   ferre manum in prœlia, que intendere
Eryx had been accustomed to bear his hand in battle, and   to stretch

brachia duro tergo. Animi obstupuere,   septem
his arms in the hard skin. Their minds were amazed;   , seven

ingentia terga tantorum boum rigebant   insuto plumbo que
great   skins of such huge oxen were stiffened with inserted lead and

ferro. Dares ipse stupet ante omnes, que longè recusat,
iron. Dares himself stands amazed before all,   and utterly   refuses

que magnanimus Anchisiades versat huc   illuc
to fight, and the high minded son of Anchises turns over this way and that

et pondus, et ipsa immensa volumina vinclorum.   Tum
both the weight, and the   immense   folds   of the gauntlets.   Then

senior   referebat tales voces pectore: Quid si quis
the aged man   uttered   these words from his breast What if any one

vidisset cæstus et arma Herculis ipsius que   tristem
had seen the gauntlets and armour of Hercules himself and   the sad

pugnam in hoc ipso litore? Tuus germanus Eryx quondam
contest on this very shore? Your   brother Eryx   formerly

gerebat hæc arma. Cernis   adhuc infecta sanguine que
bore these arms. You see *them* even now stained with blood and

sparso cerebro. His   stetit contra magnum Alciden; ego
scattered brains. With these he stood against the great Hercules; I

suetus   his, dum melior sanguis dabat   vires,
have been accustomed to these, when my better blood gave strength,

nec dum æmula senectus   canebat   sparsa   geminis
nor yet had envious age turned me gray being sprinkled on both

temporibus. Sed si Troïus Dares recusat hæc nostra arma, que
my temples. But if Trojan Dares refuses these our arms, and

id sedet   pio Æneæ, si Acestes auctor   probat,
it is determined by the pious Eneas, if Acestes our adviser approves

æquemus pugnas, remitto tibi   terga Erycis; solve   metus;
et us equal the fight. I yield to you the skins of Eryx; banish fear;

et tu exue Trojanos cæstus. Fatus hæc   rejecit
and do you put off the Trojan gauntlets. Speaking those *words* he threw back

ex humeris duplicem amictum, et exuit magnos   artus
from his shoulders his double dress, and stript the great joints

membrorum, magna ossa que lacertos, atque ingens consistit
of his limbs, his great bones and arms, and great he stood forth

mediâ arenâ: Tum pater   satus   Anchisâ extulit
in the midst of the sand Then the father descended from Anchisa raised

æquos cæstus et innexuit palmas amborum paribus armis.
the equal gauntlets and bound the hands of both with equal arms.

Extemplo uterque constitit arrectus in digitos, que interritus
Forthwith each stood erect on his toes, and undismayed

extulit brachia ad superas auras. Retro abduxere ardua
raised his arms to the lofty air. Backward they drew their towering

capita longè ab ictu, que immiscent manus manibus, que
heads far from the blow, and intermingle hands with hands, and

lacessunt pugnam, ille melior motu   pedum, que fretus
provoke the contest, the one better in the motion of his feet, and relying

juventâ; hic valens membris et mole, sed tarda genua
on his youth; the other powerful in limbs and size, but his weak knees

labant trementi: æger anhelitus quatit vastos artus. Viri
fail *him* trembling. a sickly panting shakes his vast joints. The men

jactant multa vulnera inter   se   nequicquam; ingeminant
hurl many wounds among themselves in vain: they redouble

multa cavo lateri, et dant vastos sonitus pectore, que
many on their hollow sides, and cause great sounds from their breasts, an

crebra manus errat circum aures et tempora: malæ
the frequent hand wanders around their ears and temples: their jaws

crepitant sub duro vulnere. Entellus stat gravis,   que
crash under the severe blows. Entellus stands heavy, and

immotus eodem nisu, modò corpore atque vigilantibus
unmoved in the same posture only with his body and watchful

oculis exit   tela. Ille velut qui oppugnat celsam
eyes he avoids the weapons. He as *one* who besieges a loft;

urbem molibus, aut sedet sub armis circum   montana
city   with engines,   or   sits down under   arms   around   a mountain

castella, nunc arte pererrat hos, nunc illos aditus, que
fort,   now   with art   wanders over these,   now   those approaches,   and

omnem locum: et irritus urget   variis assultibus. Entellus
all   the place; and baffled presses on with various   assaults.   Entellus

insurgens ostendit dextram, et altè extulit: ille   velox
rising   shows   his right hand, and on high raises it.   he (*Dares*) quickly

prævidit ictum venientem à vertice, que celeri corpore
foresaw   the blow   approaching   from   above,   and with his active   body

elapsus cessit.
escaping   withdraws.

Entellus effudit vires in ventum; et ipse gravis   que
Entellus   spent his strength on   the wind; and himself heavy   and

ultro concidit graviter ad terram vasto pondere;   ut
forthwith falls   heavily   to the earth with vast   weight;   as

quondam cava pinus eruta radicibus concidit   aut in
sometimes   a hollow pine   torn up   by the roots   falls   either on

Erymantho, aut magnâ Idâ. Teucri et Trinacria   pubes
Erymanthus   or   great   Ida.   The Trojan and   Sicilian   youth

consurgunt studiis: clamor it cœlo; que Acestes
arise   with anxiety;   a shout goes forth to heaven;   and   Acestes

primus accurrit, que miserans amicum æquævum attollit ab
first   runs up,   and   pitying   his friend   of equal age   lifts *him* from

humo. At heros, non tardatus que ne territus   casu,
the ground.   But the hero   not   retarded   and   not frightened   by the fall,

redit acrior ad pugnam, ac ira suscitat vim: tum pudor
returns more active to the contest, and rage arouses his violence: then   shame

incendit vires, et conscia virtus, que ardens agit   Daren
inflames his strength and conscious courage,   and   burning he drives   Dares

præcipitem toto   æquore; nunc ille ingeminans ictus
headlong   through the whole   plain;   now   he   redoubling   his blows

dextrâ, nunc sinistrâ. Nec   mora nec   requies.
on the right,   now   on the left.   Nor *is there* delay   nor   rest.

Quam multâ grandine nimbi crepitant culminibus,   sic
As   with much   hail   showers   rattle   on the house tops,   thus

densis ictibus heros creber pulsat que versat   Dareta
with thick   blows   the hero frequently   strikes   and   turns   Dares

utraque manu. Tum pater Æneas haud   passus   iras
with each   hand   Then   father   Æneas   did not   suffer   his anger

procedere longiùs, et Entellum sævire acerbis animis;   sed
to proceed   further,   and   Entellus   to rage · with bitter anger   but

imposuit finem pugnæ, que eripuit Dareta fessum, mulcens
he put   an end to the battle, and   snatched   Dares   wearied soothing him

dictis, ac fatur talia: Infelix!   quæ tanta dementia
with words, and he speaks these *things:* Unhappy *man!* what great   madness

cepit   animum? non sentis alias vires, que numina
hath possessed your mind? do you not perceive other powers,   and that the Gods

conversa? cede Deo. Que dixit, et diremit proelia
are changed? yield to the God. And he spoke, and ended the battle

voce. Ast fidi æquales ducunt illum ad naves,
with his voice. But his faithful companions lead him to the ships.

trahentem ægra genua que jactantem caput utroque
dragging his feeble knees and throwing his head on each side

que ejectantem crassum cruorem ore, que dentes
and throwing up clotted blood from his mouth, and teeth

mistos in sanguine; que vocati accipiunt galeam que ensem;
were mingled in blood; and called in they receive the helmet and sword,

relinquunt palmam que taurum Entello. Hìc victor
they leave the palm and bull to Entellus. Here the conqueror

superans animis, que superbus tauro, inquit, Nate Deâ,
elated in mind, and proud of his bull, said, O born of a Goddess,

que vos Teucri cognoscite hæc, et quæ vires fuerint
and you ye Trojans know these things, and what strength has been

mihi in juvenili corpore, et à quâ morte servetis
to me in my youthful body, and from what death you have saved

Dareta revocatum. Dixit, et stetit contra ora juvenci
Dares recalled. He said, and stood opposite the front of the bullock

adversi, qui adstabat donum pugnæ; que arduus dextrâ
opposite, which stood the prize of the contest; and high with his right hand

reductâ libravit duros cæstus inter media, cornua
drawn back he poised the hard gauntlets between the horns

que illisit in ossa, cerebro effracto. Bos sternitur, que
and dashed them into the bones, the brains being broken. The ox is struck down, and

tremens procumbit humi exanimis. Ille super effudit
trembling falls on the ground lifeless. He over him uttered

pectore tales voces: Eryx, persolvo hanc meliorem
from his breast these words: Eryx, I pay this a better

animam tibi pro morte Daretis; hìc victor
soul to you in the place of the death of Dares; and here a conqueror

repono cæstus que artem. Protinus Æneas invitat qui
I lay down my gauntlets and my art. Forthwith Æneas invites those who

fortè velint certare celeri sagittâ, et ponit
by chance might wish to contend with the swift arrow, and lays down

præmia; que ingenti manu erigit malum de nave
the rewards; and with his great hand erects a mast taken from the ship

Seresti, et suspendit ab alto malo volucrem columbam in
of Serestus, and hangs from the lofty mast a swift dove upon

fune trajecto, quò tendant ferrum. Viri convenêre:
the rope thrust through, whither they might direct their dart. The men assembled,

que ærea galea accepit dejectam sortem; et locus
and the brazen helmet received the cast lot; and the place

Hippocoöntis Hyrtacidæ exit primus ante omnes
of Hippocoon the son of Hyrtacus came out first before all

secundo clamore; quem Mnestheus modò victor navali
with favouring shout; whom Mnestheus now victorious in the naval

certamine consequitur, Mnestheus evinctus viridi oliva.
contest   follows.   Mnestheus   bound with the green olive.

Tertius Eurytion, tuus frater, ô clarissime Pandare, qui,
The third Eurytion, thy brother O most renowned Pandarus, who,

quondam jussus confundere fœdus, torsisti telum primus in
formerly commanded to confound the treaty, hurled the dart first into

medios Achivos—Acestes subsedit extremus que imâ
the midst of the Greeks—Acestes settled down the last and in the bottom

galeâ, et ipse ausus manu tentare laborem
the helmet, even he daring with his hand to attempt the labour appropriate

juvenum. Tum viri quisque pro se incurvant flexos
to youth.   Then the men each one for himself bend their flexile

arcus validis viribus, et depromunt tela pharetris. Que
bows with powerful strength, and draw out darts from their quivers. And

sagitta juvenis Hyrtacidæ prima diverberat volucres
the arrow of the youth the son of Hyrtacus first cut through the swift

auras, stridente nervo, per cœlum, et venit, que infigitur
air, from the hissing string, through the sky, and came, and is fastened

arbore adversi mali. Malus intremuit, que ales
in the wood of the opposite mast. The mast trembled, and the bird

exterrita timuit pennis, et omnia sonuerunt ingenti
terrified fluttered with her wings, and all parts resounded with great

plausu. Pòst acer Mnestheus constitit arcu adducto,
applause. After brave Mnestheus stood with his bow drawn back,

petens alta; que pariter tetendit oculos que telum. Ast
aiming high; and at once directed his eyes and dart.   But

miserandus non valuit contingere ipsam avem ferro;
to be pitied he could not touch the bird with his dart;

rupit nodos et linea vincula, queis innexa pedem
he broke the knots and hempen bandages, with which being bound as to its foot

pendebat ab alto malo. Illa volans fugit in Notos
it hung from the lofty mast. It flying escaped into the south winds

atque atra nubila. Tum rapidus Eurytion, jamdudum
and black clouds. When swift Eurytion, a long time

tenens tela contenta parato arcu, vocavit fratrem in
holding his weapon outstretched in his prepared bow, invoked his brother in

vota; jam speculatus columbam lætam vacuo cœlo, et
his vows; now watching the dove joyful in the vacant sky, and

plaudentem alis, figit sub nigrâ nube. Illa decidit
flapping with her wings, pierced her beneath a black cloud She fell

exanimis, que reliquit vitam in ætheriis astris, que delapsa
lifeless, and left her life among etherial stars, and falling

refert fixam sagittam. Acestes solus superabat palmâ
brings back the adhering arrow. Acestes alone remained the prize

amissâ: qui tamen contorsit telum in ærias auras, que
being lost; who yet shot forth his dart into the etherial air, and

pariter ostentans artem que sonantem arcum. Monstrum
at once displaying his art, and sounding bow.   A prodigy

subitò, que futurum magno augurio objicitur hìc oculis:
suddenly, and about to be a great portent is presented here to their eyes

ingens exitus docuit pòst, que terrifici vates cecinerunt
the great event taught afterwards, and the terrified prophets foretold

sera omina. Namque arundo volans in liquidis nubibus
the late omens. For the arrow flying among the liquid clouds

arsit, que consumpta recessit in tenues ventos; seu sæpe
burnt, and being consumed withdrew into the light winds; as often

sidera refixa cœlo transcurrunt, que volantia ducunt
stars , unloosed from heaven fly across the sky, and flying draw

crinem. Trinacrii viri que Teucri hæsere attonitis animis
a train. The Sicilian men and Trojans remain with astonished minds

que precati Superos: nec maximus Æneas abnuit omen
and praying the Gods: nor did great Æneas deny the omen

sed amplexus lætum Acesten cumulat magnis muneribus,
but embracing joyful Acestes loads him with great rewards,

ac fatur talia: Pater, sume nam magnus Rex Olympi
and speaks these words: O Father, take them for the great King of heaven

talibus auspiciis voluit te ducere honorem exsortem.
by such auspices has willed that you draw the honour of victory out of course.

Habebis hoc munus longævi Anchisæ ipsius; cratera
You shall have this gift of the aged Anchises himself; a goblet

impressum signis; quem Thracius Cisseus olim dederat
impressed with figures, which Thracian Cisseus formerly had given

Anchisæ genitori ferre in magno munere monumentum et
to Anchises my father to bear for a great present a monument and

pignus sui amoris Fatus sic, cingit tempora viridanti
pledge of his love. Speaking thus, he surrounds his temples with a green

lauro, et appellat Acesten primum victorem ante omnes.
laurel, and proclaims Acestes first a conqueror before all.

Nec bonus Eurytion invidit prælato honori, quamvis solus
Nor does good Eurytion envy the preferred honour, although alone

dejecit avem ab alto cœlo. Ingreditur proximus
he struck down the bird from the lofty sky. He comes next

donis, qui rupit vincula; extremus qui fixit malum
in gifts. who broke the cords, he last who pierced the mast

volucri arundine.
with the swift dart.

At pater Æneas, certamine nondum misso vocat
But father Eneas, the contest not yet being dismissed calls

ad sese Epytiden custodem que comitem impubis
to himself Epydites the guardian and companion of the youthful

Iüli, et sic fatur ad fidam aurem: Vade age, ait
Iulus, and thus he speaks to his faithful ear: Proceed go, said he

et dic Ascanio, si jam habet puerile agmen paratum
and tell Ascanius, if now he has the boyish troop prepared

secum que instruxit cursus equorum, ducat
with him and has array'd the courses of the horse, that he should lead out

turmas   avo   et ostendat sese in armis. Ipse jubet
the bands to his grandfather and shows   himself in arms.   He commands

omnem populem infusum decedere longo   circo
all   the people scattered about to withdraw from the long circus.

et campos esse patentes. Pueri incedunt, que   pariter
and the plains to be   laid open. The boys march on, and   together

lucent in frænatis equis ante   ora   parentum;   quos
shine upon their reined horses before the faces of their parents; whom

euntes omnis juventus Trinacriæ que Trojæ mirata fremit.
going out all the youth of Sicily and of Troy admiring   shout.

Coma   pressa omnibus   tonsâ   coronâ   in
The hair was pressed to all with a shorn garland according to

morem.   Ferunt bina hastilia cornea præfixo ferro;
their manner. They bear two spears of cornel with pointed steel;

pars   leves pharetras humero.   Flexilis circulus
a part bear light quivers on their shoulders. A pliant   circle

obtorti auri it per collum summo pectore.   Turmæ
of twisted gold goes over the neck from the top of the breast. The troops

equitum tres numero, que terni ductores vagantur: bis
of horsemen three in number, and three leaders range about. twice

seni pueri secuti quemque fulgent partito agmine, que
six boys following each shine in a divided band,   and

paribus magistris. Una acies juvenum quam parvus
with equal leaders.   One troop of youth which little

Priamus, referens nomen   avi,   ducit ovantem,
Priam,   bearing   the name of his grandfather, leads on triumphing.

tua clara progenies, Polite   auctura Italos, quem
thy renown'd offspring, O Polites about to augment the Italians whom

Thracius equus bicolor albis maculis portat;   vestigia
a Thracian horse variegated with white spots   bears;   the steps

primi pedis alba que arduus ostentans albam frontem.
of his fore feet are white and on high displaying his white forehead.

Alter Atys, unde Latini Attî duxere genus; parvus Atys,
The other Atys, whence the Latin Atti have derived their race. little Atys,

que puer dilectus puero Iûlo. Extremus que pulcher
and the boy beloved by the boy Iulus. The last   and   beautiful

formâ ante omnes Iulus invectus et Sidonio   equo,
in form before all   Iulus is borne on a Sidonian horse,

quem candida Dido dederat esse monumentum et pignus
which the fair Dido had given to be a monument and pledge

sui amoris. Cætera pubes fertur Trinacriis equis senioris
of her love. The other youth are borne on Trinacrian horses of the aged

Accestæ. Dardanidæ plausu excipiunt pavidos, que
Acestes. The Trojans with applause receive them trembling,   and

gaudent tuentes que agnoscunt ora   veterum parentum.
rejoice beholding and they know the features of their former parents.

Postquam læti lustravere omnem concessum, qu'
After joyful they had survey'd all   the assembly,   as

oculos suorum in equis.   Epytides longè dedit
the eyes of their friends on their horses. The son of Epytus from afar gave

signum   paratis   clamore,   que insonuit   flagello.
a sign   to them prepar'd with a shout,   and sounded   with his whip.

Olli discurrere pares, atque terni solvere agmina
They   ran away in pairs,   and three by three they display   their troops

choris   diductis;   que rursus vocati convertere vias,
their bands being drawn out and again call'd they turn'd their ways

que tulere infesta tela. Inde ineunt alios cursus, qu
and bore hostile darts. Then they enter on other courses,   an

alios recursus   adversis   spatiis,   que   impediunt
other retreats in their opposite race grounds; and   entangle

alternos orbes   orbibus,   que cient simulacra pugnæ
alternate circles with circles, and represent the image of a battle

sub armis. Et nunc nudant terga fugâ nunc
under arms.   And now they expose their backs in flight now

infensi vertunt spicula, nunc pace factâ pariter
hostile they turn their darts, now peace being made · together

feruntur. Ut lanyrinthus in altâ Cretâ fertur
they are borne on. As a labyrinth   in lofty Crete   is said

quondam habuisse iter textum cæcis parietibus, que
formerly   to have had a path interwoven in its dark walls,   and

dolum ancipitem mille viis, quà indeprensus et
a maze doubtful by a thousand ways, where the intricate and

irremeabilis error falleret signa sequendi, haud aliter
inextricable winding would deceive the signs of one following; not otherwise

nati   Teucrum   impediunt vestigia   cursu,   que
the sons of the Trojans entangle   their footsteps in the course, and

ludo texunt fugas et prœlia: similes delphinûm, qui
in sport interweave flights and battles: like dolphins,   which

nando per humida maria secant Carpathium que
in swimming through the moist seas   cut the Carpathian and

Libycum que ludunt per undas.
Libian seas and sport through the waves.

Ascanius primus retulit hunc morem cursus, atque hæc
Ascanius   first restored this custom of the race, and these

certamina, cum cingeret Albam longam muris, et docuit
contests, when he surrounded Alba onga with walls, and taught

priscos Latinos celebrare: quo modò puer ipse, quò
the ancient Latins to celebrate them: as the boy himself, as

Troia pubes secum,   Albani docuere suos:
the Trojan youth with him had observed them so the Albans taught their

hinc porro maxima Roma accepit et servavit
sons, hence moreover most exalted Rome received them and preserved

patrium honorem, nunc dicitur Troja que pueri
the native honour, now it is called Troy and the boys are called

Trojanum agmen. Hactenus certamina   celebrata
the Trojan band. Thus far the contests had been celebrated

sancto patri. Hic fortuna mutata primum novavit fidem
to the holy father Here fortune shifting first changed her faith.

Dum referunt solennia tumulo variis ludis
While they celebrate the anniversary rites at the tomb by various games,

Saturnia Juno misit Irim de cœlo ad Iliacam classem, que
Saturnian Juno sent Iris from heaven to the Trojan fleet, and

aspirat ventos eunti, movens multa, necdum
favours the winds to her going, revolving many things, nor yet

exsaturata antiquum dolorem. Illa virgo celerans viam
having satisfied her ancient grief. The maid hastening her way

per arcum mille coloribus, visa nulli decurrit cito
through a bow with a thousand colours, seen by none ran along the swift

tramite. Conspicit ingentem concursum et lustrans litora,
path. She beholds a great assembly and surveying the stores,

videt que portus desertos, que classem relictam. At
sees both the harbours deserted and the fleet abandoned. But

Troades procul secretæ in solâ actâ flebant
the Trojan matrons afar off retired upon the lonely shore mourned

Anchisen amissum, que cunctæ flentes aspectabant
Anchises lost, and all weeping beheld

profundum pontum. Heu! tot vada et tantum maris
the deep sea Alas! that so many shallows and so much of the sea

superesse fessis, una vox omnibus. Orant urbem;
remains to us wearied, this one voice was to all They pray for a city;

tædet perferre laborem pelagi. Ergo haud ignara
it wearies them to endure the labour of the ocean. Therefore she not ignorant

nocendi conjecit sese inter medias, et reponit que faciem
of injuring threw herself in the midst, and laid aside both the form

que vestem Deæ. Fit Beroë, longæva conjux
and the dress of a Goddess. She becomes Beroe, the aged wife

Dorycli Ismarii, cui quondam genus et nomen que nati
of Doryclian Ismarus, to whom formerly family and name and children

fuissent. Ac sic infert se mediam matribus Dardanidum.
had been. And thus she bears herself in the midst of the matrons of the Trojans.

O miseræ inquit, quas Achaica manus non traxerit
O wretched mothers said she, whom the Achaian band had not drawn

ad lethum bello, sub mœnibus patriæ. O infelix gens:
to death by war, under the walls of my country. O unhappy nation.

cui exitio fortuna reservat te? septima æstas jam
for what destruction does fortune reserve you? the seventh summer now

vertitur post excidium Trojæ, cum ferimur, emensæ
evolves since the fall of Troy, when we are borne on, having measured

freta, omnes terras, tot inhospita saxa, que sidera, dum
the seas, all lands, so many inhospitable rocks, and climates, while

per magnum mare, sequimur Italiam fugientem, et
through the great sea, we pursue Italy flying, and

volvimur undis. Hìc fraterni fines Erycis,
we are overwhelmed in the waves. Here are the fraternal boundaries of Eryx

atque   est   hospes Acestes; quid prohibet   jacere muros,
and   there is   our   host   Acestes;   what   forbids   us to found   walls,

et dare urbem   civibus?   O patriæ   Penates   rapti
and to give a city   to our countrymen?   O my country's household gods snatched

ex hoste nequicquam; ne nulla mœnia jam dicentur Trojæ?
from the foe   in vain;   will no   walls   now   be called   Troy?

nusquam videbo Hectoreos amnes, Xanthum et Simöenta?
never   shall I behold Hector's   streams, Xanthus   and   Simois?

Quin agite et mecum exurite infaustas puppes.   Nam
But   come on and with me   burn   these unlucky   ships.   For

imago Cassandræ vatis   per   somnum visa dare mihi
the image of Cassandra the prophetess during my sleep   seemed to give to me

ardentes faces: Hìc inquit, quærite Trojam; hìc domus est
burning   torches: Here said she,   seek for   Troy;   here a home   is

vobis. Nunc tempus   res   agi.   Nec mora   tantis
for you. Now   is the time for things to be done. There is no delay   to so great

prodigiis. En quatuor aræ Neptuno: Deus ipse ministrat
prodigies.   Lo   four   altars to Neptune: The God himself   supplies

faces que animum.   Memorans hæc   prima corripit
torches and a disposition to use them. Uttering   these words first   she seizes

infensum ignem vi, que   dextrâ   sublatâ   connixa
the hostile   fire by violence, and with her right hand uplifted   struggling

procul coruscat, et jacit.
afar off she brandishes, and hurls it.

Mentes   Iliadum   arrectæ, que corda stupefacta.
The minds of the Trojan matrons were roused, and their hearts   astonished.

Hìc una è multis, quæ maxima natu, Pyrgo, regia   nutrix
Here one from many,   who   was the eldest,   Pyrgo,   the royal   nurse

tot   natorum Priami, Beröe non vobis, matres,   hæc
of so many of the sons of Priam, said Beroe is not with you O mothers,   this

non Rhœteia conjux Dorycli: notate signa divini   decoris,
is not the Rhœteian wife   of Doryclus: mark the signs of her divine   beauty,

que oculos ardentes; qui   spiritus, qui vultus   ve
and her eyes sparkling; what   fragrant breath, what a countenance   or

sonus vocis, vel gressus illi eunti! Ipsa egomet dudum
sound of her voice, or   step   to her going!   I   myself   lately

digressa reliqui Beröen ægram, indignantem quod   sola
departing   have left Beroe   sick,   and enraged because   alone

careret   tali munere, nec inferret meritos   honores
she was deprived of such an office,   nor   could pay   deserved   honours

Anchisæ.   Effata hæc;   at matres primò   spectare
to Anchises.   She said, these things; but the mothers at first   began to regard

naves   malignis oculis, ancipites, que ambiguæ,   inter
the ships with malignant eyes,   doubting,   and   wavering,   between

miserum amorem præsentis terræ, que regna   vocantia
the wretched   love   of the present land,   and the kingdoms   inviting them

fatis; cum Dea sustulit se   paribus alis per cœlum
by the fates; when the Goddess raised   herself   on equal wings through the sky

que secuit ingentem arcum sub nubibus fugâ.   Tum verò
and   cut   a great   bow under the clouds in her flight.   Then indeed

attonitæ monstris,   que actæ furore, conclamant,   que
astonished by these prodigies, and drawn by madness, they cry out,   and

rapiunt ignem penetralibus focis: pars spoliant   aras,
seize   the fire from the inmost hearths: a part strip   the altars,

conjiciunt frondem ac virgulta que faces; Vulcanus   furit
they throw   leaves and shrubs and firebrands; the fire   rages

immissis habenis per transtra, et remos, et   pictas
with uncontrolled reins through the benches, and oars, and   painted

puppes abiete. Eumelus nuncius perfert ad   tumulum
ships   of fir. Eumelus the messenger conveys to   the tomb

Anchisæ que cuneos   theatri,   naves incensas;   et
of Anchises and to the benches of the theatre, that the ships are on fire;   and

ipsi respiciunt atram favillam volitare in nimbo. Et Ascanius
they behold   the black embers fly in a cloud. And Ascanius

primus, ut lætus ducebat equestres cursus, sic acer   equo
first   as joyful he led out the equestrian courses, thus bold on his horse

petivit turbata castra;   nec exanimes magistri possunt
sought the troubled camps; neither the astonished masters are able

retinere. Inquit, Quis iste novus furor?   Heu! miseræ
to restrain him. He says, What is this new madness? Alas! wretched

cives,   quò—quò nunc   tenditis?   non uritis
countrywomen, whether—whither now do you direct your course? you do not burn

hostem, que inimica castra Argivûm,   vestras spes.
the enemy, and the hostile camps of the Greeks,   but your own hopes.

En ego vester Ascanius. Projecit   ante pedes   inanem
Lo I am your Ascanius. He cast before their feet the empty

galeam, quâ indutus ludo ciebat simulacra belli.   Simul
helmet, in which being clad, in sport he excited images of war. At once

Æneas accelerat, simul   agmina   Teucrûm.   Ast illæ
Æneas hastened, at once the troops of the Trojans. But they

metu diffugiunt passim per diversa litora; que furtim
through fear fly every where through the different shores; and by stealth

petunt sylvas, et sicubi   concava   saxa
they seek the woods, and wherever they can hide themselves in the hollow rocks.

Piget   incepti   que lucis,   que mutatæ
They loathe   their undertaking and the light, and changed,

agnoscunt suos;   que Juno excussa est   pectore. Sed
they know their friends; and Juno is shaken from their breast. But

flammæ atque incendia idcirco non posuere   indomitas
the flames and   the fires therefore had not laid aside their unconquered

vires; stuppa vivit sub udo robore, vomens tardum fumum;
strength; the tow lives under the moist wood, vomiting forth slow smoke;

que lentus vapor   est   carinas,   et   pestis descendit
and a slow   fire consumes the keels, and the contagion descends

toto   corpore; nec   vires   heroüm, que flumina
through the whole body; nor do the strength of heroes, and streams

infusa prosunt. Tum pius Æneas abscindere vestem
poured on profit. Then pious Æneas *begins* to tear his dress

humeris, que vocare Deos auxilio, et tendere
from his shoulders, and to call the Gods to his aid, and to stretch forth

palmas: Omnipotens Jupiter, si nondum exosus Trojanos
his hands: O almighty Jupiter, if not yet hating the Trojans

ad unum, si quid antiqua pietas respicit humanos labores;
to one *man*, if in any way thy ancient compassion regards human labours;

pater, da classi nunc evadere flammam, et letho eripe
O father, give to our fleet now to escape the flame, and from death snatch

tenues res Teucrûm. Vel, si mereor, tu demitte
the reduced concerns of the Trojans. Or, if I deserve it, do you send me

morti infesto fulmine; que obrue hîc tuâ
to death with your hostile thunderbolt; and overwhelm *me* here by your

dextrâ. Vix ediderat hæc, cum atra tempestas
right hand. Scarcely had he uttered these *words*, when a black storm

furit sine more effusis imbribus, que
rages without measure from the outpouring storms, and

ardua terrarum, et campi tremiscunt tonitru; imber
the high places of the earth and the plains trembled with thunder; a shower

turbidus aquâ que nigerimus densis Austris, ruit
black with water and most dark with thick rising south winds, rushes

toto æthere, que puppes super implentur; semusta
through the whole sky, and the ships from above are filled; the half-burnt

robora madescunt; donec omnis vapor restinctus, et
timbers are drenched; until all the smoke had become extinct, and

omnes carinæ servatæ a peste, quatuor amissis. At
all the ships were saved from destruction, four being lost. But

pater Æneas, concussus acerbo casu, mutabat ingentes
father Æneas, struck by the cruel misfortune revolved great

curas pectore nunc huc, nunc illuc, versans ne
cares in his breast now here, now there, reflecting whether

resideret Siculis arvis, oblitus fatorum; ne
he should settle in the Sicilian territories forgetful of the fates; or

capesserat Italas oras. Tum senior Nautes, quem
he should attempt the Italian coasts. When the elder Nautes, whom

unum Tritonia Pallas docuit, que reddidit insignem multâ
alone Tritonian Pallas had taught, and had rendered distinguished by much

arte, dabat hæc responsa, vel quæ magna ira Deûm
art, gave these replies, or what the great wrath of the Gods

portenderet, vel quæ ordo fatorum posceret. Que is
foretold or what the order of the fates might demand. And he

solatus Ænean infit his vocibus: Nate Deâ sequamur
consoling Æneas begins with these words: Son of a Goddess we follow

quò fata trahunt que retrahunt; quicquid erit, omnis
where the fates lead us on and lead us back; whatever shall be all

fortuna superanda est ferendo. Est tibi Dardanius Acestes
fortune is to be overcome by bearing it. There is to you Trojan Acestes

divinæ stirpis: cape hunc socium conciliis et conjunge
of a divine stock: take   him the companion in your councils and   join *him*

volentem.   Trade huic   qui superant,   amissis
to you a willing *friend*.   Deliver to him *those*   who   survive   from the lost

navibus et delige   quos pertæsum est   magni   incepti
ships   and choose *those*   who   are weary   of the great   undertaking

que tuarum rerum, que longævos senes,   ac matres fessas
and   of your   affairs,   and   the aged   old men,   and mothers   wearied

æquore,   et quicquid est   tecum   invalidum, que metuens
with the sea, and   whatever   is   with you   powerless,   and   fearing

pericli; et sine   fessi   habeant   mœnia   his terris:
danger;   and permit that the weary shall inhabit   towns   in these lands:

appellabunt urbem Acestam, nomine permisso.   Tum verò
they shall call   the city   Acesta,   a name   permitted.   Then indeed

incensus talibus dictis senioris amici,   animum diducitur
inflamed   by such words   of his aged   friend,   in his mind   he is divided

in   omnes curas.   Et atra nox subvecta   bigis   tenebat
among all   cares.   And black night   borne on   in her chariot   held

polum; dehinc facies   parentis Anchisæ delapsa   cœlo
the sky;   then   the form   of his father Anchises   gliding   from the sky

subitò   visa   effundere tales voces: Nate, quondam magis
suddenly seemed   to pour forth   such words: O son,   formerly   more

care mihi   vitâ   dum vita manebat;   nate, exercite Iliacis
dear   to me   than life   while life   remained;   O son, exercised in Trojan

fatis, venio   huc imperio   Jovis,   qui   depulit ignem
fates,   I come   here by command of Jove,   who   drove back   the fire

classibus,   et tandem miseratus est ab   alto cœlo. Pare
from the ships,   and at length   pitied *thee*   from   the lofty sky.   Obey

consiliis, quæ senior Nautes nunc dat pulcherrima; defer in
the counsels, which the aged   Nautes   now   gives   most excellent;   bear   to

Italiam lectos juvenes, fortissima corda.   Gens dura, atque
Italy   chosen   youth,   the stoutest   hearts.   A race   hardy,   and

aspera cultu,   debellanda est tibi   Latio.   Antè,   ta-
rude   in cultivation,   is about to contend with you in Latium.   First, neverthe-

men, accede infernas domos Ditis; et   nate,   pete meos
less,   approach the infernal domains of Pluto;   and   O son,   seek   my

congressus per   alta Averna, namque impia Tartara que
conference   through   the deep Avernus,   for   cruel Tartarus   and

tristes umbræ non habent me; sed   colo   amœna
the gloomy shades   do not possess me;   but   I dwell among the pleasant

concilia piorum que Elysium.   Casta Sibylla ducet   te
councils   of the pious and in Elysium.   The chaste   Sibyl   shall lead   thee

huc multo   sanguine nigrantium pecudum.   Tum
hither with much   blood   of black   victims.   Then

disces   omne tuum genus, et mœnia quæ   dentur; que
you shall learn   all   your   race,   and the walls which shall be given; and

jam vale humida nox torquet medios cursus, et sævus
now farewell moist night turns her middle course, and cruel

Oriens afflavit me anhelis equis.
Orion breathes on me with panting horses.

Dixerat; et fugit ceu fumus, in tenues auras. Deinde
He said; and fled as smoke, into the light air. Then

Æneas inquit: Quò ruis? quò proripis
Eneas said. Whither do you rush? where do you bear *yourself*

quem fugis? aut quis arcet te nostris complexibus?
whom do you fly? or who drives you from our embrace?

memorans hæc suscitat cinerem et sopitos ignes,
Uttering these *words* he awakens the ashes and sleepy fires.

que supplex veneratur pio farre et plenâ accerrâ
and humbly worships with a holy cake and full censer

Pergameum Larem et penetralia canæ Vestæ.
the Trojan household God, and the shrine of hoary Vestæ.

Extemplo accessit socios, que Acesten primum; et
Forthwith he calls his companions, and Acestes first; and

edocet imperium Jovis, et præcepta cari parentis, et
teaches the command of Jove and the instructions of his dear parent, and

quæ sententia nunc constet animo. Haud mora
what sentiment now is settled in his mind. There is no delay

consiliis; nec Acestes recusat jussa. Transcribunt
in his councils; nor does Acestes refuse his commands. They mark out

matres urbi; que deponunt populum volentem,
the matrons for the city; and they establish the people willing

animos, nil egentes magnæ laudis. Ipsi novant
in their minds, not desirous of great praise. They renew

transtra que reponunt navigiis robora ambesa
their benches and replace in their ships the timbers corroded

flammis, que aptant remos que rudentes; exigui numero
by the flames, and they fit oars and cables; small in number,

sed virtus vivida bello. Interea Æneas designat
but their courage is active for war. In the mean time Æneas marks out

urbem aratro, que sortitur domos: jubet hoc
a city with a plough, and allots dwellings: he orders this *to be call'd*

Ilium et hæc loca esse Trojæ. Trojanus Acestes
Ilium and those places *to be named from those* of Troy. Trojan Acestes

gaudet regno, que indicit forum, et dat jura,
rejoices in his kingdom and proclaims a court, and gives laws,

vocatis patribus. Tum sedes vicina astris fundatur
having convoked the fathers. Then a seat near to the stars is founded

Idaliæ Veneri, in Erycino vertice que sacerdos et lucus
to Idalian Venus, on Eryx's height and a priest and a grove

latè sacer additur Anchisæo tumulo, que jam omnis
far around sacred is added to Anchises tomb. and now the whole

gens epulata novem dies, et honos factus aris;
nation having feasted nine days, and honour having been paid to the altars,

placidi venti straverunt æquora et Auster creber
peaceful winds had smooth'd the waters and the south wind frequently

aspirans rursus vocat in altum. Ingens fletus exoritur per
blowing again invites to the deep. A great mourning arises along

procurva litora complexi inter se morantur que
the crooked shores embracing among themselves they delay both

noctem que diem. Jam ipsæ matres, ipsi quibus
night and day. Now they the mothers, and those to whom

quondam facies maris visa aspera et numen
formerly the appearance of the sea seem'd rough and its authority

non tolerabile, volunt ire, que perferre omnem laborem
not to be endured, desire to go, and to endure all the labour

fugæ: quos bonus Æneas solatur amicis dictis, et
of flight: whom good Æneas consoles with friendly words, and

lacrymans commendat consanguineo Acestæ. Deinde
weeping he recommends them to his relation Acestes. Then

jubet cædere tres vitulos Eryci et agnam
he commands them to slay three calves to Eryx and a lamb

tempestatibus, que funes solvi ex ordine. Ipse
to the tempests, and the ropes to be loosen'd from their place. He

evinctus caput foliis tonsæ ' olivæ, stans procul in
binding his head with leaves of shorn olive, standing far off on

prorâ, tenet pateram, que porricit exta in salsos
the prow, holds a goblet, and casts the entrails upon the salt

fluctus, ac fundit liquentia vina. Ventus surgens a
waves, and pours out the liquid wine. The wind rising from

puppi prosequitur euntes; socii feriunt mare
the stern pursues them departing; his companions strike the sea

certatim, et verrunt æquora. At Venus interea
eagerly, and sweep the waters, But Venus in the meantime

exercita curis alloquitur Neptunum, que effundit tales
exercised with cares addresses Neptune, and utters these

questus pectore. Neptune, gravis ira et
complaints from her breast. O Neptune, the cruel anger and

inexsaturabile pectus Junonis cogunt me descendere in
'unforgiving heart of Juno, compel me to descend to

omnes preces, quam nec longa dies nec ulla
all entreaties, whom neither long continued time nor any

pietas mitigat nec quiescit infracta imperio Jovis
piety softens nor will she rest subdued by the command of Jove

ve fatis. Non est satis nefandis odiis exedisse
or by the fates. It is not enough by her cruel hatred to have destroy'd

urbem de mediâ gente Phrygum, traxisse reliquias
the city from the midst of the nation of the Trojans, to have drawn its remains

per omnem pœnam; insequitur cineres atque ossa
through every suffering; she persecutes the ashes and bones

peremtæ Trojæ. Illa sciat causas tanti furoris. Tu ipse
of ruin'd Troy. She may know the causes of so great madness. You yourself

testis mihi quam molem subitò excierit nuper in
are a witness to me what a tempest suddenly she excited lately in

Libycis undis.
the Lybian waves.

Nequicquam freta Æolus procellis, miscuit omnia
In vain trusting to the Eolian storms, she has mingled all

maria cœlo; ausa hoc in tuis regnis. Proh scelus! ecce
seas with the sky; daring thus in your kingdoms. Alas the crime! lo

etiam fœdè exussit puppes, Trojanis matribus
also shamefully she has burnt the ships, the Trojan matrons

actis et subegit socios linquere
being driven on and has compelled their companions to leave *them*

ignotæ terræ, classe amissâ. Quod superest, oro
on an unknown shore, their fleet being lost. What remains, I pray

liceat tibi dare vela tuta per undas; liceat
it may be allowed to you to give *to them* sails safe through the waves: it may be

attingere Laurentem Tybrim, si peto concessa, si
allowed to reach the Laurentian Tyber, if I seek things allowed, if

parcæ dant ea mœnia. Tum Saturnius domitor alti
the destinies give those walls. Then the Saturnian ruler of the deep

maris edidit hæc: Cytherea, est fas te fidere
sea uttered these words: O Venus, it is lawful for you to trust

omne meis regnis, unde ducis genus: merui
every thing to my kingdoms, whence you derive your race: I have deserved *it*

quoque, sæpe compressi furores, et tantam rabiem que
also, often I have restrained the rage, and great madness both

cœli que maris. Nec minor cura mihi tui Æneæ
of the heaven and the sea. Nor less care to me of your Eneas *was there*

in terris, testor Xanthum que Simöenta. Cùm Achilles
in the land, I call to witness Xanthus and Simois. When Achilles

sequens Troïa agmina exanimata impingeret muris
pursuing the Trojan bands terrified drove them against the walls

daret multa millia letho, que amnes repleti gemerent, nec
and gave many thousand to death, and the rivers being filled groaned, nor

possit Xanthus reperire viam atque evolvere se in mare;
could Xanthus find out a way and roll itself into the sea;

tunc ego eripui cavâ nube Ænean congressum forti
then I snatched in a hollow cloud Eneas engaged with the brave

Pelidæ; nec æquis Dîs nec viribus; cum cuperem ab
Achilles; nor *were there* equal Gods nor strength; when I had desired from

imo vertere mænia perjuræ Trojæ structa meis
the foundation to overturn the walls of perjured Troy built by my

manibus. Nunc quoque eadem mens perstat mihi; pelle
hands. Now also the same mind remains with me; banish

timorem; tutus accedet portus Averni quos optas.
fear; safely he shall approach the harbours of Avernus which you desire.

Tantùm erit unus quem quæret amissum gurgite,
Only there shall be one whom he shall seek lost in the sea.

unum caput dabitur pro multis.   Ubi genitor
one   life shall be given for many.   When the father *of the sea*

permulsit læta pectora Deæ   his dictis,   jungit
had soothed the joyful breast of the Goddess with these words, he joins

equos   auro, que addit spumantia   fræna
his horses *to his chariot of* gold, and puts the foaming   bits

feris,   que effundit omnes habenas manibus. Volat
in their fierce *mouths*, and lets loose all the reins from his hands. He flies

levis in cæruleo curru per summa æquora,   undæ subsidunt,
light in his azure car over the surface of the sea, the waves subside,

que tumidum æquor sternitur aquis sub tonante axe,
and the swelling sea is smoothed by the waters under the thundering axle,

nimbi fugiunt   vasto æthere. Tum   variæ facies
the clouds fly through the vast sky. Then *appear the* various forms

comitum immania cete, et senior chorus Glauci, que Inous
of his companions huge whales, and the elder band of Glaucus, and Inous

Palæmon que citi Tritones, que omnes exercitus Phorci. Thetis
Palemon and the swift Tritons, and all the army of Phorcus. Thetis

et Melite tenent læva,   que virgo Panopea. Nesæe, que Spio
and Melite hold the left *places*, and the maid Panopea. Nesæe, and Spio

que Thalia, que Cymodoce. Hìc blanda gaudia vicissim
and .Thalia, and Cymodoce.   Here pleasant joys   in turn

pertentant suspensam mentem patris Æneæ. Ocyùs jubet
thrill   the doubting mind of father Eneas. Quick he orders

omnes malos attolli, brachia intendi   velis.   Omnes
all   the masts to be raised, the yards to be stretched to the sails.   All

fecere pedem unà, que pariter solvere sinistros nunc
work   the halser together, and together they loosen the left   now

dextros sinus; unà   torquent   que detorquent ardua
the right sails; together they move forward and turn back   the lofty

cornua: sua flamina ferunt classem. Palinurus   princeps
sail yards: favourable gales move the fleet. Palinurus   chief

ante omnes agebat densum agmen: alii   jussi contendere
before all led the close squadron· the others commanded to direct

cursum ad hunc, que jam humida nox contigerat ferè
their course to him, and now the moist night had reached almost

mediam metam cœli; nautæ fusi per dura sedilia sub
the middle boundary of heaven; the sailors stretched along the hard benches under

remis laxârant membra placidâ quiete; cum Somnus
the oars relaxed their limbs with peaceful rest; when Sleep

levis delapsus ab ætheriis astris dimovit tenebrosum æra,
gently gliding from the ætherial stars removed the darkened   air

et dispulit umbras; petens te, Palinure, portans tristia
and scattered the shadows; seeking thee, O Palinurus, bearing   sad

somnia tibi insonti; que Deus consedit in altâ pupp
dreams to thee innocent; and the God sat upon the high stern,

similis Phorbanti, que fudit has loquelas   ore: Palinure
like to Phorbas, and uttered these words from his mouth. O Palinurus

Iaside, ipsa æquora ferunt classem; auræ spirant æquatæ
son of Iasus, the   waters   bear   the fleet: the gales breathe   equally

hora datur quieti, pone caput, que furare fessos
the hour is devoted to rest, lay down your head, and steal your wearied

oculos labori.
eyes from labour.

Ego ipse   paulisper   inibo   tua munera pro te.
I   myself   for a little while will undertake your duties   for you.

Cui Palinurus vix attollens lumina fatur;   jubesne
To whom Palinurus scarcely raising his eyes speaks; will you order

me ignorare   vultum   placidi   salis—que quietos
me to be ignorant of the face of the peaceful sea—and the quiet

fluctus? me confidere huic monstro? Quid enim credam
waves? shall I trust to this prodigy?   Why even shall I trust

Ænean fallacibus Austris, et toties deceptus   fraude
Ænean to the deceitful south winds, and so often deceived by the fraud

sereni cœli?   Dabat talia dicta; que affixus et hærens
of the serene sky? He uttered these words; and fastened and cleaving

nusquam amittebat clavum, que tenebat oculos sub astra.
never   did he let go the helm, and he directed his eyes to the stars.

Ecce! Deus quassat ramum madentem Lethæo rore, que
Lo!   the God shakes a branch dripping with the Lethean dew, and

soporatum Stygiâ vi, super utraque tempora que solvit
rendered sleepy by Stygian power, over both temples and relaxes

natantia lumina cunctanti.   Inopina quies vix laxaverat
his swimming eyes to him delaying. Unwished-for sleep scarcely had relaxed

primos artus, et super incumbens projecit in liquidas undas,
his first limbs, and over him leaning hurled him into the clear waters,

cum   parte puppis   revulsâ,   que cum gubernaculo,
with   a part of the ship torn off, and with the helm

præcipitem, ac sæpe vocantem socios nequicquam: ipse
headlong, and after calling on his companions in vain: he

volans ales sustulit se in tenues auras. Classis currit
flying as a bird raised himself to the light air. The fleet ran

iter æquore non secius tutum que fertur interrita
its way on the sea not less safe and is borne on fearless

promissis patris Neptuni, que jam adeo advecta subibat
by the promises of father Neptune, and now thus advancing it entered

scopulos Sirenum,   quondam difficiles, que albos
among the rocks of the Sirens, formerly difficult, and white

ossibus   multorum—(tum rauca saxa longè sonabant
with the bones of many—(then the hoarse rocks far off resound

assiduo   sale;) cum pater   sensit ratem errare
with the continual sea;) when father Æneas perceived the ship to wander

fluitantem, magistro amisso, et ipse rexit in nocturnis
floating about, its master being lost, and he guides it in the nightly

undis, gemens multa, que concussus animum   casu
waves, groaning much, and shaken in his mind by the loss

amici: Palinure, nimium confise sereno cœlo et pelago,
of his friend: O Palinurus, too much confiding in the clear sky and the sea,

nudus jacebis in ignotâ arenâ!
naked you shall lie on the unknown sand!

ÆNEID.

BOOK SIXTH.

Sic fatur lacrymans, que immittit habenas classi; et
Thus he speaks weeping, and loosens the sails to the fleet; and

tandem allabitur Euboicis oris Cumarum. Obvertunt
at length glides along the Eubean coasts of Cumæ. They turn

proras pelago; tum anchora fundabat naves tenaci dente,
the prows to the sea; then the anchor moored the ships with its grasping flook

et curvæ puppes prætexunt litora. Ardens manus
and the bending sterns line the shores. A zealous band

juvenum emicat in Hesperium litus; pars quæret semina
of young men leap upon the Italian shore; a part seek the elements

flammæ abstrusa in venis silicis; pars rapit sylvas, densa
of flame concealed in the veins of flint; a part ravage the woods, the thick

tecta ferarum, que monstrat flumina inventa. At pius
coverts of wild beasts; and point out streams discovered. But pious

Æneas petit arces quibus altus Apollo præsidet, que
Æneas seeks the towers over which high Apollo rules, and

immane antrum, secreta Sibyllæ horrendæ procul;
the dreadful cave, the retreat of the Sibyl awful at a distance;

cui Delius vates inspirat magnam mentem que
to whom the Delian prophet Apollo inspires a great mind and

animum, que aperit futura; jam subeunt lucos,
soul, and opens to her future things; now they enter the groves,

atque aurea tecta Triviæ. Dædalus, ut est fama, fugiens
and golden roofs of Diana. Dædalus, as is the report, flying

Minoia regna, ausus credere se cœlo præpetibus
Mino's kingdoms, dared to trust himself to the sky on swift

pennis, enavit ad gelidas Arctos per insuetum iter, que
wings, swam to the cold North through an unused way, and

tandem levis adstitit super Chalcidicâ arce. Redditus
at length light stood upon the Chalcidian tower. Returned

his terris primùm, sacravit tibi, Phœbe, remigium
to these lands first, he consecrated to you, O Apollo, the steerage

alarum, que posuit tibi immania templa. In foribus
of his wings, and placed to you an immense temple. On the doors

Iethum Androgeo; tum Cecropidæ jussi quotannis
was displayed the death of Androgeos; then the Athenians commanded   yearly

pendere pœnas (miserum!) septena corpora natorum;
to pay   penalties (O wretched!) seven   bodies of their children;

urna stat ductis sortibus. Gnossia tellus elata   mari
the urn stands with drawn lots.   The Gnossian land raised high in the sea

respondit   contrá.   Hic crudelis amor tauri, que
corresponds on the other side. Here the cruel love of the bull, and

Pasiphäe supposta furto, que Minotaurus inest—mistum
Pasiphae   substituted by stealth, and the Minotaur is present—a mingled

genus que biformis proles, monumenta nefandæ Veneris.
race   and two-formed offspring, monuments   of impious   love.

Hìc ille labor domus, et inextricabilis error: sed enim
Here are that labour of the house, and inextricable   maze: but even

Dædalus miseratus magnum amorem reginæ,   ipse
Dedalus   compassionating the great love of the queen, himself

resolvit dolos que ambages tecti, filo regens cæca
unravels the mazes and windings of the palace, by a thread guiding his blind

vestigia: Icare, tu quoque   haberes magnam partem in
footsteps: O Icarus, you also   should have had a distinguished part   in

tanto opere, dolor sineret. Bis conatus erat   effingere
this great work, had grief allowed. Twice had he attempted to represent

casus   in auro; patriæ manus bis cecidere. Quin
his misfortunes in gold; his paternal hands twice failed him.   But

protinus   perlegerent omnia   oculis,   ni Achates
from afar *the Trojans* would observe all things with their eyes, unless Achates

præmissus jam afforet, atque unà   sacerdos
sent before now had been present, and   together *with him* the Priestess

Phœbi que Triviæ, Deiphobe   Glauci, quæ fatur
of Apollo and Diana, Deiphobe the *daughter* of Glaucus, who addresses

regi   talia: Hoc tempus non poscit sibi ista
the king in these words: This   time   does not demand to itself these

spectacula. Nunc præstiterit mactare septem juvencos
shows.   Now it would be better to sacrifice seven   · bullocks

de intacto grege, totidem lectas bidentes de   more.
from the untouched herd, as many chosen ewes according to the custom.

Sacerdos affata Ænean talibus: (nec viri morantur
The priestess addressed Æneas *in these* words: (nor do the men delay

sacra   jussa)   vocat Teucros in alta templa. Ingens
the sacred commands) she calls the Trojans into the lofty temple. The great

latus Euboicæ rupis excisum in antrum; quò centum lati
side of a Eubœan rock is cut in the cave; where an hundred broad

aditus ducunt, centum ostia, unde totidem voces ruunt,
entrances lead,   an hundred doors, whence as many voices rush,

responsa Sibyllæ. Ventum erat   ad limen, cum
the responses of the Sibyl. They had arrived   at the entrance, when

virgo ait: Tempus poscere fata; Deus, ecce, Deus!
he maid said: It is time to inquire your fate; a God, behold a God

Cui fanti talia ante fores, subitò non vultus
To whom speaking these *words* before the doors, suddenly neither was her coun-

non color unus, comæ non mansere comtæ; sed
tenance nor her colour the same, her hair did not remain smoothed; but

pectus anhelum, et fera corda tument rabie: videri
her breast *was* panting, and her savage heart swells with rage: she appears

major, nec sonans mortale, quando jam afflata est
larger, nor uttering mortal sound, since now she is inspired

propriore numine Dei. Tros Ænea, ait, cessas in
by the nearer influence of the God. O Trojan Eneas, said she, do you hesitate in

vota que preces? cessas? enim neque magna ora
your vows and prayers? do you hesitate? for neither shall the great gate

attonitæ domûs dehiscent antè.
of the astonished mansion open before *you offer them.*

Et fata talia conticuit. Gelidus tremor cucurrit
And having said these *words* she was still. A cold trembling ran

per dura ossa Teucris; que rex fudit preces ab
through the hard bones of the Trojans; and the king utter'd prayers from

imo pectore: Phœbe, semper miserate graves
his inmost breast: O Apollo, ever pitying the mournful

labores Trojæ, qui dirêxti Dardana tela que manus
labours of Troy, who hast directed Trojan darts and the hands

Paridis in corpus Æacidæ, te duce
of Paris against the body of Achilles, you being my guide

intravi tot maria obeuntia magnas terras; que
I have enter'd so many seas flowing around extensive lands; and

gentes Maassylûm penitus repostas, que arva prætenta
the nations of the Massylians afar off removed, and the regions set around

Syrtibus. Jam tandem prendimus oras Italiæ fugientis.
by quicksands. Now at last we grasp the coasts of Italy retreating.

Hactenus Trojana fortuna secuta fuerit que omnes
Thus far Trojan fortune has followed *us* and all

Dì que Deæ quibus Ilium obstitit, et ingens gloria
the Gods and Goddesses by whom Ilium has stood, and the great glory

Dardaniæ; jam est fas vos quoquè parcere Pergameæ genti:
of Troy; now it is right for us likewise to spare the Trojan nation:

que tu ô sanctissima vates præscia venturi, da
and you O most holy prophetess foreknowing what is to come, grant

Teucros que errantes Deos que agitata numina
to the Trojans and the wandering Gods and persecuted Deities

Trojæ considere Latio (non posco regna indebita
of Troy to settle in Latium (I do not ask kingdoms not destined

meis fatis.) Tum instituam Phœbo et Triviæ templa de
by my fates.) Then I will place to Apollo and Diana temples of

solido marmore, que festos dies de nomine Phœbi. Magna
solid marble, and feast days from the name of Apollo. Great

penetralia manent te quoquè nostris regnis nam
shrines await thee likewise in our kingdoms for

ego ponam hìc tuas sortes, que arcana fata dicta meæ
I   will place here your lots,   and the secret fates declared to my

genti; que   sacrabo   lectos viros alma   tantùm
nation: and I will consecrate chosen men O kind *Goddess*   only

ne manda tua carmina ` foliis ne turbata   volent
do not commit your verses to leaves lest disturbed they should fly

ludibria rapidis ventis: oro   ipsa   canas.
the sport of the swift winds: I pray you yourself   will utter *them.*

Dedit finem loquendi   ore.   At vates   nondum
He made an end of speaking with his mouth. But the Prophetess not yet

patiens Phœbi, immanis bacchatur in antro   si
enduring the *power* of Apollo, outrageous raves in the cave *striving* if

possit pectore excussisse magnum Deum: tanto
she can *thus* from her heart shake off the powerful God: so much

magis ille fatigat rabidum   os   domans fera corda
the more he wearies her mad countenance subduing her savage heart

que fingit   premendo.   Que jam centum
and moulds *her to his will* by restraining her. And now an hundred

ingentia ostia domûs   patuere   suâ   sponte; que
great   doors of the house fly open of their own accord; and

ierunt responsa   vatis   per   auras; O tandem
bear the responses of the prophetess through the air; O at last

defuncte magnis perîclis pelagi! sed graviora terrâ
having endured the great perils of the sea! but more severe on land

manent. Dardanidæ venient in regna Lavinî (mitte
remain. The Trojans shall come to the kingdom of Lavinium (dismiss

hanc curam de   pectore) sed et   volent   non
this care from *your* breast) but also they shall wish that they had not

venisse. Cerno bella horrida bella,   et   Tybrim
come.   I behold wars horrid wars, and   the Tyber

spumantem multo sanguine. Non Simois nec Xanthus,
foaming with much blood. Neither Simois nor Xanthus,

nec Dorica castra defuerint tibi; alius Achilles jam
nor the Doric camps shall be wanting to you; another Achilles even now

partus in Latio, et ipse natus Deâ: nec Juno
is born in Latium, and he born of a Goddess: nor Juno

addita Teucris usquam aberit: cùm in egenis
added to the Trojans ever shall be from *them:* when in desperate

rebus quas gentes Italûm, aut quas urbes non tu
circumstances what nations of the Italians, or what cities will not you

supplex oraveris? Conjux hospita iterum erit causa
humbly supplicate? A wife a hostess again shall be a cause

Teucris tanti mali;   que externi thalami iterum
to the Trojans of a great misfortune; and a foreign marriage again

Ne tu   cede   malis   sed contrà
produce great woe. Do not yourself yield to your misfortunes but rather

ito audentior quàm tua fortuna   sinet.
advance more boldly as your fortune shall permit you.

Prima vıa salutis pandetur ab Graiâ urbe, quod
The first way of safety shall be opened from a Grecian city, which

minimè reris. Cumæa Sibylla canit horrendas ambages
very little you suppose. The Cumæan Sibyl uttered her dreadful ambiguities

ex adyto talibus dictis, que remugit antro involvens
from her shrine with these words, and rebellows in her cave involving

vera obscuris: Apollo concutit ea fræna furenti, et
truth with darkness: Apollo shakes the reins over her raging, and

vertit stimulos sub pectore: Ut primùm furor cessit, et
turns the goads beneath her breast: As first her rage ceased, and

rabida ora quiêrunt, heros Æneas incipit. O virgo,
her maddening mouth was at rest, the hero Eneas begins. O maid,

non ulla facies laborum surgit mihi nova ve inopina:
not any appearance of labours arises to me new or unexpected:

præcepi atque antêperegi omnia mecum animo.
I have anticipated and first acted over all things by myself in my mind.

Oro unum, quando janua inferni regis dicitur hìc,
I pray one thing since the gate of the infernal king is said to be here.

et tenebrosa palus Acheronte refuso, contingat ire
and the dark marsh from Acheron overflowing, that it may happen to me to go

ad conspectum et ora cari genitoris; doceas
to the sight and countenance of my dear father; do you teach

iter, et pandas sacra ostia. Ego eripui illum his
the way, and open the sacred doors. I snatched him on these

humeris per flammas et mille tela sequentia, que recepi
shoulders through flames and a thousand darts pursuing, and I rescued

ex medio hoste: ille comitatus meum iter,
him from the midst of the foe: he accompanying my journey,

invalidus ferebat omnia maria mecum, atque omnes minas
helpless endured all seas with me, and all the threats

que pelagi que cœli, ultra vires que sortem senectæ.
both of the sea and the sky, beyond the strength and lot of old age.

Quin, idem orans, dabat mandata ut supplex peterem
But, the same entreating, gave orders that humbly I should seek

te, et adirem tua limina. Alma precor miserere
thee, and that I should go to your temple. O kind maid I pray you pity

que nati que patris: namque potes omnia; nec Hecate
both a son and father: for you can do all things; nor did Hecate

nequicquam præfecit te Avernis lucis. Si Orpheus potuit
in vain place you over the Avernian groves. If Orpheus could

arcessere manes conjugis, fretus Threiciâ citharâ que
call back the shade of his wife, trusting to his Thracian harp and

canoris fidibus, si Pollux redemit fratrem alternâ morte, que
tuneful strings, if Pollux redeemed his brother from eternal death, and

it que redit viam toties; quid memorem Thesea; quid magnum
goes and returns the way so often; why shall I mention Theseus; why great

Alciden? et mi genus ab Jove summo. Orabat talibus
Hercules? and my race is from Jove supreme. He prayed in these

dictis, que tenebat aras. Tum vates orsa sic loqui:
words, and held the altars. Then the prophetess began thus to speak:

Tros Anchisiade, sate sanguine Divûm, descensus
O Trojan son of Anchises, descended from the blood of the Gods, the descent

Averni facilis, janua atri Ditis patet noctes atque dies; sed
of Avernus is easy, the gate of gloomy Pluto lies open night and day; but

revocare gradum, que evadere ad superas auras, hoc opus,
to recall our step, and to escape to the lofty air, this is a work,

hic est labor. Pauci quos æquus Jupiter amavit, aut ardens
this is a labour. A few whom friendly Jupiter has loved, or glowing

virtus evexit ad æthera, geniti Dîs potuere.
courage has raised to the skies, descended from Gods could do it.

Sylvæ tenent omnia media, que Cocytus labens
The woods hold all the intermediate ways, and Cocytus gliding

circumfluit atro sinu. Quòd si tantus amor, si
flows around with its black stream. But if there is so great love, if

tanta cupido est menti, bis innare Stygios lacus, bis
so great a desire is in your mind, twice to swim over the Stygian lakes, twice

videre nigra Tartara, et juvat indulgere insano labori,
to behold black Tartarus, and it delights you to indulge the mad labour,

accipe quæ prius peragenda.
receive what first must be done.

Ramus aureus et foliis et lento vimine latet opacâ
A branch golden both in its leaves and slender twig lies hid in the dark

arbore, dictus sacer infernæ Junoni: omnis lucus tegit
tree, declared sacred to infernal Juno: all the grove covers

hunc, et umbræ claudunt obscuris convallibus. Sed non
this, and shades inclose it with dark vales. But it is not

datur subire operta telluris ante quam quis decerpserit
given to enter the dark places of the earth before that any one shall pluck

auricomos fetus arbore. Pulchra Proserpina instituit hoc
the golden fruit from the tree. Beautiful Proserpine has ordained this

suum munus ferri sibi. Primo avulso, alter aureus
her own present to be borne to herself. The first being torn up, another of gold

non deficit, et virga frondescit simili metallo. Ergo
does not fail, and a twig puts forth leaves of like metal. Therefore

vestiga oculis altè, et manu ritè carpe,
search with your eyes high raised, and with your hand in order pluck it,

repertum; namque ipse volens que facilis sequetur, si fata
when found; for willingly and easily will follow, if the fates

vocant te; aliter non poteris vincere ullis viribus, nec
call thee; otherwise you could not overcome it with any strength, nor

convellere duro ferro.
tear it with hard iron.

Præterea corpus amici exanimum jacet tibi, (heu
Besides the body of your friend lifeless lies by you, (alas!

nescis) que incestat totam classem funere, dum petis
you know not) and pollutes all the fleet with his corse, while you seek

consulta, que pendes in nostro limine. Antè refei
the decrees of Heaven, and loiter at my gate. First beat

hunc suis sedibus, et conde sepulcro. Duc nigras
him to his seats, . and bury him in the tomb. Lead out the black

pecudes: ea sunto prima piacula. Sic demum aspicies
flocks: let these be the first offerings. Thus at length you shall behold

Stygios lucos, regna invia vivis. Dixit, que
the Stygian groves, realms impassable to the living. She said, and

obmutuit, ore presso. Æneas, linquens antrum,
was dumb, her mouth being closed. Æneas, leaving the cave,

ingreditur mœsto vultu defixus lumina, que volutat
walks on with sad countenance casting down his eyes, and revolves

cæcos eventus secum animo; cui fidus Achates it
the dark events with himself in his mind; to whom the faithful Achates goes

comes, et paribus curis figit vestigia. Serebant
as a companion, and with equal cares places his footsteps. They treat of

multa inter sese vario sermone; quem exanimum
many things among themselves in varied discourse; what lifeless

socium vates diceret, quod corpus humandum.
companion the prophetess had spoken of, what body was to be buried.

Atque ut illi venêre, vident Misenum in sicco litore perem-
And as they came, they see Misenus on the dry shore destroy-

tum indignâ morte; Misenum Æoliden, quo non
ed by an unworthy death; Misenus the son of Æolus, than whom not

alter præstantior ciere viros ære que accendere
another was more skilled to arouse men by the trumpet and to enkindle

Martem cantu. Hic fuerat comes magni Hectoris, et
war by its sound. He had been a companion of great Hector, and

obibat pugnas circum Hectora, insignis et lituo
he resorted to the battle around Hector, distinguished both by the trumpet

et hastâ. Postquam victor Achilles spoliavit illum vitâ
and spear. After the conqueror Achilles had deprived him of life

fortissimus heros addiderat sese socium Dardanio
this very brave hero had added himself a companion to Trojan

Æneæ, secutus non inferiora. Sed tum forté dum
Æneas, following not inferior arms. But then by chance while

demens personat æquora cavâ conchâ, et cantu
mad he sounded over the waters with his hollow trumpet, and by his song

vocat Divos in certamina, æmulus Triton, si est dignum
he calls the Gods to contest, the jealous Triton, if it is worthy

credere, spumosâ undâ immerserat virum exceptum
to believe, on the foaming wave had plunged the man caught

inter saxa. Ergo omnes fremebant circum magno
among the rocks. Therefore all murmured around him with great

clamore, præcipuè pius Æneas: tum flentes festinant
noise, especially pious Æneas: then weeping they hasten to exe

jussa Sibyllæ, haud mora, que certan
cute the commands of the Sibyl, there is no delay, and they conten

congerere que educere cœlo   aram sepulcri arboribus.
to heap up   and to raise to heaven the altar of the tomb with trees.

Itur in antiquam sylvam, alta stabula ferarum: piceæ
They go into an ancient wood, the deep retreats of wild beasts; the pitch trees

procumbunt: ilex icta securibus sonat; que fraxineæ
fall: the holm struck with axes resounds; and   ashen

trabes, et fissile robur scinditur cuneis: advolvunt ingentes
timbers, and the yielding oak is divided by wedges: they roll   great

ornos montibus. Nec non Æneas primus hortatur
wild ashes from the mountains. . Also   Eneas first   exhorts

socios   inter talia opera, que accingitur paribus armis.
his companions amidst these labours, and is girt   with equal arms.

Atque ipse volutat hæc   cum suo tristi corde, aspectans
And   he revolves these things with his sad heart,   beholding

immensam sylvam, et sic precatur ore: Si ille aureus
the immense wood,   and thus he prays with his mouth: If that golden

ramus arbore nunc ostendat se nobis in tanto nemore!
branch from the tree now shews itself to us in this great grove!

quando vates locuta est omnia verè, heu! nimium
since the prophetess has spoken all things truly, alas! too much so

de   te, O Misene!   Vix fatus erat ea,   cùm
concerning thee, O Misenus! Scarcely had he spoken these things, when

geminæ columbæ fortè venêre volantes cœlo sub ipsa
two _ doves by chance came flying in the sky under the

ora viri, et sedere viridi solo. Tum maximus heros
face of the hero, and sat on the green soil. Then the great hero

agnoscit maternas aves, que lætus precatur: O este duces,
knew his mother's birds, and joyful prays: O be ye guides,

si est qua via que per auras dirigite cursum in lucos,
if there is any way and along the sky direct your course to the groves

ubi dives ramus opacat pinguem humum, que tu,
where the rich branch overshades the fertile ground, and thou.

ô diva parens, ne defice dubiis rebus! Effatus
O divine parent, do not fail me in my doubtful concerns! Having spoken

sic, pressit vestigia, observans quæ signa ferant, quò
thus, he restrains his footsteps, watching what signs they offer, whither

pergant tendere. Illæ pascentes prodire tantum
they attempt to direct their course. They feeding proceed as much

volando, quantum oculi sequentum possent servare
by flying, as the eyes of those pursuing can keep them

acie. Inde ubi venêre ad fauces grave olentis
in their sight Then when they had come to the mouth of noisome

Averni, tollunt se celeres, que lapsæ per liquidum
Avernus, they raise themselves swift, and gliding through the liquid

aëra, sidunt geminæ super arbore optatis sedibus, unde
air, they sit down both upon the tree in their desired seats, whence

discolor aura auri refulsit per ramos. Quale viscum,
the variegated gleam of gold shone through the branches. As the misletoe

quod sua arbos non seminat, solet sylvis, virere novâ
which its own tree does not germinate, used in the woods to flourish with new

fronde brumali frigore, et circumdare teretes truncos
leaves in the wintry cold, and to surround the tapering trunks

croceo fetu; talis erat species auri fondentis
with yellow fruit; such was the appearance of the gold putting forth leaves

opacâ ilice; bractea sic crepitabat leni vento. Ex-
on the shady holm; the tinsel thus rattled with the light wind. Forth-

templo Æneas corripit. que avidus refringit cunctantem, et
with Eneas seized, and greedily breaks it lingering, and

portat sub tecta vatis Sibyllæ. Nec minùs Trojani
bears it to the dwelling of the prophetess the Sibyl. Nevertheless the Trojans

interea flebant Misenum in litore, et ferebant suprema
in the interim mourned Misenus on the shore, and paid their last *offices*

ingrato cineri. Principio struxere ingentem pyram
to his mournful ashes. In the first place they built a great funeral pile

pinguem tædis et secto robore, cui latera intexunt
rich with torches and cut oak, whose sides they interweave

atris frondibus, et ante constituunt ferales cypressos,
with mournful branches, and first they placed funeral cypresses,

que super decorant fulgentibus armis. Pars expediunt
and above they adorn it with shining arms. A part prepare

calidos latices, et ahena undantia flammis; que lavant
warm water, and brazen vessels bubbling from the flames; and they wash

et ungunt corpus frigentis. Gemitus fit: tum reponunt
and anoint · the body *of him* cold. Lamentation is made: then they place

toro membra, defleta; que super conjiciunt purpureas
on a couch his limbs, bewailed; and upon *it* they cast purple

vestes, nota velamina. Pars subiere ingenti pheretro,
dresses, his known clothing. A part support his great bier,

triste ministerium; et aversi tenuere facem subjectam
a sad office; and turning away they held a torch put under

more parentum. Thurea dona congesta
after the manner of their parents. Frankincense gifts collected

cremantur, dapes, crateres fuso olivo. Postquam cineres
are burnt, banquets, goblets of out-poured olive oil. After the ashes

collapsi, et flamma quievit, lavère reliquias et bibulam
had fallen down, and the flame had ceased, they bathe the remains and absorbing

favillam vino; que Chorinæus texit lecta ossa aheno
embers with wine; and Chorinæus covers the collected bones in a brazen

cado. Idem ter circumtulit socios purâ undâ.
cask. Also thrice he went around his companions with pure water

spargens levi rore et ramo felicis olivæ; que
sprinkling *them as* with light dew and branch of the fortunate olive; and

lustravit viros, que dixit novissima verba. At pius Æneas
he purified the men, and uttered the last words. But pious · Eneas

imponit sepulcrum ingenti mole, que sua arma viro,
built a tomb of great size, and *laid* his own arms by the man

que remum, que tubam sub aërio monte, qui nunc
and *his* oar,   and   trumpet beneath an airy mountain, which   now

dicitur Misenus ab illo, que tenet nomen æternum   per
s called Misenus from him, and retains his name   forever   through

secula.   His   actis propere exsequitur præcepta
ages.   These *things* being done hastily   he performs the commands

Sibyllæ. Fuit spelunca alta, que immanis   vasto
of the Sibyl. There was a cave deep, and dreadful with an extended

hiatu, scrupea, tuta nigro lacu que tenebris nemorum;
mouth, stony, protected by a black lake and the darkness of the groves

super quam haud ullæ volantes impunè poterant tendere
over which not any flying creatures in safety were able to direct

iter pennis; talis halitus effundens atris faucibus fereba
their way by wings; such a blast issuing from its black jaws   bore

sese ad supera convexa; unde Graii dixerunt locum
itself to the upper convex sky; whence the Greeks called   the place

nomine Aornon. Hìc sacerdos primùm constituit quatuor
by name Aornon.   Here the priestess first   placed   four

juvencos nigrantes terga, que invergit vina   fronte;
bullocks   black in their backs, and pours out wine on *their* forehead.

et carpens summas setas inter media cornua,   imponit
and plucking the longest hairs between   the horns,   places *them*

sacris ignibus, prima libamina, voce   vocans Hecaten
in the sacred fires, *as* first offerings, with her voice invoking Hecate

potentem cœlo que Erebo. Alii supponunt cultros, que
powerful in heaven and hell.   Others apply   knives,   and

pateris suscipiunt tepidum cruorem.
in bowls receive   the warm blood.

Æneas ipse ense   ferit agnam atri velleris
Æneas   himself with his sword strikes a lamb of black fleece *offering it to*

matri Eumenidum, que magnæ sorori que sterilem
the mother of the furies, and to her great sister (the earth) and a barren

vaccam tibi, Proserpina. Tum inchoat nocturnas aras
heifer to thee, O Proserpine. Then he renews the nightly   altars

Stygio regi; et imponit flammis solida viscera taurorum,
to the Stygian king; and places on the flames the entire entrails of bulls,

que fundens pingue oleum super ardentibus extis. Autem
and pouring out rich oil   upon the burning entrails.   But

ecce sub lumina et ortus primi solis, solum
lo beneath the light and the beams of the rising sun, the ground

mugire sub pedibus, et juga cœpta moveri,
began to groan under their feet, and the mountain tops began to be moved,

que canes visæ ululare per umbram sylvarum, Deâ
and the dogs seem'd to howl through the shade of the woods, the Goddess

adventante. Vates conclamat, O profani procul, procul
approaching. The prophetess exclaimed, ye profane far off,   far off

este, que absistite toto luco que tu   invade
be ye, and withdraw from the whole grove and do you   urge forward

viam quæ eripe ferrum vaginâ;   Æneas nunc
your march, and snatch the sword from the sheath;   O Æneas now

opus animis, nunc firmo pectore. Effata tantum,
there is need for courage, now for a firm breast. Having spoken thus much,

furens immisit se aperto antro. Ille æquat ducem
raging she cast herself into the open cave. He equals his guide

vadentem haud timidis passibus. Dî quibus est
advancing not with fearful steps. Ye Gods to whom is

imperium animarum, silentes umbræ, et Chaos et Phlegethon,
the empire of souls, ye silent shades, and Chaos and Phlegethon,

loca latè silentia nocte, sit fas mihi loqui audita;
places far around silent by night, let it be lawful for me to speak *things* heard;

sit vestro numine pandere res mersas altâ
may it *be allowed* by your authority to lay open things plunged in the deep

terrâ et caligine. Ibant obscuri per umbram sub solâ
earth and darkness. They went dark through the shade beneath the lonely

nocte, que per vacuas domos Ditis et inania regna; quale
night, and through the vacant dwellings of Pluto and empty kingdoms; such

iter est in sylvis per incertam lunam sub malignâ luce
a way is in the woods by the uncertain moon under a malignant light

ubi Jupiter condidit cœlum umbrâ et atra nox abstulit
when Jupiter has hid the sky in shade and black night has taken away

colorem rebus. Ante ipsum vestibulum que in primis
colour from *all* things. Before the porch and in the first

faucibus Orci, Luctus et ultrices Curæ posuere cubilia;
jaws of Hell, Grief and revengeful cares have placed their couches;

que pallentes Morbi habitant, que tristis Senectus et Metus.
and pale diseases dwell, and sad · old age and fear,

et malesuada Fames, et turpis Egestas formæ terribiles
and ill advising hunger, and degrading poverty forms terrible

visu; que Lethum que Labor; tum Sopor consanguineus
to be seen; and death and labour; then sleep related

Lethi, et mala Gaudia mentis, que in limine adverso
to death and the wicked joys of the mind, and in the threshold opposite

mortiferum Bellum, que ferrei thalami Eumenidum,
death bearing war, and the iron bed chambers of the furies,

et demens Discordia innexa vipereum crinem cruentis
and mad Discord binding her viperous hair with bloody

vittis. In medio ingens ulmus opaca pandit ramos
fillets. In the midst a great elm dark opens its branches

que annosa brachia, quam sedem vulgò ferunt vana
and aged arms, which seat commonly they say vain

Somnia tenere, que hærent sub omnibus foliis, que
dreams possess, and remain under all the leaves, and

præterea multa monstra variarum ferarum; Centauri
besides many prodigies of various wild beasts; Centaurs

stabulant in foribus, que biformes Scyllæ, et Briareus
stable in the gates, and two-formed Scylla, and Briareus

centumgeminus, ac bellua Lernæ stridens horrendùm
having an hundred hands, and the monster of Lerna hissing dreadfully

que Chimæra armata flammis; Gorgones que Harpyiæ et
and Chimera armed with fires: Gorgons and Harpies and

forma umbræ tricorporis. Hìc Æneas trepidus
the form of the shade having three bodies. Here Æneas trembling

subitâ formidine corripit ferrum que offert strictam aciem
with sudden fear seized his sword and offers its drawn . point

venientibus: et irruat et frustra diverberet umbras
to them approaching: and rushes on and in vain had beaten the shades

ferro, ni docta comes admoneat tenues
with his sword, unless his skilful companion admonished him that the light

vitas volitare sine corpore sub cavâ imagine formæ,
ghosts fly about without a body under the empty image of a form.

Hinc via, quæ fert ad undas Tartarei Acherontis; hìc
Hence is the way, which leads to the waves of Tartarean Acheron; here

gurges turbidus cœno que vastâ voragine æstuat, atque
a gulf turbid with mud and a great whirlpool boils, and

eructat omnem arenam Cocyto. Portitor Charon horrendus
throws out all the sand into Cocytus. The ferryman Charon horrid

terribili squalore servat has aquas et flumina, cui plurima
with terrible filth guards these waters and the rivers, whose abundant

canities jacet inculta mento; lumina flammæ stant; sordidus
gray hair lies neglected on his chin; his eyes of flame stand out; a filthy

amictus nodo dependet ex humeris. Ipse subigit ratem
dress · in a knot hangs from his shoulders. He guides the boat

conto, que ministrat velis, et subvectat corpora
with a pole, and supplies it with sails, and carries over the bodies

ferrugineâ cymbâ, jam senior; sed cruda que viridis senectus
in an iron coloured boat, now old; but fresh and green old age

Deo. Huc omnis turba effusa ruebat ad ripas;
belong to the God. Hither all the crowd pouring forth rushed to the banks;

matres atque viri, que corpora magnanimûm herōum defuncta
mothers and men, and bodies of high-minded heroes deprived

vitâ, pueri que innuptæ puellæ, que juvenes impositi
of life, boys and unmarried maids, and youths placed

rogis ante ora parentum; quàm multa folia lapsa
on funeral piles before the faces of their parents; as many leaves withered

cadunt in sylvis primo frigore autumni, aut quàm multæ
fall in the woods in the first cold of autumn, or as many

aves glomerantur ab alto gurgite, ubi frigidus annus
birds gather from the deep sea, when the cold year

fugat trans pontum, et immittit apricis terris. Stabant
drives them across the sea, and sends them to sunny lands. They stood

orantes transmittere cursum primi, que tendebant manus
entreating to pass over the course first, and stretched out their hands

amore ulterioris ripæ; sed tristis navita nunc accipit
with the love of the farther bank: but the sad boatman now receives

hos, nunc illos: ast   arcet   alios longè summotos   arenâ.
those, now   those: but he drives away others afar off removed from the sand.

Æneas ait (enim   miratus que motus tumultu) O virgo,
Æneas says (for   he wondered at and was moved by the tumult) O   maid,

dic quid vult concursus ad amnem? ve quid   animæ
say what means this crowd   at the river? or what   do these souls

petunt?   ve quo discrimine   hæ   linquunt ripas,   illæ
seek?   or by what difference   do these leave   the banks, those

remis verrunt livida vada?   Longæva sacerdos breviter
with oars sweep   the blue flood?   The aged   priestess   shortly

fata est olli sic: Generate   Anchisâ certissima   proles
addressed him thus: O descended from Anchises the most sure   offspring

Deûm, vides alta stagna Cocyti, que Stygiam paludem,
of the Gods, you see the deep pools of Cocytus. and the Stygian   marsh,

cujus numen Dî timent jurare et fallere. Omnis hæc
whose divinity the Gods fear to swear by and to deceive. All   this

turba quam cernis est inops que inhumata, ille portitor
crowd which you see is destitute and unburied,   the   ferryman

Charon; hi quos unda vehit, sunt sepulti. Nec datur
Charon;   those whom the wave bears, are   buried.   Nor is it allowed

transportare   horrendas ripas, nec rauca fluenta,
to transport them over the dreadful banks, nor hoarse flowing streams,

priusquam ossa quiêrunt sedibus.   Errant centum
before   their bones have rested in their seats. They wander an hundred

annos, que volitant circum hæc litora: tum demum admissi
years,   and   fly   around   these shores: then at length admitted

revisunt stagna exoptata.   Satus Anchisâ constitit, et
they revisit the pools beloved.   He descended from Anchises stopped,   and

pressit vestigia, putans multa que animo miseratus
restrained his footsteps, thinking many things and in his mind   pitying

iniquam sortem. Ibi cernit mœstos,   et   carentes
their unequal lot.   There he sees those mournful, and   deprived

honore mortis, Leucaspim, et Orontem ductorem Lyciæ
of the honour of death. Leucaspis,   and Orontes   the leader of the Lycian

classis; quos   simul vectos â Trojâ per ventosa æquora,
fleet;   whom at the same time driven from Troy through the windy   seas,

auster obruit   aquâ involvens que navem   que
the south wind overwhelmed in the water overturning both   ship   and

viros. Ecce gubernator Palinurus agebat sese, qui nuper
men.   Lo   the pilot   Palinurus introduced himself, who lately

in Libyco cursu, dum servat sidera exciderat   puppi,
in the Libyan course, while he observes the stars had fallen from the ship,

effusus in mediis undis. Ubi vix cognovit hunc mœstum
plunged in the midst of the waves. When scarcely he knew him   mournful

in multâ umbrâ, prior alloquitur sic: Palinure
in the extended shade.   first he addresses him thus·   O Palinurus

quis Deorum eripuit te nobis, que mersit sub
what one of the Gods has snatched thee from us, and plunged you beneath

medio æquore? age dic.
the midst of the sea? come say.

Namque Apollo haud antè repertus mihi fallax, hoc uno
For Apollo not heretofore found by me deceitful, by this only

responso delusit animum; qui canebat te fore
answer deluded my mind; who prophesied that you should be

incolumem ponto, que venturum Ausonios fines:
unhurt on the sea, and should come to the Ausonian boundaries:

en est hæc fides promissa? Autem ille Dux
lo is this the faith promised to me? But he said O Leader

Anchisiade neque cortina Phœbi fefellit te, nec Deus
son of Anchises neither the oracle of Apollo has deceived thee, nor has a God

mersit me æquore; namque præcipitans traxi mecum
plunged me in the sea; for falling headlong I drew with me

gubernaclum fortè revulsum multâ vi cui datus
the helm by chance torn by much violence to which being given

custos hærebam que regebam cursus. Juro aspera
as keeper I clung and ruled my course. I swear by the stormy

maria me non cepisse ullum tantum timorem pro me,
seas that I did not conceive any so great fear for myself,

quàm ne tua navis, spoliata armis, excussa magistro
as lest your ship, deprived of her tackle, dispossessed of her master

deficerit, tantis undis surgentibus, Violentus Notus
should sink, while so great waves were rising. The violent south wind

aquâ vexit me tres hibernas noctes per immensa
on the water bore me three wintery nights through the extended

æquora: vix quarto lumine prospexi Italiam,
seas: scarcely on the fourth day I beheld Italy,

sublimis ab summâ undâ. Paulatim adnabam terrræ, et
nigh from the lofty wave. By degrees I swam to the land, and

jam tenebam tuta ni crudelis gens ferro invassiset
now I held a safe place had not a cruel people with the sword attacked me

gravatum cum madidâ veste, que prensantem uncis
oppress'd with my wet dress, and grasping with crooked

manibus aspera capita montis, que ignara
hands the rough tops of the mountain and they ignorant

putasset me prædam. Nunc fluctus habet me, que venti
thought me plunder. Now the wave has me, and the winds

versant in litore. Quòd oro te per jucundum lumen
toss me on the shore. But I pray thee by the pleasant light

cœli et auras, per genitorem per spem surgentis Iuli,
of heaven and the air, by my father by the hope of the rising Iulus,

eripe me his malis, invicte; aut tu
snatch me from these misfortunes, O unconquered man; or do you

injice terram mihi namque potes, que require Velinos
cast earth on me for you can, and seek the Veline

portus aut, si est qua via si Diva creatrix ostendit
harbours or,   if there is any way if your divine mother has shewn

quam tibi, enim neque credo paras innare tanta
any   to you, for neither do I believe you prepare to swim over so great

flumina que Stygian paludem sine numine Divûm,
rivers   and the Stygian marsh without the will of the Gods,

tu da dextram misero et tolle me tecum per
do you give your right hand to me wretched and bear me with you through

undas, ut saltem quiescam placidis sedibus in morte.
the waves, that also I may rest in peaceful seats in death.

Fatus erat talia, cum vates cœpit
He had spoken these words, when the prophetess began

talia. O Palinure, unde tibi hæc tam dira
to speak these in reply. O Palinurus, · whence to you is this so dread

cupido? tu inhumatus aspicies Stygias aquas que
desire? will you unburied behold the Stygian waters and

severum amnem Eumenidum? ve injussus adibis
the cruel river of the Furies? or without orders will you approach

ripam. Desine sperare fata Deûm flecti precando:
the bank. Cease to hope the fates of the Gods are influenced by praying:

sed memor cape dicta solatia duri casus.
but mindful take these words the consolation of your hard misfortune.

Nam finitimi acti cœlestibus prodigiis longè que
For the neighbouring people driven by heavenly prodigies far and

latè piabunt ossa per urbes, et statuent tumulum
wide shall expiate your bones through the cities, and shall build a tomb

et mittent solemnia tumulo; que locus habebit
and shall present anniversary rites on the tomb; and the place shall possess

æternum nomen Palinuri. His dictis curæ
the eternal name of Palinurus. With these words his cares

emotæ, que dolor parumper pulsus tristi corde:
were removed, and grief by degrees was banished from his sad heart.

gaudet terrâ cognomine. Ergo peragunt
he rejoices in the land with his own name. Therefore they complete

inceptum iter, que propinquant fluvio: quos ut navita
their begun journey, and approach the river: whom as the boatman

jam inde ab Stygiâ undâ prospéxit ire per tacitum
now even from the Stygian wave had seen to advance through the silent

nemus, que advertere pedem ripæ, sic prior
grove, and to turn their foot to the bank, thus first

aggreditur dictis, atque ultro increpat;
he addresses them in these words, and voluntarily chides them.

Quisquis es, qui tendis ad nostra flumina armatus,
Whoever you are, who advance to our streams armed,

age fare, quid venias; et jam istinc comprime gressum.
come say, why do you come; and now from hence restrain your step.

Hic est locus umbrarum, Somni, que soporæ Noctis:
This is the place of shades, of sleep, and of drowsy night·

nefas vectare viva corpora Stygiâ carinâ. Nec vero
it is a crime to bear living bodies in the Stygian boat. Nor indeed

sum lætatus me lacu accepisse Alciden euntem,
am I rejoiced that I on the lake received Hercules *hither* coming,

nec Thesea, que Pirithoum, quanquam essent geniti
nor Theseus, and Pirithous, although they were descended from

Dîs, atque invicti viribus. Ille manu petivit Tartareum
Gods, and invincible in strength. He with his hand sought the Tartarean

custodem in vincla, que traxit trementem solio
keeper *and bound him* in chains, and dragged him trembling from the throne

Regis ipsius; hi adorti deducere dominam
of the king himself; these attempted to carry off the mistress

thalamo Ditis. Contra quæ Amphrysia
from the marriage chamber of Pluto. In reply to which *words* the Amphyrsian

vates breviter fata est. Nullæ tales insidiæ hîc; absiste
prophetess briefly spoke. No such snares *are* here; cease

moveri, nec tela ferunt vim: licet ingens
to be moved, nor do these weapons bear violence: it is allowed that the great

janitor ætenùm latrans antro terreat exsangues
porter forever barking in the cave may frighten off bloodless

umbras; ut casta Proserpina servet limen patrui.
shades; that chaste Proserpine may preserve the threshold of her uncle.

Troius Æneas, insignis pietate et armis, descendit ad
Trojan Æneas, distinguished for piety and arms, descends to

genitorem, ad imas umbras Erebi. Si nulla imago
his father, to the deepest shades of hell. If no image

tantæ pietatis movet te, at agnoscas hunc ramum
of such distinguished piety moves yôu, yet may you know this branch

(aperit ramum qui latebat sub veste.) Tum corda
(she displays the branch which lay hid beneath her dress.) Then his heart

residunt ex tumidâ irâ; nec plura his.
ceased from swelling anger; nor *were spoken* more words *than* these.

Ille, admirans venerabile donum fatalis virgæ, visum
He, admiring the venerable gift of the fatal rod, seen

post longo tempore, advertit cæruleam puppim, que
after a long time, turns his azure boat, and

propinquat ripæ. Inde deturbat alias animas, quæ sedebant
draws near to the bank. Then he drives off other souls, which sat

per longa juga, que laxat foros. Simul accipit
along the extended seats, and opens the hatches. At the same time he receives

ingentem Ænean alveo. Sutilis cymba gemuit sub
the great Æneas in the boat. The patched boat groaned under

pondere, et rimosa accepit multam paludem.
the weight, and full of cracks receives much *water* from the lake.

Tandem exponit que vatem que virum incolumes trans
At length he lands both the prophetess and the hero unharmed across

fluvium in informi limo, que glaucâ ulvâ. Ingens
the river upon the shapeless slime, and green sedge. Huge

Ceroerus personat hæc regna trifauci latratu,
Cerberus sounds through these realms with his triple jawed barking,

recubans immanis in adverso antro: cui vates
reclining immense in the opposite cave: to whom the prophetess

videns colla jam horrere colubris, objicit offam
beholding his neck now *begin* to bristle with snakes, throws a cake

soporatam melle et medicatis frugibus. Ille, pandens tria
rendered sleepy by honey and medicated fruits. He, opening his triple

guttura, rabidâ fame, corripit objectam, atque fusus
throat, with mad hunger snatches *it* thrown, and extended

humi, resolvit immania terga, que extenditur
on the ground, relaxes his enormous back, and is spread

ingens toto antro. Æneas occupat aditum, custode
huge through the whole cave. Æneas seizes the entrance, the guard

sepulto, que celer evadit ripam irremeabilis
being buried *in sleep*, and swift escapes from the bank of the never-returning

undæ. Continuò voces auditæ, et ingens vagitus, que
wave. Immediately voices are heard, and a great wailing, and

animæ infantum flentes in primo limine; quos exsortes
the souls of infants weeping in the first entrance; whom deprived

dulcis vitæ, et raptos ab ubere, atra dies abstulit, et
of sweet life, and snatched from the breast, black time bore away, and

mersit acerbo funere: juxta hos damnati mortis falso
plunged in bitter death: near to these those condemned to death for a false

crimine. Nec verò hæ sedes datæ sine sorte, sine
crime. Nor indeed are these seats given without lot, without

judice. Quæsitor Minos movet urnam: ille que vocat
a judge. The Inquisitor Minos moves the urn: he likewise convokes

concilium silentum, que discit vitas et crimina. Deinde
a council of silent shades, and learns their lives and their crimes. Then

mœsti, qui insontes peperere lethum
those mournful shades, who guiltless *of other crimes* procured death

sibi manu, que perosi lucem projecere animas,
to themselves by their hand, and hating the light threw away their lives,

tenent proxima loca.
hold the nearest places.

Quàm vellent nunc perferre et pauperiem et duros
How would they now endure both poverty and hard

labores in alto æthere! Fata obstant, que inamabilis
labours in the upper region! The fates oppose, and the dismal

palus alligat tristi undâ, et Styx novies interfusa
marsh binds them with its sad wave, and the Styx nine times flowing between

coercet. Nec procul hinc monstrantur fusi in omnem
constrains *them*. Not far from this are shewn scattered over every

partem lugentes campi, sic dicunt illos nomine. Hìc
part the mournful plains, thus they call them by name. Here

secreti calles celant, et myrtea sylva circum tegit quos
secret paths conceal, and a myrtle grove around covers *those* whom

durus amor peredit crudeli tabe: curæ non relinquunt in
cruel love corrodes by cruel consumption: cares do not leave *them* in

morte ipsâ. Cernit Phædram que Procrin his locis, que
death itself. He sees Phædra and Procris in these places, and

mœstam Eriphylen monstrantem vulnera crudelis nati,
mournful Eriphyle pointing out the wounds of her cruel son

que Evadnen, et Pasiphæn: Laodamia it comes his;
and Evadne, and Pasiphæa: Laodamia goes a companion to these·

Cæneus, quondam juvenis, nunc femina, et rursus revoluta
Cæneus, formerly a boy, now a woman, and again changed back

fato in veterem figuram. Inter quas Phœnissa Dido,
by fate into his ancient figure. Among whom Phœnician Dido,

recens a vulnere, errabat in magnâ sylvâ; juxta quam
fresh from her wound, wandered in a great grove; near to whom

ut primùm Troius heros stetit, que agnovit per obscuram
as first the Trojan hero stood, and knew *her* through the dark

umbram (qualem qui aut videt aut putat vidisse lunam
shade (such as one who either sees or thinks he has seen the moon

surgere per nubila primo mense,) demisit lacrymas,
to arise through the clouds in the first of the month,) he shed tears

que affatus est dulci amore: Infelix Dido! ergo verus
and addressed her with sweet love: Wretched Dido! therefore a true

nuncius venerat mihi extinctam, que ferro
message had come to me *that you* had been killed, and by the sword

secutam extrema?. Heu! fui causa funeris tibi!
you had attained the end *of life*? Alas! I have been the cause of death to you!

juro per sidera, per Superos, et si est qua fides
I swear by the stars, by the Gods above, and if there is any faith

sub imâ tellure, invitus cessi de tuo litore,
beneath the lowest earth, *that*, unwilling I withdrew from your shore,

regina. Sed jussa Deûm quæ nunc cogunt ire
O queen. But the commands of the Gods which now compel *me* to go

per has umbras, per loca senta situ, que profundum
through these shades, through places overrun by filth, and *through* deep

noctem, egere me suis imperiis; nec quivi credere me
night, have forced me by their commands; nor could I believe that I

ferre hunc tantum dolorem tibi discessu. Siste gradum
brought this so great grief to you by my departure. Restrain your step

que ne subtrahe te nostro aspectu. Quem fugis?
and do not withdraw yourself from my sight. Whom do you fly?

hoc est extremum quod alloquor te fato. Æneas
this is the last time which I address you *permitted* by fate. Æneas

lenibat animum ardentem et tuentem torva, talibus
soothed her mind burning with *rage* and looking sternly, with these

dictis, que ciebat lacrymas. Illa, aversa, tenebat
words, and he excited *his own* tears. She, turning away, held

oculos fixos solo; nec magis movetur vultum
her eyes fastened on the ground; nor more is she moved in her countenance

incepto sermone, quàm si stet dura silex aut
by his begun discourse, than if he should stand a firm flint or

Marpesia cautes. Tandem proripuit sese atque inimica
Marpesian cliff. At length she hurries herself away and hostile

fugit in umbriferum nemus, ubi pristinus conjux
flies into the shady grove, where her former husband

Sichæus respondet illi curis, que æquat amorem.
Sicheus responds to her by his cares, and equals her love.

Nec minus Æneas, percussus iniquo casu,
Nevertheless Æneas, struck by her unjust misfortune

prosequitur longè lacrymans, et miseratur euntem. Inde
pursues her afar weeping, and pities her departing. Then

molitur datum iter; que jam tenebant ultima arva,
he continues the appointed way; and now they had reached the remotest fields,

quæ secreti, clari bello frequentant. Hìc Tydeus,
which being retired, men distinguished in war resort to. Here Tydeus

hìc Parthenopæus inclytus armis, et imago
appears to him here Parthenopæus renowned in arms, and the image

pallentis Adrasti occurrit illi. Hìc Dardanidæ multum
of pale Adrastus meets him. Here the Trojans much

fleti ad superos, que caduci bello; quos omnes,
lamented among the living, and those falling in war; whom all,

ille cernens longo ordine, ingemuit; que Glaucum que
he beholding in long array, groans: and Glaucum and

Medonta, que Thersilochum, tres Antenoridas que
Medon, and Thersilochus, the three sons of Antenor and

Polybœten, sacrum Cereri, que Idæum, etiam tenentem
Polybetes, sacred to Ceres, and Idæus, also holding

currus, etiam arma. Animæ circumstant frequentes
his chariot, also his arms. Souls stand around in great numbers

dextrâ que lævâ. Nec est satis vidisse semel:
on the right and on the left. Nor is it enough to have seen him once:

juvat usque morari et conferre gradum, et
it delights them for a long time to delay him and to accompany his step, and

poscere causas veniendi. At proceres Danaûm, que
to demand the causes of his coming. But the leaders of the Greeks, and

Agamemnoniæ phalanges, ut vidêre virum, que fulgentia
Agamemnon's battalions, as they beheld the hero, and his glittering

arma per umbras, trepidare ingenti metu; pars
arms through the shades, they began to tremble with great fear a part

vertere terga, ceu quondam petiêre rates; pars tollere
to turn their backs, as formerly they sought the ships; a part to raise

exiguam vocem, inceptus clamor frustratur hiantes.
their slender voice, the incipient cry deceives them gasping.

Atque hìc vidit Deiphobum Priamiden laniatum toto
And here he beheld Deiphobus, the son of Priam, torn in his whole

corpore, et crudeliter laceratum ora; ora que ambâs
body, and cruelly mangled in his face; his face and both

manus, que tempora populata auribus raptis, et nares
his hands, and his temples lacerated his ears torn off, and his nostrils

truncas inhonesto vulnere. Adeo vix agnovit him
mutilated by a disgraceful wound. Thus scarcely did he know him

pavitantem et tegentem dira supplicia, et ultro
trembling and concealing his dreadful tortures; and forthwith

compellat notis vocibus: Deiphobe armipotens,
he addresses him with his well-known words: O Deiphobus powerful in arms,

genus ab alto sanguine Teucri, quis optavit sumere
whose descent is from the ennobled blood of Teucer, who has desired to take

tam crudeles pœnas, cui licuit tantum
such cruel punishments, to whom has it been allowed to exercise so great

de te? Fama tulit mihi, te, supremâ nocte,
cruelty on you? Fame brought to me, that you, on the last night,

fessum vastâ cæde Pelasgûm, procubuisse super
wearied with great destruction of the Greeks, had fallen upon

acervum confusæ stragis. Tunc egomet constitui inanem
a heap of confused slaughter. Then I myself built an empty

tumulum in Rhœteo litore, et ter vocavi Manes
tomb on the Rhœtian shore, and thrice I called upon your remains

magnâ voce. Nomen et arma servant locum. Nequivi
with a great voice. Your name and arms preserve the place. I could not

conspicere te, amice, et, decedens, ponere patriâ terrâ.
behold you, O friend, and, departing, lay you in your native earth

Atque hìc Priamides: O amice, nihil relictum tibi.
And here the son of Priam said: O friend, nothing was left undone by you

solvisti omnia Deiphobo, et umbris funeris. Sed
you have paid every respect to Deiphobus, and to the shade of his corpse. But

mea fata, et exitiale scelus Lacænæ mersere me
my own fates, and the deadly crime of Lacedemonian Helen have plunged me

his malis: illa reliquit hæc monumenta. Namque
in these misfortunes: she has left these monuments of herself For

novisti ut egerimus supremam noctem inter falsa gaudia,
you know that we passed the last night amidst false joys,

et est necesse nimium meminisse cum fatalis equus venit
and it is necessary too well remember when the fatal horse came

saltu super ardua Pergama, et gravis attulit armatum
with a bound, over our high citadel, and teeming brought an armed

peditem alvo. Illa simulans chorum, ducebat
foot-soldiery in its womb. She feigning a dance, led out

Phrygias evantes circum orgia: ipsa media tenebat
the Phrygian women howling around their orgies: she in the midst held out

ingentem flammam, et vocabat Danaos ex summâ arce.
a great torch, and called to the Greeks from the high tower.

Tum infelix thalamus habuit me confectum curis que
Then my unhappy marriage chamber held me worn down by cares and

gravatum somno, que dulcis et alta quies, que simillima
oppressed by sleep, and sweet and deep slumber and most like

placidæ morti, pressit jacentem. Interea   egregia
to peaceful death, restrained *me* lying.   In the meantime   my excellent

conjux emovet omnia arma   tectis,   et   subduxerat
wife   removed   all   arms from the palace and had withdrawn

fidum   ensem capiti: vocat Menelaum intra tecta, et
my faithful sword from my head: she invites Menelaus within the palace, and

pandit limina, scilicit sperans id fore magnum munus
opens   the gates, truly hoping that would be a great   favour

amanti, et sic famam veterum malorum posse extingui.
to a lover, and thus the fame of her former crimes   might be   destroyed

Quid moror? irrumpunt   thalamo.   Æolides,
Why do I delay? they break into the marriage chamber.   The son of Eolus,

nortator scelerum, additur comes   unà.   Dî
he adviser of crimes, is added as a companion together *with them.* Ye Gods

instaurate talia   Graiis,   si reposco   pœnas
repay   these *atrocities* to the Greeks, if I demand   punishment

pio   ore.
with a pious mouth.

Sed age, fare vicissim, qui casus   attulerint te vivum.
But come, speak in turn, what misfortunes have brought you   alive.

Ne   venis   actus   erroribus   pelagi,   an
Whether do you come driven on by the wanderings of the sea,   or

monitu   Divûm? an quæ fortuna fatigat te   ut
by the admonition of the Gods? or what fortune urges you that you

adires   tristes domos sine sole,   turbida loca.
should approach the sad dwellings without a sun, *these* disturbed places.

Hac   vice   sermonum   Aurora roseis quadrigis
In this interchange of conversation the sun in his roseate   chario

jam trajecerat medium   axem   æthereo cursu; et
now   had passed over the middle heaven in his etherial course; and

fors   traherent   omne tempus datum per talia
perhaps they would have spent all the time allowed in such *discourse*

sed Sibylla   comes admonuit que breviter affata est
but   the Sybil his companion admonished and shortly   addressed

Ænea, nox ruit   nos ducimus horas   flendo.
him thus. O Æneas, night rushes on *and* we   spend   the hours in weeping.

Hìc est locus ubi via findit se in ambas partes:
Here is the place where the way separates itself into two   parts:

dextera quæ tendit sub mœnia magni Ditis; hâc   iter
the right which leads beneath the walls of great Pluto; by this *is* the way

nobis Elysium; at læva exercet pœnas malorum et
for us to Elysium; but the left exercises the punishment of the wicked and

mittit   ad impia Tartara.   Contrà   Deiphobus
sends *them* to wicked Tartarus.   On the other hand   Deiphobus *said*

Magna sacerdos, ne sævi; discedam,   explebc
O great   Priestess, do not be angry; I will depart,   I will fill up

numerum   que   reddar   tenebris. I nostrun
the number *of ghosts* and I shall be restored to darkness. Go   on

decus, i, utere melioribus fatis. Effatus tantum, et in
glory, go, be accustomed to better fates. He spoke thus much, and on

verbo torsit vestiga. Æneas respicit subitò, et
the word he turn'd back his footsteps. Eneas looks back suddenly, and

sub rupe sinistrâ videt lata mœnia circumdata triplici
beneath a rock on the left beholds the ample ramparts surrounded by a triple

muro, quæ rapidus amnis Tartareus Phlegethon ambit
wall, which the swift river Tartarean Phlegethon surrounds

torrentibus flammis, que torquet sonantia saxa. Ingens
with rapid flames, and hurls along the resounding rocks. A great

porta adversa que columnæ solido adamante, ut nulla
gate is opposite and columns of solid adamant, so that no

vis virûm non cœlicolæ ipsi valeant exscindere
strength of men nor the Gods themselves are able to destroy them

ferro. Ferrea turris stat ad auras; que Tisiphone
with the sword. An iron tower stands raised high in the air; and Tisiphone

sedens succincta cruentâ pallâ, exsomnis servat
sitting girded with a bloody cloak, sleepless preserves

vestibulum que noctes que dies. Gemitus exaudiri hinc,
the porch both night and day. Groans are heard from hence,

et sæva verbera sonare; tum stridor ferri, que tractæ
and cruel blows resound; then the rattling of steel, and drawn

catenæ. Æneas constitit, que exterritus hausit strepitum.
chains. Æneas stopt, and frightened listened to the noise.

O virgo, effare; quæ facies scelerum ve quibus
O maid, speak; what forms of crimes are these or with what

pœnis urgentur? quis tantus plangor ad
punishment are they chastised? what is this great wailing which rises to

auras? Tum vates orsa loqui sic: Inclyte dux
the skies? Then the prophetess began to speak thus: Renowned leader

Teucrûm, fas nulli casto insistere sceleratum
of the Trojans, it is right for no chaste person to tread the accursed

limen; sed Hecate ipsa cum præfecit me Avernis
threshold; but Hecate herself when she placed me over the Avernian

lucis, docuit pœnas Deûm, que duxit per
groves, taught me the punishment of the Gods, and led me through

omnia. Gnosius Rhadamanthus habet hæc durissima
every division. Gnossian Rhadamanthus possesses these most cruel

regna que audit que castigat dolos; que subigit fateri
kingdoms and hears and chastises frauds; and compels them to confess

quæ piacula commissa quis apud superos distulit
what crimes committed each one among the regions above had put off

in seram mortem, lætatus inani furto.
unrepented to late death, exulting in the vain deceit.

Continuò Tisiphone ultrix accincta flagello, quatit
Immediately Tisiphone avenging girded with a whip, shakes it over

sontes insultans, que intentans torvos angues
the guilty insulting them, and stretching out her direful snakes.

sinistrâ   vocat   sæva   agmina   sororum.   Tum demum
in her left hand she calls the cruel bands   of her sister *Furies*. Then   at length

sacræ   portæ   stridentes   horrisono   cardine, panduntur
the sacred gates   creaking   on their horrid sounding   hinge,   are thrown open.

Cernis,   qualis   custodia   sedeat   vestibulo?   quæ   facies   servet
You see,   what   a guard   sits   in the porch?   what a form   guards

limina?   Sævior   Hydra,   immanis quinquaginta   atris
the gates?   A more dreaded Hydra,   loathsome   with fifty   black

hiatibus,   habet   sedem   intus.   Tum Tartarus   ipse   patet
mouths,   holds   her seat   within.   Then   Tartarus   itself lies open

bis tantum in præceps, que tendit sub   umbras,   quantus
twice as much   in its descent,   and extends beneath the shades,   as much as

suspectus ad   ætherium Olympum Cœli.   Hìc   antiquum
its ascent   *is* to the celestial   height   of heaven.   Here   the ancient

genus Terræ,   Titania   pubes,   dejecti   fulmine,
race   of the earth, the Titanian youth,   hurled down   by a thunderbolt,

volvuntur in imo fundo.   Hìc vidi et   geminos
are overwhelmed in   the lowest abyss.   Here I beheld also   the two sons

Aloidas, immania corpora, qui aggressi rescindere magnum
of Aloeus,   those huge   bodies,   who attempted   to tear down   the ample

cœlum   manibus, que detrudere Jovem superis   regnis.
sky   with their hands, and   to hurl   Jupiter from his exalted kingdoms.

Vidi   et   Salmonea   dantem   crudeles   pœnas,   dum
I saw   likewise Salmoneus   undergoing   cruel   punishments,   while

imitatur flammas Jovis et sonitus Olympi.   Hic invectus
he imitates the flames of Jupiter and the sounds of Olympus.   He   borne on

quatuor equis, et quassans lampada, ibat ovans   per populos
by four   horses, and shaking   a torch,   went shouting through the people

Graiûm,   que   per   urbem mediæ Elidis, que poscebat
of the Greeks,   and   through   the city   of the midst of Elis,   and   demanded

honorem   Divûm   sibi;   demens! qui   simulaverat
the honour   of the Gods to himself;   mad *man!*   who   had counterfeited

nimbos, et fulmen non imitabile,   ære et   cursu
the storms, and   thunder   not to be imitated, by brass   and   the course

cornipedum equorum.   At omnipotens pater   contorsit
of the horn-footed   horses.   But the omnipotent father   hurled

elum inter densa nubila (ille   non   faces,   nec lumina
his dart among the thick clouds   (he   did not *hurl* firebrands,   nor   lights

umea   tædis) que adegit præcipitem immani   turbine.
smoking from torches) and drove *him*   headlong   with a dreadful whirlwind.

Et nec non   erat   cernere Tityon, alumnum omniparentis
And   also   there was to be seen   Tityon,   the foster son of the all-producing

erræ, cui corpus porrigitur per novem tota jugera; que
earth,   whose body   is extended   over   nine   whole acres;   and

immanis vultur tundens immortale jecur, que   viscera
a huge   vulture   beating   his immortal liver,   and   his entrails

fecunda   pœnis   adunco rostro, que   rimatur
fruitful   in punishments, with her hooked beak   and   she searches]

epulis, que habitat sub alto pectore; nec ulla requies
for her food, and dwells beneath his deep breast; nor is any rest

datur fibris renatis. Quid memorem Lapithas,
given to nis fibres growing afresh. Why should I mention the Lapithæ,

Ixiona, que Pirithoum, super quos atra silex jam, jam
Ixion, and Perithous, over whom a black flint now, now

lapsura, que assimilis cadenti imminet. Aurea fulcra
about to fall, and like to one falling overhangs. Golden pillars

lucent altis genialibus toris, que epulæ paratæ ante
shine to the high genial couches, and feasts prepared before

ora regifico luxu; maxima Furiarum accubat juxtà, et
their faces with royal luxury; the greatest of the Furies sits near by, and

prohibet contingere mensas manibus, que exsurgit
forbids them to touch the tables with their hands, and she rises

attollens facem atque intonat ore.
uplifting her torch, and thunders with her mouth.

Hìc quibus fratres invisi dum vita manebat, ve
Here are those by whom brothers are hated while life remained, or

parens pulsatus, et fraus innexa clienti; aut qui
a parent was beaten, and fraud had been contrived against a client; or who

soli incubuere divitiis repertis, nec posuere partem suis;
alone brooded over wealth discovered, nor laid by a part for their friends,

quæ est maxima turba: que qui cæsi ob adulterium; que
which is the greatest crowd: and who were killed for adultery; and

qui secuti impia arma, nec veriti fallere dextras
who had followed impious arms, nor did they fear to violate the faith

dominorum; inclusi expectant pœnam. Ne quære
pledged to their masters; shut up they await their punishment. Do not ask

doceri quam pœnam, aut quæ forma ve fortuna mersit
to be taught what punishment, or what form or fortune overwhelmed

viros. Alii volvunt ingens saxum, pendent districti
the men. Others roll a great rock, they hang stretched

radiis rotarum. Infelix Theseus sedet, que sedebit
on the spokes of wheels. Wretched Theseus sits, and will sit

æternûm; que miserrimus Phlegyas admonet omnes, et
forever; and most miserable Phlegyas admonishes all, and

testatur per umbras magnâ voce; Moniti discite
bears witness through the shades with a great voice; Admonished learn

justitiam, et non temnere Divos. Hic vendidit patriam
justice and not despise the Gods. This man sold his country

auro, que imposuit potentem dominum; fixit atque refixit
for gold, and imposed a powerful master over it; he made and unmade

leges pretio. Hic invasit thalamum natæ, que
laws for a price. This one invaded the marriage chamber of his daughter, and

vetitos hymenæos: omnes ausi immane nefas, que potiti
forbidden nuptial rites: all had dared some dreadful crime, and executed

auso. Si sint mihi centum linguæ; que centum
what they dared. If there should be to me an hundred tongues; and an hundred

ora, ferrea vox non possim comprendere omnes formas
mouths, an iron voice, I could not comprehend all the forms

scelerum, percurrere omnia nomina poenarum. Ubi
of their crimes, run through all the names of their punishments. When

longæva sacerdos Phœbi dedit hæc dicta, ait, Sed jam
the aged priestess of Apollo had uttered these words, she said, But now

age, carpe viam, et perfice susceptum munus;
come on, take the way, and accomplish the begun duty;

acceleremus: conspicio mœnia educta caminis
let us hasten: I behold the walls of Pluto wrought in the forges

Cyclopum, atque portas adverso fornice, ubi præcepta
of the Cyclops, and the gates with the opposite arch, where our orders

jubent nos deponere hæc dona. Dixerat: et pariter gressi
command us to deposit these offerings. She said: and together walking

per opaca viarum, corripiunt medium spatium, que
through the dark passages of the way, they seize the intermediate space, and

propinquant foribus. Æneas occupat aditum, que spargit
approach the doors. Æneas reaches the entrance, and sprinkles

corpus recenti aquâ, que figit ramum in adverso limine.
his body with fresh water, and places the branch in the opposite gate.

His demum exactis, munere perfecto
These things at length being completed, the offering being accomplished

Divæ devenere lætos locos et amœna vireta,
to the Goddess they approached the joyful places and the pleasant green retreats,

que beatas sedes fortunatorum nemorum. Hìc largior
and the blessed seats of the happy groves. Here a more ex-

æther vestit campos, et purpureo lumine; nôrunt
tensive atmosphere clothes the plains, and with purple light; they know

suum solem, sua sidera. Pars exercent membra in
their own sun, and their own stars. A part exercise their limbs on

gramineis palæstris; contendunt ludo, et luctantur
the grassy wrestling grounds; they strive in sport, and struggle

fulvâ arenâ: pars plaudunt choreas pedibus, et dicunt
on the yellow sand: a part beat dances with their feet, and sing

carmina. Nec non Threicius sacerdos, cum longâ
songs. Likewise Orpheus the Thracian priest, with his long

veste, obloquitur septem discrimina vocum numeris: que
robe, recites seven varieties of words in numbers: and

pulsat eadam jam digitis, jam eburno pectine.
strikes out the same now with his fingers, now with his ivory quill.

Hìc antiquum genus Teucri, pulcherrima proles
Here is the ancient race of Teucer, the most beautiful offspring

magnanimi heroes nati melioribus annis; que Ilus que
high minded heroes born in better years; and Ilus and

Assaracus, et Dardanus auctor Trojæ. Miratur procul
Assaracus, and Dardanus the founder of Troy. He admires afar off

arma, que inanes currus virorum. Hastæ stant defixæ
the arms, and empty chariots of the men Spears stand fastened

terrâ que equi soluti pascuntur passim per campos.
ın the earth and the horses let loose feed every where through the plains.

Quæ gratia curruum que armorum fuit vivis, quæ cura
What fondness of chariots and of arms was to them living, what care

pascere nitentes equos eadem sequitur repositos tellure.
to feed the shining horses the same follows them buried in the earth.

Ecce conspicit alios, dextrâ que lævâ vescentes
Lo he beholds others, on the right hand and the left feeding

per herbam, que canentes lætum pæana choro, inter
through the grass, and singing a joyful hymn in a band, amidst

odoratum nemus lauri; unde supernè plurimus amnis
a fragrant grove of laurel; whence from above the extensive river

Eridani volvitur per sylvam. Hìc manus passi
of Eridanus rolls through the wood. Here were bands who had suffered

vulnera pugnando ob patriam; que qui casti sacerdotes
wounds in fighting for their country; and who were chaste priests

dum vita manebat; que qui pii vates et locuti
while life remained; and who were pious poets and spoke *things*

digna Phœbo; aut qui excoluere vitam per inventas artes,
worthy of Apollo; or who had adorned life by discovered arts,

que qui fecere alios memores sui merendo;
and who had made others mindful of themselves by deserving;

tempora cinguntur omnibus his niveâ vittâ. Quos
their temples are surrounded to all these by a snow white fillet. Whom

circumfusos Sybilla affata est sıc, Musæum ante omnes;
gathered around the Sybil addrest thus, Museus before all;

nam plurima turba habet hunc medium, atque suspicit
for a great crowd held him in the midst, and she beholds him

exstantem altis humeris; Felices animæ que tu optime
standing above with his lofty shoulders; Ye happy souls and thou most excellent

vates, dicite, quæ regio, quis locus habet Anchisen?
poet, say, what region, what place holds Anchises?

venimus ergo illius, et tranavimus magnos amnes
we have come therefore for him, and swam over the great streams

Erebi. Atque ita heros reddidit responsum huic paucis:
of Hell. And thus the hero returned an answer to her in a few words:

certa domus nulli; habitamus opacis lucis que
there is a certain abode to none; we inhabit the shady groves and

incolimus toros riparum et prata recentia rivis,
we rest upon the couches of the banks and meadows fresh with streams,

sed si ita voluntas fert corde, vos superate hoc
but if thus your will influences your heart, do you pass over this

jugum et sistam vos facili tramite. Dixit, et
height and I will place you in an easy path. He said, and

tulit gressum ante que desuper ostentat nitentes campos;
advanced his step before and from above shews the shining plains;

dehinc linquunt summa cacumina. At pater Anchises
then they leave the lofty summit *of the mountain.* But father Anchises

lustrabat animas, penitus inclusas virenti convalle, que
survey'd the souls, far off secluded in a green valley, and

ituras ad superum lumen, recolens studio, que fortè
about to go to the upper light, reviewing with care, also by chance.

recensebat omnem numerum suorum, que caros
he was counting all the number of his *descendants*, and dear

nepotes que fata que fortunas virorum, que mores
offspring and the fates and fortunes of the men, and their manners

que manus.
and actions.

Que is, ubi vidit Ænean tendentem adversùm per
And he, when he beheld Æneas proceeding towards *him* through

gramina, alacris tetendit utrasque palmas, que lacrymæ
the grass, joyful he stretched forth both his hands, and the tears

effusæ genis, et vox excidit ore:
poured down his cheeks, and this speech proceeded from his mouth:

Venisti tandem? que tua pietas, exspecta parenti,
Have you come at last? and has your piety, long experienced by your parent,

vicit durum iter? Nate, datur tueri tua ora, et
overcome the arduous journey? O son, it is allowed to behold your face, and

audire, et reddere notas voces? Sic equidem dinumerans
to hear, and return well known words? Thus indeed counting

tempora ducebam animo, que rebar futurum; nec mea
the times I thought in my mind, and supposed it would be; nor has my

cura fefellit me. Quas terras, et per quanta
care disappointed me. *Through* what lands, and through *what* extensive

æquora accipio te vectum, quantis periculis jactatum,
seas do I receive thee borne, by *what* great dangers · tost,

nate: quàm metui, ne regna Libyæ nocerent tibi
O son: how have I feared, lest the kingdoms of Libya might injure you

quid. Autem ille Genitor tua, tua tristis imago
by some means. But he *said* O father your, your sad image

occurrens sæpius, adegit me tendere hæc limina. Classes
meeting *me* often, has forced me to approach these mansions. The ships

stant Tyrrheno sale. Genitor, da jungere dextram,
remain in the Tyrrhene sea. O father, permit *me* to join my right hand

da; neque subtrahe te nostro amplexu. Sic
with yours, permit *me*; nor withdraw yourself from my embrace. Thus

memorans, simul rigabat ora largo fletu.
speaking, at the same time he watered his face with abundant weeping.

Ibi ter conatus circumdare brachia collo; ter
There thrice he attempted to throw his arms around his neck; thrice

imago frustra comprensa effugit manus, par lævibus
his image in vain grasped escaped his hands, equal to the light

ventis, que simillima volucri somno. Interea Æneas
winds, and most like to a swift dream. In the mean time Æneas

videt seclusum nemus in reductâ valle, et virgulta sonantia
beholds a retired grove in a secluded valley, and shrubbery resounding

.n sylvis, que Lethæum amnem, qui prænatat placidas
in the woods, and the Lethæan stream, which glides through the peaceful

domos. Innumeræ gentes que populi volabant circum hunc
dwellings. Countless nations and people flew around this *river*

ac veluti in pratis, ubi apes insidunt variis floribus
and as in the meadows, when bees sit on the varied flowers

serenâ æstate, et funduntur circum candida lilia, omnis
in the clear summer, and pour around the white lilies, all

campus strepit murmure. Æneas horrescit subito visu,
the plain buzzes with their murmur. Æneas shuddered at the sudden sight,

que inscius requirit causas; quæ sint porro ea flumina,
and unconscious inquires the causes; what may be moreover these streams,

quive viri compleverint ripas tanto agmine. Tum pater
or what men have filled the banks with so great a crowd. Then father

Anchises, Animæ, quibus altera corpora debentur fato,
Anchises *said*, the souls, to which other bodies are destined by fate,

potant securos latices et longa oblivia ad undam
drink care-expelling waters and long forgetfulness at the wave

Lethæi fluminis. Equidem jampridem cupio memorare
of the Lethean stream. Indeed long since I desire to relate

tibi, atque ostendere has coram, et enumerare hanc
to you, and to show these *things* before *you*, and to count up this

prolem meorum, quò magis mecum lætere Italiâ
progeny of my descendants, that the more * with me you may rejoice Italy

repertâ. O pater, anne est putandum aliquas sublimes
being found. O father, whether is it to be thought that any exalted

animas ire hinc ad cœlum, que iterum reverti ad tarda
souls go hence to heaven, and again to return to *their* sluggish

corpora? quæ tam dira cupido lucis miseris?
bodies? what so direful a desire of life *is there* to these wretched *creatures*?

Anchises suscipit: Equidem dicam, nec tenebo te
Anchises replied: Indeed I will declare, nor will I hold thee

suspensum, nate; atque pandit singula ordine.
in doubt, O son; and he laid open every thing in order

Principio, spiritus intus alit cœlum ac terras, que
In the first place, a spirit within cherishes the heaven and earth, and

liquentes campos, que lucentem globum Lunæ, que
liquid plains, and the shining orb of the moon, and

Titania astra; que mens infusa per artus, agitat
Titanian stars; and intelligence diffused through their members, moves

totam molem, et miscet se magno corpore. Inde
the whole mass, and mingles itself with the great body. Thence

genus hominum, que pecudum, que vitæ volantium quæ
the race of men, and of flocks, and the lives of birds, whatever

monstræ, pontus fert sub marmoreo æquore. Est
monsters, the sea produces beneath its marble surface. There is

igneus vigor et cœlestis origo ollis seminibus, quantam
a fiery strength and heavenly origin to these first principles, so much so *that*

noxia   corpora non tardant,   que terreni artus que
destructive   bodies   do not clog *them*,   and earthy limbs and

moribunda membra hebetant.   Hinc metuunt, que cupiunt,
dying   members   blunt *them*.   Hence they fear, and   desire,

dolent que gaudent; neque respiciunt auras,   clausæ
grieve and rejoice;   nor   do they behold the skies,   shut up

tenebris et cæco carcere.   Quin et cum vita reliquit
in darkness and a blind prison.   But   also when life   has left *them*

supremo lumine; tamen non omne malum, nec omnes corporeæ
with its last light;   yet   not every impurity, nor   all   corporeal

pestes funditus excedunt   miseris;   que est penitus
pollutions entirely departs from *these* unhappy *creatures*; and it is   entirely

necesse multa   diu   concreta   inolescere
necessary that many *things* for a long time compounded *with the soul*   should

miris modis. Ergo   exercentur   pœnis,
cling to it in wonderful modes.   Therefore they are exercised   by punishments,

que expendunt   supplicia veterum malorum.   Aliæ
and   they pay   the penalties of their former   sins.   Others

panduntur suspensæ ad inanes ventos; infectum   scelus
are hung up   suspended   to the empty winds;   the unwrought wickedness

eluitur   aliis sub vasto gurgite, aut exuritur igni.
is washed out from others under a vast abyss,   or   is burnt up by fire.

Patimur quisque suos Manes (exinde mittimur   per
We suffer   each one of us in his own remains (then   we are sent   through

amplum Elysium; et pauci tenemus læta arva,) donec
spacious Elysium; et a few   hold   these joyful fields,)   until

longa   dies exemit concretam labem, orbe temporis
long extended time has taken away the habitual stain, the circle   of time

perfecto,   que reliquit ætherium sensum purum, atquè
being accomplished, and   has left   the etherial   sense   pure,   and

ignem simplicis aurai.   Deus evocat omnes has   ubi
the fire of the simple soul.   God   calls   all   these when

volvêre   rotam per mille annos, ad Lethæum fluvium
they had rolled the wheel for a thousand years,   to the Lethean   stream

magno agmine, scilicet ut immemores   revisant
in a great band,   so   that unmindful *of the past*   they might revisit

supera convexa, et rursus incipiant velle reverti in
the upper convex world, and again   shall begin to wish to be restored to

corpora. Anchises dixerat; que trahit natum que Sibyllam
their bodies. Anchises   said;   and   led   his son and   the Sibyl

una in medios conventus, que sonantem turbam; et capit
together into the midst of the assembly, and the sounding crowd;   and takes

tumulum, unde posset legere omnes adversos longo ordine,
the hill,   whence he can observe all *those* opposite in a long   rank

et discere vultus   venientium. Nunc, age, expediam
and learn the countenances of those coming.   Now, come on, I will unfold

dictis, quæ gloria deinde sequatur Dardaniam prolem, qui
by words what glory hereafter shall follow the Trojan   race,   what

nepotes maneant de Italâ gente, illustres animas, que
descendants remain from the Italian nation, illustrious souls, and

ituras in nostrum nomen, et docebo te tua fata.
about to go to our name, and I will teach you your own fates.

Ille juvenis, vides? qui nititur purâ hastâ tenet proxima
That youth, do you see? who leans on his naked spear he holds the nearest

loca lucis sorte; primus, commixtus Italo sanguine,
places of light by lot; first, mingled with Italian blood,

surget, Sylvius, Albanum nomen, tua postuma proles;
shall arise, Sylvius, an Alban name, thy last offspring,

quem serum Lavinia conjux sylvis educet tibi longævo
whom late Lavinia *your* wife in the woods shall bear to you an aged man,

regem, que parentem regum; unde nostrum genus
himself a king, and a parent of kings; hence our race

dominabitur longâ Albâ. Ille proximus Procas, gloria
shall rule over long Alba. He next *is* Procas, the glory

Trojanæ gentis; et Capys, et Numitor; et Sylvius Æneas,
of the Trojan race; and Capys, and Numitor; and Sylvius Æneas,

qui reddet te nomine, pariter egregius pietate vel armis,
who shall represent thee by his name, equally renowned by piety or arms,

si unquam acceperit Albam regnandam. Qui juvenes,
if ever he shall receive Alba to govern. Which youths,

aspice, quantas vires ostentant! at qui gerunt tempora
behold, how great strength they shew! but those who wear their temples

umbrata civili quercu; hi Nomentum, et
shaded with a civic oaken *crown:* these *shall build* Nomentum, and

Gabios, que urbem Fidenam tibi; hi imponent Collatinas
Gabii, and the city Fidena for you; these shall place the Collatine

arces montibus, Pometios, que Castrum Inui, que Bolam,
towers on the mountains, Pometii, and Castrum Inui, and Bola,

que Coram. Tum hæc erunt nomina, nunc sunt terræ sine
and Cora. Then these shall be their names, now they are lands without

nomine. Quin et Mavortius Romulus, quem Ilia mater,
a name. But also Martial Romulus, whom Ilia the mother

sanguinis Assaraci educet, addet sese comitem
of the race of Assaracus shall bear, will add himself a companion

avo. Videsne, ut geminæ cristæ stant
to his grandfather. Do you see, how two crests stand

vertice, et jam Pater Superorum ipse signat
on his head, and now the Father of the Gods himself distinguishes *him*

suo honore? En, nate, hujus auspiciis, illa inclyta
with his own honour? Lo, my son, by his auspices, this renowned

Roma æquabit imperium terris, animos Olympo; et una
Rome shall equal its empire to the earth, its courage to heaven; and at once

circumdabit septem arces sibi muro, felix prole virorum;
shall surround seven towers to itself by a wall, happy in a race of heroes;

qualis Berecynthia mater turrita invehitur curru per
s the Berecynthian mother turreted is borne in her chariot through

Phrygias urbes, læta partu Deûm. complexa centum
the Phrygian cities, joyful in the birth of Gods, embracing an hundred

nepotes,   omnes   cœlicolas   omnes tenentes supera
grand children,   all   inhabitants of heaven, all   holding   exalted

alta.   Huc, huc flecte geminas acies aspice hanc
high places. Here, here bend   both   your eyes behold   this

gentem, que   tuos   Romanos.   Hic Cæsar, et omnis
nation,   and your own Romans.   Here is Cæsar, and   all

progenies Iuli, ventura sub magnum axem cœli. Hic,
the race of Iulus, about to come under the great axle of the sky. This.

hic est vir, quem sæpius audis promitti tibi, Augustus
this is the man, whom often you hear is to be promised to you, Augustus

Cæsar, genus   Divi, qui rursus condet   aurea secula
Cæsar, the offspring of a God, who again shall build up the golden age

Latio,   per arva quondam regnata Saturno, et
in Latium,   through lands formerly ruled   by Saturn, and

proferet imperium super Garamantas et Indos: tellus
shall extend his empire   over   the Garamantes and Indians: their land

jacet extra sidera,   extra vias   anni que solis, ubi
lies   beyond the stars, without the ways of the year and the sun, where

cœlifer   Atlas humero torquet axem aptum ardentibus
heaven-bearing Atlas on his shoulder turns the heavens studded with burning

stellis.   In adventum hujus jam nunc et Caspia regna
stars.   In the approach of him even now   also the Caspian kingdoms

horrent responsis. Divûm, et Mæotica tellus, et   trepida
shudder at the replies of the Gods, and the Mæotic land, and the trembling

ostia septemgemini Nili turbant.
mouths of sevenfold Nile are disturbed.

Nec vero   Alcides obivit tantum telluris licet fixerit
Nor   indeed did Hercules pass over so much land although he pierced

æripedem cervam, aut pacaverit nemora Erymanthia,
the brassfooted hind   or   quieted   the groves   of Erymanthus

et tremefecerit Lernam   arcu: nec Liber, qui
and made to tremble Lerna with his bow: nor   Bacchus, who

victor flectit juga   pampineis   habenis, agens
victorious guides his chariot with his vine bound reins,   driving

tigres de celso vertice Nysæ. Et dubitamus adhuc
tigers from the lofty top of Nysa. And do we hesitate yet

extendere virtutem factis? aut metus prohibet consistere
to extend   our virtue by deeds? or does fear forbid   to settle

Ausoniâ   terrâ? Autem quis ille procul insignis ramis
in the Ausonian land? But   who is he afar off distinguished by branches

olivæ, ferens sacra   nosco crines que incana menta
of the olive, bearing sacred utensils, I know the locks and hoary chin

Romani regis, qui primus fundabit urbem legibus, missus
of the Roman king, who first shall found the city by laws,   sent

in magnum imperium parvis Curibus et paupere terrâ:
to great   authority from little Cures, and from a poor land

cui deinde Tullus subibit, qui rumpet otia patriæ,
whom afterwards Tullus shall succeed, and shall break the peace of his country,

que movebit resides viros in arma, et agmina jam
and shall move slothful men to arms, and troops now

desueta triumphis; quem juxtà jactantior Ancus sequitur,
unused to triumphs; whom nearly vain boasting Ancus follows,

jam nunc quoque nimium gaudens popularibus auris. Vis
even now also too much rejoicing in popular gales. Will

videre et Tarquinios reges, que superbam animam ultoris
you see also the Tarquin kings, and the proud soul of the avenger

Bruti, que faces receptos? Hic primus accipiet
Brutus, and the rods recovered? He first shall receive

imperium consulis, que sævas secures; que infelix pater,
the authority of a consul, and the cruel axes; and an unhappy father

pro pulchrà libertate, vocabit natos, moventes nova bella,
for sweet liberty, shall call his sons, stirring up new wars,

ad pœnam: utcunque minores ferent ea facta, amor
to punishment: however posterity shall endure these acts, the love

patriæ, que immensa cupido laudum vincet. Quin
of country, and the immeasurable desire of praise shall conquer. But

aspice Decios, que Drusos procul, que Torquatum sævum
behold the Decii, and Drusi afar off, and Torquatus cruel

securi, et Camillum referentem signa Autem illæ
with his axe, and Camillus bearing back the standards. But those

animæ quas cernis fulgere in paribus armis, concordes nunc
ghosts whom you see to shine in equal arms, harmonious now

et dum premuntur nocte, heu quantum bellum que
and while they are oppressed by night, alas how great a war and

quantas acies que stragem ciebunt inter se si
how great battles and slaughter shall they stir up among themselves if

attigerint lumina vitæ! socer descendens Alpinis
they should reach the light of life! the father-in-law descending from the Alpine

aggeribus, atque arce Monœci; gener instructus
mounds, and tower of Monecus; the son-in-law furnished with

Eois adversis. Pueri, ne, ne assuescite tanta bella
his eastern opposed *soldiers.* Young men do not, do not accustom so great wars

animas; neu vertite validas vires in viscera
to your minds; nor turn your powerful strength against the bowels

patriæ, que tu prior tu parce, qui ducis genus
of your country, and do you first do you forbear, who derive your race

Olympo; projice tela manu, meus sanguis!
from heaven; throw away darts from your hand. *Cæsar!* O my blood!

Ille, Corintho triumphatâ, victoi aget currum ad
He, Corinth being triumphed over, victorious shall drive his chariot to

alta Capitolia, insignis cæsis Achivis. Ille eruet
the lofty Capitol, distinguished for slaughtered Greeks. He shall overturn

Argos, que Agamemnonias Mycenas, que Æaciden
Argos, and Agamemnon's Mycenas, and the descendant of Eacus

ipsum,   genus Achillei armipotentis ultus avos Trojæ,
himself,   of the race of Achilles powerful in arms avenging the ancestors of Troy,

et temerata templa Minervæ.   Quis relinquat te tacitum,
and the violated temple of Minerva.   Who   shall leave thee   in silence.

magne Cato; aut te Cosse?   quis genus Gracchi?   aut
O great   Cato;   or   thee O Cossus?   who   the family of Gracchus?   or

geminos Scipiadas, duo fulmina belli,   cladem Libyæ;
the two   Scipios,   two thunderbolts of war,   the destruction of Lybia;

que Fabricium potentem   parvo?   vel te serentem   sulco,
and   Fabricius   powerful   with a little?   or thee sowing in the furrow

Serrane?   Fabii,   quò   rapitis   fessum?   Tu es ille
O Serranus?   Ye Fabii,   whither do you bear me   wearied?   You   are that

maximus,   qui unus restitues   rem   nobis
Fabius, called   the greatest,   who   alone   restores   our affairs   to us

cunctando.   Alii excudent molliùs   spirantia   æra,
by delaying.   Others   may form   more delicately the breathing   trumpets,

equidem credo;   ducent vivos   vultus de marmore;
indeed   I believe;   they can draw out living countenances from   marble;

orabunt causas melius; que describent meatus   cœli
they shall plead causes   better;   and shall describe the wanderings   of the sky

radio, et dicent surgentia   sidera: tu,   Romane
with a rod, and   shall sing   the rising   constellations: thou,   O Roman

memento regere populos   imperio;   hæ erunt artes   tibi;
remember   to rule   nations by your authority: these shall be arts   for you;

que imponere morem   pacis,   parcere subjectis,   et
and   to impose   the manner   of peace,   to spare   the humble,   and

debellare superbos.   Pater Anchises sic,   atque   addit
war against   the proud.   Father   Anchises spoke thus, and   added

hæc   mirantibus: Aspice ut Marcellus ingreditur
these things to them wondering: See   how   Marcellus   walks along

insignis opimis spoliis, que victor supereminet omnes
distinguished   by rich spoils,   and victorious   towers above   all

viros!   Hic eques sistet Romanam rem, magno tumultu
the men!   He   a knight shall place the Roman   estate, a great   tumult

turbante;   sternet   Pœnos,   que rebellem Gallum;
raging,   he shall prostrate the Carthaginians,   and the rebellious   Gaul:

que suspendet tertia capta arma patri Quirino.   Atque
and   shall hang up   triple captured arms to father Quirinus.   And

hìc Æneas   (namque videbat juvenem egregium   formâ
here   Eneas says (for   he saw   a youth   distinguished   for beauty

et fulgentibus armis, ire unà   sed frons   parum
and   shining   arms,   to go together with him, but his front was   little

læta, et lumina   dejecto   vultu.)   Pater quis ille
joyous, and his eyes were set   in his dejected countenance.) O father who   is he,

qui sic comitatur virum euntem? filius anne alìquis de
who thus accompanies   the hero   departing!   his son   or   some one of

magnâ stirpe   nepotum?   Quis strepitus   comitum
the great   race   of his grandchildren?   What   a noise   of companions

circa; quantum instar est in ipso. sed atra
around him; how much of likeness is there in him *to the other!* but black

nox circumvolat caput tristi umbrâ. Tum pater Anchises
night flies around his head with its sad shade. Then father Anchises

ingressus lacrymis obortu: ô nate, ne quære ingentem
began the tears arising: O son, do not inquire into the great

luctum tuorum: Fata tantùm ostendent hunc terris,
grief of your friends: The fates only will show him on the earth,

que ne sinent esse ultra. Romana propago visa vobis,
and will not permit him to exist longer. The Roman stock would seem to you

Superi, nimium potens, si hæc dona fuissent propria.
O ye Gods, too powerful, if these gifts had been perpetual.

Quantos gemitus virûm ille campus aget ad
What groans of men shall that plain send forth near to

magnam urbem Mavortis! vel quæ funera, Tiberine,
the great city of Mars! or what deaths. O Tiber,

videbis cum præterlabere recentem tumulum! Nec
shall you behold, when you shall glide by his fresh tomb! Nor

quisquam puer de Iliacâ gente tollet Latinos avos in
did any boy from the Trojan nation exalt the Latin ancestors to

tantum spe; nec quondam Romula tellus jactabit
so great *a height* by hope; nor ever shall the Roman land boast

se tantum ullo alumno. Heu, pietas! heu, prisca
itself so much in any foster child. Alas, his piety! alas, his ancient

fides! que dextra invicta bello! non quisquam obvius
faith! and his right hand invincible in war! nor has any one encountering

tulisset se illi armato impunè, seu cùm pedes iret
presented himself to him armed with impunity, either when on foot he went

in hostem, seu foderet armos spumantis equi
against the foe, or pierced the flanks of his foaming horse

calcaribus. Heu puer miserande! si qua
with his spurs. Alas boy to be pitied! if by any means

rumpas aspera fata, tu eris Marcellus. Date lilia
you can break through cruel fate, you shall be Marcellus. Give lilies

plenis manibus; spargam purpureos flores, que saltem
with full hands; let me scatter purple flowers, and at least

accumulem animam nepotis his donis, et fungar
let me heap on the shade of my grandchild with these gifts, and let me perform

inani munere. Sic vagantur passim totâ regione
this useless duty. Thus they wander every where through the whole region

in latis campis aëris, atque lustrant omnia; per quæ
in the broad plains of air, and they survey all things; through which

singula, postquam Anchises duxit natum, que incendit
particulars, after Anchises had led his son, and had inflamed

animum amore venientis famæ, exin memorat viro
his mind with the love of approaching fame, then he relates to the hero

quæ bella deinde gerenda; que docet
what wars afterwards were to be waged; and instructs *him respecting*

Laurentes populos, que urbem Latini; et quo modo que
the Laurentian people,   and the city of Latinus; and by what mode he both

fugiat que ferat quemque laborem. Sunt geminæ portæ
shall shun and shall bear   each   labour.   There are two   gates

Somni; quarum altera fertur cornea, quâ facilis exitus
of Sleep; of which the one is said to be of horn, by which an easy departure

datur veris umbris: altera nitens, perfecta candenti
is given to true   shades: the other glittering,   wrought with shining

elephanto; sed Manes mittunt falsa insomnia ad cœlum.
ivory;   but the infernal Gods send forth false visions to the upper world.

Tum ubi Anchises prosequitur natum que Sibyllam unà
Then when Anchises had followed up his son and   the Sybil together

      his dictis, que emittit   eburnâ portâ, ille secat
with these words, and had sent them out by the ivory door, the hero directs

viam ad naves, que revisit socios; tum fert se
his way to the ships, and revisits his associates; then he bears himself

     recto litore ad portum Caietæ. Anchora jacitur de
along the direct shore to the harbour of Caieta. The anchor is cast from

prorâ, puppes stant litore.
the prow, the ships remain by the shore.

ÆNEID.

BOOK SEVENTH.

Tu quoque Caieta, Æneia nutrix, moriens dedisti æternam
Thou also O Caieta, Æneas' nurse, dying hast given eternal

famam nostris litoribus; nunc tuus honos servat   sedem,
fame   to our   shores; now   your honour preserves this situation,

que nomen signat   ossa in magnâ Hesperiâ, si ea est
and the name points out your bones in great   Italy;   if this is

qua gloria. At pius Æneas exsequiis ritè   solutis,
any glory.   But pious Æneas the funeral rites in order being performed,

aggere tumuli   composito, postquam alta æquora
the mound of the tomb being adjusted, after   the deep   waters

quieverunt, tendit   iter   velis,   que relinquit
had become calm, directs his course by the sails, and   leaves

portum. Auræ aspirant in noctem; nec candida luna
the harbor. The breezes favour him at night; nor does the bright moon

negat cursum; pontus splendet sub tremulo lumine.
oppose his progress; the sea shines beneath her trembling light.

Litora proxima Circææ terræ raduntur; ubi dives
The shores nearest to the Circean land are coasted along; where the rich

filia Solis resonat inacessos lucos assiduo
laughter of the sun resounds through the impervious groves with unremitting

cantu, que superbis tectis urit odoratum cedrum in
song, and in her august palace burns odorous cedar for

nocturna lumina, percurrens tenues telas arguto
nocturnal lights, running over her light web with her shrill sounding

pectine. Hinc gemitus exaudiri, que iræ leonum
shuttle. Hence groans began to be heard, and the rage of lions

recusantium vincla, et rudentium sub serâ nocte; que
refusing their chains, and roaring in the late night; and

setigeri sues atque ursi sævire in præsepibus, ac formæ
bristly boars and bears growl in their cells, and the forms

magnorum luporum ululare; quos sæva Dea Circe
of great wolves howl; whom the dread Goddess Circe

potentibus herbis induerat ex facie hominum in
by powerful plants had changed from the appearance of men into

vultus ac terga ferarum; quæ talia monstra ne pii
the aspect and limbs of wild beasts; which like prodigies lest the pious

Troës, delati in portus, paterentur, neu subirent
Trojans, borne in these harbours, might endure, or enter

dira litora; Neptunus implevit vela secundis ventis,
these direful shores; Neptune had filled their sails with prosperous winds,

atque dedit fugam, et vexit præter fervida
and had aided their flight, and had carried them beyond the glowing

vada. Que jam mare rubescebat radiis, et
shallows. And now the sea blushed with the rays of the sun, and

lutea Aurora fulgebat in roseis bigis ab alto æthere;
the saffron Morning shone in her roseate chariot from the lofty sky;

cum venti posuere que omnis flatus repentè
when the winds laid aside their violence and every blast suddenly

resedit et tonsæ luctantur in lento marmore. Atque hìc
ceas'd and the oars struggle in the gentle surface of the sea. And here

Æneas prospicit ingentem lucum ex æquore. Inter hunc
Æneas beholds a great grove from the sea. In the midst of this

Tiberinus amœno fluvio, rapidis vorticibus, et flavus
the Tiber with its pleasant stream, with swift whirlpools, and yellow

multâ arenâ, prorumpit in mare, que circùm que suprà
with much sand, rushes forward into the sea, and around and above

variæ volucres assuetæ ripis, et alveo fluminis, mulcebant
various birds accustom'd to the bank, and channel of the river, soothed

æthera cantu, que volabant luco. Imperat sociis
the air with their song, and flew about the grove. He orders his associates

flectere iter, que advertere proras terræ; et lætus
to direct their course, and to turn their prows to the land; and joyful

succedit opaco fluvio. Nunc age, Erato expediam
he enters the dark stream. Now come, Erato, muse of love, I will explain

qui reges, quæ tempora, quis status rerum fuerit
who were the kings, what times, what condition of things has been

antiquo Latio, cum primùm advena exercitus appulit
in ancient Latium, when first   a strange army   brought

classem Ausoniis oris; et revocabo exordia   primæ
their fleet to the Ausonian shores; and I will recall the commencement of the first

pugnæ.
battle.

Tu, tu, Diva, mone vatem. Dicam horrida bella,
Thou, thou, O Goddess, advise your poet.   I will sing of dreadful wars,

dicam acies, que reges actos animis in funera, que
I will sing of armies, and kings driven by their passions to death,   and

Tyrrhenammanum que totam Hesperiam coactam sub arma.
the Tuscan   band and all   Italy   united under arms.

Major ordo rerum nascitur mihi; moveo majus opus. Rex
A greater order of things arises   to me; I undertake a greater work.   King

Latinus, jam senior, regebat arva, et placidas urbes in
Latinus,   now an old man, ruled the fields, and peaceful cities in

longâ pace. Accipimus hunc genitum Fauno,   et
long continued peace.   We receive   him   descended from Faunus,   and

Maricâ Laurente Nymphâ. Picus pater Fauno; que is
Marica a Laurentian Nymph.   Picus was father to Faunus; and he

refert te parentem, Saturne; tu   ultimus   auctor
declares thee his parent,   O Saturn; thou art the most distant   founder

sanguinis. Fuit huic filius, fato Divûm, que nulla virilis
of his race. There was to him no son, by the decree of the Gods, and no   male

proles, que   oriens   erepta est   primâ juventâ.
offspring, and each one growing up was snatched away in the first dawn of youth.

Sola filia servabat domum et tantas sedes, jam matura
An only daughter preserved his house and these large seats, now ripe

viro, jam nubilis plenis annis. Multi petebant illam
for a husband, now marriageable with full years. Many   sought   her

e magno Latio, que totâ Ausoniâ. Turnus   petit,
from great Latium, and all Ausonia.   Turnus sought her,

pulcherrimus ante omnes alios, potens   avis   que
the most beautiful before all others,   powerful in grandfathers and

atavis, quem regia conjux properabat miro amore
great grandfathers, whom the royal spouse hastened with wonderful love

adjungi   generum: sed portenta   Deûm
to be joined to her daughter as a son-in-law: but the prodigies of the Gods

obstant variis terroribus. Erat laurus medio tecti,
oppose with various terrors.   There was a laurel in the midst of the palace,

in altis penetralibus, sacra comam, que servata metu
in the deep recesses,   sacred as to its foliage, and preserved through fear

per multos annos; quam   inventam pater Latinus   ipse
for many years;   which when discovered father Latinus   himself

ferebatur sacrâsse Phœbo, cum conderet primas arces,
is said to have consecrated to Apollo, when he built the first towers,

que posuisse nomen Laurentis colonis ab eâ. Densæ
and to have established their name to the Laurentian colonists from it.   Thick

apes (mirabile dictu) vectæ ingenti stridore trans
gathering bees (wonderful to be told) borne on with great noise across

liquidum æthera, obsedêre summum apicem hujus et
the clear sky, settled down on the highest summit of it and

pedibus nexis per mutua, subitum examen pependit
with feet connected together, a sudden swarm hung down

frondente ramo. Continuò vates inquit: Cernimus
from the leafy branch. Immediately the prophet said: We behold

externum virum adventare, et agmen petere easdem partes
a foreign man to approach, and an army to seek the same parts

ex îsdem partibus, et dominari summâ arce. Præterea
from the same parts, and to rule in the lofty palace. Besides

dum virgo Lavinia adolet altaria castis tædis, et adstat
while the maid. Lavinia perfumes the altars with chaste torches, and stands

juxta genitorem, visa nefas! comprendere ignem
near to her father, she seemed O horrible! to catch the fire

longis crinibus, atque cremari omnem ornatum
with her long hair, and to be burnt in all her ornaments

crepitante flammâ; que accensa regales comas, accensa
in the noisy flame; and inflamed *as to* her royal locks, inflamed

coronam insignem gemmis; tum fumida involvi
as to her crown distinguished with jewels; then covered with smoke to be involved

fulvo lumine, ac spargere Vulcanum totis tectis.
in dazzling light, and to scatter fire through the whole palace.

Id verò ferri horrendum, ac mirabile visu; namque
This indeed is esteemed terrible, and wonderful to be seen; for

canebant ipsam fore illustrem famâ que fatis, sed
they foretold that she would be illustrious by fame and fates, but

portendere magnum bellum populo. At rex, solicitus
threatened great war to the people. But the king, anxious

monstris, adit oracula Fauni fatidici genitoris,
for these prodigies, went to the oracles of Faunus the fate-declaring father,

que consulit lucos sub altâ Albunea, quæ, maxima
and consults the groves beneath lofty Albunea, which the greatest

memorum, sonat sacro fonte, que opaca exhalat
of groves, resounds with a sacred fountain, and dark breaths forth

sævam mephitim. Hinc Italæ gentes, que omnis Œnotria
a cruel stench. Hence the Italian nations, and all the Œnotrian

tellus, petunt responsa in dubiis. Cùm sacerdos tulit
land, seek replies in their doubts. When the priest had brought

dona huc et incubuit stratis pellibus cæsarum ovium sub
gifts here and lay down on spread skins of slain sheep in

silenti nocte, que petivit somnos; videt multa simulacra
the still night, and had sought sleep; he beholds many ghosts

volitantia miris modis, et audit varios voces, que
flying about in a wonderful manner, and hears various voices, and

fruitur colloquio Deorum, atque affatur Acheronta imis
enjoys the converse of the Gods, and addresses Acheron in the deepest

Avernis. Tum hìc et pater Latinus ipse, petens responsa
regions below Then here even father Latinus himself, seeking replies

mactabat rìtè centum lanigeras bidentes, atque jacebat
sacrificed in order an hundred wool-bearing sheep, and lay

effultus tergo que stratis velleribus harum. Subita vox
supported on the skins and spread fleeces of these. A sudden voice

est reddita ex alto luco, O mea progenies, ne pete
is sent forth from the deep grove, O my offspring, do not seek

sociare natam Latinis connubiis neu crede paratis
to unite your daughter in Latin wedlock, nor trust to prepared

thalamis. Externi generi venient qui ferent nostrum
marriage rites. Foreign sons-in-law shall come who shall raise our

nomen in astra sanguine, que a stirpe quorum nepotes
name to the stars by their blood, and from the stock of whom our offspring

videbunt omnia que verti que regi sub pedibus, quà
shall see all things both subdued and ruled beneath their feet, where

recurrens sol aspicit utrumque oceanum. Latinus ipse
the returning sun beholds each ocean. Latinus himself

non premit suo ore hæc responsa patris Fauni, que
does not confine in his mouth these responses of father Faunus, and

monitus datos silenti nocte; sed jam fama, volitans latè
admonitions given in the silent night; but now fame, flying far

circùm, tulerat per Ausonias urbes, cum Laomedontia
around, had borne them through the Ausonian cities, when the Laomedon

pubes religavit classem ab gramineo aggere ripæ.
youth had fastened the fleet near by the grassy mound of the bank.

Æneas, que primi duces, et pulcher Iulus, deponunt
Æneas, and the chief leaders, et beautiful Iulus, recline

corpora sub ramis altæ arboris; que instituunt dapes,
their bodies beneath the branches of a high tree; and prepare a feast,

et per herbam subjiciunt adorea liba epulis, (sic Jupiter
and along the grass they place fine wheaten cakes for food, (thus Jupiter

ipse monebat,) et augent Cereale solum agrestibus
himself admonished them) and they heap Ceres' soil with rustic

pomis Hìc fortè aliis consumptis, ut penuria edendi
fruits. Here by chance other things being consumed as scarcity of food

adegit vertere morsus in exiguam Cererem, et
compelled them to turn their teeth upon the small cake, and

violare orbem fatalis crusti manu, que audacibus malis
to break the crust of the fated cake with their hands, and greedy jaws,

nec parcere patulis quadris; Iulus alludens inquit, Heus!
nor to spare the broad quadrants; Iulus sporting said, Ho!

consumimus etiam mensas; nec plura. Ea vox
we consume also our tables; nor did he say more. This word

audita prima tulit finem laborum; que pater eripuit
being heard first brought an end of their labours; and his father took it up

primam ab ore loquentis; ac stupefactus numine
first from the mouth of him speaking; and astonished by the divine impulse

pressit.   Continuò   Salve, tellus debita mihi   fatis,
restrained *his voice*. Forthwith *he cried* Hail,   land   destined to me by the fates,

que vos salvete, ò fidi   Penates Trojæ! Hic   domus,
and ye   hail,   O faithful   household Gods of Troy! This *is our* house,

hæc est patria.   Genitor   Anchises (namque nunc
this is   our country. My father   Anchises   (for   now

repeto)   reliquit talia arcana fatorum mihi. Nate, cum
I call it to mind   left   such   secrets of the fates to me. O son, when

fames coget te,   vectum ad ignota litora, consumere
hunger shall compel thee,   borne to unknown shores,   to consume

mensas, dapibus accisis,   tum   defessus memento
your tables,   your food being eaten up, then   wearied out   remember

sperare domos, que ibi locare   prima tecta   manu,
to hope for homes, and then place   your first dwellings with your hands,

que moliri   aggere.   Hæc erat illa fames,   hæc
and   fortify *them*   by a wall.   This was that famine,   these

suprema   manebant nos positura modum   exitiis.
last *circumstances*   remained to us about to place an end to our sorrows.

Quare agite, et, cum primo lumine solis, læti vestigemus
Wherefore come on, and, with the first light of the sun, joyful let us search

quæ loca,   ve qui homines habeant, ubi mœnia
what places *these are*, or what   men   hold them, where *are* the cities

gentis, et petamus diversa   a   portu. Nunc libate
of the nation, and let us seek different ways from the harbour. Now   pour out

pateras Jovi, que vocate Anchisen genitorem precibus, et
goblets to Jupiter, and   invoke Anchises   *my* father   by prayers, and

reponite vina mensis.   Sic effatus, deinde, implicat
replace   wine on the tables.   Thus having spoken, next,   he binds

tempora frondenti ramo, et precatur que Genium   loci,
his temples with a leafy branch, and entreats both the Genius of the place,

que Tellurem primam Deorum, que Nymphas, et flumina
and   the earth   the first of the Gods, and the Nymphs, and the streams

adhùc ignota; tum invocat Noctem, que orientia   signa
as yet unknown; then he invokes Night,   and the rising   constellations

noctis, que Idæum Jovem, que Phrygiam matrem
of night, and   Idean   Jupiter, and the Trojan   mother *Cybele*,

ex ordine, et duplices parentes que Cœlo que Erebo. Hìc
in order, and his double parents   both in heaven and   in hell.   Here

omnipotens pater intonuit ter clarus ab alto cœlo,   que
the almighty . father thundered thrice clearly from the lofty heaven,   and

ipse ostendit ab æthere nubem ardentem radiis lucis et
he   exhibits from the sky a cloud   glowing   with rays of light and

auro,   quatiens manu.   Hìc subitò   rumor diditur
with gold, brandishing with his hand. Here suddenly   a report is spread

per Trojana agmina, diem advenisse, quo   condant
through the Trojan troops,   that the day had arrived, when they should build

debita mœnia. Certatim instaurant epulas, atque   læti
the destined walls.   Eagerly   they renew the feast, and   rejoicing

magno omine statuunt crateras, et coronant vina. Cùm
in the great omen they place the goblets, and crown the wine. When

postera dies orta lustrabat terras primâ lampade,
the next day arising surveyed the earth with its first light,

diversi explorant urbem, et fines, et litora
separating they explore the city, and boundaries, and shores

gentis: hæc stagna fontis Numici, hunc fluvium
of the nation: these are the pools of the fountain Numicus, this the river

Tybrim, fortes Latinos habitare hìc. Tum satus
Tyber, the brave Latins dwell here. Then he descended

Anchisâ, jubet centum oratores, delectos ab omni
from Anchises, commands an hundred orators, chosen from every

ordine, ire ad augusta mœnia regis, omnes velatos
rank, to go to the proud walls of the king, all veiled

ramis Palladis; que ferre dona viro, que exposcere
with the branches of Minerva; and to bear gifts to the hero, and ask

pacem Teucris. Haud mora: jussi festinant, que
peace for the Trojans. There is no delay: commanded they hasten, and

feruntur rapidis passibus: ipse designat mœnia
are borne on with rapid steps: Æneas himself marks out the walls

humili fossâ, que molitur locum, que cingit primas
with an humble ditch, and plans out the place, and surrounds the first

sedes in litore pinnis, atque aggere in morem
seats upon the shore with pickets, and a rampart in the manner

castrorum: que jam juvenes, emensi iter,
of camps: and now the young men, having measured their way,

cernebant turres ac ardua tecta Latinorum; que subibant
beheld the turrets and lofty roofs of the Latins, and approached

muro. Ante urbem pueri, et juventus primævo flore,
the wall. Before the city boys, and youth in primeval bloom,

exercentur equis, que domitant currus in pulvere aut
are exercised on horses, and guide chariots in the dust or

tendunt acres arcus, aut contorquent lenta spicula
stretch their strong bows, or hurl their slender darts

lacertis, que lacessunt cursu que ictu, cùm
with their arms, and challenge each other in the race and in striking, when

nuncius, prævectus equo, reportat ad aures, longævi regis,
a messenger, borne before on a horse, reports to the ears, of the aged king,

ingentes viros advenisse in ignotâ veste. Ille imperat
that great men had come in an unknown dress. He commands them

vocari intra tecta, et consedit medius avito solio.
to be called within the palace, and sat down in the midst on his ancient throne.

Fuit augustum tectum, ingens, sublime centum columnis,
There was a proud palace, large, high with an hundred columns,

summâ urbe, regia Laurentis Pici, horrendum
in the highest part of the city, the royal abode of Laurentian Picus, dreaded

sylvis et religione parentum. Erat omen
for its woods and the superstition of the fathers of the nations. It was a usage

regibus accipere sceptra hìc, et attollere primos   fasces:
to kings to receive their sceptres here, and to take   the first badges of power:

hoc templum,   curia   illis;   hæ sedes sacris epulis:
this *was* a temple, *this* a senate-house to them; these their seats for sacred feasts:

hìc patres, ariete cæso,   soliti considere perpetuis
here the fathers, a ram being slain, were accustomed to sit   at their long

mensis.
tables.

Quin etiam effigies veterum avorum ex ordine è
But   also   the images of their ancient forefathers in   order   of

antiquâ cedro; que Italus que pater Sabinus, que senex
ancient   cedar; and Italus and father Sabinus, and   old

Saturnus, vitisator, servans curvam falcem sub imagine;
Saturn   the vineplanter, holding a crooked sickle beneath his image;

que imago bifrontis Jani adstabant vestibulo: que alii
and the figure of the two-faced Janus stood   in the porch: and other

reges ab origine,   qui passi martia vulnera pugnando
kings from the origin *of the race*, who had suffered martial wounds   in fighting

ob patriam que multa arma præterea pendent in sacris
for their country and many arms   besides   hung   on the sacred

postibus, captivi currus que curvæ secures, et   cristæ
posts,   captive chariots and crooked axes,   and   crests

capitum, et ingentia claustra portarum, que spicula, que
of their heads, and great   bars   of gates,   and   darts,   and

clypei, que rostra erepta carinis. Picus ipse, domitor
shields, and prows torn from ships. Picus himself,   the tamer

equûm, sedebat Quirinali lituo, que succinctus parvâ
of horses,   sat   with his augurial wand, and girt   with a short

trabeâ, que gerebat ancile lævâ   quem percussum
robe,   and   he bore a shield in his left hand whom   struck

aureâ virgâ que versum venenis, conjux Circe, capta
with a golden wand and changed by poisons, his wife Circe, overcome

cupidine fecit avem, que sparsit alas coloribus. Latinus
by lust   had made a bird, and specked his wings with colours. Latinus

sedens intus tali templo Divûm, que patriâ   sede
sitting within this temple of the Gods, and on his paternal seat

vocavit Teucros ad sese in   tecta; atque prior placido
called   the Trojans to him within the palace; and   first   with mild

ore edidit hæc   ingressis: Dardanidæ enim neque
address he uttered these *words to them* having entered: Ye Trojans for   neither

nescimus et urbem, et genus, que   auditi
are we ignorant both of your city, and race,   and   we have heard

advertitis cursum   æquore, dicite quid petitis? quæ
that you have turned *your* course hither on the sea, say what do you seek? what

causa vexit rates aut egentes cujus   ad Ausonium
cause has borne your ships or wanting what *have you come* to the Ausonian

litus per tot cærula vada? Sive acti errore   viæ,
shore through so many azure   waves? Whether driven by mistake of *your* way

sive tempestatibus (multa qualia nautæ patiuntur in alto
or   by tempests   (many such *calamities* sailors endure   on the deep

mari) intravistis ripas fluminis que sedetis portu;
sea) you have entered the banks of the river, and have settled in our harbour;

ne fugite hospitium, neve ignorate Latinos, gentem
do not avoid *our* friendship, nor be ignorant of the Latins,   a race

Saturni, æquam haud vinculo nec legibus, suâ sponte,
of Saturn,   just with no bonds nor laws, *ruled* by their own will,

que tenentem se more veteris Dei. Atque
and restraining themselves by the law of their ancient God.   And

equidem memini (fama est obscurior annis) Auruncos
indeed   I remember (report is more obscure by years) *that* the Auruncan

senes ferre ita, ut Dardanus, ortus his agris, penetravit
old men relate thus, that Dardanus, sprung from these territories, penetrated

ad Idæas urbes Phrygiæ que Thraciam Samum, quæ nunc
to the Idean cities of Phrygia and Thracian Samos, which now

fertur Samothracia. Nunc aurea regia stellantis cœli
is called Samothracia.   Now the golden palace of the starry heaven

accipit illum solio, profectum hinc ab Tyrrhenâ sede
has received him on its throne, having departed hence from his Tuscan   seat

Coriti, et altaribus auget numerum Divorum. Dixerat,
of Coritus, and by his altars he augments the number of the Gods. He said,

et Ilioneus secutus dicta voce sic: Rex, egregium
and Ilioneus followed in these words with his voice thus: O King, renowned

genus Fauni nec atra hiems subegit actos fluctibus,
offspring of Faunus neither the dark tempest compelled us driven by the waves,

succedere vestris terris; nec sidus ve litus fefellit
to approach your lands: nor the constellation or the shore deceived us

regione viæ. Omnes afferimur hanc urbem consilio
from the region of the way. We all are borne to this   city by design

que volentibus animis; pulsi regnis quæ sol veniens
and willing minds; banished from realms which the sun approaching

extremo Olympo, aspiciebat quondam maxima.
from the extremity of heaven, beheld formerly   the greatest.

Principium generis ab Jove; Dardana pubes gaudet
The origin of our race *is* from Jove; the Trojan youth rejoice in

Jove avo rex ipse, Troius Æneas de supremâ
Jove their ancestor our king himself, Trojan Æneas *sprung* from the high

gente Jovis, misit nos ad tua limina. Quanta tempestas
race of Jupiter, sent us to your palace. How great   a storm

effusa sævis Mycenis, ierit per Idæos campos, quibus
let loose from dread Mycenæ, has passed over the Idean plains, by what

fatis uterque orbis Europæ atque Asiæ concurrerit audivit,
fates each circle of Europe and Asia has conflicted he has heard.

et si quem extrema tellus submovet refuso oceano,
if *such there be* whom the most remote land has removed by the intervening ocean,

et si quem plaga iniqui solio extenta in medio
and whom the region of the unequal sun stretching into the midst

quatuor plagarum dirimit.
of four climates has separated.

Vecti ex illo diluvio per tot vasta æquora; rogamus
Borne from this deluge through so many extended seas, we ask

exiguam sedem, que innocuum litus patriis Dîs, et
a small settlement, and a safe shore for our country Gods, and

que undam que auram patentem cunctis. Non erimus
both water and air open to all. We will not be

indecores regno; nec vestra fama feretur levis,
disgraceful to your kingdom, nor shall your fame be esteemed light,

que gratia tanti facti abolescet: nec pigebit Ausonios
and the favour of so great a deed be effaced: nor shall it repent the Ausonians

excepisse Trojam gremio. Juro per fata Æneœ,
to have received Troy to their bosoms. I swear by the fates of Æneas,

que potentem dextram, sive quis expertus est fide,
and his powerful right hand, whether any one has experienced it in faith

seu bello, et armis; multi populi, multæ gentes (ne
or in war, and arms; many people, many nations (do not

temne quòd ultro præferimus vittas manibus et
despise us because willingly we bear before us fillets in our hands and

verba precantia) et petiêre, et voluere adjungere
words entreating peace) both have sought, and have wished to unite us

sibi. Sed fata Deûm egere nos suis
to themselves. But the fates of the Gods have compelled us by their

imperiis exquirere vestras terras. Dardanus ortus hinc,
commands to seek your lands. Dardanus sprung from hence,

repetit huc, que Apollo urget ingentibus jussis ad
returns here, and Apollo urges us by his great commands to

Tyrrhenum Tybrim, et sacra vada fontis Numici.
the Tuscan Tyber, and the sacred streams of the fountain Numicus.

Præterea dat tibi parva munera prioris fortunæ, reliquias
Besides he gives to you small presents of his former fortune, relics

receptas ex ardente Trojâ. Pater Anchises libabat
recovered from burning Troy, Father Anchises performed libations

ad aras hoc auro: hoc erat gestamen Priami cùm
at the altars from this golden bowl: this was the sceptre of Priam when

daret jura populis vocatis more, que sceptrum
he gave laws to the people convoked in their manner, and a mace

que sacer tiaras, que vestes, labor Iliadum. Talibus
and sacred crown, and dresses, the labour of Trojan matrons. With such

dictis Ilionei, Latinus tenet ora defixa obtutu,
words of Ilionius. Latinus holds his countenance fixed in firm regard,

que hæret immobilis solo, volvens intentos oculos.
and remains unmoved on the ground, rolling his attentive eyes.

Nec picta purpura movet regem, nec Priameia
Neither the painted purple moves the king, nor does Priam's

sceptra movent eum tantùm, quantùm moratur in
sceptre move him so much, as he dwells upon

connubio que thalamo natæ, et volvit sortem
the marriage and marriage rites of his daughter, and he revolves the lot

veteris Fauni sub pectore: hunc illum generum
of ancient Faunus in his heart: that this is the son-in-law

profectum ab externâ sede fatis portendi, que vocari
proceeding from a remote seat by the fates foretold, and call'd

paribus auspiciis in regna; hinc futuram progeniem
by equal auspices to his kingdom; that hence would be a race

egregiam virtute et quæ viribus occupet totum orbem.
renowned for courage and which by power shall possess the whole globe

Tandem lætus ait: Dî secundent nostra incepta,
At length joyful he says: May the Gods favour our undertaking,

que suum augurium. Trojane, dabitur quod
and their own augury. O Trojan, it shall be given which

optas: nec sperno munera. Uber divitis agri,
you ask; nor do I despise your gifts. The richness of the fertile land,

que opulentia Trojæ non deerit vobis Latino
and the wealth of Troy shall not be wanting to you while Latinus

rege. Modò Æneas ipse adveniat (si est tanta cupido
is king. Provided Æneas himself will come (if there is so great a desire

nostrî, si properat jungi hospitio, que vocari socius)
of us, if he hastens to be united in friendship, and to be call'd an ally)

neve exhorrescat amicos vultus. Erit pars
nor let him dread our friendly countenance. It shall be the part

pacis mihi tetigisse dextram tyranni. Vos contrà
of peace to me to have touched the right hand of the prince. You on the other

nunc referte mea mandata regi: Est mihi
hand now bear back my commands to your king: There is to me

nata quam sortes ex patrio adyto, plurima
a daughter whom the oracles from my paternal shrine, whom many

monstra cœlo non sinunt jungere viro nostræ gentis:
prodigies from heaven do not permit me to unite to a husband of our nation:

canunt hoc restare Latio, generos affore ab
they prophecy that this awaits Latium, that sons-in-law will be here from

externis oris, qui sanguine ferant nostrum nomen
foreign coasts, who by their blood will raise our name

in astra. Et reor et opto (si mens augurat quid
to the stars. And I suppose and desire it (if my mind augurs any thing

veri) fata poscere hunc illum
of truth) the fates demand this man himself.

Pater effatus hæc, eligit equos omni numero
The father having spoken these words, selected horses from all the number

ter centum nitidi stabant in altis præsepibus:
three hundred shining steeds stood in the lofty sta ls

extemplo jubet alipedes, instratos ostro que
forthwith he commands the wing-footed horses overspread with purple and

pictis tapetis, duci omnibus Teucris ordine. Aurea
painted trappings, to be led out for all the Trojans in order. Golden

monilia pendent demissa pectoribus; tecti auro
martingales hang depending from their breasts; covered with gold

mandunt fulvum aurum sub dentibus; currum que
they champ the yellow gold beneath their teeth, a chariot and

geminos jugales ab æthereo semine, spirantes ignem
two match-horses from the ethereal race, breathing forth fire

naribus absenti Æneæ: de gente illorum, quos
from their nostrils, for the absent Æneas: from the race of those, which

Dædala Circe, furata patri creavit nothos de
Dædalian Circe, having stolen from her father produced a spurious race from

supposità matre. Æneadæ, talibus donis que dictis Latini
a substituted mother. The Trojans, with such gifts and words of Latinus

redeunt sublimes in equis, que reportant pacem. Autem
return proud on their horses, and bring back peace. But

ecce! sæva conjux Jovis referebat sese ab Inachiis
lo! the dread wife of Jupiter brought back herself from Inachian

Argis, que invecta tenebat auras: et longè ab æthere,
Argos, and borne on she possessed the air: and far from the sky,

ab usque Siculo Pachyno, prospexit lætum Ænean, que
from even Sicilian Pachinus, she beheld joyful Æneas, and

Dardaniam classem. Videt jam moliri
the Trojan fleet. She beholds the Trojans already begin to build

tecta, jam sidere terræ, deseruisse rates. Stetit fixa
houses, already to settle on the land, to desert their ships. She stood pierced

acri dolore; tum quassans caput, effudit hæc dicta
with sharp grief: then shaking her head, she poured out these words

pectore: Heu! invisam stirpem, et fata Phrygum
from her breast: Ah! hateful race, and fates of the Trojans

contraria nostris fatis! num occumbere Sigëis
opposed to our fates! whether could I overthrow them on the Sigean

campis? Num capti potuere capi? num incensa
plains? Whether conquered could they be conquered? whether has conflagrated

Troja cremavit viros? invenere viam medias
Troy burnt these men? they have found a way through the midst

acies, que per medios ignes. At, credo, mea numina
of armies, and through the midst of fires. But, I believe, my divinity

tandem jacent fessa; aut exsaturata odiis, quievi.
at length lies wearied; or satisfied with hatred, I have rested.

Quin etiam infesta ausa sequi excussos patrià
But even hating I dared to follow them driven from their country

per undas, et opponere me profugis toto ponto
through the waves, and to oppose myself to the fugitives through the whole sea

Vires que cœli que maris absumptæ in Teucros.
The powers both of heaven and the sea are consumed against the Trojans.

Quid Syrtes, aut Scylla, quid vasta Charybdis
What did quicksands, or Scylla, what did the vast Charybdis

profuit mihi: conduntur optato alveo Tybridis, securi
profit me. they are moored in the desired channel of the Tyber, careless,

pelagi atque mei. Mars valuit perdere immanem gentem
of the ocean and of me. Mars could destroy the huge race

Lapitharum; genitor Deûm ipse concessit antiquam
of the Lapithæ; the father of the Gods himself yielded ancient

Calydona in iras Dianæ: quod tantum scelus Lapithis,
Calydon to the anger of Diana: what so great crime *was* to the Lapithæ,

aut Calydone merente? Ast ego, magna conjux Jovis,
or was Calydon deserving? But I, the great wife of Jupiter,

quæ potui linquere nil inausum, quæ infelix verti
who could leave nothing undared, who unhappy have turned

memet in omnia, vincor ab Æneâ. Quòd si mea
myself to all *expedients*, am overcome by Æneas. What if my

numina non sunt satis magna, equidem haud dubitem
divinity is not sufficiently great, indeed I will not hesitate

implorare quod est usquam: si nequeo flectere Superos,
to implore that which is any where: if I cannot bend the Gods,

movebo Acheronta. Esto, non dabitur
I will move hell. Be it so, *that* it shall not be granted to *me*

prohibere Latinis regnis, atque Lavinia manet conjux
to forbid *him* the Latin kingdoms, and Lavinia remains *his* wife

immota fatis: at licet trahere, atque addere moras
fixed by the fates: but it is permitted to prolong, and to add delays

tantis rebus; at licet excindere populos amborum
to these great events; but it is permitted to cut off the people of both

regum. Gener atque socer coëant hâc mercede
kings. Let the son-in-law and father in-law unite at this price

suorum. Virgo, dotabere Trojano et Rutulo
of their *friends*. O maid, you shall be endowed with Trojan and Rutulian

sanguine; et Bellona pronuba manet te: nec tantùm
blood; and Bellona a bridesmaid shall remain to thee: nor alone

Cisseis prægnans face enixa jugales ignes quin
did Hecuba teeming with a firebrand bear nuptial fires but

suus partus Veneri idem, et alter Paris, que tedæ
her own offspring shall be to Venus the same, and another Paris, and torches

iterum funestæ in recidiva Pergama.
again *shall be* deadly against new rising Troy.

Ubi dedit hæc dicta, horrenda petivit terras. Ciet
When he uttered these words, dread she sought the earth. She calls up

luctificam Alecto ab sede dirarum sororum, que infernis
mournful Alecto from the seat of the direful sisters, and infernal

tenebris; cui cordi tristia bella, que iræ, que insidiæ,
darkness; in whose heart are mournful wars, and wrath, and fraud,

et noxia crimina. Et pater Pluton ipse odit. Tartareæ
and hurtful crimes. And father Pluto himself hates *her*. The Tartarean

sorores odere monstrum; vertit sese in tot ora
sisters hate the monster; she turns herself into so many features

tam sævas facies, atra   pullulat tot   colubris.   Quam
so many cruel forms, black *she* sprouts forth so many snakes.   Whom

Juno acuit   his   verbis, ac fatur talia: Virgo,   sata
Juno provoked with these words, and speaks these things: O Maid,   born

Nocte, da mihi hunc proprium laborem, hanc operam;
from Night, give to me this   appropriate   labour,   this   work;

ne noster honos, ve infractra fama cedat   loco,   neu
let not our   honour,   or   mutilated   fame   yield on this occasion,   nor

Æneadæ possint ambire Latinum connubiis, ve   obsidere
let the Trojans be able to circumvent Latinus by marriage,   or   besiege

Italos   fines. Tu   potes armare unanimes fratres in
the Italian boundaries. You   can   arm   harmonious   brothers to

prœlia, atque versare   domos odiis; tu   inferre verbera
battle   and   overturn families by hatred; you *can* bear   stripes

que funereas faces tectis; tibi   mille nomina,   mille
and   deadly   firebrands to houses; to you *are* a thousand names,   a thousand

artes nocendi: concute fecundum pectus, disjice compositam
arts of injuring; strike   your prolific   breast,   break   this established

pacem, sere crimina   belli: juventus velit,   que simul
peace,   sow   crimes *the seeds* of war; the youth   wish,   and   at once

poscat, que   rapiat   arma.   Exin   Alecto, infecta
demand it, and   let them seize upon arms.   Forthwith   Alecto,   stain'd

Gorgoneis venenis, principio petit Latium et celsa
with Gorgonian   poisons,   in the first place sought Latium and the lofty

tecta   Laurentis tyranni, que obsedit tacitum limen
palace of the Laurentine prince,   and besieg'd   the silent   gate

Amatæ quam ardentem super adventu Teucrûm   que
of Amata whom   raging   about   the coming   of the Trojans   and

nymenæis   Turni que femineæ curæ que iræ coquebant.
the marriage rites of Turnus both female   cares and passions   inflamed,

Dea   conjicit huic unum anguem de cæruleis
The Goddess   cast   on her   one   snake   from   her azure

crinibus, que subdit in   sinum   ad intima præcordia,
locks,   and   it sunk into her bosom   to   her inmost   heart,

quo monstro furibunda permisceat omnem domum.
by which monster   raging   she may disturb   all   her family.

Ille lapsus inter   vestes et lêvia pectora volvitur nullo
It   gliding between her dress and smooth   breast   rolls on   with no

attactu, que fallit furentem, inspirans viperam animam:
impression, and deludes   her raging,   inspiring   a viperous   soul:

ingens coluber fit   tortile aurum   collo,   fit
the great   snake   becomes wreathed   gold   for *her* neck; it becomes

tænia longæ   vittæ que innectit   comas, et lubricius
a wreath of a long   fillet and   binds   *her* hair.   and   gliding

errat   membris. Ac dum prima lues,   sublapsa
wanders over   her limbs.   And   while the first infection,   gliding under

udo veneno, pertentat sensus, atque implicat ignem
with moist poison,   thrills through her senses, and   implants   fire

ossibus, necdum animus percepit flammam toto
in her bones, nor yet did her mind feel the flame through all

pectore: locuta est mollius et de solito more
her heart: she spoke more gently and according to the usual mode

matrum, lacrymans multa super natâ que Phrygiis
of mothers, weeping much about her daughter and the Trojan

hymenæis: O genitor, ne Lavinia datur ducenda Teucris
nuptials: O father, shall Lavinia be given to be married to Trojan

exsulibus? nec miseret te que natæ que tui? nec
exiles? nor do you pity both your daughter and yourself? nor

miseret matris quam perfidus prædo relinquet primo
do you pity her mother whom this treacherous robber will abandon with the first

Aquilone, petens alta, virgine abductâ? An non
north wind, seeking the deep, the maid *being* carried off? Did not

Phrygius pastor sic penetrat Lacedæmona, que vexit
the Trojan shepherd *Paris* thus enter Lacedemon, and bear off

Ledæam Helenam ad Trojanas arces? Quid tua
Leda's Helen to the Trojan towers? What avails your

sancta fides, quid antiqua cura tuorum, et dextera
holy faith, what the ancient regard for your friends, and your right *hand*

data toties consanguineo Turno? Si gener petitur
pledged so often to your relation Turnus? If a son-in-law is sought

Latinis de externâ gente, que id sedet, que jussa
by the Latins from a foreign nation, and this is determined, and the commands

parentis Fauni premunt te: equidem reor omnem
of *your* father Faunus restrain you: indeed I think every

terram externam, quæ libera nostris sceptris dissidet;
land is foreign, which free from our authority is separated from *us*,

et Divos dicere sic.
and the Gods declare thus.

Et si prima origo domus repetatur, Inachus que Acrisius
And if the first origin of his family be demanded, Inachus and Acrisius

patres Turno, que mediæ Mycenæ, Ubi
were ancestors to Turnus, and the midst of Mycenæ *is his country.* When

videt Latinum stare contra, experta nequicquam
she beholds Latinus to stand opposed *to her*, having tried in vain

his dictis, que furiale malum serpentis lapsum penitus
with these words, and maddening mischief of the serpent gliding deeply

in viscera, que pererrat totam; tum verò
into her entrails, and had wandered through her whole *frame*; then indeed

infelix excita ingentibus monstris, lymphata furit per
the hapless *woman* aroused by *these* great prodigies; frantic rages through

immensum urbem sine more: ceu quondam turbo volitans
the extensive city beyond measure: as whenever a top flying

sub torto verbere, quem pueri intenti ludo, exercent in
beneath a wreathed lash, which boys intent on play, exercise in

magno gyro circum vacua atria: ille actus habenâ fertur
a great circle around the empty halls: it drawn by the thong is borne

curvatis   spatiis: inscia turba stupet, que impubes
in circling   spires: the ignorant crowd stand amazed, and the youthful

manus   mirata   volubile buxum: dant   animos   plagæ.
band   admiring the whirling   wood: they give their sou.s to the blow.

Agitur non segnior   illo cursu, per   medias
The queen is driven on not more slowly than this course, through   the midst

urbes, que feroces populos. Quin etiam adorta   majus
of cities, and   fierce   people.   But   even   advancing to a greater

nefas que orsa majorem furorem evolat in sylvas,   simulato
evil   and rising to a greater madness she flies into the woods, having feigned

numine Bacchi, et abdit natam frondosis   montibus,
the divinity of Bacchus, and hides her daughter in the leafy   mountains,

quò eripiat thalamum Teucris, que moretur   tædas;
that she may snatch marriage from the Trojans, and delay the nuptial torches

fremens Evoë Bacche, vociferans te solum   dignum
crying out Evœ Bacchus,   declaring   that you alone   are worthy

virgine; etenim sumere molles thyros tibi, lustrare   te
of the maid;   for she has taken soft   spears for you, she encircles   thee

choro, pascere sacrum crinem tibi. Fama volat,   que
with a dance, preserves her sacred locks   for you. Fame flies,   and

simul idem ardor agit omnes matres, accensas   Furiis
at once the same zeal urges   all   the mothers, inflamed by the Furies

pectore, quærere nova tecta. Deseruere domos; dant
in their breasts, to seek   new dwellings. They desert their homes; they give

colla que comas ventis. Ast aliæ complent   æthera
their necks and hair   to the winds. But others   fill   the skies

tremulis ululatibus, que incinctæ pellibus gerunt pampineas
tremulous   cries,   and covered with skins they bear the vine bound

hastas; ipsa fervida sustinet flagrantem pinum inter medias
spears;   she   raging   upholds   a burning   pine   in the midst

ac canit hymenæos   natæ   que Turni,   torquens
and sings the nuptial song of her daughter and Turnus,   rolling

sanguineam aciem que repentè clamat torvùm: Io
her bloody   eye-ball and suddenly cries out in a stern manner: O

Latinæ matres, audite, ubiquæque,   si qua   gratia
ye Latin mothers,   hear,   wheresoever you are, if any   regard

infelicis Amatæ manet   piis animis, si cura   materni
of the wretched Amata dwells in your pious minds,   if care   of a mother's

juris remordet,   solvite crinales vittas, capite orgia
right   corrodes your hearts, loosen   your hairy fillets,   take up the orgies

mecum. Alecto agit reginam talem stimulis   Bacchi,
with me.   Alecto urges the queen   thus   with the goads   of Bacchus,

undique inter sylvas, inter deserta ferarum. Postquam
on every side among the woods, among the deserts of wild beasts.   After

visa   acuisse   primos furores satis,   que
she seemed to have provoked her first madness sufficiently,   and

vertisse   consilium que omnem domum Latini, protinus
to have overturned the counsel and   all   the house of Latinus, forthwith

tristis Dea tollitur hinc fuscis alis ad muros audacis
the sad Goddess is borne from hence on mournful wings to the walls of the daring

Turni: quam urbem Danaë, delata præcipiti Noto dicitur
Turnus: which city Danae, borne on the swift south wind is said

fundavisse Acrisioneis colonis. Locus quondam
to have been founded for her Acrisian colonists. The place was formerly

dictus Ardua avis, et nunc Ardea manet magnum
called Ardua by our ancestors and now Ardea remains a great

nomen; sed fortuna fuit.
name; but *its* fortune has been.

Hìc in altis tectis Turnus jam carpebat mediam quietem
Here in the lofty palace Turnus now enjoyed his midnight sleep

nigrâ nocte. Alecto exuit torvam faciem et furialia
in the black night. Alecto put off her grim countenance and Fury's

membra; transformat sese in aniles vultus, et arat
limbs; transforms himself into an old woman's looks, and ploughs

obscœnam frontem rugis; induit albos crines cum
her filthy forehead with wrinkles; puts on white hair with

vittâ, tum innectit ramum olivæ: fit Calybe
a fillet, then she binds on the bough of an olive; she becomes Calybe,

anus Junonis, que sacerdos templi; et offert se
an old woman of Juno, and a Priestess of the temple; and offers herself

juveni ante oculos cum his vocibus: Turne, patiere
to the youth before his eyes with these words: O Turnus, will you suffer

tot labores fusos incassùm, et tua sceptra transcribi
so many labours wasted in vain, and shall your sceptre be transferred

Dardaniis colonis? Rex abnegat conjugium tibi, et dotes
to the Trojan colonists? The king denies marriage to you, and dowries

quæsitas sanguine; que externus hæres quæritur in regnum,
gain'd by blood; and a foreign heir is sought for the kingdom.

I nunc, irrise, offer te ingratis periculis; I,
Go, now, scorn'd man, present yourself to ungrateful dangers; Go,

sterne Tyrrhenas acies; tege Latinos pace. Adeó
prostrate the Tuscan armies; protect the Latins by peace. Thus

omnipotens Saturnia lapsa jussit me fari
the all powerful *daughter* of Saturn gliding down commanded me to speak

hæc palam tibi, cum jaceris placidâ nocte. Quare
these words openly to you, when you lay in the peaceful night. Wherefore

age, et lætus para pubem armari, que moveri
come on, and joyful prepare the youth to be armed, and to be removed

portis in arma: et exure Phrygios duces, qui
from the gates to war: and burn the Trojan leaders, who

consedere pulchro flumine, que pictas carinas. Magna
have settled by this fair stream, and painted ships. The great

vis cœlestium jubet sic: Rex Latinus ipse, ni
power of the Gods commands thus; let King Latinus himself, unless

fatetur dare conjugium, et parere dicto, sentiat,
he agrees to grant the marriage, and to comply with his word. know

et tandam experiatur Turnum in armis. Hìc juvenis
and at length experience Turnus in arms. Here the youth

irridens vatem sic vicissim refert   ore
scoffing the prophetess thus in turn replies   with *his* mouth *to what*

orsa: Nuncius non effugit meas aures, ut rere,
she had begun *to say*: the news has not escaped my ears, as you suppose.

classes invectas alveo Tybridis. Ne finge
that ships have been wafted to the channel of the Tiber. Do not feign

tantos metus mihi, nec est regia Juno immemor nostrî.
so great fears to me, nor is royal Juno unmindful of us.

Sed, ô mater, senectus victa situ que effœta veri,
But, O mother, old age overcome by its rust and powerless of truth,

nequicquam exercet te caris, et inter arma regum,
in vain exercises you with cares, and amid the arms of kings,

ludit vatem falsâ formidine. Tibi cura tueri
mocks the prophetess with deceptive fear. To you *is* the care to guard

effigies et templa Divûm; viri gerant bella que pacem
the images and temples of the Gods; let men manage wars and peace

queis bella gerenda. Alecto exarsit in iras talibus
by whom wars are to be conducted. Alecto kindled into wrath by these

dictis. At subitus tremor occupat artus juveni oranti,
words. But a sudden trembling seizes the limbs of the youth *while* speaking,

oculi diriguere: Erinnys sibilat tot hydris, que
his eyes stiffened: The Fury hisses with so many snakes, and

tanta facies aperit se: tum torquens flammea lumina
so great a form discloses itself then turning her flaming eyes

et repulit cunctantem, et quærentem dicere plura,
both repelled him delaying, and seeking to say many things,

et erexit geminos angues crinibus, que insonuit
and she rais'd two snakes from her hair, and sounded

verbera, que addidit hæc rabido ore: En ego
her lash, and superadds these *words* with her maddening mouth: Lo I

victa situ, quam senectus effœta veri ludet falsâ
overcome by the rust *of age*, whom old age powerless of truth mocks by false

formidine inter arma regum. Respice ad hæc: adsum
fear amidst the arms of kings. Look back to these *things*: I am here

ab sede dirarum sororum; gero bella que lethum manu.
from the seat of the direful sisters; I bear wars and death in my hand.

Effata sic, conjecit facem juveni et fixit tædas
Speaking thus, she cast a firebrand at the youth and planted the torches

fumantes atro lumine sub pectore. Ingens
smoking with blackening light beneath his breast. Great

pavor rupit olli somnum que sudor proruptus toto
fear broke his sleep and sweat bursting from his whole

corpore, perfudit ossa et artus. Amens fremit arma
body, bathes his bones and limbs. Mad he raves for arms.

requirit arma   toro   que   tectis.   Amor ferri,
he seeks   arms in the bed and through the palace.   The love of the sword

et scelerata insania belli,   supèr ira   sævit.
and execrable madness of war, moreover anger rages.

Veluti cum virgea flamma suggeritur costis   aheni
  As   when an osier flame is placed under the sides of a brass vessel

undantis magno   sonore, que latices exsultant   æstu;
boiling   with great noise,   and the liquids boil over   with heat;

vis   aquæ   furit intus, atque fumidus amnis exuberat
the violence of the water rages within,   and   the smoking stream effervesces

spumis   altè; nec jam unda   capit se: ater
with foam   on high;   nor now does the water restrain itself: the blackening

vapor volat ad auras.   Ergo   indicit   iter   primis
steam   flies into the air.   Therefore   he directs the way to the chiefs

juvenum ad regem Latinum, pace pollutâ, et jubet
of the youth to king   Latinus, the peace being violated, and orders

arma   parari,   tutari Italiam, detrudere hostem
arms to be prepared, to protect Italy,   to drive out   the foe

finibus;   se venire satis ambobus, que Teucris
from his boundaries; declaring that he comes sufficient for both, both the Trojans

que Latinis. Ubi   dedit   hæc dicta, que vocavit Divos
and   Latins. When he had uttered these words, and had invoked the Gods

in vota, Rutuli exhortantur sese   certatim in arma.
in his prayers, the Rutulians exhort   each other   eagerly to   arms.

Egregium decus formæ atque juventæ movet hunc,
The remarkable beauty of his form   and   youth   move this one,

atavi   reges   hunc, dextera claris factis
his ancestor kings influence another,his right hand for renowned deeds distinguished

hunc.   Dum Turnus implet Rutulos audacibus
moves   this one. While Turnus fills the Rutulians with daring

animis, Alecto concitat se Stygiis alis   in Teucros;
courage, Alecto raises herself on Stygian wings against the Trojans;

speculata locum novâ arte, quo litore pulcher Iúlus
watching   the place with renewed fraud, on which shore beautiful Iulus

agitabat feras insidiis que cursu. Hìc Cocytia virgo
hunted   wild beasts by snares and the chase. Here the infernal maid

objicit subitam rabiem canibus, et contingit nares
casts   sudden   madness on the dogs,   and   touched their nostrils

noto   odore, ut ardentes agerent cervum; quæ fuit
with the known scent, as glowing they drove the stag; which was

prima causa malorum,   que accendit agrestes animos
the first cause of their misfortunes, and inflamed the rustic minds

bello.   Erat cervus præstanti formâ, et ingens cornibus,
to war. There was a stag of excelling beauty, and large in horns;

quem, raptum ab ubere matris,   Tyrrheidæ pueri
which, snatched from the dugs of its mother,   Tyrrheus' sons

nutribant, que Tyrrheus pater cui regia armenta
nursed,   and Tyrrheus their father whom the royal herds

parent, et custodia campi   latè credita. Sylvia   soror
obey,   and the keeping of the plain far around is entrusted. Sylvia their sister

ornabat ferum, assuetum imperiis,   omni curâ, intexens
adorned the beast, accustomed to her commands, with every care, intertwining

cornua mollibus sertis, que pectebat, que lavabat in
its horns with soft garlands, and she combed it, and washed it in

puro fonte. Ille patiens manum, que assuetus heríli
the clear fountain. He enduring the hand, and accustomed to his master's

mensæ, errabat sylvis; que rursus ipse ferebat se
table, wandered in the woods; and again he withdrew himself

domum ad nota limina, quamvis serâ nocte. Rabidæ
home to the known gates, however late at night. The maddening

canes venantis Iuli commovêre hunc errantem procul, cùm
dogs of hunting Iulus roused him wandering afar off, when

fortè deflueret secundo fluvio, que evaret æstus
by chance he swam down the prosperous stream, and relieved the heat

viridante ripâ. Etiam Ascanius, succensus amore eximiæ
on the green bank. Also Ascanius, inflamed with love of distinguished

laudis, ipse direxit spicula curvo cornu; nec Deus
praise, himself directed his darts from his crooked bow; nor was the God

abfuit erranti dextræ, que arundo acta multo sonitu,
absent from his erring right hand, and the reed driven on with much noise,

venit, que per uterum, que per ilia. At quadrupes
came, both through his stomach, and through his flank. But the animal

saucius refugit intra nota tecta, que gemens
wounded flew back within its known dwelling, and groaning

successit stabulis; que cruentus atque similis imploranti,
came up to the stables; and bloody and like to one entreating,

replevit omne tectum questu. Sylvia soror prima
filled the whole house with complaints. Sylvia the sister first

percussa lacertos palmis, vocat auxilium, et conclamat
striking her arms with her hands, calls assistance, and calls together

duros agrestes. Olli improvisi adsunt (enim aspera pestis
the hardy rustics. They unexpectedly are present (for the cruel plague

latet tacitis sylvis;) hic armatus obusto torre,
lies hid in the silent woods;) this one armed with a burnt brand,

hic modis gravidi stipitis: ira facit telum, quod
this with the knots of a heavy club: anger produces a weapon, whatever

repertum cuique rimanti. Tyrrheus spirans immanè,
is found by each searching. Tyrrheus breathing forth wrathfully,

securi raptâ, vocat agmina, ut fortè scindebat quercum
an axe being seized, calls the troops, as by chance he cut up the oak

quadrifidam coactis cuneis.
split in four parts with driven wedges.

At sæva Dea, nacta è speculis tempus
But the cruel Goddess, having found from the watch-towers a time

nocendi, petit ardua tecta stabuli, et de summe
for doing injury, sought the high roof of the stable; and from the lofty

culmine canit pastorale signum, que intendit Tartaream
height sings forth the shepherd's signal, and stretches her hellish

vocem recurvo cornu; quâ protinus omne nemus
voice with the crooked horn; by which from afar all this grove

contremuit, et profundæ sylvæ intonuere. Et lacus Triviæ
trembled, and the deep woods thundered. And the lake of Diana

longè audivit; amnis Nar, albus sulfureâ aquâ, audivit,
afar off heard; the river Nar, whitened with sulphureous water, heard it,

que fontes Velini; et trepidæ matres pressêre natos ad
and fountains of Velinus: and the trembling mothers press their children to

pectora. Tum verò ad vocem, quâ dira buccina dedit
their breasts. Then indeed at the voice, by which the direful trumpet gave forth

signum, indomiti agricolæ celeres concurrunt undique
the signal, the unconquered farmers swift run together on every side

telis raptis; necnon et Troia pubes effundit auxilium
with weapons seized; likewise both the Trojan youth pour forth assistance

Ascanio apertis castris. Direxere acies; non agitur
to Ascanius from the open camps. They drew up their troops; they are not engaged

jam agresti certamine duris stipitibus ve præustis sudibus·
now in rustic strife with hard clubs or burnt stakes;

sed decernunt ancipiti ferro, que atra seges strictis
but they contend with the doubtful sword, and a direful crop with drawn

ensibus horrescit latè que æra lacessita sole fulgent,
swords bristles up far around and the brazen *armor* being struck by the sun shines,

et jactant lucem sub nubila: utì cum fluctus cœpit
and throws the light beneath the clouds: as when the wave begins

albescere primo vento, mare tollit sese paulatim, et
to grow white with the first wind, the sea raises itself by degrees, and

erigit undas altiùs, inde consurgit imo fundo ad æthera.
elevates the waves higher, then it rises from the lowest depths to the skies.

Hic juvenis Almon, qui fuerat maximus natorum Tyrrhei,
Here the youth Almon, who was the eldest of the sons of Tyrrheus,

sternitur ante primam aciem stridente sagittâ; enim vulnus
is overthrown before the first rank with a hissing arrow; for the wound

hæsit sub gutture et inclusit iter udæ vocis, que
stuck fast under his throat and stopped up the passage of his soft voice, and

tenuem vitam sanguine. Multa corpora virûm circà que
slender life with blood. Many bodies of heroes *fall* around and

senior Galæsus dum offert se medium paci; qui unus
the elder Galesus *falls* while he offers himself in the midst for peace: and alone

fuit justissimus, que olim ditissimus Ausoniis arvis
was the most just, and formerly the richest in the Ausonian fields.

Quinque greges balantum, quina armenta redibant illi,
Five flocks of bleating *sheep*, five herds of cattle returned to him

et vertebat terram centum aratris. Atque dum ea
and he turned up the earth with an hundred ploughs. And while these things

geruntur æquo Marte per campos, Dea facta
are done in the equal contest through the plains, the Goddess being made

potens promissi, ubi . imbuit bellum sanguine, et
powerful of her promise, when she had stained the war with blood,   and

commisit funera primæ pugnæ, deserit Hesperiam, et
had sent death to the first contest, deserts Italy,   and

convexa per auras cœli, victrix affatur Junonem
borne through the air of heaven, a conqueror she addresses Juno

superbâ voce. En discordia perfecta tibi tristi bello!
with a proud voice. Behold the discord wrought for you in this sad war!

dic coant in amicitiam, et jungant fœdera quandoquidem
say that they unite in friendship, and join treaties since

respersi Teucros Ausonio sanguine. Addam hoc etiam
I have sprinkled the Trojans with Ausonian blood. I will add this also

his; si tua voluntas certa mihi, feram finitimas urbes
to them; if your will is sure to me, I will drive the neighbouring cities

in bella rumoribus, que accendam animos amore insani
to war by rumours, and I will inflame their minds with the love of mad

Martis, ut veniant undique auxilio; spargam arma
war, that they may assemble on every side with aid: I will scatter arms

per agros. Tum contra Juno Est abundè
through the fields. Then on the other hand Juno said. There is enough

terrorum et fraudis: causæ belli stant; pugnatur
of terrors and of fraud: the causes of the war remain; let them fight

armis cominus; novus sanguis imbuit arma, quæ prima
with arms hand to hand; new blood has stained their arms, which the first

fors dedit. Egregium genus Veneris, et rex Latinus
chance has given. The renowned son of Venus, and king Latinus

ipse celebrent talia connubia et tales hymenæos. Pater
himself shall celebrate these marriages and such nuptial rites. The father

ille regnator summi Olympi, haud velit te errare
himself the ruler of high heaven, is not willing that you wander

licentiùs super ætherias auras. Cede locis.
at liberty about the etherial skies. Withdraw to your place.

Si qua fortuna laborum superest ego ipsa regam.
If any fortune of labour remains to us I myself will manage it.

Saturnia dederat tales voces. Autem illa attollit
Saturnian Juno had uttered these words. But she raised

alas stridentes anguibus, que petit sedem Cocyti, linquens
her wings hissing with snakes, and seeks the seat of Cocytus, leaving

supera ardua. Est locus, sub altis montibus medio
the exalted high places. There is a place, beneath the lofty mountains in the centre

Italiæ, nobilis, et memoratus famâ in multis oris, valles
of Italy, renowned, and commemorated by fame in many coasts, the vales

Amsancti: latus nemoris atrum densis frondibus, urget
of Amsanctus, the side of the grove black with thick leaves, incloses

hunc utrimque que medio fragosus torrens dat sonitum
it on each side and in the midst a noisy torrent gives a sound

saxis et torto vortice. Hîc specus horrendum et
with rocks and a whirling pool. Here a cave horrid in its aspect and

spiracula sævi Ditis, monstrantur; que ingens vorago
the breathing *places* of dread Pluto, are shown; and a huge gulf

Acheronte rupto, aperit pestiferas fauces; queis Erinnys,
Acheron bursting, opens its pestiferous jaws; in which Erynnys

invisum numen condita levabat terras que cœlum.
the hateful fury being hid relieved the earth and sky.

Nec minus interea Saturnia regina imponit extremam
Nevertheless in the meantime the Saturnian queen places her last

manum bello. Omnis numerus pastorum ruit ex
hand to the war. The whole number of shepherds rushed out from

acie in urbem; que reportant cæsos, Almonem puerum,
the army to the city; and bring back the slain, Almon the youth,

que ora fœdati Galæsi: que implorant Deos, que
and the features of the defiled Galesus: and they intreat the Gods, and

obtestantur Latinum. Turnus adest, que in medio
implore Latinus *for revenge.* Turnus is present, and in the midst

crimine cædis, et ignis ingeminat terrorem, Teucros
of the crime of murder, and of fire redoubles the alarm, that the Trojans

vocari in regna, Phrygiam stirpem admisceri
are called to the kingdom, *that* the Trojan race is to be intermingled *with the*

se pelli limine. Tum quorum matres,
Latins that he is banished from the palace. Then *they* whose mothers,

attonitæ Baccho, insultant thiasis avia nemora,
astounded *by the rites* of Bacchus, leap about in dances in the pathless groves,

(enim neque nomen Amatæ leve,) collecti undique
for neither is the name of Amata of light *concern,*) assembled on every side

coëunt, que fatigant Martem. Ilicet cuncti poscunt
unite, and provoke the war. Forthwith all demand

perverso numine, infandum bellum, contra omina,
by the perverted deity, dreadful war, against the omens,

contra fata Deûm. Certatim circumstant tecta regis
against the fates of the Gods. Eagerly they stand around the palace of the king

Latini. Ille resistit, velut immota rupes pelagi: ut
Latinus. He withstands *them* as an unmoved rock of the ocean as

rupes pelagi, quæ magno fragore veniente, tenet sese
a rock of the ocean, which with great noise approaching, holds itself

mole, multis undis circùm latrantibus: nequicquam
by its mass, many waves around howling: in vain

scopuli et spumea saxa fremunt circùm que alga illisa
the cliffs and foaming rocks roar around and the sea weed uptorn

lateri refunditur. Verùm ubi nulla potestas datur
on its side is thrown back But when no power is granted

exsuperare cæcum consilium, et res eunt nutu sævæ
to overcome the blind counsel, and affairs proceed by the will of dread

Junonis, pater inanis testatus Deos que auras multa,
Juno, the father in vain attesting the Gods and the air much

inquit, Heu! frangimur fatis, que ferimur procellâ,
says, Alas! we are broken down by the fates, and borne off by the storm

O miseri! ipsi pendetis has pœnas sacrilego sanguine.
O wretched men! you   shall pay these penalties with your sacrilegious blood.

Turne, te, nefas, triste supplicium manebit; que
O Turnus, thee, disaster, *and* mournful punishment   shall await;   and

venerabere Deos seris votis. Nam quies est parta
you shall entreat the Gods by late prayers. For   rest   is obtained

mihi, que omnis portus in limine: spolior
for me, and all the harbour *of my cares is* in view: am deprived

felici funere. Nec locutus plura, sepsit se tectis,
of a happy burial.   Nor did he speak more, he shut himself in his palace,

que reliquit habenas rerum. Erat mos in Hesperio
and left   the reins of affairs. *There* was a custom in Hesperian

Latio, quem Albanæ urbes protinus coluere sacrum, nunc
Latium, which the Alban cities long since have honoured as sacred, now

Roma maxima rerum colit, cum movent Martem in prima
Rome the greatest of things honours, when they excite Mars to the first

prœlia; sive parant manu inferre lacrymabile bellum
contests; whether they prepare with the hand to wage mournful   war

Getis. ve Hyrcanis, ve Arabis, seu tendere
against the Getians, or the Hyrcanians, or the Arabians, or to march

ad Indos, que sequi Auroram, que reposcere Parthos
against the Indians, and to follow the morning, and redemand of the Parthians

signa.
standards.

Sunt geminæ portæ belli (sic dicunt nomine) sacræ
There are two gates of war (thus they call *them* by name) sacred

religione et formidine sævi Martis. Centum ærei vectes,
by religion and the fear of dread Mars.   An hundred brazen bolts,

que æterna robora ferri claudunt nec Janus custos
and the eternal strength of iron close *them* nor does Janus the keeper

absistit limine. Ubi certa sententia pugnæ sedet
withdraw from the gate. When the sure sentence of war is settled

patribus, consul ipse, insignis Quirinali trabeâ que
by the fathers, the consul himself, distinguished by a Roman robe and

Gabino cinctu, reserat stridentia limina; ipse vocat
Gabinian cincture, unlocks the creaking gates;   he invites

pugnas: tum cætera pubes sequitur que ærea cornua
the contest. then the other youth follows and the brazen trumpets

conspirant rauco assensu. Et tum Latinus jubebatur
resound   with hoarse concord. And then Latinus was commanded

indicere bella Æneadis hoc more, que recludere
to proclaim war against the Trojans in this manner, and to lay open

tristes portas. Pater abstinuit tactu, que aversus
the mournful gates. Father *Latinus* withdrew from the touch, and turning away

refugit fœda ministeria, et condidit se cæcis umbris.
fled from the foul employment, and concealed himself in the dark shades.

Tum Saturnia regina Deûm, delapsa cœlo ipsa
Then the Saturnian queen of the Gods, gliding down from heaven she

impulit morantes portas manu, et cardine verso,
pushed open the delaying gates with her hand, and the hinge being turn'd,

rupit ferratos postes belli. Ausonia, inexcita atque immobils
burst the iron posts of war. Ausonia at rest and unmoved

antè, ardet. Pars parat ire pedes campis; pars arduus
before, is inflamed A part prepare to go on foot to the plains; a part proud

altis equis pulverulentus furit; omnes
on their high horses involved in dust rush furiously on: all

requirunt arma. Pars tergunt lêves clypeos, et
agerly demand arms. A part cleanse their light shields, and

lucida spicula pingui arvinâ, que subigunt secures in
shining spears with fat tallow, and sharpen their axes on

cote: que juvat ferre signa que audire
the whetstone and it delights them to bear the standards and to hear

sonitus tubarum. Adeo quinque magnæ urbes, incudibus
the sounds of trumpets. Thus five great cities, their anvils

positis, novant tela, potens Atina que superbum
being placed, renew their weapons, powerful Atina and proud

Tibur, Ardea que Crustumeri et turrigeræ antemnæ.
Tibur, Ardea and Crustumeri and turret bearing antemnæ.

Cavant tuta tegmina capitum, que flectunt salignas
They hollow out safe coverings of their heads, and bend the willow

crates umbonum: alii ducunt ahenos thoracas, aut leves
hurdles of their shields: others draw out brazen breastplates, or light

ocreas lento argento. Honos vomeris et
greaves from ductile silver. The honour of the ploughs are and

falcis huc, omnis amor aratri cessit, huc recoquunt
sickle yields here, all love of the harrow yields here, they reforge

patrios enses fornacibus, que jam classica sonant,
their paternal swords in furnaces, and now the trumpets sound.

tessera it signum bello. Hic trepidus rapit
the die goes forth a signal for the war. This man trembling seizes

galeam tectis: ille cogit frementes equos ad juga,
a helmet from the roof: this one joins the neighing horses to the yoke,

que induitur clypeum, que loricam trilicem auro,
and puts on the shield, and coat of mail triple with gold.

que accingitur fido ense. Deæ nunc pandite
and is girded with a faithful sword. Ye Goddesses now open

Helicona, que movete cantus; qui reges exciti
Helicon, and direct my song; what kings have been aroused

bello; quæ acies secutæ quemque compleverint
by the war; what troops following each leader have filled

campos; quibus viris jam tum alma Itala terra floruerit,
the plains; by what men even then the fair Italian land flourished,

quibus armis arserit: enim Divæ et meministis,
with what arms it was inflamed: for ye Goddesses ye both remember

et potestis memorare: vix tenuis aura famæ
and ye can commemorate these things: scarcely has a light breath of fame

perlabitur ad nos Asper Mezentius contêmtor Divûm,
glided by to us. Cruel Mezentius the despiser of the Gods,

primus init bellum ab Tyrrhenis oris, que armat agmina.
first enters the war from the Tuscan coasts, and arms his troops.

Huic juxtà filius Lausus, quo non fuit
Next to him near at hand his son Lausus, than whom there was not

alter pulchrior, corpore Laurentis Turni excepto.
another more beautiful, the form of Laurentine Turnus being excepted.

Lausus domitor equorum, que debellator ferarum, ducit
Lausus the tamer of horses, and destroyer of wild beasts, leads on

mille viros, secutos nequicquam ex urbe Agyllinâ
a thousand men, following him in vain from the city Agylla

dignus qui esset lætior patris imperiis, et
a worthy youth who should have been more joyful in a father's commands, and

cui Mezentius haud esset pater.
to whom Mezentius should not have been a father.

Post hos pulcher Aventinus, satus pulchro Hercule,
After these beautiful Aventinus, sprung from fair Hercules,

ostentat currum insignem palmâ, que victores equos
displays his chariot distinguished by the palm, and his victorious horses

per gramina: que clypeo gerit paternum insigne,
through the grass: and on his shield he bears his father's emblem,

centum angues que hydram cinctam serpentibus; quem
an hundred snakes and a hydra surrounded by serpents; whom

Rhea Sacerdos, mulier mixta Deo, partu edidit furtivum
Rhea the priestess, a woman uniting with a God, at a birth bore secretly

sub auras luminis sylvâ Aventini collis, postquam
into the etherial light in a wood of the Aventine hill, after

Tirynthius victor attigit Laurentia arva, Geryone
Hercules a conqueror had reached the Laurentine fields, Geryon

exstincto, que lavit Iberas boves in Tyrrheno flumine.
being destroyed, and bathed his Iberian heifers in the Tuscan stream.

Manu gerunt pila que sævos dolones in bella, et
In their hand they bear darts and cruel daggers for the war, and

pugnant tereti mucrone, que Sabello veru. Ipse pedes
they contend with the tapering blade, and Sabine dart. He on foot

torquens immane tegmen leonis, impexum terribili setâ
shaking the huge skin of a lion, untrimmed with frightful bristles

cum albis dentibus, indutus capiti; sic subibat regia
with white teeth, placing this on his head; thus entered the royal

tecta horridus que innexus humeros Herculo amictu.
palace horrid to the view and covered as to his shoulders with Hercules' dress.

Tum gemini fratres linquunt Tiburtia mœnia; gentem
Then the two brothers leave the Tiburtian ramparts; the nation

dictam cognominé fratris Tiburti, que Catillus que acer
is called by the name of their brother Tibertus, both Catillus and brave

Coras, Argiva juventus: et feruntur ante primam aciem
Coras, Argive youth; and they are borne before the first troop

inter densa   tela: ceu duo Centauri   nubigenæ,   cùm
amidst thick *flying* darts: as two   Centaurs descendants of the clouds, when

descendunt ab alto vertice montis, linquentes Omolen,
they come down from the lofty top of a mountain, leaving   Omole,

que nivalem Othryn rapido cursu; ingens sylva dat
and snowy   Othrys in their swift course; the great wood gives

locum euntibus, et virgulta cedunt magno fragore.
place   to them going and the shrubbery withdraws with great   noise.

Nec Cæculus, fundator Prænestinæ urbis, defuit; quem
Nor was Cæculus, the founder of the Prænestine city, absent;   whom

regem omnis ætas credidit genitum Vulcano inter agrestia
as king every age believed descended from Vulcan amidst the rustic

pecora, que inventum focis. Agrestis legio comitatur
flocks,   and   found by the fires. A rustic legion accompanies

hunc latè: que viri qui colunt altum Præneste que qui
him from afar: and the men who inhabit high Præneste and   who

arva Gabinæ Junonis, que gelidum Anienem, et
inhabit the fields of Gabinian Juno, and the cold Anio, and

Hernica saxa roscida rivis: quos dives Anagnia, pascis,
the Hernican rocks watered with rivers: whom O rich Anagnia, you feed,

quos   pater Amasene. Non omnibus illis arma,
whom *also you feed* O Father Amasenus. Not to all these do arms,

nec clypei ve currus sonant: maxima pars spargit glandes
nor   shields or chariots sound: the greatest part scatter balls

liventis plumbi, pars gestat bina spicula manu, que habet
of livid   lead,   a part bear two darts in their hand, and have

fulvos galeros de pelle lupi, tegmen capiti; instituere
yellow caps from the skin of a wolf, a covering for their head; they form

vestigia sinistri pedis nuda: crudus pero tegit altera. At
the prints of their left foot naked: a raw shoe protects the other. But

Messapus, domitor equorum, Neptunia proles, quem neque
Messapus, the ruler of horses, Neptune's offspring, whom neither

fas cuiquam sternere igni nec ferro, subitò vocat
was it allowed to any one to prostrate by fire nor sword, suddenly calls

populos jampridem resides que agmina desueta bello, in
the people long since at rest, and the troops unaccustomed to war, to

arma, que retractat ferrum. Hi   Fescennias acies,
arms, and resumes the sword. These *command* the Fescennine troops,

que æquos Faliscos; hi habent arces Soractis, que
and just Falisci; these possess the towers of Soractes, and

Flavinia arva, et lacum Cimini, cum monte, que
the Flavinian fields, and the lake of Ciminus, with the mountain, and

Capenos lucos. Ibant æquati numero, que canebant
the Capenian groves. They went uniform in number, and sang *praises to their*

regem: ceu quondam nivei cycni inter liquida nubila, cùm
king: as when snowy swans amid the liquid clouds, when

referunt sese e pastu, et dant canoros modos
they withdraw themselves from the pasture, and give forth tuneful measures

per longa colla· amnis, et Asia palus pulsa longè
through their long necks; the river *Cayster* and the Asian lake struck from afar

sonat.
resounds.

Nec quisquam putet æratas acies misceri ex
Nor would any one think *them* brass clad troops intermingled from

tanto agmine, sed æriam nubem raucarum volucrum urgeri
so great a band, but an airy cloud of hoarse birds driven on

ab alto gurgite ad litora. Ecce! Clausus, de prisco
from the deep sea to the shores. Lo! Clausus, from the ancient

sanguine Sabinorum, agens magnum agmen, que ipse
blood of the Sabines, leading a great troop, and himself

instar magni agminis; a quo et Claudia tribus et gens
like a great troop; from whom also the Claudian tribe and nation

diffunditur per Latium, postquam· Roma data in
is spread through Latium, after Rome was surrendered in

partem Sabinis. Unà ingens Amiterna cohors, que
part to the Sabines. Together *with them* great Amiterna's band, and

prisci Quirites, omnis manus Ereti que Mutuscæ
the ancient Quirites, all the troop of Eretus and Mutusca

oliviferæ: qui urbem Nomentum, qui
abounding in olives; *those* who *inhabit* the city Nomentum, who *inhabit*

rosea rura Velini, qui colunt horrentes rupes Tetricæ,
the roseate fields of Velinus, who inhabit the frightful rocks of Tetrica,

que montem Severum, que Casperiam, que Forulos et
and the mountain Severus, and Casperia, and Foruli and

flumen Himellæ: qui bibunt Tyberim que Fabarim; quos
the river of Himella: *those* who drink the Tyber and Fabar; whom

frigida Nursia misit, et Hortinæ classes, que Latini populi;
cold Nursia sent, and the Hortine ships, and Latin nations;

que quos Allia, infaustum nomen, secans interluit: quàm
and whom Allia, inauspicious name, dividing flows between: as

multi fluctus volvuntur Libyco marmore, ubi sævus
many waves are rolled along on the Libyan sea, where severe

Orion conditur hibernis undis; vel quot densæ aristæ
Orion is hid by the wintry billows; or as many thick set ears of corn

torrentur novo sole, aut campo Hermi, aut flaventibus
are burnt by the early *summer* sun, either on the plain of Hermus, or the yellow

arvis Lyciæ. Scuta sonant, que tellus excita tremit
fields of Lycia. Their shields resound, and the earth excited trembles

pulsu pedum. Hinc Agamemnonius Halesus, hostis
by the tread of their feet. Hence Agamemnon's Halesus, the enemy

Trojani nominis, jungit equos curru, que rapit mille
of the Trojan name, joins *his* horses to *his* chariot, and draws a thousand

feroces populos Turno, qui rastris vertunt Massica
fierce people to Turnus; *those* who with harrows turn up the Massic *plains*

felicia Baccho, et quos Aurunci patres misere de altis
fruitful in wine, and whom the Auruncian fathers sent from the high

collibus, que juxtà Sidicina æquora que qui linquunt Cales,
hills,   and *those* near by the Sidicinian plains and who   leave   Cales,

que accola vadosi amnis Vulturni, què pariter asper
and the vicinage of the shallow stream Vulturnus,   and likewise   rude

Saticulus que manus Oscorum. Teretes aclides sunt   tela
Saticulus   and the band of the Osci. Tapering darts   are   weapons

illis; sed est   mos aptare hæc lento flagello. Cetra
to them; but it is *their* custom to fit these to a slender thong. A target

tegit illis lævas; falcati enses   cominus.
covers their left *arms*; hooked swords *are theirs with which they fight* hand to hand.

Nec tu, Œbale, abidis indictus nostris carminibus, quem
Nor shall you, O Œbale, pass off unmentioned in our   verses,   whom

Telon fertur generavisse   nymphâ Sebethide, cùm
Telon   is said to have begotten with the nymph Sebethis,   when

jam senior teneret   Capreas, regna Teleboûm; sed et
now an old *man* he held Caprea, the kingdom of the Teleboans; but also

filius, non contentus   patriis arvis, jam tum   latè
the son, not   content   with *his* paternal lands, even then   far around

premebat populos Sarrastes   ditione, et æquora quæ
oppressed   the people *called* Sarrastes by *his* authority, and the plains which

Sarnus rigat; que qui tenent Rufas, que Batulum, atque
Sarnus waters; and who hold Rufas, and   Batulum,   and

arva Celennæ, et   quos mœnia maliferæ Abellæ
the fields of Celenna, and *those* whom the walls of fruit-bearing Abella

despectant; soliti torquere   cateias Teutonico ritu;
look down upon; accustomed to hurl *their* darts in the Teutonic manner;

queis tegmina capitum cortex raptus de subere,   que
whose coverings of their heads was bark torn   from the cork-tree,   and

æratæ peltæ micant, et æreus ensis micat. Et montosæ
their brazen shields glitter, and the brazen sword shines.   And mountainous

Nursæ misere te, Ufens, in prœlia, insignem famâ et
Nursæ   sent   you, O Ufens, to battle,   distinguished by fame, and

felicibus armis; cui præcipuè Æquicola duris glebis,
successful arms; to whom especially *are* the Æquicolæ with their hardy soil,

horrida gens, que assueta multo venatu nemorum, armati
a frightful nation,   and accustomed to much hunting of the groves,   armed

exercent terram, que semper juvat   convectare recentes
they till   the earth, and   ever it delights *them*   to bear off   fresh

prædas et vivere rapto.
plunder and to live by violence.

Quin et fortissimus Umbro venit missu   regis
But   also most brave, Umbro came by the sending   of king

Archippi, sacerdos de Marrubiâ gente, comtus super
Archippus,   a priest   from the Marrubian nation, adorned   upon

galeam fronde et felici olivâ, qui solebat spargere
his helmet with the leaf and happy olive, who was accustomed to scatter

somnos vipereo generi, et hydris graviter spirantibus, que
sleep   on the viperous race,   and hydras dreadfully   breathing,   both

cantu que manu, que mulcebat iras, et levabat
by charming and with the hand, and he soothed their rage, and relieved

morsus arte. Sed non evaluit medicari ictum Dardaniæ
their stings by his art. But he could not cure the blow of a Trojan

cuspidis; neque somniferi cantus et herbæ quæsitæ in Marsis
spear; neither sleep bearing charms and herbs sought in the Marsian

montibus, juvere eum in vulnera. Nemus Angitiæ
mountains, assisted him against those wounds. The grove of Angitea

te, Fucinus vitreâ undâ te, liquidi lacus
lamented thee, Fucinus with glassy wave lamented thee, the liquid lakes

flevere te. Et Virbius proles Hippolyti pulcherrima
lamented thee. And Virbius the offspring of Hippolytus most beautiful

ibat bello, quem insignem mater Aricia misit,
marched to the war, whom illustrious his mother Aricia sent,

eductum lucis Egeriæ, circum humentia litora, ubi
brought up in the groves of Egeria, around the moistened shores, where

pinguis et placabilis ara Dianæ. Namque ferunt famâ,
the rich and placable altar of Diana is. For they report by fame

Hippolytum, postquam occiderit arte novercæ, que
that Hippolytus, after he had fallen by the art of his stepmother, and

distractus turbatis equis, expleverit patrias pœnas
drawn apart by frightened horses, had satisfied his father's punishment

sanguine, venisse rursus ad ætheria sidera, et sub superas
by blood, had come again to the celestial stars, and beneath the superior

auras cœli, revocatum Pæoniis herbis, et amore Dianæ.
airs of heaven, recovered by Pæonian herbs, and the love of Diana.

Tum omnipotens pater, indignatus aliquem mortalem
Then the almighty father, enraged that another mortal could

surgere ab infernis umbris ad lumina vitæ, ipse
rise from the infernal shades to the lights of life, himself

fulmine detrusit Phœbigenam repertorem talis
with his thunderbolt hurled the son of Apollo the discoverer of such

medicinæ et artis ad Stygias undas. At alma Trivia
medicine and art to the Stygian waves. But fair Diana

recondit Hippolytum secretis sedibus, et relegat nymphæ
concealed Hippolytus in secret seats, and transferred him to the nymph

Egeriæ que nemori, ubi solus, ignobilis, exigeret ævum
Egeria and the grove, where alone, unhonoured, he passed his life

in Italis sylvis, que ubi esset Virbius nomine verso:
among the Italian woods, and where he was Virbius his name being changed:

unde etiam cornipedes equi arcentur templo que
whence also the horn-footed horses are driven from the temple and

sacratis lucis Triviæ, quòd pavidi marinis monstris
consecrated groves of Diana, because frightened by sea monsters

effudere currum et juvenem litore. Filius haud
they overturned the chariot and the youth on the shore. His son not

segniùs exercebat ardentes equos æquore campi,
more slothfully exercised his glowing horses on the surface of the plain.

que ruebat curru in bella. Turnus ipse præstanti
and rushed in his chariot to the war. Turnus himself of beautiful

corpore vestitur inter primos, tenens arma, et est supra
body is exercised among the chiefs, grasping his arms, and is above

toto vertice: cui alta galea, crinita triplici jubâ,
the others by a whole head: whose lofty helmet, plumed by a triple crest,

sustinet Chimæram effantem Ætnæos ignes faucibus: illa
upholds a Chimera breathing Ætnean fires from her jaws: she

fremens tam magis, et effera tristibus flammis, quàm
raging so much the more, and savage with mournful flames, as

pugnæ magis crudescunt effuso sanguine. At Io,
the contest the more becomes fierce with flowing blood. But Io,

cornibus sublatis, insignibat levem clypeum auro, jam
with horns upraised, distinguished his light shield with gold, now

obsita setis, jam bos (ingens argumentum) et Argus
covered with bristles, now a heifer (a great device) and Argus

custos virginis, que pater Inachus fundens amnem
the keeper of the maid, and father Inachus pouring out a river

cælatâ urnâ. Nimbus peditum insequitur, que
from his engraved urn. A cloud of foot soldiers followed, and

clypeata agmina densantur totis campis; que Argiva
shielded troops condense through all the plains; and the Argive

pubes, que Auruncæ manus, Rutuli, que veteres Sicani,
youth, and Auruncian bands, the Rutulians, and ancient Sicanians,

et Sacranæ acies, et Labici picti scuta: qui arant
and Sacranian troops, and the Labici painted as to their shields: who plough

tuos saltus, Tiberine, que sacrum litus Numici, que
your lawns, O Tiber, and the sacred shore of Numicus, and

exercent. Rutulos colles vomere, que Circæum
cultivate the Rutulian hills with the ploughshare and the Circæan

jugum; queis avis Anxurus Jupiter præsidet, et Feronia
mount; over whose fields Anxurian Jupiter presides, and Feronia

gaudens viridi luco; quà atra palus Saturæ jacet, que
rejoicing in her green grove; where the black marsh Satura lies, and

gelidus Ufens quærit iter per imas valles, atque conditur
the cold Ufens seeks its way through deep vales, and is lost

in mare.
in the sea.

Super hos Camilla bellatrix, advenit de Volscâ
Beside these Camilla a female warrior, came from the Volscian

gente, agens agmen equitum et catervas florentes ære.
nation, leading on a troop of horsemen and companies flourishing with brass.

Illa non assueta femineas manus colo ve calathis
She had not accustom'd her feminine hands to the distaff or baskets

Minervæ; sed virgo pati dura prœlia, que
of Minerva; but a maid she had learnt to endure severe warfare, and

prævertere ventos cursu pedum. Illa volaret vel per
to outstrip the wind in the swiftness of her feet. She flew either over

summa gramina segetis intactæ, nec læsisset teneras
the highest blades of corn untouched, nor did she injure the tender

aristas cursu; vel ferret iter per medium mare,
ears in her course; or she bore her way through the midst of the sea,

suspensa tumenti fluctu, nec tingeret celeres plantas
sustained by the swelling wave, nor did she dip her swift feet

æquore. Omnis juventus effusa tectis que agris
in the sea. All the youth pouring out from the houses and fields

que turba matrum miratur, et prospectat illam euntem,
and the crowd of matrons admire and regard her going,

inhians attonitis animis; ut regius honos velet leves
gaping with astonished minds; as the royal honour veils her smooth

numeros ostro, ut fibula internectat crinem auro;
shoulders with purple, as the buckle intertwines her hair with gold;

ut ipsa gerat Lyciam pharetram, et pastoralem myrtum
as she wears her Lycian quiver, and shepherd's myrtle

præfixâ cuspide.
on her pointed spear.

ÆNEID.

BOOK EIGHTH.

Ut Turnus extulit signum belli ab Laurenti arce, et
As Turnus raised the standard of war from the Laurentine tower, and

cornua strepuerunt rauco cantu; que ut concussit acres
the trumpets resounded with harsh din; and as he aroused the swift

equos, que ut impulit arma, extemplo animi turbati;
horses, and as he struck the arms, immediately all minds were agitated;

simul omne Latium conjurat trepido tumultu que effera
at the same time all Latium conspires with trembling tumult and the eager

juventus sævit. Primi ductores, Messapus et Ufens, que
youth rage. The first leaders, Messapus and Ufens, and

Mezentius, contemtor Deûm, cogunt auxilia undique,
Mezentius, the despiser of the Gods, collect their forces from every side,

et vastant latos agros cultoribus. Et Venulus mittitur
and lay waste the broad fields for the cultivators. And Venulus is sent

ad urbem magni Diomedis, qui petat auxilium, et edoceat
to the city of great Diomede, who may ask assistance, and inform

Teucros consistere Latio; Ænean advectum classi
that the Trojans are established in Latium; that Æneas had arrived with his fleet

que referre victos   Penates, et dicere se   posci
and   brings the conquered household Gods, and declares himself to be demanded

regem fatis; que multas gentes adjungere se Dardanio
king by the fates; and *that* many nations   join themselves to the Trojan

viro, et   nomen increbescere latè Latio. Quid   struat
hero, and *that* his name   spreads   wide in Latium. What he may purpose

his cæptis; quem eventum pugnæ cupiat, si fortuna
by these attempts; what   event   of war he may desire, if   fortune

sequatur, apparere manifestiùs ipsi   quàm regi Turno aut
favours,   appears   more clear   to himself than to king Turnus   or

regi Latino. Talia   per Latium; cuncta quæ
to king Latinus. Such *things were done* through Latium;   all   which

Laomedontius heros videns, fluctuat magno æstu curarum,
the Trojan   hero   seeing,   fluctuates with a great tide   of cares,

atque dividit celerem animum nunc huc, nunc illuc, que
and   divides his active   mind   now here, now there, and

rapit   in varias partes que versat per   omnia,   sicut
bears it away to various subjects and turns *it* through   all *things*,   as

ubi tremulum lumen aquæ ahenis labris, repercursum sole,
when the tremulous light of water in brazen vessels,   reflected   by the sun

aut imagine radiantis lunæ, pervolitat omnia loca   latè
or by the image of the glowing moon,   flits over   all   places far around

que jam erigitur sub auras, que ferit laquearia summi
and now   is raised near to the skies, and strikes   the ceiling of the lofty

tecti. Erat nox, et altus sopor habebat fessa animalia
roof.   It was night, and deep sleep   possessed wearied   animals

per omnes terras, genus alituum que pecudum; cùm pater
through all   lands, the race of birds and   flocks;   when father

Æneas, turbatus pectora tristi bello, procubuit in ripâ que
Æneas,   disturbed in *his* breast by sad war,   lay   on the bank and

sub axe gelidi ætheris que dedit seram quietem   per
under the pole of the cold sky   and   gave   late   rest   through

membra. Deus ipse   loci, senior Tiberinus, amæno
his limbs.   The God himself of the place, the aged   Tiber, by the pleasant

fluvio, visus huic attollere se inter populeas frondes;
stream, seemed to him   to raise himself among   poplar   leaves;

tenuis carbasus velabat eum glauco amictu, et umbrosa
a light   sail   covered him with a sea-green dress,   and   shady

arundo tegebat crines. Tum   affari sic et demere curas
reed   protected his locks. Then *he began* to speak thus and to banish   cares

his dictis: O sate   gente Deûm qui revehis   nobis
by these words: O sprung from the race of Gods who   bringest back   to us

Trojanam urbem ex hostibus, qui servas æterna   Pergama,
the Trojan   city from *our* enemies, who preservest the eternal citadel of Troy,

expectate Laurenti solo que Latinis arvis; hìc certa
looked for on the Laurentian soil   and   Latian   fields;   here *is* a certain

domus tibi, certi Penates;   ne absiste, neu   terrere
home   for you,   sure household Gods: do not withdraw,   or   be frightened

mınis belli. Omnis tumor et iræ Deûm concessere, que'
by the threats of war.   All   the rage and anger of the Gods have ceased,   and

jam ne   putes   somnum fingere hæc vana,   ingens
now lest you should think *that* sleep   feigns   these vain *things*,   a great

sus inventa tibi   sub   litoreis   illicibus, enixa   fetus
sow discovered by you under the shore-broidering oaks, having borne   a litter

triginta capitum, jacebit; alba, recubans   solo;   albi
of thirty   head,   shall lie; white, reclining on the ground;   her white

nati   circum ubera. Hic erit locus urbis, ea certa requies
offspring around   her dugs.   This shall be a place of a city, this a sure   rest

laborum; ex quo   ter denis annis redeuntibus, Ascanius
of labours; from which *time* thrice ten   years   returning,   Ascanius

condet   urbem Albam clari cognominis. Haud cano
shall build   the city   Alba of renowned   name.   Neither do I sing *things*

incerta.   Nunc adverte, docebo paucis,   quâ ratione
doubtful.   Now   attend,   I will teach   in a few *words* by what means

victor   expedias   quod instat.   Arcades,   genus
a conqueror you may accomplish what   is to be done.   The Arcadians,   a race

profectum a Pallante, qui comites regem Evandrum, qui
descended   from Pallas,   who *as* companions to king   Evander,   who

secuti signa,   delegêre locum his oris, et in montibus
following his banners, have chosen   a place in these coasts, and on the mountains

posuere urbem Pallanteum de nomine Pallantis   proavi.
have placed a city   Pallanteum . from the name   of Pallas   *their* ancestor.

Hi ducunt bellum assiduè cum Latinâ gente; adhibe hos
They   wage   war   continually with the Latin nation;   take   them

socios   castris, et junge fœdera.   Ego ipse ducam te
associates to your camps, and unite   in a treaty.   I   myself will lead you

ripis   et recto flumine, ut subvectus superas adversum
by the banks and direct   stream, so that upborne you may overcome the opposing

amnem remis. Age, surge, nate Deâ, que primis astris
river   with oars.   Come,   arise,   born of a Goddess, and with the first stars

cadentibus fer preces ritè Junoni, que supera iram que
declining   offer prayers formally to Juno,   and surmount *her* anger   and

minas supplicibus votis.   Victor   persolves honorem mihi.
threats   by humble   vows.   A conqueror you shall pay   honour   to me.

Ego sum, quem cernis stringentem ripas pleno flumine,
I   am *he*, whom   you see   grazing   the banks with full   stream,

et secantem pinguia culta,   cæruleus Tibris, amnis
and separating   the rich   cultivated *fields*, azure   Tiber,   a river

gratissimus cœlo. Hìc mihi magna domus: caput exit
most grateful to heaven. Here   to me *is* a great house: my source proceeds

celsis urbibus. Fluvius dixit, deinde condidit se   alto
from lofty cities. The river   *God* said,   then   concealed himself in the deep

lacu, petens ima;   nox que somnus reliquit Æncan.
lake,   seeking the bottom; night   'and   sleep   abandoned   Æneas.

Surgit, et spectans orientia lumina ætherii solis sustulit
He arises, and surveying   the rising   lights of the celestial sun   raised

undam   rite   cavis palmis de flumine, ac effudit tales
water   formally in his hollow hands from the river, and uttered these

voces ad æthera: Nymphæ, Laurentes nymphæ,   unde
words to the skies: Ye nymphs, ye Laurentian   nymphs, from whence

est genus amnibus; que tu, O Tybri genitor, cum tuo
is the origin to rivers; and thou, O Tyber father, with thy

sancto flumine: accipite Ænean, et tandem arcete periculis.
holy stream: receive Æneas, and at last free him from dangers.

Quocunque fonte lacus   tenet te miserantem nostra
In whatever fountain your lake detains you compassionating ou

incommoda, quocunque solo pulcherrimus exis, celebrabere
misfortunes, from whatever soil most beautiful you proceed you shall

    semper meo honore, semper donis, corniger fluvius,
honoured ever by my regard, ever by gifts, horn-bearing river,

regnator Hesperidum aquarum; O tandem adsis, et propriùs
ruler of the Italian waters; O at length be present, and kindly

firmes tua numina. Sic memorat, que legit geminas
confirm thy divinity. Thus he speaks, and selects two

biremes de classe,   que aptat   remigio;   simul
galleys from the fleet, and prepares them for rowing; at the same time

instruit   socios   armis.
he furnishes his companions with arms.

Autem ecce subitum monstrum atque mirabile oculis,
But   lo   a sudden prodigy and wonderful to the eyes;

candida sus concolor cum   albo fœtu, procubuit per
a white sow of one colour with her white litter, lay   in

sylvam que conspicitur in viridi litore; quam pius
the wood and is seen on the verdant shore; which pious

Æneas mactat tibi, enim tibi, maxima Juno, ferens
Æneas offers to thee, even to thee, supreme Juno, offering

sacra et sistit ad aram cum grege. Tybris lenivit
sacrifices and places it at the altar with the flock. Tiber sooth'd

tumentem fluvium eâ nocte, quàm longa est, et refluens
his swelling stream that night, however long it is, and flowing back

ita substitit tacitâ   undâ, ut sterneret   æquor
'thus stood with its silent wave, as he smooth'd the surface

    aquis in morem mitis stagni que placidæ paludis
with its waters in the manner of a gentle pool and a peaceful lake

ut luctamen   abesset   remo. Ergo celerant
so that struggling was absent from the oar. Therefore they hasten

inceptum iter secundo rumore. Uncta abies labitur
their begun journey with favouring shout. The anointed boat glides

vadis et undæ mirantur; nemus insuetum
on the waves, and the surges admire; the grove unused to these things

miratur scuta virûm   fulgentia longè que pictas carinas
admires the shields of men shining from far and the painted keels

innare fluvio. Olli fatigant que noctem que   diem
swim over the river. They weary both night and day

remigio, et superant longos flexus, que teguntur variis
with rowing, and they overcome the long windings, and are protected by various

arboribus, que secant virides sylvas placido æquore.
trees, and cut the green woods *reflected* on the peaceful water.

Igneus sol conscenderat medium orbem cœli, cùm
The fiery sun had ascended the middle circle of heaven, when

vident muros que arcem procul, et rara tecta
they behold the walls and citadel afar off, and scattered roofs

domorum, quæ nunc Romana potentia equavit cœlo:
of the houses, which now Roman power has equalled with the sky:

tum Evandrus habebat inopes res. Advertunt proras
then Evander possess'd his poor estates. They turn *their* prows

ociùs que propinquant urbi. Forté illo die rex Arcas
quickly and approach the city. By chance on that day king Arcas

ferebat solennem honorem magno Aphitryoniadæ, que
offered an annual honour to the great son of Amphitryon, and

Divis in luco ante urbem. Pallas filius unà, omnes
to the Gods in the grove before the city. Pallas his son together, all

primi juvenum unà, que pauper senatus, dabant
the chief of the youth together, and the poor senate, offered

thura huic; que tepidus cruor fumabat ad aras. Ut
frankincense to him; and the warm blood smoked at the altars. As

vidêre celsas rates atque allabi inter opacum nemus,
they saw the lofty ships both to glide among the dark forest.

et incumbere tacitis remis, terrentur subito
and *the sailors* to lean on their silent oars, they are alarmed at the sudden

visu, que cuncti consurgunt mensis relictis; quos
sight, and all arise the tables being abandoned; whom

audax Pallas vetat rumpere sacra que ipse, telo
daring Pallas forbids to interrupt the sacrifices and he, his weapon

rapto, volat obvius, et procul è tumulo inquit:
being seized, flies to meet *them*, and) far from the tomb said.

Juvenes, quæ causa subegit tentare ignotas vias? quò
Young men, what cause compels *you* to attempt unknown ways? whither

tenditis? qui genus? unde domo? ne fertis
do you steer? who *are you as to your* race? where *your* home? do you bring

pacem an arma? Tum Pater Æneas sic fatur ab altâ
peace or arms? Then Father Æneas thus speaks from the lofty

puppi que prætendit ramum paciferæ olivæ manu: vides
ship and extends a branch of peaceful olive in his hand: you see

Trojugenas, ac tela inimica Latinis, quos profugos illi
the sons of Troy, and weapons hostile to the Latins, whom fugitives they

egêre superbo bello. Petimus Evandrum. Ferte hæc
have made by proud war. We seek Evander. Bear these *things*

et dicite lectos duces Dardaniæ venisse, rogantes socia
and say *that* chosen leaders of Troy have come, asking friendly

arma. Pallas perculsus tanto nomine obstupuit; ait,
arms. Pallas struck by so great a name stood amaz'd; he said

O quicunque   es,   egredere que alloquere coram parentem
O whoever   you are, approach and   speak   before   my father

ac hospes succede nostris Penatibus. Que accepit manu,
and a guest approach our   household gods. And he took him by the hand,

que amplexus   dextram   inhæsit; progressi   subeunt
and embracing his right hand clung to him; advancing they enter

luco, que relinquunt fluvium Tum Æneas affatur regem
the grove, and leave   the river. Then Æneas addresses the king

amicis dictis: Optime   Grajugenûm, cui   fortuna
with friendly words: O best of the sons of the Greeks, to whom fortune

voluit   me precari, et prætendere ramos   comptos
has willed that I pray, and hold out branches   adorned

vittâ: Equidem   non   extimui,   quòd
with the fillet   Indeed   neither   had I feared, because

ductor Danaûm et Arcas, que quòd a   stripe
a leader of the Greeks and an Arcadian, and because from your origin

fores conjunctus geminis Atridis; sed mea virtus,
you were united with the two sons of Atreus; but my own courage,

et sancta oracula Divûm, que cognati patres, tua fama
and the holy oracles of the Gods, and our related fathers, your own fame

didita terris, conjunxere me tibi; et egere   me
spread over the earth, had united me to you; and   made   me

volentem fatis; Dardanus primus pater et auctor
obedient to the fates; Dardanus the first parent and founder

Iliacæ urbis, cretus Electrâ Atlantide, ut Graii
of the Trojan city, born from Electra daughter of Atlas, as Greeks

perhibent, advehitur Teucros; Maximus Atlas, qui
relate,   is borne on   to the Trojans; All powerful Atlas,   who

sustinet ætherios orbes humero, edidit   Electram.
upholds   the celestial spheres with his shoulder, begot   Electra.

Mercurius est pater vobis, quem conceptum candida
Mercury   is father to you, whom being conceived fair

Maia fudit gelido vertice Cyllenes. At, si credimus
Maia bore on the cold top of Cyllene. But, if we believe

quicquam auditis, Atlas, idem Atlas, qui tollit sidera
any thing in things is heard, Atlas, the same Atlas, who supports the stars

cœli, generat Maiam. Sic genus amborum scindit se
of heaven, begat Maia. Thus the race of both divides   itself

ab uno sanguine. Fretus his, non pepigi legatos,
from one blood. Trusting to these, I did not resort to ambassadors,

neque prima tentamenta tui per artem: ipse objeci
nor   the first trials of you by art: I have exposed

me, me, que meum caput, et supplex veni ad limina.
myself, myself, and my own life, and humbly have come to your gates.

Eadem Daunia gens, quæ insequitur te crudeli bello; si
The same Daunian race, which persecutes you by cruel war; 11

pellant nos, credunt nihil abesse, quin mittant
they should banish us, they believe nothing is wanting, but they will send

omnem Hesperiam penitùs sub sua juga, et teneant mare,
till   Italy   far   under their yokes, and will hold the sea,

quod alluit suprà, que quod infrà. Accipe que da
which flows   above, and which is beneath. Receive and impart

fidem.   Sunt nobis pectora fortia bello, sunt animi, et
confidence. These are to us breasts brave for war, these are minds, and

juventus spectata rebus. Æneas dixerat; ille jamdudum
youth   experienced in deeds. Æneas   said;   he   long

lustrabat os que oculos loquentis, et totum corpus lumine
had surveyed the face and eyes of him speaking, and his whole body with his eye

Tunc refert pauca sic: ut libens accipio que
Then he responds in a few words thus: how willingly I receive and

agnosco te, fortissime Teucrûm! ut recordor verba,
acknowledge you, most brave of the Trojans! how I call to mind the words,

et vocem que vultum magni parentis Anchisæ; nam
and voice and looks of your great father Anchises; for

memini Laomedontiaden Priamum, visentem regna
I remember that Laomedon's son Priam   visiting the kingdoms

sororis Hesiones, petentem Salamina, protinùs invisere
of his sister Hesione, seeking Salamis, from afar came

gelidos fines Arcadiæ.
to the cold boundaries of Arcadia.

Tum prima juventa vestibat mihi genas flore: que
Then early youth clothed my cheeks with its flower: and

mirabar Teucros duces, et mirabar Laomedontiaden ipsum;
I admired the Trojan leaders, and I admired the son of Laomedon himself;

sed Anchises ibat altior cunctis. Mens ardebat mihi
but Anchises walked higher than all. My mind glowed to me

juvenili amore compellare virum, et conjungere dextram
with youthful love to address the hero, and unite my right hand

dextræ. Accessi, et cupidus duxi sub mœnia Phenei.
to his right hand. I approached, and anxiously I led him to the walls of Pheneus.

Ille discedens dedit mihi insignem pharetram, que Lycias
He departing gave to me a splendid quiver, and Lycian

sagittas que chlamydem intertextam auro que bina aurea
arrows, and a cloak interwoven with gold and two golden

frœna, quæ meus Pallas nunc habet. Ergo et dextra
bridles, which my Pallas now has. Therefore both my right hand

quam petitis est juncta mihi fœdere, et cum primùm
which you ask is joined by me in treaty, and when first

crastina lux reddet se terris, dimittam lætos auxilio
to-morrow's light shall restore itself to the earth, I will send you joyful with aid

que juvabo opibus. Interea, quando venistis
and I will assist you with my wealth. In the mean time since you have come

huc amici, faventes nobiscum celebrate hæc annua sacra
here friends, rejoicing with us celebrate these annual sacrifices

quæ nefas differe et jam—nunc—assuescite mensis
which it is wrong to put off and now—now— be accustomed to the tables

sociorum. Ubi hæc   dicta,   jubet dapes et pocula
of your friends.   When these *things* were said, he orders feasts   and   bowls

sublata reponi   que ipse locat viros gramineo sedile: que
borne in   to be replaced and   ne   places the men on the grassy   seat: and

accepit præcipuum Ænean   toro,   et pelle villosi leonis,
receives   distinguished   Æneas   on a couch, and the skin of a shaggy   lion,

que invitat   acerno solio.   Tum lecti juvenis que sacerdos
and   invites *him to* a maple throne.   Then chosen   youth   and   the priest

aræ   certatim ferunt tosta viscera taurorum que onerant
of the altar eagerly   bear   roasted entrails   of bulls   and   load

dona laboratæ cereris canistris, que ministrant Bacchum.
the gifts of prepared   corn   in baskets,   and   supply   wine.

Æneas et simul Trojana juventus, vescitur tergo perpetui
Æneas   and at once the Trojan   youth,   fed   on the chine of a whole

bovis et lustralibus extis. Postquam fames exempta, et
ox   and the consecrated entrails.   After   hunger was overcome, and

amor edendi compressus, rex Evandrus ait: Non
the love of eating   repressed,   the king   Evander   said: Not

superstitio vana que ignara veterum Deorum, imposuit hæc
superstition   vain   and ignorant of the ancient gods,   has imposed these

solennia nobis, has dapes   ex   more, hanc   aram
solemnities   on us,   these feasts according to our manner, this   altar

tanti numinis, Trojane hospes, servati sœvis periculis,
of so great   a god,   O Trojan   guest,   preserved from cruel   dangers.

facimus que novamus meritos honores. Jam primùm aspice
we perform and   renew   deserved honours.   Now   first   see

hanc rupem suspensam saxis—ut moles disjecta   procul.
this   rock   suspended   by cliffs—as the mass scattered   far around,

que domus montis   stat deserta, et scopuli   traxere
and the house of the mountain stands abandoned, and the rocks have drawn down

ingentem ruinam.   Hìc fuit spelunca submota vasto
great   destruction.   Here has been   a cave   removed   into a vast

recessu, quam, inaccessam radiis solis,   dira   facies
recess,   which,   inaccessible to the rays of the sun, the direful   form

Caci semihominis tenebat: que semper humus tepebat
of Cacus   half human   held: and   always   the ground was warm

recenti cœde; que ora   virûm affixa superbis   foribus
with fresh slaughter; and the faces of men   fastened to the proud   doors

pendebant pallida tristi tabo. Vulcanus erat pater   huic
hung   pale   with sad gore.   Vulcan   was father   to this

monstro; vomens illius atros ignes ferebat   se   magnâ
monster;   belching   his   black flames he bore   himself   with his vast

mole. Aliquando ætas attulit et auxilium que adventum
bulk.   At length   time   brought both   aid   and   the advent

Dei nobis optantibus. Nam Alcides aderat,   maximus
of a God to us   desiring.   For   Hercules was present, *our*   great

ultor superbus   nece   que spoliis tergemini   Geyronis,
avenger   e ated   by the death and   spoils of the triple-formed   Geyron,

que victor agebat ingentes tauros hàc: que boves tenebant
and a conqueror drove his great bulls here: and the heifers possessed

vallem que amnem. At mens Caci effera furiis, ne
the vale and the river. But the mind of Cacus brutal through rage, lest

quid ve sceleris ve doli fuisset inausum aut
any thing either of crime or fraud should have been not dared or

intractatum, avertit quatuor tauros præstanti corpore a
unattempted, turned away four bulls of beautiful form from

stabulis, totidem juvencas superante formâ: atque
the stables, and as many heifers of excelling beauty: and

occultabat hos opaco saxo, tractos in speluncam caudâ,
hid them in a dark cliff, dragged into the cave by the tail,

que raptos versis indiciis viarum ne forent qua
and drawn by the inverted tracks of the paths lest there should be any

vestigia rectis pedibus. Nulla signa ferebant quærentem
marks of direct feet. No signs led him seeking

ad speluncam. Interea cùm jam Amphitryoniades
to the cave. In the mean time when now Hercules

moveret saturata armenta stabulis, que pararet abitum
moved the full fed flocks from the stables, and prepared to depart

boves mugire discessu, atque omne nemùs impleri
the heifers began to low at their departure, and all the grove to be filled

querelis, et colles relinqui clamore, Una boum
with complaints, and the hills to be left with a cry. One of the heifers

reddidit vocem, que mugivit sub vasto antro, et custodita
returned the cry, and bellowed under the vast cave, and guarded

fefellit spem Caci. Hìc verò dolor atro felle exarserat
deceived the hope of Cacus. Here indeed grief with black gall inflamed

Alcidæ furiis: rapit arma manu, que robur gravatum
Hercules' rage: he seizes arms in his hand, and a club heavy

nodis, et petit ardua aërii montis cursu. Tum primùm
with knots, and seeks the height of an airy mountain in his course. Then first

nostri videre Cacum timentem que turbatum oculis.
our friends beheld Cacus fearing and disturbed in his eyes.

Ilicit fugit ocior Euro, que petit speluncam; timor
Forthwith he flies swifter than the east wind, and seeks the cave; fear

addidit alas pedibus. Ut inclusit sese, que catenis ruptis
added wings to his feet. As he inclosed himself, and the chains being burst

dejecit immane saxum, quod pendebat ferro, et
he threw down the huge rock, which hung suspended by iron, and

paternâ arte, que emuniit postes fultos obice; ecce!
his father's art, and fortified the posts supported by a bolt; lo!

Tirynthius, furens animis, aderat que lustrans omnem
Hercules, raging in his feelings, was present and surveying all

accessum, ferebat ora huc et illuc, infrendens dentibùs.
the approach; cast his eyes here and there, gnashing with his teeth.

Fervidus irâ, ter lustrat totum montem Aventini; ter
Glowing with rage, thrice he surveys all the mountain of Aventine; thrice

nequicquam tentat saxea limina: ter fessus   resedit
in vain   he tries the rocky gates: thrice wearied he sat down

valle. Acuta silex stabat saxis præcisis undique,
in the vale. A sharp cliff stood with rocks cut off on every side,

insurgens dorso speluncæ, altissima visu, domus opportuna
rising   on the back of the cave, very high to view, an abode   fit

rudis dirarum volucrum.
for nests of direful birds.

Dexter, nitens in adversum,   concussit hanc,
On the right bending against the opposing *rock*, he shook   it,

ut prona incumbebat jugo ad amnem lævum, et
so *that* inclining it leaned against the mountain to the river on the left, and

solvit avulsum imis radicibus; inde repentè impulit;
broke *it* torn up from its lowest roots;   then suddenly he hurled *it* down;

quo impulsu maximus æther insonat, ripæ dissultant
by which effort the wide-extended air resounds, the banks leap apart

que amnis exterritus refluit. At specus, et ingens regia
and the river terrified flows back. But the den, and great palace

Caci detecta apparuit, et ambrosæ cavernæ penitus
of Cacus uncovered appeared, and the shady caverns deeply

patuere; non secus ac si terra, penitus dehiscens quâ
were exposed; not otherwise than if the earth, deeply opening by any

vi, reseret infernas sedes, et recludat pallida regna,
violence, should unlock the infernal seats, and lay open the pale kingdoms,

invisa Dîs; que immane barathrum cernatur super, que
hated by the Gods; and the dreadful abyss should be seen from above, and

manes trepident lumine immisso. Ergo Alcides premit
the shades tremble light being admitted. Therefore Hercules pierced *him*

telis desuper repentè deprensum in insperatâ luce, que
with darts from above suddenly seized in the unhoped-for light, and

inclusum cavo saxo, atque rudentem insueta, que
shut up in the hollow rock, and braying forth unaccustomed *sounds*, and

advocat omnia arma, et instat ramis que vastis
calls on every kind of arms, and presses *him* with branches and vast

molaribus. Autem ille enim neque jam ulla fuga periculi
mill-stones, But he for neither now any flight of danger

superest evomit ingentem fumum faucibus, mirabile dictu!
remained vomits much smoke from his jaws, wonderful to be told!

que involvit domum cæcâ caligine, eripiens prospectum
and overwhelms the house with black smoke, snatching the prospect

oculis; que glomerat fumiferam noctem sub antro,
from our eyes; and gathers smoky night under the cave,

tenebris commixtis igne. Alcides animis non tulit,
darkness mingled with fire. Hercules in his rage did not bear *it*,

que ipse jecit se per ignem præcipiti saltu, quà
and he cast himself through the fire with headlong leap, where

plurimus fumus agit undam, que ingens specus æstuat
the abundant smoke drives out its wave, and the huge den undulates

atrâ nebulâ. Hic corripit Cacum, vomentem vana
with a black cloud. He seizes Cacus, vomiting vain

incendia in tenebris, complexus in nodum, et inhærens
fires in darkness, grasping *him* in a knot, and seizing

angit elisos oculos, et guttur siccum sanguine. Extemplo
he squeezes his forced out eyes, and throat dry of blood. Forthwith

atra domus panditur foribus revulsis; que abstractæ boves
the black house is opened the doors being torn off; and the stolen heifers

que abjuratæ rapinæ, ostenduntur cœlo: que informe cadaver
and forsworn plunder, are exposed to heaven; and the deformed corse

protrahitur pedibus. Corda nequeunt expleri tuendo
is drawn out by the feet. Our hearts cannot be satisfied with beholding

terribiles oculos, vultum que pectora semiferi villosa
the terrible eyes, face and breast of the half-monster shaggy

setis, atque ignes extinctos faucibus. Ex illo
with bristles, and the fires extinguished in his jaws. From that *time*

honos celebratus, que læti minores servavere diem;
his fame *is* celebrated, and joyful posterity have observed the day,

que primus auctor Potitius, et Pinaria domus custos
and *our* first founder Potitius, and the Pinarian family the keeper

Herculei sacri, statuit hanc aram luco, quæ semper
of the Herculean sacrifice, has established this altar in the grove, which ever

erit maxima. Quare agite, O juvenes, in munere tantarum
shall be greatest. Wherefore come on, O young men, in the favour of so great

laudum cingite comas fronde, et porrigite pocula
praises encircle your hair with the leaf, and hold out goblets

dextris; que vocate communem Deum, et volantes
in your right hands; and invoke *our* common God, and willing

date vina. Dixerat, cùm populus vicolor velâvit comas
give wine. He said, when the poplar variegated veiled his locks

Herculeâ umbrâ, que pependit, innexa foliis: et sacer
with Hercules' shade, and hung, bound with leaves: and the sacred

scyphus implevit dextram. Omnes ociùs læti libant
cup filled his right hand. All quick joyful make libation

in mensam, que precantur Divos. Interea Vesper
on the table, and entreat the Gods. In the meantime the evening

fit proprior devexo Olympo: que jam sacerdotes, que
becomes nearer in the declining sky: and now the priests, and

primus Potitius, ibant cincti pellibus in morem,
first Potitius, went covered with skins according to *their* manner,

que ferebant flammas. Instaurant epulas, et ferunt grata
and bore flames. They renew the feasts, and bear grateful

dona secundæ mensæ, que cumulant aras oneratis lancibus.
gifts to the second table, and heap the altars with loaded dishes.

Tum Salii evincti tempora populeis ramis, adsunt ad
Then the Salii bound about their temples with poplar branches, are present at

cantus, circum incensa altaria; hic chorus juvenum, ille
the songs, around the burning altars; this band of young men, that

senum, qui ferunt Herculeas laudes et facta carmine; ut
of old men, who   extol   Hercules'   praises and deeds   in song; how

premens eliserit prima monstra   novercæ,   que geminos
strangling he tore the first monsters of his step-mother, and   her two

angues manu;   ut idem disjecerit urbes que Trojam, que
snakes with his hand; how the same overthrew cities both Troy,   and

Œchaliam egregias bello; ut pertulerit mille duros labores
Œchalia   renowned in war; how he endured a thousand severe labours

sub rege Eurystheo, fatis iniquæ Junonis. Tu invicte
nder king Eurystheus, by the fates of unjust Juno.   You unconquered

bìmembres nubigenas, que Hylæum que Pholum
slay the double limbed sons of the clouds, both Hylæus and Pholus

manu;   tu mactas Cressia prodigia, et vastum leonem
with your hand; you   slay   the Cretan monsters, and the vast   lion

sub rupe Nemeæ. Stygii lacus tremuere te. Janitor
under the rock of Nemea. The Stygian lakes trembled for you. The keeper

Orci, recubans cruento antro super semesa ossa,   te,
of hell, reclining in his bloody cave upon half-eaten bones,   for you

nec ulla facies   non arduus Typhæus
trembles, nor did any forms terrify you, nor did lofty Typheus

ipse, tenens arma terruit te; Lærnæus anguis turbâ
himself, holding arms terrify you; the Lærnean snake with his host

capitum, circumstetit te non egentem rationis. Salve vera
of heads, stalked around you not deprived of reason. Hail true

proles Jovis, addite decus Divis: dexter adi et nos et
offspring of Jove, add honour to the Gods: kindly visit both us and

tua sacra secundo pede. Celebrant talia carminibus:
your sacrifices with favouring foot. They celebrate these things with songs:

super omnia adjiciunt speluncam Caci, que ipsum spirantem
above   all   they add   the cave of Cacus, and himself   breathing

ignibus. Omne nemus consonat strepitu que colles
in fires. All the grove resounds with the noise and the hills

resultant.
rebound.

Exin divinis rebus   perfectis,   cuncti referunt
Then these divine actions being accomplished,   all   withdraw

se ad urbem. Rex ibat obsitus   ævo;   et
themselves to the city. The king went oppress'd with age; and

ingrediens tenebat Ænean comitem que natum juxtà.
walking he held Æneas as a companion and his son near by.

Que levabat viam vario sermone. Æneas miratur
And he relieved the way with various discourse. Æneas admires

que fert faciles oculos circum omnia, que capitur
and moves his nimble eyes around all things, and is captivated

locis,   et lœtus que exquirit que audit singula
with the places, and joyful both he seeks and hears   all

monumenta priorum virûm. Tum Rex Evandrus conditor
the monuments of former men. Then the king Evandrus the builder

Romanæ arcis: Fauni que Nymphæ indiginæ, que gens
of the Roman tower *spoke:* The Fauns and Nymphs   natives,   and a race

virûm nata truncis   et duro robore, tenebant hæc nemora,
of men born in trunks *of trees* and hard   oak,   possessed   these   groves,

queis erat neque mos neque cultus;   nec nôrant
to whom was neither manners nor cultivation;   nor did they know

jungere tauros, aut componere opes, aut   parcere
to yoke   bulls,   or   to gather wealth, or   to spare

parto;   sed rami atque asper venatus victu
what they had obtained: but branches and   savage hunting   with food

alebat.   Saturnus primus venit ab ætherio Olympo.
cherished *them.* Saturn · first   came from celestial   Olympus.

fugiens arma Jovis, exul regnis ademptis.   Is
flying   the arms of Jove, an exile his kingdoms being taken away.   He

composuit genus indocile ac dispersum altis montibus,
formed   a race untaught and scattered in the lofty mountains,

que dedit leges; que maluit vocari Latium, quoniam
and gave laws; and chose to be called Latiam,   since

latuisset tutus in his oris. Aurea secula, quæ perhibent,
he lay conceal'd safe in these coasts. The golden ages, which they speak of,

fuerunt sub illo rege; sic regabat populos in placidâ pace;
had been under this king; thus he ruled the people in tranquil peace;

donec paulatim deterior et decolor ætas, et rabies belli,
until by degrees a worse and varied age, and the madness of war,

et amor habendi successit. Tum Ausonia manus, et
and the love of possessing succeeded. Then the Ausonian band,   and

Sicanæ gentes venere; et sæpius Saturnia tellus posuit
the Sicilian nations came, . and often the Saturnian land   laid aside

nomen. Tum reges que asper Tibris immani corpore;
its name. Then *came* kings and cruel Tiber of immense   body;

a quo post Itali diximus fluvium Tibrim cognomine;
from whom afterwards the Italians called the river Tiber   by name,

vetus Albula amisit verum nomen. Omnipotens fortuna
old   Albula lost her true name.   Omnipotent   fortune

et ineluctabile fatum posuere me his locis, pulsum
and inevitable   fate   have placed me in these places, banished

patriâ,   que sequentem extrema pelagi; que tremenda
from my country, and following the extremity of the ocean; and   dreadful

monita Carmentis Nymphæ matris, et Deus Apollo
admonitions of Carmentis the Nymph *my* mother, and the God   Apollo

auctor, egere. Vix ea dicta, progressus dehinc,
our patron, urged us on. Hardly these *words* were said, proceeding   thence,

monstrat et aram, et Carmentalem portam Romano
he points out both the altar, and the Carmentalian gate *call'd* by a Roman

nomine, quam memorant priscum honorem Carmentis
name,   which they declare *to be* the ancient honour of the Carmental

Nymphæ fatidicæ vatis, quæ prima cecinit Æneados
Nymph   the fate declaring prophetess, who first foretold *that* the Trojans

futuros magnos et Pallanteum nobile. Hinc ingentem
would be great and Pallanteum noble. Hence *he shows* a great

ucum, quem acer Romulus retulit asylum, et monstrat
grove, which brave Romulus made a sanctuary, and shews

Lupercal sub gelidâ rupe; dictum de Parrhasio more
the Lupercal under the cold rock, call'd from the Arcadian manner

Lycæi—Panos. Nec non et monstrat nemus sacri Argileti,
of Lycean Pan, Likewise also he points out the grove of sacred Argiletus,

que testatur locum, et docet lethum hospitis Argi. Hinc
and calls to witness the place, and teaches the death of his guest Argus. Hence

ducit ad Tarpeiam sedem et Capitolia, nunc aurea,
he leads to the Tarpean seat and the. Capitol, now golden,

olim horrida sylvestribus dumis. Jam tum dira
formerly rough with wild bushes. Even then the dreadful

religio loci terrebat pavidos agrestes; jam tum tremebant
religion of the place frightened the fearful rustics; even then they trembled

sylvam que saxum. Inquit, Deus (est incertum quis Deus)
at the wood and the rock. He says, a God (it is doubtful what God)

habitat hoc nemus, hunc collem frondosâ vertice. Arcades
inhabits this grove, this hill with leafy top. The Arcadians

credunt se vidisse Jovem ipsum cùm sæpe concuteret
believe they have seen Jupiter himself when often he had shaken

nigrantem Ægida dextrâ, que cieret nimbos.
his blackening shield with his right hand, and aroused the clouds.

Præterea vides hæc duo oppida muris disjectis, reliquias
Besides you see these two towns the walls being overthrown, the reliques

que monumenta veterum virorum: pater Janus condidit
and monuments of former men: father Janus built

hanc, Saturnus hanc urbem, Janiculum fuerat nomen
this, Saturn that city, Janiculum has been the name

huic, Saturnia illi. Talibus dictis inter se subibant
to this, Saturnia to that. With such words among themselves, they arrived

ad tecta pauperis Evandri; que videbant armenta passim
at the palace of poor Evander; and saw the herds every where

mugire Romano foro, et lautis Carinis. Ut ventum
to low in the Roman forum, and proud *street* Carinæ. As they came

ad sedes, inquit, Alcides victor subivit hæc limina; hæc
to the seats, he said, Hercules a conqueror entered these gates; this

regia cepit illum: hospes, aude contemnere opes, et finge
palace received him; O guest, dare to despise riches, and render

te quoque dignum Deo que veni non asper egenis
yourself also worthy a God and come not churlish to our poor

rebus. Dixit, et duxit ingentem Ænean subter fastigia
possessions. He said, and lead great Æneas beneath the roof

angusti tecti, que locavit stratis, effultum foliis et
of his humble house, and placed *him* on a couch, supported by leaves and

pelle Libystidis ursæ. Nox ruit, et amplectitur tellurem
the skin of a Lybian bear. Night rushes on, and embraces the earth

fuscis alis. At Venus mater, haud nequicquam exterrita
with gloomy wings. But Venus *his* mother, not in vain alarmed

animo, mota que minis Laurentum, et duro
in her mind, moved also by the threats of the Laurentians, and direful

tumultu, alloquitur Vulcanum, que incipit hæc aureo
tumult, addresses Vulcan, and begins these *words* in the golden

thalamo conjugis, et aspirat divinum amorem
marriage chamber of her husband, and inspires divine love

dictis. Dum Argolici reges vastabant bello debita
by her words. While the Grecian kings laid waste by war the destined

Pergama que arces casuras inimicis ignibus, non
walls of Troy and towers about to fall by hostile fires, neither

rogavi illum auxilium miseris, non arma tuæ
did I ask that aid for *my* wretched *friends*, nor arms of your

artis que opis, nec volui exercere te, carissime
art and aid, nor have I wished to exercise you, O dearest

conjux, ve tuos labores incassum. Quamvis et deberem
husband, or your labours in vain. Although even I had owed

plurima natis Priami, et sæpe flevissem durum laborem
many things to the sons of Priam, and often I had mourned the cruel labour

Æneæ. Nunc constitit oris Rutulorum imperiis
of Æneas. Now he has landed on the coasts of the Rutulians by the commands

Jovis: ergo, eadem venio supplex et genetrix nato,
of Jove: therefore the same I come humble and a mother for a son,

rogo arma numen sanctum mihi. Filia Nerei
ask arms of your deity sacred to me. The daughter of Nereus

potuit flectere te, Tithonia conjux te lacrymis.
could influence you, Tithonus' wife *could influence* you with tears.

Aspice qui populi coëant, quæ mænia acuant ferrum
Behold what people unite, what towns sharpen the sword

portis clausis in me que excidium meorum!
their gates being closed against me and the ruin of my *friends!*

Diva dixerat, et niveis lacertis hinc atque hinc
The Goddess spoke, and with snowy arms on this side and that

fovet cunctatem molli amplexu: ille repentè accepit
she fondles *him* delaying in her soft embrace. he suddenly catches

solitam flammam que notus calor intravit medullas,
the accustomed flame and the known warmth entered his marrow,

et cucurrit per labefacta ossa; non secus atque olim
and ran through his agitated bones; not otherwise than as sometime

cum ignea rima rupta corusco tonitru, micans percurrit
when a fiery flash bursting from glittering lightning, shining runs over

nimbos lumine. Conjux læta dolis, et conscia formæ
the clouds with light. His wife rejoiced by the fraud, and conscious of beauty,

sensit. Tum pater, devinctus æterno amore, fatur
perceived *it*. Then the father, bound by eternal love, says

Quid petis causas ex alto? quó fiducia mei cessit
Why do you seek causes from afar? whether has confidence of me ceas'd

tibi Diva? si   fuisset similis cura, tum quoque fuisset
to you O Goddess? if *there* had been a like care, then also it had been

fas nobis armare Teucros. Nec omnipotens pater, nec
lawful for me to arm the Trojans. Nor the Almighty father, nor

fata vetabant Trojam stare, que Priamum superesse
the fates did forbid Troy to stand, and Priam to survive

per alios decem annos. Et nunc si paras bellare atque
through other ten years, And now if you prepare to fight and

est tibi hæc mens, quidquid curæ in meâ arte possum
there is to you this disposition, whatever of care *there is* in my art I can

promittere, quid potest fieri ferro ve liquido electro,
promise, what can be done by iron or liquid amber,

quantum ignes que animæ valent; absiste indubitare
whatever fires and blasts can effect; cease to doubt

tuis viribus precando. Locutus ea verba, dedit
your own powers in praying. Having spoken these words, he gave

optatos amplexus; que infusus gremio conjugis petivit
the desired embraces; and stretched on the bosom of his wife he sought

placidum soporem per membra. Inde ubi prima quies
peaceful sleep through his limbs. Then when the first rest

expulerat somnum; medio curriculo noctis jam abactæ,
had banished sleep; in the midst of the circle of night now pass'd away,

cum fœmina cui primum tolerare vitam colo
when the female to whom *it is* a first *duty* to support life by the distaff

que tenui Minervâ, suscitat cineram impositam
and the graceful *arts* of Minerva, awakens the ashes covered up

et sopitos ignes, addens noctem operi, que exercet
and the sleeping fires, adding night to her labour, and exercises

famulas ad lumina longo penso, ut possit servare
her female servants by the lights with a long task, that she may preserve

cubile conjugis castum, et educere parvos natos; haud
the bed of her husband chaste, and bring up her little children; not

secus ignipotens, nec segnior illo tempore
otherwise the fire powerful God, not more slothful at that time

surgit e mollibus stratis ad fabrilia opera. Insula erigitur
arises from his soft couch to his mechanical labours. An island arises

juxta Sicanium latus que Eoliam Liparen, ardua
near to the Sicilian side and Eolian Lipare, high

fumentibus saxis; subter quam specus, et Etnea antra,
with smoking rocks; beneath which a den, and Etnean caves,

exesa caminis Cyclopum, tonant, que validi ictus
perforated by chimneys of the Cyclops, thunder, and powerful blows

incudibus auditi referunt gemitum que stricturæ chalybum
on anvils heard re-echo the groan and bars of steel

stridunt cavernis, et ignis anhelat fornacibus; domus
hiss in the caverns, and the fire pants in the furnaces; the house

Vulcani, et Vulcania tellus nomine. Tunc Ignipotens
of Vulcan, and the Vulcanian land by name. Then the fire powerful *God*

descendit huc ab alto cœlo. Cyclopes que Brontes que
descended   here from the high heaven. The Cyclops and   Brontes   and

Steropes et Pyræmon nudus   membra, excercebant
Steropes   and   Pyræmon   naked *as to* his limbs,   exercised

ferrum in vasto   antro. Erat his manibus   fulmen
the iron   in   the vast   cave. *There* was in these hands   a thunderbolt

informatum, quæ plurima genitor dejecit   toto   cœlo in
informed,   which many the father sent   from the whole heaven to

terras,   parte jam politâ; pars manebat imperfecta.
the earth,   a part now being polished, a part remained   unwrought.

Addiderunt tres radios torti imbris, tres aquosæ nubis,
They added   three rays of wreathed storm, three of the watery cloud

tres rutili ignis et alitis Austri. Nunc misceban
three of glittering lightning and the swift south wind. Now   they mingled

operi   terrificos fulgores que sonitum que metum,
in their labour   terrific   corruscations and   noise   and   fear,

que iras   sequacibus flammis.   Aliâ parte instabant
and rage with persecuting   flames.   *From* another part they press on

Marti que currum que volucres rotas, quibus ille excitat
for Mars   both the chariot and swift   wheels, by which he arouses

viros, quibus urbes; que certatim polibant horriferam
men,   by which cities;   and   eagerly they polished the dread bearing

Ægida arma turbatæ Palladis,   squamis serpentum que
shield the arms of troubled Minerva,   with scales of serpents   and

auro, que angues connexos que Gorgona ipsam in pectore
gold,   and snakes intertwined and the Gorgon itself in   the breast

Divæ vertentem lumina   desecto   collo. Inquit,
of the Goddess turning   its eyes to its dissevered neck.   He says,

Ætnei Cyclopes, tollite cuncta que auferte   cæptos
ye Etnean Cyclops,   take away all things and   bear off   your begun

labores, et advertite mentem huc.
labours, and   turn   your mind   here.

Arma facienda   acri viro; nunc usus viribus, nunc
Arms are to be made for a brave man; now there is need for strength, now

rapidis manibus, nunc omni magistrâ arte. Præcipitate
for rapid hands,   now for all your masterly art.   Banish

moras. Nec effatus plura. At omnes illi ociùs incubuere
delays. Nor *did he* speak more. But all   they soon ply their work

que pariter sortiti laborem. Æs que metallum auri fluit
and equally assort the labour. Brass and the metal of gold flows

rivis; que vulnificus chalybs liquescit vastâ fornice.
in streams; and the wounded steel   melts   in the vast furnace

Informant ingentem clypeum, unum contra omnia tela
They form   a great   shield,   alone against all   the darts

Latinorum, que impediunt septenos orbes orbibus. Alii
of the Latins, and interweave seven fold circles with circles. Others

accipiunt que reddunt auras ventosis follibus; alii tingunt
receive   and   return blasts from windy bellows; others   dip

æra stridentia lacu; antrum gemit incudibus impositis.
the metal hissing in the trough; the cave resounds anvils being placed.

Illi tollunt brachia inter sese, multâ vi in numerum,
They raise *their* arms among themselves, with much force in regular number.

que versant massam tenaci forcipe. Dum Lemnius pater
and they turn the mass with grasping tongs. While the Lemnian father

properat hæc Æoliis oris, alma lux et matutini
hastens these things on the Æolian coasts, the cheering light and morning

cantus volucrum sub culmine suscitat Evandrum ex
songs of birds under his roof arouses Evander from

humili tecto. Senior consurgit que inducitur tunicâ
his humble mansion. The old man arises and equips with a coat

artus, et circumdat Tyrhena vincula plantis pedum:
his limbs, and girds Tyrhene bandages to the soles of his feet:

tum subligat Tegæum ensem lateri, atque humeris,
then he binds a Tegæan sword to his side, and shoulders,

retorquens terga pantheræ demissa ab lævâ. Nec non et
turning back the skin of a panther suspended from his left side. Likewise

gemini canes custodes procedunt ex alto limine que
two dogs *his* guards proceed from the high gate and

comitantur herilem gressum. Heros petebat sedem et
accompany their master's step. The hero sought the seat and

secreta hospitis Æneæ, memor sermonum et promissi
retreats of his guest Æneas, mindful of his words and promised

muneris. Nec minus Æneas matutinus agebat se. Pallas
favour. Nevertheless Æneas early aroused himself. Pallas

filius ibat comes huic, Achates olli. Congressi
the son went as companion to the one, Achates to the other. Meeting

jungunt dextras, que resident mediis ædibus,
they join right hands, and sit down in the midst of the rooms,

et tandem fruuntur licito sermone. Rex prior hæc.
and at length enjoy uninterrupted discourse. The king first *said* these

Maxime ductor Teucrorum, quo sospite equidem
things. Greatest leader of the Trojans, who being safe indeed

nunquam fatebor res Trojæ aut regna victas.
never will I confess the affairs of Troy or her kingdoms to be conquered.

Nobis exiguæ vires ad auxilium belli pro tanto nomine:
To us are slender powers for aid of war for so great a name:

hinc claudimur Tusco amni, hinc Rutulus premit,
on this side we are surrounded by the Tuscan river, on this the Rutulian presses,

et circumsonat murum armis. Sed ego paro jungere
and sounds around our wall with arms. But I prepare to unite

ingentes populos tibi; que castra opulenta regnis, quam
great people to you; and camps rich in kingdoms, which

salutem inopina fors ostentat; affers te huc fatis
succour unexpected chance presents; you bring yourself here the fates

poscentibus. Haud procul hinc sedes urbis Agyllinæ,
demanding. Not far hence the seat of the city Agylla,

fundata vetusto saxo, ·incolitur; ubi quondam Lydia
founded   on an ancient rock, is inhabited; where formerly the Lydian

gens, præclara bello insedit Etruscis jugis. Deinde
nation, renowned in war settled down on the Etruscan mountains. Afterwards

rex Mezentius tenuit hanc, florentem multos annos, superbo
the king Mezentius held this,   flourishing many years,   in proud

imperio, et sævis armis   Quid memorem   infandas
rule   and cruel arms.   Why should I relate his dreadful

cœdes? quid effera facta tyranni?   Dii   reservent
murders? why the savage deeds of the tyrant? May the Gods reserve them

ipsius capiti que generi. Quin etiam jungebat mortua corpora
for his head and race.   For even he united dead   bodies

vivis, componens manus manibus, atque ora oribus, genus
to living.   placing hands to hands, and faces to faces, a kind

tormenti et sic necabat   fluentes sanguine que tabo in
of torture and thus he slew them dripping with blood and gore in

misero complexu longâ morte. At tandem   cives
wretched embrace by a prolonged death. But at last his countrymen

fessi, armati circumsistunt que ipsum furentem infanda
wearied out, armed surround   both him raging unutterable

que domum; obtruncant socios, jactant ignem ad
things and his family; they butcher his associates, they cast fire to his

fastigia. Ille elapsus inter cædes confugere in agros
roof.   He escaping amidst the slaughter fled to the territories

Rutulorum, et defendi armis Turni hospitis. Ergo
of the Rutulians, and was defended by the arms of Turnus his host. Therefore

omnis Etruria surrexit justis furiis præsenti marte reposcunt
all   Etruria arose in just wrath in present war they redemand

regem ad supplicium. Ænea ego addam te ductorem
the king for punishment. Æneas I will add you a leader

his millibus. Namque puppes condensæ fremunt
to these thousands. For   the ships gathered   rage

toto litore que jubent ferre signa. Longævus
through the whole shore and order to unfold the standards. The aged

aruspex canens fata retinet. O delecta juventus Mæoniæ
prophet foretelling fates restrains them. O chosen youth of Mæonia

flos que virtus veterum virum quos justus dolor fert
the flower and strength of ancient heroes whom a righteous grief bears

in hostem et Mezentius accendit meritâ irâ fas
against the foe and Mezentius inflames with deserved anger it is lawful

nulli Italo subjungere tantam gentem; optate externos duces.
for no Italian to subdue this great nation; chose foreign leaders.

Tum Etrusca acies resedit hoc campo exterrita monitis
Then the Tuscan army sat down on this plain frightened by the admonition

Divûm. Tarchon ipse misit oratores que coronam
of the Gods. Tarchon himself sent orators and the crown

regni cum sceptro ad me que mandat insignia:
of the kingdom with the sceptre to me and commends these standards.

succedam   castris que capessam Tyrrhena regna.   Sed
that I would come to the camps and   possess   the Tuscan kingdoms.   But

senectus tarda ' gelu   que effeta seculis invidet mihi
old age · restrained by *its frost* and powerless by time envies   me

imperium, que vires   seræ ad fortia.   Exhortarer
the empire,   and my strength *too* late for brave *deeds envies me.* I would exhort

natum, ni mixtus Sabellâ matre traheret   partem
my son, unless mixed with a Sabine mother derives   a part

patriæ hinc.   Tu, cujus et annis et generi fatum
of his country from hence. You, whom both in years and race   fate

indulget, quem numina poscunt, ingrederê ô fortissime
indulges,   whom the Gods demand, proceed O thou bravest

ductor Teucrorum atque Italorum.   Præterea adjungam
leader of the Tuscans and   Italians.   Besides   I will join

Pallanta hunc tibi, spes et solatia   ostri: sub te
Pallas   himself to you, the hope and consolation of me: under you

magistro assuescat tolerare militiam et grave opus
his master he shall be accustomed to endure warfare and the severe labour

Martis, cernere tua facta et miretur te ab primis annis.
of Mars, to behold your deeds and to admire you from his first years.

Dabo bis centum Arcadas equites huic, lecta robora
I will give two hundred Arcadian horsemen to him, the chosen strength

pubis, que Pallas   totidem tibi   suo nomine.   Vix
of *our* youth, and Pallas *will give* as many to you in his own name.   Scarcely

fatus erat ea   que Æneas Anchisiades et fidus
had he spoken these *words* both Æneas the son of Anchises and faithful

Achates tenebant ora defixi, que putabant multa
Achates held their countenances unmoved, and thought many

dura cum suo tristì corde, ni Cytherea dedisset signum
hard things in their sad hearts, unless Venus had given a signal

aperto cœlo; namque improvisó fulgor, vibratus ab
in the open sky; for unexpectedly lightning, glittering from

æthere, venit cum sonitu; et omnia visa ruere repentè
the air, came with a sound; and all things seemed to rush suddenly

que Tyrrhenus clangor tubæ mugire per æthera.
and the Tuscan clangor of the trumpet to rattle through the heavens.

Suspiciunt iterum atque iterum ingens fragor intonat;
They look up again and again a great sound thunders forth;

vident arma inter nubem rutilare per sudum in serenâ
they see arms within the cloud to glitter through the clear sky in the serene

regione cœli, et pulsa   tonare. Alii obstupuere
region of heaven, and clashed *together* to thunder Others were astonished

animis; sed Troius heros agnovit sonitum, et promissa
in their minds; but the Trojan hero knew the sound, and the promises

Divæ parentis. Tum memorat, hospes, ne verò, ne profectò
of his divine mother Then he says, · O host, do not indeed do not indeed

quære quem casum portenta ferant: ego poscor Olympo.
ask what event these prodigies bring: I am demanded by heaven

Diva creatrix cecinit missuram hoc signum si bellum
My divine mother foretold she would send this signal if war

ingrueret, que laturam Vulcania arma per auras
should attack me, and that she would bear Vulcanian arms through the skies

auxilio. Heu quantæ cædes instant miseris Laurentibus?
to my aid. Alas how great slaughter threatens the wretched Laurentines?

quas pœnas dabis mihi Turne? quam multa scuta virorum,
what penalties shall you give to me O Turnus? how many shields of men,

que galeas et fortia pectora, volves sub undas Pater
and helmets and brave breasts, will you roll under your waves O Father

Tybri! Poscant acies, et rumpant fœdera. Ubi dedit
Tiber! Let them demand armies, and break treaties. When he uttered

hæc dicta, tollit se ab alto solio; et primùm excitat
these words, he raises himself from the lofty throne; and first arouses

sopitas aras Herculeis ignibus, que lætus adit Larem,
the sleeping altars with Hercules' fires, and joyful approaches the household God,

hesternum que parvos Penates: mactat lectas bidentes
worshipped yesterday and the little household Gods: he sacrifices chosen sheep

de more; Evandrus pariter, Trojana juventus
according to custom; Evander also, the Trojan youth

pariter. Post hinc graditur ad naves, que revisit
in like manner. After this he walks to the ships, and revisits

socios; de numero quorum legit præstantes virtute,
his companions; from the number of whom he selects those excelling in courage,

qui sequantur sese in bella: cætera pars fertur pronâ
who may follow him to the wars: the other part is borne on the declining

aquâ, que segnis defluit secundo amni, ventura nuncia
water, and slow flow down the favouring stream, about to come bearing tidings

Ascanio que rerum que patris. Equi dantur Teucris
to Ascanius both of his affairs and his father. Horses are given to the Trojans

petentibus Tyrrhena arva: ducunt exsortem Æneæ, quem
seeking the Tuscan fields: they lead a chosen one for Æneas, which

obit fulva pellis leonis, præfulgens aureis unguibus,
covers the tawny skin of a lion, shining with golden claws,

totum. Subitò fama vulgata volat per parvam urbem,
all over. Suddenly fame spread abroad flies through the little city,

equites ire ocyùs ad litora Tyrrheni regis. Matres
that horsemen were going quickly to the shores of the Tuscan king. The mothers

duplicant vota metu; que timor it propius periculo,
redouble their vows through fear; and fright goes nearer to the danger,

et imago martis apparet major. Tum Pater Evandrus
and the image of war appears greater. Then Father Evander

complexus dextram euntis, hæret lacrymans
embracing the right hand of him going, hangs to him weeping

inexpletum, ac fatur talia; O si Jupiter referat præteritos
immeasurably, and speaks these words: O if Jupiter would restore my past

annos mihi! qualis eram, cum stravi primam aciem sub
years to me! such as I was, when I threw down the first band under

ipsâ Præneste, que victor incendi acervos scutorum, et
even Præneste, and a conqueror I burnt piles of shields, and

hâc dextrâ misi regem Herilum sub Tartara; cui
with this right hand I sent the king Herilus under Tartarus; to whom

nascenti mater Feronia dederat tres animas, horrendum
when born his mother Feronia had given three lives, dreadful

dictu; terna arma movenda; erat ter sternendus letho;
to be told; triple arms to be moved; he was thrice to be overthrown by death:

cui tamen tum hæc dextra abstulit omnes animas,
from whom nevertheless then this right hand took away all his lives,

et exuit totidem armis! nunc ego non divellerer
and stripped him of as many arms! now I neither had been torn

usquam tuó dulci amplexu, nate; neque unquam
ever from your sweet embrace, O son; nor ever

finitimus Mezentius, insultans huic capiti, dedisset tot
should my neighbour Mezentius, insulting this head, have given so many

sæva funera ferro, viduasset urbem tam multis civibus.
cruel deaths by the sword, have deprived the city of so many citizens

At vos, O Superi, et tu maxime rector Divûm Jupiter,
But you, O ye Gods, and thou the greatest ruler of the Gods Jupiter,

quæso miserescite Arcadii regis, et audite patrias preces:
I pray you pity the Arcadian king, and hear a father's prayers:

si vestra numina, si fata reservant Pallanta incolumem
if your deity, if the fates preserve Pallas unharmed

mihi, si vivo visurus eum, et venturus in unum oro
to me, if I live to see him, and to come in my only son, I pray

vitam, et patiar durare quamvis laborem. Sin, fortuna,
for life, and I will bear to undergo any labour. But if, O fortune,

minaris aliquem infandum casum, O nunc, nunc
you threaten any unspeakable misfortune, O now, now

liceat abrumpere crudelem vitam, dum curæ ambiguæ,
may it be allowed to break through this cruel life, while cares are doubtful,

dum spes futuri incerta; dum teneo te complexu,
while hopes of the future are uncertain; while I hold thee in my embrace,

care puer, mea sera et sola voluptas, ne gravior nuncius
O dear boy, my late and only pleasure, lest a more cruel message

vulneret aures. Genitor fundebat hæc dicta supremo
should wound my ears. The father poured forth these words at his last

digressu; famuli ferebant collapsum in tecta. Que adeo
departure; his servants bore him fainting to the palace. And thus

jam equitatus exierat apertis portis; Æneas et fidus
ow the cavalry had departed from the open gates; Æneas and faithful

Achates inter primos; inde alii proceres Trojæ, Pallas ipse
Achates among the first; then other nobles of Troy, Pallas himself

in medio agmine, conspectus chalmyde et in pictis armis;
in the midst of the band, conspicuous in a cloak and in painted arms;

qualis ubi Lucifer, perfusus undâ oceani, quem Venus
as when Lucifer bathed in the wave of the ocean whom Venus

diligit ante alios ignes astrorum, extulit sacrum   os
loves   before other fires of stars,   has raised his sacred countenance

cœlo que resolvit tenebras.
in heaven and banished darkness.

Matres stant pavidæ in muris, que sequuntur pulveream.
The mothers stood frightened on the walls, and   follow   the dusty

nubem oculis, et catervas fulgentes ære. Olli armati
cloud with their eyes, and the bands shining with brass. They armed

tendunt per dumos quá meta viarum   proxima.
march through the bushes where the end of the ways is nearest.

Clamor   it   et agmine facto, ungula quatit putrem
A shout goes forth and a band being formed, the hoof shakes the mouldering

campum quadrupedante sonitu. Est ingens lucus prope
plain   with a four footed sound. There is a great grove near

gelidum amnem Cæritis, sacer latè religione   patrum;
the cold stream of Cæris, sacred far around by the religion of our fathers;

cavi colles inclusere undique, et cingunt nemus nigrâ
hollow hills inclose it on each side, and surround the grove with black

abiete. Est fama   veteres   Pelasgos, qui primi
fir.   There is a report that the ancient Pelasgi, who first

aliquando habuere Latinos fines, sacravisse que lucum
long since held the Latin boundaries, consecrated both the grove

que diem Sylvano, Deo arvorum que pecoris. Haud
and day to Sylvanus, the God of fields and the flock.   Not

procul hinc Tarcho et Tyrrheni tenebant castra tuta
far from hence Tarcho and the Tuscans held their camps safe

locis: que jam omnis legio poterat videri de
in these places and now all the legion could be seen from

célso colle, et tendebat in latis arvis. Pater Æneas
the high hill, and march'd into the broad fields. Father Æneas

et juventus lecta bello succedunt huc, que fessi
and the youth selected for war come here, and weary

curant et   equos et corpora. At Venus, candida
provide for both their horses and bodies. But Venus, the fair

Dea aderat, ferens dona inter ætherios nimbos; que
Goddess was present, bearing gifts within the celestial clouds, and

ut vidit natum secretum procul egelido flumine in
as she saw her son retired afar by the cold stream in

reductâ valle   affata est talibus dictis, que
a secluded vale   addressed him in these words, and

obtulit se uItro. En munera perfecta promissâ arte
offered herself voluntarily. Lo gifts wrought by the promised aid

mei conjugis, nate, ne mox dubites poscere aut superbos
of my husband. O son, do not now hesitate to demand either the proud

Laurentes aut acrem Turnum in prœlia Cytherea dixit.
Laurentines or the brave Turnus to battle. Venus said,

et petivit amplexus nati; posuit radiantia arma sub
and sought the embraces of her son; she placed the glittering arms beneath

adversâ quercu. Ille, lætus donis Deæ, et tanto
an opposite oak. He, joyful with the gifts of the Goddess, and so great

honore, nequit expleri, atque volvit oculos per singula,
an honour, could not be satisfied, and rolls his eyes over every thing,

que miratur, que inter manus et brachia versat galeam
and admires *them*, and between his hands and arms he turns his helmet

terribilem cristis que vomentem flammas, que fatiferum
terrible with crests, and throwing out flames, and his fatebearing

ensem, loricam ex ære rigentem, sanguineam, ingentem,
sword, *his* coat of mail of brass stiff, bloody, huge.

qualis cum cærula nubes inardescit radiis solis, que
as when an azure cloud glows with the rays of the sun, and

refulget longè: tum lêves ocreas electro que auro recocto
shines afar: then the light boots of amber and gold reforged

que hastam et non enarrabile textum clypei. Ignipotens
and the spear and indescribable texture of the shield. The fire-powerful

haud ignarus vatum que inscius ævi venturi
God not ignorant of the prophet and unconscious of time to come

fecerat illic Italas res que triumphos Romanorum;
had made there the Italian affairs and the triumphs of the Romans;

illic omne genus stirpis futuræ ab Ascanio, que
there all the generation of his race about to proceed from Ascanius, and

bella pugnata in ordine. Et fecerat fetam lupam
wars fought in their order. And he had made a teeming wolf

procubuisse in viridi antro Mavortis; geminos pueros
to recline within the green cave of Mars; the two children

ludere huic pendentes circum ubera, impavidos lambere
to sport by her hanging around her dugs, fearless to lick

matrem; illam reflexam tereti cervice mulcere
their mother; her turning back with her tapering neck to lick *them*

alternos et fingere corpora linguâ. Nec procul hinc
by turns and form their bodies with her tongue. Nor far from hence

addiderat Romam et Sabinas raptas sine more
he had added Rome and the Sabine maids ravished without law

concessu caveæ, magnis Cercensibus actis, que
in the crowd of the theatre, the great Cercensian games being performed, and

subitò novum bellum consurgere Romulidis que seni
suddenly a new war to arise to the Romans and to old

Tatio que severis Curibus. Pòst idem reges, certamine
Tatius and the severe Cures. Afterwards the same kings, the contest

inter se posito, armati stabant ante aras Jovis
among them being laid aside, armed stood before the altars of Jupiter

que tenentes pateras et porcâ cæsa, jungebant
and holding goblets and a sow being sacrificed, they joined

federa. Haud procul inde citæ quadrigæ distulerant
treaties. Not far from thence swift chariots tore

Metium in diversa, at Albane tu maneres
Metius in different *parts*, but O Alban you should have adhered

díctis,   que Tullus raptabat vicera mendacis viri
to your promises, and Tullus dragged   the entrails of the deceitful man

per sylvam et vepres sparsi sanguine rorabant. Necnon
through the wood and the briers sprinkled with blood dripped.   Also

Porsenna jubebat   accipere Tarquiniun ejectum que
Porsenna   commanded *the Romans* to receive Tarquin   rejected   and

premebat urbem ingenti obsidione. Æneadæ ruebant in
oppressed   the city with a great siege.   The Romans rushed   on

ferrum pro libertate. Aspiceres   illum   similem
the sword for   liberty.   You might have seen him   like

indignanti que similem ninanti,   quòd Cocles audéret
one enraged and   like to one threatening, because Cocles   had dared

vellere pontem et Clœlia innaret fluvium vinculis
to tear down the bridge and Clœlia   swam   the river   her chains

ruptis. In summo Manlius custos Tarpeiæ arcis stabat
being broken. On the top Manlius the keeper of the Tarpean citadel stood

pro templo, et tenebat celsa Capitolia que recens regia
before the temple, and guarded the lofty Capitol   and the new palace

horrebat Romuleo culmo. Atque híc argenteus anser
was rough with Romulean   straw.   And here   a silver   goose

volitans per auratis porticibus canebat Gallos adesse in
flying   through the gilded porches . declared   the Gauls were present at

limine. Galli aderant per dumos que tenebant arcem
the gate. The Gauls advanced through the bushes and   held   the tower,

defensi tenebris et dono opacæ noctis. Ollis aurea cæsaries
defended by darkness and favor of the gloomy night. On them golden   hair

atque aurea vestis lucent virgatis sagulis; tum lactea
and   a golden dress shine with variegated cloaks; then their milk white

colla innectuntur auro; coruscant quisque duo Alpina
necks are bound   with gold; they brandish each one two   Alpine

gæsa manu, protecti   corpora   longis scutis, Hic
darts in their hand, protecting   their bodies with long shields.   He

extuderat exsultantes Salios, que nudos Lupercos, que
had engraved the dancing Salii,   and the naked Luperci,   and

lanigeros apices et ancilia lapsa cœlo; castæ matres
their woollen caps and shields fallen from heaven; the chaste matrons

in mollibus pilentis ducebant sacra per urbem.
in   *their* soft   sedans led on   the sacrifices through the city.

Procul hinc addit etiam Tartareas sedes alta ostia Ditis
Far from thence he adds also the Tartarean seats the deep doors of Pluto

et pœnas   scelerum, et te Catalina pendentem
and the punishment of crime, and thee O Cataline   hanging

minaci scopulo que trementem ora Furiaram;
from a threatening rock   and trembling   at the faces of the Furies;

que pios secretos,   Catonem dantem jura his.
and the pious separated *from the wicked*, Cato administering laws to them.

Inter hæc aurea imago maris latè tumidi ibat,
Among   these the golden image of the sea far around swelling went.

sed cærula spumabant cano fluctu et delphines
out the azure *waters* foamed with hoary waves; and dolphins

clari argento verrebant æquora circùm in orbem
bright with silver swept through the waters around in a circle

caudis que secabant æstum. In medio erat cernere
with *their* tails and cut the tide. In the midst was to be seen

æratas classes, Actia bella, que videres totum
brazen *prow'd* ships, Actian wars, and you might see all

Leucaten fervere instructo Marte, que fluctus effulgere auro.
Leucate to glow with arrayed war, and the waves to glitter in gold.

Hinc Cæsar Augustus agens Italos in prœlia cum
Here Cæsar Augustus leading on the Italians to battle with

patribus que populo, Penatibus et magnis Dîs, stans
the fathers and the people, the household Gods and great Gods, standing

in celsâ puppi, cui læta tempora vomunt geminas flammas,
on the lofty stern, whose joyful temples pour forth double flames,

que patrium sidus aperitur vertice. Aliâ parte
and his paternal star is exhibited from his head. In another part

Agrippa, ventis et Dîs secundis, arduus agens agmen
Agrippa, the winds and Gods being propitious, boldly leading on his fleet

cui tempora fulgent rostratâ navali coronâ superbum
whose temples glitter with a beaky naval crown a proud

insigne belli. Hinc victor Antonius barbaricâ
ensign of war. On this side victorious Anthony with foreign

ope que variis armis vehit Ægyptum, que vires Orientis,
aid and various arms bears Egypt, and the powers of the east,

et ultima Bactra secum, ab populis Auroræ et rubro
and the most remote Bactra with him, from the people of the east and the red *sea*

litore que nefas! Ægyptia conjux sequitur. Omnes ruere
shore and O disgrace! his Egyptian wife follows. All rush

unâ ac totum æquor spumare convulsum remis reductis,
together and all the sea foams torn oars drawn back,

que tridentibus rostris. Petunt alta credas
and trident beaks. They seek the deep *waters* you would believe

Cycladas revulsas innare pelago aut altos montes
that the Cylades torn up swam on the sea or *that* high mountains

concurrere montibus: viri instant turritis puppibus
rushed against mountains: the men press on in their towering ships

tantâ mole. Stuppea flamma spargitur manu que
with the great mass. The hempen flame is scattered by the hand and

volatile ferrum telis. Neptunia arva rubescunt novâ
the flying steel with darts. Neptune's territories blush with new

cæde. In mediis regina vocat agmina
slaughter. In the midst *Cleopatra the Egyptian* queen calls her bands

patrio sistro. Necdum etiam respicit geminos
with her native trumpet. Nor yet even does she look back on the two

angues a tergo, que monstra omnigenûm Deûm, et
snakes from behind, and the monsters of every kind of Gods and

Anubis latrator. tenent tela contra Neptunum et
Anubis the barker, wield their darts against Neptune and

Venerem que contra Minervam. Mavors cælatus ferro
Venus and against Minerva. Mars engraved on steel

sævit in medio certamine que tristes Diræ ex æthere; et
rages in the midst of the contest and the sad Furies from the sky; and

Discordia vadit gaudens scissâ pallâ, quam Bellona
Discord walks rejoicing with her torn cloak, whom Bellona

sequitur cum sanguineo flagello. Actius Apollo cernens
follows with a bloody whip. Actian Apollo beholding

hæc desuper intendebat arcum; eo terrore omnis
these things from above was stretching his bow: with this terror all

Ægyptus, Indi et omnis Arabs, omnes Sabæi vertebant
Egypt, the Indians and every Arab, all the Sabeans were turning

terga. Regina ipsa videbatur dare vela ventis vocatis,
their backs. The queen herself seemed to give sails the winds being invoked,

et jam que jam immittere laxos funes. Ignipotens
and now and now to relax the loosened ropes. The fire powerful *God*

fecerat illam inter cædes pallentem morte futurâ—
had made her amidst the slaughter pale with death approaching—

ferri undis et Iapyge—autem contra
to be borne on by the waves and west wind—but opposite *he had formed*

Nilum magno corpore mœrentem, que pandentem sinus
the Nile with his great body mourning, and opening his robes

et totâ veste vocantem victos in cæruleum
and with all his dress *thrown open* inviting the conquered into his azure

gremium que latebrosa flumina. At Cæsar invectus Romana
bosom and his dark streams. But Cæsar borne to the Roman

mœnia triplici triumpho sacrabat immortale votum
walls by a threefold triumph consecrated his immortal vow

Italis Dîs, ter centum delubra per totam urbem.
to the Italian Gods, three hundred temples through the whole city

Viæ fremebant lætitiâ que ludis que plausu. In omnibus
The streets resounded with joy and sports and applause. In all

templis chorus matrum; omnibus aræ. Ante aras
the temples *is* a band of matrons; in all *are* altars. Before the altars

cæsi juvenci stravere terram. Ipse sedens niveo
slain bullocks overspread the earth. *Cæsar* himself sitting in the snow white

limine candentis Phœbi recognoscit dona populorum que
gate of glowing Apollo counts up the gifts of the people and

aptat superbis postibus. Victæ gentes incedunt longo
fits *them* to proud posts. Conquered nations march on in long

ordine, quâm variæ linguis tam habitu vestis et
array, as various in languages as in the form of their *dress* and

armis. Hìc Mulciber genus Nomadum et
in arms. Here Vulcan *had engraved* the race of the Numidians and

discinctos Afros; hìc finxerat Lelegas que Caras que
loosely dressed Africans; here he had engraved the Lelegians and Carians and

sagittiferos Gelonos. Euphrates, ibat jam molliot   undis
Arrow-bearing Geloni.   The Euphrates, went now more gently with *ts* waves,

que Morini extremi, hominum, que   bicornis Rhenus,
and the Morini the most distant   of men,   and the double-horned   Rhine.

que Dahæ indomiti, et Araxes indignatus pontem. Miratur
and the Dahæ unconquered, and Araxes spurning   a bridge. *Æneas* admires

talia dona   parentis   per clypeum Vulcani: que gaudet
these gifts of *his* mother *displayed* over the shield   of Vulcan; and   rejoices

    imagine   rerum   ignarus, que attollens famam
in the representation of these things *altho'* ignorant, and bearing   the fame

et fata nepotum   humero.
and fates of his offspring on his shoulder.

ÆNEID.

BOOK NINTH.

Atque dum   ea   geruntur penitus diversâ parte,
And   while these things are done   in a far distant   part.

Saturnia Juno misit Irim de cœlo ad audacem Turnum.
Saturnian Juno despatched Iris from heaven to the daring   Turnus.

Tum fortè Turnus sedebat   luco   parentis Pilumni
Then by chance Turnus   sat   in the grove of his parent Pilumnus

sacratâ valle; ad quem Thaumantias sic locuta est
in a hallowed vale; to   whom the daughter of Thaumas thus   spoke

roseo   ore: Turne en volvenda dies attulit   ultro, quod
with rosy mouth: O Turnus, lo revolving time has brought voluntarily, what

nemo Divûm auderet promittere optanti! Æneas, urbe, et
no one of the Gods would dare to promise to me desiring! Æneas, the city, and

sociis,   et classe relictâ, petivit sceptra que sedem
his companions and   fleet being abandoned has sought the sceptre and   seat

Palatini Evandri.   Nec   satis; penetravit ad
of Palatine Evander.   Nor was   this enough; he has made his way to

extremas urbes Coriti, armat manum Lydorum que agrestes
the most distant cities of Coritus, he arms a band of Lydians and   rustics

collectos. Quid dubitas? nunc tempus poscere equos,
collected.   Why do you hesitate? *it is* now   time to demand horses,

nunc currus. Rumpe omnes moras, et arripe turbata castra.
now   chariots. Banish all delays, and seize on the troubled camps.

Dixit, et sustulit se   in cœlum   paribus alis, que
She said, and raised herself towards heaven   with equal wings, and

fugâ secuit ingentem arcum sub nubibus. Juvenis
n *her* flight she cut a great bow under the clouds. The youth

agnovit que sustulit duplices palmas ad sidera, ac
knew *her* and raised both *his* hands to the stars, and

secutus est fugientem tali voce: Iri, decus cœli,
followed *her* flying with this address: O Iris, *thou* glory of heaven

quis detulit te actam nubibus mihi in terras! unde
who commissioned thee sent from the clouds to me on the earth! whence

hæc tempestas tam repentè clara? Video medium cœlum
this storm so suddenly bright? I see the midst of heaven

discedere—que stellas palantes polo. Sequor tanta
separate— and the stars wandering through the sky. I follow these great

omina, quisquis vocas in arma. Et effatus sic,
omens, whoever *you are who* call me to arms. And having spoken thus,

processit ad undam, que hausit lymphas de summo gurgite,
he proceeded to the stream, and drew water from the surface of the pool;

orans Deos multa; que oneravit æthera votis. Que jam
praying the Gods many *things*; and loaded the air with vows. And now

omnis exercitus ibat apertis campis, dives equorum, dives
all the army went to the open plains, rich in horses, rich

pictaï, vestis et auri. Messapus primas acies,
in painted dress, and gold. Messapus *leads on* the first bands,

juvenes Tyrrhidæ cœrcent postrema: dux Turnus
the sons of Tyrrhus urge on the last: the commander 'Turnus

vertitur medio agmine, tenens arma, et est supra
moves in the midst of the band, holding arms, and is above *all*

toto vertice. Ceu altus Ganges surgens per tacitum
by a whole head. As the deep Ganges arising in its peaceful

septem sedatis amnibus; aut Nilus pingui
fountain with *its* seven quiet streams; or the Nile with rich

flumine, cùm refluit campis, et jam condidit se
stream, when it flows from the plains, and now has hid itself

alveo. Hic Teucri prospiciunt subitam nubem glomerari
in its channel. Here the Trojans behold a sudden cloud to be gathered

nigro pulvere, ac tenebras insurgere campis. Caïcus
from black dust, and darkness to arise on the plains. Caicus

primus conclamat ab adversâ mole; O cives, quis
first cries out from the opposite mound; O my countrymen, what

globus volvitur atrâ caligine? Citi, ferte ferrum, date
mass *of men* is rolled on in gloomy darkness? Quick, bring the sword, give

tela, scandite muros: hostis adest, eia. Teucri condunt
weapons, climb the walls: the enemy is present, ho. The Trojans shut up

se ingenti clamore per omnes portas, et complent
themselves with great clamour within all the gates, and fill

mœnia: namque Æneas, optimus armis, discedens
the walls: for Æneas, most excellent in arms, departing

præceperat ita; si interea fuisset qua fortuna. ne
had commanded thus; if in the meantime *there* should be any chance, they

auderent struere aciem, neu credere campo; modò
should not dare to array the army, nor to trust to the plain; only

servarent castra et mûros tutos aggere. Ergò,
they should secure the camps and the walls guarded by a rampart. Wherefore,

etsi pudor que ira monstrat conferre manum,
although shame and rage urges *them* to join *their* hand,

tamen objiciunt portas et facessunt præcepta, que
nevertheless they bar the gates and accomplish their orders, and

armati expectant hostem cavis turribus. Turnus ut
armed await the foe in the hollow towers. Turnus as

antevolans præcesserat tardum agmen, comitatus vìginti
flying before had anticipated the slow band, accompanied by twenty

lectis equitum, et improvisus adest urbi; quem Thra-
chosen *men* of the cavalry, and unexpected is present at the city; whom a Thra-

cius equus albis maculis portat, que aurea galea rubrâ
cian horse with white spots bears, and a golden helmet with a ruddy

cristâ tegit. Juvenes, ecquis erit, qui primus
crest covers. O young men, what one *of you* will there be who first *will march*

in hostem mecum? En! ait, et intorquens jaculum,
against the enemy with me? Lo! he says, and casting his dart,

emittit in auras, principium pugnæ; et arduus infert
he hurls it into the air, the commencement of the fight; and boldly bears

sese campo. Socii excipiunt clamore, que
himself to the plain. His companions receive *him* with a shout, and

sequuntur horrisono fremitu; mirantur inertia corda
follow *him* with horrid sounding noise; they wonder at the sluggish hearts

Teucrorum, viros non dare se æquo campo,
of the Trojans, *that* the men do not give themselves to the equal plain,

non ferre obvia arma, sed fovere castra. Turbidus
that they do not bear opposing arms, but cherish the camps. Troubled

lustrat muros huc atque huc equo, que quærit aditum
he surveys the walls on this side and that from his horse, and seeks an approach

per avia. Ac veluti lupus, insidiatus pleno ovili, cùm
through the fields. And as a wolf, having ensnared a full sheepfold, when

fremit ad caulas, perpessus ventos et imbres, super media
he rages at the pens, enduring winds and storms, at mid

nocte; agni tuti sub matribus exercent balatum; ille
night; the lambs being safe under their dams exert · their bleating; he

asper et improbus irâ, sævit in absentes: rabies edendi
savage and cruel; with anger, rages against them absent; the madness of eating

collecta ex longo fatigat et fauces siccæ sanguine;
contracted from long *abstinence* wearies *him*, and his jaws are dry from blood·

haud aliter iræ ignescunt Rutulo tuenti muros et castra,
not otherwise rage inflames the Rutulian gazing on the walls and camps;

et dolor ardet duris ossibus, quâ ratione tentet
and grief burns in his hard bones, by what means he may attempt

aditus, et quâ via excutiat Teucros clausos
their approaches, and by what way he may drive out the Trojans inclosed

valıo, atque effundat in æquor. Invadit classem, quæ
by a wall, and force *them* out into *he plain. He attacks the fleet, which

llatebat adjuncta lateri castrorum, circumseptam aggeribus
lay concealed adjoining the side of the camps, surrounded by ramparts

et fluvialibus undis; que poscit ovantes socios
and river waters; and commands his rejoicing associates *to bring*

incendia; atque fervidus implet manum flagrante pinu.
fire; and glowing he fills his hand with a burning pine.

Tum vero incumbunt; præsentia Turni urget atque
Then indeed they press on; the presence of Turnus urges *them* and

omnis pubes accingitur atris facibus. Diripuere focos;
all the youth are furnished with black firebrands. They tear up the hearths;

fumida tæda fert piceum lumen et vulcanus commixtam
the smoking torch bears on a pitchy light and the fire *raises* the mingled

favillam ad astra. O Musæ, quis Deus avertit tam sæva
embers to the stars. O ye Muses, what God averted such cruel

incendia Teucris? . quis depulit tantos ignes
fires from the Trojans? who drove these great conflagrations

ratibus? dicite. Prisca fides facto, sed fama
from the ships? say. *There* is ancient faith for the deed, but its fame *is*

perennis. Quo tempore primùm Æneas formabat classem
eternal. At that time when first Æneas built his fleet

in Phrygiâ Idâ, et parabat petere alta pelagi, Berecynthia
on the Trojan Ida, and prepared to seek the depths of the sea, Berecynthia

ipsa, genetrix Deûm, fertur affata magnum Jovem
herself, the mother of the Gods, is said to have addressed great Jupiter

his vocibus: Nate, da petenti, quod tua cara parens
in these words: O son, grant *to me* asking, what your fond parent

poscit te, Olympo domito. Pinea sylva delecta mihi
demands of you, Olympus being conquered. A pine wood beloved by me

per multos annos, fuit lucus in summâ arce, quò
for many years, has been a grove on a high mountain, where

ferebant sacra, obscurus nigrante piceâ que acernis
they offered sacrifices, gloomy with blackening pitch and maple

trabibus: læta dedi has Dardanio juveni, cùm egeret classis:
branches: joyful I gave these to the Trojan youth, when he wanted a fleet

nunc anxius timor angit solicitam. Solve metus, atque
now solicitous fear tortures my anxious *mind*. Banish dread, and

sine parentem posse hoc precibus, ne
allow a parent to be able *to obtain* this by her prayers, that

vincantur quassatæ ullo cursu, neu turbine
they may not be overcome disabled in any course, nor by the raging

venti: prosit ortas in nostris montibus.
of the wind: may it profit *that* they grew in our mountains.

Contrà filius, qui torquet sidera mundi,
On the other hand, *her* son, who turns the stars of the *heavenly* world,

huic: O genetrix, quò vocas fata? aut quid
said to her O mother, whither do you invoke the fates? or what

petis   istis;   ne carinæ factæ mortali manu habeant
do you seek from these; shall ships   made   by a mortal hand   have an

immortale   fas?   que Æneas certus lustret   incerta
immortal   right?   and Æneas assured survey   uncertain

pericula?   cui Deo   tanta   potestas permissa?   Imò, ubi
perils?   to what God is so great authority   allowed?   Nay, where

defunctæ   tenebunt   finem   que Ausonios
having passed all perils they shall attain to their destination and the Ausonian

portus, quæcunque   olim   evaserit   undis,   que
harbours, whatsoever   hereafter shall have escaped the waves,   and

vexerit Dardanium ducem Laurentia arva,   eripiam
shall have borne the Trojan leader to the Laurentian fields, I will snatch away

mortalem formam que   jubebo   esse Deas magni
from them this mortal form and will command them to be Goddesses of the great

æquoris; qualis Nerïea Doto et Galatea secant spumantem
ocean;   such as the Nereian Doto and Galatea they shall cut the foaming

pontum pectore.   Dixerat; que annuit id ratum per
sea   with their breast.   He said;   and affirmed it ratified by

flumina Stygii fratris, per ripas torrentes pice, que
the rivers of his Stygian brother, by the banks boiling over with pitch, and

atrâ voragine, et tremefecit totum Olympum nutu;
the black whirlpool, and   shook   all   heaven   with his nod.

ergò promissa dies aderat et Parcæ   complêrant
therefore the promised day was present and the Destinies   had fulfilled

debita tempora, cùm injuria Turni   admonuit
their allotted times, when the injury of Turnus   admonished

matrem   depellere tædas   sacris ratibus. Hìc
the mother of the Gods to drive back the firebrands from the sacred ships.   Here

primùm nova lux effulsit oculis et ingens nimbus visus
first   a new light shone on their eyes and a great cloud   seemed

transcurrere cœlum ab Aurora, que   Idæi   chori:
to run across   the sky from the east,   and with it   the Idean   bands

tum vox horrenda excidit per auras et   complet agmina
then a voice to be dreaded passed through the air and   fills   the bands of

Tröum que Rutulorum;   Teucri   ne   trepidate
the Trojans and of the Rutulians with fear; O my Trojans do not   fear

defendere meas naves, neve armate manus;   dabitur
to defend   my   ships,   nor   arm   your hands; it shall be given

Turno exurere maria antèquàm sacras pinus.   Vos
to Turnus to burn   seas   rather than the sacred pines.   Do you

solutæ   ite. Ite Deæ   pelagi: Genitrix
freed from restraint depart. Go ye Goddesses of the sea: The mother of the Gods

jubet, et continuò quæque puppes abrumpunt sua vincula
commands, and immediately   all   the ships   break   their   cables

ripis,   que petunt tuta æquora, rostris   demersis
from the bank, and   seek   the safe waters,   with bows   plunged

modo delphinum   Hinc totidem virginæ   facies
in the manner of dolphins   Hence as many   virgin   forms

mirabile monstrum, reddunt   se   que feruntur   ponto
a wonderful   miracle,   exhibit themselves and are borne on the dee,

quot æratæ proræ priùs steterunt ad litora.
as   brazen   prows before they had stood at the shores.

Rutuli   obstupuere   animis; Messapus ipse conter
The Rutulians were astonished in their minds; Messapus   himself is fright

ritus, equis   turbatis; et amnis Tiberinus sonans   rauca
ened, his horses being terrified; and the river   Tiber   sounding   hoarse.

cunctatur, que revocat pedem ab alto. At fiducia   non
is restrained, and withdraws his foot from the sea. But confidence did not

cessit audaci Turno; tollit animos dictis, ultro,   atque
cease to the daring Turnus; he arouses their minds by his words, voluntarily, and

increpat   ultro.   Hæc monstra petunt Trojanos.
rebukes them voluntarily.   These   prodigies   regard   the Trojans

Jupiter ipse eripuit solitum auxilium his;   non
Jupiter himself has snatched their accustomed aid from them; they do not

expectant tela nec Rutulos ignes. Ergò maria   invia
await   darts nor Rutulian   fires. Therefore seas are impassable

Teucris,   nec   ulla   spes fugæ; altera pars   rerum
to the Trojans, nor is there any hope of flight; another part of their affairs

adempta est; autem terra in nostris manibus: Italæ
is taken from them; but the land is in our   hands: The Italian

gentes ferunt   tot millia   arma.   Fatalia responsa
nations bring to us so many thousand arms. The fatal responses

Deorum, si Phryges jactant quæ præ   se   terrent
of the Gods, even if the Trojans should boast any for themselves   terrify

me nil.   Sat   datum   fatis que Veneri quòd
me in nothing.   Enough has been given to the fates and to Venus that

Tröes   tetigere arva fertilis Ausoniæ. Et sunt mihi
the Trojans have reached the fields of fertile Italy.   And there are to me

mea fata   contrâ,   exscindere sceleratum gentem
my own fates on the other hand, to destroy the accursed   nation

ferro, conjuge   præreptâ,   nec iste dolor tangit
with the sword, my wife being stolen from me, nor does this grief affect

Atridas   solos, que licet   Mycenis solis capere
the sons of Atreus alone, and it is allowed to the Mycenians alone to take up

arma. Sed est satis periise semel; fuisset satis peccare
arms.   But it is enough to have perished once; it had been enough for them to sin

antè;   modò   non penitus perosos omne femineum
before;   provided they had not entirely hated   all   the female

genus. Quibus hæc fiducia   medii   valli   que
race.   To whom this confidence of the midst of the rampart and

moræ fossarum parva discrimina lethi, dant animos:
the defences of the ditches small difference of death, give courage:

an non viderunt mœnia Trojæ, fabricata manu Neptuni,
have they not seen the walls of Troy, wrought by the hand of Neptune,

considere in ignes? Sed vos, O lecti,   quis apparat
o setttle down into the fire? But you, O chosen men, say, who will appear

scindere vallum ferro, et invadit trepidantia castra
to cut down the rampart with the sword, and invade their trembling camps

mecum: non est opus mihi armis Vulcani, non mille
with me *there* is no need to me of the arms of Vulcan, nor a thousand

carinis in Teucros. Omnes Etrucii addant se protinus
ships against the Trojans. Let all the Tuscans add themselves forthwith

socios; ne timeant tenebras et inertia furta
as companions; let them not fear darkness and the disgraceful theft

Palladii, custodibus summæ arcis cæsis; nec condemur
of the Palladium, the guards of the lofty tower being slain; nor will we be concealed

in cæco alvo equi; certum circumdare muros, igni
in the dark womb of the horse; it is determined to surround the walls, with fire

palam luce. Faxo haud putent esse rem sibi
openly by day. I will cause they shall not think there is a controversy to them

cum Danais, et Pelasgâ pube, quos Hector distulit in
with the Greeks, and the Pelasgan youth, whom Hector put off to

decimum annum. Nunc, nunc adeò quoniam melior pars
the tenth year. Now, now thus since the better part

diei acta, quod superest, viri, læti procurate corpora
of the day is past, what remains, O men, joyful provide for your bodies

rebus gestis bene, et parati sperate pugnam.
your affairs being accomplished well, and prepared await the fight.

Interea cura datur Messapo obsidere portas
In the mean time the care is allotted to Messapus to besiege the gates

excubiis vigilum, et cingere mœnia flammis. Bis septem
with guards of watches, and to surround the walls with flames. Twice seven

Rutuli delecti, qui servent muros milite; ast centeni
Rutulians *are* selected, who shall keep the walls with the soldiery; but an hundred

juvenes, purpurei cristis que corusci auro, sequuntur
youths, purple with crests and glittering with gold, follow

illos quemque; discurrunt que variant vices, que fusi
them each; they run out and vary *their duty* in turn, and stretched

per herbam indulgent vino que vertunt ahenos crateras.
along the grass indulge in wine and turn up the brazen goblets,

Ignes collucent, custodia ducit insomnem noctem ludo.
Fires shine, the guard spend the sleepless night in play.

Trões prospectant hæc e vallo super, et tenent
The Trojans observe these *things* from the wall from above, and hold

alta armis; nec non trepidi formidine explorant
the high places by arms; likewise trembling with fear they watch

portas, que jungunt pontes et propugnacula; gerunt tela.
the gates, and unite the bridges and bulwarks; they bear arms.

Mnestheus que acer Serestus instant; quos pater Æneas
Mnestheus and brave Serestus press on; whom father Æneas

dedit esse rectores juvenum et magistros rerum, si
appointed to be guides of the youth and directors of their concerns, if

quando adversa vocarent. Omnis legio sortita
at any time hostile *circumstances* should call them. All the legion having cast lots

periculum, excubat per muros, que exercet   vices,
for the danger, watch   along the walls, and   exercise   *their* allotments,

quod   est cuique tuendum.   Nisus,   Hyrtacides, erat
whatever   is   for each   to be protected.   Nisus,   the son of Hyrtacus, was

custos portæ, acerrimus armis, quem Ida,   venatrix,
keeper of the gate,   most bold   in arms,   whom   Ida,   devoted to hunting.

miserat comìtem Æneæ; celerem jaculo que levibus
had sent   a companion to Æneas;   swift   with the dart and   light

sagittis; et juxtà comes Euryalus,   quo   non fuit
arrows;   and near by his associate   Euryalus,   *than* whom there was not

alter Æneadum, nec   induit Trojana arma, pulchrior;
another of the Trojans, nor *any one that* wore   the Trojan arms, more beautiful;

puer signans intonsa ora primâ   juventâ.   Erat
a boy   marking his unshaved face   with the first   youthful bloom.   *There* was

his unus amor, que pariter ruebant in bella; tum quoque
to them one   love,   and together they rushed to the wars; then   also

tenebant portam communi statione. Nisus ait, Euryale,
they kept   the gate   in a common station.   Nisus said, O Euryalus,

ne   Dî addunt hunc ardorem mentibus? an   sua
whether do the Gods add   this   ardour   to *our* minds? or does his own

dira cupido fit Deus cuique. Jamdudum mens agitat
ardent   desire become a God to each one.   Even now   my mind   drives

mihi aut invadere pugnam, aut aliquid magnum; nec est
me   either to press to   the fight,   or   something   great;   nor   is it

contenta placidâ quiete. Cernis quæ fiducia   rerum
contented   with peaceful   rest.   You see what   confidence of *their* affairs

habeat Rutulos; lumina micant rara;   procubuere
possesses the Rutulians; their lights shine   scattered around;   they lie

soluti somno que vino; loca latè silent.   Porro
relaxed   by sleep   and   wine; the places   around are still.   Moreover

percipe quid dubitem, et quæ sententia nunc surgat animo.
observe   what I doubt,   and what sentiment   now   arises   in my mind.

Omnes que populus, que patres, exposcunt Ænean
All   both   the people,   and the fathers,   demand   Æneas

accire; que viros mitti qui reportent certa.   Si
te be called; and men   to be sent   who should report   our true *condition.* If

promittunt tibi, quæ posco (nam   fama   facti   est
they promise to you, what   I demand (for   the reputation of the deed   is

sat mihi) videor posse. reperire viam ad muros et
enough for me)   I seem   to be able   to find out   a way   to   the walls and

Pallantea mænia sub illo tumulo. Euryalus obstupuit,
Pallantean   ramparts under that   hill.   Euryalus   stood amazed

perculsus magno amore laudum;   simul   affatur
struck   with the great   love   of praise; at the same time he addresses

ardentem amicum his;   Igitur Nise   ne   fugis
his glowing   friend in these *words*;   Wherefore O Nisus   will you refuse

adjungere me   socium   summis   rebus? mittam te
to join - me   as a companion   in your great   concerns? shall I send you

solum in tanta percula? Non ita genitor Opheltes
alone to so great dangers? Not thus your father Opheltes

assuetus bellis, erudiit me sublatum inter Argolicum
accustomed to wars, taught me brought up amidst Grecian

terrorem que labores Trojæ; nec gessi talia
terror and the labours of Troy; nor have I performed such things

tecum secutus magnanimum Æneam et extrema fata.
with you following high minded Æneas and his extreme fates.

Est hìc, est animus contemtor lucis, et qui credat
There is here, there is a soul the despiser of life, and which believes

istum honorem quò tendis bene emi vitâ.
that honour whither you direct your course well bought with life.

Nisus ad hæc: Equidem verebar nil tale de
Nisus to these things said: Indeed I feared nothing like this concerning

te, nec fas. Non; ita magnus Jupiter aut quicunque
you, nor is it right I should. No; so may great Jupiter or whatever

aspicit hæc æquis oculis, referat me ovantem
God regards these things with equal eyes, shall restore me triumphing

tibi. Sed si quis, si quis ve casus ve Deus rapiat
to you. But if any one, if any either chance or God should bear me

in adversum (quæ vides multa tali discrimine) velim
to adversity (which you see many times in such danger) I could wish

te superesse: tua ætas dignior vitâ. Sit qui
you to survive: your age is more worthy of life. Let there be one who

mandet me solitâ humo, raptum pugnâ, redemtum
shall commit me to my destined earth, borne from the fight, or redeemed

pretio; aut si qua fortuna vetabit id, ferat inferias
by a price; or if any fortune should forbid that, should pay funeral rights

absenti, que decoret sepulchro; neu sim causa tanti
to me absent, and should honour my tomb; nor can I be the cause of so great

doloris miseræ matri, quæ sola ausa e multis matribus
grief to your unhappy mother, who alone daring from so many mothers

prosequitur te puer, nec curat mœnia magni Acestæ.
follows you O boy, nor cares for the ramparts of great Acestes.

Autem ille, Nequicquam nectis inanes causas; nec
But he said, In vain you contrive vain causes; nor

jam mea sententia mutata cedit loco: acceleremus
now does my opinion changed yield to the occasion: let us hasten

ait; simul excitat vigiles. Illi succedunt que
said he; at the same time he awakes the guards. They come up and

servant vices: statione relictâ ipse graditur comes
observe their turns: the station being abandoned he walks on a companion

Niso que requirunt regem. Cætera animalia per omnes
to Nisus and they seek the king. The other animals through all

terras laxabant curas somno et corda oblita laborum.
lands relaxed their cares in sleep and their hearts forgetful of labours.

Primi ductores Teucrûm et delecta juventus habebant
The first leaders of the Trojans and select youth held

consilium ۱e summis rebus regni; quid facerent;
a council about the chief concerns of the kingdom; what they should do;

quisve jam esset nuncius Æneæ. Stant adnixi
or who now should be a messenger to Æneas. They stand leaning

longis hastis et tenentes scuta medio castrorum
on *their* long spears and holding *their* shields in the midst of *their* camps

et campi.
and the plain.

Tum Nisus et Euryalus unà alacres orant admitti
Then Nisus and Euryalus together eagerly pray to be admitted

confestim; rem magnam que fore
immediately; *that* their business was of great consequence and would be

pretium moræ. Iülus primus accepit trepidos, ac jussit
a compensation for delay. Iulus first receives *them* trembling, and commands

Nisum dicere. Tunc Hyrtacides sic: O Æneadæ audite
Nisus to speak. Then son of Hyrtacus thus *spoke:* O associates of Æneas hear

æquis mentibus, neve hæc quæ ferimus
with impartial minds, nor let these *things* which we have brought

spectentur ab nostris annis. Rutuli conticuere sepulti
be regarded by our years. The Rutulians are at rest buried

somno que vino; ipsi conspeximus locum insidiis, qui
in sleep and wine; we have seen a place for *our* stratagems, which

patet in bivio portæ quæ proxima ponto. Ignes
lies in a corner of the gate which is nearest to the sea. The fires

interrupti, que ater fumus erigitur ad sidera. Si
are interrupted, and black smoke is raised to the stars. If

permittitis uti fortunâ, cernetis Ænean quæsitum ad
you will allow *us* to use fortune, you shall see Æneas sought at

Pallantea mœnia mox, affore hìc cum spoliis, ingenti
the Pallantean ramparts, soon to be present here with spoils, a great

cæde peractâ: nec via fallit nos euntes; vidimus
slaughter being accomplished: nor does the way deceive us going; we have seen

primam urbem sub obscuris vallibus assiduo venatu, et
the first *part of* the city in the dark valleys in our continued hunting, and

cognovimus totum amnem. Hìc Alethes gravis annis, atque
we know all the river. Here Alethes grave in years, and

maturus animi, Patrii Dî sub quorum numìne
ripened in intellect, *said,* O my country's Gods under whose authority

Troja est semper, tamen non paratis delere Teucros
Troy is ever, nevertheless you do not prepare to destroy the Trojans

omnino, cum tulistis tales animos juvenum et tam
entirely, since you have produced such minds of youth and so

certa pectora.
resolved breasts.

Memorans sic tenebat humeros que dextras amborum
Speaking thus he held the shoulders and right hands of both

et rigabat vultum atque ora lacrymis. Viri quæ,
and bathed his countenance and face with tears. Ye heroes what *rewards,*

quæ digna præmia rear posse solvi vobis pro talibus
what worthy rewards shall I suppose can be paid to you for such

ausis? primùm Di que vestri mores dabunt
daring deeds? first the Gods and your own manners will give

pulcherrima; tum pius Æneas actutùm reddet cætera atque
the fairest; then pious Æneas forthwith shall pray the rest and

Ascanius integer ævi non unquam immemor tanti meriti.
Ascanius ripe in age never will be unmindful of so great merit.

Ascanius excipit, imò ego cui sola salus genitore
Ascanius adds, truly I whose only safety consists in my father's

reducto, obtestor vos ô Nise, per magnos Penates que
being restored, entreat you O Nisus, by the great household Gods and

Larem Assaraci et penetralia canæ Vestæ,
the domestic God of Assaracus and sacred shrines of hoary Vesta,

quæcunque fortuna que fides est mihi pono in vestris
whatsoever fortune and faith is to me I place in your

gremiis; revocate parentem, reddite conspectum: nihil
bosoms; recall my parent, restore his presence to me: nothing

triste, illo recepto. Dabo bina pocula perfecta
can be sad, he being recovered. I will give two bowls wrought

argento, atque aspera signis quæ genitor cepit devictâ
from silver, and rough with figures which my father took from vanquished

Arisbâ; et geminos tripodas, duo magna talenta auri,
Arisba; and two tripods, two great talents of gold

antiquum cratera, quem Sidonia Dido dat. Si vero
an ancient goblet, which Sidonian Dido gave me. If indeed

contigerit victori capere Italiam que potiri sceptris,
it should happen to me a conqueror to possess Italy and enjoy the crown,

et ducere sortem prædæ, vidisti quo equo, in quibus
and to draw the lot of spoil, have you seen on what horse, in what

armis Turnus aureus ibat? excipiam illum clypeum
arms Turnus glittering in gold went? I will exempt that shield

ipsum, que rubentes cristas sorti, jam nunc tua præmia,
itself, and crimsoned crests from the lot, even now your rewards

Nise. Præterea genitor dabit bis sex lectissima
O Nisus. Besides my father shall give twice six chosen

corpora matrum que captivos que sua arma omnibus:
bodies of matrons and captives and their own arms which belonged to all.

insuper his, campi quod rex Latinus ipse
besides these, those fields which king Latinus himself

habet. Accipio te verò venerande puer, quem mea
possesses. I receive you indeed most regarded boy, whom my own

ætas insequitur propioribus spatiis, jam toto pectore et
age follows in nearer space, now with all my heart and

complector comitem in omnes casus. Nulla gloria
I embrace you as a companion in all my fortunes. No glory

quæretur meis rebus sine te; seu geram pacem seu
shall be sought in my concerns without thee; whether I make peace or

ɒella, tıbı maxima fides rerum que verborum.
war, to you *shall* be the chief confidence of my affairs and words.

Quem contra Euryalus fatur talia. Nulla dies
To whom on the other hand ' Euryalus speaks these *words*. No day

arguerit me dissimilem tam fortibus ausis, tantum
shall prove me unworthy of so brave enterprizes, only *let*

fortuna cadat secunda, haud adversa. Sed oro te unum
fortune fall out prosperous, not hostile. But I pray thee one thing

super omnia dona, est mihi genetrix de vetustâ gente
above all gifts, *there* is to me a mother from the ancient race

Priami, quam miseram excedentem mecum, non Ilia
of Priam, whom miserable departing with me, not *even* the Trojan

tellus tenuit, non mœnia regis Acestæ. Ego nunc linquo
land restrained, nor the walls of king Acestes. I now leave

hanc ignaram hujus periculi quodcunque est; que insalutatam;
her ignorant of this danger whatever it is; and unsaluted;

nox et tua dextera testis quod nequeam perferre lachrymas
night and your right hand are witness that I cannot endure the tears

parentis, at oro tu solare inopem, et succurre relictæ.
of *my* mother, but I pray you solace *her* destitute, and relieve *her* abandoned.

Sine me ferre hanc spem tui; ibo audentior in omnes
Permit me to bear this hope of you; I shall go more boldly into all

casus. Dardanidæ dederunt lacrymas mente
misfortunes. The Trojans shed tears *there* minds

perculsâ; ante omnes pulcher Iülus; atque imago patriæ
being affected; before all beautiful Iulus; and the image of this paternal

pietatis strinxit animum. Tum sic effatur. Spondeo
piety struck *his* mind. Then thus he speaks. I promise

omnia digna tuis ingentibus cœptis. Namque ista erit
all *things* worthy of your great attempts. For she shall be

genetrix mihi, que nomen Creusæ solum defuerit;
a mother to me, and the name of Creusa alone shall be wanting *to her*;

nec parva gratia manet talem partum, que quicun
nor shall small favour remain to such an offspring, and whatever

casus sequetur factum juro per hoc caput, per quod pater
chance may follow the deed I swear by this life, by which my father

solebat jurare ante, hæc eadem quæ polliceor tibi
was accustomed to swear formerly, these same *things* which I promise to you

reduci que secundis rebus manebunt que tuæ matri,
returning and in prosperous circumstances shall remain also to your mother,

que generi. Sic ait illacrymans simul exuit
and *her* family. Thus he said weeping at the same time he took off

auratum ensem humeri quem Gnossius Lycaon fecerat
his gilded sword from his shoulder which Gnossan Lycaon had made

mirâ arte, atque aptaverat habilem eburnâ vaginâ.
with wonderful art, and fitted *it* conveniently to an ivory sheath.

Mnestheus dat pellem Niso, que exuvias horrentis leonis·
Mnestheus gives a skin to Nisus, and the spoils of a rough lion·

fidus   Alethes,   permutat galeam.   Protinus armati
faithful Alethes, exchanges his helmet. Forthwith armed

incedunt; quos euntes omnis manus primorum, que
they march; whom proceeding all the band of the chiefs. both

juvenum que senum, prosequitur votis ad portas;
young and old, follows with prayers to the gates;

nec non et pulcher Iülus, gerens que virilem animum que
likewise also beautiful Iulus, bearing both a manly mind and

curam ante annos; dabat multa mandata portanda patri;
concern beyond his years; gave many commands to be borne to his father;

sed auræ discerpunt omnia, et donant irrita nubibus.
but the winds scatter them all, and give them useless to the clouds.

Egressi superant fossas, que petunt inimica castra per
Departing they pass the trenches, and seek the hostile camps through

umbram noctis; tamen futuri exitio multis antè.
the shade of night; nevertheless about to be destruction to many first.

Vident corpora fusa passim vino que somno per
They see bodies scattered every where by wine and sleep along

herbam, currus arrectos litore, viros inter lora que
the grass, chariots raised on the shore, men among the reins and

rotas, simul arma jacere, simul vina.
wheels, at the same time arms to lie about, at the same time wine.

Hyrtacides prior locutus sic ore: Euryale,
The son of Hyrtacus first speaks thus with his mouth: O Euryalus,

     audendum dextrâ; nunc res ipsa vocat.
there must be daring with the right hand; now the affair itself calls.

Iter est hàc; tu custodi et consule longè, ne qua manus
Our way is here; do you guard and watch from afar, lest any band

possit attollere se nobis a tergo. Ego dabo
can raise itself against us from behind. I will render

hæc vasta, et ducam te lato limite. Sic memorat,
these things waste, and will lead you by a broad path of death. Thus he speaks,

que premit vocem; simul aggreditur superbum
and restrains his voice; at the same time he attacks the proud

Rhamnetem ense; qui, fortè extructus altis tapetibus,
Rhamnes with his sword, who, by chance raised on high carpets,

proflabat somnum toto pectore; idem rex, et augur
snored out sleep from his whole breast; the same a king, and soothsayer

gratissimus regi Turno; sed potuit non depellere
most grateful to king Turnus; but he could not keep off

pestem augurio. Juxtá premit tres famulos jacentes
destruction by prophesy. Near by he kills three servants lying

temerè inter tela, que armigerum Remi, que aurigam
at random among the darts, and the armor-bearer of Remus, and the charioteer

nactus sub equis ipsis, que secat pendentia colla
having found him under the horses themselves, and cuts off their hanging necks

ferro; tum aufert caput domino ipsi, que relinquit
with the sword; then he cuts off the head of his master himslf, and leaves

truncum singultantem sanguine; terra tepefacta que tori
his trunk   spouting   with blood; the earth was warmed and couches

madent atro cruore. Necnon que Lamyrum que Lamum,
dripped with black gore. Likewise both Lamyrus and Lamus,

et juvenem Serranum, qui, insignis facie, luserat
and the youth Serranus, who, distinguished for beauty, had sported

plurima illâ nocte, que jacebat victus membra
much that night, and lay overcome in his limbs

multo Deo; felix, si protinus æquavisset illum
with the powerful God of wine; happy, if still he had equalled that

ludum nocti, que tulisset in lucem. Ceu leo impastus
play to the night, and had prolonged it to the day. As a lion unfed

turbans per plena ovilia (enim vesana fames suadet,)
raging through the full sheepfolds (for mad hunger induces,)

que mandit que trahit pecus molle que mutum metu;
and he tears and drags the flock feeble and dumb with fear;

fremit cruento ore: nec cædes Euryali minor: et
he rages with bloody mouth: nor was the slaughter of Euryalus less: and

ipse incensus perfurit, ac subit multam plebem sine
he inflamed rages, and comes up to a numerous crowd without

nomine in medio, que Fadum que Hebesum que Rhætum
name in the midst, both Fadus and Hebesus and Rhætus

que Abarim, ignaros: Rhætum vigilantem, et videntem
and Abaris, unknown; Rhætus watching, and seeing

cuncta; sed metuens tegebat se post magnum cratera:
all things; but fearing he hid himself behind a great goblet

cui assurgenti condidit totum ensem cominus in
to whom rising he buried the whole sword forthwith in

adverso pectore, et recepit multâ morte. Ille vomit
his opposing breast, and received him with abundant death. He vomits out

purpuream animam, et moriens refert vina mista cum
his crimsoned life, and dying throws up wine mixed with

sanguine. Hic fervidus instat furto. Que jam
blood. He glowing presses on by stealth. And now

tendebat ad socios Messapi, ubi videbat extremam
he directed his course to the companions of Messapus, where he saw the last

ignem deficere, et equos religatos ritè carpere gramen,
fire to fail, and the horses fastened in order to crop the grass,

cùm Nisus breviter (enim sensit ferri nimiâ
when Nisus briefly (for even he perceived that they were borne on too much

cæde atque cupidine,) ait, talia: Absistamus; nam
slaughter and ardour.) said, these words: Let us withdraw; for

mimica lux propinquat. Satis pœnarum est exhaustum;
the hostile light approaches Enough of punishment is accomplished;

via facta per hostes. Relinquunt que multa arma virûm,
a way is made through our foes, They leave also many arms of men,

perfecta solido argento, que simul crateras que
wrought from solid silver, and at the same time goblets, and

pulchros tapetas. Euryalus phaleras Rhamnetis, et
beautiful carpets. Euryalus *seizes* the ornaments of Rhamnes, and

cingula aurea bullis, quæ dona ditissimus Cadicus
girdles golden with bosses, which gifts the very wealthy Cadicus

olim mittit Tiburti Remulo, cùm absens jungeret
formerly sent to Tiburtine Remulus, when absent he had united

hospitio; ille moriens dat suo nepoti habere:
with him in friendship; he dying allows his grandson to have *them*:

post mortem Rutuli potiti bello que prædâ: rapit hæc,
after his death the Rutulians enjoyed the war and plunder: he seizes these,

atque nequicquam aptat fortibus humeris. Tum induit
and in vain fits *them* to his strong shoulders. Then he puts on

galeam Messapi habilem, que decoram cristis. Excedunt
the helmet of Messapus convenient, and beautiful with crests. They leave

castris, et capessunt tuta. Interea equites
the camps, and possess the safe *places*. In the meantime the horsemen

præmissi ex Latinâ urbe, dum cætera legio moratur
sent before from the Latin city, while the other legion delays

instructa campis, ibant, et ferebant responsa regi
drawn up on the plains, went, and bore replies to king

Turno; tercentum, omnes scutati, Volcente magistro.
Turnus; three hundred, all wearing shields, Volcens being their leader.

Que jam propinquabant castris, que subibant muro,
And now they approached the camps, and approached the wall,

cùm cernunt hos procul flectentes lævo limite; et
when they see these afar off winding along the left path; and

galea prodidit Euryalum immemorem in sublustri umbrâ
his helmet betrayed Euryalus unmindful in the light shade

noctis, que adversa radiis refulsit. Haud temerè est
of night, and opposed to the rays *of the moon* gleamed. Not plainly was

visum; Volscens conclamat ab agmine; Viri, state: quæ
it seen; Volscens cries out from the troop; Men, stand: what *is*

causa viæ? ve qui estis in armis? ve quò
the cause of your march? or who are you in arms? or whither

tenetis iter? Illi tendere nihil contrà; sed
do you direct *your* march? They attempt nothing on the other hand; but

celerare fugam in sylvas, et fidere nocti.
begun to hasten *their* flight into the woods, and to trust to the night.

Equites objiciunt sese ad nota divortia hinc atque
The horsemen oppose themselves to the known turnings on this side and

hinc, que coronant omnem aditum custode. Fuit
that, and they surround all the entrance with a guard. *There* was

sylva horrida latè dumis atque nigrâ ilice, quam
a wood horrid far around with bushes and gloomy oak, which

densi sentes compleverant undique: rara semita
entangled thorns had filled up on every side: here and there a path

ducebat per occultos calles. Tenebræ ramorum que
led *them* through the secret ways. The darkness of the branches and

onerosa præda impediunt Euryalum, que timor fallit
loaded plunder hinder Euryalus, and fear misleads *him*

regione viarum. Nisus abit; que jam imprudens
from the region of the ways. Nisus departs; and now thoughtless

evaserat hostes atque lacus; qui dicti Albani de nomine
had escaped the foes and the lakes; which called Albanian from the name

Albæ; tum rex Latinus habebat alta stabula. Ut stetit,
of Albæ; then king Latinus had *there* his lofty stables. As he stood,

et frustra respexit absentem amicum: Infelix Euryale,
and in vain looks back for his absent friend: Unhappy Euryalus,

quâ regione reliqui te? ve quâ sequar? Rursus
in what region have I left you? or whither shall I follow *you*? Again

revolvens omne perplexum iter fallacis sylvæ, simul
unwinding all *his* perplexed path of the deceiving wood, at the same time

et legit vestigia observata retro, que errat silentibus
also marks *his* footsteps observed backwards, and wanders through the silent

dumis: audit equos, audit strepitùs, et signa sequentium.
bushes: he hears the horses, he hears the noise, and signals of those following.

Nec longum tempus in medio, cùm clamor pervenit ad
Nor *is* a long time intermediate *there*, when a shout comes to

aures, ac videt Euryalum, quem jam omnis manus rapit
his ears, and he sees Euryalus, whom now the whole band seizes

oppressum fraude loci et noctis, subito tumultu
overcome by the fraud of the place and of the night, a sudden tumult

turbante, et conantem plurima frustra. Quid faciat? quâ
raging, and attempting many things in vain. What can he do? by what

vi, quibus armis audeat eripere juvenem? An
violence, by what arms shall he dare to seize the youth? Whether

moriturus inferat sese in medios hostes et properet
about to die shall he bear himself to the midst of his foes and hasten

pulchram mortem per vulnera? Ocyùs torquens hastile
honourable death by wounds? Quickly turning *his* spear

lacerto adducto, suspiciens altam Lunam, sic
his arm being drawn back, gazing on the lofty moon, thus

precatur voce: Tu, Dea, tu præsens succurre
he prays with his voice: Thou, O Goddess, thou kindly relieve

nostro labori, Latona, decus astrorum, et custos nemorum:
our labour, Latona, thou glory of the stars, and keeper of the groves:

si unquam pater Hyrtacus tulit qua dona tuis aris
if ever *my* father Hyrtacus has borne any gifts to your altars

pro me: si ipse auxi qua meis venatibus, ve suspendi
for me: if I have added any by my hunting, or suspended *them*

tholo, aut fixi ad sacra fastigia: sine me
from the ceiling, or have fastened *them* to thy sacred roof: permit me

turbare hunc globum, et rege tela per auras.
to rout this crowd, and guide *my* darts through the air.

Dixerat, et connixus toto corpore conjicit ferrum.
He said, and struggling with his whole body he hurled *his* dart

Hasta volans diverberat umbras noctis, et venit in
The spear flying strikes through the shadows of night, and comes against

tergum Sulmonis adversi: que ibi frangitur ac
the back of Sulmon opposed to *him*: and there is broken and

transit præcordia fisso ligno. Ille frigidus volvitur,
passes through his breast with the broken wood. He cold *in death* rolls over,

vomens calidum flumen de pectore, et pulsat ilia
vomiting forth a warm stream from *his* breast, and strikes *his* sides

longis singultibus. Diversi circumspiciunt. Ecce
with long drawn sobs. Different ways they look around. Lo

idem, acrior hoc, librat aliud telum ab summâ
the same *Nisus*, more active with this, poises another dart from the top

aure, dum trepidant. Stridens hasta iit per utrumque
of *his* ear, while they tremble. The hissing spear passed through each

tempus Tago, que tepefacta hæsit trajecto cerebro. Atrox
temple of Tagus, and warmed remained in *his* pierced brain. Cruel

Volscens sævit, nec conspicit auctorem teli usquam,
Volscens raged, nor did he behold the author of the dart any where,

nec quô ardens possit immittere se. Tamen, inquit, tu
nor where glowing he can throw himself. Yet, he said, do you

interea persolve pænas amborum mihi calido
in the mean time pay the penalties of both to me with *your* warm

sanguine: simul ibat in Euryalum, recluso ense.
blood: at the same time· he went against Euryalus, with drawn sword.

Tunc vero Nisus exterritus, amens conclamat; nec potuit
Then indeed Nisus frightened, mad cried out; nor could

celare se tenebris amplius, aut perferre tantum dolorem:
he conceal himself in darkness any longer, or endure so much grief:

me, me, adsum qui feci; O Rutuli, convertite
on me, on me, I am here who have done *it*; O Rutulians, turn

ferrum in me: omnis fraus mea: iste nihil, nec
your dart on ·me: all the fraud *is* mine: he has done nothing, nor

ausus, nec potuit: testor hoc cœlum, et conscia sidera:
dared he, nor could he: I call to witness this heaven, and conscious stars:

tantùm nimiùm dilexit infelicem amicum.
that only too much he loved *his* unhappy friend.

Dabat talia dicta: sed ensis adactus viribus
He uttered these words: but the sword thrust with violence

transadigit costas, et rumpit candida pectora. Euryalus
pierced through *his* ribs, and broke *his* fair breast. Euryalus

volvitur letho, que cruor it per pulchros artus, que
rolls in death, and blood flows through *his* beautiful limbs, and

cervix collapsa recumbit in humeros: veluti cum purpureus
his neck falling leans on *his* shoulders: as when a purple

flos succisus aratro languescit moriens, ve papavera
flower cut down by the plough faints dying, or poppies

demisere caput lasso collo cum fortè gravantur
hang down *their* head with wearied neck when by chance they are oppressed

pluviâ. At Nisus ruit in medios, que petit Volscentem
with rain. But Nisus rushed into the midst, and sought Volscens

solum per omnes, moratur in Volscente solo; circum quem
alone through all, he stays for Volscens alone: around whom

hostes glomerati hinc atque hinc cominus proturbant.
the enemies gathering on this side and that instantly drive *him away*.

Instat ' non secius, ac rotat fulminum ensem, donec
He presses on not the less and rolls his thundering sword, until

condidit in adverso ore clamantis Rutuli, et moriens
he has hid *it* in the hostile mouth of the bawling Rutulian, and dying

abstulit animam hosti. Tum confossus projecit sese
he took away life from the foe. Then pierced he cast himself

super exanimum amicum, que ibi demum quievit placidâ
upon *his* lifeless friend, and there at last rested in peaceful

morte.
death.

Fortunati ambo! si mea carmina possunt quid, nulla dies
Happy both! if my verses can effect any thing, no day

unquam eximit vos memori ævo: dum domus Æneæ
ever shall exempt you from this memorable time: while the house of Æneas

accolet immobile saxum Capitolii que Romanus pater
shall occupy the immoveable rock of the capitol and the Roman father

habebit imperium. Rutuli victores, potiti prædâ, que
shall possess the empire. The Rutulians victorious, enjoying the plunder, and

spoliis, flentes ferebant exanimum Volscentem in castra,
the spoils, weeping bore the lifeless Volscens into the camps.

nec minor luctus in castris, Rhamnete reperto exsangui,
nor *was there* less grief in the camps, Rhamnes being found lifeless,

et tot primis peremtis unâ cæde, que Serrano que
and so many chiefs being destroyed in one slaughter, both Serranus and

Numâ. Ingens concursus ad corpora ipsa, que
Numa. A great crowd *collects* at the bodies themselves, and

seminece's viros, que locum tepidum recenti cæde, et
dying heroes, and the place warm with fresh slaughter, and

rivos plenos spumanti sanguine. Agnoscunt inter se
rivers full of foaming blood. They recognise among them

spolia, que nitentem galeam Messapi et phaleras
the spoils, and shining helmet of Messapus and the trappings

receptas multo sudore. Et jam prima Aurora, linquens
recovered with much sweat. And now the early morning, leaving

croceum cubile Tithoni, spargebat terras novo lumine;
the saffron bed of Tithonus, sprinkled the earth with new light,

sole jam infuso, jam rebus retectis
the rays of the sun now being diffused, now *all* things being made manifest

luce. Turnus suscitat viros in arma, ipse circumdatus armis,
by his light. Turnus arouses the men to arms, he being surrounded by arms

que quisque cogit suas æratas acies in prœlia, que acuunt
and each one forces his brazen clad bands to battle. and they provoke

iras variis rumoribus.   Quin præfigunt ipsa capita
their wrath by various reports.   But   they fasten   the very heads

Euryali et Nisi in hastis arrectis, miserabile visu, et
of Euryalus and Nisus on spears erected,   miserable to be seen, and

sequuntur multo clamore.   Duri Æneadæ opposuere
they follow with great outcry.   The hardy Trojans   opposed *to them*

aciem in sinistrâ parte murorum (nam dextera cingitur
their band on the left part of the walls (for   the right   is surrounded

amni) que tenent ingentes fossas, et mœsti stant
by the river) and they hold   the deep   ditches, and mournful they stand

altis turribus, simul videbant ora virûm præfixa,
on the high towers, as soon as   they saw the heads of the men   fixed up,

nimis nota   miseris   que fluentia atro   tabo.
too well known to *their* wretched *friends* and   flowing with black   blood.

Interea pennata Fama, volitans per pavidam urbem
In the mean time winged Fame, flying through the frightened city

ruit nuncia, que allabitur aures matris Euryali; ac
rushes on a messenger, and glides to the ears of the mother of Euryalus; and

subitus calor reliquit ossa   miseræ.   Radii
suddenly warmth left   the bones of the unhappy *woman*. The shuttles

excussi manibus, que pensa revoluta. Infelix evolat,
falling from her hands, and her task is unravelled. Unhappy she flies,

et femineo ululatu, scissa comam, amens petit muros,
and with female wailing, tearing her hair, mad   she seeks the walls,

atque prima agmina cursu. Illa non memor virûm,
and the first bands in *her* course. She *was* not mindful of the men,

non illa periculi que telorum; dehinc implet cœlum
nor *was* she of danger and darts; then she fills the heaven

questibus; Euryale, ego aspicio te hunc? Ne tu illa
with *her* cries; O Euryalus, do I behold you thus? Whether *art* thou that

sera requies meæ senectæ? Crudelis potuisti linquere
late consolation of my old age? Cruel could *you* leave *me*

solam? nec copia data   miseræ matri affari te
alone? nor was permission given to *your* wretched mother to address *you*

extremùm, missum sub tanta pericula! Heu! jaces
for the last time, sent   to so great dangers! Alas! you lie

ignota terrâ, data præda Latinis canibus que alitibus!
in an unknown land, given up as a prey to the Latin dogs and   birds!

nec mater produxi te tua funera, ve pressi oculos, aut
nor *I your* mother prepared you for your funeral, or have closed *your* eyes, or

lavi vulnera, tegens veste quam festina urgebam
washed *your* wounds, shrouding *you* with the dress which hastening I urged on

noctes que dies tibi, et solabar aniles curas telâ.
by night and day for you, and consoled *my* aged anxieties with the loom.

Quò sequar? aut quæ tellus nunc habet artus,
Where shall I follow *you*? or what land now possesses *your* limbs,

que avulsa membra, et lacerum funus? nate, refers,
and lacerated members, and violated corpse? O son, do you bring

hoc mihi de te? hoc sum secuta, que terrâ que
this to me of yourself? for this have I followed thee, both by land and

mari? Figite me (si qua pietas est?)   O Rutuli, conjicite
sea? Pierce me (if any piety belongs to you) O Rutulians, hurl

omnia tela in me; absumite me primam ferro? aut
all your darts on me; cut me off first by the sword? or

tu, magne pater Divûm, miserere, que detrude hoc invisum
thou, great father of the Gods, pity, and cast this hated

caput sub Tartara tuo telo, quando nequeo
head to Tartarus with your thunderbolt, since I cannot

abrumpere crudelem vitam aliter. Animi
destroy this cruel existence in any other way. Their minds

concussi hoc fletu, que mœstus gemitus it per omnes.
were agitated by this wailing, and mournful grief extends through all.

Vires infractæ torpent ad prælia. Idæus et Actor,
Their strength broken, is powerless in battle. Ideus and Actor,

monitu Ilionei et Iüli lacrymantis multùm, corripiunt
by the advice of Ilioneus and Iulus weeping much, bear away

illam incendentem luctus, que inter manus reponunt
her inflaming their grief, and between their hands they replace her

sub tecta. At tuba increpuit terribilem sonitum procul
within the house. But the trumpet sounded a terrible noise afar

canoro ære. Clamor sequitur, que cœlum remugit.
with tuneful brass. A noise follows, and the sky re-echoes.

Volsci accelerant pariter, testudine actâ, et parant
The Volscians hasten together, a testudo being formed, and prepare

implere fossas, ac vellere vallum. Pars quærunt
to fill the ditches, and to tear down the wall. A part seek

aditum, et ascendere muros scalis, quâ acies est
access, and to ascend the walls with ladders, where the line is

rara, que corona non tam spissa viris interlucet. Contrà,
thin, and the circle not so dense with men is seen through. On the other

Teucri effundere omne genus telorum, ac
hand, the Trojans pour forth every kind of weapons, and

detrudere duris contis, assueti defendere muros longo
push them down with hard poles, accustomed to defend the walls in the pro-

bello. Volvebant quoque saxa infesto pondere,
longed war. They rolled down also rocks with hostile weight,

si quâ possunt perrumpere aciem tectam;
if by any means they can break through the army protected by their shields:

cùm tamen libet ferre omnes casus subter densâ
when yet it pleases them to endure all chances beneath the crowded

testudine. Nec jam sufficiunt; nam, quâ ingens globus
testudo. Nor now do they endure it; for, where the great mass

imminet, Teucri que volvunt que ruunt immanem
hangs over, the Trojans both roll and push down an immense

molem, quæ stravit Rutulos latè, que resolvit tegmina
rock, which overthrows the Rutulians far around, and breaks the coverings

armorum. Nec audaces Rutuli curant contendere
of *their* arms. Nor did the daring Rutulians care to contend

ampliùs cæco Marte, sed certant pellere vallo
any longer in blind war, but attempt to drive *them* from the wall

missilibus. Aliâ parte Mezentius, horrendus visu,
with flying darts. In another part Mezentius, dreadful in *his* aspect,

quassabat Etruscam pinum, et infert fumiferos ignes. At
shook *his* Tuscan pine, and scatters the smoking fires. But

Messapus, domitor equorum, Neptunia proles, rescindit
Messapus, the tamer of horses, Neptune's offspring, cut down

vallum et poscit scalas in mœnia. Vos, O Calliope,
the ramparts, and demands ladders against the walls. You, O Calliope,

precor, aspirate canenti, quas strages, quæ funera Turnus
I pray, favour *me* singing, what slaughters, what deaths Turnus

tum ediderit ibi ferro, quem virum quisque demiserit
then had effected there with the sword, what hero each one sent

orco; et mecum evolvite ingentes oras belli: Divæ,
to hell; and with me unfold the great outlines of the war; ye goddesses,

enim, et meministis, et potestis memorare. Erat
for, you both remember, and you can commemorate *them*. *There* was

turris vasto suspectu, et altis pontibus, opportuna loco,
a tower of lofty aspect, and high stages, convenient in its location,

quam omnes Itali certabant expugnare summis
which all the Italians contended to overcome with the greatest

viribus, que evertere summâ vi opum;
force, and to overturn with the utmost power of *their* strength;

contrà, Troës defendere saxis, que densi
on the other hand, the Trojans *attempted* to defend *it* with stones, and in close

intorquere tela per cavas fenestras. Turnus
array to hurl darts through the hollow windows. Turnus

princeps conjecit ardentem lampada, et affixit flamman
foremost hurled a burning rocket, and fastened the flame

lateri, quæ plurima vento, corripuit tabulas, et
in the side *of the tower*, which being increased by the wind, seized the boards, and

hæsit postibus adesis. Turbati, trepidare intus, que
cleaved to the posts *till* destroyed. Troubled, *they began* to tremble within, and

frustra velle fugam malorum. Dum glomerant
in vain to wish for escape *from their* misfortunes. While *they* gather

se, que residunt retro in partem quæ caret
themselves, and withdraw back into *that* part which *is* free from

peste, tum turris procubuit subitò pondere, et omne
contagion, then the tower fell suddenly with weight, and all

cœlum tonat fragore: seminneces veniunt ad terram,
heaven thunders with the noise: half dead they come to the earth,

ımmani mole secutâ, que confixi suis telis, et transfossi
a huge mass following, and pierced with their darts, and transfixed

    pectora duro ligno.
in their breasts with the hard wood.

Vix Helenor unus et Lycus elapsi, quorum Helenor
Hardly Helenor alone and Lycus escaped, of whom Helenor

primævus (quem serva Licymnia furtim sustulerat Mæonio
the elder (whom the slave Licymnia secretly had borne to the Lydian

regi que miserat ad Trojam vetitis armis) levis
king and had sent to Troy with forbidden arms) was lightly armed

nudo ense, que inglorius albâ parmâ. Que ubi is
with a naked sword, and unhonoured with a blank shield. And when he

videt se inter media millia Turni; Latinus acies
sees himself in the midst of the thousands of Turnus; The Latin forces

adstare hinc, atque acies hinc; ut fera, quæ
to oppose on this side, and the troops on that; as a wild beast, which

septa densâ coronâ venantium, furit contra tela,
hedged in by a thick circle of hunters, rages against their weapons,

que haud nescia injicit sese morti, et fertur saltu supra
and not ignorant casts himself on death, and is borne by a leap above

venabula; haud aliter juvenis moriturus, irruit in
their hunting spears; not otherwise the youth about to die, rushes into

medios hostes, et tendit quâ vidit tela densissima. At
the midst of foes, and marches where he sees darts thickest. But

Lycus longè melior pedibus, et inter hostes, et inter arma,
Lycus far better on foot, and amidst foes, and amidst arms,

tenet muros fugâ, que certat prendere alta tecta manu,
attains the walls by flight, and strives to seize the lofty roof with his hand,

que attingere dextras sociorum; quem Turnus secutus
and to reach the right hand of his associates; whom Turnus following

pariter cursu que telo, victor increpat his:
likewise in his course and with a dart, victorious rebukes with these words:

ne demens speravisti te posse evadere nostras manus?
whither madmen have you hoped that you could escape my hands?

Simul arripit ipsum pendentem, et revellit cum
At the same time he seizes him hanging, and tears him down with

magnâ parte muri; quales ubi armiger Jovis,
a great part of the wall; as when the armour bearer of Jupiter,

petens alta, sustulit aut leporem, aut cycnum candenti
seeking the lofty air, has raised either a hare, or swan of white

corpore, uncis pedibus; aut Martius lupus rapuit agnum
body, in his crooked feet; or a Martial wolf has seized a lamb

a stabulis, quæsitum matri multis balatibus. Clamor
from the stalls, sought by the mother with many bleatings. A shout

tollitur undique. Invadunt, et complent fossas
arises on every side. They press on, and fill the ditches

aggere; alii jactant ardentes tædas ad fastigia.
with a heap of earth; others throw burning torches to the roofs.

Ilioneus saxo atque ingenti fragmine montis
Ilioneus with a rock and with a great portion of a mountain overthrows

Lucetium; subeuntem portæ, que ferentem ignes; Liger sternit
Lucetius, coming up to the gate, and bearing fires; Liger overthrows

Emathiona, Asylas Chorinæum, hic bonus jaculo,
Emathion, Asylas *prostrates* Chorinæus, this one skilful with the dart,

hic, sagittâ fallente longè; Cæneus Ortigium
that one, with the arrow deceiving from afar; Cæneus *conquers* Ortygius,

Turnus Cænea victorem, Turnus Itys, que Clonium,
Turnus *kills* Cæneis the conqueror, Turnus *overthrows* Itys, and Clonius,

Dioxippum, que Promulum, et Sagarim, et Idam stantem
Dioxippus, and Promulus, and Sagaris, and Idas standing

pro summis turribus; Capys Privernum. Levis
upon the lofty towers; Capys *conquers* Privenus. The light

hasta Themillæ strinxerat hunc primò; ille demens,
spear of Themilla had graz'd him first; he mad,

tegmine projecto, tulit manum ad vulnus; ergo sagitta
his shield being cast aside, placed *his* hand on the wound; therefore an arrow

allapsa alis et manus infixa est lævo lateri que abdita
came gliding on wings and *his* hand was fastened to *his* left side and penetrating

intus rupit spiramenta animæ lethali vulnere. Filius
within broke the breathing *places* of his soul with a deadly wound. *His* son

Arcentis stabat in egregiis armis; pictus chlamydem
Arcentis stood *clad* in splendid arms; embellished in his cloak

acu, et clarus Iberâ ferrugine, insignis facie;
with the needle, and distinguished in Iberian purple, renowned for beauty;

quem genitor Arcens miserat Æneæ, eductum luco
whom his father Arcens had sent to Æneas, trained in the grove

Martis, circum Symætheia flumina, ubi pinguis et placabilis
of Mars, around Symæthia's streams, where the rich and peaceful

ara Palici. Mezentius ipse armis positis, egit
altar of Palicis *is*. Mezentius himself, *his* arms being laid aside, drives

stridentem fundam, habenâ adductâ ter circum caput,
a hissing sling, with a string drawn thrice around his head,

et diffidit media tempora adversi liquefacto plumbo
and rent the midst of the temple of *his* adversary with the melting lead

ac extendit porrectum multâ arenâ. Tum primùm bell,
and stretched *him* prostrated in the deep sand. Then first in the war

Ascanius dicitur intendìsse celerem sagittam, solitus
Ascanius is said to have hurled a swift arrow, accustomed

terrere fugaces feras antè, que manu fudisse
to frighten flying wild beasts before, and with his hand to have overthrown

fortem Numanum cui Remulo erat cognomen, que
strong Numanus to whom Remulus was a surname, and

nuper sociatus thalamo, habebat minorem germanam
lately united in marriage, he had the younger sister

Turni. Is ante primam aciem vociferans digna atque
of Turnus. He before the first troop crying out *things* worthy and

indigna relatu que tumidus præcordia novo regno
unworthy to be spoken and swelling in *his* heart with *his* new kingdom

ibat et ferebat sese ingenti clamore Non pudet
went and conducted himself with great noise. Does *it* not shame you

Phryges bis capti, iterum teneri obsidione que vallo
ye Trojans twice conquered, again to be detained by siege and a wall

et prætendere muros morti. En qui poscunt nostra
and to interpose ramparts to death. Lo those who demand our

connubia sibi bello. Quis Deus, quæ dementia adegit
intermarriage with them by war. What Deity, what madness drove

vos Italiam?
you to Italy?

Atridæ non hìc, nec Ulysses fictor fandi,
The sons of Atreus are not here, nor Ulysses the dissembler of speaking,

durum genus a stirpe. Deferimus natos ad
but a hardy race from their stock. We carry our children to

flumina primùm, que duramus sævo gelu et undis.
the rivers first, and we harden them by the severe frost and waters.

Pueri invigilant venatu que fatigant sylvas; ludus
Our sons are watchful in hunting and they range the woods; it is their sport

flectere equos et tendere spicula cornu. At juventus
to turn their horses and to send arrows from the bow. But our youth

patiens operum que assueta parvo, aut domat terram
patient of labour and accustomed to economy, either subdue the earth

rastris aut quatit oppida bello. Omne ævum teritur
with harrows or shake the towns in war. Our whole life is worn out

ferro; que fatigamus terga juvencûm versâ hastâ,
with the sword; and we goad the backs of bullocks with the inverted spear,

nec tarda senectus debilitat vires animi que mutat
nor does slow old age weaken our powers of mind and change

vigorem. Premimus canitiem galeâ que juvat
our activity. We press down our grey hair with the helmet and it delights us

semper convectare recentes prædas et vivere rapto. Vobis
ever to bear together fresh spoils and to live by plunder. Your

vestis picta croco et fulgenti murice; desidiæ cordi;
dress is painted with saffron and glittering purple; sloth is in your heart

juvat vos indulgere choreis et tunicæ habent manicas
it delights you to indulge in dances and your tunics have sleeves

et mitræ redimicula. O verè Phrygiæ que ne enim
and your caps ribands. O truly Trojan women and not truly

Phryges, ite per alta Dindyma ubi tibia dat
Trojan men, go through lofty Dindymus where the pipe gives forth

biforem cantum assuetis. Tympana que Berecynthia
the discrepant note to you accustomed. The tymbrel and Berecynthian

buxus Idææ matris vocat vos: sinite arma viris et cedite
flute of the Idæan mother call you: yield arms to men and retire from

ferro. Ascanius non tulit jactantem talia dictis
the sword. Ascanius did not endure him boasting these things in words

ac canentem dira, que obversus contendit telum
and singing forth direful cries, and turning he extended his arrow

equino nervo, que ducens brachia diversa constitit
on the horse hair string, and drawing his arms apart he stood

supplex precatus Jovem per vota antè. Omnipotens Jupiter
humbly praying Jupiter by vows first. Almighty Jove

annue audacibus cœptis. Ipse feram solemnia dona tibi,
favour my daring attempt. I will bear solemn gifts to you,

ad tua templa et ante aram statuam candentem juvencum
to your temples and before your altar I will place a white bullock

auratâ fronte, que ferentem caput pariter cum matre;
with gilded forehead, and bearing his head equally with his mother

qui jam petat cornu et spargat arenam pedibus.
who now strikes with his horn and scatters the sand with his feet.

Genitor audivit, et de serenâ parte cœli intonuit
The Father of the Gods heard, and from the serene part of heaven thundered

lævum. Fatifer arcus sonat unà; et sagitta elapsa
on the left. The fate-bearing bow sounds at once; and the arrow discharged

fugit stridens horrendùm que venit per caput Remuli et
flies hissing dreadfully and comes through the head of Remulus and

trajicit cava tempora ferro. I illude virtutem superbis
pierces the hollow temples with the steel. Go mock courage by proud

verbis. Phryges bis capti remittant hæc responsa
words. The Trojans twice captured send back these replies

Rutulis. Ascanius hæc tantùm. Teucri sequuntur
to the Rutulians. Ascanius said these things only. The Trojans follow

clamore, que fremunt lætitiâ que tollunt animos ad sidera.
with a shout, and applaud with joy and raise their minds to the stars.

Tum fortè crinitus Apollo in ætherea plagâ desuper
Then by chance golden haired Apollo in the celestial region from above

videbat Ausonias acies que urbem, sedens nube, atque
saw the Ausonian armies and city, sitting on a cloud, and

affatur Iulum victorem his: Macte novâ virtute,
addresses the Iulus conqueror in these words: Prosper in your new virtue,

puer; sic itur ad astra; genite Diis, et geniture
O boy; thus heroes ascend to the stars; descended from Gods, and about to generate

Deos. Omnia bella ventura fato, jure resident sub
Gods. All wars about to come by fate, in justice shall terminate under

gente Assaraci; nec Troja capit te. Simul effatus
the race of Assaracus; nor can Troy contain thee. At the same time having said

hæc, mittit se ab alto æthere, dimovit spirantes
these things, he casts himself from the lofty sky, moves through the breathing

auras, que petit Ascanium; tum formâ oris
gales, and seeks Ascanius; then in the form of his countenance

vertitur in antiquum Buten. Hic fuit armiger
he is changed into ancient Butes. He had been armour-bearer

Dardanio Anchisæ antè, que fidus custos ad limina; tum
to Trojan Anchises formerly, and a faithful keeper at the gate; then

pater addidit comitem Ascanio. Apollo ibat similis
his father united him as a companion to Ascanius. Apollo went resembling

longævo omnia, que vocem, que colorem, et albos crines,
the aged man in all things, both in voice, and hue, and hoary locks,

et arma sæva sonoribus; atque affatur ardentem Iülum
and arms harsh in their sound; and he addresses the glowing Iulus

his dictis: Æneide, sit satis Numanum oppetivisse
with these words: Son of Æneas, let it be enough that Numanus has fallen

tuis telis impunè: magnus Apollo concedit
by your darts without *injury to yourself:* great Apollo has yielded

hanc primam laudem tibi, et non invidet paribus armis.
this first praise to you, and does not envy *you* equal arms.

Cætera parce bello puer; Apollo sic orsus, reliquit
For the rest abstain from war, *noble* boy; Apollo thus having said, laid aside

mortales aspectus medio sermone, et evanuit procul ex
his mortal appearance in the midst of his discourse, and vanished far from

oculis in tenuem auram. Dardanidæ Proceres agnovere
their eyes into thin air. The Trojan Chiefs knew

Deûm, que divina tela, que sensere sonantem pharetram
the God, and his divine darts, and perceived the sounding quiver

fugâ.
in *his* flight.

Ergo prohibent Ascanium avidum pugnæ, dictis
Therefore they forbid Ascanius anxious for the fight, by the words

ac numine Phœbi: ipsi rursus succedunt in certamina,
and divine influence of Apollo; they again march on to the contest,

que mittunt animas in aperta pericula. Clamor it per
and expose *their* lives to open dangers. A cry goes through

propugnacula totis muris; intendunt acres arcus, que
the bulwarks around all the walls; they direct the strong bows, and

torquent amenta. Omne solum sternitur telis; tum
hurl the slings. All the ground is spread with darts: then

scuta que cavæ galeæ dant sonitum; flictu, aspera
shields and hollow helmets give forth a sound; in *their* conflict, a cruel

pugna surgit; quantus imber veniens pluvialibus
slaughter arises; such a shower proceeding from the rainy

Hædis ab occasu verberat humum; quàm multâ grandine
Hædi from the west beats the ground; as with much hail

nimbi præcipitant in vada, cùm Jupiter, horridus
storms rush down upon the waves, when Jupiter, terrible

Austris, torquet aquosam hyemem, et rumpit cava
with *his* south winds, hurls the watery tempest, and bursts the hollow

nubila cœlo. Pandarus et Bitias creti Idæo Alcanore,
clouds in the sky. Pandarus and Bitias sprung *from* Idean Alcanor,

quos sylvestris Hiera eduxit luco Jovis, juvenes
whom rustic Hiera brought up in the grove of Jupiter, young men

æquos patriis abietibus et montibus, recludunt portam,
equal to *their* native firs and mountains, open the gates

quæ commissa imperio ducis, freti armis,
which had been entrusted to the command of *their* leader, trusting to *their* arms,

que mœnibus ultro invitant hostem. Ipsi intus adstant
and from the walls gladly challenge the enemy. They within stand

pro turribus   dextrâ   ac lævâ, armati   ferro,   et
upon the towers on the right *hand* and the left, armed with the sword, and

corusci   alta capita cristis: quales geminæ aëriæ quercus
glittering on *their* lofty heads with crests: as   two   tall   oaks

consurgunt circum liquentia flumina, sive ripis   Padi,
arise   about   the flowing streams, either on the banks of the Po,

seu propter amænum Athesim, que attollunt   intonsa
or   near to the pleasant Athesis, and   lift *their* untrimmed

capita cœlo, et nutant sublimi   vertice.   Rutuli
heads to heaven, and nod with *their* lofty   head.   The Rutulians

irrumpunt, ut videre aditus patentes. Continuò Quercens
rush in,   as they beheld the entrance open. Forthwith Quercens,

et Equicolus pulcher armis, et Tmarus præceps animi, et
and Equicolus beautiful in arms, and Tmarus rash   in mind, and

mavortius Hæmon, aut versi   dedere   terga,   totis
warlike   Hæmon, either repulsed turned *their* backs, with all

agminibus, aut posuere vitam in limine ipso portæ.
their bands, or laid down their life at the entrance itself of the gate.

Tum iræ magis increscunt discordibus animis; et jam
Then rage the more increases in *their* discordant minds; and now

Troës collecti glomerantur eòdem,   et audent conferre
the Trojans collected gather to the same places, and dare engage

manum, et procurrere longius. Nuncius perfertur Turno,
their hand, and to advance farther. A message is brought to Turnus,

ductori furenti in diversâ parte, que turbanti viros;
the leader raging in a different part, and disturbing the men;

hostem fervere novâ   cæde, et præbere portas
that the foe burned with unprecedented destruction, and rendered *their* gates

patentes. Deserit inceptum, atque concitus immani irâ,
open.   He deserts *his* purpose, and aroused with dreadful rage,

ruit ad Dardaniam portam, que superbos fratres; et
he rushes to the Trojan gate,   and proud   brothers; and

primum jaculo conjecto sternit,   Antiphaten,
first,   *his* arrow being thrown, he prostrates Antiphates,

nothum alti Sarpedonis de Thebanâ matre;
the spurious offspring of the proud Sarpedon from a Theban mother;

enim is primus agebat se.   Itala cornus volat per
for he first showed himself. The Italian arrow flies through

tenuem aëra, que infixa stomacho, abit sub altum pectus;
the thin air, and piercing *his* stomach, enters beneath *his* deep breast,

specus atri vulneris reddit spumantem undam et
the orifice of the deep wound sends forth a foaming wave *of blood*, and

ferrum tepescit in fixo pulmone. Tum Meropem atque
the sword warms in *his* pierced lungs. Then Merops and

Erymantha manu, tum sternit Aphidnum, tum Bitian
Erymas with *his* hand, then he overthrows Arphidnus, then Bitias

ardentem oculis, que frementem animis; non jaculo,
flashing fire from *his* eyes, and raging in *his* mind; not with the dart.

enim neque ille dedisset vitam jaculo; sed contorta
for neither would he have yielded *his* life to the dart; but a brandished

phalarica stridens magnùm venit, acta modo
fiery javelin hissing much came, driven on in the manner

fulminis, quam nec duo taurea terga, nec fidelis
of a thunderbolt, which neither two bulls' hides, or *his* faithful

lorica duplici squamâ et auro, sustinuit: immania
coat of mail double with scales and gold, sustained: *his* huge

membra ruunt collapsa.
limbs fall fainting.

Tellus dat gemitum, et ingens intonat super clypeum.
The earth gives a groan, and huge he thunders *falling* upon his shield.

Qualis, in Euboico litore Baiarum, quondam saxea pila
As, on the Eubean shore of Baiæ, sometimes a rocky mass

cadit, quam, constructam ante magnis molibus, jaciunt
falls, which, built up before of great size, they place

ponto; sic illa prona trahit ruinam, que penitus
in the sea; thus it inclining draws down destruction, and deeply

recumbit illisa vadis. Maria miscent se, et
falls dashed against the shallows. The seas intermingle themselves, and

nigræ arenæ attolluntur. Tum alta Prochyta tremit sonitu, que
the black sands are upraised. Then high Prochyta trembles with the sound, and

Inarime imposita Typhæo, durum cubile, imperiis
Inarime placed on Typheus, a hard bed, by command

Jovis. Hìc Mars armipotens addidit animum que vires
of Jupiter. Here Mars powerful in arms has added courage and strength

Latinis, et vertit acres stimulos sub pectore, que immisit
to the Latins, and turned sharp goads *in their* breast, and cast

fugam, que atrum timorem Teucris. Conveniunt
flight, and black dread on the Trojans. *The Latins* assemble

undique; quoniam copia pugnæ data que bellator
from every side; since an occasion of fighting is given and the warrior

Deus incidit animo. Pandarus, ut cernit germanum
God glides into *their* mind. Pandarus, as he sees *his* brother

corpore fuso, et quo loco fortuna sit, qui casus
his body being overthrown, and in what place fortune is, what chance

agat res, torquet portam multâ vi cardine
Influences *his* affairs, hurls back the gate with much violence on the hinge

converso, obnixus latis humeris, que linquit multos
turned, opposing with *his* broad shoulders, and leaves many

suorum exclusos mœnibus, in duro certamine; ast
of *his friends* excluded from the walls, in the hard contest; but

includit alios cum se, que recipit ruentes; demens!
he includes others with himself and receives *them* rushing; mad man!

qui non viderit Rutulum regem in medio agmine
who had not seen the Rutulian king in the midst of the troops

irrumpentem que ultro incluserit urbi, veluti immanem
rushing in and anxiously inclosed *him* in the city as a savage

tigrim inter inertia pecora. Continuò nova lux effulsit
tiger amidst the helpless flocks. Forthwith a new light shone

oculis, et arma sonuere horrendùm; sanguineæ cristæ
from his eyes, and his arms sounded horridly; his bloody crests

tremunt in vertice, que mittit micantia fulgura clypeo.
tremble on his head, and sends glittering lightnings from his shield.

Æneadæ turbati subitò agnoscunt invisam faciem atque
The Trojans disturbed suddenly recognize his hated face and

immania membra. Tum ingens Pandarus emicat et
immense limbs. Then great Pandarus springs forth and

fervidus irâ fraternæ mortis affatur: hæc non dôtalis
glowing with rage for his brother's death cries out: this is not the dowry

regia Amatæ, nec media Ardea cohibet Turnum
palace of Amata, nor does the midst of Ardea contain Turnus

patriis muris. Vides inimica castra; nulla potestas
in his father's walls. You behold hostile camps; there is no power

exire hinc. Turnus subridens olli sedato pectore:
to escape from hence. Turnus smiling on him with settled breast says:

incipe, si qua virtus animo, et consere dextram;
begin, if any courage is in your soul, and engage my right hand;

narrabis Priamo Achillem inventum hìc etiam. Dixerat
you shall say to Priam that Achilles is found here also. He said.

Ille intorquet hastam rudem nodis et crudo cortice
He hurled his spear rough with knots and green bark.

adnixus summis viribus. Auræ excepere vulnus;
struggling with all his strength, The air received the wound:

Saturnia Juno veniens detorsit, que hasta infigitur portæ.
Saturnian Juno approaching turned it, and the spear is fastened in the gate.

At non effugies hoc telum, quod mea dextera versat
But you shall not escape this dart, which my right hand hurls

vi, enim neque auctor teli, nec vulneris is.
with strength, for neither is the author of the dart, nor of the wound the same.

Sic ait, et consurgit altè in ensem sublatum, et ferro
Thus he said, and rises high on his sword uplifted, and with its blade

dividit mediam frontem inter gemina tempora, que
he divides the midst of his forehead between his two temples, and

impubes malas immani vulnere; sonus fit, tellus est
youthful cheeks with a deep wound; a sound is made, the earth is

concussa ingenti pondere. Moriens sternit humi
shaken with his great weight. Dying he stretches on the ground

collapsos artus, atque arma cruenta cerebro; atque caput
his fainting limbs, and arms bloody with brains; and his head

pependit illi æquis partibus huc atque illuc ex
hangs down from him with equal parts hither and thither from

utroque humero. Tröes versi trepidâ formidine
each shoulder. The Trojans turning with trembling fear

diffugiunt: et si continuò ea cura subivisset victorem
fly: and if immediately this care had occurred to the conqueror.

rumpere claustra manu que immittere socios
to break open the enclosures with *his* hand and to admit *his* companions

portis, ille dies fuisset ultimus bello que genti; sed
by the gates, that day had been the last to the war and to the nation; but

furor que insana cupido cædis egit ardentem in
rage and a mad desire of slaughter drove *him* on raging against

adversos. Principio excepit Phalarim, et Gygen poplite
his foes. At first he intercepts Phalaris, and Gyges *his* ham

succiso; hinc ingerit hastas raptas in tergum fugientibus;
being cut; then he hurls *his* spears snatched up against the back of the flying,

Juno ministrat vires que animum.
Juno supplies strength and courage.

Addit Halyn comitem, et Phegea parmâ confixâ: deinde
He adds Halys as a companion, and Phegeas *his* shield being pierced; then

ignaros in muris, que cientes martem, que Alcandrum,
those ignorant on the walls, and exciting war, and Alcander,

que Halium que Nöemana, que Prytanim. Connixus
and Halius and Noeman, and Prytanis. Struggling

dexter ab aggere occupat Lyncea tendentem contra
on the right from the wall he seizes Lynceus approaching against him

que vocantem socios, vibranti gladio; huic caput
and calling out to his companions, with glittering sword; his head

cominus dejectum uno ictu jacuit longè cum galeâ; inde
forthwith struck off with one blow, fell far off with his helmet; then

Amycum, vastatorem ferarum; quo non alter felicior
Amycus, the destroyer of wild beasts; *than* whom not another *was* more skilful

ungere tela manu, que armare ferrum veneno; et
to anoint the darts with the hand, and to arm its steel with poison; and

Clytum Æoliden, et Cretea, amicum Musis, Cretea
Clytus the son of Æolus, and Creteus, a friend to the Muses, Creteus

comitem Musarum, cui carmina semper et citharæ
a companion of the Muses, to whom *were* songs ever and harps

cordi, que intendere numeros nervis; semper canebat
for a delight, and to direct numbers on the strings; ever he sung

equos, atque armâ virorum, que pugnas. Tandem Teucri
of horses, and the arms of men, and battles. At last the Trojan

ductores, Mnestheus, que acer Serestus, cæde suorum
leaders, Menestheus, and brave Serestus, the slaughter of his friends

auditâ conveniunt; que vident socios palantes, que
being heard, assemble; and they see their companions wandering about, and

hostem receptum. Et Mnestheus inquit: Quò deinde
the enemy received in. And Mnestheus says: Whither then

fugam? quò tenditis? quos alios muros, quæ mœnia
shall I fly? where do you direct *your course?* what other walls, what ramparts

jam habetis ultra? O cives, unus homo, septus
now have you beyond? O my countrymen, shall one man, surrounded

vestris aggeribus undique, ediderit tantas strages per
by your ramparts on every side, have given so great destruction through

urbem impunè? miserit tot primos juvenum Orco?
the city unpunished? shall he send so many of the first of our youth to hell?

non que miserit que pudet, segnes infelicis patriæ.
are you not both moved with pity and shame, ye slothful for your unhappy country

que veterum Deorum, et magni Æneæ? Accensi talibus,
and your ancient Gods, and great Æneas? Inflamed by such words

firmantur et consistunt denso agmine. Turnus paulatim
they are animated and they stand in thick array. Turnus by degrees

excedere pugnâ, et petere fluvium, ac partem quæ cingitur
departs from the battle, and seeks the river, and the part which is surrounded

amni. Teucri acriùs hoc incumbere magno
by the river. The Trojans more boldly for this press on with great

clamore, et glomerare manum: ceu cùm turba premit sævum
shout, and collect a band: as when a crowd presses a cruel

leonem infensis telis; at ille territus, asper, tuens acerba,
lion with hostile darts; but he terrified, bold, looking sternly,

redit retro; et neque ira aut virtus patitur dare terga;
retires backwards; and neither anger or courage suffers him to give back;

nec ille est potis tendere contra, per tela que viros,
nor he is able to proceed against them through darts and men,

cupiens quidem hoc; haud aliter Turnus dubius refert
desiring indeed this; not otherwise Turnus doubtful bears

improperata vestigia retro; et mens exæstuat irâ. Quin
his unhurried steps backward; and his mind burns with rage. But

etiam tum, bis invaserat hostes medios: bis
even then, twice had he attacked his enemies in the midst: twice

vertit agmina confusa fugâ per muros. Sed omnis
he turned their backs confused in flight along the walls. But all

manus coit properè e castris in unum; nec
the band unites hastily from the camps against him alone; nor

Satùrnia Juno audet sufficere vires contra; nam Jupiter
does Saturnian Juno dare to supply strength against them; for Jupiter

demisit aëriam Irim cœlo, ferentem haud mollia jussa
sent down airy Iris from heaven, bearing not gentle commands

germanæ, ni Turnus cedat altis mœnibus
to his sister, unless Turnus would withdraw from the lofty walls

Teucrorum. Ergo juvenis valet subsistere tantum, nec
of the Trojans. Therefore the youth can sustain so much, neither

clypeo nec dextrâ; sic obruitur telis injectis
with his shield, nor right hand; thus he is overwhelmed with darts cast

undique. Galea, circum cava tempora, strepit
from every side. His helmet around his hollow temples, resounds

assiduo tinnitu, et solida æra fatiscunt saxis; que
with continual ringing, and the solid brazen-armour cracks with stones; and

jubæ discussæ capiti; nec umbo sufficit ictibus: et
the plumes are struck off from his head; nor can the boss sustain the blows; both

Tröes, et fulmineus Mnestheus ipse, ingeminant
the Trojans, and thundering Mnestheus himself, redouble their attacks

hastis. Tum sudor liquitur toto corpore, et
with spears. Then perspiration runs from *his* whole body, and

agit piceum flumen, nec potestas respirare; æger
pours a pitchy stream, nor *is there* power to breathe: a feeble

anhelitus quatit fessos artus. Tum demum præceps dedit
panting shakes *their* weary limbs. Then at last headlong he gave

sese omnibus armis, saltu in fluvium. Ille accepit
himself with all *his* arms, with a leap into the river. It receives *him*

venientem cum suo flavo gurgite, ac extulit mollibus undis;
coming with *its* yellow stream, and raises *him* on the soft waves;

et remisit lætum sociis, cæde ablutâ.
and sends *him* back joyful to his companions, blood being washed *from him.*

ÆNEID.

BOOK TENTH.

INTEREA domus omnipotentis Olympi panditur
In the mean time the house of the all commanding Olympus is laid open,

que pater Divûm atque rex hominum vocat concilium in
and the father of the Gods and ruler of men calls a council in

sideream sedem, unde arduus aspectat omnes terras, que
the starry seat, whence exalted he beholds all countries, and

castra Dardanidum, que Latinos populos. Considunt
the camps of the Trojans, and the Latin people. They were seated

tectis bipatentibus; ipse incipit; magni
in apartments having folding doors; he begins; ye great

cælicolæ, quianam vobis sententia versa retro?
inhabitants of heaven, why *is* your purpose turned back?

que certatis tantùm iniquis animis? Abnueram Italiam
and do you contend so much with hostile minds? I had forbidden Italy

concurrere Teucris bello: quæ discordia contra
to engage with the Trojans in war; what *is this* discord against

vetitum? quis metus suasit, aut hos aut hos, sequi
my prohibition? what fear has persuaded, either these or those, to pursue

arma, que lacessere ferrum? Justum tempus pugnæ
arms, and to provoke the sword? A just time of war

adveniet (ne arcesssite) cùm olim fera Carthago
shall come (do not anticipate *it*) when hereafter savage Carthage

immittet magnum exitium, atque apertas Alpes, Romanis
shall send great destruction, and the opened Alps, on the Roman

arcìbus: tum   licebit   certare odiis, tum rapuisse
towers: then   it shall be allowed to contend with hatred, then   to ravage

res. Nunc sinite, et læti componite placitum fœdus.
all things.   Now   cease, and joyful   ratify   an approved   treaty.

Dixit hæc   paucis;   at aurea Venus refert,
He said these *things* in a few *words:* but beautiful Venus replies *in words.*

non pauca,   contrà. O patèr, ô æterna potestas
not   a few,   on the other hand. O father, O eternal   sovereignty

hominum que Divûm (namque quid aliud sit, quod
of men   and of Gods   (for   what   other can there be, which

jam queamus implorarè?) cernis ut Rutuli insultant
now   we can   supplicate?)   you see how the Rutulians insult   *us*

que Turnus insignis equis feratur per medios, que
and Turnus distinguished by his horses is borne through the midst, and

ruat tumidus   secundo Marte? jam   clausa mænia
rushes on swelling   with prosperous war?   now *their* enclosed ramparts

non tegunt Teucros; quin miscent prælia intra portas,
do not protect the Trojans; but they intermingle battle within the gates,

atque ipsis aggeribus murorum, et fossæ   inundant
and   the very towers   of the walls, and the ditches   swim

sanguine. Æneas ignarus abest. Ne nunquam sines
with blood.   Æneas   ignorant is absent. Will you never   allow *us*

levari obsidione? Iterum hostis imminet muris nascentis
to be relieved from siege? Again   the foe threatens the walls of rising

Trojæ, nec-non alter exercitus; atque iterum Tydides
Troy,   likewise another   army;   and again   Diomede.

surgit ab Ætolis Arpis, in Teucros. Equidem credo
arises from Ætolian Arpi, against the Trojans. Indeed   I believe

mea vulnera restant; et tua progenies, demoror mortalia
my own wounds remain; and I your own offspring,   await   mortal

arma. Si Trôes petiere Italiam sine tuâ pace, atque
arms.   If the Trojans have sought Italy without thy leave,   and

numine invito,   luant   peccata, neque juveris
thy deity forbidding, let *them* suffer for *their* faults, nor do you assist

illos   auxiliis, sin secuti tot responsa quæ Superi
them with *your* aid, but if pursuing so many prophecies which the Gods above

que Manes dabant, cur nunc potest quis quam flectere
and the Gods below gave, why now can any one turn aside

tua jussa? aut cur condere nova fata? Quid repetam
thy commands? or why contrive new destinies? Why shall I call to mind

classes exustas in Erycino litore? Quid regem
their fleets   burnt on the Erycinian shore? Why   the king

tempestatum, que furentes ventos excitos Æoliâ, aut Irim
of tempests,   and the raging winds awakened in Eolia, or   Iris

actam nubibus?   nunc etiam movet manes, (hæc
commissioned from the clouds?   now even she moves the shades, (this

sors rerum manebat intentata;) et Alecto,   repentè
chance of *your* affairs remained unattempted,) and Alecto,   suddenly

immissa   superis,   bacchata per medias urbes
sent up to tne world above,   rages through the midst of the cities

Italorum. Moveor   nil   super imperio; speravimus
of the Italians. I am moved in no way for   power;   we had hoped

ista   dum fortuna fuit;   vincant,   quos mavis
these things while fortune remained; let them conquer, whom you wish

vincere. Si   est nulla regio quam tua dura conjux
to conquer. If there is no region which your cruel   wife

det Teucris, genitor, obtestor per fumantia   excidia
will give to Trojans, O father, I pray by the smoking   remains

eversæ Trojæ,   liceat   dimittere   Ascanium
of overturned Troy, may it be lawful to send away   Ascanius

incolumem ab armis;   liceat   nepotem superesse;
unhurt   from arms: let it be allowed to my grandson to survive;

sanè Æneas jactetur in ignotis undis, et quamcunque
truly Æneas may be tossed on unknown waves,   whatever

viam fortuna dederit, sequatur;   valeam tegere hunc,
way fortune may have given, let him follow; may I be able to protect him,

et subducere   diræ   pugnæ.
and withdraw him from the dreadful fight.

Est Amathus,   est mihi celsa Paphos, atque
There is Amathus, there is to me lofty Paphos,   and

Cythera, que domus Idaliæ: inglorius exigat ævum hìc,
Cythera, and the house of Idalia: without honour let him pass his life here,

armis positis. Jubeto ut Carthago premat Ausoniam
arms being relinquished. Command that Carthage may restrain Ausonia

magnâ ditione; nihil inde obstabit Tyrñs urbibus.
with great authority; nothing hence shall oppose the Tyrian cities.

Quid juvit evadere   pestem   belli, et medium
What does it profit to escape the destruction of war, and in the midst

fugisse   per Argolicos ignes; que tot pericula
to have escaped through the Grecian fires; and so many dangers

maris que vastæ terræ exhausta, dum Teucri quærunt
of the sea and the extended land exhausted, while the Trojans seek

Latium que recidiva Pergama? non ne satiùs insedisse
Latium and new rising Pergamus? was it not better to sit down

supremos cineres patriæ, atque solum, quo Troja fuit?
on the last ashes of their country, and the soil, where Troy has been?

Oro,   redde Xanthum et Simoënta miseris;   que da
I entreat, restore Xanthus and Simois to the unhappy men; and give

Teucris,   pater, iterum revolvere Iliacos casus. Tum
to the Trojans, O father, again to endure Trojan calamities. Then

regia Juno, acta gravi furore; quid cogis me
royal Juno, inflamed by severe anger said; why do you constrain me

rumpere alta silentia, et   vulgare obductum dolorem
to break deep silence, and to spread abroad my concealed grief

verbis? Quisquam hominum que Divûm subegit Ænean
by words? Did any one of men and of Gods compel Æneas

sequi   bella, aut inferre se   hostem regi Latino? Petivit
to prosecute war,   or to offer himself an enemy to king Latinus? He sought

Italiam fatis   auctoribus: esto; impulsus furiis Cassandræ
Italy   the fates being *his* guides: be it so; driven on by the madness of Cassandra

num   hortati sumus   linquere   castra,   aut committere
whether did we advise *him* to relinquish *his* camps, or   to trust

vitam ventis? num credere summam   belli, num
his life to the winds? whether to trust the chief *conduct* of the war, whether

muros puero, ve agitare Tyrrhenam fidem, aut gentes
the walls to a boy, or to unsettle Tuscan faith, or   nations

quietas? Quis Deus, quæ dura potentia   nostra   egit
at peace? What God, what severe authority of ours has driven *him*

in fraudem? Ubi   Juno híc, ve Iris demissa nubibus? Est
to   fraud? When *was* Juno here, or Iris sent down from the clouds? It is

indignum, Italos circumdare nascentem Trojam flammis,
disgraceful for the Italians to surround   rising   Troy   with flames,

et Turnum consistere patriâ terrâ, cui Pilumnis   avus
and for Turnus to settle on his native soil, to whom Pilumnis *is* grand sire,

cui   Diva Venilia mater. Quid   Trojanos ferre vim
to whom the Goddess Venelia *is* mother. What *is it* for the Trojans to offer violence

Latinis atrâ   face, premere aliena arva jugo, atque
to the Latins with cruel warfare, to subject foreign fields to the yoke, and

avertere prædas? Quid legere soceros, et abducere
to carry off plunder? What to steal fathers-in-law, and to withdraw

pactas gremiis?   orare pacem
affianced *wives* from the bosoms *of their husbands*? to beg for peace

manu,   præfigere arma pupibus.
with *suppliant* hand, *and* to display arms on *their* ships.

Tu potes subducere Ænean manibus   Graiûm que
You can   withdraw   Æneas from the hands of the Greeks, and

obtendere nebulam et inanes ventos pro viro; et potes
interpose   mist   and empty winds instead of the man; and you can

convertere classem in totidem nymphas: est nefandum
change   the fleet into as many   nymphs: it is a dreadful *thing*

nos juvisse Rutulos aliquid contra. Æneas ignarus
for us to have aided the Rutulians in any way against *him*. Æneas ignorant

abest; et ignarus absit. Est Paphos que Idalium tibi,
is absent; and ignorant let him be absent. *There* is Paphos and Idalium to you,

sunt alta Cythera; quid tentas urbem gravidam bellis,
there *is* lofty Cythera; why do you attempt a city   teeming   with war,

et aspera corda? nos ne conamur vertere fluxas   res
and savage hearts? do we attempt to overturn the falling concerns

Phrygiæ tibi fundo?   Nos? an qui objicit
of Troy for you from *their* foundations? We? or he who exposed

miseros Troas Achivis? Quæ fuit causa que Europam
the wretched Trojans to the Greeks? Who has been the cause that both Europe

que Asiam consurgere in arma, et solvere fœdera furto?
and Asia   arose   in arms, and violated treaties by fraud?

Dardanius adulter expugnavit Spartam me duce? aut
Has a Trojan adulterer conquered Sparta, I being *his* conductor? or

ego dedi tela, ve fovi bella cupidine?
have I furnished weapons, or have I cherished wars by lust?

Tunc decuit metuisse tuis: nunc sera
Then it had become *you* to have feared for your *friends*: now *too* late

assurgis haud justis querelis, et jactas irrita jurgia.
you arise not in just complaints, and throw away vain disputes.

Juno orabat talibus; que cuncti cœlicolæ fremebant
Juno entreated in these *words*: and all the Gods murmured

vario assensu; ceu cùm prima flamina deprensa sylvis
with various assent; as when the first blasts confined in the woods

fremunt, et volutant cæca murmura, prodentia nautis
blow, and roll on in distinct murmurings, betraying to sailors

ventos venturos. Tum omnipotens pater, cui est
that winds are about to come. Then the all-powerful father, to whom is

summa potentia rerum, infit. Eo dicente, alta domus
the chief supremacy of things, begins. He speaking, the lofty palace

Deûm silescit; et tellus tremefacta solo;
of the Gods is still; and the earth *is* shaken from its foundation;

arduus æther silet: tum Zephyri posuere;
the exalted sky is still: then the west winds laid aside *their violence*;

pontus premit placida æquora. Ergo accipite atque figite
the sea restrains its peaceful waters. Therefore receive and establish

hæc mea dicta animis: quandoquidem haud est licitum
these my words in *your* minds, since it is not allowed

Ausonios conjungi Teucris fœdere, nec vestra discordia
the Ausonians to be united to the Trojans in treaty, nor your discord

capit finem; quæ fortuna est cuiquam hodie, quam spem
receive an end; whatever fortune is to each one to-day, what hope

quisque secat, fuat Tros ve Rutulus, habebo
each one may mark out, let him be Trojan or Rutulian, I will hold them

nullo discrimine; seu castra tenentur obsidione fatis
with no distinction; whether the camps are held in siege by the fates

Italorum, sive malo errore Trojæ, que sinistris
of the Italians, or• by the unfortunate error of Troy, and inauspicious

monitis. Non solvo Rutulos. Sua exorsa ferent
admonitions. Nor do I free the Rutulians. His own undertakings shall bring

laborem que fortunam cuique. Rex Jupiter idem omnibus.
suffering and fortune `to each. King Jupiter *is* the same to all.

Fata invenient viam. Annuit per flumina Stygii
The fates will find out a way. He nodded by the streams of his Stygian

fratris, per ripas torrentes pice que atrâ voragine, et
brother, by the banks overflowing with pitch and black whirlpools, and

tremefecit totum Olympum nutu. Hic finis fandi:
shook all heaven with his nod. Here *was* an end of speaking:

tum Jupiter surgit aureo solio, quem medìum Cœlicolæ
then Jupiter rises from his golden throne, whom in the midst the Gods

ducunt ad limina. Interea Rutuli omnibus portis
lead to his palace. In the mean time the Rutulians in all the gates

instant sternere viros circùm cœde, et cingere
rush on to destroy the men all around with slaughter, and to surround

mœnia flammis. Ast legio Æneadum tenetur obsessa
the ramparts with flames. But the legion of the Trojans is held besieged

vallis; nec ulla spes fugæ. Miseri stant altis
within the walls; nor is there any hope of flight. Wretched they stand on the high

turribus nequicquam, et cinxere muros rarâ coronâ.
towers in vain, and surround the walls with a thin circle.

Asius Imbracides, que Hicetaonius Thymœtes, que
Asius the son of Imbracus, and Hicetaon's son Thymœtes, and

duo Assaraci, et senior Tybris cum Castore, prima
the two sons of Assaracus, and the old Tybris with Castor, for the first

acies; ambo germani Sarpedonis, et Clarus et Hæmon, ab
band; both brothers of Sarpedon, and Clarus and Hæmon, from

altâ Lyciâ comitantur hos. Lyrnessius Acmon, minor
lofty Lycia accompany them. Lyrnessian Acmon, inferior

nec Clytio genitore, nec fratre Mnestheo, connixus
neither to Clytius his father, nor his brother Mnestheus, striving

toto corpore, fert ingens saxum haud exiguam partem
with his whole body, bears a great rock not a small part

montis. Hi certant defendere jaculis, illi saxis,
of a mountain. These strive to defend the place with darts, those with rocks.

que moliri ignem, que aptare sagittas nervo. Ecce
and to hurl fire, and to fit arrows to the string. Behold

Dardanius puer ipse, justissima cura Veneris, detectus
the Trojan boy himself, the most righteous care of Venus, uncovered

honestum caput, inter medios, micat qualis gemma, quæ
as to his honest head, in the midst, shines as a jewel, which

dividit fulvum aurum, decus aut collo aut capiti;
separates the yellow gold, an ornament either to the neck or to the head;

vel quale ebur lucet per artem inclusum buxo, aut
or as ivory shines by art inclosed in box-work, or

Oriciâ terebintho; cui lactea cervix accipit fusos
Orician ebony; whose milk white neck receives his flowing

crines, et circulus subnectit molli auro. Ismare,
hair, and a circle binds it with ductile gold. O Ismarus,

magnanimæ gentes viderunt te, quoque dirigere vulnera,
high-minded nations have seen thee, also attempt wounds,

et armare calamos veneno, generose Mæoniâ domo;
and arm reeds with poison, noble of a Lydian family;

ubi que viri exercent pinguia culta que Pactolus
where both men till the rich cultured fields and Pactolus

irrigat auro. Et Mnestheus adfuit, quem pristina
overflows them with gold. And Mnestheus was present, whom the former

gloria Turni pulsi aggere murorum tollit sublimem;
glory of Turnus driven from the mound of the walls raises high

et Capys: hinc nomen ducitur Campaniæ urbi. Illi
and Capys: hence the name is derived to the Campanian city. They

contulerant certamina duri belli inter sese; Æneas
had engaged in contests of cruel war among themselves; Æneas

secabat freta mediâ noctę. Namque ut ab Evandro adit
cut the seas at midnight. For as from Evander he goes

regem, ingressus Etruscis castris, et memorat regi
to the king, entering the Tuscan camps, and makes known to the king

que nomen que genus; ve edocet quid petat, ve quid
both his name and race; or declares what he requires, or what

ipse ferat; quæ arma Mezentius conciliet sibi, que
he brings; what arms Mezentius would procure for himself, and

violenta pectora Turni; admonet quæ fiducia sit
the violent disposition of Turnus; he admonishes him what confidence can be

humanis rebus, que immiscet preces; mora haud fit;
in human concerns, and intermingles prayers; delay does not take place;

Tarchon jungit opes que ferit fædus. Tum Lydia gens
Tarchon joins his strength and strikes up a league. Then the Lydian nation

libera fatis, conscendit classem, commissa externo duci
set free from the fates, ascends the fleet, entrusted to a foreign leader

jussis Divûm. Ænea puppis tènet prima subjuncta
by command of the Gods. Æneas' ship holds the first rank having subjoined

rostro Phrygios leones. Ida imminet super
to its beak Trojan lions. Ida's mount hangs from above

gratissima profugis Teucris. Hìc magnus Æneas sedet
most grateful to the fugitive Trojans. Here great Æneas sits

que volutat varios eventus belli secum, que Pallas
and revolves the varied events of war with himself, and Pallas

affixus sinistro lateri jam quærit sidera, iter
adhering to his left side now inquires concerning the stars, their passage

opacæ noctis; jam quæ passus que terrâ que
through the dark night: now what he had endured both on land and

mari.
the sea.

Deæ, nunc pandite Helicona que movete cantus; quæ
Ye Goddesses, now lay open Helicon and direct my song; what

manus comitetur Ænean interea ab Tuscis oris que
band accompanied Æneas, in the meantime from the Tuscan coasts and

armet rates que vehatur pelago. Massicus princeps secat
armed his ships and is borne on the sea. Massicus first cuts

æquora æratâ Tigri sub quo manus mille
the waters in the brazen-beaked Tigris, under whom a band of a thousand

juvenum, qui mœnia Clusi, que qui liquere urbem
youth, who have left the walls of Clusus, and who have left the city

Cosas, queis tela sagittæ que leves coryti humeris
Cosa, whose weapons are arrows and light quivers on their shoulders

et lethifer arcus. Torvus Abas unà huic;
and the death-bearing bow. Stern Abas goes together with him,

totum   agmen   insignibus   armis, et   puppis fulgebat
the whole troop   with distinguished arms, and   the stern glittered

auratâ   Apolline.   Populonia, mater,   dederat   illi
with a gilded Apollo.   Populonia, his mother city, had bestowed on him

sexcentos   juvenes   expertos   belli; ast   insula   Ilva
six hundred youth   experienced in war; but the island Ilva

generosa   inexhaustis   metallis chalybum   trecentos.
abounding   in unexhausted mines   of iron sent three hundred.

Tertius   Asylas,   ille   interpres hominum que   Divûm,
The third was Asylas, the interpreter of men   and   Gods,

cui   fibræ pecudum, cui sidera cœli, et linguæ
to whom the entrails of cattle, to whom the stars of heaven, and the languages

volucrum et ignes   præsagi fulminis parent;   rapit
of birds   and lightnings of prophetic thunder are obedient; he bears away

mille   densos   acie   atque horrentibus hastis. Pisæ,
a thousand condensed in a band and with frightful spears.   Pisa,

Etrusca urbs   solo   ab origine Alpheæ, jubent hos
a Tuscan city in its foundation from the origin of Alphea, command these

parere.   Pulcherrimus Astur sequitur.   Astur fidens
to obey.   Most beautiful Astur follows   Astur trusting

equo   et versicoloribus armis. Qui   domo   Cærete,
to his horse and variegated   arms. Who are of the house of Cære,

qui sunt in arvis Minionis, et veteres Pyrgi,   que
who are   in the fields of Minio, and the veteran Pyrgi,   and

intempestæ Graviscæ adjiciunt tercentum (omnibus una
the insalubrious Graviscæ   add   three hundred (to all was one

mens   sequendi.) Ego non   transiverim te, Cycne,
purpose   of following.) I   will not pass by   thee, O Cycnus,

ductor Ligurum, fortissime bello; et Cupavo   comitate
leader of the Ligurians, most heroic in war; and Cupavus accompanied

paucis, de cujus vertice olorinæ pennæ surgunt. Amor
by few,   from whose head   swans'   plumes   arise.   Love

vestrum crimen que   insigne   paternæ formæ que
was your   crime .   and the distinguished cause of your father's form also.

Nam ferunt Cycnum luctu Phætontis amati dum canit inter
For they say that Cycnus for grief of Phæton beloved while he sings among

populeas frondes que umbram sororum et solatur mœstum
the poplar leaves   and the shade of his sisters and consoles   his sad

amorem Musâ,   canentem molli plumâ duxisse senectam
love   by the muse, becoming white in his soft plumage passed   his old age

liquentem terras et sequentem sidera voce.   Filius
abandoning the earth and pursuing the stars with his voice.   His son

comitatus æquales catervas classe promovet ingentem
accompanying his equal   troops   in his fleet propels   the huge

Centaurum remis; ille instat aquæ que arduus minatur
Centaur   with oars; he stands on the water and bold threatens to hurl

immane saxum   undis   et   sulcat alta maria
a huge   rock against the waves and   ploughs the deep   seas

longâ carinâ. Etiam Ocnus ille ciet agmen ab
with *his* long keel.   Also Ocnus himself leads on a band from

patriis oris, filius fatidicæ Mantus et Tusci amnis qui
his native coasts, the son of the prophetic Mauto and the Tuscan river, who

dedit muros que nomen matris tibi Mantua; Mantua
gave walls and the name of his mother to thee, O Mantua;   Mantua

dives avis: sed non unum genus omnibus. Illi triplex
rich in ancestors: but *there is* not one race to all.   To her is a triple

gens quaterni populi sub gente—ipsa caput populis.
race four people under *one* nation—herself the capital *city* to the people

Vires de Tusco sanguine. Mezentius hinc quoque
Their strength *is* from Tuscan blood.   Mezentius hence also

armat quingentos in se, quos Mincius patre
arms five hundred against himself, whom Mincius from *his* father

Benaco velatus glaucâ arundine ducebat in æquora
Benacus crowned with sea-green reed led to the sea

infestâ pinu.
in a hostile ship.

Gravis Auletes it, que assurgens verberat fluctum
Stern Auletes goes, and rising beat the wave

centenâ arbore: vada spumant marmore verso.
with an hundred oars: the billows foam, the sea being upturned.

Immanis Triton et exterrens cærula freta conchâ
The vast Triton also frightening the azure seas with *his* shell

vehit hunc, cui nanti hispida frons præfert hominem
bears him, to whom swimming a hairy front exhibits a man

tenus laterum, alvus desinit in pristin; spumea unda
as far as the sides, *his* belly ends in a fish; the foaming wave

murmurat sub semifero pectore. Tot lecti proceres
murmurs under *his* half monstrous breast. So many chosen chiefs

ibant ter denis navibus subsidio Trojæ et secabant
went in thrice ten ships to the aid of Troy and cut

campos salis ære. Jamque dies concesserat
the plains of brine with *their* brazen prow. And now the day had departed

cœlo que alma Phœbe pulsabat medium Olympum
from the sky and the fair moon shook the midst of the sky

noctivago curru. Æneas ipse sedens, que regit
with *her* night-wandering chariot. Æneas himself sitting, both guides

clavum que ministrat velis (enim neque cura dat quietem
the helm and attends the sails (for neither does care allow rest

membris.) Atque ecce chorus suarum comitum occurrit
to *his* limbs.) And lo a band of his associates met

illi in medio spatio, Nymphæ, quas alma Cybele jusserat
him in middle space, Nymphs, whom fair Cybele had commanded

habere numen maris, que esse Nymphas e
to have divinity of the sea, and to be Nymphs from

navibus: innabant pariter, que secabant fluctus; quot
his: they swam together, and divided the billows; as many

æratæ proræ steterant prius ad litora. Agnoscunt regem
brazen prows had stood before by the shore. They know *their* king

longè que lustrant choreis: quarum Cymodocea, quæ
from afar and surrounded *him* with dances: of whom Cymodocea, who was

doctissima fandi, sequens ponè, tenet puppim
the most skilled in speaking, following behind, holds the stern

dextrâ; que ipsa eminet dorso, ac subremigat
with *her* right hand; and she rises above with her back, and rows beneath

lævâ tacitis undis. Tum alloquitur ignarum
with *her* left hand in the silent waves. Then she addresses *him* unconscious

sic: Ænea, gens · Deûm, ne vigilas? vigila, et immitte
thus: O Æneas, descendent of the Gods, are you awake? awake, and loosen

rudentes velis. Nos sumus Ideæ pinus de sacro
the cordage from the sails. We are Ida's pines from *its* sacred

vertice tua classis; nunc Nymphæ pelagi. Ut perfidus
top thy fleet; now Nymphs of the ocean. As the treacherous

Rutulus premebat nos precipites ferro que flammâ,
Rutulian oppressed us swift *sailing* with sword and fire,

invitæ rupimus tua vincula, que quærimus te per æquor.
unwilling we broke your cables, and sought thee through the sea.

Genetrix miserata refecit hanc faciem, et dedit esse
The mother *of the Gods* pitying restored this form, and allowed *us* to be

Deas, que agitare ævum sub undis. At puer Ascanius
Goddesses, and to pass *our* life beneath the waves. But the boy Ascanius

tenetur muro que fossis inter media tela atque Latinos
is detained by the wall and ditches in the midst of darts and the Latins

horrentes Marte. Jam Arcas eques, permistus forti
raging in war. Now the Arcadian cavalry intermingled with the bold

Etrusco, tenet jussa loca: est certa sententia Turno
Etruscan, holds the appointed places· it is a resolved determination to Turnus

opponere illis medias turmas, ne jungant castris.
to oppose to them his compact bands, lest they should join the camps.

Age, surge, et Aurorâ veniente, primus jube socios
Come, arise, and the morn approaching, first command *your* companions

vocari in arma; et cape clypeum, quem Ignipotens
to be called to arms; and take the shield, which the fire-powerful *God*

ipse dedit invictum, atque ambivit oras auro. Crastina
himself gave invincible, and encircled its borders with gold. To-morrow's

lux spectabit ingentes acervos Rutulæ cædis (si non
light shall behold great heaps of Rutulian slaughter (if you do not

putâris mea dicta irrita.) Dixerat, et discedens, impulit
think my words vain.) She said, and moving on, she propelled

altam puppim dextrâ, haud ignara modi: Illa
the lofty ' stern with her right hand, not ignorant of the manner: It

fugit per undas ocyor et jaculo, et sagittâ æquante
flies through the waves swifter even than a dart, and arrow equalling

ventos. Inde aliæ celerant cursus. Tros Anchisiades
the winds. Then the others hasten *their* course. The Trojan son of Anchises

ipse inscius stupet; tamen tollit animos omine.
himself unconscious stands amazed; yet he arouses *their* courage by the omen.

Tum aspectans supera convexa precatur breviter:
Then beholding the high vaulted sky he prays *thus* briefly:

Idæa, alma parens Deûm, cui Dindyma que turri-
O Idean *Goddess* bountiful parent of the Gods, to whom Dindyma and turret

geræ urbes, que liones bijugi ad fræna, cordi tu
bearing cities, and lions yoked in pairs to *your* reins, *are for* a delight be thou

nunc princeps pugnæ mihi: tu, Diva, propinques augurium
now the guide of the battle to me: do thou, O Goddess, propitiate the augury

ritè, que adsis Phrygibus secundo pede. Effatus
in form, and approach the Trojans with auspicious foot. He said

tantum; et interea dies revoluta jam ruebat maturâ
so much; and in the mean time day revolving now arose with timely

luce, que fugarât noctem. Principio edicit sociis
light, and banished night. In the first place he instructs his associates

sequantur signa, atque aptent animos armis, que parent
that they follow the signals, and prepare *their* minds for arms, and dispose

se pugnæ. Que jam habet Teucros et sua castra
themselves for the fight. And now he has the Trojans and his camps

in conspectu stans in celsâ puppi. Tum deinde extulit
in sight standing on the lofty stern. Then afterwards he raises

ardentem clypeum sinistrâ. Dardanidæ tollunt
his glowing shield on *his* left *hand.* The Trojans raise

clamorem e muris ad sidera. Spes addita suscitat iras.
a shout from the walls to the stars. Hope superadded arouses *their* rage.

Jaciunt tela manu: quales Strymoniæ grues dant signa,
They hurl darts with *their* hand: as Strymonian cranes give signals

sub atris nubibus, atque tranant æthera, cum sonitu, que
under the black clouds, and skim along the skies, with a sound, and

fugiunt notos secundo clamore. At ea videri
fly the south winds with prosperous cry. But these things seem

mira Rutulo regi que Ausoniis ducibus: donec
wonderful to the Rutulian king and the Ausonian leaders; until

respiciunt puppes versas ad litora, que totum æquor
they look back upon the ships turned to the shores, and the whole stream

allabi classibus. Apex ardet capiti que flamma
to be glided over by ships. The top *of his* *helmet* blazes on *his* head and a flame

funditur cristis a vertice, et aureus umbo vomit, vastos
is poured on *his* crest from *his* head, and a golden boss sends forth copious

ignes: not secus ac si quando sanguinei cometæ rubent
fires: not otherwise than if at any time bloody comets shine

lugubrè liquidâ nocte; aut Sirius ardor, ille ferens
mournfully in the clear night; or the dog-star's heat, itself bearing

sitim que morbos ægris mortalibus, nascitur, et contristat
thirst and diseases to sick mortals, arises, and saddens

cœlum lævo lumine.
heaven with unpropitious light.

Tamen fiducia haud cessit audaci Turno præripere
Yet confidence did not fail the bold Turnus to preoccupy

litora, et pellere venientes terrâ. Ultro tollit
the shores, and drive them off approaching from the land. Forthwith he arouses

animos dictis, atque ultro increpat: adest
their courage by his words, and forthwith he rebukes them: the time is come

perfringere dextrâ, quod optâstis votis;
to demolish with your right hand, which you have desired in your prayers;

viri, Mars ipse in manibus. Nunc, quisque esto
men, Mars himself is in your hands. Now, let each one be

memor suæ conjugis que tecti; nunc referto magna
mindful of his own wife and home; now call to mind the great

facta que laudes patrum. Ultro occurramus ad
deeds and praises of your fathers. Forthwith let us meet them at

undam, dum trepidi que prima vestigia labant egressis.
the water, while trembling and their first footsteps totter to them coming

Fortuna juvat audentes. Ait hæc, et versat
from the water. Fortune favours the daring. He said these things, and revolves

cum se quos ducere contra, vel quibus posset
with himself whom to lead against them, or to whom he may

concredere obsessos muros. Interea Æneas exponit
entrust the besieged walls. In the mean time Æneas lands

socios de altis puppibus pontibus. Multi servare
his companions from the lofty ships on bridges. Many watch

recursus languentis pelagi, et credere se brevibus
the ebb of the faintly moving sea, and trust themselves to the shallows

saltu: alii per remos. Tarchon speculatus litora,
by a leap: others by oars. Tarchon watching the shores

quâ sperat non vada, nec fracta unda
where he hopes there are no shallows, nor where the dashing wav.

remurmurat, sed mare inoffensum allabitur crescenti
remurmurs, but the sea inoffensively glides on with the increasing

æstu, advertit proras subitò, que precatur socios;
tide, turns his prows suddenly, and prays his companions

nunc, ô lecta manus, incumbite validis remis; tollite,
now, O my chosen band, press on your strong oars; arouse

ferte rates; findite hanc inimicam terram
yourselves, urge on the ships; cleave this hostile land

rostris, que carina ipsa premat sulcum sibi: nec
with your beaks, and let the keel itself press out a furrow for itself: nor

recuso frangere puppim tali statione, tellure semel
do I refuse to break the ship in such a harbour, the land once

arreptâ. Quæ talia postquam Tarchon effatus,
being seized. Which like words after Tarchon had uttered,

socii consurgere tonsis, que inferre spumantes rates
his associates arose on their oars, and bore the foaming ships

Latinis arvis, donec rostra tenent siccum, et omnes
to the Latin shore, until the beaks attain the dry land, and all.

carinæ   sedere   innocuæ: sed non tua puppis Tarchon;
the keels settle down unharmed: but not thy ship O Tarchon;

namque   inflicta   vadis   dum   pendet iniquo   dorso
for   having struck the shoals while   it hangs on the unequal   bank

sustentata   diu   anceps   que fatigat fluctus,   solvitur
upheld   for a long time in suspense and wearies the waves, it is separated

atque exponit viros   in   mediis   undis;   quos fragmina
and   throws out the men in   the midst of the waters; whom broken parts

remorum et fluitantia transtra impediunt, que   simul
of oars   and floating   benches   entangle, and at the same time

relabens unda retrahit pedes.   Nec   segnis mora
the retreating wave draws back their feet. Nor does slothful delay

retinet Turnum;   sed   acer   rapit   totam aciem in
keep back Turnus;   but   bold   he urges on his whole force against

Teucros,   et   sistit   in litore   contrà.   Canunt
the Trojans, and   places them on the shore on the other side. They call out

signa.   Æneas primus invasit agrestes turmas,   omen
their signals. Æneas   first   attacked the rustic bands, an omen

pugnæ;   que   stravit   Latinos,   Therone   occiso,   qui
of battle; and   prostrated the Latins,   Theron   being slain, who

maximus virorum,   ultro petit Ænean: haurit   huic
the largest of men, forthwith seeks Æneas: he drains his

apertum latus   gladio,   que per   ærea
open   side with his sword, and through the brazen folds of his shield

suta,   per   tunicam squalentem auro.   Inde   ferit
stitched, through his coat of mail scaled with gold. Then he strikes down

Lycon, exsectum   matre   jam peremtâ, et sacrum tibi,
Lycon,   cut out from his mother now being dead, and sacred to you,

Phœbe,   quod   licuit   parvo evadere   casus
O Apollo, because it was allowed to him young to escape the chances

ferri.   Nec longè   dejecit   durum Cissea letho, que
of the knife. Nor far off he overwhelms the strong Cisseus in death, and

immanem Gyan sternentes agmina   clavâ.   Arma
the huge Gyas hurling down troops   with a club. The arms

Herculis   illos nihil,   validæ manus juvere nil; que
of Hercules availed them nothing, their strong hands aided them not; and

genitor Melampus,   comes   Alcidæ, usque dum
their father Melampus availed them not, the companion of Hercules, even while

terra præbuit   graves labores.   Ecce intorquens jaculum
the earth supplied to him severe labours. Lo   hurling   a dart

Pharo,   dum jactat inertes voces,   sistit   in   ore
at Pharus, while he boasts idle   words, he plunges it in the mouth

clamantis.   Dum tu quoque, infelix Cydon,   sequeris
of him bawling. While thou also, unhappy Cydon, art following

Clytium, nova gaudia, flaventem malas   primâ lanugine,
Clytius, a new love, yellow as to his cheeks with their first down,

miserande   jaceres   stratus Dardaniâ dextrâ,   securus
to be pitied would have lain prostrate by the Trojan's right hand, thoughtless

amorum juvenum qui semper erant tibi, ni stipata
of the loves of boys which ever were to you, unless an attending

cohors fratrum, progenies Phorci, foret obvia; septem
band of brothers, the offspring of Phorcus, had been in the way; seven

numero, que conjiciunt septena tela: partim irrita
in number, and they hurl seven darts; partly rendered vain

resultant, galeâ que clypeo; partim alma Venus
they rebound from his helmet and shield, partly fair Venus

deflexit stringentia corpus. Æneas affatur fidum
turned them aside grazing his body. Æneas addresses the faithful

Achatem sic: Suggere tela mihi, quæ steterunt in corpore
Achates thus: Supply weapons to me, which have stood in the body

Graiorum Iliacis campis (dextra non torserit illum
of the Greeks on the Trojan plains (my right hand shall not hurl it

frustra Rutulos.)
in vain against the Rutulians.)

Tum corripit magnam hastam et jacit: illa volans
Then he seizes a great spear and hurls it: it flying

transverberat æra clypei Mæonis, et rumpit
pierces through the brass folds of the shield of Mæon, and breaks

thoraca simul cum pectore. Frater Alcanor
his breastplate at the same time with his breast. His brother Alcanor

subit huic; que sustentat fratrem ruentem dextrâ;
comes up to him; and supports his brother falling with his right hand;

protinus hasta missa, lacerto trajecto, fugit, que cruenta
far off the spear being sent, his arm being pierced, it flies, and bloody

servat tenorem; que dextera moribunda pependit
preserves its course; and his right hand dying hung

nervis ex humero. Tum Numitor, jaculo rapto
by the nerves from his shoulder. Then Numitor, the javelin being snatched

de corpore fratris, petivit Ænean: sed non est licitum
from the body of his brother, aims at Æneas: but it was not allowed to him

figere contrà, que perstrinxit femur magni Achatæ.
to pierce him on the other hand, and it grazed the thigh of great Achates.

Hìc Clausus Curibus, fidens primævo corpore, advenit,
Here Clausus from Cures, relying on his youthful frame, comes up,

et eminus ferit Dryopen rigidâ hastâ, pressâ
and from afar strikes Dryopes with his hard spear, pressed

graviter sub mentum; que pariter rapit vocem que
heavily under his chin, and at once snatches away his voice and

animam loquentis, gutture trajecto: at ille ferit terram
soul of him speaking, his throat being pierced: but he strikes the earth

fronte et vomit crassum cruorem ore. Et per
with his forehead and vomits thick blood from his mouth. Also by

varios casus sternit tres Threicios quoque, de supremâ
various chances he overthrows three Thracians likewise, from the high

gente Boreæ, et tres, quos pater Idas, et patria Ismara
race of Boreas, and three, whom his father Idas, and his country Ismara

mittit. Halæsus occurrit, que Auruncæ manus; et
sent. Halæsus meets *him*, and the Aruncian band; and

Neptunia proles, Messapus, insignis equis, subit: nunc
Neptune's offspring, Messapus, distinguished for horses, succeeds: now

hi, nunc illi, tendunt expellere.   Certatur
these, now those, attempt to drive away *each other*. *There is* a contest

in ipso limine Ausoniæ. Ceu venti discordes tollunt
in the very boundary of Ausonia. As the winds discordant raise

prælia magno æthere, æquis animis et viribus;
warfare in the extended sky, with equal rage and strength;

non ipsi inter se, non nubilæ, non mare cedit;
nor they among themselves, nor clouds, nor sea yields;

pugna anceps diu, omnia stant obnixa contra:
the contest is doubtful long, all stand conflicting against *each other:*

haud aliter Trojanæ acies que Latinæ acies concurrunt
not otherwise the Trojan armies and Latin troops rush together:

pes hæret pede, que densus vir viro. At ex aliâ partê,
foot cleaves to foot, and crowded man to man. But from another part,

quâ torrens impulerat saxa rotantia latè que arbusta
where the torrent had hurled the rocks rolling far and trees

diruta ripis, ut Pallas vidit Arcadas, insuetos
torn from the banks, as Pallas beheld the Arcadians, accustomed

inferre pedestres acies, dare terga sequaci Latio,
to engage in pedestrian battle, to turn *their* backs to pursuing Latium.

queis quando aspera natura loci suasit dimittere
whom since the rough condition of the place persuades to let loose *their*

equos nunc prece, nunc amaris dictis, (quod unum restat
horses now by entreaty, now by bitter words, (which alone remains

egenis rebus,) accendit virtutem: socii quò
in *his* desperate affairs,) *he* inflam'd *their* courage: *my* associates whither

fugitis? per vos et fortia facta, per nomen ducis
do *you* fly? by yourselves and *your* brave deeds, by the name of *your* leader

Evandri, que devicta bella que meam spem, quæ
Evander, and by *your* victorious wars and *my* own hope, which

nunc subit æmula patriæ laudis ne fidite pedibus.
now rises anxious for *my* country's praise, do not trust to *your* feet.

Via est rumpenda ferro per hostes, quâ ille
A passage is to be broken by the sword through the foes, where that

densissimus globus virûm urget: hâc alta patria
most crowded mass of men press on us: here *your* exalted country

reposcit vos et Pallanta ducem. Nulla numina premunt:
demands you and Pallas *your* leader. No Gods pursue *us:*

mortales urgemur ab mortali hoste: nobis totidem
mortals we are followed by a mortal foe: to us *there* are as many

que animæ que manus. Ecce pontus claudit nos magno
both lives and hands. See the water incloses us with its great

obice maris: jam terra deest fugæ: ne petemus pelagus,
barrier of the sea: now land is wanting for flight: whether shall we seek the sea.

Trojam.   Ait hæc,   et prorumpit medius in   densos
or Troy.   *He said these words,* and *broke in the midst upon the crowded*

hostes. Primùm Lagus, adductus iniquis fatis fit   obvius
foes.   *First* *Lagus,*   *led on* *by unequal fates, becomes opposed*

huic: figit hunc   intorto   telo, dum vellit saxum magno
to him: he stabs him *with a wreathed dart,* *while he tears up a rock* *of great*

pondere, quà   spina dedit discrimina   costis   per
weight, *where his spine causes* *a separation in his ribs* *through*

medium   dorsi: que receptat hastam hærentem   ossibus:
the middle of his back: and *draws out the spear sticking in his bones.*

quem supèr Hisbon non occupat, ille quidam sperans
whom from above Hisbon does not prevent, *he indeed desiring*

hoc; nam Pallas excipit antè, ruentem, incautum, dum
this; for Pallas seizes him first, *rushing on, unsuspecting,* *while*

furit crudeli   morte sodalis, atque recondit   ensem
he rages with the cruel death of his companion, and hides his sword

in   tumido pulmone. Hinc   petit Sthenelum   et
in his swelling lungs. *Hence he seeks Sthenelus* *and*

Anchemolum, de vetustâ gente Rhæti, ausum incestare
Anchemolus, *from the ancient race of Rhætus, daring to pollute*

thalamos   novercæ. Vos etiam gemini fratres,
the marriage chamber of his stepmother. *Ye also ye twin brothers,*

Laride que Thymber Daucia proles, cecidistis in Rutulis
Laridus *and Thymber Daucus' offspring, fell in the Rutulian*

arvis,   simillima,   indiscreta,   que   gratus
fields, *most resembling,* *undistinguished, and a grateful*

error   suis   parentibus. At nunc Pallas dedit dura
delusion to their own parents. *But now Pallas has given dreadful*

discrimina vobis: nam Evandrius ensis abstulit tibi caput,
discrimination to you: for Evander's sword bore off your head,

Thymbre; dextera   decisa quæret te suum, Laride;
O Thymber; your right hand cut off seeks thee its own, O Laridus;

que digiti semianimes micant, que retractant ferrum.
and your fingers dying quiver, and draw back the sword.

Mistus dolor et pudor, armat Arcadas accensos   monitu,
Mingled grief and shame, *arms the Arcadians inflamed by the admonition,*

et tuentes præclara facta viri, in   hostes. Tum
and beholding the renowned deeds of the hero against their enemies. *Then*

Pallas trajicit Rhœtea fugientem præter   bijugis. Hoc
Pallas pierces Rhœteus flying beyond him in his chariot. *This*

spatium, que tantum moræ fuit   Ilo: namque procul
space, *and so much of delay was granted to Ilus: for afar off*

direxerat validam hastam Ilo; quam Rhœteus medius
he had directed his powerful spear to Ilus; which Rhœteus in the midst

intercipit, fugiens te, optime Teuthra, que fratrem
intercepts, escaping thee, most excellent Teuthra, and thy brother

Tyren; que volutus   curru   semianimis cædit arva
Tyren, *and rolling from his chariot dying he beats the fields*

Rutulorum   calcibus. Ac velut ventis coortis   optato
of the Rutulians with *his* heels. And as   the winds having arisen to *his* wish

æstate,   pastor immittit incendia dispersa   sylvas;
in summer, the shepherd   casts   fires   scattered through the woods;

mediis   correptis subitò, horrida Vulcania   acies
the intermediate *trees* being seized   suddenly, the horrid Vulcanian   force

extenditur unâ per latos campos; ille victor, sedens,
is spread   at once through the broad   plains;   he victorious, sitting,

despectat ovantes flammas: non aliter omnis   virtus
looks down on the exulting   flames: not otherwise   all   the courage

sociûm coit   in   unum, que juvat te, Palla.
of *his* companions unites   in   one,   and delights thee, O Pallas.

Sed Halæsus, acer bellis, tendit in adversos, que colligit
But Halæsus,   brave in war, marches against   *his* foes,   and   collects

se   in sua arma. Hic mactat Ladona, que Phereta,
himself   upon his own arms.   He   slays   Ladon,   and   Pheres,

que Demodocum; diripit dextram   Strymonio, elatam
and   Demodocus;   he tears the right *hand* from Strymonius,   raised

in   jugulum, fulgenti ense; ferit ora Thoantis
against   his throat, with *his* glittering sword; he strikes the face   of Thoas

saxo,   que dispergit ossa permixta cruento cerebro.
with a rock, and   scatters   his bones intermingled with bloody   brains.

Genitor, canens fata, celaverat Halæsum sylvis. Ut
His father, foreseeing *his* fate, had concealed Halæsus   in the woods. As

senior solvit canentia lumina letho, Parcæ injecere
the old man relaxed *his* whitening   eyes   in death, the fates   cast

manum   que sacraverunt telis Evandri; quem Pallas
their hands *on him* and consecrated *him* to the darts of Evander; whom   Pallas

petit, sic precatus antè: Pater Tybri, nunc da fortunam
seeks, thus invoking first: O Father Tyber,   now   give   fortune

atque viam ferro, quod libro missile,   per pectus
and   a way to *my* sword, which I poise about to hurl,   through the breast

duri Halæsi: tua quercus habebit hæc arma, que exuvias
of cruel Halæsus: thy   oak   shall have these   arms,   and   the clothes

viri.   Deus audivit illa;   dum Halæsus texit Imaona,
of the hero. The God   heard   these *words*; while Halæsus protected   Imaon,

infelix dat inermum pectus Arcadio telo. At Lausus,
unhappy he offers *his* unprotected breast to the Arcadian dart.   But   Lausus,

ingens pars belli,   non sinit agmina perterrita tantâ
a great   portion of the war, does not permit *his* troops to be frightened by this great

cæde   viri Primus interimit Abantem oppositum, que
destruction of the hero. First   he kills   Abas   opposing,   both

nodum   que moram pugnæ. Proles Arcadiæ sternitur.
the strength   and   stay   of battle. The offspring of Arcadia *is* prostrate.

Etrusci sternuntur,   et vos Teucri, O corpora imperdita
The Etruscans are overthrown, and you *ye* Trojans, O ye frames not destroyed

Graiis. Agmina concurrunt, æquis que ducibus et
by the Greeks. The troops rush together, equal both in leaders and

viribus. Extremi addensent acies; nec turba
strength. The last press on the *advanced* ranks; nor does the crowd

sinit tela que manus moveri. Hinc Pallas instat et
permit weapons and hands to be moved. Hence Pallas urges and

urget; hinc contra Lausus: nec ætas discrepat
drives on the *troops;* hence opposed is Lausus: nor does *their* age differ

multùm; egregii formâ; sed queis fortuna negârat reditus
much; renowned for beauty; but to whom fortune had denied a return

in patriam. Tamen regnator magni Olympi, haud
to *their* country. Nevertheless the ruler of great Olympus, did not

passus ipsos concurrere inter se; mox sua fata
suffer them to engage together among themselves; soon their own fates

manent illos sub majore hoste. Interea alma soror
await them under a greater enemy. In the meantime *his* kind sister

monet Turnum, qui secat medium agmen volucri
admonishes Turnus, who divides the intermediate troops with *his* swift

curru, succurrere Lauso. Ut vidit socios: Tempus
chariot, to relieve Lausus. As he saw his companions, *he said,* It is time

desistere pugnæ: ego solus feror in Pallanta; Pallas
to withdraw from battle: I alone am borne against Pallas; Pallas

debetur mihi soli: cuperem parens ipse adesset
is due to me alone: I could have wished *his* father himself would be present

spectator. Ait hæc; et socii cesserunt æquore
a spectator. He said these *things;* and *his* companions withdrew from the plain

jusso. At abscessu Rutulorum, juvenis, tum
commanded. But by the departure of the Rutulians, the youth, then

miratus superba jussa, stupet in Turno; que volvit
admiring the proud commands, stood amazed on Turnus: and rolls

lumina per ingens corpus, que procul obit omnia
his eyes over *his* vast body, and from afar surveys all *things*

truci visu, et it contra dicta tyranni talibus
with grim countenance, and goes against the words of the tyrant with these

dictis: Jam ego laudabor aut opimis spoliis raptis, aut
words: Now I will be praised either for rich spoils being taken, or

insigni letho. Pater est æquus utrique sorti.
for distinguished death: My father is equal to each lot.

Tolle minas. Fatus, procedit in medium æquor.
Banish threats. Having spoken, he proceeds into the middle plain.

Frigidus sanguis coit Arcadibus in præcordia.
The cold blood congeals to the Arcadians in *their* hearts.

Turnus desiluit bijugis: pedes apparat ire
Turnus leaped from *his* chariot: on foot he appears to go to *engage him*

cominus. Que ut leo advolat, cùm ab altâ speculâ
hand to hand. And as a lion flies, when from a high watch-tower

vidit taurum stare procul campis meditantem prælia; imago
he sees a bull to stand far off on the plains resolving battle, the image

Turni venientis est haud alia. Ubi Pallas credidit hunc
of Turnus coming   is   not different. When Pallas believed   him

tore contiguum   hastæ missæ   ire prior
to be   near to   the spear sent   he began to advance first

imparibus viribus, si qua fors adjuvit ausum,   itaque
with unequal strength, if any chance should aid his daring *attempt*, therefore

latur ad magnum æthera: Alcide, precor te, per hospitium
he speaks to the lofty sky: O Hercules, I pray you, by the hospitality

patris, et mensas quas advena   adîsti,   adsis
of *my* father, and the tables which a stranger *you* resorted to,   assist

ingentibus cœptis ; cernat me rapere   cruenta arma
my great   endeavours; let him see me   strip   *his* bloody   arms

sibi semineci, que morientia lumina Turni ferant
from him dying,   and let the dying eyes of Turnus endure

victorem. Alcides audivit juvenem, que premit magnum
a conqueror. Hercules heard the youth, and repress'd   a great

gemitum sub   imo corde, que effudit inanes lacrymas
groan.   in *his* inmost heart, and pours forth useless   tears

Tum genitor affatur natum amicis dictis: sua dies sta
Then the father addresses *his* son with friendly words: his own day remains

tuique: est omnibus, breve et irreparabile tempus vitæ.
to each: *there* is to all,   a short and remediless   time of life.

sed extendere famam factis, hoc opus virtutis. To
but to prolong reputation by deeds, this is the work of virtue. So many

nati Deûm cecidere sub altis mænibus Trojæ;   quin
sons of the Gods have fallen under the lofty walls of Troy;   ever

Sarpedon, mea progenies, occidit unà: etiam
Sarpedon, *my* own offspring.   fell   together *with them:* also *his*

sua   fata vocant Turnum, que pervenit ad metas ævi
own   fates call Turnus, and he has arrived at the limits of life

dati: sic ait, atque rejicit oculos arvis Rutulorum
allowed: thus *he* said, and turns away *his* eyes from the fields of the Rutulians

At Pallas emittit hastam magnis viribus, que deripit
But Pallas sent *his* spear with great violence, and snatched

fulgentem ensem   cavâ   vaginâ. Illa volans incidit
As shining sword from the hollow sheath. It flying struck

quâ summa. tegmina surgunt humeris, atque molita
where the high armour rises on the shoulders, and wearing

viam per   oras   clypei tandem etiam strinxit de
its way through the borders of the shield, at length even gras'd from

magno corpore Turni. Hîc Turnus,   diu vibrans
the great body of Turnus. Here Turnus, for a long time brandishing

robur præfixum acuto ferro, jacit in Pallante, atque
a spear, pointed with sharp steel, hurls it against Pallas,   and

ita fatur: aspice, num nostrum telum sit magè penetrabile
thus speaks: see, whether our dart be more penetrating

Dixerat: at cuspis transverberat medium   clypeum
He said: but the spear pierced through the midst of the shield

vibranti ictu, cùm obeat tot terga ferri, tot
with quivering blow, when it passes through so many coverings of iron, so many

æris, pellis tauri cìrcumdata toties que perforat moras
of brass, the hide of a bull surrounding it so often and penetrates the obstructions

loricæ, et ingens pectus. Ille frustrâ rapit calidum
of his coat of mail, and his great breast. He in vain tears the warm

telum de vulnere: que sanguis que animus sequuntur unâ
weapon from the wound: and his blood and soul follow by one

que eâdem viâ. Corruit in vulnus; arma dedere sonitum
and the same way. He fell on his wound; his arms gave forth a sound

supèr, et moriens petit hostilem terram cruentâ ore,
from above, and dying he strikes the hostile eart' with bloody mouth,

super quem Turnus assistens, inquit: Arcades, memores
over whom Turnus standing, says: Arcadians, mindful

referte hæc mea dicta Evandro: remitto Pallanta, qualem
bear back these my words to Evander: I send back Pallas, such as

meruit. Quisquis honos tumuli, quicquid solamen
he has deserved. Whatsoever honour there is of a tomb, whatever consolation

est humandi largior. Æneïa hospitia stabant illi haud
is in being buried I grant it. Æneas's friendship shall cost him not

parvo. Et fatus talia, pressit exanimum lævo
a little. And speaking these words; he pressed his lifeless body with his left

pede, rapiens immania pondera baltei, que nefas
foot, bearing off the immense weight of his belt, and the dreadful deed

impressum, (manus juvenum cæsa fœdè sub unâ
engraved on it, (that a company of youth was slain basely in one

jugali nocte, que thalami cruenti) quæ bonus
nuptial night, and the marriage chambers were bloody) which good

Eurytion cælaverat multo auro; quo spolio nunc
Eurytion had carved in abundant gold; with which spoil now

Turnus ovat, que gaudet potitus. mens hominum
Turnus rejoices, and exults possessing it. O mind of men,

nescia fati que futuræ sortis, et servare modum, sublata
ignorant of fate and future lot, and to preserve moderation, exalted

secundis rebus! Erit tempus Turno, cùm optaverit
by prosperous affairs! There will be a time to Turnus, when he shall desire

emptum magno intactum Pallanta, et cùm oderit
to purchase at a great price uninjured Pallas, and when he shall detest

ista spolia, que diem.
these spoils, and this day.

At socii frequentes referunt Pallant', impositum
But his associates in great numbers bring back Pallas, placed

scuto, multo gemitu que lacrymis, O rediture
on a shield, with great mourning and tears, O about to return

dolor atque magnum decus parenti. Hæ d.es prima
the grief and great glory to your parent. This day first

dedit te bello, hæc eadem aufert: cùm tamen l'.quis
gave you to the war, this the same bears you away: when yet we leave

ingentes acervos Rutulorum. Nec jam fama tanti
great heaps of Rutulians *slain*. Nor now the fame of so great

mali, sed certior auctor advolat Æneæ: suos
a misfortune *alone*, but a more authentic authority flies to Æneas; that his

    esse tenui discrimine lethi; tempus succerrere
friends are in near peril of death; *that* it is time to succour

versis Teucris. Metit. quæque proxima gladio, que
the flying Trojans. He cuts down whatever is nearest with the sword, and

ardens   agit latum limitem ferro   per
burning *with revenge* he makes a broad path with the steel through

agmen, quærens te, Turne, superbum novâ cæde.
the army, seeking thee, O Turnus, elated with recent slaughter.

Pallas, Evander, omnia sunt in ipsis oculis; mensæ quas
Pallas, Evander, all *things* are before his eyes; the tables which

primas tunc advena adiit,   que dextræ datæ.
first but then a stranger he had approached, and right *hands* pledged

Hìc rapit quatuor juvenes, viventes creatos Sulmone, totidem
Here he seizes four youths, alive; sprung from Sulmo, as many

quos Ufens educat: quos immolat inferias
whom Ufens brings up: whom he sacrifices as funeral offerings

umbris que perfundat flammas rogi captivo
to the shade *of Pallas* and overflows the flames of the funeral pile with captive

sanguine. Inde cùm procul tenderet infensam hastam
blood. Next when afar off he had directed his hostile spear

Mago, ille subit astu, ac tremebunda hasta supervolat;
at Magus, he stoops with cunning, and the trembling spear flies over him:

et amplectens genua, supplex effatur talia; per patrios
and embracing *his* knees, humbly he utters these *words*; by thy father's

manes, et spes surgentis Iùli, precor te serves hanc
shades, and the hopes of the rising Iulus, I pray thee spare this

animam que nato que patri. Est alta domus, talenta
life both to the son and the father. *There* is a lofty house, talents

cælati argenti jacent penitus defossa; sunt mihi pondera
of adorned silver lie deeply buried; *there* are to me masses

auri facti que infecti: victoria Teucrûm non vertitur
of gold wrought and unwrought: the victory of the Trojans does not turn

hìc: una anima non dabìt tanta discrimina. Dixerat:
here: one life will not give so great a difference. He said.

cui   contrà Æneas reddit talia: parce
to whom on the other *hand* Æneas returned these *words:* spare

tuis natis, multa talenta argenti atque auri, quæ memoras:
for your sons, the many talents of silver and of gold, which you recount.

Turnus prior sustulit ista commercia belli, jam tum
Turnus first authorized these terms of war. even now

Pallante peremto; manes patris Anchisæ hoc,
Pallas being slain; the shades of *my* father Anchises *sanctions* this.

Iùlus sentit hoc. Fatus sic, tenet galeam lævâ,
Iulus thinks it. Speaking thus he holds his helmet with his left *hand.*

atque abdidit **ensem** tenus cápulo reflexâ cervice
and   hid   *his* sword up to   the hilt in the reclining neck

orantis. Nec Emonides procul, sacerdos Phœbi
of him praying. Nor *was* Emonides far off,   the priest   of Apollo

que Triviæ cui tempora infula redimibat sacrâ vittâ,
and Diana whose temples a mitre bound   with a sacred fillet,

totus collucens veste atque insignibus armis; quem
all   glittering with his dress and distinguished arms;   whom

congressus agit campo que superstans immolat
overtaking he drives along the plain and standing over *him* he offers *him*

lapsum que tegit ingenti umbrâ. Serestus refert
fallen   and shrouds *him* in a great shade *of death*. Serestus bears off

lecta arma humeris, trophæum tibi, Gradive Rex.
his collected arms on his shoulders, a trophy to you, O martial King.

Cœculus, creatus stirpe Vulcani, et Umbro veniens
Cœculus,   born   from the stock of Vulcan, and Umbro   coming

montibus Marsorum instaurunt acies. Dardanides
from the mountains of the Moors renew   the contest. The Trojan *hero*

furit contra; dejecerat sinistram Anxuris ense, et
rages against *them*; *Umbro* had struck off the left hand of Anxur with his sword, and

totum orbem' clypei ferro. Ille dixerat aliquid
the whole circle of his shield with his sword. He had uttered something

magnum, que crediderat vim affore verbo, que ferebat
great,   and had believed *that* force would be in his word and had raised

animum cœlo fortassè, que promiserat canitiem et longos
his soul to heaven perhaps, and had promised gray hairs and extended

annos sibi.
years to himself.

Tarquitus contrà exultans fulgentibus armis, quem
Tarquitus on the other *hand* exulting in glittering arms, whom

Nympha Dryope crearat Fauno Sylvicolæ,
the Nymph Dryope had borne to Faunus a native of the woods,

obvius obtulit sese ardenti. Ille hastâ reductâ
meeting opposed himself to *him* enraged. He *his* spear being drawn back

impedit loricam que ingens onus clypei; tum terræ
entangles his coat of mail and the great weight of his shield; then to the earth

deturbat caput orantis nequicquam, et parantis dicere
he strikes the head of him praying in vain,   and preparing to say

multa que provolvens tepentem truncum fatur hæc
many *things* and rolling over his warm   trunk he speaks these *things*

super inimico pectore; metuende, nunc jace istic.
from his hostile breast; dreaded *hero*, now lie there.

Optima mater non condet te humi, ve onerabit
Thy kind mother shall not bury thee in the earth, or   load

membra patrio sepulchro; linquere feris alitibus,
thy limbs in a native tomb;   you shall be left to the savage birds,

aut unda feret mersum gurgite, que impasti pisces
or the wave shall bear *thee* plunged in the deep, and unfed fishes

ıambent   vulnera. Protinus persequitur Antæum, et
shall suck *your* wounds. Forthwith he follows Antæus, and

Lycan, prima agmina Turni, que fortem Numam, que
Lycas, the first troops of Turnus, and brave Numa, and

Camertem fulvum   satum   magnanimo Volsccnte:
Camers, yellow *with gold* sprung from high-minded Volscens;

qui fuit   ditissimus agri Ausonidum, et regnavit
who was the richest in land of the Ausonians, and ruled

tacitis Amydis. Qualis Egæon cui dicunt centum brachia,
in silent Amydæ. As Egæon, to whom they say *were* an hundred arms,

que centenas manus, ignem arsisse quinquaginta oribus
and an hundred hands, *that* fire burnt *from his* fifty mouths

que pectoribus, cùm streperet tot paribus clypeis contra
and breasts, when he clashed on so many equal shields against

fulmina Jovis, stringeret tot enses: Sic Æneas victor
the thunders of Jove, *when* he drew so many swords: Thus Æneas victorious

desævit   in   toto   æquore, ut semel   mucro
raged through the whole plain, as once *his* blade

intepuit.   Quin ecce! tendit, in quadrijuges
had been warmed *in blood*. But lo! he marches against the chariot

equos Niphæi, que adversa pectora: atque illi, ut
horses of Nipheus, and *their* hostile breasts: and they, as

vidêre longè gradientem et frementem dira, versi
they beheld *him* far off marching and raging dreadfully, turning

metu que ruentes retro, que effundunt ducem que
with fear and rushing back, both overthrow *their* leader and

rapiunt currus ad littora. Interea   Lucagus infert
bear off the chariot to the shore. In the meanwhile Lucagus bears

se in medios albis bijugis. Que Liger frater:
himself to the midst on *his* white chariot horses. Also Liger *his* brother:

sed   frater flectit equos habenis, et acer Lucagus rotat
but *his* brother guides *his* horses with reins, and brave Lucagus whirls

strictum ensem. Æneas haud tulit   furentes   tanto
his drawn sword. Æneas could not endure *them* raging with so much

fervore: que irruit que ingens apparuit   adversâ
violence: and he rushed on and great he appeared *before them* with hostile

hastâ, cui Liger: non cernis equos Diomedis, nec currum
spear, to whom Liger *said:* you do not behold the horses of Diomede, nor the chariot

Achillis, aut campos Phrygiæ; nunc finis belli et ævi
Achilles, or the plains of Troy; now the end of the war and of *your* life

dabitur his terris. Talia dîcta volant latè vesano Ligeri: sed
shall be given to these lands. Such words fly far from mad Liger: but

et Troius heros non parat dicta contrà: nam torquet
also the Trojan hero does not prepare words in opposition: for he hurls

jaculum in hostem. Lucagus ut pronus pendens in
his dart against the foe. Lucagus as leaning forward hanging on

verbera, admonuit bijugos   telo,   dum aptat se
the lash, urged on *his* yoke-horses with the dart. while he prepares himself

pugnæ lævo pede projecto: hasta subit per imas
for battle with his left foot advanced: the spear enters through the lowest

oras fulgentis clypei, dum perforat lævum inguen,
borders of his glittering shield, while it pierces his left groin,

excussus curru, moribundus, volvitur arvis: quem pius
thrown out from the chariot, dying, he is rolled on the fields' who:n pious

Æneas affatur amaris dictis Lucage nulla segnis fuga
Æneas addresses with bitter words: Lucagus no slothful flight

equorum prodidit tuos currus, aut vana umbra vertere
of horses has betrayed your chariot, or have vain shades turned them

ex hostibus; saliens rotis ipse deseris juga. Ita fatus
from the enemy; leaping from the wheels you desert the chariot. Thus uttering

hæc, arripuit bijugos. Infelix frater, delapsus
these words, he seized the horses. His wretched brother, falling

eodem curru, tendebat inermes palmas: per
from the same chariot, stretched out his unarmed hands and said: by

te, per parentes qui genuere te talem, Trojane
thyself, by thy parents who have borne thee thus renowned, O Trojan

vir, sine hanc animam, et miserere precantis. Æneas
hero, spare this life, and pity me praying. Æneas

oranti pluribus. Haud dabas talia dicta
addresses him speaking in many words. You did not utter such words

dudum; morere, et frater ne desere fratrem. Tum
lately; die, and a brother did not abandon your brother. Then

recludit pectus, latebras animæ, mucrone. Dardanius
he opens his breast, the hiding place of his soul, with his sword. The Trojan

ductor edebat talia funera per campos, furens more
leader caused these deaths through the plains, raging in the manner

torrentis aquæ, vel atri turbinis. Tandem puer Ascanius,
of a torrent of water, or black whirlwind. At last the boy Ascanius,

et juventus obsessa, nequicquam erumpunt et relinquunt
and the youth besieged, in vain break out and abandon

castra. Interea Jupiter compellat Junonem ultro:
the camps. In the meantime Jupiter addresses Juno willingly:

O germana, atque eadem conjux gratissima mihi! ut
O sister, and also the same my wife most grateful to me! as

rebare (nec sententia fallit te) Venus sustentat
you supposed (nor does your sentiment deceive you) Venus upholds

Trojanas opes! non viris dextra vivida bello, que
the Trojan power! there is not to the men a right hand alive for the war, and

animus ferox, que patiens periculi! Cui Juno
a disposition bold, and patient of danger! To whom Juno

summissa: O pulcherrime conjux, quid sollicitas ægram,
most humbly said most accomplished husband, why do you urge me sick,

et timentem tua tristia dicta? Si foret mihi vis in
and dreading your sad words? If there could be to me that power in

amore, quæ fuerat quondam, quamque decebat essse,
love, which has been formerly, and which ought to be ever

namque non negares hoc mihi, omnipotens:
indeed you would not deny this to me, O all powerful *husband:*

quin et possem subducere Turnum pugnæ, et
but even I might be able to withdraw Turnus from the battle, and

servare incolumem Dauno parenti. Nunc pereat,
to preserve *him* unharmed for Daunus *his* father. Now let *him* perish,

que det pœnas Teucris pio sanguine. Tamen ille
and give penalties to the Trojans with *his* pious blood. Yet he

deducit nomen nostrâ origine que Pilumnus quartus
has derived *his* name from our origin and Pilumnus is a fourth *removed*

pater illi: et sæpe oneravit tuâ limina largâ manu,
father to him: and oft he has loaded your temples with his generous hand,

que multis donis. Cui rex ætherei Olympi sic fatur
and numerous gifts. To whom the king of heavenly Olympus thus speaks

breviter: Si mora præsentis lethi, que tempus oratur
briefly: If delay of present death, and time is asked

caduco juveni, que sentis me ponere hoc ita; tolle
for the falling youth, and you think fit for me to establish it thus; bear off

Turnum fugâ, atque eripe instantibus fatis.
Turnus by flight, and snatch *him* from threatening fate.

Vacat indulsisse hactenus. Sin ulla altior venia
It is allowed to have indulged *you* thus far. But if any higher favour

latet sub istis precibus, que putas totum bellum
is concealed under these prayers, and you think all the war

moveri ve mutari, pascis inanes spes. Cui Juno
to be removed or changed, you feed empty hopes. To whom Juno

illacrymans: quid si dares mente, quod gravaris
weeping *said:* what if you should grant in your mind, what you deny

voce, atque hæc vita maneret rata Turno? Nunc
with *your* voice, and this life should remain ratified to Turnus? Now

gravis exitus manet insontem; aut ego feror vana
a mournful end awaits *him* innocent; or I am esteemed ignorant

veri; quòd O ut potiùs ludar falsâ formidine, et
of the truth; but O that rather I may be deluded by false fear, and

qui potes, reflectas tua orsa in meliùs. Ubi
thou who art able, may change thy designs for the better. When

dedit hæc dicta, protinus misit se alto cœlo,
she had uttered these words, forthwith she cast herself from the lofty sky,

succincta nimbo, agens hiemem per auras, que petivit
girt with a cloud, driving tempests through the air, and sought

Iliacam aciem et Laurentia castra. Tum Dea ornat
the Trojan army and the Laurentian camps. Then the Goddess adorns

Dardaniis telis, tenuem umbram sine viribus cavâ
with Trojan arms, a light shade without substance from a hollow

nube, in faciem Æneæ (monstrum mirabile visu) que
cloud, in the form of Æneas (a monster wonderful to be seen) and

assimulat clypeum que jubas divini capitis; dat
imitates the shield and crests of *his* divine head; she gives *to it*

mania verba, dat sonum sine mente, que effingit
vain   words, sne gives sound without understanding, and feigns

gressus euntis; quales figuras fama est volitare morte
the step of him walking; such like figures report is use to fly about death

obitâ, aut somnia quæ deludunt sopitos sensus. At
having passed, or dreams which deceive the sleeping senses. Bu.

læta imago exultat ante primas acies, que irritat
the playful phantom dances before the advanced ranks, and provokes

virum telis, et lacessit voce; cui Turnus instat,
t.e hero with darts, and aggravates him with its voice; whom Turnus pursues

que conjicit stridentem hastam eminus; illa vertit vestigia
and hurls his hissing spear afar; it turns its steps

tergo dato. Tum verò ut Turnus credidit Ænean
its back being presented. Then indeed as Turnus believed that Æneas

aversum cedere, atque turbidus hausit inanem spem
turning had withdrawn, and disturbed drank in empty hope

animo: Ænea, quò fugis? ne desere pactos
in his mind: he said O Æneas, whither do you fly? do not desert plighted

thalamos: tellus quæsita per undas dabitur
marriage; the land sought through the waves shall be given

hâc dextrâ. Vociferans talia sequitur, que coruscat
by this right hand. Crying out in these words he pursues, and brandishes

strictum mucronem; nec videt ventos ferre sua
his drawn sword; nor does he observe that the winds bear away his

gaudia. Fortè ratis, conjuncta crepidine celsi saxi,
joys. By chance a ship, joined to the margin of a high rock,

stabat scalis expositis et ponte parato, quâ rex Osinius
stood with ladders placed and a bridge prepared, on which king Osinius

advectus Clusinis oris. Trepida imago Æneæ
was borne from the Clusian shores. The trembling image of Æneas

fugientis conjicit sese huc in latebras: Turnus nec
escaping casts itself hither in concealment: Turnus not

segnior instat que exsuperat moras, et transilit
more slothful presses on and rises above all obstacles, and leaps over

altos pontes. Vix attigerat proram; Saturnia rumpit
the high bridges. Hardly had he touched the prow; Juno breaks

funem, que rapit navem avulsam per revoluta æquora.
the rope, and bears away the ship torn through the rolling waters.

Autem Æneas poscit illum absentem, in prælia: demittit
But Æneas demands him absent, to the battle: he sends

multa corpora virûm obvia morti. Tunc levis imago
many bodies of heroes meeting him to death. Then the light phantom

haud quærit latebras ultra jam sed volans sublimè
does not seek concealment farther now but flying high

immiscuit se atræ nubi; cùm interea turbo
mingled itself in the black cloud; when in the mean time the whirlwind

fert Turnum medio æquore. Respicit ignarus rerum,
bears Turnus in the midst of the sea. He looks back ignorant of things

que ingratus salutis, et tendit duplices manus cum
and ungrateful for *his* safety, and stretches both hands with

voce ad sidera: Omnipotens genitor, ne
his voice towards the stars, *he said:* All powerful father, whether

duxisti me dignum tanto crimine? et voluisti
have you thought me worthy of so great a crime? and have you willed

expendere tales pœnas? quò feror? unde
that I pay such penalties? whither am I borne? whence

abivi? quæ fuga reducet me, ve quem? ne videbo
have I departed? what flight shall restore me, or to what? shall I see

Laurentes muros aut castra iterum? quid illa manus
the Laurentian walls or camps once more? what will this band

virûm, qui secuti me que mea arma? que omnes quos
of heroes *say,* who followed me and my arms? and all whom

reliqui, nefas, in infandâ morte? Et nunc
I have abandoned, O dreadful *crime,* to unutterable death? And now

video palantes, que accipio gemitum cadentûm.
I behold *them* wandering, and I receive the groans of the falling.

Quid agam? aut quæ terra jam satis ima dehiscat
What shall I do? or what land now sufficiently deep will open

mihi? Vos, ô venti, potiùs miserescite (Turnus volens
for me? You, O *ye* winds, rather pity *me* (I Turnus willingly

adoro vos;) ferte ratem in rupes, in saxo que immittite
adore you;) drive *my* ship on the cliffs, upon the rocks and sink *it*

sævis vadis syrtis, quò neque Rutuli, neque
in the cruel shallows the quicksands, where neither the Rutulians, nor

conscia fama sequatur me. Memorans hæc, fluctuat
conscious fame shall pursue me. Uttering these *words,* he waves

animo nunc huc, nunc illuc, an amens ob tantum
in *his* mind now here, now there, whether mad for so great

dedecus induat sese mucrone, et exigat crudum
a dishonour he should pierce himself with *his* blade, and drive *his* naked

ensem per costas, an jaciat mediis fluctibus,
sword through *his* ribs, or should cast *himself* into the midst of the waves,

et petat curva litora nando, que reddat se iterum
and seek the curving shores in swimming, and restore himself again

in arma Teucrûm. Conatus utramque viam ter;
against the arms of the Trojans. ◆ Attempting each way thrice,

ter maxima Juno continuit que miserata animo
thrice great Juno restrained *him* and commiserating in *her* mind

repressit juvenem. Labitur secans alta, que
she restrained the youth. He glides on dividing the deep, both

secundo fluctu que æstu; et defertur ad antiquam urbem
with favouring wave and tide; and *is* borne to the ancient city

patris Dauni. At intereâ Mezentius monitis Jovis
of *his* father Daunus. But in the interim Mezentius by the monitions of Jupiter,

ardens succedit pugnæ, que invadit ovantes
burning *with rage* comes up to the fight, and attacks the rejoicing

Teucros. Tyrrhenæ acies concurrunt, atque instant viro
Trojans. The Tuscan bands rush on together, and pursue the man

uni, uni omnibus odiis que frequentibus telis.
alone, *him* alone with all *their* hatred and numerous darts.

Ille velut rupes, quæ prodit in vastum æquor obvia
He as a rock, which projects into the vast ocean exposed

furiis ventorum que exposita ponto, perfert cunctam
to the madness of the winds and obnoxious to the sea, endures all

vim atque minas, que cœli que maris, ipsa manens
the violence and threats, both of heaven and the deep, itself remaining

immota. Sternit Hebrum prolem Dolicaonis humi;
unmoved. He prostrates Hebrus the offspring of Dolicaon on the ground,

cum quo Latagum que fugacem Palmum; sed occupat
with him Latagus and flying Palmus; but he attacks

Latagum os que adversam faciem saxo, atque ingenti
Latagus in the mouth and adverse face with a rock, and great

fragmine montis; sinit Palmum volvi segnem
fragment of a mountain; he permits Palmus to be rolled over slowly

poplite succiso; que donat Lauso habere arma
his ham being cut; and allows to Lausus to have arms

huméris, et figere cristas vertice. Nec non Phrygium
on *his* shoulders, and to place crests on *his* head. Also Trojan

Evantem, que Mimanta æqualem que comitem Paridis:
Evas *he kills* and Mimas the equal and companion of Paris;

quem Theano dedit in lucem genitori Amyco unâ nocte,
whom Theano gave to the light to *his* father Amycus the same night,

et Cissëis regina, prægnans face, creat Parin: occubat
also Hecuba the queen, pregnant with a firebrand bore Paris: he falls

paternâ urbe; Laurens ora habet Mimanta ignarum. Ac
in *his* native city; the Laurentine coast possesses Mimas unknown. And

velut ille aper, actus de altis montibus morsu canum,
as a boar, driven from the high mountains by the biting of dogs,

pastus arundineâ sylvâ (quem pinifer Vesulus defendit
having fed in the reedy wood (which the pine-bearing Vesulus had defended

multos annos, que Laurentia palus multos) postquam
for many years, and the Laurentian marsh for many) after

ventum est inter retia, substitit, que ferox infremuit, et
he had come amidst the nets, he stops, and fierce he roars, and

inhorruit armos; nec virtus cuiquam irasci, ve
bristles up *his* shoulders; nor *is there* courage in any one to display his anger, or

accedere propius, sed instant jaculis que tutis
to approach nearer, but they press on *him* with darts and safe

clamoribus procul: autem ille impavidus cunctatur in
clamours from afar: but he fearless delays *them* in

omnes partes infrendens dentibus et decutit hastas
every side gnashing with *his* teeth and shakes the spears

tergo: haud aliter, animus non ulli, quibus Mezentius
from *his* back; just so, courage *was* not to' any, to whom Mezentius

st justæ iræ, concurrere stricto ferro;
a subject of righteous indignation, to engage *him* with the drawn sword,

lacessunt longè missilibus et vasto clamore. Acron,
they provoke *him* from afar with flying *darts* and vast noise. Acron

Graius homo, venerat de antiquis finibus Coriti profugus
a Grecian man, had come from the ancient boundaries of Coritus a deserter

linquens hymenæos infectos: Ubi longè vidit hunc
leaving *his* nuptial rites unfinished: When from afar he saw him

miscentem media agmina purpureum pennis, et
intermingling in the midst of the bands glowing with the plumes, and

ostro conjugis pactæ; ceu sæpe impastus leo peragrans
purple of his wife betrothed; as often an unfed lion wandering thro'

alta stabula (enim vesana fames suadet) •si fortè conspexit
the deep retreats (for mad hunger induces *him*) if by chance he sees

fugacem capream, aut cervum surgentem in cornua,
a flying goat, or a stag rising on *his* horns,

gaudet hians immanè, que arrexit comas et hæret
he rejoices yawning hideously, and rears *his* hair, and clings fast

incumbens super visceribus: teter cruor lavit improba
bending over *his* entrails: black blood bathes *his* cruel

ora: sic Mezentius alacer ruit in densos hostes.
jaws: thus Mezentius joyful rushes against *his* thickening foes.

Infelix Æron sternitur, et expirans tundit atram humum
Unhappy Æron is overthrown, and dying beats the black ground

calcibus, que cruentat infracta tela. Atque idem haud
with *his* heels, and stains *his* broken arms. And the same did not

dignatus est sternere Oroden fugientem, nec dare cæcum
condescend to overthrow Orodes flying, nor to give a secret

vulnus jactâ cuspide; obvius que occurrit adverso
wound with the hurled spear; meeting also he engaged *his* foe

que vir contulit se viro, haud melior furto, sed
and man engaged himself to man, not superior in deceit, but

fortibus armis. Tum nixus pede posito super
in powerful arms. Then struggling with *his* foot placed upon *him*

abjectum, et hastâ: Viri, altus Orodes, pars
overthrown, and with his spear: Men (*said he*) high Orodes, a portion

belli haud temnenda, jacet. Socii conclamant
of the war not to be despised, lies here. *His* companions exclaim together

secuti lætum Pæana. Autem ille expirans: Quicunque
following a joyful Pæan. But he expiring *says:* Whoever

es, non victor nec lætabere longùm me
thou art, *thou shalt* not *live* a conqueror nor shall you rejoice long over me

inulto; paria fata prospectant te quoque, atque mox
unrevenged; like fates await thee also, and soon

tenebis eadem arva. Ad quem Mezentius subridens
you shall possess the same fields. To whom Mezentius smiling

mistâ irâ, Nunc morere, ast pater Divorum
with mingled wrath, *says,* Now die, but let the father of the Gods

atque rex hominum viderit de me. Dicens hoc eduxit
and king of men see for me. Saying this he drew

telum corpore. Dura quies et ferreus somnus
the dart from *his* body. Cruel sleep and iron slumber

urget olli oculos, lumina clauduntur in æternam
press down his eyes, *his* sight is closed in eternal

noctem. Cædicus obtruncat Aleathoum, Sacrator Hydaspen
night. Cædicus beheads Aleathous, Sacrator *kills* Hydaspes

que Rapo Parthenium, et Orsen prædurum viribus.
and Rapo Parthethius, and Orsen very hardy in *his* strength.

Messapus Clonium que Lycaonium Ericeten illum
Messapus *overthrows* Clonius and Lycaonian Erecetes/ himself

jacentem tellure lapsu infrænis equi, pedes
lying on the ground by a fall of *his* undisciplined horse, on foot

hunc peditem; et Lycius Agis processerat; quem
he attacks him on foot; and Lycian Agis had gone out *against him;* whom

tamen Valerus haud expers avitæ virtutis dejicit: Salius
yet Falerius not destitute of ancestral courage overthrows: Salius

Authronium que Nealces insignis jaculo, et sagittâ
kills Authronius and Nealces renown'd for the dart, and arrow

longè fallente Salium. Jam gravis Mavors æquabat
far deceiving *killed* Salius. Now cruel Mars equalled *their*

luctus et mutua funera; victores que victi cædebant
grief and mutual deaths; the conquerors and conquered fell

pariter que pariter ruebant. Fuga ne nota his nec
together and together rushed on. Flight *is* not known to these nor

illis. Dii in tectis Jovis miserantur inanem iram
those. The Gods in the palace of Jove pity the vain anger

amborum, et esse mortalibus tantos labores. Hinc
of both, and *that there* are to mortals so great labours. On this *side*

Venus, hinc contrà Saturnia Juno spectat. Pallida
Venus, on that on the other hand Saturnian Juno beholds. Pale

Tisiphone sævit inter media millia. At verò Mezentius
Tisiphone rages in the midst of thousands. But indeed Mezentius

quatiens ingentem hastam turbidus ingreditur campo;
brandishing *his* great spear troubled walks on the plain,

quàm magnus Orion cùm incedit pedes scindens viam
as great Orion when he marches on foot dividing the way

per maxima stagna medii Nerei, supereminet undas
through great pools of the midst of Nereus, rises above the waves

humero, aut referens annosam ornum summis
with *his* shoulder, or bearing back on aged ash from the lofty

montibus que ingreditur solo, et condit caput inter
mountains and walks on the ground, and hides *his* head amid

nubila: Mezentius talis infert se vastis armis
the clouds: Mezentius thus bears himself with *his* vast arms.

Contrà Æneas speculatus in longo agmine parat
On the other hand Æneas watching in the long rank prepares

ire obvius huic. Ille manet imperterritus opperiens
to go to meet him. He remains unfrightened awaiting

magnanimum hostem et stat suâ mole atque
his high minded foe and stands in his own bulk and

emensus oculis quantum spatium satis hastæ,
having measured with his eyes as much space as is enough for his spear,

Dextra Deus mihi et telum quod libro missile
said My right hand a God to me and the dart which I poise about to send

nunc adsint; Lause voveo te ipsum tropæum
now be friendly to me; O Lausus I vow to thee thyself the trophy

Æneæ indutum spoliis raptis e corpore prædonis.
of Æneas clothed in spoils stript from the body of the robber.

Dixit que jecit stridentem hastam eminus, at illa volans
He said and hurl'd the hissing spear afar off, but it flying

excussa est clypeo que procul figit egregium Antorem
is shaken off from the shield and afar off pierces the noble Antores

inter latus et ilia; Antorem comitem Herculis qui
between the side and the stomach; Antores the companion of Hercules who

missus ab Argis hæserat Evandro atque consederat
being sent from Argos had joined Evander and had settled down

Italâ urbe. Infelix sternitur alieno vulnere que
in an Italian city. Unhappy he is overthrown by a foreign wound and

aspicit cœlum et moriens reminiscitur dulces Argos,
looks up to heaven and dying calls to mind his beloved Argos,

Tum pius Æneas jacit hastam, illa transivit per cavum
Then pious Æneas hurls his spear, it pass'd through the hollow

orbem, triplici ære, per linea terga que opus intextum
circle, of triple brass, through the linen coverings and the work interwoven

tribus tauris que sedit imâ inguine; sed
with three bulls hides and settles down to the bottom of the groin; but

haud pertulit vires. Æneas lætus sanguine Tyrrheni
it did not retain its strength. Æneas joyful the blood of the Tuscan

viso, ocyùs eripit ensem a femore et fervidus
being seen, quickly snatches his sword from his thigh and glowing

instat trepidanti. Lausus ut vidit gravitèr ingemuit
presses on him trembling. Lausus as he saw it heavily groaned

amore cari genitoris, que lacrymæ volutæ per
through love of his dear parent, and the tears came rolling over his

ora. Si qua vetustas sit latura fidem tanto operi
face. If by any means antiquity shall give faith to so great a deed

equidem non silebo casum duræ mortis
indeed I will not be silent concerning the misfortune of thy cruel death

hîc, que tua optima facta nec te juvenis memorande.
here, and thy most worthy deeds nor thee O youth to be commemorated.

Ille referens pedem et inutilis que inligatus cedebat
He withdrawing his foot both disabled and encumbered retreated

que trahebat inimicum hastile clypeo. Juvenis prorupit
and drew the hostile spear in his shield. The youth burst forth

que immiscuit sese armis, que subiit mucronem
and cast himself on the arms, and encountered the blade

Æneæ, jam assurgentis· dextrâ, que ferentis plagam
of Æneas, now rising with his right *hand*, and aiming a blow

que sustinuit ipsum morando. Socii sequntur magno
and sustained him by delaying. *His* associates follow with a great

clamore, dum genitor protectus parmâ nati abiret;
shout, while the father protected by the shield of *his* son withdrew,

que conjiciunt tela que proturbant nostem missilibus
and they hurl darts and drive away the foe by missile *spears*

eminus. Æneas furit que tectus tenet se. Ac velut
afar off. Æneas rages and protected restrains himself. And as

si quando nimbi præcipitant grandine effusâ, omnis
if at any time the clouds rush on with hail pouring down, every

arator diffiugit campis, et omnis agricola, et viator
ploughman flies from the plains, and every farmer, and traveller

latet tutâ arce aut ripis amnis, aut fornice alti
lies hid in a safe shelter either on the banks of a river, or the recess of a high

saxi, dum pluit in terris, ut possint exercere diem
rock, while it rains on the land, that they may spend the day

sole reducto. Sic Æneas obrutus telis undique
the sun being restored. Thus Æneas overwhelmed with darts on every side

sustinet omnem nubem belli dum detonet, et increpitat
endures all the cloud of war while it thunders, and rebukes

Lausum, que minatur Lauso. Quò ruis moriture?
Lausus, and threatens Lausus. Whither do you rush about to die?

que audes majora viribus? tua pietas fallit
and *why* do you dare greater *things* than your strength? your piety deceives

te incautum. Necminus ille demens exultat que jam sævæ
you unsuspecting. Nevertheless he mad exults and now cruel

iræ surgunt altiùs Dardanio ductori, que Parcæ legunt
wrath arises higher in the Trojan leader, and the Destinies draw out

extrema fila Lauso, namque Æneas exigit validum
his last threads *of life* to Lausus,. for Æneas plunges *his* powerful

ensem per medium juvenem que recondit totum.
sword through the middle of the youth and hides *it* entirely

Mucro transit et parmam, levia arma
within him. The blade pierced both *his* shield, the light arms

minacis, et tunicam quam mater neverat molli auro
of him threatening and the coat which *his* mother had spun of ductile gold

que sanguis implevit sinum; tum vita mœsta concessit
and blood filled his bosom; then *his* life sad withdrew

per auras ad manes, que reliquit corpus. At verò ut
through the air to the shades, and abandoned *his* body. But indeed as

Anchisiades vidit vultum et ora morientis,
the son of Anchises saw the face and countenance of him dying,

ora pallentia miris modis miserans ingemuit
his countenance pale in a wonderful manner compassionating he groaned

graviter que tetendit dextram; et imago patriæ
heavily and extended his right hand; and the image of his paternal

pietatis subiit mentem. Puer miserande quid nunc
piety entered his soul. O youth to be pitied what now *is left*

tibi pro istis laudibus, quid pius Æneas dabit dignum
to you for those praises, what *can* the pious Æneas give worthy

tantâ indole. Habe tua arma quibus lætatus que
so great virtue. Take your own arms in which you rejoiced and

remitto te manibus et cineri parentum; si ea est
I restore thee to the shades and ashes of your parents; if this is

qua cura. Tamen infelix solabere miseram mortem
any care. Yet unhappy *youth* you shall console your wretched death

hoc, cadis dextrâ magni Æneæ. Increpat ultro
by this, you fall by the right *hand* of great Æneas. He chides forthwith

socios cunctantes et sublevat ipsum terrâ turpantem
his companions delaying and supports him on the ground defiling

capillos comptos de more, sanguine. Interea
his locks adorned according to the custom, with blood. In the mean time

genitor siccabat vulnera lymphis, ad undam Tiberini
his father rinsed *his* wounds with water, at the stream of Tiber's

fluminis, que levabat corpus acclinis trunco arboris.
river, and raised *his* body leaning against the trunk of a tree.

Ærea galea dependet procul ramis, et gravia arma
His brazen helmet hung afar off on the branches, and *his* heavy arms

quiescunt prato. Lecti juvenes stant circùm; ipse
rest on the meadow. Chosen youth stand around; he

æger anhelans fovet colla, fusus propexam barbam in
sick panting relieves *his* neck, spreading *his* long beard on

pectore, rogitat multa super Lauso, que remittit
his breast, he asks many *things* concerning Lausus, and sends back

multos qui revocent, que ferant mandata mœsti
many who may recall *him*, and bear the commands of *his* mournful

parentis. At socii flentes ferebant Lausum exanimum,
father. But *his* companions weeping bore Lausus lifeless,

super arma ingentem atque victum ingenti vulnere.
upon *his* arms a great *corpse* and conquered by a great wound.

Mens præsaga mali agnovit gemitum longè:
The father's mind foreknowing misfortune knew *their* groan afar off.

deformat canitiem immundo pulvere et tendit ambas
he deforms *his* gray hair with filthy dust and stretches both

palmas ad cœlum, et inhæret corpore. Nate tantane
his hands to heaven, and cleaves to the body. O *my* son has so great

voluptas vivendi tenuit me ut paterer quem
a pleasure of living withheld me that I should have suffered *him* whom

genui succedere hostili dextræ, pro me? ne
I have begotten to yield to a hostile right hand, instead of myself? whether

genitor servor per hæc tua vulnera? vivens tuâ morte?
a father am I saved by these thy wounds? living by your death?

Heu! demum mihi misero exilium infelix, nunc
Alas! at length to me miserable my exile is unhappy, now

vulnus adactum altè. Nate ego idem maculavi tuum
the wound is driven deeply. O my son I the same have stained your

nomen crimine; pulsus solio que paternis sceptris,
name with crime; banished from my throne and paternal sceptre

ob invidiam. Debueram pœnas patriæ, que ipse
on account of hatred. I owed penalties to my country, and I

dedissem sontem animam odiis meorum, per
should have given my guilty soul to the indignation of my subjects, by

omnes mortes. Nunc vivo, que ne adhuc relinquo
all deaths. Now I live, and not as yet do I abandon

homines que lucem, sed linquam. Simul
men and the light of life, but I will leave them. At the same time

dicens hæc attollit se in ægrum femur, et
saying these things he raised himself on his wounded thigh, and

quanquam vis tardat alto vulnere, haud dejectus,
although pain restrains him by a deep wound, he was not cast down,

jubet equum duci. Hoc decus illi, hoc erat
he orders his horse to be led out. This was an honour to him, this was

solamen; abibat victor hoc omnibus bellis. Alloquitur
a consolation; he departed a conqueror by this from all wars. He addresses

mœrentem et infit talibus. Rhœbe viximus diu,
him mourning and begins with these words. O Rhebus we have lived long,

si qua ulla res est diu mortalibus. Aut victor hodie
if any thing is long to mortals. Either a conqueror this day

referes illa cruenta spolia, et caput Æneæ que
you shall bear off these bloody spoils, and the head of Æneas and

eris ultor dolorum Lausi mecum aut si nulla vis
you shall be the avenger of the griefs of Lausus with me or if no power

aperit viam, occumbes pariter, enim neque fortissime
opens a way, you shall fall together with me, for neither most brave horse

credo dignabere pati aliena jussa, et Teucros
do I believe you will condescend to endure another's commands, and Trojan

dominos. Dixit et exceptus tergo, locavit membra
owners. He said and being received on his back, he placed his limbs

consueta, que oneravit ambas manus acutis jaculis,
in their accustomed seat, and loaded both hands with sharp javelins,

fulgens ære caput, que hirsutus equinâ cristâ.
shining with brass as to his head, and rough with a horse hair crest.

Sic rapidus dedit cursum in medios. Ingens pudor
Thus swift he directed his course into the midst. Deep shame

æstuat in imo corde, que insania luctu misto et
boils in his inmost heart, and madness with grief mingled and

amor agitatus furiis, et conscia virtus; atque hìc vocavit
love convulsed by madness, and conscious courage; and here he called

Ænean ter magnâ voce. Æneas agnovit eum que lætus
Æneas thrice with a loud voice. Æneas knew him and joyful

precatur: Sic ille pater Deûm, sic altus Apollo
prayed: Thus *may* the   father of the Gods, thus exalted   Apollo

faciat, incipias conferre manum. Effatus tantum,
move *you*, *that* you may begin to engage your hand *with me*.   He said so much,

et subit obvius infestâ hastâ. Autem ille
and passes on against *him* with his hostile spear.   But   he *said*

sævissime quid terres me nato erepto? hæc
most cruel *man* why do you terrify me my son being snatched from me? this

fuit sola via quâ posses perdere. Nec horremus
was the only way by which you could destroy *me.* Neither   do we fear

mortem nec parcimus ulli Divûm.
death   nor   regard any one of the Gods.

Desine, jam venio moriturus, et priùs porto hæc dona
Cease, now I come about to die, and first   I bear these gifts

tibi. Dixit, que intorsit telum in hostem, que inde
to you. He said, and hurled *his* dart against the foe, and   then

figit aliud atque aliud, que super volat ingenti
he fastens another and another, and over *the plain* he flies in a great

gyro, sed aureus umbo sustinet. Equitavit in lævos
circle, but the golden boss sustains *them.* He rode in   sinister

orbes ter circum adstantem, jaciens tela manu.
circles thrice around *him* standing, hurling darts with *his* hand.

Troius heros ter circumfert secum immanem
The Trojan hero thrice bore around with him   a great

sylvam ærato tegmine. Inde ubi tædet
forest *of darts* in *his* brazen shield.   Then when it wearies *him*

traxisse tot moras, vellere tot spicula, et
to have contrived so many delays,   to draw out so many darts, and

urgetur congressus iniquâ pugnâ movens multa
he is driven on engaging in unequal contest revolving many *things*

animo, jam tandem erumpit, et conjicit hastam inter
in *his* mind, now at last he breaks forth, and hurls *his* spear between

cava tempora bellatoris equi. Quadrupes tollit se
the hollow temples of the warrior horse. The horse raised himself

arrectum et verberat auras calcibus, que ipse secutus
upright and beat   the air with his heels, and   he following

super effusum equitem implicat que cernuus incumbit
upon the fallen rider binds *him* down and falling over lies upon

armo ejecto, que Troes que Latini incendunt cœlum
his shoulder projecting, and the Trojans and Latins   rend   the sky

clamore. Æneas advolat que eripit ensem vaginâ,
with *their* cry. Æneas flies   and snatches *his* sword from *his* sheath,

et super hæc: Ubi nunc acer Mezentius, et illa
and over *him says* these *things:* Where now *is* brave Mezentius,   and that

effera vis animi? Contra, Tyrrhenus ut suspiciens
savage violence of mind? On the other hand, the Tuscan as   beholding

cœlum hausit auras, que recepit mentem; Amare
the sky he breathes the air, and recovers *his* understanding *says;* O cruel

hostis, quid increpitas et minaris mortem? nullum
enemy, why do you rebuke and threaten death? there is no

nefas in cæde, nec sic veni ad prœlia, nec meus
crime in my destruction, nor thus have I come to battle, nor did my

Lausus pepigit mihi hæc fœdera tecum. Oro hoc
son Lausus negotiate for me these treaties with you. I pray this

unum per, si qua venia est victis hostibus, patiare
one thing by this, if any indulgence is to vanquished foes, suffer

corpus tegi humo. Scio acerba odia meorum
my body to be covered in the earth. I know the bitter hatred of my subjects

circumstare; oro defende hunc furorem et concede me
surrounds me; I pray you prevent this madness and yield me

consortem sepulcro nati. Loquitur hæc que haud
a companion to the tomb of my son. He speaks these things and hot

inscius accipit ensem jugulo que diffundit animam
ignorant he receives the sword in his throat and pours out his soul

cruore undanti in arma
blood flowing over his arms.

ÆNEID.

BOOK ELEVENTH.

Interea Aurora surgens reliquit Oceanum. Æneas
In the meantime Aurora rising left the ocean. Æneas,

victor, solvebat vota Deûm primo Eöo, quanquam curæ
victorious, paid the vows of the Gods at the first dawn, although cares

præcipitant dare tempus socios humandis, que mens
urge him to bestow his time on his companions to be buried, and his mind

est turbata funere. Constituit ingentem quercum tumulo,
is disturbed by the funeral. He placed a great oak on a mound,

ramis decisis undique, que induit fulgentia arma,
its branches being cut off on each side, and placed upon it shining arms,

exuvias ducis Mezentii: tropæum tibi, magne
the spoils of the leader Mezentius: a trophy to thee O great

Bellipotens! aptat cristas rorantes sanguine, que trunca
God powerful in war! he fits his crests dripping with blood, and the broken

tela viri, et thoraca petitum que perfossum bis sex
darts of the hero, and the breast plate indented and pierced in twice six

locis; que subligat clypeum ex ære sinistræ, atque
places; and he binds a shield of brass to his left hand, and

suspendit eburnum ensem collo. Tum hortatur
suspends *his* ivory sword from *his* neck. Then he exhorts

socios ovantes (namque omnis turba ducum stipata
his companions rejoicing (for all the band of leaders crowding

tegebat eum) incipiens sic: Viri, maxima res effecta:
surround him) beginning thus: Heroes, *our* greatest work is accomplished:

omnis timor abesto. Quod superest; hæc sunt spolia et
let all fear depart. What remains; these are the spoils and

primitiæ de superbo rege; que hic est Mezentius meis
first fruits from *this* proud king; and here is Mezentius in my

manibus. Nunc est nobis iter ad regem que Latinos
hands. Now *there* is to us a way to the king and the Latin

muros; parate arma et præsumite bellum animis, et
walls; prepare arms and anticipate the war in *your* minds, and

spe, ne qua mora impediat ignaros que sententia
hope, lest any delay should hinder *you* unprepared and *wavering* resolution

tardet segnes metu; ubi primùm Superi annuerint
retard *you* slothful through fear; when first the Gods have consented

vellere signa que educere pubem castris.
to tear up the standard and to lead out the youth from the camps.

Interea mandemus socios que inhumata
In the meantime let us commit *our* companions and *their* unburied

corpora terræ; qui est solus honos sub imo Acheronte.
bodies to the earth; which is the only honour in the lowest Acheron.

Ait, ite, decorate egregias animas, quæ peperere
He says, go, honour the illustrious souls, who have obtained

hanc patriam nobis suo sanguine, supremis muneribus;
this country for us with *their* blood, with *their* last offices;

que Pallas quem non egentem virtutis atra dies abstulit,
and Pallas whom not destitute of courage cruel time has borne off.

et mersit acerbo funere, primus mittatur ad mœstam
and plunged in bitter death, first let him be sent to the mournful

urbem Evandri. Sic ait illacrymans, que recepit gressum
city of Evander. Thus he says weeping, and withdraws his step

ad limina, ubi senior Acætes servabat positum corpus
to the gates, where the old Acætes guarded the laid out body

exanimi Pallantis; qui fuit antè armiger Parrhasio
of the lifeless Pallas; who had been formerly the armour-bearer to Parrhasian

Evandro, sed tum ibat datus comes caro alumno non
Evander, but then he went an allotted companion to *his* dear foster child not

auspiciis æque felicibus. Omnes circum, que manus
with auspices equally happy. All *collect* around *the body*, both the band

famulûm que Trojana turba, et mœstæ Iliades
of servants and the Trojan crowd, and mournful Trojan matrons

solutæ crinem de more. Verò ut Æneas
dishevelling *their* hair according to *their* manner. But as soon as Æneas

intulit sese altis foribus tollunt ingentem gemitum
presented himself at the lofty gates they raise a great groan

ad   sidera,   pectoribus   tunsis   que   regia   immugit
o   the stars, *their* breasts being beaten and the palace resounds

mæsto   luctu.   Ut ipse   vidit   fultum   caput,   et
with mournful grief.   As   he   beheld the supported head,   and

ora   nivei Pallantis   que   patens   vulnus   Ausoniæ
countenance of pale Pallas   and the opening wound of the Ausonian

cuspidis in   levi   pectore,   ita   fatur   lacrymis   obortis;
spear   in *his* smooth   breast,   thus he speaks *his* tears bursting forth;

inquit   puer   miserande,   ne   Fortuna   cùm   veniret
says he   O boy to be pitied, could   Fortune   when she approached

læta   invidit te mihi,   ne   videres   nostra regna neque
joyful envy you to me,   that you should not see my kingdom nor

veherere   victor   ad   paternas sedes; discedens,
be borne   a conqueror   to *your* father's seats;   I departing,

non   dedèram hæc promissa   parenti Evandro   de   te,
did not give   these promises to *your* father Evander concerning you,

cùm   complexus me   euntem,   mitteret   in   magnum
when   embracing me   going,   he sent *me* against   a great

imperium, que metuens moneret,   esse   acres viros
empire,   and fearing admonished *me*, that they were brave men

prœlia,   cum durâ gente.   Et nunc quidem
in contest, *that we must engage* with a hardy race.   And now   indeed

ille multùm   captus inani   spe, fors et   facit   vota
he   much   overcome with vain hope, perhaps even *now* makes *his* vows

que cumulat altaria donis; nos mœsti comitamur juvenem
and loads the altars with gifts; we mournful accompany the youth

exanimum, et jam debentem nil ullis   cœlestibus,
deprived of life, and now owing   nothing to any of the heavenly powers,

vano   honore. Infelix   videbis   crudele funus
of vain respect.   Wretched *father* you shall behold the sad   funeral

nati. Hi   nostri reditus, que expectati triumphi? hæc
of *your* son. Are these our returns,   and our expected triumphs? is this

mea magna fides? At Evandre   non aspicies pulsum
my   great confidence? But O Evander you shall not see *him*   beaten

vulneribus   pudendis;   nec   pater   optabis dirum
with wounds   to be ashamed of; nor   a father shall you desire accursed

funus   nato   sospite. Hei mihi! quantum
death *yourself* your son, *disgracefully* being saved. Alas me!   how great

præsidium Ausonia perdis et quantum   tu
a safeguard   O Ausonia you lose and how great *protection* have you *lost*

Iüle. Ubi   deflevit   hæc,   imperat   miserabile
O Iulus. When he had bewailed in these *terms* he commands the lamented

corpus tolli,   et mittit mille   viros lectos ex
corpse to be borne off, and he sends a thousand men   selected from

toto agmine, qui comitentur supremum honorem, que
the whole army, who accompany   the last   honour,   and

intersint lacrymis   patris; exigua solatia ingentis luctus,
be present to the tears of *his* father; trifling consolation of great   grief

sea debita misero patri. Alii haud segnes texunt
but   due   to an unhappy father.   Others not slothful interweave

crates et molle pheretrum arbuteis virgis et querno
hurdles and a light   bier   of arbute rods and oaken

vimine, que inumbrant exstructos toros obtentu
vine,   and they overshadow the high-raised couch with a covering

frondis. Hìc ponunt juvenem sublimem in agresti
of leaves. Here they place the youth high   on his rustic

stramine qualem florem seu mollis violæ, seu languentis
bed   as   a flower either of the soft violet, or the drooping

hyacinthi, demessum virgineo pollice, cui que
hyacinth, plucked by a virgin's thumb, from which also

ne fulgor adhuc, necdum sua forma recessit; jam
neither brightness as yet, nor its own beauty has departed; now

mater tellus non alit, que ministrat vires. Tum Æneas
its mother earth does not feed it, and supply strength. Then Æneas

extulit geminas vestes, rigentes que auro que ostro,
brought out two   vests,   stiff   both with gold and purple,

quas Sidonia Dido ipsa læta laborum, quondam fecerat
which Sidonian Dido herself rejoicing in the labour, formerly had made

illi suis manibus, et discreverat telas tenui auro.
for him with her own hands, and had separated the web by slender gold.

Mœstus induit unam harum juveni supremum honorem
Mournful he put on one of these to the youth his last honour

que obnubit comas assuras amictu. Que præterea
and shrouds his hair about to be burnt in a veil. And besides

aggerat multa præmia Laurentis pugnæ, et jubet
he adds   many prizes of the Laurentian battle, and commands

prædam duci longo ordine. Addit equos et tela
the plunder to be brought out in long array. He adds horses and darts

quibus spoliaverat hostem. Et vinxerat manus
of which he had stripped the enemy. And bound the hands of those

post terga, quos mitteret inferias umbris,
behind their backs, whom he would send as funeral offerings to his shade,

sparsuros flammam cæso sanguine; que jubet
about to sprinkle the funeral flame with slaughtered blood; and commands

duces ipsos ferre truncos indutos hostilibus armis,
the chiefs themselves to bear trunks of trees covered with hostile arms,

que inimica nomina figi. Infelix Accœtes
and their hostile names to be marked upon them. Wretched Accœtes

confectus ævo ducitur fœdans nunc pectora pugnis
worn down by age is led out disfiguring now his breast with his fists

nunc ora unguibus et sternitur terræ projectus
now his face with his nails and he is thrown on the earth extended

toto corpore. Et ducunt currus perfusos Rutulo
with his whole body. And they lead out chariots bathed with Rutulian

sanguine. Pòst Æthon bellator equus it lacrymans
blood.   Next Æthon his warrior horse goes weeping

insignibus positis que humectat ora grandibus
his trappings *being laid aside* *and* *he moistens his face* *with heavy*

guttis. Alii ferunt hastam que galeam; nam Turnus
drops of tears. *Others bear* *his spear* *and helmet;* *for* *Turnus*

victor habet cætera. Tum mœsta phalanx que
victorious *possesses* *the rest.* *Then the mourning* *band* *both*

Teucri que Tyrrheni duces et Arcades armis versis
the Trojan and *Tuscan* *leaders and* *the Arcadians with arms* *reversed*

sequuntur. Postquam omnis ordo comitum præcesserat
follow. *After* *the whole band of companions* *had advanced*

longê, Æneas substitit que addidit hæc alto gemitu.
far *Æneas* *stopt* *and* *added* *these words* *with a deep* *groan:*

Eadem horrida fata belli vocant nos hinc ad alias lacrymas.
The same *dreadful fates of war* *call* *us* *hence to other* *griefs.*

Salve æternum maxime Palla que vale æternùm.
Farewell *forever.* *most noble Pallas* *and farewell* *forever.*

Nec affatus plura; tendebat ad altos muros que ferebat
Nor *speaking more,* *he marched to the lofty walls* *and* *withdrew*

gressum in castra. Que jam oratores aderant ex Latinâ
his step *to the camps.* *And* *now* *orators* *had come* *from the Latin*

urbe, velati ramis oleæ que rogantes veniam;
city, *crowned with branches* *of the olive and* *entreating* *favour;*

redderet corpora quæ jacebant fusa ferro
that he would give up *the bodies which* *lay* *scattered by the sword*

per campos; ac sineret succedere tumulo terræ;
through *the plains;* *and would permit them* *to be placed* *in a tomb of earth;*

nullum certamen cum victis, et cassis æthere;
that there is no *contest* *with the conquered, and those deprived* *of life;*

parceret quondam vocatis hospitibus, que soceris.
that he would spare those *formerly* *called* *guests,* *and associates.*

Quos precantes haud aspernanda bonus Æneas
To whom *asking* *these favours* *not* *to be despised* *good* *Æneas*

prosequitur veniâ et insuper addit hæc verbis:
answers *with kindness and* *moreover* *adds* *these to his words:*

Latini, quænam indigna fortuna implicuit vos tanto
Ye Latins, *what* *unworthy fortune* *has entangled* *you so great*

bello, qui fugiatis nos amicos. Ne oratis pacem exanimis
a war, *who shun* *us your friends.* *Do you ask* *peace* *for the dead*

et peremptis sorte Martis? equidem vellem concedere
and those destroyed by the lot of war? *indeed* *I would wish* *to yield it*

et vivis. Nec veni nisi Fata dedissent locum que
also to the living. *Nor had I come unless the fates* *had granted a place* *and*

sedem nec gero bellum cum gente. Rex
settlement to me. *nor* *do I wage* *war* *with the nation.* *Your king*

reliquit nostra hospitia et potiùs credidit se
has abandoned *our* *friendship* *and in preference has trusted himself*

armis Turni. Fuerat æqius Turnum opponere se
to the arms of Turnis *It had been* *more just* *for Turnus* *to oppose* *himself*

huic morti. Si apparat finere bellum manu, si
to this death.　If he prepares to terminate the war with *his* hand, if *he intends*

pellere Teucros, decuit concurrere his telis mecum
to drive out the Trojans, it became *him* to engage with these weapons with me.

Vixisset cui Deus aut sua dextra dedisset
He would have lived to whom God or his own right hand should have given

vitam. Nunc ite et supponite ignem, .miseris
life.　Now go and apply the fire to your wretched

civibus. Æneas dixerat. Olli silentes obstupuere, que
countrymen Æneas said.　They silent stood amaz'd, and

conversi tenebant oculos atque ora inter se.
turning held · *their* eyes and *their* faces towards each other

Tum senior Drances infensus juveni Turno, odiis
Then the aged Drances hostile to the youth Turnus, in hatred

et crimine, sic vicissim refert orsa, ore;
and crimination, thus in turn returns *these* words, with his mouth;

O Trojane vir ingens famâ, ingentior armis, quibus
O Trojan hero great in fame, greater in arms, by what

laudibus, æquem te cœlo? ne priùs mirer
praises, shall I equal you to heaven? whether first shall I admire *thy*

justitiæ, ne laborum belli? Verò nos grati referemus
justice, or the labours of the war? But we grateful will bear back

hæc ad patriam urbem; et, si qua fortuna dederit
these *things* to our native city; and, if any fortune shall give

viam, jungemus te regi Latino. Turnus quærat
a way, we will unite thee to king Latinus.　Let Turnus seek out

fœdera sibi. Quin et juvabit attollere fatales
treaties for himself. But even it will delight *us* to raise up the fate decreed

moles murorum, que subvectare Trojana saxa
masses of *your* walls, and to uplift Trojan rocks

humeris. Dixerat hæc, que omnes fremebant
on our shoulders.　He said these *things*, and all murmured

uno ore eadem. Pepigere bis senos dies; et
with one mouth the same.　*They* bargained *peace* for twice six days; and

pace sequestrâ, Teucri que Latini misti erravere impunè
a truce intervening, the Trojans and the Latins mingling wandered unharm'd

per sylvas jugis. Fraxinus sonat icta ferro
through the woods on the mountains.　The ash sounds struck with the iron

bipenni; evertunt pinus actas ad sidera, nec cessant
axe;　*they* overturn pines rais'd to the stars, nor do *they* cease

scindere cuneis robora et olentum cedrum, nec vectare
to cleave with wedges the oak and fragrant cedar, nor to bear off

ornos gementibus plaustris. Et jam fama volans,
the mountain *ashes* in groaning wagons. And now fame flying,

prænuncia tanti luctus, complet Evandrum que domos
a forerunner of great grief, fills Evander and the house

Evandri, et mænia; quæ modò ferebat Latio Pallanta
of Evander, and the city; which now bore to Latium that Pallas

victorem.   Arcades ruêre ad portas, et   rapuere
was victorious.   The Arcadians rushed to the gates, and   seized

funereas fasces de   vetusto more.   Via lucet
the funeral torches according to   the ancient manner.   The way shines

longo ordine flammarum et discriminat agros   latè.
with a long train   of flames   and marks out   the fields far around.

Contrà   turba Phrygum veniens jungit plangentia
On the other hand a crowd of Trojans approaching joins   the mourning

agmina: quæ postquam matres viderunt succedere tectis,
troops: which   after   the mothers· saw   to enter   the palace,

incendunt mæstam urbem clamoribus. At non ulla vis
they inflame the mournful   city   with cries.   But not   any force

est potis tenere Evandrum, sed venit in medios. Feretro
is able to restrain   Evander,   but he comes into the midst.   The bier

reposito,   procumbit super Pallanta, atque hæret
being set down,   he falls   upon   Pallas,   and   hangs to him

que lacrymans que gemens; et vix tandem via laxata est
both weeping   and groaning;   and hardly at last   a way   is opened

voci dolore;   O Palla   non   dederas   hæc
to his voice   for grief;   O Pallas   you had not   given   these

promissa parenti, ut velles credere te   cautiùs
promises   to your parent, that you would trust   yourself more cautiously

sævo Marti. Haud eram ignarus, quantum nova gloria
to cruel war.   Neither was I   ignorant,   how much new   fame

in armis posset, et prædulce decus primo certamine.
in   arms   can do,   and very pleasant glory   in a first   contest.

Miseræ primitiæ juvenis, que dura rudimenta   propinqui
O wretched first fruits   of youth,   and cruel first lessons   of approaching

belli! et vota exaudita nulli Deorum, que meæ preces!
war!   and vows   heard   by no one of the Gods,   and my   prayers!

que tu O sanctissima conjux, felix tuâ morte, neque
and   thou O   most holy   wife,   happy in thy death,   not

servata in hunc dolorem!   Contrà ego   vici   mea
reserved for this   wretchedness! On the contrary I   have conquered my own

fata vivendo, ut genitor restarem superstes. Rutuli
fates   by living,   that a father   I should remain surviving.   The Rutulians

obruerunt   telis, secutum socia   arma
should have crushed me with their weapons,   following   associated   arms

Trôum; ipse   dedissem   animam, atque hæc pompa
of the Trojans; I   should have surrendered my life,   and   this   pomp

referret me non Pallanta, domum. Ne arguerim vos
should have borne me not   Pallas,   home.   Nor might I have accused you

Teucri nec   fædera, nec dextras   quas   junximus
O Trojans nor   your treaties,   nor the right hand   which we have united

hospitio: ista sors erat debita nostræ senectæ. Quòd si
in friendship: this   fate   was   destined to my   old age.   But   it

immatura mors manebat natum, juvabit cecidisse
untimely   death   remained   to my son,   it will delight me   that he fell

ducentem Teucros in Latium, millibus Volscorum cæsis
leading   the Trojans into Latium,   thousands of the Volscians being slain

antè. Quin ego non dignor te Palla,   alio   funere quàm
first.   But   I will not honour you O Pallas, with any other funeral   than

pius Æneas, et quám magni Phryges, que quàm Tyrrheni
pious Æneas, and than the heroic Trojans,   and than   the Tuscan

duces et omnis exercitus Tyrrhenum.   Ferunt
leaders and all   the army of the Tuscans *have prepared.* They bear

magna trœphea   quos tua dextera dat letho. Tu
great   trophies *from those* whom thy right *hand* gives to death. You

quoque Turne, nunc   stares   immanis truncus in
also   O Turnus, now should have stood a huge   trunk   in

armis, si   esset   par ætas, et idem robur ab annis.
arms, if *there* had been equal age, and the same strength from *my* years.

Sed quid infelix demoror Teucros ab armis? vadite, et
But   why unhappy do I withhold the Trojans from arms? march, and

memores, referte hæc mandata regi: qùod moror
mindful   bear back these commands to your king; that if I drag out

invisam vitam, Pallante perempto, tua dextera est causa;
a hated life, Pallas being slain, thy right hand is the cause;

quam vides debere Turnum que nato que patri
which you see owes Turnus   both to the son and to the father

meritis. Hic locus solus vacat tibi que fortunæ. Non
by *its* deserts. This method alone is open to you and fortune. I do not

quæro guadia vitæ, nec fas;   sed perferre   sub
ask   the joys of life, nor is it right *I should*; but to bear *this*   to

imos Manes nato.
the lowest shades to *my* son.

Interea   Aurora extulerat almam lucem miseris
In the mean time the morning had introduced the cheering light to wretched

mortalibus, referens opera atque labores. Jam pater Æneas
mortals,   renewing *their* works and labours. Now father Æneas,

jam Tarchon, constituere pyras in curvo litore. Huc
now   Tarchon,   built up funeral piles on the winding shore. Hither

tulere corpora suorum, quisque more patrum;
they bore the bodies of their *friends*, each one in the manner of his fathers:

que atris ignibus subjectis, altum cœlum conditur in
and black fires being applied. the lofty sky is hid in

tenebras caligine. Cincti fulgentibus armis decurrêre ter
darkness by the smoke. Arrayed in shining arms ran thrice

circum accensos rogos;   ter lustravere mæstum
around   the burning funeral piles; thrice they surrounded the mournful

iguen funeris in equis que dedere ulutatus ore.
fire of the funeral on horses and uttered wailings with *their* mouths.

Et tellus spargitur lacrymis, et arma sparguntur
And the earth is sprinkled with *their* tears, and *their* arms are bedewed

Que clamor virùm que clangor tubarum it cœlo. Hinc
And the cry of men and the blast of the trumpets goes to the sky. Hence

alii conjiciunt igni spolia direpta occisis Latinis,
others   into the fire spoils   torn   from the slain Latins,

galeas que decoros enses, que fræna, que ferventes
helmets and   decorated swords, and bridles, and   glowing *chariot*

rotas; pars munera nota, clypeos ipsorum, et tela non
wheels; part   gifts well known, shields of their own, and darts not

felicia. Multa corpora boûm circà mactantur morti; que
fortunate. Many bodies   of oxen around are sacrificed to death; and

jungulant setigeros sues, que pecudes raptas ex omnibus
they butcher   bristly swine, and sheep snatched from   all

agris in flammam: tum   toto litore spectant ardentes
the fields in the flame: then along the whole shore they behold *their* burning

socios, que servant semusta busta; neque possunt
companions, and guard the half burnt funeral piles; nor   can they

avelli, donec humida nox invertit cœlum aptum
be torn away until   moist   night turns round the sky   studded

fulgentibus stellis; nec minus et miseri Latini struxere
with glittering stars;   nevertheless also the wretched Latins   raised

pyras in diversâ parte; et partim infodiunt multa corpora
funeral piles in a different part; and partly they bury many   bodies

virûm terræ; que partim tollunt avecta in finitimos
of men in the earth; and   partly they carry them borne off into the neighbouring

agros, que remittunt urbi. Cremant cœtera, que
fields,   and send them back to the city. They burn the others, and

ingentem acervum confusæ cædis, nec numero nec
a great   pile   of mingled slaughter, without number   or

honore; tunc undique vasti agri collucent certatim
honour;   then on every side the extensive fields shine   in rival *splendor*

crebris ignibus. Tertia lux dimoverat gelidam umbram
with frequent fires.   The third day had removed the cold   shade

cœlo; mœrentes ruebant altum cinerem et ossa
from the sky; mournful   they piled up the deep   ashes   and the bones

confusa focis, que onerabant tepido aggere terræ.
intermingled in the fires, and they loaded them with a warm mound of earth.

Jam verò præcipuus fragor, et longè maxima pars luctûs
Now indeed the chief noise, and far the greatest part of the mourning *are*

in urbe, tectis prædivitis Latini. Hìc matres, que
in the city, *and* palace of the rich Latinus. Here the mothers, and

miseræ nurus, hìc cara pectora mœrentûm sororum,
wretched daughters-in-law, here the fond breasts of mourning   sisters,

que pueri orbi parentibus, exsecrantur dirum bellum,
and boys deprived of their parents, curse   the dreadful war,

que hymenæos Turni; jubent ipsum armis, que ipsum
and the nuptials of Turnus; they command him by arms, and himself

ferro, decernere qui poscat regnum Italiæ et
by the sword, to conclude *the war* who demands the kingdom of Italy and

primos honores sibi. Sævus Drances ingravat hæc, que
the first honours for himself. Furious Drances aggravates these, and

testatur Turnum solum vocari, solum posci in certamina
testifies that Turnus alone is called, alone demanded for   the contest

Contrà   multa sententia   simul   variis dictis pro
On the other hand a general sentiment at the same time in various words   for

Turno, et magnum nomen reginæ obumbrat;   multa
Turnus, and the great   name   of the queen overshadows *him*; *his* extensive

fama sustentat virum meritis tropæis. Inter hos   motus,
fame   sustains   the hero by merited trophies.   Among these commotions,

in medio tumultu flagrante, ecce   super mœsti legati
in the midst of the tumult   raging,   lo   moreover mournful delegates

ferunt responsa ab magnâ urbe Diomedis; nihil   actum
bear   replies   from the great city of Diomede; that nothing was done

omnibus impensis tantorum operum; dona   nil, nec
by all   the expense of so great   labours; that gifts *availed* nothing, nor

aurum, nec magnas preces valuisse; alia arma   quærenda
gold,   nor   did great entreaties   prevail; other arms were to be sought

Latinis aut pacem petendam   ab Trojano rege. Rex
by the Latins or   peace was to be sought from the Trojan king.   King

Latinus ipse deficit ingenti luctu.
Latinus himself faints with great grief.

Ira   Deûm admonet, que recentes tumuli ante
The anger of the Gods admonishes *him*, and the newly-made graves   before

ora   fatalem Ænean ferri manifesto numine.
his face *admonish* that fated   Æneas is led on by a manifest   deity.

Ergo   cogit magnum concilium que primos suorum
Therefore he collects a great   council   and the chiefs of *his* friends

accitos imperio   intra alta limina. Olli convenere que
called   by his command within the lofty palace. They   assemble   and

fluunt ad regia tecta   plenis   viis. Latinus sedet
rush   to the royal palace through the crowded ways. Latinus   sits

in mediis et maximus ævo et primus sceptris, haud
in the midst both greatest   in age and   first   in power,   not

lætâ fronte. Atque hìc jubet   legatos remissos
with happy front.   And   here he commands ambassadors   sent back

ex Ætolâ urbe fari quæ   referant,   et reposcit
from the Ætolian city . to tell what they might have brought, and he demands

cuncta responsa suo ordine. Tunc silentia facta
all   *their* answers in their   order.   Then   silence was made

linguis,   et Venulus parens dicto infit farier ita:
to *their* tongues, and Venulus   obeying *his* command begins to speak thus:

O cives,   vidimus   Diomedem que Argiva castra,
O my countrymen, we have seen   Diomede   and   the Grecian camps,

atque emensi   iter   superavimus omnes   casus,
and having measured our way we have surmounted all   misfortunes,

que contigimus manum quâ   Ilia tellus concidit. Ille
and we have touched the hand by which the Trojan land   fell.   He

victor   condebat urbem Argyripam cognomine   patriæ
victorious   built up   the city Argyripa   with the name of *his* native

gentis arvis Gargani Japygis. Postquam   introgressi
race in the territory of Garganian Japyx.   After   we had been introduced

et copia fandi coram   data,   præferimus munera;
and leave of speaking before *the prince* was given, we first offer   our gifts,

docemus   nomen que patriam; qui intulerint bellum, quæ
we announce   our name and country; who had conducted the war, what

causa attraxerit Arpos. Auditis ille reddidit hæc
cause had drawn us to Arpos. Being heard he   uttered   these *words*

    placido ore: O fortunatæ gentes, Saturnia   regna,
from *his* placid mouth: O happy   nations, Saturnian   kingdoms,

antiqui Ausonii, quæ fortuna solicitat vos quietos que
ancient Ausonians, what fortune disturbs you at rest   and

suadet   lacessere ignota bella. Quicunque violavimus
persuades *you* to provoke unknown wars. Whoever *of us* have violated

Iliacos   agros   ferro   (mitto   quæ
the Trojan territories with the sword (I omit *those things* which *were*

    exhausta   bellando sub altis muris; quos viros ille
sustained to the utmost in fighting under the lofty walls; those heroes that

Simois   premat)   expendimus   infanda   supplicia
Simois   overwhelmed)   we have endured unspeakable ·punishments

per   orbem et omnes   pœnas   scelerum; manus
through the globe and all   the penalties of our crimes;   a band

miseranda vel Priamo. Triste   sidus Minervæ scit
to be pitied   even by Priam. The mournful star of Minerva knows

et Euboicæ cautes que ultor Caphareus. Adacti ex
and the Euboian cliffs   and the avenger Caphareus.   Driven from

illâ militiâ ad diversum litus, Menelaus Atrides   exulat
that war to a different shore, Menelaus the son of Atreus goes to exile

usque ad columnas Protei. Ulysses vidit Ætnæos Cyclopas.
even   at the columns of Proteus. Ulysses saw the Ætnean   Cyclops.

Referam   regna   Neoptolemi que Penates   versos
Shall I relate the kingdoms of Neoptolemus and household Gods overturned

Idomenei? ne Locros habitantes Libyco litore? Mycenacus
of Idomeneus? or the Locri 'inhabiting the Lybian shore? the Mycenæan

ductor magnorum Achivorum ipse oppetiit intra prima
leader of the mighty Greeks   himself fell within *his* first

limina   dextrâ   infandæ conjugis; adulter subsedit
gates by the right hand of *his* cruel wife;   the adulterer settled down

Asiam devictam: Deos invidisse mihi ut redditus   patriis
in Asia subdued: The Gods had envied me that returned to *my* native

aris   viderem   optatum conjugium .et pulchram
altars I might see *my* beloved   wife   and   beauteous

Calydona. Nunc etiam portenta horribili visu sequuntur
Calydon.   Now   also portents of horrible vision. follow *me*

et   socii amissi petierunt æthera pennis; aves
and *my* companions lost   have sought the skies on wings; as birds

vagantur   fluminibus (heu dira supplicia meorum)
they wander about the streams (alas! dreadful punishments of my *friends*)

et implent scopulos lacrymosis vocibus. Adeo jam
and they fill the rocks with tearful cries. Thus now

hæc fuerunt speranda mihi ex illo tempore cùm
these *things* have been expected by me from that time when

demens appetii cœlestia corpora ferro, et violavi
mad I attacked heavenly bodies with the sword, and violated

dextram Veneris vulnere. Ne verò, ne impellite
the right hand of Venus by a wound. Do not indeed, do not drive

me ad tales pugnas, nec mihi ullum bellum cum
me to such contests, nor to me let there be any war with

Teucris pòst Pergama eruta; nec memini, ve
the Trojans since the Trojan city is overthrown; nor have I remembered, or

lætor veterum malorum. Vertite munera ad
do I rejoice in *their* former misfortunes. Return *your* presents to

Ænean quæ potâstis ab patriis oris ad me. Stetimus
Æneas which you have borne from *your* native coasts to me. We have stood

contra aspera tela que contulimus manus.
against *his* cruel darts and we have fought against *his* bands.

Credite experto; quantus assurgat in clypeum, quo
Give credit to an experienced man; how great he rises on *his* shield, with what

turbine torqueat hastam. Si Idæa terra tulisset duo
fury he hurls *his* spear. If the Idean land could have borne two

tales viros præterea, Dardanus venisset ultro ad
such men besides, the Trojan had come unmolested to

Inachias urbes et Græcia lugeret fatis versis.
the Inachian cities and Greece had mourned *her* fates reversed.

Quicquid cessatum est apud mœnia duræ Trojæ, victoria
Whatever was yielded at the walls of obstinate Troy, the victory

Graiûm hæsit manu Hectoris que Æneæ, et retulit
of the Greeks remained in the hand of Hector and Æneas, and restrained

vestigia in decimum annum. Ambo insignes animis,
its footsteps to the tenth year. Both distinguished for courage,

ambo præstantibus armis; hic prior pietate. Dextræ
both for excelling arms; he first in piety. Let *your* right hands

coëant in fœdera, quà datur; ast cavete arma
unite in treaties, in any way it is allowed: but beware *lest* arms

concurrant armis. Optime rex regum, simul audîsti
engage with arms. O most worthy king of kings, at once you have heard

et quæ responsa sint et quæ sententia sit magno bello.
both what *his* replies are and what *his* opinion is of this great war.

Vix legati ea, que varius fremor cucurrit
Hardly *had* the ambassadors *said* these *words*, and a varied murmuring ran

per turbata ora Ausonidûm; ceu cùm saxa morantur
through the troubled mouths of the Ausonians; as when rocks block up

rapidos amnes, murmur fit gurgite clauso, que
rapid rivers, a noise is made the stream being closed, and

vicinæ ripæ fremunt crepitantibus undis. Ut primùm
the neighbouring banks resound by the noisy waves. As first

animi placati et trepida ora quierunt rex,
their minds were appeased and their trembling mouths rested, the king

præfatus Divos, infit ab alto solio: equidem Latini,
having first addressed the Gods, begins from his lofty throne: indeed ye Latins

et vellem et fuerat melius statuisse antè
even I could wish and it had been better to have determined before

de summâ re; non cogere concilium tali
concerning this great affair; not to assemble a council at such

tempore; cùm hostis obsidet muros. Cives, gerimus
a time; when the enemy besieges our walls. My countrymen, we wage

importunum bellum cum gente Deorum que invictis viris
inconvenient war with a nation of the Gods and unconquered men

quos nulla prœlia fatigant, nec victi possunt absistere
whom no battles fatigue, nor vanquished can they abstain

ferro. Ponite spem, si habuistis quam in accitis
from the sword. Lay aside hope, if you have had any in the invited

armis Ætolûm; quisque sibi spes, sed videtis
arms of the Etolians; each one must be to himself a hope, but you see

quam angusta hæc. Quâ ruinâ cætera rerum
how narrow this is. In what destruction the rest of our concerns

perculsa jaceant, omnia sunt ante oculos que inter
struck down lie prostrate, all things are before your eyes and within

vestras manus. Nec incuso quemquam; plurima virtus,
your hands. Nor do I blame any one; the greatest courage,

quæ potuit esse, fuit; certatum est toto
which could be, has been; there has been contending with the whole

corpore regni. Adeo nunc expediam quæ sententia
body of the kingdom. Thus now I will unfold what sentiment

sit dubiæ menti; et docebo paucis (adhibete animos.)
is in my doubtful mind: and I will teach in few words (lend me your attention.)

Est mihi antiquus ager proximus Tusco amni,
There is to me an ancient territory near to the Tuscan river,

longus in occasum, usque super Sicanos fines; Arunci
far to the west, even beyond the Sicanian limits; the Aruncians

que Rutuli serunt, et exercent duros colles
and Rutulians sow it, and they work the hard hills

vomere, atque asperrima horum pascunt. Omnis
with the plough share, and the roughest parts of these they pasture. All

hæc regio, et pinea plaga celsi montis cedat amicitiæ
this region, and pine tract of the lofty mountain shall yield to the friendship

Teucrorum, et dicamus æquas leges fœderis, que
of the Trojans, and let us declare equal conditions of compact, and

vocemus socios in regna. Considant, si
let us invite them as allies to our kingdoms. Let them settle down, if there is

tantus amor, et condant mœnia. Sin est animus
so great desire, and let them build towns. But if there is a disposition

ᴄapessere alios fines que aliam gentem, que possunt
to possess   other   limits and another nation,   and   they can

decedere nostro solo, texamus bis denas naves Italo
withdraw from our soil, let us build twice ten ships of Italian

robore, seu plures, valent   complere; omnis materies
wood, or   more, if they are able to fill them; all   the materials

jacet ad undam; ipsi præcipiunt que numerum que
lie   by the water; they may prescribe both the number and

modum carinis; nos demus æra, manus,   navalia.
the fashion of the ships; we will give brass, hands, naval stores.

Præterea placet   centum Latinos oratores de primâ
Besides it is our desire that an hundred Latin orators from the first

gente ire, qui ferant dicta et firment fœdera, que
of the nation go, who may bear our words and confirm our treaties, and

prætendere ramos pacis manu, que portantes munera
hold out branches of peace in their hand, and bearing presents

eboris que talenta auri et sellam   que trabeam,
of ivory and talents of gold and the chair of office and   robe,

insignia nostri regni. Consultite in medium succurrite
the ensigns of our authority. Consult for our common interest, relieve

fessis rebus.
our distressed affairs.

Tum Drances infensus (idem quem gloria Turni
Then Drances hostile (the same whom the glory of Turnus

agitabat obliquâ invidiâ, que amaris stimulis largus
aroused with oblique envy, and with bitter goads abounding

opùm et melior linguâ, sed dextera frigida bello
in wealth and better in language, but his right hand was cold in war

habitus non futilis auctor consiliis, potens seditione;
esteemed not a useless adviser in councils, powerful in sedition;

materna nobilitas dabat huic superbum genus, ferebat
his maternal nobility gave to him a proud race, he derived

incertum de patre,) surgit et onerat   his dictis;
a doubtful one from his father,) rises and loads Turnus with these words;

atque aggerat iras. O bone rex consulis   rem
and provokes anger against him. O kind king you consult about an affair

obscuram nulli, nec egentem nostræ vocis. Cuncti fatentur
dark to none, nor wanting my voice. All must confess

se scire quid fortuna populi ferat, sed mussant
that they know what the fortune of our people demands, but they hesitate

dicere.   Det libertatem fandi que remittat flatus
to declare it. Let him grant liberty of speaking and relax his pride

ob cujus infaustum auspicium, que sinistros mores
for whose unhappy influence, and unfortunate manners

(equidem dicam licet minetur arma que mortem
(indeed I will speak although he should threaten arms and death

mihi) videmus lumina tot ducum cecidisse, que
to me) we see the lights of so many leaders to have gone out, and

totam urbem cònsedisse luctu, dum tentat Troia
the whole city to have set down in mourning, while he tempts the Trojan

castra, fidens fugæ et territat cœlum, armis. Qptime
camps, trusting to flight and terrifies heaven with arms. Most excellent

regum, adjicias unum etiam unum istis donis, quæ
of kings, will you add one thing even one to these favours, which

plurima jubes mitti, que dari Dardanidis; nec
in great numbers you command to be sent, and to be given to the Trojans; nor

violentia ullius vincat te, quin pater, des
let the violence of another overcome thee but O father, give

natam egregio genero, que dignis hymenæis, et
your daughter to this renowned son-in-law, and honourable nuptials, and

jungas hanc pacem æterno fœdere. Quòd si tantus
confirm this peace by an eternal treaty. But if so great

terror habet mentes et pectora, obtestemur ipsum, que
dread possesses your minds and souls, let us entreat him, and

oremus veniam ab ipso; cedat proprium jus regi,
let us beg favour from him; that he will yield his own right to the king,

que remittat patriæ. Quid projicis miseros cives
and forego it for his country. Why do you drive your wretched countrymen

toties, in aperta pericula? ô caput et causa horum
so often, to open dangers? O fountain and cause of these

malorum Latio! Nulla salus bello; omnes poscimus
misfortunes to Latium! There is no safety in war; we all demand

te, Turne, pacem, simul solum inviolabile pignus
of thee, O Turnus, peace, at the same time the only unbroken pledge

pacis. En! ego primus (quem tu fingis invisum tibi, et
of peace. Lo! I first (whom you pretend am hostile to you, and

nil moror esse) supplex venio; miserere
in no way do I hesitate to be) humbly approach you; pity

tuorum; pone animos, et pulsus abi. Fusi
your countrymen; lay aside your anger, and beaten depart. Routed

vidimus sat funera, et desolavimus ingentes agros.
we have seen enough deaths, and we have desolated extensive territories.

Aut, si fama movet, si concipis tantum robur pectore,
Or, if fame moves you, if you feel so great courage in your breast,

et si adeo dotalis regia est cordi; aude, atque fidens
and if thus a dotal palace is in your heart;. dare, and confident

fer adversum pectus in hostem. Scilicet, ut regia
bear your opposing breast against the foe. For, that a royal

conjux contingat Turno, nos, viles animæ, turba
bride shall fall to Turnus, shall we, despicable souls, a mob

inhumata que infleta sternamur campis? Et jam tu,
unburied and unwept be laid prostrate on the plains? And now you,

si tibi qua vis, si habes quid patrii Martis
if to you is any courage, if you have any thing of your country's warlike spirit

aspice illum contrà, qui vocat. Violentia Turni
behold him opposed to you, who challenges you. The rage of Turnus

exarsit talibus dictis; dat gemitum, que rumpit has
glows at these words; he utters a groan, and breaks out in these

voces imo pectore: Drance, tibi quidem semper
words from his inmost heart: O Drances, there is to you indeed ever

larga copia fandi, tunc cùm bella poscunt manus;
a copious abundance of speaking, even then when wars demand active hands;

que patribus vocatis primus ades; sed curia est
and the fathers being convoked first you are present, but now the court is

non replenda verbis, quæ magna volant tibi tuto,
not to be filled with words, which large escape from you in safety,

dum agger murorum distinet hostem, nec fossæ inundant
while the mound of our walls keeps off the foe, nor do the ditches flow

sanguine. Proinde tona eloquio, solitum tibi, que tu
with blood. Therefore thunder forth in eloquence, accustomed to you, and you

Drance, argue me timoris, quando tua dextra dedit
Drances, accuse me of fear, since thy right hand has given

tot acervos stragis Teucrorum, que passim insignis
so many heaps of the slaughter of the Trojans, and every where you mark

agros tropæis. Licet experiare quid vivida virtus
the field with trophies. It is allowed you to try what lively courage

possit: scilicet nec hostes quærendi nobis longè;
can do: for neither are our enemies to be sought by us far hence;

circumstant muros undìque. Imus in adversos? quid
they surround the walls on every side. Do we go against our enemies? why

cessas? An Marvors erit tibi semper in ventosâ
do you withdraw? Whether will Mars be to you ever on your windy

linguâ, que istis fugacibus pedibus? Ego pulsus? aut
tongue, and in these flying feet? Am I beaten? or

quisquam fœdissime, merito arguet pulsum, qui
will any one thou most foul wretch, justly accuse me of being beaten, who

videbit tumidum Tybrim crescere Iliaco sanguine, et
shall see the swelling Tyber increase with Trojan blood, and

totam domum Evandri cum stirpe procubuisse, atque
all the house of Evander with his race to have fallen, and

Arcades exutos armis? Bitias et ingens Pandarus
Arcadians deprived of their arms? Bitias and great Pandarus

haud ita experti me, et mille, quos victor misi
not thus have experienced me, and a thousand, whom victorious I sent

sub Tartara die, inclusus muris, que septus hostili
under Tartarus in a day, inclosed by walls, and hedged in by a hostile

aggere. Nulla salus bello? demens, cane talia
rampart. Is there no safety in war? madman, tell such things

Dardanio capiti, que tuis rebus. Proinde ne cessa
to the Trojan chief, and to your own concerns. Wherefore do not cease

turbare omnia magno metu atque extollere vires
to confuse all things by great fear and boast the strength

gentis   bis   victæ;   contrà   premere arma
of the nation twice conquered; on the other hand to restrain the arms

Latini. Nunc et proceres Myrmidonum tremiscunt Phrygia
of Latinus. Now also the chiefs of the Myrmidons tremble at Trojan

arma! nunc et Tydides et Larissæis Achilles! et amnis
arms! now also Dromede and Larissean Achilles! and the river

Aufidus retro fugit Adriacas undas! vel cùm scelus
Aufidus backwards flies from the Adriatic waves! even when the guilt

artificis fingit se pavidum contra mea jurgia, et
of the deceiver feigns himself fearful against my threats, and

acerbat crimen formidine. Numquam amittes talem animam
embitters crime with dread. Never will you lose such a soul

hâc dextrâ; (absiste moveri;) habitet cum te, et sit
with this right hand (cease to be moved;) it shall dwell with thee, and be

in isto pectore. Nunc revertor ad te, pater, et tua magna
in that breast. Now I return to thee, O father, and thy great

consulta. Si ponis nullam spem ultrà in nostris armis;
decrees. If you place no hope farther in our arms;

si sumus tam deserti, et occidimus funditus, agmine semel
if we are so abandoned, and we fall entirely, our army once

verso, neque Fortuna habet regressum; oremus
being overcome, nor our Fortune has a return; we will pray for

pacem, et tendamus dextras inermes. Quanquam ô
peace, and we will extend our right hands unarmed. Although O

si quicquam solitæ virtutis adesset! Ille mihi
if something of accustomed courage was present! He *seems* to me

que fortunatus laborum, que egregius animi ante alios,
both fortunate in *his* labour, and distinguished in mind before others,

qui ne videret quid tale, procubuit moriens
who *that* he might not see any such *thing*, fell dying

et semel momordit humum ore. Sin et opes, et
and at once bit the ground with *his* mouth. But if even wealth, and

juventus adhuc intacta, que Italæ urbes que populi
youth as yet untouched, and Italian cities end people

supersunt nobis auxilio; sin et gloria venit Trojanis cum
remain to us for aid; but if also glory comes to the Trojans with

multo sanguine; sunt illis sua funera, que par
much blood; there are to them *their* own deaths, and an equal

tempestas per omnes; cur indecores deficimus in
storm *rages* through all; why disgraced do we fail in

primo limine? cur tremor occupat artus
the first entrance *of the war?* why does trembling possess *our* limbs

ante tubam?
before *we hear* the trumpet?

Dies, que varius labor mutabilis ævi retulit multa
Time, and the varied labour of changeful life have restored many *things*

in melius; fortuna alterna revisens lusit multos,
to a better condition; fortune alternately revisiting has deceived many.

et rursus locavit in solido. Ætolus non erit
and again has placed *them* on firm *ground.* The Etolian *prince* will not be

auxilio nobis, et Arpi; at Messapus erit, que felix
aid to us, and Arpis; but Messapus will be, and happy

Tolumnius, et duces quos tot populi misere; nec
Tolumnius, and the leaders whom so many people have sent; nor

parva gloria sequetur delectos Latio et Laurentibus
shall small glory follow the chosen *bands* from Latium and the Laurentian

agris, et est Camilla de egregiâ gente Volscorum,
fields, and *there* is Camilla from the renowned nation of the Volsci

agens agmen equitum, et catervas florentes ære. Quòd
leading on a troop of horse, and bands flourishing with brass. But

si Teucri poscunt me solum in certamina, que id placet,
if the Trojans demand me alone in combat, and this pleases,

que obsto communibus bonis tantùm; victoria non adeo
and I oppose the common good so much; victory not thus

fugit has manus, exosa, ut recusem tentare
escapes these hands, hateful, that I should refuse to attempt

quicquam pro tanto spe. Ibo animis contra,
any thing for so great a hope. I will go with resolution against *Æneas,*

licèt ille præstet vel magnum Achillem, que induat
though he should excel even great Achilles, and should put on

paria arma, facta manibus Vulcani. Ego Turnus haud
equal arms, wrought by the hands of Vulcan. I Turnus not

secundus ulli veterum virtute, devovi hanc animam
second to any of the ancients in courage, have devoted this life

vobis, que socero Latino. Æneas vocat solum? et
to you, and to my father-in-law Latinus. Does Æneas call *me* alone? and

oro vocet. Nec potiùs Drances luat morte, sive hæc
I pray he may call. Nor rather shall Drances suffer death, whether this

est ira Deûm; sive est virtus et gloria tollat.
is the anger of the Gods; or it is *that* courage and glory shall bear *me* off.

Illi certantes agebant hæc inter se dubiis
They contending discuss these *things* among themselves in their doubtful

rebus. Æneas movebat castra, que aciem. Ecce
concerns. Æneas advanced the camp, and army. Lo

nuncius ruit ingenti tumultu per regia tecta, que
a messenger rushes out with great tumult through the royal apartments, and

implet urbem magnis terroribus; Teucros
fills the city with great fears; *announcing that* the Trojans

instructos acie, que Tyrrhenam manum, descendere a
drawn out in array, and the Tuscan band, descended from

Tiberino flumine totis campis. Extemplo animi
Tiber's stream from all the plains. Forthwith *their* minds

turbati, que pectora vulgi concussa, et iræ
were disturbed. and the breasts of the crowd were shaken, and *their* anger

arrectæ haud mollibus stimulis. Trepidi poscunt arma
aroused not by gentle provocations. Trembling they demand arms

manu; juventus fremit arma; patres mœsti flent que
in hand; the youth rage for arms; the fathers mournful weep and

mussant. Hìc magnus clamor undique tollit se in
mutter. Here a great shout from every side raises itself into

auras vario dissensu: haud secus atque cùm fortè
the air with varied discord: not otherwise as when by chance

catervæ avium consedêre in alto luco, ve rauci cynci dant
troops of birds alight in a deep grove, or hoarse swans utter

sonitum piscoso amne Padusæ per loquacia stagna.
their noise along the fishy stream of Padusa through the noisy pools.

Turnus, tempore arrepto, ait imo, ô cives, cogite
Turnus, the opportunity being seized, said nay, O my countrymen, assemble

concilium, et sedentes laudate pacem; illi ruunt
a council, and sitting *at ease* applaud peace; *while* they rush

armis in regno. Nec locutus plura, corripuit sese, et
in arms against *our* kingdom. Nor speaking more, he hurried himself, and

citus extulit altis tectis. Tu, Voluse, edice maniplis
quick withdrew from the lofty palace. You, O Volusus, command your bands

Volscorum armari; et duc Rutulos; ait: Messap is
of Volscians to be armed; and lead on the Rutulians; he says: *You* Messap is

et Coras cum fratre, diffundite equitem in armis
and Coras with your brother, pour out your cavalry in arms *throu h*

latis campis: pars firment aditus urbis, qu
the broad plains; let a part strengthen the entrances of the city, a t

capessant turres; cætera manus inferat arma mecup
guard the towers; let the other band bring up arms with m

quâ jusso. Ilicet discurritur in muros, totâ urbe
where I command. Forthwith there is a running to the walls, through all the city

Pater Latinus ipse deserit concilium, et magna incepta
Father Latinus himself abandons *his* council, and *his* great purpose

ac turbatus tristi tempore, differt; que incusat se
and disturbed by the sad occasion, withdraws; he blames himsel

multa, qui non ultro acceperit Dardanium Ænean
much, *that* he did not forthwith receive Trojan Æneas

que asciverit generum urbi.
and invite *him* as his son-in-law to the city.

Alii præfodiunt portas, aut subvectant saxa, que sudes
Others dig *trenches* before the gates, or upraise rocks, and stakes

rauca buccina dat cruentum signum bello: tun
the shrill *sounding* trumpet gives a bloody signal for the war: the

matronæ que pueri cinxere muros variâ coronâ
the matrons and boys surrounded the walls with a varied circle

ultimus labor vocat omnes. Nec non regina magnâ
the last effort invites all. Also the queen with a great

caterva matrum subvehitur ad templum que ad summas
company of matrons is borne to the temple and to the lofty

arces Palladis ferens dona; que juxtà virgo Lavinia
towers of Minerva bearing gifts; and near by the maid Lavinia

comes, causa tanti mali, atque dejecta decoras
her companion, the cause of so great a misfortune, and casting down *her* beautiful

oculos. Matres succedunt, et vaporant templum
eyes. The mothers come up, and perfume the temple

thure; et fundunt mœstas voces de alto limine.
with incense; and pour out *their* mournful voices from the lofty entrance.

Tritonia virgo armipotens præses belli, frange
O Tritonian maid powerful in arms, sovereign of the war, break

telum Phrygii prædonis manu, et sterne ipsum
the darts of the Trojan robber with *your* hand, and stretch him

pronum solo, que effunde sub altis portis.
prostrate on the ground, and overthrow *him* under the lofty gates.

Turnus ipse furens certatim, cingitur in prœlia que
Turnus himself raging anxiously, is girt for battle and

jam adeo indutus Rutulum thoraca horrebat ahenis
now thus having put on *his* Rutulian breastplate looks terrible in brazen

squamis; que incluserat suras auro, adhuc nudus
scales; and he had inclosed *his* legs in gold, as yet naked

tempora; que accinxerat ensem lateri, que fulgebat
as to *his* temples; and he had girded a sword to *his* side, and he shone

aureus decurrens altâ arce; que exsultat animis, et
in gold hastening from the high citadel; and exults with courage, and

jam præcipit hostem spe; qualis equus ubi fugit
now anticipates the enemy in *his* hope; as a horse when he escapes

præsepia vinculis abruptis, tandem liber que potitus
from the stalls, *his* fastenings being broken, at length free and enjoying

aperto campo; ille aut tendit in pastus, que armenta
the open plain; he either directs *his* course to the pastures, and herds

equarum, aut assuetus perfundi noto flumine
of mares, or accustomed to be bathed in the known stream

aquæ, emicat que luxurians fremit cervicibus arrectis
of water, springs forth and wantoning neighs with *his* neck raised

altè; que jubæ ludunt per colla, per armos. Cui
high; and *his* mane sports over *his* neck, along *his* shoulders. Whom

Camilla acie Volscorum comitante obvia occurrit,
Camilla with *her* troop of Volscians accompanying meeting encounters,

que regina desiluit ab equo sub portis ipsis; quam
and the queen leaped from *her* horse under the gates themselves; whom

tota cohors imitata defluxit ad terram equis relictis.
all the troop imitating leaped down on the ground *their* horses being left.

Tum fatur talia: Turne, si qua fiducia sui
Then she speaks these *words:* O Turnus, if any confidence of one's self

meritò est forti, audeo, et promitto occurrere turmæ
deservedly is to the brave, I dare, and I promise to encounter the host

Æneadum, que sola ire obvia contra Tyrrhenos equites.
of Trojans, and alone to go opposed against the Tuscan horse.

Sine me tentare prima pericula belli manu; tu
Allow me to attempt the first dangers of the war with my hand; do you

pedes subsiste ad muros et serva mœnia. Turnus
on foot stay by the walls and preserve the ramparts. Turnus

fixus oculos in horrendâ virgine ad hæc:
fastening *his* eyes on the dreadful maid *responds* to these *things:*

O virgo, decus Italiæ, quas grates parem dicere,
O maid, ornament of Italy, what thanks can I prepare to express,

ve quas referre! sed nunc, quando iste animus est supra
or what to return! but now, since this *thy* mind is above

mnia, partire laborem mecum. Ut fama que
ll *dangers,* divide the labour with me. As report and

exploratores missi reportant fidem, improbus Æneas
our spies sent out bring back confidence, cruel Æneas

præmisit levia arma equitum quaterent campos;
has sent before light arms of horse *that* they may shake the plains;

per ardua deserta montis adventat ad urbem. Paro
through the high deserts of the mountain he approaches to the city. I prepare

furta belli, in convexo tramite sylvæ, ut obsidam
stratagems of war, in a winding path of the wood, that I may besiege

bivias fauces armato milite. Tu excipe Tyrrhenum
the double straits with armed soldiery. Do you encounter the Tuscan

equitem signis collatis. Acer Messapus erit tecum
cavalry *our* signals being compared. Brave Messapus shall be with you

que Latinæ turmæ que manus Tiburti; et tu concipe
ind the Latin troops and band of Tiburtus; and do you take

curam ducis. Sic ait, et paribus dictis hortatur
the charge of a leader. Thus he said, and with like words he exhorts

Messapum que socios duces in prœlia, et pergit in
Messapus and the associate leaders to battle, and he marches against

hostem. Est vallis curvo anfractu accommoda fraudi
the foe. *There* is a valley in a crooked winding fitted for fraud

que dolis armorum; quam atrum latus urget utrimque
and the deceits of arms; which a gloomy side encloses on each side

densis frondibus; quò tenuis semita ducit, que angustæ
with thick leaves; where a narrow path guides, and narrow

fauces que maligni aditus ferunt. Super hanc, in
straits and malignant entrances lead. Over this, on

speculis que in summo vertice montis, ignota
the height and upon the loftiest summit of a mountain, a concealed

planities jacet, que tuti receptus; seu velis occurrere
plain lies, and safe retreats; whether you wish to engage

pugnæ dexterâ que lævâ, sive instare jugis et
in battle on the right and left, or to press *the enemy* from the heights and

volvere grandia saxa. Juvenis fertur huc notâ
to roll down large rocks. The youth *Turnus* is borne hither by the known

regione viarum, que arripuit locum et insedit
egion of the ways, and seiz'd the place and sat down

iniquis sylvis.
in the unequal forests.

Interea   in superis sedibus Latonia compellabat velocem
In the mean time in the highest seats.   Diana   address'd   swift

Opim, unam ex   sociis   virginibus que   sacrâ   catervâ
Opis,   one of *her* associated   maids   and consecrated   band

et dabat has voces   tristi   ore.   O virgo, Carmilla
and uttered these   words from *her* mournful mouth.   O nymph,   Camilla

graditur ad crudele bellum, et nequicquam cingitur nostris
goes out   to   cruel   war,   and in vain   is girt   with our

armis; cara mihi ante alias: enim neque iste   amor   novus
arms;   dear to me before others: for   neither *is* this affection   new

venit Dianæ que movit   animum   subitâ dulcedine.
which comes to Diana   and influences *my* mind   with sudden   fondness.

Cùm Metabus   pulsus   regno ob invidiam,   que
When Metabus   banished from *his* kingdom for   envy,   and

superbas vires excederet   antiquâ urbe   Priverno,
haughty   authority had departed from *his* ancient city   Privenus,

fugiens inter media   prœlia   belli, sustulit   infantem
escaping   in the midst   of the contests of war,   he bore off   the infant

comitem exilio,   que vocavit   Camillam,   nomine
his companion   in exile,   and   called *her*   Camilla,   the name

matris Casmillæ parte   mutatâ. Ipse portans præ se
of *his* m *ther*   Casmilla   in part being changed. He bearing *her* before him

sinu petebat   longa   juga solorum nemorum; sæva
in *his* bosom sought   the long   heights of the lonely groves;   cruel

tela   premebant   undique   et Volsci   volitabant
darts   press'd *him*   on every side   and the Volscans   flew about

milite   circumfuso.   Ecce medio   fugæ, Amasenus
the soldiery   pouring around *him*.   Lo   in the midst   of *his* flight,   Amasenus

abundans spumabat summis ripis; tantus imber ruperat
overflowing   foamed over *its* highest   banks;   so great a shower   had burst

se   nubibus; ille parans innare tardatur   amore
itself   from the clouds;   he   preparing to swim   is hindered   by *his* love

infantis, que timet   caro oneri.   Vix hæc sententia
of the infant, and   fears   for *his* dear   load. Scarcely had this   sentiment

subitò sedit   versanti omnia   secum.   Immane
suddenly settled *in his mind* revolving all *things* with himself.   *There was* a huge

telum quod fortè bellator gerebat validâ manu, solidum
dart   which by chance the warrior wielded   in *his* strong   hand,   firm

nodis et cocto robore: implicat natam huic clausam
with knots and seasoned oak: he binds *his* daughter to this   inclosed

libro et sylvestri subere, atque circumligat   habilem
with bark and sylvan   cork,   and fastens *her around* dexterously

mediæ   hastæ: quam librans   ingenti dexterâ ita
to the midst   of the spear: which poising   in *his* great   right hand thus

fatur ad æthera: Virgo Latonia alma cultrix nemorum,
he speaks to heaven: Virgin   Diana   fair   inhabitant   of groves

ipse pater voveo hanc famulam tibi: supplex   fugit
I   a father devote   his   handmaid to you: suppliant   she flies

hostem per auras prima tenens tua tela: Diva
the foe through the air first holding thy weapons. O Goddess

testor accipe tuam quæ nunc committitur dubiis
I entreat you receive your own who now is entrusted to the doubtful

auris. Dixit et immittit contortum hastile lacerto
winds. He said and hurled the wreathed dart his arm

adducto: undæ sonuere: infelix Camilla fugit in
being drawn back: the waves resounded: hapless Camilla flies on

stridente jaculo, super rapidum amnem. At Metabus
the hissing dart, above the rapid stream. But Metabus

magnâ catervâ jam urgente propius dat sese fluvio,
a great troop now pursuing him nearer gives himself to the stream.

atque, victor vellit hastam, donum Triviæ, cum virgine
and, a conqueror plucks the dart, the gift of Diana, with the maid

de gramineo cespite. Non ullæ urbes accepere illum
from the grassy turf. No other cities received him

tectis non mœnibus; neque ipse dedisset manus
in their dwellings nor walls; nor did he yield his hands

feritate: at exegit ævum pastorum
to the arts of life through wildness: but underwent the life of shepherds

solis montibus. Hic nutribat natam in dumis
In the solitary mountains. Here he nourished his daughter among the bushes

que inter horrentia lustra, mammis armentalis equæ
and among the frightful haunts of beasts, by the teats of a brood mare

et ferino lacte, immulgens ubera teneris labris. Que
and wild animal milk, milking her udder with her tender lips. And

ut infans institerat vestigia primis plantis pedum,
as the infant had mark'd her footsteps with the first prints of her feet,

oneràvit palmas acuto jaculo, que suspendit
he loaded her hands with the sharp dart, and suspended

spicula et arcum ex humero parvæ.
arrows and a bow from the shoulder of the little maid.

Pro crinali auro, pro tegmine longæ pallæ,
In place of a fillet of gold, in place of a dress of a long cloak,

exuviæ tigridis pendent a vertice per dorsum. Jam tum
the skin of a tiger hangs from her head over her back. Even then

torsit puerilia tela tenerâ manu, et egit
she hurled childish darts with her tender hand, and whirled

fundam tereti habenâ, circum caput, que dejecit
a sling with tapering thong, around her head, and struck down

Strymoniam gruem, aut album olorem. Multæ matres per
a Strymonian crane, or white swan. Many mothers through

Tyrrhena oppida frustra optavere illam nurum.
the Tuscan towns in vain desired her as a daughter-in-law.

Contenta Dianâ solâ intemerata colit æternum.
Contented with Diana alone unviolated she cultivates the eternal

amorem telorum. et virginitatis. Vellem haud fuisset
love of weapons, and maidenhood. I could wish she had not been

correpta. tali militiâ, conata lacessere Teucros
orne away by this war, attempting to provoke the Trojans

foret cara mihi que una mearum comitum nunc.
she might have been dear to me and one of my companions now.

Verùm age, nympha, quandoquidem urgetur acerbis
But come, O nymph, since it is settled by the cruel

fatis, labere polo que invise Latinos fines, ubi tristis
fates, glide from the sky and visit the Latin coasts, where the sad

pugna committitur infausto omine. Cape hæc que
contest is fought with hapless omen. Take these *weapons* and

deprome ultricem sagittam pharetrâ. Quicunque
draw forth a revengeful arrow from *my* quiver. Whoever

violaverit sacrum corpus vulnere, Tros ve Italus,
shall violate *her* sacred body with a wound, Trojan or Italian,

det pœnas mihi sanguine pariter hâc. Pòst
let *him* give penalties to me with *his* blood equally by this. Hereafter

ego feram cavâ nube corpus miserandæ et
I will bear off in a hollow cloud the body of the unfortunate *maid* and

arma inspoliata ab tumulo, que reponam patriæ.
her arms uninjured from the tomb, and I will restore *her* to *her* country

Dixit: at illa demissa per leves auras cœli
She said: but she casting *herself* through the light airs of heaven

insonuit, circumdata corpus nigro turbine. At
sounded, surrounding *her* body with a black whirlwind. But

interea Trojana manus propinquat muris que Etrusci
in the meantime the Trojan band approached the walls and the Tuscan

duces que omnis exercitus equitum compositi in turmas
leaders and all the army of the horse *were* arranged in bands

numero. Insultans sonipes fremit toto æquore et
in order. The bounding horse neighs through all the plain and

pugnat habenis pressis, obversus huc et huc: tum ferreus
fights *his* reins being restrained, turning here and there: then an iron

ager horret late hastis, que campi ardent sublimibus
field bristles up far around with spears, and the plains glow with upraised

armis. Nec non contrà Messapus que celeres Latini
arms. Also on the other hand Messapus and the active Latins

et Coras cum fratre et ala virginis Camillæ apparent
and Coras with *his* brother and wing of the maid Camilla appear

adversi campo que protendunt hastas longè
opposed *to them* on the plain and protrude *their* spears far *before*

dextris reductis, et vibrant spicula: que
their right hands being drawn back, and they brandish *their* darts: and

adventus virorum, que fremitus equorum, ardescit.
the coming of the men, and the neighing of the horses, grows warm.

Jamque uterque progressus intra jactum teli
And now each *army* having advanced within the cast of a dart,

substiterat: erumpunt subito clamore, que exhortantur
halted: they burst forth with sudden shout, and encourage

frementes equos; simul fundunt. crebra tela undique
their neighing   horses;   at once they pour forth thickening darts on every side

ritu   nivis, que cœlum obtexitur umbrâ.   Continuô
in the manner of snow, and the sky   is covered with *their* shade.   Immediately

Tyrrhenus et acer Aconteus connixi   incurrunt adversis
Tyrrhenus   and bold   Aconteus   struggling   rush together with hostile

hastis, que primi dant ruinam ingenti sonitu, que rumpunt
spears,   and   first   cause destruction with great noise,   and   they dash

pectora quadrupedantum perfracta pectoribus. Aconteus,
the breasts   of *their* horses   striking   against breasts.   Aconteus,

excussus in morem fulminis aut ponderis acti
thrown off   in the manner   of a thunderbolt   or   a weight   sent forth

tormento, præcipitat longè et dispergit vitam in auras.
from an engine, is hurried   far off and scatters   *his* life   in   the air.

Extemplo acies turbatæ que Latini versi rejiciunt
Forthwith   the troops are disordered and   the Latins   turned   throw back

parmas et vertunt   equos ad mœnia.   Troes agunt;
their shields   and turn   *their* horses   to the walls.   The Trojans drive on;

princeps Asylas inducit turmas, que jam propinquabant
the chief   Asylus   leads on   the troops, and   now   they approached

portis; que rursus Latini tollunt clamorem, et reflectunt
the gates; and   again the Latins   raise   a shout,   and   turn back

mollia colla: hi fugiunt que referuntur, habenis
their flexile   necks: these   fly   and   are carried back,   the reins

penitus datis: qualis ubi pontus procurrens   alterno
entirely being given up: as   when   the sea   running   with alternate

gurgite nunc ruit ad terras, que spumeus jacit undam
tide   now   rushes to the land,   and   foaming   casts   *its* wave

super scopulos, que   perfundit extremam arenam
upon   the rocks,   and   bathes   the extreme   sand

sinu.   Nunc rapidus atque resorbens saxa
with *its* curling wave.   Now   swift   and   swallowing up the rocks

revoluta   æstu,   fugit retro que relinquit litus,
rolled back   with the tide,   it hastens back   and   leaves   the shore,

vado labente. Bis Tusci egere Rutulos versos ad
the current gliding back.   Twice the Tuscans drove the Rutulians turned   to

mœnia; bis rejecti respectant   tegentes   terga
the walls; twice driven back   they regard *their* foes   covering   *their* backs

armis. Sed postquam congressi in tertia   prœlia,
with *their* arms.   But   after   meeting   in the third   engagement,

implicuere totas acies inter   se, que vir legit
hey entangle *their* whole   forces   among   themselves, and   man selects

virum; tum verò et gemitus morientum que arma que
his man;   then   indeed   even the groans   of the dying   and   arms   and

corpora et semianimes equi permisti   cæde virorum,
bodies   and   expiring   horses intermingled with the slaughter of men,

volvuntur in alto sanguine; aspera pugna surgit. Orsilochus
are rolled   in deep   blood;   a cruel   contest arises.   Orsilochus

'ntorsit hastam equo Remuli, quando horrebat
hurled *his* spear against the horse of Remulus, when he shuddered

adire ipsum, que reliquit ferrum sub aure; quo ictu
to approach him, and left the steel under *his* ear; by which blow

sonipes furit arduus, que impatiens vulneris, jactat
the horse raged high *leaping*, and impatient of the wound, throws out

crura alta pectore arrecto. Ille excussus volvitur
his legs high, *his* breast being upraised. He shaken off is rolled

humi. Catillus dejicit Iolam que Herminium ingentem
on the ground. Catillus strikes down Iolas and Herminius great

corpore et armis; cui fulva cæsaries nudo vertice
in body and in arms; whose yellow hair *flowed* on *his* uncovered head

que humeri nudi. Nec vulnera terrent: patet
and *his* shoulders *were* uncovered. Nor did wounds terrify *him*: he is exposed

tantus in arma. Hasta, acta per huic latos armos, tremit, que
so much in arms. The spear, driven through his broad shoulders, trembles, and

transfixa duplicat virum dolore. Ater cruor funditur
piercing doubles the hero with pain. Black blood is poured out

ubique; certantes dant funera ferro que petunt
on every side; contending they cause death by the sword and seek

pulchram mortem per vulnera. At inter medias cædes
honourable death by wounds. But in the midst of the slaughter

Amazon pharetrata Camilla exsultat exserta unum latus
the Amazon quiver bearing Camilla marches forth baring one side

pugnæ, et nunc spargens lenta hastilia manu
to the battle, and now scattering *her* slender spears with *her* hand

denset, nunc indefessa rapit validam bipennem
she thickens *them around*, now untired she seizes the strong axe

dexterâ. Aureus arcus sonat ex humero et arma
with *her* right-hand. *Her* golden bow sounds from *her* shoulder and the arms

Dianæ. Illa etiam siquando pulsa recessit in
of Diana. She even if at any time repulsed *she* withdrew in

tergum dirigit fugientia spicula arcu converso.
retreat directed *her* flying darts *her* bow being turned.

At circum lectæ comites, que Larina virgo que
But around *her went her* chosen companions, both Larina a maid and

Tulla et Tarpeia quatiens æratam securim; Italides
Tulla and Tarpeia shaking *her* brazen axe; daughters of Italy

quas dia Camilla ipsa delegit, decus sibi, que
whom divine Camilla herself had chosen, an ornament to herself, and

ministras bonæ pacis que belli: quales Threiciæ
handmaids of pleasant peace and of war; such like Thracian

Amazones cùm pulsant flumina Thermodoontis, et bellantur
Amazonians when they beat the streams of Thermodoon, and fight

pictis armis; seu circum Hyppolyten; seu cùm martia
with painted arms; or around Hyppolyte; or when martial

Penthesilea refert se curru, que magno tumultu
Penthesilea brings back herself in *her* chariot, and with great tumult

ululante, feminea agmina exultant lunatis peltis. Aspera
screaming, the female troops exult with crested shields. O true

virgo quem primum, quem postremum dejicis
maid whom first, whom last did you overthrow

telo? aut quot morientia corpora fundis
with *your* darts? or how many dying bodies did you stretch

humi? Primum Eumenium Clytio patre, apertum
on the ground? First Eumenius Clytius *being his* father, the open

pectus cujus adversi transverberat longâ abiete.
breast of whom opposite she transfixed with *her* long *spear* of fir.

Ille cadit vomens rivos sanguinis atque mandit cruentam
He falls vomiting streams of blood and bites the bloody

humum, que moriens versat se in suo vulnere. Tum
ground, and dying turns himself on his wound. Then

super Lirin que Pagasum; quorum alter dum revolutus
besides *she slew* Liris and Pagasus; of whom the one while rolling

equo suffosso colligit habenas, alter dum
from *his* horse stabbed beneath he collects the reins, the other while

subit ac tendit inertem dextram labenti,
he comes up and reaches out *his* unarmed right hand to *his* falling *friend*,

ruunt præcipites que pariter. Addit Amastrum, Hippotaden
they fall headlong and together. She adds Amastrus, the son of Hippotas

his, que incumbens sequitur eminus hastâ, que Terea
to them, and pressing on she follows afar off with *her* spear, and Tereus

que Harpalycum et Demophoonta que Chromin; que quot
and Harpalycus and Demophoon and Chromis; and as many

spicula emissa manu virgo contorsit; tot Phrygii
darts as sent forth from *her* hand the maid hurled; as many Trojan

viri cecidere. Ornytus venator fertur procul ignotis
heroes fell. Ornytus the hunter is borne afar with unusual

armis et Iapyge equo cui latos humeros pellis erepta
arms and an Apulian horse whose broad shoulders a skin torn from

pugnatori juvenco operit; ingens hiatus oris, et malæ
a fighting bullock covers; the great opening of the mouth, and the jaws

lupi cum albis dentibus texere caput, que agrestis sparus
of a wolf with white teeth covered *his* head, and a rustic dart

armat manus. Ipse vertitur in mediis catervis, et est
arms *his* hands. He is exercised in the midst of the troops, and is

supra toto vertice. Illa trajicit hunc exceptum, (enim
above *them* by a whole head. She pierces him intercepted, (for

neque labor agmine verso) et fatur hæc super
neither *was there* labour the band being routed) and speaks these *things* over *him*

inimico pectore: Tyrrhene putâsti te agitare feras
with unfriendly breast: O Tuscan did you suppose yourself to hunt wild

sylvis? Dies advenit qui redarguerit vestra verba
beasts in the woods? The day has arrived which shall disprove your words

muliebribus armis: tamen referes hoc nomen haud
by female arms: yet you shall bear back this name not

leve manibus ·patrum, cecidisse telo Camillæ.
trifling to the shades to your fathers, that you have fallen by the dart of Camilla.

Protinus Orsilochrum et Buten duo maxima corpora
Next she attacks Orsilochus and Butes the two greatest bodies

Teucrûm: sed figit Buten adversum cuspide inter
of the Trojans: but she pierces Butes opposed with her spear between

loricam que galeam, quà colla sedentis lucent, et
his coat of mail and helmet, where the neck of him sitting shines, and

parma dependet lævo lacerto: fugiens Orsilochum
his shield hangs from his left arm· flying she deceives Orsilochus

que agitata per magnum orbem, interior gyro eludit
and driving through a great circle, within a circle she mocks him

que sequitur sequentem. Tum insurgens altior congeminat
and follows him following her. Then rising higher she redoubles

validam securim que per arma que per ossa · viro
her strong axe both through the arms and through the bones of the man

oranti et precanti multa; vulnus rigat ora calido
praying and entreating much; the wound flows over on his face with warm

cerebro.
brains.

Bellator filius Auni, Apenninicolæ, haud
The warrior son of Aunus, an inhabitant of the Appennines, not

extremus Ligurum, dum fata sinebant fallere, indicit
the last of the Ligurians, while the fates permitted him to deceive, encountered

huic, que territus subito aspectu hæsit; que is ubi cernit
her, and terrified by the sudden sight paused; and he when he perceives

jam posse evadere pugnâ nullo cursu, que ne
now that he can escape from the contest by no flight, and neither

avertere reginam instantem, ingressus versare dolos
turn aside the queen pressing on, attempting to practice fraud

consilio et astu incipit hæc: Quid tam egregium
by design and cunning begins in these words: What is there so distinguished

si femina fidis forti equo? dimitte fugam, crede te
if a woman you confide in a brave horse? lay aside flight, trust yourself

cominus mecum æquo solo, que accinge pedestri
hand to hand with me on the level ground, and prepare for pedestrian

pugnæ: jam nosces cui ventosa gloria ferat fraudem.
contest: soon you shall know to whom windy glory shall bring loss.

Dixit: at illa furens que accensa acri dolore tradit
He said: but she furious and inflamed with fierce resentment delivers

equum comiti, que assistit in paribus armis pedes,
her horse to a companion, and stands in equal arms on foot,

interrita nudo ense que purâ parmâ. At juvenis,
undismayed with the naked sword and spotless shield. But the youth,

ratus vicisse dolo, ipse avolat (haud mora,)
supposing that b. nad conquered by fraud, himself flies (there was no delay,

que fugax aufertur habenis conversis, que fatigat citum
and flying is borne off his reins being turned, and wearies his swift

quadrupedem ferratâ calce. Vane Ligur, que frustra
horse with his iron spur. Vain Ligurian, and fruitlessly

elate superbis animis, lubricus nequicquam tentasti
elated with proud presumption, deceitful in vain you have attempted

patrias artes; nec fraus perferet te incolumem
your native arts; nor shall fraud restore you unharmed

fallaci Auno. Virgo fatur hæc, et ignea
to your dishonest father Aunus. The maid uttered these words and inflamed

pernicibus plantis transit equum cursu, que
with rage on her swift feet she passes his horse in the course, and

frænis prehensis adversa congreditur, que sumit pœnas
his reins being grasped conflicting she meets him, and takes penalties

ab inimico sanguine; quàm facile accipiter, ales sacer
from his hostile blood; as easily a hawk, a bird sacred to Mars

ab alto saxo, consequitur pennis columbam sublimem in
from a high rock, pursues with wings a dove high in

nube, que tenet comprensam, que eviscerat uncis
a cloud, and holds her grasped, and disembowels her with his crooked

pedibus; tum cruor, et vulsæ plumæ labuntur ab æthere.
claws; then blood, and torn feathers fall down from the sky.

At, sator hominum atque Deorum, observans hæc non
But, the sire of men and of Gods, observing these things not

nullis oculis, sedet altus summo Olympo. Genitor
with regardless eyes, sits high on lofty Olympus. The celestial father

suscitat Tarchontem Tyrrhenum in sæva prœlia, et incitat
arouses Tarchon the Tuscan to cruel battle, and provokes

iras, haud mollibus stimulis. Ergo, inter cædes
his anger, not with gentle provocations. Therefore, amidst slaughter

que cedentia agmina, Tarchon fertur equo, que instigat
and retreating troops, Tarchon is borne away by his horse, and urges

alas variis vocibus, vocans quemque nomine; que reficit
the troops with varied words, calling each one by name; and rallies

pulsos in prœlia. O Tyrrheni, nunquam dolituri,
the vanquished to battle. O Tuscans, never to be excited,

O semper inertes, quis metus, quæ tanta ignavia venit
O ever slothful what fear, what so great cowardice has come

animis? Femina agit palantes, atque vertit hæc
to your minds? Does a woman drive you wandering, and turn aside these

agmina? Quo ferrum? ve quid gerimus hæc tela
troops? In what does the sword profit? or why do we wield these weapons

irrita dextris? At non segnes in Venerem, que
useless in our right hands? But you are not slothful in love, and

nocturna bella, aut ubi curva tibia indixit choros Bacchi
nocturnal wars, or when the winding pipe proclaims the choirs of Bacchus,

expectare dapes, et pocula plenæ mensæ. Hic amor:
to await for feasts, and bowls of the full table. This is your love:

noc studium dum secundus aruspex nunciet sacra, ac
this *your* delight, while the favouring augur announces sacred rites, and

pinguis hostia vocet in altos lucos. Effatus hæc, ipse
the fat *?* victim calls you to the deep groves. Speaking these *things*, he

et moriturus concitat equum in medios, et turbidus infert
also about to die spurs on *his* horse into the midst, and disturbed bears

se adversum Venulo; que complectitur hostem
himself against Venulus; and seizes the foe

dexterâ dereptum ab equo, et concitus multâ
with *his* right hand torn from *his* horse, and moved with much

vi aufert ante suum gremium. Clamor tollitur in
violence he bears *him* off before his bosom. A shout is raised to

cœlum; que cuncti Latini convertere oculos. Igneus
heaven; and all the Latins turned *their* eyes. Fiery

Tarchon volat æquore, ferens arma que virum; tum
Tarchon hastens through the plain, bearing arms and the man; then

diffringit ferrum ab summâ hastâ ipsius, et rimatur
he breaks the steel from the top of the spear of him, and searches out

apertas partes, quâ ferat lethale vulnus. Contrà ille
the open parts, where he may strike a deadly wound. On the other hand he

repugnans sustinet dextram a jugulo, et exit vim
contending keeps off *his* right hand from *his* throat, and avoids violence

viribus, que ut cùm fulva aquila volans altè, fert draconem
by violence, and as when a tawny eagle flying high, bears a serpent

raptum, que implicuit pedes, atque hæsit unguibus: at
seized, and entwines *its* feet, and cleaves to *him* with *its* claws: bu

serpens saucius versat sinuosa volumina, que horret
the serpent wounded turns *its* winding folds, and appears terrible

squamis arrectis, et sibilat ore, insurgens arduus;
with *his* scales erect, and hisses with *its* mouth, rising high;

illa haud minùs urget luctantem obunco rostro,
she not the less presses *him* struggling with hooked beak,

simul verberat æthera alis: haud aliter
at the same time beats the air with *her* wings: not otherwise

Tarchon ovans portat prædam ex agmine Tiburtum.
Tarchon rejoicing bear off *his* prey from the army of the Tiburtines.

Mæonidæ, secuti exemplum que eventum ducis,
The Tuscans, following the example and success of *their* leader.

incurrunt. Tum Aruns, debitus fatis, prior circuit
rush on. Then Aruns, destined by the fates, first moves round

velocem Camillam, jaculo et multâ arte, et tentat quæ
the swift Camilla, with *his* dart and much skill, and tries what

fortuna sit facillima. Quacunque furens virgo tulit se
opportunity may be the most easy. Whenever the raging maid offered herself

medio agmine, Aruns subit hàc, et tacitus lustrat
in the midst of the troops, Aruns advances here, and silently surveys

vestigia. Quà illa victrix redit, que reportat pedem
her footsteps. Wherever she victorious returns, and withdraws *her* foo

ex hoste juvenis furtim detorquet celeres habenas hàc.
from the foe the youth by stealth turns *his* swift reins there.

Pererrat hos aditus, que jam hos aditus, que
He passes over these approaches, and now those approaches, and

omnem circuitum undique, et improbus quatit certam
the whole circuit on each side, and devoted to evil he shakes *his* sure

hastam. Fortè Chloreus, sacer Cybelæ, que olim
spear. By chance Chloreus, sacred to Cybele, and formerly

sacerdos, insignis fulgebat longè in Phrygiis armis, que
her priest, distinguished shone from afar in Trojan arms, and

agitabat spumantem equum; quem pellis conserta ahenis
urged on *his* foaming horse; which a skin braced together with brazen

squamis auro, plumam tegebat. Ipse, clarus peregrinâ
scales *and* gold, *as* a plume covered. He, bright in foreign

ferrugine et ostro, torquebat Gortynia spicula Lycio
blue and purple, hurled *his* Gortynian arrows from *his* Lycian

cornu. Aureus arcus sonat ex humeris, et aurea
bow. A golden bow sounds from *his* shoulders, and a golden

cassida vati; tum collegerat que croceam chlamydem
helmet *was* to the priest; then he had collected both *his* yellow cloak

que carbaseos sinus crepantes, in nodum, fulvo auro,
and lawn robes rustling, in a knot, with yellow gold,

pictus acu tunicas et barbara tegmina crurum.
being embroidered with a needle *as to his* tunic and the foreign coverings of *his* legs.

Virgo, sive ut præfigeret Troïa arma templis, sive
The maid, whether that she might hang up Trojan arms in the temple, or

ut venatrix ferret se in captivo auro, cæca
that as a huntress she might bear herself in captive gold, blind

sequebatur unum ex omni certamine pugnæ; que incauta
she pursued *him* alone from all the contest of the fight; and fearlessly

ardebat per totum agmen femineo amore prædæ et
she raged through the whole army with a female's love of plunder and

spoliorum; cum tandem Aruns, tempore capto, conjicit
spoils; when at length Aruns, the opportunity being taken hurled

telum ex insidiis, et precatur Superos sic voce: Summe
his dart from ambush, and prays the Gods above thus with *his* voice: Greatest

Deûm, Apollo, custos sancti Soractis, quem primi colimus,
of Gods, Apollo, keeper of holy Soracte, whom first we worship,

cui pineus ardor pascitur acervo; et cultores,
whose pine fire is fed *from our* heap: and we worshippers,

freti pietate, premimus vestigia multa pruna per
trusting to *our* piety, press *our* footsteps on many coals through

medium ignem; omnipotens pater, da hoc dedecus aboleri
the midst of fire; O almighty father, grant this disgrace to be effaced

nostris armis. Non peto exuvias ve tropæum, aut ulla spolia
from our arms. I do not ask for spoils or a trophy, or any spoils

pulsæ virginis: cætera facta ferent laudem mihi.
of the vanquished maid: let other deeds award praise to me.

Dum hæc dira pestis pulsa cadat meo vulnere,
Provided that this direful plague struck down may fall by my wound,

inglorius remeabo patriam urbem. Phœbus audit et
without honour I will return to my native city. Apollo heard him and

dedit partem voti succedere mente; dispersit partem
granted a part of his wish to succeed in his mind; he scattered a part

in volucres auras. Annuit oranti, ut sterneret
in the swift air. He consented to him praying, that he might overthrow

Camillam turbatam subitâ morte; non dedit, ut
Camilla overwhelmed by sudden death; he did not grant, that his

alta patria viderit reducem, que procellæ vertêre vocem
exalted country should see him restored, and the storms turned his prayer

in notos. Ergo ut hasta missa manu, dedit
to the south winds. Therefore as his spear sent from his hand, caused

sonitum per auras, acies convertêre animos, que
a sound through the air, the armies turned their minds, and

cuncti Volsci tulere oculos ad reginam. Ipsa nihil
all the Volscians directed their eyes to the queen. She was nothing

memor nec auræ nec sonitus, aut teli venientis ab
mindful neither of the air nor of the sound, or of the dart coming from

æthere, donec hasta, perlata sub exsertam papillam,
the sky, until the spear, driven under her naked breast,

hæsit, atque altê bibit virgineum cruorem; trepidæ
remained, and deeply drunk her virgin blood; her trembling

comites concurrunt, que suscipiunt dominam ruentem.
companions rush together, and receive their mistress falling.

Aruns exterritus fugit ante omnes, lætitiâ que metu
Aruns frightened flies before all, with joy and fear

misto; nec jam ampliùs audet credere hastæ, nec
commingled; nor now any more dared he to trust to his spear, nor

occurrere armis virginis. Ac velut ille lupus, priusquam
to encounter the arms of the maid. And as a wolf, before

inimica tela sequantur, continuò, avius abdidit sese in
hostile darts pursued him, forthwith, secretly concealed himself in

altos montes, pastore, ve magno juvenco occiso
the lofty mountains, the shepherd, or great bullock being slain,

conscius audacis facti; que remulcens pavitantem caudam,
conscious of the daring deed; and clinging his cowardly tail,

subjecit utero, que petivit sylvas: haud secus
placed it under his belly, and sought the woods: not otherwise

turbidus Aruns abstulit se ex oculis, que contentus
frightened Aruns withdrew himself from their eyes, and contented

fugâ immiscuit se mediis armis. Illa moriens
with flight intermingled himself in the midst of arms. She dying

trahit telum manu; sed ferreus mucro stat ad costas
draws out the dart with her hand; but its iron point stands in the ribs

,nter ossa alto vulnere. Labitur exsanguis, lumina
amidst the bones in a deep wound. She falls bloodless; her eyes

laburitur frigida letho; color quondam purpureus reliquit
fail cold in death; her colour formerly blooming has left

ora. Tum exspirans sic alloquitur Accam, unam ex
her face. Then dying thus she addresses Acca, one of

æqualibus, quæ sola fida Camillæ ante alias, quicum
her equals, who alone faithful to Camilla before others, with whom

partiri curas; atque ita fatur hæc: Soror Acca,
she divided her cares; and thus she speaks these things: O sister Acca,

potui hactenus, nunc acerbum vulnus conficit,
I have been able to act thus far, now a cruel wound destroys me.

et omnia circum nigrescunt tenebris. Effuge, et perfer
and all things around blacken with darkness. Fly, and bear

hæc novissima mandata Turno; succedat pugnæ,
these my last commands to Turnus; let him advance to the battle,

que arceat Trojanos urbe; que jam vale. Simul,
and drive off the Trojans from the city; and now farewell. At once

his dictis, linquebat habenas, fluens ad terram
with these words, she relinquishes the reins, falling to the earth

non sponte; tum frigida paulatim exsolvit se
not with her own accord; then cold by degrees she relaxed herself

toto corpore, que posuit lenta colla, et caput
in her whole body, and inclined her slender neck, and head

captum letho, relinquens arma: que vita indignata fugit
overcome by death, leaving her arms: and life not enduring fled

cum gemitu sub umbras. Tum verò immensus clamor
with a groan under the shades. Then indeed a great cry

surgens ferit aurea sidera. Camillâ dejectâ, pugna
arising strikes the golden stars. Camilla overthrown, the contest

crudescit. Densi incurrunt, simul omnis copia Teucrûm;
grows bloody. Thick they rush on, together all the force of the Trojans;

que duces Tyrrhenûm, que alæ Evandri Arcadis. At
and leaders of the Tuscans, and the troops of Evander the Arcadian. But

Opis, custos Triviæ, jamdudum sedet alta in summis
Opis, a keeper of Diana, for a long time sits high on the loftiest

montibus, que interrita spectat pugnas. Ut procul
mountains, and undismayed beholds the battles. As afar off

prospexit Camillam, multatam tristi morte, in medio
she beheld Camilla, overthrown by sad death, in the midst

clamore juvenum furentum, que ingemuit, que dedit has
of the shout of the youth raging, she both groaned, and uttered these

voces imo pectore: heu! virgo, luisti nimium,
words from her inmost breast: alas! O maid, you have suffered too,

nimium crudele supplicium, conata lacessere Teucros
too cruel punishment, attempting to provoke the Trojans

bello! nec profuit tibi desertæ in dumis coluisse
to the war! nor had it profited you deserted in the wilds to have honoured

Dianam, aut gessisse nostras pharetras humero: tamen
Diana,   or to have wielded   our   quivers on *your* shoulder.   yet

tua regina non relinquet te indecorem jam in extremâ
your queen shall not   leave   you dishonoured   now   in   extreme

morte; neque hoc lethum erit sine nomine per
death;   nor   shall this   death   be   without   a name   through

gentes, aut patieris famam inultæ: nam
the nations, or   shall you endure the reputation of being unrevenged: for

quicunque violavit tuum corpus vulnere luet meritâ
whosoever   shall violate your   body by a wound shall expiate *it* by deserved

morte.
death.

Sub alto monte fuit ingens bustum antiqui Laurentis
Under a high mountain was a great   tomb of the ancient Laurentian

regis Dercenni ex terreno aggere, que tectum opacâ
king   Dercennus   from an earthen mound,   and   covered by a gloomy

ilice. Hìc primùm pulcherrima Dea sistit se rapido
holm.   Here   first   the most beautiful Goddess   placed herself by a rapid

nisu, et speculatur Aruntem ab alto tumulo. Ut vidit
effort, and   watches   Aruns   from the high tomb.   As she beheld *him*

fulgentem armis ac tumentem vana, inquit:
shining.   in arms   and   swelling   with vain *importance*, she said:

Cur abis diversus? dirige gressum huc, veni huc
Why do you go a different way? direct   your step   hither,   come   hither

periture, ut capias præmia digna Camillæ. Ne tu
about to die, that you may take rewards   due   to Camilla. Whether will you

etiam moriere telis Dianæ! Dixit, et Threissa
also   die   by the darts of Diana! She said, and   the Thracian *maid*

depromsit volucrem sagittam auratâ pharetrâ, que infensa
drew out   a swift   arrow from *her* gilded quiver,   and   hostile

tetendit cornu, et duxit longè, donec capita curvata
stretch'd *her* bow,   and   drew *it* far out, until   the points   curved

coirent inter se, et jam tangeret æquis manibus, lævâ
met   together, and now she touched *them* with equal   hands, with the left

aciem ferri, dexterâ que nervo papillam. Extemplo
the point of the dart, with *her* right   and the string   *her* breast.   Forthwith

Aruns audiit stridorem teli, que sonantes auras unâ,
Aruns   heard   the hissing of the dart, and the sounding air   together,

que ferrum hæsit in corpore. Socii obliti
and   the iron weapon   stuck in   *his* body.   *His* companions forgetful

linquunt illum expirantem, atque gementem extrema,
left   him   dying,   and   groaning *his* last   *agonies*,

in ignoto pulvere camporum: Opis aufertur pennis ad
in the unknown dust   of the plains;   Opis   is borne   on wings and

ætherium Olympum. Levis ala Camillæ prima fugit,
he etherial   heaven.   The light   wing of Camilla   first   flies,

dominâ amissâ; Rutuli turbati fugiunt; acer
their mistress   being lost; The Rutulians disturbed   fly;   bold

Atinas fugit; que disjecti duces, que manîpli desolati
Atinas flies; and the scattered leaders, and the companies deserted

petunt tuta, et aversi tendunt equis ad mœnia.
seek safe *quarters*, and turning they advance on horses to the ramparts

Nec quisquam valet sustentare telis, aut sistere contra
Nor *is* any one able to sustain with darts, or to stand against

Teucros instantes, que ferentes lethum; sed · referunt
the Trojans pressing on, and causing death; but they bear back

laxos arcus languentibus humeris, que ungula
their relaxed bows on *their* fainting shoulders, and the hoof

quadrupedum quatit putrem campum cursu. Pulvis
of the horses shakes the mouldering plain in *their* course. The dust

turbidus, atrâ caligine volvitur ad muros; et matres,
disturbed, in black darkness is roll'd to the walls; and the mothers,

percussæ pectora tollunt, è speculis, femineum
striking *their* breasts raise, from the watch towers a female

clamorem ad sidera cœli. Qui primi irrupere patentes
shout to the stars of heaven. Who first break the opening

portas cursu, inimica turba premit hos misto
gates in *their* course, an unfriendly throng presses them in a mingled

agmine super: nec effugiunt miseram mortem, sed
band upon *them:* nor do they escape wretched death, but

confixi in limine ipso, in patriis mœnibus, atque
pierced in the threshold itself, within *their* native walls, and

inter tuta domorum, expirant animas. Pars
amidst the safe *shelter* of *their* houses, they breathe out *their* souls. A part

claudere portas; audent nec aperire viam sociis,
close the gates; they dare neither to open a way to *their* friends.

nec accipere orantes mœnibus; que miserrima
nor to receive *them* praying *for entrance* to the walls; and a most wretched

cædes oritur defendentûm aditus armis, que ruentiûm
slaughter arises of those defending the entrances with arms, and rushing

in arma. Exclusi pars volvitur præcipites in
on arms. *Those* shut out a part are rolled headlong into

fossas, ruinâ urgente, ante oculos que ora
the ditches, destruction pressing *them*, before the eyes and . faces of *their*

parentum lacrymantum; pars cæca et concita frænis
parents weeping; a part blinded and excited *their* reins

immissis arietat in portas et postes duros
being let oose forcibly beat against the gates and posts made fast

obice. Summo certamine, ut matres ipsæ vidêre
by bolts. In the greatest contest, as the mothers themselves saw

Camillam de muris (verus amor patriæ monstrat,)
Camilla from the walls (true love of country directs *them*.)

trepidæ jaciunt tela manu, ac præciptes imitantur
trembling they cast *their* darts with *their* hands, and quick rushing they imitate

ferrum duro robore, stipitibus que obustis sudibus, que
the sword with hard oak, clubs and burnt stakes, and

ardent primæ mori pro mœnibus. Interea
they burn first to die before the walls. In the mean time

sævissimus nuncius implet Turnum in sylvis, et Acca
this most cruel news encounters Turnus in the woods, and Acca

fert ingentem tumultum juveni; acies Volscorum
reports the great disturbance to the youth; that the bands of the Volscians

deletas, Camillam cecidisse, infensos hostes ingruere
were destroyed, Camilla had fallen, the hostile foes attacked

et corripuisse omnia secundo Marte; jam metum
and seized all things by favourable warfare; that now fear

ferri ad mœnia. Ille furens deserit obsessos colles,
was borne to the walls. He raging deserts the besieged hills,

linquit aspera nemora (nam sæva numina Jovis
leaves the rugged groves (for the stern purposes of Jupiter

poscunt sic.) Vix exierat è conspectu,
demand it to be thus.) Hardly had he withdrawn from their view,

que tenebat campum, cùm pater Æneas, ingressus
and attained the plain, when father Æneas, entering

apertos saltus, que exsuperat jugum, que evadit opacâ
the open lawns, both passes over the height, and escapes from the dark

sylvâ. Sic ambo feruntur rapidi que toto agmine,
wood. Thus both are borne on swift and with their whole army

ad muros; nec absunt longis passibus inter se.
to the walls; nor are they separated by long paces between them.

Ac simul Æneas prospexit longè campos fumantes
As soon as Æneas beheld from afar the plains smoking

pulvere, que vidit Laurentia agmina; et Turnus agnovit
with dust, and saw the Laurentian bands; also Turnus knew

sævum Ænean in armis, que audivit adventum pedum,
the stern Æneas in arms, and heard the coming of feet,

que flatus equorum. Continuò ineant pugnas,
and the breathing of the horses. Immediately they would enter on battles,

et tentent prœlia, ni jam roseus Phœbus tingat
and attempt the contest unless now the rosy sun should dip

fessos equos Ibero gurgite, que reducat noctem die
his wearied horses in the Iberian sea, and restore night the day

labente. Considunt castris ante urbem, et
withdrawing. They sit down in their camps before the city, and

vallant mœnia.
fortify the ramparts.

ÆNEID.

BOOK TWELFTH.

Ut Turnus videt Latinos infractos adverso Marte
As Turnus sees that the Latins broken down by hostile war

defecisse: sua promissa nunc reposci, se
had become faint: that his promises now were demanded, himself

signari oculis; ultrò, implacabilis, ardet, que attollit
marked out by the eyes of men; keenly, resentful he burns, and arouses

animos. Qualis ille leo in arvis Pœnorum saucius
his courage. As a lion in the fields of the Carthaginians wounded

pectus gravi vulnere venantum, tum demum movet
in the breast by a severe wound of the hunters, then at last he exerts

arma, que gaudet, excutiens comantes toros cervice,
his valour, and rejoices, shaking the hairy muscles on his neck,

que impavidus frangit fixum telum latronis, et fremit
and fearless he breaks the piercing dart of the hunter, and rages

cruento ore; haud secus violentia gliscit accenso
with bloody mouth; not otherwise violence urges on the inflamed

Turno. Tum sic affatur regem, atque ita turbidus
Turnus. Then thus he addresses the king, and thus disturbed

infit: Nulla mora in Turno; est nihil quod ignavi
he begins: No delay is in Turnus; there is nothing for which the cowardly

Æneadæ retractent dicta; nec recusent quæ pepigere;
Trojans shall revoke their words; nor refuse what they have promised;

Congredior; pater, fer sacra, et concipe fœdus.
I join battle; O father, command the sacred rites, and devise a treaty.

Aut mittam Dardanium, desertorem Asiæ, sub Tartara
Either I will send the Trojan, the fugitive of Asia, under Tartarus

hac dexterâ, (Latini sedeant que spectent) et solus
with this right hand, (the Latins shall set by and behold it) and alone

refellam commune crimen ferro; aut habeat
I will disprove the common reproach with the sword; or he shall hold us

victos, Lavinia conjux cedat. Latinus respondit olli,
vanquished, Lavinia his wife shall yield. Latinus replied to him,

sedato corde: O juvenis, præstans animi, quantum ipse
with composed heart: O youth, excelling in mind, as much as you

exsuperas feroci virtute, tanto impensius est æquum
abound in fierce courage, so much more solicitously is it right

me consulere atque metuentem expendere omnes
for me to provide for you and fearing to weigh all

casus.   Sunt tibi   regna   patris Daüni,
the chances *of the* contest. *There* are to you the kingdoms of *your* father Daunus.

sunt multa oppida   capta   manu; nec non   est que
there are many   towns   captured by *your* hand; likewise *there* is both

aurum que animus Latino.   Sunt aliæ innuptæ
gold   and   courage   with Latinus. *There* are other   unmarried *maids*

Latio,   et Laurentibis agris;   nec   indecores
in Latium,   and   the Laurentine   territories;   nor   *are they* dishonourable

genus. Sine me aperire hæc   haud mollia   fatu,
in *their* race. Permit   me to lay open these *things* not   gentle to be uttered

dolis sublatis,   simul   hauri hæc   animo. Erat
deceit being laid aside, at the same time receive these *things* in *your* mind. It was

fas   me sociare   natam nulli   veterum procorum;
lawful for me   to unite *my* daughter to no one of *her* former   lovers,

que omnes que Divi que homines canebant id.   Victus
and   all   both Gods and   men   foretold this.   Subdued

amore tui,   victus   cognatâ   sanguine, et lacrymis
by love of thee,   overcome   by *our* related   blood,   and   the tears

mœstæ conjugis, rupi omnia vincula; eripui
of *my* mourning wife,   I broke all   bonds;   I snatched *my daughter*

promissam   genero;   sumpsi impia   arma.   Turne,
promised   from my son-in-law;   I took up impious   arms.   O Turnus,

vides qui   casus,   quæ bella sequantur me   ex   illo;
you see what misfortunes, what wars   pursue   me   from that *time*;

quantos labores   primus patiare.   Victi   bis magnâ,
how great exertions *you* especially undergo.   Conquered twice in a great

pugnâ,   vix   tuemur   Italas   spes urbe; Tyberina
battle,   scarcely do we guard our Italian   hopes   in the city;   Tyber's

fluenta   adhuc recalent nostro sanguine, que ingentes
flowing *waters* even now *are* warm   with *our*   blood,   and   the great

campi albent   ossibus.   Quò   referor   toties,   quæ
plains are white with *our* bones.   Where am I borne back so often,   what

insania mutat mentem? Si sum paratus accire
madness   changes *my* mind?   If   I am   prepared to invite *the Trojans*

socios, Turno   extincto,   cur potiùs   non tollo certamina,
as *my* allies, Turnus being destroyed, why rather   do I not banish   contests,

incolumi?   Quid consanguinei   Rutuli,   quid
he being unharmed?   What will *our* relations   the Rutulians *say*, what will

cætera Italia dicet, si prodiderim te ad mortem,   (fors
the rest of Italy say,   if I should betray thee to   death,   (may fortune

refutet dicta) petentem   natam et nostra   connubia?
refute *my* words)   seeking   *my* daughter and our   nuptial alliance?

Respice   varias   res   bello; miserere   longævi
Look back   on the varied   concerns in war;   pity   *your* aged

parentis, quem nunc mæstum patria Ardea dividit
parent,   whom even now   sad   *his* native   Ardea   separates

longè.   Violentia Turni haudquaquam flectitur   dictis:
far from *you*. The violence of Turnus by no means   is controlled by *these* words.

exsuperat magis, que ægrescit medendo. Ut primùm
he strives more, and sickens by being cured. As first

potuit fari, sic institit ore: Optime,
he was able to speak, thus he pursues *the subject* with *his* mouth: Most excellent

precor pro me deponas hanc curam, quam
king, I pray you, for me lay aside this anxiety, which

geris pro me, que sinas me pacisci lethum pro
you experience on account of me, and suffer me to bargain death for

laude. Et nos, pater, spargimus tela, que ferrum haud
praise. And we, O father, wield darts, and the sword not

debile dexterâ; et sanguis sequitur de nostro
with a powerless right hand; and blood follows from our

vulnere. Dea mater erit longè illi, quæ tegat
wound. *His* Goddess mother will be far from him, who may conceal

fugacem femineâ nube, et occulat sese vanis umbris.
her flying *son* with a female cloud, and hide herself in vain shades.

At regina, conterrita novâ sorte pugnæ, flebat, et
But the queen, alarmed by the new lot of battle, wept, and

moritura, tenebat ardentem generum: Turne, te
about to die, held *her* daring son-in-law: O Turnus, *I entreat* thee

per has lacrymas, per Amatæ, si quis honos
by these tears, by *your love* of Amata, if any respect *for her*

tangit animum: tu nunc una spes senectæ, tu
touches *your* mind: you now the only hope of *my* old age, you

requies miseræ; decus que imperium Latini penes
the repose of *my* wretched *self*; the glory and power of Latinus *is* with

te; omnis domus inclinata recumbit in te: oro unum,
thee; all *our* house inclining rests on thee: I pray one *thing*.

desiste committere manum Teucris. Quicunque casus
forbear to engage *your* hand with the Trojans. Whatsoever misfortunes

manent te, Turne, isto certamine, manent et me,
remain to thee, O Turnus, in this contest, remain likewise with me,

simul, relinquam hæc invisa lumina, nec captiva
at the same time I will leave this hated light, nor a captive

videbo Æneam generum. Lavinia, accepit vocem
will I see Æneas *my* son-in-law. Lavinia, receives the address

matris, perfusa lacrymis, flagrantes genas; cui plurimus
of *her* mother, bathed with tears, as to *her* burning cheeks; whose profuse

rubor subjecit ignem, et cucurrit per calefacta
blushing supplied the glow, and ran through *her* heated

ora. Veluti si quis violaverit Indum ebur sanguineo
countenance. As if any one had stained Indian ivory with bloody

ostro; vel ubi alba lilia, mixta multâ rosâ rubent;
purple; or when white lilies, intermingled with many roses blush:

virgo dabat tales colores ore. Amor turbat illum, que
the maid gave such colours from *her* face. Love distracts him, and

figit vultus in virgine. Ardet magis in arma, que
he fastens *his* looks on the maid. He burns more for arms, and

affatur Amatam paucis. O mater, quæso ne
addresses Amata with a few *words*. O mother, I pray *you*, do not

prosequere me lacrymis, neve tanto omine, euntem in
pursue me with tears, nor so great an omen, going into

certamina duri Martis: enim mora mortis neque libera
contests of hard war: for the putting off of death *is* not allowed

Turno. Idmon, nuncius, refer hæc mea dicta Phrygio
to Turnus. Idmon, my *trusty* messenger, bear back these my words to the Trojan

tyranno, haud placitura: cùm primùm crastina
tyrant not about to please *him*: when first to-morrow's

Aurora, invecta puniceis rotis, rubebit cœlo, non
dawn, borne up on crimson wheels, shall redden in the sky, let him not

agat Teucros in Rutulos; arma Teucrûm et Rutulûm
lead out the Trojans against the Rutulians; the arms of the Trojans and Rutulians

quiescant; bellum dirimatur nostro sanguine; conjux
shall rest; the war shall be determined by our blood; the bride

Lavinia quæratur illo campo. Ubi dedit hæc dicta,
Lavinia shall be sought on that plain. When he had uttered these words,

que rapidus recessit in tecta, poscit equos, que
and quick had withdrawn to the palace, *he* demands *his* horses, and

gaudet, tuens frementes ante ora; quos Orithyia ipsa
rejoices, seeing *them* neighing before *his* face; which Orithyia herself

dedit decus Pilumno; qui anteirent nives candore,
gave an honour to Pilumnus; which surpassed the snows in whiteness,

auras cursibus. Properi aurigæ circumstant, que
the winds in the race. The hasty charioteers stand around, and

lacessunt pectora plausa cavis manibus, et pectunt
excite *their* breasts clapped with hollow hands, and comb

comantia colla. Dehinc ipse circumdat loricam
their flowing manes. Then he wraps *his* coat of mail

humeris, squalentem auro que albo orichalco;
about *his* shoulders, scaled with gold and white mountain brass;

simul aptat habendo que ensem que clypeum, et
at the same time he fits for wearing both *his* sword and shield, and

cornua rubræ cristæ; ensem, quem ignipotens Deus
the points of *his* blushing crest; the sword, which the fire-powerful God

ipse fecerat Dauno parenti et tinxerat candentem
himself had made for Daunus *his* parent and dipped glowing hot

Styiâ undâ.
in the Stygian wave.

Exin corripit validam hastam vi, quæ astabat in
Then he seized *his* strong spear with violence, which stood in

mediis ædibus adnixa ingenti columnæ, spolium
the midst of the palace leaning on a *great* column, the spoil

Aurunci Actoris, que quassat trementem, vociferans:
of Auruncian Actor, and shook *t* trembling, crying out:

Nunc, ô hasta, nunquam frustrata meos vocatus, nunc
Now, O spear, never disappointing my calls, now

tempus adest: maximus Actor   te,   nunc dextra
the time   is present: the most heroic Actor   *bore* thee,   now the right hand

Turni gerit te: da   sternere corpus, que lacerare
of Turnus bears thee: grant *me* to overthrow *his* body,   and   to tear

  loricam   semiviri Phrygis, revulsam validâ manu,
the coat of mail of the effeminate Trojan,   stripped by *my* powerful band,

et fœdare crines in pulvere, vibratos calido ferro, que
and defile *his* hair in the dust,   curled with a hot iron, and

madentes myrrhâ.   Agitur his furiis, que scintillæ
flowing   with myrrh. He is agitated by these furies, and   sparks

absistunt ab   toto   ore   ardentis;   ignis micat
fly off   from the whole countenance of him glowing; fire glitters

 acribus oculis: veluti cùm taurus ciet terrificos mugitus
in *his* fierce eyes: as when a bull excites dreadful bellowings

in prima prœlia, atque tentat irasci in cornua,
in the first contests,   and attempts to vent *his* rage on *his* horns,

 obnixus trunco arboris; que lacessit ventos ictibus, et
pushing against the trunk of a tree; and strikes the winds with blows, and

proludit ad pugnam arenâ sparsâ.   Nec minus
preludes to the fight the sand being scattered.   Nevertheless

 interea   Æneas, sævus in maternis armis, acuit
in the mean time Æneas, stern in *his* maternal arms, provokes

Martem, et suscitat se irâ, gaudens   bellum
war,   and arouses himself with anger, rejoicing *that* the war

componi fœdere oblato. Tum solatur socios,
was to be determined by the treaty offered. Then he consoles *his* companions,

que metum mœsti Iuli, docens fata; que jubet
and the fear of the mournful Iulus, teaching *them* the fates; and commands

viros referre certa responsa regi Latino, et
the men to take back *his* determined replies to king Latinus, and

dicere leges   pacis. Vix postera dies orta
to pronounce the conditions of peace. Scarcely the next day arising

spargebat summos montes lumine, cùm primùm equi
had sprinkled the highest mountains with light, when first the horses

 solis tollunt se   alto gurgite,   que efflant
of the sun raise themselves from the deep gulf *of the sea,* and breathe forth

lucem elatis naribus. Rutuli que Teucri viri
light from *their* elevated nostrils. The Rutulian and Trojan men

 dimensi campum ad certamen parabant; sub mœnibus
having measured the plain for the battle made it ready; under the walls

magnæ urbis, que in medio   focos et gramineas
of the great city, and in the midst *they raised* hearths and grassy

aras communibus Dîs: alii ferebant que fontem que ignem
altars to *their* common Gods: others brought both water and fire

velati lino et vincti   tempora verbenâ.   Legio
veiled with linen and bound *as to their* temples with vervain. The legion

Ausonidum procedit, que pilata agmina fundunt se
of Ausonians proceeds, and the dart bearing troops pour themselves

plenis portis: hinc omnis Troïus, que Tyrrhenus
from the full gates: on this side all the Trojan, and Tuscan

exercitus ruit variis armis, haud secus instructi
army rush on in varied arms, not otherwise furnished

ferro, quàm si aspera pugna Martis vocet. Nec non
with the sword, than if the cruel battle of Mars should call *them*. Also

mediis millibus ductores ipsi volitant decori auro,
in the midst of thousands the leaders themselves fly adorned in gold,

que ostro; et Mnestheus, genus Assaraci, et fortis
and purple; and Mnestheus, the offspring of Assaracus, and bold

Asylas, et Messapus, domitor equorum, Neptunia proles.
Asylas, and Messapus, the tamer of horses, Neptune's progeny.

Utque quisque recessit in sua spatia signo dato,
And as each one withdrew into his own space a signal being given,

defigunt hastas tellure, et reclinant scuta. Tum
they plant *their* spears in the ground, and lean upon *their* shields. Then

matres effusæ studio, et inermum vulgus, que
the mothers pouring out with zeal, and the unarmed populace, and

invalidi senes, obsedêre turres et tecta domorum: alii
powerless old men, besiege the towers and roofs of the houses: others

astant sublimibus portis. At Juno prospiciens ex summo
stand by the lofty gates. But Juno looking from the high

tumulo, qui nunc habetur Albanus (tunc erat neque
hill, which now is called Albanus (then *there* was neither

nomen, honos, aut gloria monti,) spectabat campum,
name, honour, or glory to the mountain,) beheld the plain,

et ambas acies Laurentûm que Troûm, que urbem
and both the armies of the Laurentines and Trojans, and the city

Latini. Extemplo sic affata est sororem Turni, Diva
of Latinus. Forthwith thus she addressed the sister of Turnus, a Goddess

Deam, quæ presidet stagnis, que sonoris fluminibus:
to a Goddess, who presides over pools, and sounding streams;

Jupiter, altus rex ætheris sacravit hunc honorem illi
Jupiter, the high king of the sky consecrated this honour to her

pro virginitate ereptâ. Nymphâ decus fluviorum,
for *her* virginity ravished. O Nymph, ornament of rivers,

gratissima nostro animo, scis, ut prætulerim te unam
most grateful to my mind, you know that I had preferred thee alone

cunctis, quæcunque Latinæ ascendêre ingratum cubile
to all, whatever Latin maids ascended the ungrateful bed of

magnanimi Jovis, que libens locârim in parte
high-minded Jupiter, and willingly I have placed *thee* in a part

cœli: Juturna, disce tuum dolorem ne incuses me.
of heaven: O Juturna, learn your grief lest you should accuse me.

Quâ fortuna visa est pati, que Parcæ sinebant
Wherever fortune appeared to allow, and the destinies permitted

rès cedere Latio, texi Turnum, et tua
her concerns to succeed to Latium, I have guarded Turnus and your

mœnia: nunc video juvenem concurrere imparibus fatis;
city: now   I see   the youth   encounter   with unequal fates,

que dies Parcarum et inimica vis propinquat. Non possum
and the day of the Destinies and hostile power approaches.   I   cannot

aspicere hanc pugnam   oculis, non fœdera.   Si   tu
behold   this   battle   with my eyes, nor this treaty.   If   thou

audes quid præsentius pro germano, perge: decet:
darest any thing more favourable for thy brother, proceed: it will become you:

forsan meliora sequentur   miseros.   Vix   ea
perhaps better things will follow   your unhappy friends. Scarcely these things

        cùm Juturna profudit lacrymas   oculis, terque
were said, when Juturna   shed   tears   from her eyes, and thrice

que quater percussit honestum pectus manu. Saturnia
and four times struck   her fair   breast with her hand. Saturnian

Juno ait, hoc non tempus lacrymis; accelera et eripe
Juno says, this is not a time for tears; hasten   and snatch

fratrem   morti,   si   quis modus: aut tu cie
your brother from death, if there is any way: or do you excite

bella, que excute conceptum fœdus. Ego auctor
wars,   and break   the contracted treaty. I am   authority

audendi. Sic exhortata reliquit incertam, et turbatam
for your daring. Thus having advised she left her in doubt,   and   disturbed

tristi vulnere mentis.   Interea   reges,   Latinus
by sad remorse of mind. In the mean time the kings proceed,   Latinus

ingenti mole vehitur quadrijugo curru, circum   cui
with a great crowd is borne in his four horse   chariot,   around   whose

fulgentia tempora bis sex aurati radii cingunt, specimen
shining   temples twice six golden rays encircle,   an emblem

Solis   avi; Turnus it in bigis   albis
of the sun his ancestor; Turnus goes out in a chariot with two white horses,

crispans bina hastilia lato ferro   manu. Hinc pater
brandishing two spears with broad steel in his hand. On this side father

Æneas, origo Romanæ stripis, flagrans   siderec
Æneas,   the founder of the Roman race.   burning   with his starry

clypeo et cœlestibus armis, et juxtà Ascanius, altera spes
shield   and heavenly   arms, and near by Ascanius, the other hope

magnæ Romæ, procedunt castris: que sacerdos in purâ
of great Rome,   go out   from the camps: and the Priest in a spotless

veste attulit fœtum setigeræ suis, que   bidentem
dress brought out the offspring of a bristly swine, and   a two year old sheep

intonsam que admovit pecus flagrantibus aris. Illi,
unshorn   and removed   the flock to the burning altars. They,

conversi lumina ad surgentem solem, dant salsas fruges
turning   their eyes   to the rising   sun,   offer salted   cakes

        manibus, et notant summa tempora   pecudum
with their hands,   and mark   the high   temples   of the victims

ferro, que libant altaria   pateris.   Tum pius
with the sword, and pour out on the altars from goblets of wine. Then pious

Æneas, ense stricto, precatur sic: Nunc Sol, et hæc
Æneas, with sword drawn, prays thus: Now O sun, and this

terra, propter quam potui perferre tantos labores,
land, for which I have been able to endure so great labours,

esto testis mihi precanti; et omnipotens pater, et tu
be witness to me praying, and O Almighty father, and thou

Saturnia Juno, O Diva, jam jam melior, precor; que
Saturnian Juno, O Goddess, now now more kind, I pray; and

tu, inclyte Mavors, qui pater, torques cuncta bella sub
thou, renowned Mars, who as our father, directest all wars under

tuo numine: voco que fontes que fluvios, que quæ
thy divinity: I invoke you also ye fountains and ye streams, and whatever

religio alti ætheris, et quæ numina sunt cæruleo
is the religion of the lofty sky, and whatever duties are in the azure

ponto. Si fors victoria cesserit Ausonio Turno,
deep. If by chance victory should fall to Ausonian Turnus,

convenit victos discedere ad urbem Evandri.
it is agreed that the conquered shall depart to the city of Evander.

Iülus cedet agris: nec pòst Æneadæ rebelles
Iulus shall leave these lands: nor hereafter shall the Trojans rebellious

referent ulla arma, ve lacessent hæc regna ferro.
again bear any arms, or disturb these kingdoms with the sword.

Sin victoria annuerit Martem nobis nostrum, (ut
But if victory should yield war to us in our favour, (as

potiùs reor, et potiùs Dî firment numine,) ego
rather I suppose, and rather may the Gods confirm by their authority,) I

non jubebo, nec Italos parere Teucrìs, nec peto
will not command, neither the Italians to obey the Trojans, nor do I ask

regna mihi: ambæ gentes invictæ mittant se
kingdoms for myself: both nations unconquered shall yield themselves

paribus legibus in æterna fœdera. Dabo sacra
to equal laws in eternal leagues. I will grant their sacred observances

que Deos: socer Latinus habeto arma, socer
and Gods: let my father-in-law Latinus possess his arms, my father-in-law

solenne imperium. Teucri constituent mœnia mihi,
his accustomed authority. The Trojans shall build a city for me,

que Lavinia dabit nomen urbi. Æneas prior sic:
and Lavinia shall give a name to the city. Æneas first thus spoke:

deinde Latinus sic sequitur, suspiciens cœlum que
afterwards Latinus thus follows, looking up to heaven and

tendit dextram ad sidera: Ænea, juro hæc eadem
stretches his right hand to the stars: O Æneas, I swear by these same

terram, mare, sidera, duplex genus Latonæ,
authorities the earth, the sea, the stars, the double offspring of Latona,

que bifrontem Janum, que infernam vim Deûm,
and doublefaced Janus, and the infernal power of the Gods below,

et sacraria diri Ditis.
and the courts of direful Pluto.

Genitor, qui sancit fœdera fulmine, audiat
May the father, who sanctifies *our* treaties by *his* thunder, hear

hæc. Tango aras, que testor medios ignes
these *things*. I touch the altars, and call to witness the intermediate . fires

et numina; nulla dies rumpet hanc pacem, nec fœdera
and deities; no day shall break this peace, nor treaties

Italis, quocunque res cadent; nec ulla vis
with the Italians, whatever events may happen; nor any authority

avertet me volentem, non si effundat tellurem
turn me willingly *from them*, not if it should overwhelm the earth

in undas, miscens diluvio, ve solvat cœlum in
in the waves, mingling *them* in a deluge, or break down heaven into

Tartara. Ut hoc sceptrum, (nam fortè gerebat sceptrum
hell. At this sceptre, (for by chance he bore a sceptre

dexterâ) nunquam fundet virgulta nec umbras
in *his* right hand) never shall spread out branches nor shades

levi fronde, cùm semel recisum de imo stirpe in
with *its* light foliage, since once cut up from *its* low stem in

sylvis caret matre, que posuit comas et brachia
the forest it is deprived of *its* mother, and has laid down *its* leaves and branches

ferro; olim arbos, nunc manus artificis inclusit
to the axe; formerly a tree, now the hand of the artist has enclosed *it*

decoro ære, que dedit Latinis patibus gestare.
with beauteous brass, and has given *it* to the Latin fathers to bear.

Talibus dictis firmabant fœdera inter se in medio
With such words they confirmed *their* treaties among themselves in the midst

conspectu proçerum; tum ritè jugulant sacratas pecudes
of the view of the elders; then in order they butcher the consecrated victims

in flammam et eripiunt viscera vivis, que cumulant
in the flame and they take out the entrails from them alive, and . heap

aras oneratis lancibus. At verò ea pugna jamdudum
the altars with loaded dishes. But indeed this contest at last

videri Rutulis impar, et pectora misceri vario
seemed to the Rutulians unequal, and *their* breasts were mingled with various

motu; tum magis ut propiùs cernunt non æquis
emotion; then more as more nearly they see *they are* not of equal

viribus. Turnus adjuvat progressus tacito incessu,
strength. Turnus increases *this impression* proceeding with silent walk,

et suppliciter venerans aram demisso lumine, que
and humbly worshipping the altar with downcast eyes, and

tabentes genæ, et pallor in juvenili corpore. Quem
his consumptive cheeks, and the paleness on *his* youthful body. Which

sermonem simul ac Juturna soror vidit crebrescere, et
discourse as soon as Juturna *his* sister saw to spread around, and

labantia corda vulgi variare; assimulata formam Camerti
the fainting hearts of the crowd to waver; counterfeiting the form of Camertus

(cui erat ingens genus a proavis, que clarum
(to whom was a great race from *his* ancestors, and the distinguished

.iomen paternæ virtutis, et ipse acerrimus armis,)   dat
name   of his father's courage, and he   most bold   in arms,) she throws

sese in medias   acies,   haud nescia rerum,   que serit
.erself into the midst of the bands, not   ignorant of affairs,   and scatters

varios rumores, ac fatur talia.   Non   pudet
various   reports,   and speaks these *words*. Does it not   shame   *you*

O Rutuli, objectare unam animam pro cunctis talibus?
O ye Rutulians, to expose   one   life   for   all   these?

sumus nonne æqui numero an viribus? En! omnes et
are we   not   equal in number or strength? Lo!   all   both

Troës et Arcades sunt hìc, que Etruria infensa Turno
Trojans and Arcadians are here, and Etruria *is* hostile to Turnus

fatalis manus: vix   habemus hostem, si alterni
a fatal   band: scarcely   have we   an enemy, if one by one

congrediamur. Ille quidem famâ succedet ad Superos,
we should engage.   He   indeed   by fame   shall arise to   the Gods

quorum aris devovet se,   que feretur vivus per
to whose altars he devotes himself, and shall be borne living   in

ora;   nos,   patriâ amissâ, cogemur parere
the mouths *of men*; we,   *our* country being lost, are compelled   to obey

superbis dominis, qui nunc   lenti consedimus arvis.
proud   masters, who now at *our* ease   sit down   on the fields.

Jam sententia juvenum est magis atque magis incensa
Now   the opinion of the youth is   more   and   more   inflamed

talibus dictis, que murmur serpit per agmina. Laurentines
by these words. and a murmur creeps through the troops. The Laurentines

ipsi   mutati, que Latini ipsi, qui jam sperabant
themselves are changed, and the Latins themselves, who but now   hoped for

requiem pugnæ   sibi,   que salutem rebus, nunc
rest   from fighting for themselves, and success in *their* affairs,   now

volunt arma, que precantur fœdus infectum: et miserantur
they wish for arms, and   pray   the treaty unmade: and   they pity

iniquam sortem Turni. Juturna adjungit aliud   majus
the unequal lot of Turnus. Juturna adjoins another *thing* greater

his et dat signum alto cœlo, quo non ullum
to these and gives a signal from lofty heaven, *than* which not   any

præsentius turbavit Italas mentes, que fefellit   monstro.
more readily   disturbed Italian minds, and deluded *them* by a prodigy.

Namque fulvus ales Jovis, volans in rubrâ æthrâ
For   the tawny bird of Jupiter, flying in the reddening   sky

agitabat litoreas aves, que sonantem turbam aligeri
drove about the shore frequenting birds, and a noisy crowd of a winged

agminis, cùm subitò lapsus ad undas, improbus rapit
troop,   when suddenly gliding to the waves   cruel   he seizes

excellentem cycnum uncis pedibus.
a beautiful   swan, in *his* crooked claws.

Itali   arrexere   animos; que cunctæ volucres
The Italians aroused   *their* minds; and   all   the birds

convertunt fugam clamore, mirabile visu! que
turn *their* flight with a shout wonderful to be seen! and

obscurant æthera pennis, que premunt hostem per
darken the air with *their* wings, and press the foe through

auras nube factâ; donec ales victus vi et
the skies a cloud being formed; until the bird overcome by violence and

pondere ipso, deficit, que projecit prædam ex unguibus
the weight itself, fails. and casts *its* prey from *its* claws

fluvio, que penitus fugit in nubila. Tum verô
into the river. and afar off flies into the clouds. Then indeed

Rutuli salutant augurium clamore, que expediunt manus:
the Rutulians salute the omen with a shout, and draw out *their* bands:

que Tolumnius augur primus inquit: Hoc erat, hoc
and Tolumnius the soothsayer first says: This was, this *was that*

quod sæpe petivi votis; accipio que agnosco
for which often I sought in *my* prayers; I receive *it* and acknowledge

Deos: me, me duce, corripite ferrum, ô Rutuli,
the Gods: I, I being your leader, seize the sword, O Rutulians,

quos improbus advena territat bello, ut invalidas aves, et
whom *this* cruel stranger frightens by war, as powerless birds, and

populat vestra litora vi. Ille petet fugam, que penitus
lays waste your shores with violence. He shall seek flight, and afar off

dabit vela profundo. Vos unanimi densate catervas, et
shall give sail to the deep. Ye of one mind close *your* bands, and

pugnâ defendite regem raptum vobis. Dixit, et
with battle defend *your* king snatched from you. He said, and

procurrens contorsit telum in adversos hostes: stridula
hastening hurled *his* weapon against *his* adverse foe; the hissing

cornus dat sonitum, et certa secat auras. Simul hoc,
arrow gives a sound, and sure cuts the air. At once this *is done*,

simul ingens clamor, omnes cunei turbati, que
at once a great cry *arises*, all the ranks are disturbed, and

corda calefacta tumultu. Hasta volans, ut fortè
their hearts are warmed by the tumult. The spear flying, as by chance

novem pulcherrima corpora fratrum constiterant contrâ,
nine most beautiful bodies of brothers stood opposed.

quos tot una fida Tyrrhena conjux creârat
whom *though* so many one faithful Tuscan wife had borne

Arcadio Gilippo; transadigit costas unum horum juvenum
to Arcadian Gilippus; pierces through the ribs of one of these young men

egregium formâ et fulgentibus armis, ad medium quâ
distinguished for beauty and shining arms, in the middle where

sutilis balteus teritur alvo, et fibula mordet juncturas
the sewed belt *is* worn into the stomach, and the buckle corrodes the joints

laterum, que effundit fulvâ arenâ. At fratres, phalanx
of the sides, and stretches *him* on the yellow sand. But the brothers, a band

animosa, que accensa luctu, pars stringunt gladios
animated, and inflamed with grief, a part draw *their* swords

manibus,　　pars corripiunt missile ferrum, que cæci ruunt;
in *their* hands,　a part　　seize　　the flying　steel,　　and blind rush on;

contra　quos agmina Laurentum procurrunt: hinc rursus
against　whom the troops of the Laurentines　rush out:　here　again

　densi　Troës,　que Agyllini, et Arcades　　pictis
the thickening Trojans,　and Agyllenians, and Arcadians　with painted

armis inundant. Sic unus amor habet omnes decernere
arms　overflow.　Thus one　love possesses　all　　to contend

ferro.　Diripuere　　aras; turbida tempestas telorum
with the sword. They teardown *their* altars; a thick　tempest　of darts

it　toto　　　cœlo, ac ferreus imber ingruit;　　ferunt
goes thro' the whole sky,　and an iron shower thickens around; they bear off

que crateras que focos. Latinus ipse fugit　referens
both goblets　and hearths. Latinus himself flies,　bearing back

pulsatos　　Divos,　fœdere infecto.　Alii infrænant
the repulsed　Gods,　the treaty being broken.　Others　rein in

　currus,　aut subjiciunt corpora saltu in　equos,
their chariots,　or　cast　*their* bodies with a leap on *their* horses,

et adsunt strictis ensibus. Messapus, avidus confundere
and are present with drawn swords.　Messapus,　eager　to break

fœdus,　proterret Tyrrhenum Aulesten regem, que
the treaty, strikes against Tuscan　Aulestes　a king,　and

gerentem insigne regis,　adverso equo; ille recedens
wearing　the ensign of a king, with *his* opposing horse; he　withdrawing

ruit,　et miser involvitur aris oppositis à tergo in
falls,　and wretched rolls over the altars opposing *him* from behind upon

caput, que in　humeros. At fervidus Messapus advolat
his head, and on *his* shoulders. But glowing　Messapus　flies

　hastâ que altus　desuper equo, graviter ferit,
with *his* spear and high　from above on *his* horse, heavily　strikes *him*,

orantem multa,　　trabali　telo, atque ita　fatur:
praying　many *things* with *his* heavy wooden dart, and　thus　he speaks:

Habet　hoc: hæc melior victima data magnis　Divis.
Let him have this: this a better　victim　offered up to the great　Gods.

Itali　concurrunt que spoliant calentia membra. Chorinæus
The Italians rush together and strip　*his* warm　limbs.　Chorinæus

corripit ambustum torrem ab arâ, et, obvius Ebuso
seized　a burning　brand　from the altar, and　meeting Ebusus

venienti, que ferenti plagam, occupat os　flammis.
coming up,　and aiming　a blow,　strikes *his* face with the flames

Ingens barba reluxit illi, que ambusta dedit nidorem.
His great beard　shone　to him, and　burning gave forth　a stench.

Ipse super secutus, corripit cæsariem turbati hostis
He　from above following,　seized　the hair of *his* disturbed enemy

　lævâ,　que nitens genu impresso, applicat ipsum
with *his* left hand, and struggling *his* knee being pressed, fastens　him

terræ;　sic ferit latus rigido ense. Podalirius
to the earth; thus he strikes *his* side with *his* hard　sword.　Podalirius

sequens,   nudo ense, Alsum pastorem, que ruentem per
following, with *his* naked sword,   Alsus the shepherd,   as   rushing through

ela primâ   acie, superimminet, ille disjicit medium
darts in the front of the army, towers above *him*,   he   strikes   the midst

frontem,   que mentum adversi securi   reductâ,   et
of the forehead, and   chin   of *his* foe   *his* axe being drawn back, and

rigat   arma cruore sparso latè. Dura quies, et ferreus
moistens *his* arms with blood scattered far around. Cruel   rest, and   iron

somnus urget oculos, olli; lumina clauduntur in æternam
sleep   closes *his* eyes, for him;   *his* eyes   are shut   in   eternal

noctem.   At pius Æneas tendebat   dextram inermem,
night   But the pious Æneas   stretched forth *his* right hand   unarmed,

capite nudato, atque vocabat suos   clamore: Quò
his head being bare, and   called   his *friends*   with a shout: Whither

ruitis?   ve quæ ista repens discordia   surgit? O cohibete
do you rush? or what *is* this   sudden   discord   *which* arises?   O restrain

iras! jam fœdus ictum, et omnes leges   compositæ;
your anger! now   a treaty   *is* made, and   all   the conditions   are settled

mihi soli   jus   concurrere; sinite me, atque auferte metus;
to me alone *is* the right to engage;   suffer   me,   and   banish   *your* fears;

ego faxo fœdera firma manu; hæc sacra jam debent
I will make treaties   firm with *my* hand; these sacred rites   now   owe

Turnum mihi. Inter has voces, inter media talia
Turnus   to me. Among   these words,   in the   midst of these

verba,   ecce stridens sagitta allapsa est alis   viro,
exhortations,   lo   a hissing   arrow   glided   on wings to the hero,

incertum quâ manu pulsa, quo turbine adacta, quis,
it is doubtful by what   hand   it was sent, by what   violence it was hurled, who,

ne   casus, ne Deus, attulerit   tantam laudem
whether   chance,   or   a God,   had obtained   so great   praise

Rutulis;   insignis gloria facti est pressa; nec
for the Rutulians; the distinguished glory   of the deed   is   concealed;   nor

quisquam jactavit sese   vulnere Æneæ. Ut Turnus
did any one   boast   himself   of the wound of Æneas.   As   Turnus

vidit Ænean cedentem ex agmine, que   duces   turbatos,
saw   Æneas   withdrawing from the army, and *that* the leaders were troubled,

fervidus ardet subitâ spe;   simul   poscit equos
glowing   he burns with sudden hope; at the same time he demands horses

atque arma, que superbus   emicat   saltu   in currum,
and   arms,   and   proud   he springs forth with a bound into   *his* chariot,

et molitur habenas manibus. Volitans dat multa fortia
and guides   the reins with *his* hands.   Flying   he gives many   brave

corpora virorum letho; volvit multos semineces, aut
bodies   of men   to death; he rolls over   many   half-dead,   or

proterit agmina   curru,   aut ingerit hastas raptas
tramples   troops   with *his* chariot,   or   hurls   spears   snatched

fugientibus. Qualis cùm sanguineus Mavors, concitus apud
at those flying.   As   when   bloody   Mars,   excited   at

flumina gelidi Hebri, increpat ciypeo, atque movens
the streams of cold Hebrus, rattles on *his* shield, and moving

bella immittit furentes equos: Illi volant aperto æquore
war lets loose *his* raging horses: They fly *through* the open plain

ante Notos, que Zephyrum. Ultima Thracia gemit
before the south winds, and the west wind. Remotest Thrace groans

pulsu pedum, que circum ora atræ Formidinis, que
by the beating of *their* feet, and around *him* the faces of black fear, and

Iræ, que Insidiæ, comitatus Dei, aguntur. Talis Turnus
rage, and stratagem, the retinue of the God, are scattered. Thus Turnus,

alacer inter media prœlia, quatit equos fumantes sudore,
joyful in the midst of battle, provokes *his* horses foaming with sweat

miserabilè insultans cæsis hostibus; rapida ungula,
wretchedly insulting *his* slain foes; the rapid hoof,

spargit sanguineos rores, que cruor calcatur mistâ
scatters the bloody dews, and blood *is* trodden down mingled

arenâ. Que jam dedit que Sthenelum, que Thamyrim,
with sand. And now he gave both Sthenelus, and Thamyris,

que Pholum ne ci, congressus hunc et hunc, illum eminus;
and Pholus to death, engaging this and that *hand to hand*, the other afar off;

ambo Imbrasidas eminus, Glaucum atque Laden,
he slew also both sons of Imbrasus at a distance, Glaucus and Lades,

quos Imbrasus ipse nutrierat Lyciâ; que oneraverat
whom Imbrasus himself had nourished in Lycia; and had burdened

paribus armis, vel conferre manum, vel prævertere
with equal arms, either to engage hand to hand, or to outstrip

ventos equo. Aliâ parte, Eumedes fertur in media
the winds on the horse. In another part, Eumedes is borne into the midst

prœlia, proles antiqui Dolonis præclara bello, referens
of the battle, the offspring of ancient Dolon renowned in war, restoring

avum nomine, parentem animo, que
his grandfather by *his* name, *his* father by *his* courage, and *deeds wrought by his*

manibus; qui quondam, ut speculator adiret castra
hands; who formerly, as a spy approached the camps

Danaûm ausus poscere currus Pelidæ pretium sibi:
of the Greeks daring to demand the chariot of Achilles as a reward to himself

Tydides affecit illum alio pretio pro talibus ausis; nec
Diomede punished him with another reward for such daring; nor

aspirat equis Achillis.
did he aspire to the horses of Achilles.

Ut Turnus conspexit hunc procul aperto campo, antè
As Turnus beheld him afar off on the open plain, first

secutus per longum inane levi jaculo, sistit
having pursued *him* through the long void with a light arrow, he stops

bijuges equos, et desilit curru, atque supervenit
his yok'd horses, and leaps from *his* chariot, and comes up to *him*

semianimi que lapso; et collo impresso pede, extorquet
half dead and fallen; and *his* neck being press'd with *his* foot, he wrenches

mucronem dextræ, et tingit fulgentem alto jugulo,
the blade from *his* right hand, and dips it shining in *his* deep throat,

atque insuper addit hæc. En, Trojane, jacens metire
and moreover he adds these *words*. Lo, Trojan, stretch'd out measure

agros et Hesperiam, quam petîsti bello: ferunt
the lands and Italy, which you have sought in war: they bear off

hæc præmia, qui ausi tentare me ferro: sic condunt
these rewards, who dare to tempt me with the sword: thus they build up

mœnia. Mittit huic comitem Buten, cuspide
walls. He sends to him for a companion Butes, *his* spear

conjectâ; que Chlorea, que Sybarim, que Dareta, que
being hurled; and Chloreas, and Sybaris, and Dares, and

Thersilochum, et Thymœten, lapsum cervice sternacis
Thersilochus, and Thymætes, fallen from the neck of *his* plunging

equi. Ac velut, cùm spiritus Edoni Boreæ insonat alto
horse. And as, when the breath of Thracian Boreas resounds on the deep

Ægæo, que sequitur fluctus ad litora, quâ venti
Ægean *sea*, and pursues the waves to the shores, where the winds

incubuere, nubila dant fugam cælo; sic agmina
hover round, the clouds give flight in the sky; thus the troops

cedunt Turno, quacunque secat viam, que acies
withdraw from Turnus. wherever he cuts *his* way, and the armies

conversæ ruunt: impetus fert ipsum, et aura quatit
turn'd rush out: impetuosity bears him on, and the wind shakes

cristam volantem adverso curru. Phegeus non
his crest flying against the opposing chariot. Phegeus did not

tulit instantem, que frementem animis: objecit sese ad
endure *him* pressing on, and raging with anger; he opposed himself to

currum, et dextrâ detorsit ora citatorum
the chariot, and with *his* right hand turned the mouths of the swift

equorum spumantia frænis, Dum trahitur, que pendet
horses foaming on the reins. While he is borne on, and hangs

jugis, lata lancea consequitur hunc retectum, que
from the chariot, *his* broad lance follows him unprotected, and

infixa rumpit bilicem loricam, et degustat summum
fastened breaks *his* double plated coat of mail, and grazes the surface

corpus vulnere. Tamen ille conversus ibat clypeo
of *his* body with a wound. Yet he turning went with *his* shield

objecto in hostem, et petebat auxilium ducto mucrone;
opposed to the foe, and sought aid with *his* drawn blade;

cùm rota et axis concitus procursu, impulit præcipitem,
when the wheel and axis moving on in its course, hurled *him* headlong,

que effudit solo; que Turnus secutus inter imam
and overthrew *him* on the ground; and Turnus following between the lowest

galeam, et oras summi thoracis, abstulit caput
part of the helmet, and the borders of the highest corslet, cut off *his* head

ense, que reliquit truncum arenâ. Atque dum
with *his* sword, and left *his* trunk on the sand. And while

Turnus victo dat ea funera campis, interea
Turnus victorious causes these deaths on the plains; in the mean time

Mnestheus, et fidus Achates, que Ascanius comes,
Mnestheus, and faithful Achates, and Ascanius, his companion,

statuere Ænean cruentum castris, nitentem alternos
placed Æneas bloody in the camp, supporting his alternate

gressus longâ cuspide. Sævit, et luctatur eripere telum
footsteps with a long spear. He rages, and struggles to tear out the dart

arundine infractâ, que poscit viam auxilio, quæ
the reed being fractured, and he demands a way for aid, which is

proxima; ut secent vulnus lato ense, que
nearest; that they should cut the wound with a broad sword, and

recindant latebram teli penitus, que remittant sese in
lay open the concealment of the dart deeply, and restore him to

bella. Que jam Iapyx Iasides, dilectus Phœbo ante
the war. And now Iapyx the son of Iasius, beloved by Apollo before

alios, aderat; cui quondam Apollo ipse, captus acri
others, was present; to whom formerly Apollo himself, overcome by powerful

amore, lætus dabat suas artes, sua munera, augurium,
love, joyfully imparted his arts, his gifts, prophecy

que citharam, que celeres sagittas. Ille, ut proferret
and music, and the swift arrows. He, that he might prolong

fata depositi parentis, maluit scire potestates
the fates of his dying parent, choose to know the powers

herbarum, que usum medendi et inglorius agitare
of herbs, and the use of healing and without honour to practise

mutas artes.
dumb arts.

Æneas stabat fremens acerbâ, nixus in ingentem hastam,
Æneas stood raging bitterly, leaning on his great spear,

immobilis magno concursu, que lacrymis juvenum et
unmoved by the great crowd, and the tears of the youth and

mœrentis Iüli. Ille senior succinctus amictu in Pæonium
the mourning Iulus. The old man girt with a dress in the Pæonian

morem, nequicquam trepidat multa medicâ manu, que
manner, in vain trembles much with his healing hand, and

potentibus herbis Phœbi; nequicquam solicitat spicula
the powerful herbs of Apollo in vain he urges the darts

dexterâ, que prensat ferrum tenaci forcipe. Nulla
with his right hand, and seizes the steel with grasping pincers. No

fortuna regit viam; Apollo auctor subvenit nihil; et
success guides his way; Apollo his patron relieves him in nothing; and

sævus horror crebrescit magis ac magis in campis, que
cruel dread increases more and more in the plains, and

malum est propius. Jam vident cœlum stare pulvere;
the evil is nearer. Now they see the sky to stand thick with dust:

equites subeunt, et densa spicula cadunt mediis
the horsemen succeed and the thick flying darts fall in the midst

castris: tristis   clamor bellantum juvenum, et cadentum,
cf the camp a saddening shout   of warring   youth,   and of those falling,

sub duro Marte,   it ad æthera.   Hìc Venus genetrix
in   cruel   war,   goes to the sky.   Here Venus   his mother

concussa   indigno   dolore   nati, carpit dictamnum ab
moved   by the unworthy distress of her son, plucks   dittany   from

Cretæâ Idâ,   caulem   puberibus   foliis, et   comantem
Cretan   Ida,   the stalk   with full grown leaves, and   waving

purpureo flore: illa gramina non incognita feris capris,
with a purple flower: these plants are not unknown to the wild goats,

cùm volucres sagittæ hæsere   tergo.   Venus circumdata
when   swift   arrows have stuck in their backs.   Venus   surrounded

faciem obscuro   nimbo, detulit hoc: hoc   inficit
as to her face with a dark   cloud,   bore   this: with this she tinctured

fuscum amnem splendentibus labris, medicans occultè,
the dark   water   in the shining   vats,   medicating it   secretly,

que   spargit   salubres   succos ambrosiæ, et odoriferam
and she sprinkles the healthful   juices   of ambrosia, and   scented

panaceam.   Longævus Iapyx, ignorans,   fovit vulnus
panacea.   Aged   Iapyx,   ignorant of its value, bathes the wound

eâ lymphâ;   que subitò   quippe omnis dolor fugit   de
with this water;   and suddenly   indeed   all   pain had fled from

corpore, omnis sanguis stetit   imo   vulnere, que jam
his body,   all   the blood remained in the deep wound,   and   now

sagitta,   secuta   manum, excidit, nullo cogente, atque novæ
the arrow, following   his hand,   fell out, no one   forcing it,   and   new

vires rediere in pristina.   Citi properate arma   viro;
strength returned into its former state. Quick   hasten   arms for the hero;

quid   statis? Iapyx   conclamat,   que primus   accendit
why do you stand? Iapyx   cries,   and   first   he inflames

animos   in   hostes: Hæc   non proveniunt humanis
their minds against the foe.   These things do not   proceed   from human

opibus, non magistrâ arte, neque mea   dextera   servat
aid,   nor   a master   art,   nor   does my right hand preserve

te,   Ænea; major Deus agit, atque remittit ad majora
thee, O Æneas; a greater God   does it,   and   remands you to   greater

opera. Ille, avidus pugnæ, incluserat suras auro,   hinc
labours. He,   anxious   for combat,   had enclosed his legs in gold, on this side

atque hinc, que odit moras, que coruscat hastam. Postquam
and   that,   and hates delays, and brandishes his spear.   After

clypeus est habilis lateri, que lorica   tergo, complectitur
his shield   is   fitted   to his side, and his corslet to his back,   he embraces

Ascaniun: armis   fusis   circum,   que delibans summa
Ascanius,   his armour being spread around him,   and   kissing   the tip

oscula   per   galeam,   fatur: Puer, disce virtutem
of his mouth through   his helmet, he speaks thus: My boy,   learn   courage

que verum laborem ex me, fortunam ex aliis. Nunc
and   true   occupation from me,   fortune   from others.   Now

mea dextera dabit te defensum bello, et ducet inter
my right hand shall render thee defended in war, and lead *thee* amid

magna præmia. Tu facito, sis memor, mox cùm
great rewards. Do you cause, *that* you be mindful, soon when

matura ætas adoleverit; et te, et pater Æneas, et
timely age shall have ripened; and thee, let both your father Æneas, and

avunculus Hector excitet repetentem exempla tuorum
your uncle Hector excite recalling the examples of your *friends*

animo. Ubi dedit hæc dicta, ingens extulit sese
to *your* mind. When he had uttered these words, lofty he withdrew himself

portis, quatiens immane telum manu; simul que
from the gates, shaking *his* immense dart in *his* hand; at once also

Anteus, que Mnestheus, ruunt denso agmine, que omnis
Anteus, and Mnestheus, rush out in close array, and all

turba fluit castris relictis: tum campus miscetur
the crowd pours out from the camps abandoned: then the plain is confused

cæco pulvere, que tellus excita pulsu pedum
by blinding dust, and the earth moved by the beating of *their* feet

tremit. Turnus videt venientes ex adverso aggere;
trembles. Turnus sees *them* approaching from the opposite hill;

Ausonii vidêre que gelidus tremor cucurrit per
the Ausonians beheld and a cold trembling ran through

ima ossa.
their inmost bones.

Juturna prima audiit ante omnes Latinos, que agnovit
Juturna first heard before all the Latins, and knew

sonum, et tremefacta refugit. Ille volat, que rapit
the sound, and trembling fled back. He (*Æneas*) flies, and drives

atrum agmen aperto campo. Qualis ubi nimbus, sidere
his dark band on the open plain. As when a storm, a constellation

abrupto, it per medium mare ad terras: heu! corda,
setting, passes over the midst of the sea to the land: alas! hearts.

præscia longè, horrescunt miseris agricolis! ille dabit
foreseeing far, shudder to the wretched farmers! *knowing* it will bring

ruinas arboribus, que stragem satis, que ruet omnia
destruction on the trees, and ruin on the corn-fields, and overturn all things

latè: venti antevolant, que ferunt sonitum ad litora: talis
far around *he winds fly before, and bear the sound to the shores: thus

Rhæteius ductor agit agmen in adversos hostes: densi
Rhæteus the leader drives on *his* troop against *his* hostile foes: close

quisque agglomerant se cuneis coactis. Thymbræus
each gather themselves in battalions condensed. Thymbræus

ferit gravem Osirim ense, Mnestheus obtruncat
strikes stern Osiris with *his* sword, Mnestheus beheads

Archetium, Achates Epulonem, que Gyas Ufentem.
Archetius, Achates *kills* Epulon, and Gyas Ufens.

Tolumnius ipse augur cadit, qui primus torserat telum
Tolumnius himself the prophet falls who first hurled the dart

in adversos hostes. Clamor tollitur in cœlum; que
against the hostile foes. A shout is raised to heaven; and

Rutuli versi vicissim dant pulverulenta terga
the Rutulians wheeling round in their turn give their dusty backs

fugâ per agros. Ipse neque dignatur sternere
in the flight through the fields. He neither condescends to prostrate

aversos morti; nec insequitur congressos æquo pede,
those turning in death; nor does he follow them engaging in equal fight,

nec ferentes tela; vestigat Turnum solum,
nor those throwing darts; he searches for Turnus alone

lustrans in densâ caligine; poscit solum certamina.
pursuing him in the thick cloud; he demands him alone to the contest

Virago Juturna, concussa mentem hoc metu,
The maid Juturna, affected in mind with this fear,

excutit Metiscum aurigam Turni inter media lora, et
strikes down Metiscus the charioteer of Turnus in the midst of the reins, and

relinquit lapsum, longè temone. Ipsa subit que flectit
leaves him fallen, far from the beam. She comes up and guides

undantes habenas manibus, gerens cuncta, que vocem et
the flowing reins with her hands, assuming all, both the voice and

corpus et arma Metisci. Velut cùm nigra hirundo pervolat
form and arms of Metiscus. As when a black swallow flies over

magnas ædes divitis domini, et lustrat alta atria pennis,
the spacious palace of a rich lord, and surveys the lofty halls on wings,

legens parva pabula, que escas loquacibus nidis; et
picking up scanty nourishment, and food for her noisy young; and

sonat nunc vacuis porticibus, nunc circum humida stagna:
twitters now thro' the empty porches, now around the moist pools:

Juturna, similis fertur equis per medios hostes, que
Juturna, in like manner is borne by her horses through the midst of foes, and

volans obit omnia rapido curru; que jam hìc, que jam
flying passes over all things in her swift chariot; and now here, and now

hìc, ostendit germanum ovantem, nec patitur cor ferre
there, exhibits her brother triumphing, nor allows him to engage

manum; volat avia longè. Haud minùs Æneas
his hand; she flies through retired places far off. Not less Æneas

oovius, legit tortos orbes, que vestigat virum, et vocat
opposing, follows his winding circuits, and seeks out the hero, and calls him.

magnâ voce per disjecta agmina. Quoties conjecit
with a loud voice through scattered troops. As often as he turned

oculos in hostem, que cursu tentavit fugam alipedum
his eyes upon the foe, and in his course tried the speed of his swift-footed

equorum; toties Juturna retorsit aversos currus. Heu,
horses; so often Juturna turned back the retreating chariot. Alas,

quid agat? nequicquam fluctuat vario æstu, que
what can he do? in vain he fluctuates with a varied tide of feeling, and

diversæ curæ vocant animum in contraria. Messapus,
conflicting cares call his mind to opposite purposes. Messapus

uti fortè levis cursu gerebat lævâ   duo lenta hastilia
as by chance swift in *his* course he bore in his left *hand* two slender spears

præfixa ferro, contorquens unum horum certo ictu,
pointed with steel, hurling one of these with a sure blow

dirigit huic. Æneas substitit, et collegit se in arma.
he directs at him. Æneas stopt, and contracted himself within *his* arms.

subsidens poplite: tamen hasta incita tulit summum
sitting down on *his* hams: yet *his* spear hurled carried the highest

apicem, que excussit summas cristas vertice. Tum
tuft, and shook off the loftiest crests from *his* head. Then

verò iræ assurgunt; que subactus insidiis, ubi
indeed anger arises; and compelled by the snares *of his foe*, when

sensit equos que currum diversos, referre testatur
he perceived *his* horses and chariot turned aside, were borne back, he swears

multa Jovem, et aras læsi fœderis. Jam tandem
many *things* to Jove, and the altars of *his* broken treaty. Now at last

invadit medios,. et terribilis secundo Marte, suscitat
he presses into the midst, and terrible with prosperous war, he provokes

sævam cædem nullo discrimine, que effundit omnes
direful slaughter with no discrimination, and gives loose all

habenas irarum. Nunc quis Deus, quis expediat mihi
the reins of *his* passions. Now what God, who can unfold to me

carmine tot acerba, diversas cædes, que obitum
in song so many bitter *evils*, various slaughters, and the death

ducum, quos nunc Turnus, que nunc Troïus heros invicem
of chiefs, whom now Turnus, and now the Trojan hero by turns

agit toto æquore? Jupiter, ne placuit gentes,
drives through the whole plain? O Jupiter, whether does it please *thee* that nations

futuras in æternâ pace, concurrere tanto motu?
about to be in eternal peace, should conflict in so great commotion?

Æneas, haud moratus multa, excipit Rutulum Sucronem
Æneas, not delaying much, strikes Rutulian Sucro

in latus (ea pugna prima statuit loco Teucros
in the side (this contest first restrained in *their* place the Trojans

ruentes) et quà fata celerrima, adigit crudum ensem
rushing on) and where fates *are* most active, he plunges *his* naked sword

trans costas et crates pectoris. Turnus, pedes
through *his* ribs and grated openings of *his* breast. Turnus, on foot

congressus Amycum dejectum equo, que fratrem
attacking Amycus thrown from *his* horse and *his* brother

Diorem, ferit hunc venientem longâ cuspide ferit
Diores, strikes the one coming up with *his* long spear, he stabs

hunc mucrone; que suspendit abscissa capita duorum
the other with *his* sword; and hangs the dissevered heads of the two

curru, et portat rorantia sanguine. Ille mittit
from *his* chariot and bears *them off* bedewed with blood. He dispatches

Talon que Tanaim neci, que fortem Cethegum, tres
Talon and Tanais to death, and brave Cethegum, the three

uno congressu, et mœstum Onyten; Echionium nomen,
in one   attack,   and mournful Onytes;   an Echionian   name,

que genus   matris Peridiæ.   Hic   fratres missos
and the race of *his* mother Peridia.   He (*Turnus*) *kills his* brothers   sent

Lyciâ   et   agris Apollinis, et Menœten Arcada juvenem
from Lycia and the territories of Apollo, and Menœtes an Arcadian   youth

nequicquam exosum bella; cui ars, que pauper domus
in vain   detesting wars; whose arts, and   poor   dwelling

fuerat circum flumina piscosæ Lernæ; nec   limina
had been around   the streams of fishy Lerna;   nor *were* the gates

potentum nota,   que pater serebat conductâ tellure.
of the powerful known *to him*, and *his* father sowed on rented   land.

Ac velut ignes immissi diversis partibus in arentem
And as   fires   let loose from different parts   in   the dry

sylvam, et virgulta lauro sonantia; aut ubi spumosi
wood,   and shrubbery with laurel rustling; or when   foaming

amnes, rapido decursu de altis montibus, dant sonitum,
streams, in *their* swift descent from the high mountains, cause a sound,

et currunt in æquora, quisque populatus suum iter, non
and run into the sea, each one laying waste its own path; not.

segniùs ambo Æneas que Turnus, ruunt per prœlia;
more slothfully both Æneas and Turnus, rush through   battles;

nunc, nunc ira fluctuat intus: pectora nescia vinci
now, now rage fluctuates within: *their* breasts ignorant to be conquered

rumpuntur;   nunc itur totis   viribus in vulnera.
are burst *with anger*; now they go with all *their* strength to   wounds.

Hic   scopulo atque turbine ingentis saxi, excutit
This *one* with a rock and   the whirling of a great stone,   strikes

præcipitem, que effundit solo Murranum, sonantem
headlong,   and throws out upon the ground Murranus, sounding forth

atavos et antiqua nomina avorum, que omne genus
his ancestors and the ancient names of *his* progenitors, and *his* whole   race

actum per Latinos reges; rotæ provolvêre hunc subter
derived through Latin   kings; the wheels   rolled   him   under

lora et juga; et, supèr, ungula equorum, nec memorum
the reins and yoke; and, moreover, the hoof of the horses, not   mindful

domini, incita proculcat   crebo pulsu.
of *their* master, excited treads *him* down by *its* frequent blow.

Ille   occurrit Ilo ruenti que frementi immanâ
He (*Turnus*) meets Ilus rushing on and   raging   dreadfully

animis, que torquet telum ad aurata tempora; hasta
in *his* mind, and hurls *his* dart at *his* gilded temples;   the spear

stetit olli cerebro fixo per galeam, nec tua dextera
stands in his brains pierced through the helmet, nor did thy right hand

eripuit te Turno, Creteu, fortissime Graiûm; nec
snatch thee from Turnus, O Creteus, the bravest of the Greeks;   nor

sui   Dî texere Cupencum, Æneâ veniente. Dedit
did *his* own Gods protect   Cupencus,   Æneas coming up. He yielded

pectora obvia ferro: nec mora æris clypei
his breast to meet the sword: nor did the obstruction of his brazen shield

profuit misero. Laurentes campi viderunt te
profit its wretched owner. The Laurentine plains beheld thee

quoque Æole, oppetere, et consternere terram latè
likewise O Æolus, fall, and spread the earth far around

tergo. Occidis, quem Argivæ phalanges non potuere
with your back. You fall, whom the Grecian bands could not

sternere, nec Achilles eversor regnorum Priami. Hìc
prostrate, nor Achilles the overturner of the kingdoms of Priam. Here

erant tibi metæ mortis: alta domus sub Idâ,
were to you the limits of your death: a proud palace under mount Ida,

alta domus Lyrnessi; sepulcrum Laurente solo. Adeo
a proud palace in Lyrnessus; your tomb is on the Laurentian soil. Thus

totæ acies conversæ; que omnes Latini, omnes Dardanidæ:
all the troops are turned: both all the Latins, all the Trojans:

Mnestheus, que acer Serestus, et Messapus, domitor
Mnestheus, and bold Serestus, and Messapus, the tamer

equûm, et fortis Asylas, que phalanx Tuscorum, que alæ
of horses, and brave Asylas, and a band of Tuscans, and troops

Evandri Arcadis, viri, quisque pro se, nituntur
of Evander the Arcadian, heroes, each one for himself, struggle

summâ vi opum; nec mora, nec requies;
with the greatest effort of their strength; there is no delay, nor rest;

tendunt vasto certamine. Hìc pulcherrima genetrix
they strive with a great effort. Here his most beauteous mother

misit mentem Æneæ, ut iret ad muros, que
influenced the mind of Æneas, that he should go to the walls, and

adverteret agmen urbi ocyùs, et turbaret Latinos
bring back his army to the city quickly, and should confound the Latins

subitâ clade. Ille, ut circumtulit acies huc atque
by sudden slaughter. He, as he turned around his eyes here and

huc, vestigans Turnum per diversa agmina, aspicit
there, searching for Turnus through the different troops, beholds

urbem immunem tanti belli, atque quietam impunè.
the city free from so great a war, and undisturbed at rest.

Continuò imago majoris pugnæ accendit; vocat Mnesthea
Forthwith the image of a greater battle inflames him; he calls Mnestheus

que Sergestum, que fortem Serestum ductores, que capit
and Sergestus, and brave Serestus leaders, and takes

tumulum quô cætera legio Teucrûm concurrit, nec
the hill where the other legion of the Trojans run together, nor

densi deponunt scuta aut spicula; stans medius
crowded do they lay down their shields or darts; standing in the midst

fatur celso aggere; nec esto qua mora meis
he speaks from the lofty mound; let there be not any hinderance to my

dictis; Jupiter stat hâc, neu quis ito segnior mihi
words Jupiter stands on this side, nor let any one proceed more slothful to me

ob subitum inceptum. Hodie eruam urbem
on account of the sudden purpose. This day I will upturn the city

causam belli, regna ipsa Latini, ni victi
the cause of the war. the kingdom itself of Latinus, unless vanquished

fatentur accipere frænum, et parere, et ponam
they shall consent to receive our reins of authority, and to obey us, and I will lay

culmina fumantia æqua solo. Scilicet exspectem
their towers smoking even with the ground. Truly shall I wait

dum libeat Turno pati nostra prælia, que victus
while it shall please Turnus to endure our battle, and vanquished

rursus velit concurrere? ô cives, hic caput, hæc
again will he encounter me? O my countrymen, this is the head, this

summa nefandi belli. Ferte faces properè, que
the chief cause of the accursed war. Bring firebrands quickly, and

reposcite fœdus flammis.
redemand the treaty with flames.

Dixerat: atque animis pariter certantibus omnes dant
He said: and their minds together contending all form

cuneum, que feruntur ad muros densâ mole. Improvisô
a battalion, and are borne to the walls in a close mass. Unexpectedly

scalæ, que subitus ignis apparuit. Alii discurrunt ad
ladders, and a sudden fire appear. Some run to

portas, que trucidant primos: alii torquent ferrum,
the gates, and butcher the first they encounter: others hurl the steel,

et obumbrant æthera telis. Æneas ipse, inter primos,
and darken the sky with darts. Æneas himself, among the first,

tendit dextram sub mœnia, que incusat Latinum
stretches forth his right hand beneath the walls, and accuses Latinus

magnâ voce; que testatur Deos, cogi iterum
with a loud voice; and calls to witness the Gods, that he is forced again

ad prælia; Italos jam bis hostes, hæc altera
to battle; that the Italians now are twice his enemies, that these other

fœdera rumpi. Discordia exoritur inter trepidos cives:
leagues are broken. Discord arises among the trembling citizens:

alii jubent reserare urbem, et pandere portas Dardanidis,
some command to unlock the city, and to open the gates to the Trojans

que trahunt regem ipsum in mœnia. Alii ferunt arma, et
and they draw the king himself to the walls. Others bear arms, and

pergunt defendere muros, Ut cùm pastor vestigavit apes
proceed to defend the walls, As when a shepherd has searched out bees

inclusas in latebrosâ pumice, que implevit amaro fumo;
inclosed in a dark cliff, and filled it with bitter smoke;

discurrunt per cerea castra, que acuunt iras
they run around through their waxen camps, and excite their rage

magnis stridoribus: ater odor volvitur tectis; tum
with great buzzing: a black stench is rolled through their cells; then

saxa intus sonant cæco murmure; fumus it ad vacuas
the rocks within resound with blind murmuring; smoke goes to the vacant

auras. Hæc fortuna etiam accidit   fessis   Latinis, quæ
airs.   This fortune also happened to the wearied Latins, which

funditus, concussit totam urbem luctu.   Ut regina
to *its* foundation shook the whole city with grief. As the queen

prospicit hostem venientem   tectis,   muros   incessi,
beheld   the enemy approaching to the houses, the walls to be attacked.

ignes volare ad tecta; Rutulas acies nusquam contrà,
fires to fly to the roofs; The Rutulian armies no where in opposition,

nulla agmina Turni;   infelix credit juvenem
no   troops of Turnus *to be seen;* wretched she believes the youth

exstinctum in certamine pugnæ, et, turbata mentem subito
is killed   in the conflict of battle, and, distracted in mind by sudden

dolore, clamat,   se causam, que crimen, que caput
grief,   she cries out, *that* she *is* the cause, and the crime, and the fountain

malorum;   que demens effata multa   per·
of *their* misfortunes; and distracted she utters many *things* through

mæstum furorem, moritura discindit purpureos amictus
mournful madness, about to die she tears *her* purple robes

manu, et nectit nodum informis lethi ab altâ trabe,
with *her* hands, and ties a knot of haggard death from a lofty beam,

Quam cladem postquam miseræ Latinæ accepere,
Which murder after the wretched Latin women had received,

filia Lavinia prima furit, laniata   flavos   crines et
her daughter Lavinia first rages, torn *as to her* beautiful locks and

roseas genas; tum cætera turba circùm; ædes resonant
roseate cheeks: then the other crowd around; the palace resounds

latè plangoribus. Hinc infelix fama vulgatur per
far around with cries. Hence the unhappy report is spread through

totam urbem. Demittunt   mentes. Latinus it scissâ
the whole city. They cast down *their* minds. Latinus goes out with torn

veste. Attonitus fatis   conjugis, que · ruinâ   urbis,
dress. Amazed by the fate of *his* wife, and the destruction of the city,

turpans canitiem perfusam immundo pulvere; que incusat
defiling *his* grey hair overspread with filthy dust; and accuses

se multa,   qui non acceperit Dardanium
himself of many *things, that* he had not received Trojan

Ænean antè, que asciverit generum ultro. Interea
Æneas before, and invited *him* as a son-in-law willingly. In the mean time

bellator Turnus sequitur paucos palantes in extremo
.the warrior Turnus follows a few wandering about in the extremity of the

æquore, jam segnior; atque jam minùs atque minùs
plain, now more listless; and now less and less

lætus successu equorum. Aura attulit illi hunc
joyful by the success of *his* horses. The wind brought to him this

clamorem commixtum cæcis terroribus, que sonus
ery   commingled with blind terrors, and the sound

confusæ urbis, et illætabile murmur impulit arrectas
of the confused city, and the joyless murmuring struck *his* attentive

aures. Hei mihi! quid   mœnia   turbantur tanto luctu?
ears.   Alas me! why are our walls disturbed by so great grief?

ve quis tantus clamor ruit ab   diversâ   urbe?
or what great noise rushes from a distant part of the city?

Sic ait, que amens subsistit habenis adductis; atque
Thus he said, and mad stopt   his reins being drawn up: and

soror, ut, conversa in faciem Metisci aurigæ, regebat que
his sister, as being changed into the form of Metiscus the charioteer, guided both

currum et equos et lora, accurrit huic talibus dictis:
the chariot and horses and the reins, replied to him in these words:

Turne, sequamur Trojugenas hàc, quà victoria prima
O Turnus, let us pursue the sons of Troy here, where victory first

pandit viam.   Sunt alii qui possunt defendere   tecta
opens a way There are others who can   defend   the dwellings

manu: Æneas ingruit Italis, et miscet prœlia. Et
with their hand: Æneas attacks the Italians, and intermingles battle. And

nos mittamus sæva funera Teucris   manu,
let us send   direful death to the Trojans with our hand,

recedes   nec inferior numero, nec honore pugnæ.
you shall withdraw neither inferior in number, nor honour of battle.

Turnus   ad hæc: O soror, et dudum agnovi, cùm
Turnus replied to these things: O sister, even at length I have known, when

prima turbâsti fœdera per artem, que dedisti   te
first you disturbed our leagues by art, and you have yielded yourself

in hæc bella; et nunc Dea nequicquam fallis. Sed quis
to these wars; and now a Goddess in vain you deceive. But who

voluit te demissam Olympo ferre tantos labores? an ut
has wished you sent down from heaven to endure so great labours? or that

videres   crudele lethum miseri fratris? nam quid
you might see the cruel death of your wretched brother? for what

ago? aut quæ fortuna jam spondet salutem? Ipse   vidi
can I do? or what fortune now promises safety?   I have seen

Murranum, quo non alter superat carior mihi,
Murranus, than whom not another survives more dear to me,

vocantem me voce, ingentem atque victum ingenti
calling me with his voice, a great man and vanquished by a great

vulnere, oppetere ante meos oculos. Infelix Ufens occidit,
wound, to fall before my eyes.   Unhappy Ufens fell,

ne aspiceret nostrum dedecus: Teucri potiuntur corpore
nor did he behold our dishonour The Trojans possess his body

et armis. Perpetiarne domos exscindi? id unum defuit
and arms. Shall I suffer our houses to be destroyed? this alone was wanting

rebus;   nec refellam dicta Drancis   dextrâ?
to our affairs; nor shall I refute the words of Drances with my right hand?

Dabo terga? et hæc terra videbit Turnum fugientem?
Shall I give my back? and shall this land behold Turnus flying?

Est ne usque, adeo miserum   mori? O vos manes
Is it even,   so dreadful a thing to die? O ye shades

este boni mihi, quoniam voluntas Superis aversa.
be ye kind to me, since the will of the Gods is hostile.

Descendam ad vos sancta anima, atque inscia istius
I will descend to you a holy soul, and unconscious of this

culpæ, haud unquam indignus magnorum avorum. Vix
fault, not ever unworthy of my great ancestors. Scarcely

erat fatus ea; ecce! Sages, vectus spumante
had he spoken these things; when lo! Sages, borne on his foaming

equo volat per medios hostes, saucius ora adversa
horse flies through the midst of the foes, wounded in his face opposed

sagittâ, que ruit implorans Turnum nomine:
to him, with an arrow, and rushed on entreating Turnus by name:

Turne, suprema salus in te; miserere tuorum. Æneas
O Turnus, our last safety is in thee; pity your friends. Æneas

fulminat armis; que minatur dejecturum summas
thunders in arms; and threatens that he will throw down the lofty

arces Italorum, que daturum excidio, que jam faces
towers of the Italians, and will give them to destruction, and now firebrands

volant ad tecta. Latini ora in te; referunt oculos
fly to the roofs. The Latins turn their faces on thee; they turn their eyes

in te; rex Latinus ipse mussat quos vocet generos, aut
on thee; king Latinus himself hesitates whom he shall call sons-in-law, or

ad quæ fœdera flectat sese. Præterea regina ipsa,
to what treaties he shall yield himself. Besides the queen herself,

fidissima tui, occidit suâ dexterâ, que exterrita fugit
most faithful to you, has fallen by her own right hand, and terrified flies

lucem. Messapus et acer Atinas soli sustentant aciem
the light. Messapus and bold Atinas alone sustain the battle

pro portis. Densæ phalanges stant utrinque circum
before the gates. The crowded battalions stand on each side around

hos, que ferrea seges horret strictis mucronibus:
these, and an iron harvest bristles up with drawn sword: yet

tu versas currum in deserto gramine. Turnus, confusus
you turn your chariot on the desert grass. Turnus, confounded

variâ imagine rerum, obstupuit et stetit tacito
by this varied image of things, stood amazed and remained in a silent

obtutu. Ingens pudor æstuat in imo corde, que insania
posture. Great shame boils in his inmost heart, and madness

misto luctu, et amor agitatus furiis et conscia virtus.
with mingled grief, and love agitated by rage and conscious courage.

Ut primùm umbræ discussæ, et lux est reddita menti,
As first the shades were dispelled, and light is restored to his mind,

turbidus torsit ardentes orbes oculorum ad mœnia, èque
troubled he turned the glowing balls of his eyes to the walls, and from

rotis respexit ad magnam urbem. Autem ecce! vortex
the wheels looked back to the great city. But lo! a torrent

flammis volutus inter tabulata undabat ad cœlum, que
with flames rolled on among the planks ascended to heaven, and

tenebat turrim; quam turrim ipse eduxerat compactis
held the tower; which tower he had raised with compact

trabibus, que subdiderat rotas, que instraverat altos
timbers, and had placed under it wheels, and had spread over it high

pontes. Soror, jam Fata superant; absiste . morari,
bridges. O sister, *he says*, now the Fates rule; forbear to delay me,

sequamur quò Deus et quò dura fortuna vocat; stat
let us follow where God and where cruel fortune calls; it is determined

conferre manum Æneæ; stat pati quidquid
to engage the hand with Æneas; it is determined to suffer any thing

acerbi est morte: nec germana, videbis me indecorem
of cruelty *there* is in death: nor O sister, shall you behold me disgraced

ampliùs. Oro, sine me furere hunc furorem antè.
any longer. I pray *you*, permit me to rage out this madness first.

Dixit, et dedit saltum ocyùs e curru arvis; que
He said, and gave a leap quickly from *his* chariot on the fields: and

ruit per hostes, per tela, que deserit mœstam sororem;
rushed through foes, through darts, and deserts *his* mournful sister;

ac rumpit media agmina rapido cursu. Ac veluti
and breaks through the midst of the troops with rapid course. And as

cùm saxum ruit præceps de vertice montis, avulsum
when a rock rushes headlong from the top of a mountain, torn up

vento, seu turbidus imber proluit, aut vestustas
by the wind, whether a raging storm has washed *it*, or antiquity

sublapsa solvit annis; improbus mons fertur in
undermining loosened *it* by years; the destructive mass is borne along

abruptum magno actu, que exsultat solo, involvens
the abyss with great violence, and rebounds on the ground, overwhelming

sylvas, amenta, que viros secum: sic Turnus ruit per
woods, herds, and men with itself: thus Turnus rushed through

disjecta agmina ad muros úrbis, ubi plurìma terra
.he scattered bands to the walls of the city, where the extensive land

madet sanguine fuso, que auræ strident hastilibus.
is moist with blood shed, and the breezes hiss with darts.

Que significat manu, et simul incipit magno ore:
And he signifies by *his* hand, and at once begins with a great voice:

Rutuli, jam parcite, et vos, Latini, inhibite tela,
O Rutulians, now cease, and you, Latins, prohibit weapons,

quacunque fortuna est, est mea: veriùs me unum
whatsoever fortune *there* is, is mine: it is more fit for me alone

luere fœdus pro vobis, et decernere ferro. Omnes
to expiate the league for you, and contend with the sword. All

medii discessêre, que dedere spatium. At pater
in the midst withdrew, and surrendered the space. But father

Æneas, nomine Turni audıto, et deserit muros, et
Æneas, the name of Turnus being heard, both deserts the walls, and

deserit summas arces, que præcipitat omnes moras·
deserts the lofty towers, and banishes all delays:

rumpit   omnia   opera,   exsultans lætitiâ, que intonat
he breaks through all *their* works,   exulting   with joy, and   thunders

horrendùm armis; quantus Athos, aut quantus Eryx,
dreadfully   in arms;   as great as   Athos,   or   as great as   Eryx

aut quantus pater Apenninus ipse, cùm fremit, coruscis
or as great as father   Apenninus   himself, when he rages, with waving

ilicibus, que gaudet attollens   se   nivali vertice ad
oaks,   and   rejoices uplifting   himself   with *his* snowy top   to

auras.   Jam verò et Rutuli certatim, et Troës, ct
the skies.   Now   indeed also the Rutulians   eagerly,   and the Trojans, an

omnes Itali   convertêre   oculos, que   qui tenebant
all   the Italians   turned   *their* eyes,   both *they* who   retained

alta mœnia,   que   qui pulsabant imos   muros
the lofty walls,   and   *they* who   beat   the lowest   wall

ariete: que   deposuere   arma   humeris.
with the battering ram.   and   they laid aside *their* arms from *their* shoulders.

Latinus ipse stupet, ingentes viros, genitos diversis
Latinus   himself   is amazed, *that* great men,   born   in different

partibus orbis,   coiisse   inter se   et cernere
parts   of the globe, should have united among themselves even   to contend

ferro.   Atque illi ut que campi patuerunt   vacuo
with the sword.   And   they as also the spaces were made clear in the vacant

æquore,   hastis conjectis eminus rapido   procursu,
plain,   *their* spears   being cast   far off   with rapid   projection.

invadunt Martem clypeis atque sonoro ære.   Tellus
they press on   the war   with shields and   resounding brass.   The earth

dat gemitum: tum congeminant crebros ictus   ensibus.
gives a groan: then   they redouble *their* frequent blows with *their* swords.

Fors et virtus miscentur in unum. Ac velut ingenti
Chance and courage are commingled in one.   And as   on great

Silâ ve summo Taburno cùm duo tauri incurrunt frontibus
Sila or lofty Taburnus when two   bulls rush together *their* fronts

conversis in inimica prœlia, pavidi magistri   cessere:
being turned to   hostile   battle, the frightened   masters have withdrawn;

omne pecus stat mutum metu, que juvencæ mussant,
all   the flock stands dumb with fear, and   the heifers   low,

quis imperitet pecori,   quem tota   armenta
doubting who   shall rule   the flock,   whom the whole   herds

sequantur: illi miscent vulnera inter   se   multâ
shall follow: they intermingle   wounds   among themselves with much

vi, que obnixi infigunt cornua, et lavant   colla
violence, and struggling they entangle *their* horns,   and bathe *their* necks

que armos   largo   sanguine: omne nemus remugit
and shoulders with copious   blood: the whole grove   rebellows

gemitu.   Haud aliter Tros Æneas et Daunius heros
with groaning.   Not otherwise Trojan Æneas and the Daunian   hero

concurrunt clypeis: Ingens fragor complet æthera.
encounter   with *their* shields: A great   noise   fills   the air.

Jupiter ipse sustinet duas lances æquato examine, et
Jupiter himself sustains two scales with equal weight, and

imponit diversa fata duorum: quem labor damnet
places in them the different fates of the two: whom labour may condemn

et quo pondere lethum vergat. Hìc Turnus emicat,
and by what weight death may decline. Here Turnus springs forward,

et toto corpore consurgit in ensem sublatum altè,
and with his whole body rises on his sword lifted high,

putans impunè, et ferit. Troës exclamant,
thinking he could do it safely, and strikes. The Trojans exclaim,

que Latini trepidi, que acies amborum arrectæ. At
and the Latius are trembling, and the armies of both are aroused. But

perfidus ensis frangitur, que deserit ardentem in
his treacherous sword is broken, and abandons him burning in

medio ictu, ni fuga subeat subsidio, Fugit
the midst of the blow, unless flight would succeed to his relief. He flies

ocyor Euro, ut aspexit capulum ignotum que
swifter than the east wind, as he beheld a hilt unknown and

dextram inermem. Est fama cùm conscendebat
his right hand unarmed. There is a report that when he mounted

equos junctos in prima prœlia, patrio mucrone
his horses yoked in the first contests, his father's sword

relicto, dum trepidat, præcipitem rapuisse ferrum
being left, while he trembles with anxiety, hurried he snatch'd the sword

aurigæ Metisci, que id suffecit diu, dum Teucri
of his charioteer Metiscus, and that supplied him long, while the Trojans

dabant palantia terga: postquam ventum est ad
gave their retreating backs: after it came to

Vulcania arma Dei, mortalis mucro dissiluit ictu,
the Vulcanian arms of the God, the mortal blade snapt asunder with a blow,

ceu futulis glacies: fragmina resplendent fulvâ arenâ.
as brittle ice: the fragments glitter on the yellow sand.

Ergo Turnus, amens, petit diversa æquora fugâ, et
Therefore Turnus, mad, seeks different plains by flight, and

implicat incertos orbes; nunc huc, indehuc. Enim
winds about in doubtful circles; now here, then there. For

Teucri inclusere undique densâ coronâ, atque
the Trojans surrounded him on each side by a dense circle, and

hinc vasta palus, hinc ardua mœnia cingunt.
on this side an extended marsh, on that high walls enclose him.

Nec minus Æneas insequitur, quanquam genua, tardata
Nevertheless Æneas pursues, although his knees, impeded

sagittâ, interdum impediunt que recusant cursum, que
by an arrow, sometimes restrain him and refuse speed, and

fervidus urget pede pedem trepidi. Veluti
glowing he presses on with his foot to the foot of his trembling foe. As

si quando venator canis, nactus cervum, inclusum in
if when a hunting dog, having found a stag, enclosed by

flumine, aut septum formidine puniceæ   pennæ,   instat
a river,   or hedged in   by the fear of the crimson   wing,   presses on

ei   cursu et latratibus: autem ille,   territus   insidiis
to him in the chase and with barking: but   he, affrightened by the snares

et altâ ripâ, fugit, et refugit   mille   vias: At vividus
and a high bank, flies on, and flies back a thousand ways: But   the lively

Umber   hians hæret   que jam tenet que jam similis
Umbrian *dog*   gaping hangs to *him* and   now holds *him* and now   like

tenenti increpuit   malis, que elusus est   inani
to one holding chides with *barking* jaws, and is mocked   with delusive

morsu: tum verò clamor exoritur, que ripæ que lacus
bite: then indeed   a cry   is raised, and the banks and   lakes

circà responsant, et omne cœlum tonat tumultu.   Ille
around   reply,   and now the heaven thunders with tumult.   He

simul   fugiens,   simul   increpat omnes Rutulos,
at the same time escaping, at the same time rebukes   all the Rutulians,

vocans quemque nomine, que efflagitat   notum ensem.
calling   each one   by name, and demands *his* well known   sword.

Æneas   contrà   minatur mortem que præsens exitium,
Æneas   on the other hand threatens death   and present destruction,

si quisquam adeat;   que   terret   trementes,
if   any one should approach *him*; and   terrifies *them*   trembling,

minitans   excisurum   urbem, et saucius instat.
threatening *that* he will tear down   the city, and wounded presses on.

Explent quinque orbes cursu, que retexunt totidem
They accomplish five   circles in the race, and unravel   as many

huc,   illuc. Enim nec levia aut ludicra præmia petuntur:
hither, *and* thither. For neither light · or trifling   rewards are sought

sed certant de vitâ et sanguine Turni. Fortè oleaster
but they contend for the life and blood   of Turnus. By chance a wild olive

amaris foliis, sacer Fauno, steterat hìc, olim lignum
with bitter leaves, sacred to Faunus, had stood here, formerly a wood

venerabile nautis, ubi servati ex undis,   solebant
venerated by sailors, when preserved from the waves, they were accustomed

figere   dona Laurenti Divo, et suspendere   votas
to place *their* gifts to the Laurentian God, and to suspend-   *their* votive

vestes. Sed Teucri sustulerant   sacrum   stirpem
garments. But the Trojans had borne away· the sacred   stock

nullo   discrimine, ut possent concurrere   puro
with no   distinction,   that they might   engage in *warfare* in the open

campo Hasta Æneæ stabat hìc, impetus detulerat
field.   The spear of Æneas stood   here, *his* impetuosity had hurled

illam fixam huc, et tenebat in lentâ radice. Dardanides
it   fastened here, and held *it*   in the tough root.   The Trojan

incubuit,   que voluit convellere ferrum   manu;
applied *himself*, and wished to tear out   the steel with *his* hand;

que seoui   telo, quem non poterat prendere cursu.
and to follow *him* with the dart, whom he could not overtake in the chase.

Tum   verò   Turnus   amens   formidine,   inquit: Faune,
Then   indeed   Turnus   mad   with fear,   said;   O Faunus,

precor, miserere; que   tu,   optima   terra,   tene   ferrum,
I pray you,   pity me;   and thou, most indulgent   earth,   hold fast   the steel,

si   semper   colui   vestros   honores,   quos   Æneadæ
if   ever   I have observed   your   honours,   which   the Trojans

contrà   fecere   profanos bello.   Dixit, que vocavit
on the other hand have rendered   profane   by war.   He said, and   invoked

opem   Dei   in vota non cassa.   Namque Æneas luctans
the aid of the God   in vows not   vain.   For   Æneas   struggling

diu,   que   moratus   in   lento   stirpe,   haud   valuit
long,   and   delaying   on   the tough   root,   was not   able

discludere   morsus   roboris   ullis   viribus.   Dum   acer
to disengage   the grasp   of the wood   by any   strength.   While   bold

nititur   et instat, rursus   Daunia   Dea   mutata
he struggles and   urges,   again   the Daunian   Goddess Juturna   changed

in   faciem   aurigæ   Metisci,   procurrit, que reddit
into the appearance of the charioteer   Metiscus,   runs on,   and restores

ensem   fratri: quod   Venus   indignata   licere
the sword to her brother;   which   Venus   enraged   that it was allowed

audaci   nymphæ,   accessit, que revellit   telum ab   altâ
to the daring   nymph,   approached and   torn up   the dart   from the deep

radice.   Olli sublimes,   refecti   armis   que animis,   hic
root.   They   elated,   refurnished   with arms   and courage,   he

fidens   gladio, hic   acer et arduus   hastâ, adsistunt
trusting to his sword, this one   bold and   daring   with his spear,   they stand

contrà,   anheli   certamine   Martis.   Interea   rex
opposed,   panting   for the contest   of Mars.   In the meantime   the king

omnipotentis Olympi alloquitur Junonem, tuentem   pugnas
of all-powerful   heaven   addresses   Juno,   regarding   the battles

de   fulvâ nube: Quæ erit finis jam conjux? quid denique
from a golden   cloud: What will be the end   now   O wife?   what   finally

restat?   ipsa   scis,   et   fateris   scire   Ænean
remains?   you   know,   and   you confess yourself to know   that Æneas

indigetem deberi   cœlo,   que   tolli   Fatis ad sidera.
as a demigod   is due   to heaven,   and to be borne off by the fates to   the stars.

Quid   struis   aut   quâ   spe   hæres   in gelidis nubibus?
What do you purpose or with what hope do you remain in the cold   clouds?

Ne decuit   Divum violari   mortali vulnere? aut ensem
Was it becoming for a God to be violated by a mortal   wound?   or   a sword

ereptum   reddi Turno, et   vim   crescere   victis?
taken away   to be restored to Turnus, and violence   to increase to the vanquished?

(enim quid   valeret   Juturna   sine   te?)   Jam   tandem
(for   what   could   Juturna   do without you?)   Now   at last

desine, que   flectere   nostris   precibus: nec   tantus   dolor
cease,   and be influenced   by our   prayers   nor   let so great   grief

edat   te tacitam, et tuæ tristes curæ sæpe recursunt mihi
corrode you   in silence, and your   sad   cares   often   recur   to me

ex tuo dulci ore. Ventum est ad supremum.
(from your sweet mouth. We have come to the last:

potuisti agitare Trojanos terris, vel undis;
you have been able to drive the Trojans from the earth, or the waves,

accendere infandum bellum, deformare domum
to enkindle the dreadful war, to dishonour the house of Latinus

et miscere hymenæos luctu: veto tentare ulteriùs.
and to intermix marriage with grief: I forbid you to proceed farther.

Sic Jupiter orsus: Contrà Saturnia Dea sic
Thus Jupiter began: On the other hand the Saturnian Goddess thus spoke

submisso vultu: Magne Jupiter, quia quidem ista
with humble countenance: O great Jove, because indeed this

tua voluntas nota mihi, invita reliqui et Turnum, et
your will was known to me, unwillingly I left both Turnus, and

terras. Nec tu videres me nunc solam æriâ sede pati
the earth. Nor had you seen me now alone on an airy seat to suffer

digna indigna; sed, cincta flammis, starem sub
things worthy and unworthy; but, girt with flames, I had stood at

aciem ipsam, que traherem Teucros in inimica prœlia.
the battle itself, and I would have led the Trojans to hostile strife.

Fateor, suasi Juturnam succurrere misero fratri, et
I confess, I have persuaded Juturna to relieve her wretched brother, and

probavi audere majora pro vitâ; tamen non
I approved that she should dare greater things for his life; yet not

ut tela, non ut contenderet arcum, adjuro
that she should hurl darts, nor that she should stretch her bow, I swear it

implacabile caput Stygii fontis, quæ una superstitio
by the merciless source of the Stygian fountain, which is the only religious dread

reddita Divis superis. Et nunc cedo equidem, que
yielded to the Gods above. And now I yield indeed, and

exosa pugna relinquo. Obtestor te illud pro Latio,
detesting battles I yield them up. I entreat of you this for Latium,

pro majestate tuorum, quod tenetur nullâ lege
for the majesty of your blood, which is held back by no law

fati: cùm jam component pacem felicibus connubiis,
of fate: when now they shall establish a peace by happy nuptials,

esto, cùm jam jungent leges et fœdera, ne jubeas
let it be, when now they shall unite in laws and treaties, you will not

Latinos indigenas mutare vetus nomen, neu
command the Latin natives to change their ancient name, nor

fieri Troas, que vocari Teucros, aut viros mutare
to become Trojans, and to be called Teucri, or the men to change

vocem, aut vertere vestes.
their language, or to alter their dress.

Sit Latium, sint Albani reges per secula; sit
Let it be Latium, let them be Alban kings through ages; let

Romana propago potens Italâ virtute. Troja occidit.
the Roman stock be powerful in Italian courage. Troy has fallen,

que sinas occiderit cum nomine. Repertor hominum
and permit it may have fallen with its name. The founder of men

que rerum, subridens olli, Et germana Jovis, que
and things, smiling on her, said, O thou both sister of Jove, and

altera proles Saturni, volvis tantos fluctus irarum
another offspring of Saturn, why do you revolve so great waves of anger

sub pectore? Verùm age, et submitte furorem
in your breast? But come on, and yield your madness

inceptum frustra: Do quod vis; et que victus que
entertained in vain: I grant what you wish; and both vanquished and

volens, remitto me. Ausonii tenebunt patrium
willing, I submit myself. The Ausonians shall retain their native

sermonem que mores: que nomen erit ut est; tantùm
language and manners: and the name shall be as it is; only

Teucri commisti corpore subsident: adjiciam
the Trojans intermingled in their whole nation shall settle in Latium: I will add

morem, que ritus sacrorum, que faciam omnes
the custom, and rituals of their sacred things, and I will make them all

Latinos uno ore. Videbis genus hinc, quod
Latins with one language. You shall see a race arise from hence, which

mistum Ausonio sanguime, surget ire supra homines,
mingled with Ausonian blood, shall rise to advance above men,

supra Deos pietate; nec ulla gens quæ æquè
above the Gods in piety; nor is there any nation which equally

celebrabit tuos honores. Juno annuit his, et
shall celebrate your honours. Juno assents to these declarations, and

lætata retorsit mentem. Interea excedit
rejoiced regained her tranquil mind. In the mean while she withdrew from

cœlo, que reliquit nubem. His actis, genitor
the sky, and left the cloud. These things being done, the father of Gods

ipse volutat aliud secum, que parat dimittere
himself revolves another project by himself. and prepares to send away

Juturnam ab armis fratris. Dicuntur geminæ
Juturna from the arms of her brother. There are said to be two

pestes, diræ cognomine; quas et tartaream Megæram,
plagues, direful in their name; whom with hell-born Megæra,

intempesta nox tulit uno que eodem partu, que revinxit
untimely night bore at one and the same birth, and bound

paribus spiris serpentum, que addidit ventosas alas. Hæc
with equal folds of serpents, and added swift wings. These

apparent ad solium Jovis, que in limine sævi regis,
appear at the throne of Jove, and in the court of the cruel king,

que acuunt metum ægris mortalibus, si quando
and they sharpen fear in sickly mortals, if at any time

rex Deûm molitur horrificum luctum que morbos,
the king of the Gods prepares dread causing grief and diseases,

aut territat meritas urbes bello. Jupiter demisit unam
or terrifies guilty cities by war Jupiter sent on

harum celerum ab summo æthere, que jussit
of these swift from the lofty sky, and commands her

occurrere Jûturnæ in omen. Illa volat, que
to encounter Juturna for an omen. She flies, and

fertur ad terram, celeri turbine: non secus ac
is borne to the earth, by a swift whirlwind: not otherwise than

sagitta impulsa nervo per nubem, quam armatam
an arrow propelled from the string through a cloud, which armed

felle sævi veneni immedicabile telum, Parthus—
with the gall of direful poison a cureless dart, a Parthian—

(Parthus sive Cydon,) torsit stridens, et incognita
(a Parthean or Cydonian,) hurled hissing, and undistinguished

transilit celeres umbras. Talis sata nocte, tuli
passes through the swift shades. Like this she born from night, raised

se, que petivit terras. Postquam videt Iliacas
herself, and sought the earth. After she beholds the Trojan

acies, atque agmina Turni, subitò collecta in figuram
armies, and the troops of Turnus, suddenly contracted into the form

parvæ alitis, quæ quondam sedens nocte in bustis, aut
of the little bird, which sometimes sitting by night on graves, or

desertis culminibus, importuna canit serùm per
abandoned roofs, untimely sings her late strain among

umbras: pestis versa in hanc faciem, sonans que
the shades: the plague changed into this appearance, hooting both

fert que refert se ad ora Turni, que everberat
advances and bears back herself before the face of Turnus, and beat

clypeum alis. Novus torpor solvit illi membra
his shield with her wings. An unusual numbness relaxed his limbs

formidine, que comæ arrectæ horrore, et vox hæsit
with fear, and his hair stood erect with horror, and his voice clave

faucibus. At, ut infelix soror Juturna procul agnovit
to his jaws. But, as his unhappy sister Juturna from afar knew

stridorem et alas Diræ, scindit solutos crines,
the hoarse sound and the wings of the fury, she tore her dishevelled locks,

fœdans ora unguibus, et pectora pugnis. Turne,
defiling her face with her nails, and her breast with her hands. O Turnus,

quid nunc potest tua germana juvare te? at quid jam
what now can your sister advantage you? but what now

superat mihi miseræ? quâ arte morer lucem tibi?
remains to me wretched? by what art shall I extend your life to you?

posumne opponere me tali monstro? jam, jam linquo
can I oppose myself to such a prodigy? now, now I leave

acies. Obscœnæ volucres, ne terrete me timentem:
the armies. Ye filthy birds, do not frighten me alarmed:

nosco verbera alarum, que lethalem sonum nec
I know the beating of your wings, and the deadly sound of your cries, nor

superba jussa magnanimi Jovis fallunt. Reponit
do the proud commands of high-minded Jove deceive me. Has he reaped

hæc   pro   virginitate?   Quo   dedit   æternam
these *rewards* for   my virginity?   For what did he give *to me*   eternal

vitam? cur est conditio mortis ademta?   nunc certe
life?   why is the condition of death taken away? now   truly

possem finire tantos dolores, et ire comes   misero
I could finish so great griefs, and go a companion to *my* wretched

fratri per umbras.   Ego immortalis? aut   erit
brother through the shades. Am I immortal?   or will *there* be

quicquam meorum, frater, dulce mihi sine te? O quæ
any thing of mine, O brother, pleasant to me without thee? O what

terra satis alta dehiscat mihi, que demittat Deam ad
land sufficiently deep will open on me, and send *me* a Goddess to

imos Manes? effata tantùm, Dea contexit caput glauco
the lowest shades? speaking thus, the Goddess covered *her* head with a green

amictu, gemens multa,. et condidit se   alto fluvio.
veil,   groaning much, and hid herself in the deep stream

Contrà   Æneas instat, que coruscat ingens arboreum
On the other hand Æneas persists, and brandishes *his* great wooden

telum, et sic fatur sævo pectore. Nunc deinde quæ
spear, and thus speaks from *his* stern breast. Now then what

est mora? aut quid jam retractas, Turne. Non est
is the delay? or why now do you decline *battle*, O Turnus. It is not

certandum cursu, sævis armis cominus. Verte
for us to contend in the race, *but* with cruel arms hand to hand. Turn

tete in omnes facies et contrahe quidquid vales,
yourself into all forms and collect whatever. *aid* you can,

sive animis, sive arte; opta sequi ardua astra
either from your courage or art; desire to follow the lofty stars

pennis, que condere te   clausum cavâ   terrâ.
on wings, and to conceal yourself inclosed in the hollow earth.

Ille, quassans caput,   Ferox tua fervida dicta
He, moving *his* head *answers*, Cruel *foe*, your glowing words

non terrent me; Dî et Jupiter hostis terrent me.
do not frighten me; The Gods and Jupiter *my* enemy frighten me.

Nec effatus plura, circumspicit ingens saxum, antiquum
Nor speaking more, he looks around upon a great stone, an ancient

saxum, ingens, quod fortè jacebat campo, positus
rock, large, which by chance lay on the plain, placed

limes agro, ut discerneret litem arvis.
as a boundary in the field, that it might decide controversy in the fields.

Vix   bis sex lecti qualia corpora hominum   tellus
Scarcely twice six chosen *men*, such bodies of men *as* the earth

nunc producit, subirent illud cervice. Ille heros,
now produces, could support it on *their* neck. The • hero,

insurgens altior et concitus cursu, torquebat raptum
rising higher and accelerated in *his* course, he hurled *it* snatched

trepidâ manu in hostem. Sed neque cognoscit
with a trembling hand against the foe. But neither did he know

se currentem, nec euntem, ve tollentem que moventem
himself running, nor going, or raising and moving

immane saxum. Genua labant; gelidus sanguis concrevit
the huge rock. His knees fail; his chilled blood congealed

frigore. Tum lapis ipse, volutus per vacuum inane,
with cold. Then the stone itself, rolled through the vacant void,

nec evasit totum spatium viri nec pertulit ictum. Ac
neither passed over the whole space of the man nor effected a blow, And

velut in somnis, ubi languida quies pressit oculos nocte,
as in sleep, when weakening sleep has closed the eyes by night,

nequicquam videmur velle extendere avidos cursus, et
in vain do we seem to wish to extend our anxious race, and

ægri succidimus in mediis conatibus; lingua
disappointed we sit down in the midst of our efforts; the tongue

non valet, notæ vires non sufficiunt corpore,
cannot effect any thing, the known strength does not supply the body,

nec vox, aut verba sequuntur: sic dira Dea
nor does the voice, or do words follow: thus the direful Goddess

negat successum Turno quâcunque virtute petivit viam.
denies success to Turnus with whatever courage he sought the way.

Tum varii sensus vertuntur pectore: Aspectat
Then varied feelings are revolved in his breast: He looks upon

Rutulos et urbem; que cunctatur metu; que tremescit
the Rutulians and the city; and delays through fear; and trembles

telum instare. Nec quò eripiat
lest his dart should reach him. Nor knows he by what means he shall rescue

se, nec quâ vi tendat in hostem, nec videt
himself, nor by what power he should march against the foe, nor does he see

currus usquam, ve aurigam sororem. Æneas coruscat
the chariot any where, or the charioteer his sister. Æneas brandishes

fatale telum cunctanti, sortitus fortunam oculis,
the fatal dart against him delaying, selecting fortune with his eyes,

et eminus intorquet toto corpore. Saxa concita
and from afar he hurls it with the whole force of his body. Rocks hurled

murali tormento nunquam sic fremunt, nec tanti
from a warlike engine never thus resound, nor have so great

crepitus desultant fulmine. Hasta, ferens dirum
claps burst from thunder. The spear, bearing dread

exitium, volat instar atri turbinis, que recludit oras
destruction, flies like a black whirlwind, and tears open the borders

loricæ, et extremos orbes septemplicis clypei; stridens
of his corslet, and the extreme folds of his sevenfold shield; hissing

transit per medium femur. Ingens Turnus ictus incidit
it passes through the midst of his thigh. Heroic Turnus struck falls

ad terram duplicato poplite. Rutuli consurgunt gemitu
to the earth on his doubled ham. The Rutulians arise with a groan

que totus mons circùm remugit, et alta nemora
and the whole mountain around re-echoes, and the high groves

remittunt vocem, latè. Ille, humilis que supplex
send back the voice, far around. He, humble and suppliant

protendens oculos que dextram precantem, inquit:
stretching forth *his* eyes and *his* right hand entreating, said:

Equidem merui, nec deprecor; utere tuâ
Indeed I have deserved *it*, nor do I pray against *it*; use your

sorte. Si qua cura miseræ parentis potest tangere te, oro,
fortune. If any care of a wretched parent can affect thee, I pray

miserere senectæ Dauni (fuit et tibi talis genitor
pity the old age of Daunus (*there* has been also to you such a father

Anchises;) et redde me, seu mavis, corpus spoliatum
Anchises;) and restore me, or if you choose, *my* body deprived

lumine meis. Vicisti, et Ausonii vidêre
of life to my *friends*. You have conquered, and the Ausonians have seen

victum tendere palmas: Lavinia est tua conjux, Ne
me vanquished to stretch out *my* hands: Lavinia is your wife. Do not

tende ulteriùs odiis. Æneas, acer in armis, stetit, volvens
advance farther in *your* hate. Æneas, bold in arms, stood, rolling

oculos, que repressit dextram, et jam que jam sermo
his eyes, and drew back *his* right hand, and now and now *his* address

cœperat flectere magis cunctantem, cùm infelix balteus
had begun to move *him* more delaying, when the unfortunate belt

pueri Pallantis apparuit alto humero, et cingula
of the youth Pallas, appeared on *his* high shoulder, and, the girdle

fulserunt notis bullis; quem victum Turnus
shone with the known boss; whom vanquished Turnus

straverat vulnere, atque gerebat inimicum insigne
had slain *with a cruel* wound, and had worn the unfriendly ensign

humeris. Postquam ille hausit oculis monumenta
on *his* shoulders. After he had received with *his* eyes the monuments

sævi doloris que exuvias, accensus furiis et
of *his* cruel grief and the spoils *of his friend*, inflamed with rage and

terribilis irâ Tune indute spoliis meorum
dreadful in wrath *he said*. Will you clothed in the spoils of *my friends*

eripiare hinc mihi? Pallas, Pallas immolat te hoc
be snatched hence from me? Pallas, Pallas sacrifices thee with this

vulnere et sumit pœnam ex scelerato sanguine. Dicens
wound and takes *this* penalty from your accursed blood. Saying

hoc fervidus condit ferrum sub adverso pectore. Ast
this, glowing he hides *his* sword within *his* hostile breast. But

illi membra solvuntur frigore, que vita indignata fugit cum
his limbs are relaxed with cold, and *his* life indignant fled with

gemitu sub umbras.
a groan to the snades.

THE

BUCOLICS AND GEORGICS

OF

VIRGIL,

WITH AN

INTERLINEAR ENGLISH TRANSLATION;

AS CLOSELY LITERAL AS THE IDIOMATIC DIFFERENCE OF THE
LANGUAGES WILL ALLOW.

BY LEVI HART.

"*Every thing*, of itself, is difficult to children, and the great use and skill of a
teacher is to *make all as easy as he can.*"—LOCKE.

THE BUCOLICS

OF

PUBLIUS VIRGILIUS MARO.

ECLOGUE I.

MELIBÆUS.—TITYRUS.

MELIBÆUS.

TITYRE, tu, recubans sub tegmine patulæ fagi,
TITYRUS, you, recumbent beneath the shade of a spreading beech,

meditaris silvestrem Musam tenui avenâ: nos
meditate *your* rustic Muse on a slender pipe: we

linquimus fines patriæ, et dulcia arva; nos
abandon the boundaries of *our* country, and *our* pleasant fields; we

fugimus patriam: tu, Tityre, lentus in umbrâ, doces
fly *our* country: you, O Tityrus, at ease in the shade, teach

silvas resonare formosam Amaryllida.
the woods to resound fair Amaryllis.

TITYRUS.

O Melibæe, Deus fecit hæc otia nobis; namque ille
O Melibæus, God has granted this leisure to us; for he

erit semper Deus mihi: sæpe tener agnus, ab nostris
shall be ever a God to me: often a tender lamb, from our

ovilibus, imbuet illius aram. Ille permisit meas boves
sheepfolds, shall stain his altar. He permits my heifers

errare, ut cernis, et ipsum ludere quæ vellem, 10
to wander, as you see, and myself to play what I will,

agresti calamo.
on my rural reed.

MELIBÆUS.

Equidem non invideo, miror magis; turbatur usque
Indeed I do not envy *you*, I wonder rather; there is trouble thus

adeò totis agris undique. En ipse, æger, ago capellas
far in all the fields on every side. Lo I. sick, drive *my* kids

3

protenùs : Tityre, etiam vix duco hanc : namque
far off: O Tityrus, even scarcely do I lead this : for

modò connixa gemellos, spem gregis, hic inter densas
just now yeaning twins, the hope of the flock, here among the thick

corylos, ah! reliquit in nudâ silice. Memini quercus,
hazels, alas! she left them on the naked rock. I remember the oaks,

tactas de cœlo, sæpe prædicere hoc malum nobis, si
struck from heaven, often foretold this misfortune to us, if my

mens non fuisset læva : sæpe sinistra cornix prædixit
mind had not been foolish: often the unlucky crow foretold it

ab cavâ ilice. Sed tamen, Tityre, da nobis, qui iste
from the excavated oak. But yet, O Tityrus, tell us, who this

Deus sit?
God may be?

TITYRUS.

20   Melibææe, ego stultus putavi urbem, quam dicunt
    O Melibæus, I foolish have thought the city, which they call

Romam, similem huic nostræ quò pastores sæpe so-
Rome, like to this of ours whither we shepherds often are

lemus depellere teneros fetus ovium. Sic nôram
accustomed to drive the tender offspring of our sheep. Thus I have known

catulos similes canibus, sic hœdos matribus ; sic
whelps like to dogs, thus kids like to their mothers; thus

solebam componere magna parvis. Verûm
I was accustomed to compare great things with small. But

hæc extulit caput inter alias urbes tantum, quantum
this city has raised her head among other cities as much, as

cupressi solent inter lenta viburna.
the cypresses used to do among the slender shrubbery.

MELIBÆUS.

Et quæ fuit tibi tanta causa videndi Romam ?
And what has been to you so great a cause of seeing Rome?

TITYRUS.

Libertas : quæ sera, tamen respexit inertem ;
Liberty: which though late, yet looked back on me inactive,

postquam candidior barba cadebat tondenti : tamen respexit
after my whiter beard fell on me shaving; yet she regarded

et venit longo tempore post ; postquam Amaryllis
me, and came a long time after; since Amaryllis

30   habet nos, Galatea reliquit. Namque, dum Gala-
    holds us, Galatea has left us. For, while Gala-

tea tenebat me (enim fatebor) erat nec spes libertatis,
tea held me (for I will confess it) there was neither hope of liberty

nec cura peculi. Quamvis multa victima exiret meis
nor care of my stock. Although many a victim departed from my

septis, et pinguis caseus premeretur ingratæ urbi;
folds. and rich cheese was pressed for the ungrateful city;

dextra non unquam redibat mihi domum gravis
my right hand never returned to me home heavy

ære.
with money.

MELIBÆUS.

Amaryllis, mirabar quid tu mœsta vocares Deos;
Amaryllis, I wondered why you mournfully invoked the Gods;

cui patereris poma pendere in suà arbore. Tityrus
to whom you suffered the apples to hang on their own tree. Tityrus

aberat hinc: Tityre, pinus ipsæ te,
was absent from hence: O Tityrus, the pines themselves *invoked* thee,

fontes ipsi, hæc arbusta ipsa vocabant te.
the fountains themselves, these groves themselves invoked thee. 40

TITYRUS.

Quid facerem? neque licebat me exire servitio,
What could I do? neither was it permitted me to depart from slavery,

nec cognoscere tam præsentes Divos alibi. Melibæe,
nor to know so favouring Gods elsewhere. O Melibæus,

hic vidi illum juvenem, cui nostra altaria fumant bis
here I have seen that youth, for whom our altars smoke twice

senos dies quotannis. Hic ille primus dedit responsum
six days yearly. Here he first gave a reply

mihi petenti; Pueri, pascite boves, ut antè, submittite
to me entreating; Boys, feed *your* heifers, as before, compel

tauros.
your bulls *to labour.*

MELIBÆUS.

Fortunate senex, ergo tua rura manebunt, et magna
Happy old *man*, therefore your fields shall remain, and extensive

satis tibi: quamvis nudus lapis, que palus obducat
enough for you: although the naked stone, and marsh covers

omnia pascua limoso junco: insueta pabula non ten-
all *your* pastures with slimy bulrush: unusual food shall not

tabunt graves fetas: nec mala contagia
injure your heavy teeming *ewes:* nor dire contagion 50

vicini pecoris lædent. Fortunate senex, hic
of the neighbouring flock shall hurt *them.* Happy old *man,* here

inter nota flumina, et sacros fontes, captabis
amid the *well* known streams, and sacred fountains, you shall enjoy

opacum frigus. Hinc sepes, quæ, ab vicino limite,
the shady cold. Here a hedge, which, from the neighbouring path.

semper depasta florem salicti Hyblæis apibus,
ever feed upon as to the flower of the willow by Hyblæan bees.

sæpe suadebit tibi inire somnum levi susurro.
often shall persuade you to go to sleep by its gentle whispering.

Hinc frondator canet ad auras: sub alta rupe. Tamen
Here the pruner shall sing to the skies: beneath a lofty rock. Yet

interea nec raucæ palumbes, tua cura, nec
in the mean time neither shall the hoarse wood-doves, your care, nor

turtur cessabit gemere ab aëriâ ulmo.
the turtle shall cease to coo from the airy elm.

TITYRUS.

60 Antè ergo leves cervi pascentur in æthere,
Sooner therefore swift stags shall feed upon air,

et freta destituent pisces nudos in litore; ante, aut
and the sea shall leave the fish naked on the shore; sooner, either

Parthus exul bibet Ararim, aut Germania Tigrim,
the Parthian exile shall drink the Saone, or Germany the Tigris,

finibus amborum pererratis, quàm illius vultus
the boundaries of both being wandered over, than his countenance

labatur nostro pectore.
shall glide from my breast.

MELIBÆUS.

At nos hinc, ibimus alii sitientes Afros: pars veniemus
But we hence, shall go some to the thirsty Africans: a part will come

Scythiam et rapidum Oaxem Cretæ, et Britannos penitùs
to Scythia and the swift Oaxes of Crete, and the Britons entirely

divisos toto orbe. En, unquam videns mirabor
separated from the whole globe. Lo, ever beholding *again* shall I admire

patrios fines longo tempore post, et culmen pauperis
my native boundaries a long time after, and the roof of my poor

tuguri congestum cespite, post aliquot aristas,
cottage covered with turf, *standing* behind some ears of corn,

70 mea regna? impius miles habebit hæc tam
my own kingdoms? shall a wicked soldier possess these so

culta novalia? Barbarus has segetes?
highly cultivated newly *ploughed* fields? A barbarian these corn fields?

En, quo discordia perduxit miseros cives! En,
Lo, whither has discord led *my* wretched countrymen! Lo,

queis consevimus agros ! Melibæe, nunc insere
for whom have we sown our fields! O Melibæus, now ingraft

pyros : pone vîtes ordine. Ite, ite meæ capellæ,
your pear trees place your vines in order. Go, go my goats,

quondam felix pecus. Ego, projectus in viridi antro,
formerly a happy flock. I, reclined within a verdant grotto,

non videbo vos posthac pendere procul de dumosâ
shall not behold you hereafter hang afar off from the bushy

rupe. Canam nulla carmina; capellæ non carpetis
rock. I may sing no songs; O ye goats, ye shall not crop

florentem cytisum et amaras salices, me pascente.
the flowery cytisus and bitter willows, *while* I am feeding *you*.

TITYRUS.

Hic tamen poteris requiescere hanc noctem 80
Here nevertheless you can rest this night

mecum super viridi fronde. Sunt nobis mitia poma,
with me upon the verdant leaves. There are to us mellow apples,

molles castaneæ, et copia pressi lactis. Et jam summa
soft chestnuts, and plenty of pressed milk. And now the highest

culmina villarum procul fumant, que majores umbræ cadunt
tops of the villas afar off smoke, and the larger shades fall

de altis montibus.
from the high mountains.

ECLOGUE II.

ALEXIS.

Pastor Corydon ardebat formosum Alexin, delicias
The shepherd Corydon ardently loved the beautiful Alexis, the darling

domini; nec, habebat quid speraret. Tantùm
of his master; nor, had he any thing he could hope for. Only

veniebat assiduè inter densas fagos umbrosa cacumina;
he came continually among the thick beeches *having* shady tops;

ibi solus jactabat hæc incondita montibus
there alone he threw away these unstudied *complaints* to the mountains

et silvis inani studio: O crudelis Alexi, curas nihil
and the woods with vain regard: O cruel Alexis, you care nothing

mea carmina; nil miserere nostri; denique coges me
for my songs; you do not pity me; finally you will compel me

mori. Nunc, etiam, pecudes captant umbras et frigora,
to die. Now, also, the flocks enjoy the shade and cold;

nunc etiam spineta occultant virides lacertos; et Thesty-
now even the brambles conceal the green lizards; and Thesty-

lis contundit allia que serpyllum, olentes herbas, mes-
lis pounds garlic and thyme, sweet smelling herbs, for the

soribus fessis rapido æstu. At, dum lustro 10
reapers weary with swift *descending* heat. But, whilst I survey

tua vestigia, arbusta resonant raucis cicadis mecum
your footsteps, the groves resound with hoarse grasshoppers with me

sub ardenti sole. Nonne fuit satiùs pati tristes iras
beneath the burning sun. Was it not better to endure the cruel anger

Amaryllidis, atque superba fastidia?   Nonne
of Amaryllis,   and   her proud disdain?   Was it not *better to endure*

Menalcan? quamvis ille niger, quamvis tu esse candidus
Menalcas?   although he *was* black, although you are   fair

O formose puer, ne crede nimiùm colori.   Alba ligustra
O beauteous boy, do not trust too much to complexion. White   privets

cadunt, nigra vaccinia leguntur.   Sum despectus tibi,
fall.   black hyacinths are gathered. 1 am   despised by you

    Alexi, nec quæris qui sim? quàm dives   nivei
O Alexis, nor do you inquire who I may be?   how   rich in the snowy

20 pecoris, quàm abundans lactis. Meæ mille agnæ
     flock, how abundant in milk.   My thousand lambs

errant in Siculis montibus. Novum lac defit mihi non
wander upon the Sicilian mountains.   New milk is wanting to me not

æstate, non frigore.   Canto, quæ Dircæus Amphion
in summer, nor in the cold *of winter*. I sing, what Dircæan   Amphion

erat solitus   in Actæo Aracyntho, si quando vo-
was accustomed *to sing* upon Actæon Aracynthus, if at any time he

cabat   armenta. Nec sum adeò informis; nuper in
called together *his* herds.   Nor am I so deformed; lately upon

litore vidi me, cùm mare staret placidum ventis.
the shore I beheld myself, when the sea stood   peaceful by the winds.

Ego non metuam Daphnin, te judice,. si imago
I   will not fear   Daphnis. you being judge, if *my* likeness

nunquam fallat. O tantum libeat tibi habitare mecum
never   shall deceive *me*. O at length will it please you to inhabit with me

sordida rura atque humiles casas, et figere cervos, que
the dirty fields and   humble cottages, and to pierce the stags, and

compellere gregrem hædorum viridi hibisco! Imita-
to drive together a flock   of kids with a green bulrush! You shall

30 bere Pana canendo unà mecum in silvis. Pan
     imitate Pan in singing together with me in the woods Pan

primus instituit conjungere plures calamos cerà: Pan
first   taught   to unite   many   reeds   with wax· Pan

curat oves, que magistros ovium. Nec pœniteat te
provides for sheep, and the masters of sheep. Nor let it ashame you

trivisse labellum calamo. Quid faciebat Amyntas non
to have worn your lip with the reed.   What did   Amyntas   not

   ut sciret hæc eadem?   Est mihi fistula
accomplish that he might know these same things? There is to me a pipe

compacta septem disparibus cicutis, quam Damætas
joined   with seven unequal   reeds, which   Damætas

olim dedit mihi dona, et moriens dixit: Nunc ista
formerly has given to me as a gift, and dying   said Now   this

habet te secundum.   Damætas dixit; stultus Amyntas
has you for its second *owner* Damætas said;   foolish   Amyntas

40 invidit. Præterea duo capreoli reperti mihi nec
     envied *me*   Besides two little goats found   by me   nor

tutâ valle, etiam nunc pellibus sparsis albo, siccant
in a safe vale, even now their skins being sprinkled with white, they drain

bina ubera ovis die; quos servo tibi. Jampridem
two udders of a sheep in a day: which I keep for you. Long since

Thestylis orat abducere illos à me; et faciet:
Thestylis prays to take them from me; and let her do it;

quoniam nostra munera sordent tibi. Ades huc, O for-
since my gifts disgust you. Come hither, O beau-

mose puer: ecce Nymphæ ferunt lilia tibi plenis calathis:
tiful boy: behold the Nymphs bear lilies to you in full baskets:

candida Nais, carpens palentes violas et summa papavcra
fair Nais, plucking pale violets and the highest poppies

tibi, jungit narcissum et florem bene olentis anethi.
for you, she joins the narcissus and the flower of the sweet smelling anise.

Tum intexens casiâ atque aliis suavibus herbis, pingit
Then interweaving cassia and other sweet herbs, she paints

mollia vaccinia luteolâ calthâ. Ego ipse legam 50
soft hyacinths with yellow marygold. I myself will gather

cana mala tenerâ lanugine, que castaneas nuces, quas
hoary apples with tender down, and chestnuts, which

mea Amaryllis amabat. Addam cerea pruna: et honos
my Amaryllis loved. I will add waxen plums: and honour

erit huic pomo quoque: et carpam vos, ô lauri, et
shall be to this fruit also: and I will pluck you, O ye laurels, and

te, myrte, proxima; quoniam sic positæ miscetis
thee, O myrtle, nearest; since thus disposed you mingle

suaves odores. Corydon, es rusticus, nec Alexis
your sweet odours. Corydon, you are a clown, nor does Alexis

curat munera: nec Iolas concedat, si certes
care for your gifts: nor would Iolas yield, if you should contend

muneribus. Eheu, quid volui mihi misero! perdi-
with gifts. Alas, what have I wished for myself wretched! lost

tus immisi Austrum floribus, et apros
man I have let loose the south-wind among the flowers, and the boars

liquidis fontibus. Ah, demens! quem fugis? Di
to the liquid fountains. Alas, mad man! whom do you fly? The gods

quoque, que Dardanius Paris habitârunt silvas. 60
even, and Trojan Paris have inhabited the woods.

Pallas ipsa colat arces quas condidit: silvæ
Let Minerva herself inhabit towers which she has built: the woods

placeant nobis ante omnia. Torva leæna sequitur
please us before all things. The stern lioness pursues

lupum, lupus ipse capellam; lasciva capella sequitur
the wolf, the wolf himself the goat; the wanton goat follows

florentem cytisum; Corydon te, ô Alexi. Sua
the flowering cytisus; Corydon pursues you, O Alexis His own

voluptas trahit quemque. Aspice, juvenci referunt
pleasure draws aside each one. See, the bullocks bring back

aratra suspensa jugo, et sol decedens duplicat
the ploughs hanging from the yoke, and the sun withdrawing redoubles

crescentes umbras; tamen amor urit me. Enim quis
the increasing shades; yet love burns me. For what

modus adsit amori? Ah, Corydon, Corydon! quæ de-
limit is there to love? Alas, Corydon, Corydon! what mad-

mentia cepit te? Est tibi semiputata vitis in frondosâ
ness possesses you? There is to you an unpruned vine upon the leafy

70 ulmo. Quin tu potiùs para detexere aliquid sal-
elm. But do you rather prepare to interweave something at

tem, usus quorum indiget viminibus que molli junco?
least, the utility of which is required of vines and soft bulrush?

invenies alium Alexin, si hic fastidit te.
you shall find another Alexis, if this one scorns you.

ECLOGUE III.

MENALCAS.

Damæta, dic mihi cujum pecus? an Melibæi?
O Dametas, tell me whose is this flock? whether Melibæus's?

DAMÆTAS.

Non; verùm Ægonis. Ægon tradidit mihi nuper.
No; but Egon's. Ægon delivered it to me lately.

MENALCAS.

Oves, semper infelix pecus! dum ipse fovet
O sheep, always an unhappy flock! whilst he cherishes

Neæram, ac veretur ne illa præferat me sibi; hic
Næera, and fears lest she should prefer me to him; here

alienus custos mulget oves bis in horâ; et succus
a strange keeper milks the sheep twice in an hour; and nourishment

subducitur pecori, et lac agnis.
is withdrawn from the flock, and milk from the lambs.

DAMÆTAS.

Tamen memento ista objicienda viris parcius.
Yet remember these things are to be charged to men more cautiously.

Et novimus qui te, hircis tuentibus transversa
And we have known who betrayed you, the goats gazing obliquely

et quo sacello, sed faciles nymphæ risere.
and in what chapel, but the gentle nymphs laughed.

MENALCAS.

Credo, tum, cùm videre me incidere arbustum 10
I believe it, then, when they beheld me cut down the grove

Myconis, atque novellas vites malâ falce
of Mycon, and the new vines with a mischievous sickle.

DAMÆTAS.

Aut hic ad veteres fagos, cum fregisti arcum et
Or here by the ancient beeches, when you broke the bow and

calamos Daphnidis, quæ tu, perverse Menalca, cùm
reeds of Daphnis, which you, O morose Menalcas, when

vidisti donata puero, et dolebas, et mortuus esses
you saw them presented to the boy, you both grieved, and would have died

si non nocuisses aliquâ.
if you had not injured him in some way.

MENALCAS.

Quid domini faciant, cùm fures audent talia? non
What will masters do, when thieves dare such things? have

ego vidi te, pessime, excipere caprum Damonis
I not seen you, most felonious wretch, seize the goat of Damon

insidiis, lyciscâ latrante multum? et cum clamarem;
by stratagem, the mongrel barking much? and when I cried out;

Quo nunc ille proripit se? Tityre, coge pecus;
Whither now does he snatch himself? O Tityrus, collect your flock;

tu latebas post carecta.
you lay hid behind sedges. 20

DAMÆTAS.

An non ille, victus cantando, redderet mihi
Whether shall not he, overcome in singing, restore to me

caprum, quem mea fistula meruisset carminibus?
the goat, which my pipe may have deserved by its songs?

si nescis, ille caper fuit meus; et Damon ipse fate-
if you know it not, this goat has been mine; and Damon himself con-

batur mihi, sed negabat posse reddere.
fessed it to me, but he denied that he was able to repay it.

MENALCAS.

Tu illum cantando? aut unquam fuit tibi
You conquer him in singing? or ever has there been to you

fistula juncta cerâ? non tu, indocte, solebas dis-
a pipe united with wax? were not you, ignorant dunce, accustomed to

perdere miserum carmen stridenti stipulâ in tri-
torture a wretched song on a creaking straw in the cross

viis?
roads?

DAMÆTAS.

Vis,   ergo,   vicissim   experiamur   inter   nos
Are you willing, therefore,   in turn   that we try   among ourselves

quid uterque possit?   Ego depono hanc vitulam (ne forte
what   each   can do?   I   pledge   this   heifer   (lest perhaps

recuses,   bis venit ad mulctram, alit binos fetus
you may refuse, twice she comes to   the milk pail, she feeds two   offspring

30   ubere)   tu   dic,   quo   pignore   certes
    with her udder) do you   say,   with what   pledge   you will contend

mecum.
with me.

MENALCAS.

Non   ausim deponere quicquam de   grege   tecum;
I do not   dare   to pledge   any thing   from   the flock   with you

namque est   mihi pater domi,   est injusta noverca:
for   there is   to me   a father at home, there is an unjust stepmother

que bis   die   ambo numerant pecus, et alter hædos
and   twice in the day both   count   the flock, and   one   the kids.

Verùm, quoniam libet tibi insanire,   ponam   id, quod
But,   since   it pleases you to be mad,   I will pledge this,   which

tute ipse   fatebere majus, fagina pocula, cælatum opus
you yourself shall confess greater, beechen bowls, the wrought work

divini   Alcimedontis: quibus lenta vitis, superaddita
of the divine   Alcimedon: to which a slender vine,   added

facili   torno, vestit corymbos diffusos pallente hedera.
by a skilful turner, decks   clusters   overspread with the pale   ivy.

In medio   duo signa, Conon: et quis fuit alter, qui
In the midst are two statues,   Conon: and who was the other, he who

40   descripsit totum orbem gentibus   radio;   quæ,
    described   the whole globe to the nations with a wand;   what

tempora messor, quæ   curvus   arator   haberet? nec-
seasons   the reaper,   what the bending ploughman should have?   nor

dum admovi labra illis, sed   servo   condita.
yet   have I moved my lips to them, but   I keep them preserved.

DAMÆTAS.

Et idem Alcimedon fecit duo pocula nobis, et am-
And the same   Alcimedon   made two   bowls   for us, and he em-

plexus est ansas circum molli   acantho: que posuit
braced   the handles around with the soft bearsfoot: and he placed

Orphea in medio, que silvas sequentes.   Necdum
Orpheus in the midst, and the woods following.   Nor yet

admovi   labra illis, sed   servo   condita. Si spec-
have I moved my lips to them, but   I keep them stored up.   If you will

tes ad vitulam, est nihil   quod   laudes   pocula.
ook at the calf, there is nothing for which you should praise the bowls.

MENALCAS.

Nunquam effugies hodiè: veniam quocunque vo-
By no means shall you fly me to day: I will come wherever you

câris. Tantùm vel qui venit audiat hæc.
shall call Only even let him who comes attend to this *controversy*.

Ecce, Palæmon: efficiam ne lacessas 50
See here, is Palæmon: I will cause that you shall not provoke

quemquam voce posthàc.
any one with *your* voice hereafter.

DAMÆTAS.

Quin age, si habes quid; non erit ulla
But come on, if you have any thing; there shall not be any

mora in me: nec fugio quemquam. Tantùm, vicine
delay in me: nor do I avoid any one. Only, neighbour

Palæmon, reponas hæc imis sensibus, res
Palæmon, do you lay up these *things* in your inmost senses, the affair

est non parva.
is not small.

PALÆMON.

Dicite; quandoquidem consedimus in molli herba:
Say; since we have sat down upon the soft grass:

et nunc omnis ager, nunc omnis arbos parturit, nunc silvæ
and now every field, now every tree produces, now the woods

frondent, nunc annus formosissimus. Incipe, Damæta,
put forth leaves, now the year is most fair. Begin, Damætas,

tu deinde sequere, Menalca. Dicetis alternis.
you afterwards follow, O Menalcas. You shall sing in alternate *verse*

Camenæ amant alterna.
The Muses love alternate *verses*.

DAMÆTAS.

Musæ, principium ab Jove: omnia 60
Ye Muses, our beginning *is* from Jove: all *things*

plena Jovis: ille colit terras, mea carmina illi curæ
are full of Jove: he cultivates the earth, my songs *are* his care.

MENALCAS.

Et Phœbus amat me: sunt, Phœbo, semper apud me
And Apollo loves me: there are, for Apollo, ever with me

sua munera, lauri, et suave rubens hyacinthus.
his own gifts, laurels, and the sweetly blushing hyacinth.

DAMÆTAS.

Galatea, lásciva puella, petit me malo, et
Galatea, a wanton maid, strikes me with an apple, and

fugit ad salices, et cupit se videri antè.
flies to the willows, and desires that she be seen first

MENALCAS.

At meus ignis Amyntas offert sese mihi ultro ; ut
But my flame Amyntas offers himself to me willingly ; so that
non Delia sit notior nostris canibus.
not *even* Delia is more known to our dogs.

DAMÆTAS.

Munera sunt parta meæ veneri ; namque ipse notavı
Gifts are provided for my love ; for I have noted
locum, quo aëriæ palumbes congessere.
the place, where the airy wood doves have built *their nests.*

MENALCAS.

Misi decem aurea mala puero, lecta ex sil-
I have sent ten golden apples to my boy, plucked from the
70 vestri arbore, quod potui : cras mit-
wild tree, what I could do, *I have done :* to-morrow I will
tam altera.
send others.

DAMÆTAS.

O quoties, et quæ Galatea locuta est nobis !
O how often, and what *things* Galatea has spoken to us !
venti, referatis aliquam partem ad aures divûm.
ye winds, bear back some part to the ears of the gods.

MENALCAS.

Quid prodest, Amynta, quod ipse non spernis
What does it profit, O Amyntas, that you do not despise
me animo, si ego servo retia, dum tu sectaris
me in your mind, if I keep the nets, while you pursue
apros ?
the boars ?

DAMÆTAS.

Iola, mitte Phyllida mihi, est meus natalis. Cum
Iola, send Phyllis to me, it is my birthday. When
faciam vitulâ, pro frugibus, ipse venito.
I shall *make sacrifice*, with a heifer, for the fruits, do you come.

MENALCAS.

Iola, amo Phyllida ante alias, nam flevit me discedere ;
O Iolas, I love Phyllis before others, for she wept when I departed·
et inquit Formose, vale longum, vale.
and said, O fair *youth*, farewell for a long *time*, farewell.

DAMÆTAS.

Lupus triste stabulis ; imbres maturis frugibus ;
The wolf is a sad *thing* to the stables; showers to the ripe fruits

venti arboribus ; iræ Amaryllidis nobis. 86
winds to trees; tne anger of Amaryllis to us.

MENALCAS.

Humor dulce satis ; arbutus de-
Moisture is a pleasant *thing* to corn planted ; the strawberry tree to the

pulsis hædis ; lenta salix fœto pecori : Amyntas
weaned kids; the slender willow to the teeming flock : Amyntas

solus mihi.
alone to me.

DAMÆTAS.

Pollio amat nostrum musam ; quamvis sit rustica.
Pollio loves my muse ; although she be rustic.

Pierides, pascite vitulam vestro lectori.
Ye Muses, feed a heifer for your reader.

MENALCAS.

Et Pollio ipse facit nova carmina : pascite
And Pollio himself makes rare verses ; feed *for him*

taurum, jam petat cornu, et qui spargat arenam
the bull, now he strikes with his horn, and he scatters the sand

pedibus.
with his feet.

DAMÆTAS.

Qui amat te, Pollio, veniat quò gaudet
He who loves thee, O Pollio, let him arrive where he rejoices

te. Quoque, mella fluant illi, et as-
that you *have reached*. Also, may honey flow to him, and may the

per rubus ferat amomum.
rough bramble produce spikenard.

MENALCAS.

Qui non odit Bavium, amet tua carmina, 90
He who does not hate Bavius, shall love thy verses,

Mævî; atque idem jungat vulpes, et mulgeat hircos.
O Mævius: and the same shall yoke foxes, and shall milk he goats.

DAMÆTAS.

O pueri, qui legitis flores, et fraga nascentia humi,
O boys, who gather flowers, and strawberries growing on the ground,

fugite hinc, frigidus anguis latet in herbâ.
fly from hence, a cold snake lies hid in the grass.

MENALCAS.

Oves, parcite procedere nimiùm; non bene creditur
Ye sheep, cease to proceed too far; it is not well trusting

ripæ. etiam aries ipse nunc siccat vellera.
to the bank: even the ram himself now dries *his* fleece.

DAMÆTAS.

Tityre, reice pascentes capellas à flumine:
O Tityrus, drive back the feeding goats from the river

ipse, lavabo omnes in fonte, ubi erit tempus.
I, will wash *them* all in the fountain, when it shall be time.

MENALCAS.

Pueri, cogite oves; si æstus præceperit lac
Ye boys, collect *your* sheep; if the heat shall have dried up the milk

ut nuper, frustra pressabimus ubera palmis.
as *it did* lately, in vain shall we press the udders with *our* hands.

DAMÆTAS.

100 Eheu! quam macer mihi taurus est in pingui arvo!
Alas! how lean my bull is in the rich field

idem amor est exitium pecori, que magistro pecoris.
the same love is destruction to the flock, and to the master of the flock.

MENALCAS.

Certè neque amor est causa his: vix
Truly neither love is the cause to them *of leanness:* scarcely

hærent ossibus; nescio quis oculus fascinat mihi
they hang together by their bones; I know not what eye bewitches my

teneros agnos.
tender lambs.

DAMÆTAS.

Dic, in quibus terris, spatium cœli pateat tres ulnas,
Say, in what lands, the space of heaven spreads out three ells,

non amplius, (et eris magnus Apollo mihi.)
and no more, (and you shall be a great Apollo to me.)

MENALCAS.

Dic, in quibus terris flores nascantur, inscripti
Say, in what lands flowers grow, having written on them

nomina regum; et solus habeto Phyllida.
the names of kings; and alone possess Phyllis.

PALÆMON.

Non est nostrum componere tantas lites inter
It is not our *office* to settle so great controversies among

vos: et tu dignus vitulâ, et hic; et quisquis aut
you: and you are worthy of the heifer, and he; and whosoever either

metuet dulces, aut experietur amaros amores. Jam, 110
has feared pleasant, or experienced bitter loves. Now,

pueri, claudite rivos: prata biberunt sat.
boys, shut up the rivers: the meadows have drunk enough.

ECLOGUE IV.

SICELIDES Musæ, canamus paulo majora
YE Sicilian Muses, let us sing in strains a little more exalted

Arbusta, que humiles myricæ, non juvant omnes. Si
Groves, and humble tamarisks, do not delight all. It

canimus silvas, silvæ sint dignæ consule. Jam ul-
we sing of woods, let the woods be worthy of a consul. Now the

tima ætas Cumæi carminis venit; magnus ordo
last age of the Cumæan song has arrived; a great order

seculorum nascitur ab integro. Et jam virgo redit, Sa-
of ages arises anew. And now the virgin returns, Sa-

turnia regna redeunt: jam nova progenies demittitur
turn's kingdoms return: now a new race is sent down

alto cœlo. Tu modò, casta Lucina, fave nascenti
from high heaven. Do you now, O chaste Lucina, favour the infant

puero, quo ferrea primùm desinet, ac aurea gens
boy, by whom the iron age first shall end, and the golden age

surget toto mundo: jam tuus Apollo 10
shall arise through the whole world: now your own Apollo

regnat. Que adeò hoc decus ævi inibit, te, Pollio,
reigns. And thus this glory of the age shall enter, you, O Pollio,

te consule; et magni menses incipient procedere.
you being consul; and the great months shall begin to advance.

Te duce, si qua vestigia nostri sceleris manent,
You being chief, if any marks of our crime shall remain,

irrita solvent terras perpetuâ formidine. Ille
rendered vain they shall free the earth from perpetual fear. He

accipiet vitam deorum, que videbit heroas permistos
shall receive the life of gods, and shall behold heroes mingled

divis, et ipse videbitur illis; que reget pacatum
with gods, and he shall be seen by them; and he shall rule the peaceful

orbem patriis virtutibus. At tellus prima
globe by his father's virtues. But the earth first shall pour out

munuscula tibi, puer, nullo cultu, errantes hederas,
her offerings to you. O boy, with no cultivation wandering ivy

20 passim cum baccare, que fundet colocasia,
every where with lady's-glove, and shall produce Egyptian beans,

mista ridenti acantho; capellæ ipsæ referent domum
mingled with smiling acanthus; the goats themselves shall bring home

ubera distenta lacte; nec armenta metuent magnos
their udders swelled out with milk; nor shall the herds fear the great

leones. Cunabula ipsa fundent blandos flores tibi.
lions. Cradles themselves shall pour forth pleasant flowers to you.

Et serpens occidet, et fallax herba veneni occidet;
And the serpent shall die, and the deceiving herb of poison shall die

Assyrium amomum nascetur vulgò; at simul poteris
Assyrian spikenard shall grow every where; but as soon as you can

jam legere laudes heroum, et facta parentis, et
now read the praises of heroes, and the deeds of *your* father, and

cognoscere quæ virtus sit; campus flavescet paulatim
know what virtue is; the plain shall grow yellow by degrees

molli aristâ, que rubens uva pendebit incultis
with the soft ears of corn, and the blushing grape shall hang on the rude

30 sentibus, et duræ quercus sudabunt roscida mella.
brambles, and the hardy oaks shall perspire dewy honey

Tamen pauca vestigia priscæ fraudis suberunt, quæ
Yet a few footsteps of ancient fraud shall survive, which *shall lead*

tentare thetim ratibus, quæ cingere oppida
men to explore the sea in ships, which *shall induce them* to surround towns

muris, quæ jubeant infindere sulcos telluri.
with walls, which shall command *them* to cleave furrows in the earth.

Tum erit alter Tiphys, et altera Argo, quæ
Then shall there be another Tiphys, and another Argo, which

vehat delectos heroas; etiam altera bella erunt; atque
shall transport chosen heroes; also other wars shall be; and

magnus Achilles mittetur iterum ad Trojam. Hinc, ubi
great Achilles shall be sent again to Troy. Hence, when

jam firmata ætas fecerit te virum, et vector ipse
now confirmed age shall have made you a man, and the sailor himself

cedet mari; nec nautica pinus mutabit merces:
shall withdraw from the sea; nor shall the marine boat exchange merchandise:

omnis tellus feret omnia. Non humus patietur
every land shall produce every thing. Nor shall the ground endure

40 rastros, non vinea falcem: jam quoque robustus
harrows, nor the vineyard the sickle: now also the strong

arator solvet juga tauris. Nec lana disce·
ploughman shall loosen the yokes from the bulls. Nor shall wool learn

mentiri varios colores; sed aries, ipse, in pratis,
to counterfeit various colours; but the ram, himself, in the meadows,

mutabit vellera, jam suave rubenti murice, jam
shall exchange *his* fleece, now with the sweetly blushing purple, now

croceo luto. Sandyx vestiet pascentes agnos suâ sponte.
with yellow dye. Crimson shall clothe the feeding lambs spontaneously.

Parcæ, concordes stabili numine fatorum, dixerunt
The fates, harmonious in the firm will of the destinies, have said

suis fusis, talia sæcla currite. O clara soboles deûm,
to their spindles, let these ages run on. O bright offspring of gods,

magnum incrementum Jovis, aggredere magnos honores,
great descendant of Jupiter, approach thy great dignities,

jam tempus aderit. Aspice mundum convexo 50
now the time has arrived. Behold the world with its vaulted

pondere nutantem, que terras, que tractus maris, que
weight nodding, and the lands, and the regions of the sea, and

profundum cœlum; aspice, ut omnia lætentur sæclo
exalted heaven; behold, how all things rejoice in the age

venturo. O ultima pars tam longæ vitæ maneat
about to come. O that the last part of so long a life would remain

mihi, et spiritus, quantum erit sat dicere tua facta!
to me, and breath, as much as will be enough to sing your deeds!

non vincet me carminibus, nec Thracius Or-
not any one shall excel me in songs, neither Thracian Or-

pheus, nec Linus; quamvis mater, Calliopea, adsit
pheus, nor Linus; although his mother, Calliopea, shall assist

huic Orphei, atque pater, formosus Apollo, huic
him Orpheus, and his father, fair Apollo, shall aid him

Lino. Si etiam Pan certet mecum, Arcadiâ judice,
Linus. If even Pan should contend with me, Arcadia being judge,

etiam Pan dicat se victum, Arcadiâ judice.
also Pan shall declare himself conquered, Arcadia being judge.

Parve puer, incipe cognoscere matrem risu: 60
Little boy, begin to know your mother by her smile:

decem menses tulerunt longa fastidia matri,
ten months have brought long-continued pains on your mother

Incipe, parve puer; cui parentes non risere, nec
Begin, little boy; on whom your parents have not smiled, nor

deus hunc mensâ, nec dea dignatâ est kin
a god honoured him with his table, nor a goddess honoured kin

cubili.
with her bed.

ECLOGUE V.

MENALCAS.

Mopse, quoniam convenimus, ambo boni, tu
O Mopsus, since we have assembled, both good men, you
inflare leves calamos, ego dicere versus, cur non conto blow the light reeds, I to sing verses, why do we not
sedimus hic inter ulmos mistas corylis?
sit down here among the elms mingled with hazels?

MOPSUS.

Tu major; est æquum me parere tibi, Menalcas;
You are the elder; it is right for me to obey you,: O Menalcas;
sive sub incertas umbras, zephyris motantibus, sive
either beneath the uncertain shades, the west winds moving, or
potius succedimus antro; aspice, ut silvestris labrusca
rather we enter the grotto; see, how the rural wild vine
sparsit antrum raris racemis.
sprinkles the cave with scattered clusters.

MENALCAS.

In nostris montibus Amyntas solus certet tibi.
In our mountains Amyntas alone shall contend with you.

MOPSUS.

Quid si idem certet superare Phœbum canendo?
What if the same should strive to excel Apollo in singing?

MENALCAS.

Mopse, prior incipe, si habes aut quos ignes Phyllidis,
O Mopsus, first begin, if you have either any flames of Phyllis,
10 aut laudes Alconis, aut jurgia Codri; incipe, Ti-
or praises of Alcon, or quarrels of Codrus; begin, Tityrus servabit pascentes hædos.
tyrus shall keep the feeding kids.

MOPSUS.

Imo, experiar hæc carmina quæ descripsi nuper viridi
Nay, I will try these songs which I have written lately on the green
cortice fagi, et modulans notavi alterna: dein-
bark of the beech tree, and tuning I have noted them by turns: after-
de tu jubeto Amyntas certet.
wards you command that Amyntas should contend.

MENALCAS.

Quantum lenta salix cedit pallenti olivæ, quantum
As much as the slender willow yields to the pale olive, as much as

humilis saliunca puniceis rosetis; tantum Amyntas
the lowly lavender to the crimson rose beds; so much Amyntas

cedit tibi nostro judicio.
yields to you in my judgment.

MOPSUS.

Sed, puer, tu desine plura: successimus antro.
But, O boy, do you cease to utter more: we have entered the grotto

Nymphæ flebant Daphnin extinctum crudeli funere: 20
The nymphs mourned Daphnis destroyed by cruel death;

vos, coryli, et flumina, testes nymphis: cum mater
you, ye hazels, and ye streams, are witnesses to the nymphs: when the mother

complexa miserabile corpus sui nati, vocat atque deos
embracing the wretched body of her son, she calls both the gods

atque astra crudelia Daphni, non ulli egere pastos
and the stars cruel. O Daphnis, not any swains drove their fed

boves ad frigida flumina illis diebus: nulla quadrupes
oxen to the cool streams on those days: no quadruped

neque libavit amnem, nec attigit herbam graminis Daphni,
neither tasted the stream, nor touched a blade of grass. O Daphnis,

que feri montes que silvæ loquuntur, etiam Pœ-
both the savage mountains and the woods speak, also the

nos leones ingemuisse tuum interitum. Daphnis
Carthagenian lions mourned your death. Daphnis

et instituit subjungere Armenias tigres curru, Daph-
likewise taught to join Armenian tigers to the chariot, Daph-

nis inducere thiasos Baccho, et intexere lentas 30
nis taught to lead out dances to Bacchus, and to intertwine slender

hastas mollibus folliis. Ut vitis est decori arboribus, ut
spears with soft leaves. As the vine is the glory to the trees, as

uvæ vitibus, ut tauri gregibus, ut segetes pingui-
the grapes to the vines, so the bulls are to the flocks, as the corn to the

bus arvis; tu omne decus tuis. Postquam
rich fields; so you are all the glory of your friends. After

fata tulerunt te, Pales ipsa, atque Apollo ipse reliquit
the fates bore you off, Pales herself, and Apollo himself left

agros. Sæpe, sulcis quibus mandavimus grandia
the fields. Often, in the furrows to which we have committed the large

hordea, infelix lolium, et steriles avenæ dominantur. Pro
barley, unhappy darnel, and barren oats prevail. Instead of

molli violâ, pro purpureo narcisso, carduus et paliurus
the soft violet, instead of the purple narcissus, the thistle and thorn

surgit. acutis spinis. Pastores, spargite humum folliis,
arises with sharp prickles. Ye shepherds, spread the ground with leaves

40 inducite umbras fontibus; Daphnis mandat talia
lead on the shades to the fountains; Daphnis commands suck

fieri sibi. Et facite tumulum, et superaddite
things to be done for him. And make a tomb, and superadd

carmen tumulo; Ego, Daphnis, notus in silvis, hinc
a verse to the tomb; I, Daphnis, known among the woods, hence

usque ad sidera, custos formosi pecoris, ipse formosior.
even to the stars, the keeper of a fair flock, myself more fair.

MENALCAS.

Divine poëta, tuum carmen tale nobis, quale sopor fessis
O divine poet, your song is such to us, as sleep to the wearied

in gramine, quale per æstum restinguere sitim saliente
upon the grass, as in the heat to extinguish thirst from a springing

rivo dulcis aquæ. Nec æquiparas magistrum calamis
rivulet of sweet water. Nor do you equal your master with the reeds

solùm, sed voce. Fortunate puer, nunc tu eris alter,
only, but with the voice. Happy boy, now you will be another,

50 ab illo, Tamen nos dicemus hæc nostra tibi
from him. Nevertheless we will sing these our *verses* for you

vicissim, que tollemus tuum Daphnin ad astra; feremus
in turn, and we will extol your Daphnis to the stars; we will raise

Daphnin ad astra: Daphnis amavit nos quoquè.
Daphnis to the stars: Daphnis loved us also.

MOPSUS.

An sit quicquam majus nobis tali munere?
Whether can there be any thing greater to us than such a favour?

et puer ipse fuit dignis cantari; et jampridem Stimicon
and the boy himself was worthy to be sung; and long since Stimicon

laudavit ista carmina nobis.
had praised these songs to us.

MENALCAS.

Daphnis, candidus, miratur insuetum limen olympi,
Daphnis, in white, admires the unaccustomed court of heaven

que videt nubes et sidera sub pedibus. Ergo alacris
and beholds the clouds and the stars beneath his feet. Therefore joyous

voluptas tenet silvas et cætera rura, que Pana, que
pleasure holds the woods and other fields, and Pan, and

pastores, que Dryadas puellas. Nec lupus insidias
the shepherds, and the Dryad maids. Nor does the wolf *meditate* snares

pecori, nec ulla retia meditantur dolum cervis:
against the flock, nor do any nets meditate fraud to the stags:

60 bonus Daphnis amat otia. Intonsi montes
good Daphnis loves retirement. The unshorn mountains

ipsi jactant voces ad sidera lætitiâ: jam rupes
themselves throw their voices to the stars with joy: now the rocks

ipsæ carmina, arbusta ipsa sonant.
themselves *re-echo these* songs, the groves themselves resound *them*

Menalca, Deus, ille Deus. O sis bonus que felix tuis
Menalcas, a God, this is a God. O be thou good and happy to your

en quatuor aras; ecce duas tibi, Daphni, que duo
friends! lo four altars; behold two for you, O Daphnis, and two

altaria Phæbo, statuam bina pocula spumantia novo
altars for Apollo, I will place two bowls foaming with new

lacte quotannis, que duos crateras pinguis olivi tibi: et
milk yearly, and two goblets of rich oil for you and

imprimis hilarans convivia multo Baccho, ante focum,
especially enlivening the feasts with much wine, before the hearth.

si erit frigus, si messis, in umbrâ fundam 70
if it shall be winter, if harvest, in the shade, I will pour out

Arvisia vina, novum nectar, calathis. Damætas et Lyctius
Arvisian wine, new nectar, in baskets. Damætas and Lyctian

Ægon cantabunt mihi; Alphesibæus imitabitur saltantes
Ægon shall sing to me; Alphesibæus shall imitate the dancing

Satyros. Hæc semper erunt tibi, et cum reddemus
Satyrs. These ever shall be thine, both when we offer up

solennia vota Nymphis, et cum lustrabimus agros.
our annual vows to the Nymphs, and when we survey the fields.

Dum aper juga montis, dum piscis amabit
While the boar *shall love* the heights of the mountain, while the fish shall love

fluvios; que dum apes pascentur thymo, dum cicadæ
the rivers; and while bees shall feed *upon* thyme, while the grass-

rore; semper honos, que tuum nomen, que
hoppers on dew; for ever *your* honour, and your name, and

laudes manebunt. Agricolæ facient vota tibi quotannis
praises shall remain. The farmers shall pay their vows to you yearly

sic, ut Baccho que Cereri; tu quoquè damnabis 80
thus, as to Bacchus and to Ceres; you also shall compel

votis.
them to their vows.

MOPSUS.

Quæ, quæ dona reddam tibi pro tali carmine? nam
What, what gifts shall I pay to you for such a song? for

neque sibilus venientis austri me tan-
neither do the whispers of the approaching south wind *delight* me so

tum, nec litora percussa fluctu tam juvant, nec flu-
much, nor the shores struck by the billow so delight *me* nor the

mina, quæ decurrunt inter saxosas valles.
rivers which run among the rocky vallies.

MENALCAS.

Nos donabimus te ante hâc fragili cicutâ. Hæc
We will present thee first with this brittle reed. This

nos, "Corydon ardebat formosum Alexin:" hæc
has taught us, "Corydon loved the beautiful Alexis:" this

eadem docuit, "cujum pecus?" an
same has taught us, "whose flock is this?" whether is it the flock
Melibæi?
of Melibæus?

MOPSUS.

At Menalca, tu sume pedum, formosum paribus
But O Menalcas, do you take your crook, beautiful with equal
nodis; atque ære, quod Antigenes non tulit, cum sæpe
knots; and with brass, which Antigenes did not obtain, when often
rogaret me, (et tum erat dignus amari.)
he entreated me for it, (and then he was worthy to be loved.)

ECLOGUE VI.

SILENUS.

Nostra Thalia prima dignata est ludere Syracosio
My muse at first condescended to sport in Syracusian
versu; nec erubuit habitare silvas. Cum canerem
verse; nor has she blushed to inhabit the woods. When I would have sung
reges et prælia, Cynthius vellit aurem, et admonuit:
of kings, and battles, Apollo pulled my ear, and admonished
Tityre, oportet pastorem pascere pingues oves,
me thus: O Tityrus, it becomes a shepherd to feed his fattening sheep
dicere deductum carmen. Nunc ego meditabor
and to sing an humble song. Now I will meditate
agrestem musam tenui arundine, (namque super-
my rustic muse on a slender reed, (for there will
erunt tibi, Vare, qui cupiant dicere tuas laudes, et
remain to you, O Varus, those who desire to sing your praises, and
condere tristia bella.) Non cano injussa; tamen,
to describe mournful wars.) I do not sing unbidden subjects; yet,
si quis, si quis captus amore leget hæc
if any one, if any one captivated by love of verse will read these
10 quoquè; Vare, nostræ myricæ te, omne
even; O Varus, our tamarisks shall sing of thee, every
nemus canet te: nec est ulla pagina gratior Phœbo
grove shall sing of thee: nor is any page more grateful to Apollo
quàm quæ præscripsit nomen Vari sibi. Pierides,
than that which has prefixed the name of Varus on it. Ye Muses,
pergite: Chromis et Mnasylus, pueri, videre Sile-
proceed: Chromis and Mnasylus, playful boys, beheld Sile-
num jacentum somno in antro, inflatum venas hesterno
nus lying in sleep in a cave, blown up as to his veins with yester

Iaccho ut semper.　　　　　Serta, tantùm delapsa
day's wine, as ever　　he is.　His garlands, just now　fallen

capiti,　jacebant procul;　et gravis cantharus pende-
from his head,　lay　at a distance; and his weighty　tankard　hung

bat attritâ ansâ. Aggressi, injiciunt　　vincula ex
by its worn handle. Approaching, they cast over　him　chains　from

ipsis sertis·(nam sæpe senex luserat ambo　　spe
these wreaths (ror　often the old man had beguiled　both with the hope

carmiuis). Ægle addit　se　　sociam,　que su-　20
of a song).　Ægle　adds　herself　as a companion, and came

pervenit　　timidis　　Ægle pulcherrima Naïa-
up　to them　alarmed by her approach,　Ægle the most beautiful of the

dum,　que pingit frontem et tempora jam　videnti
fountain nymphs, and　paints his forehead and temples　just now　looking

sanguineis　moris.　Ille, ridens,　　dolum,
on them　with bloody　mulberries.　He,　laughing,　at the deceit,

inquit,　Quò nectitis　vincula?　solvite me, pueri:
says,　Why　do you bind these　chains?　loose　me,　boys:

est satis　　potuisse　videri.　　Cognoscite
it is enough　to have been suffered　to be beheld thus.　　Hear

carmina quæ vultis: carmina　vobis;　erit aliud
the songs　which you wish: the songs　are　for you; there　shall be another

mercedis huic. Simul ipse incipit. Tum verò videres
reward　for her. At once he　begins.　Then indeed you might

que Faunos que　feras ludere　　in nume-
have seen both Fauns　and wild beasts to sport about him in regulated

rum;　tum rigidas quercus motare cacumina. Nec Par-
measure; then the hardy　oaks　to move　their tops.　Nor does the

nassia rupes tantùm gaudet Phœbo, nec Rhodope et Isma-
Parnassian rock so much rejoice Apollo, nor Rhodope and Isma-

rus tantùm miratur Orphea. Namque canebat, uti　30
rus so much　admire　Orpheus.　For　he sang, how

semina　que terrarum, que animæ, que maris, et　si-
the elements both of the earth,　and　of the air,　and of the sea, and at the

mul　liquidi　ignis, fuissent coacta per magnum
same time of the unmixed fire,　had been　united through　the great

inane: ut　his primis　　omnia exordia,
void:　how from these first　principles are　all　the causes of things,

ut tener orbis mundi　ipse　concreverit.　Tum
how the tender globe of the world　itself　had become hardened.　Then

solum cœperit durare,　et discludere Nerea　ponto,
the soil had begun to become firm, and　to set apart　the waters　in the sea,

et sumere formas rerum paulatim. Jamque ut　terræ
and to take　the forms of things　by degrees.　And now how the lands

stupeant　　novum solem　lucescere, atque imbres
were amazed when　the new　sun　began　to shine,　and　showers

cadant,　nubibus　submotis　altiùs: cum primùm
all.　from the clouds　being removed　higher·　when　first!

silvæ incipiunt surgere, que cum rara animalia errent
the woods begin to arise, and when few animals wander

40 per ignotos montes. Hic refert jactos lapides
through unknown mountains. He relates the cast stones

Pyrrhæ, Saturnia regna, que Caucaseas volucres, que
of Pyrrha, Saturn's kingdom, and the Caucasian birds, and

furtum Promethei. Adjungit his, quo fonte nautæ
the theft of Prometheus. He adjoins to these, in what fountain the sailors

camâssent relictum Hylan: ut omne litus sonaret,
had called aloud on the lost Hylas: how every shore resounded

Hyla, Hyla. Et solatur Pasiphæn amore nivei
Hylas, Hylas. And he consoles Pasiphæ with the love of a snowy

juvenci: fortunatam, si armenta nunquam fuissent. Ah,
bullock: happy, if herds never had been. Alas,

infelix virgo, quæ dementia cepit te? Prætides
unhappy maid, what madness possesses thee? The daughters of Prætus

implerunt agros falsis mugitibus; at tamen non ulla
filled the fields with false lowings· but yet not any one

secuta est tam turpes concubitus pecudum, quamvis timu-
followed so base cohabitation of flocks, although she might

50 isset aratrum collo, et sæpe quæsivisset cornua
fear the plough on her neck, and often she had sought for horns

in levi fronte. Ah, infelix virgo, nunc tu erras
upon her smooth forehead. Alas, unhappy maid, now you wander

in montibus! ille, fultus niveum latus molli hy-
upon the mountains! he, supporting his snowy side on the soft hy

acintho, ruminat pallentes herbas sub nigrâ illice.
acinth, chews the pale herbs beneath the black oak,

aut sequitur aliquam in magno grege. Nymphæ,
or follows another heifer in the great herd. Ye nymphs,

Dictææ nymphæ, claudite, jam claudite saltus nemo-
ye Dictæan nymphs, shut up, now shut up the lawns of the

rum: si forte qua errabunda vestigia bovis, obvia,
groves: if perhaps any wandering footsteps of the bullock, in the way,

ferant sese nostris oculis. Forsitan aliquæ vaccæ
may offer themselves to my eyes. Perhaps other heifers

perducant illum ad Gortynia stabula, aut captum viridi
will lead him to the Gortynian stalls, or captivated by the green

60 herbâ, aut secutum armenta. Tum canit puellam
grass, or pursuing the herds. Then he sings of the maid

miratam mala Hesperidum: tum circumdat Phæ-
admiring the apples of the Hesperides: then how he surrounds the daugh-

tontiadas musco amaræ corticis, atque eriget
ters of Phæton with the moss of the bitter bark, and raises them

proceras alnos solo. Tum canit, ut una sororum
tall alders from the ground. Then he sings, how one of the sisters

duxerit Gallum errantem ad flumina Permessi in Aonas
ed Gallus wandering to the streams of Permessus on the Aonian

montes; que ut omnis chorus Phœbi assurexerit viro;
mountains; and how all the band of Apollo arose to the man:

ut Linus, pastor, ornatus crines floribus atque
how Linus, the shepherd, ornamented as to his locks with flowers and

amaro apio, dixerit hæc illi divino carmine:
bitter parsley, said these things to him in divine verse:

Musæ dant tibi hos calamos, en, accipe, quos ante
The Muses present to you these reeds, lo, take *them*, which before

    seni Ascræo; quibus ille solebat de- 70
they gave to the old Ascrian; with which he was accustomed to

ducere rigidas ornos montibus cantando. Origo
lead out the hardy wild ashes from the mountains by singing. Let the origin

Grynæi nemoris dicatur tibi his; ne sit quis
of the Grynean grove be sung by you on these; that there be not any

lucus, quo Apollo jactet se plus. Quid loquar,
grove, in which Apollo may boast himself more. Why should I speak

    aut Scyllam Nisi? quam,
of what he said, either of Scylla *the daughter* of Nisus? *or of her* whom,

succinctam candida inguina latrantibus monstris,
girt as to her snow white waist with barking monsters,

fama secuta est vexâsse Dulichias rates, et, in
fame has handed down to have vexed the Dulachian ships, and, in

alto gurgite, ah, lacerâsse timidos nautas marinis
the deep whirlpool, alas, to have torn the frightened sailors with sea

canibus? aut ut narraverit artus Terei mutatos?
dogs? or how he related that the limbs of Tereus were changed?

quas dapes, quæ dona Philomela paraverit illi? quo
what festivals, what gifts Philomela had prepared for him? with

    cursu petiverit deserta, et quibus alis in- 80
what swiftness he sought the deserts, and with what wings the

felix supervolitaverit tecta ante sua? ille
wretched *prince* flew above the palace formerly his own? he

canit omnia, quæ beatus Eurotas audiit, Phœbo
sung all *these things*, which joyful Eurotas heard, Apollo

quondam meditante, que jussit lauros ediscere:
formerly having played them, and commanded the laurels to learn;

pulsæ valles referunt ad sidera. Donec vesper
the stricken vales re-echo *them* to the stars. Until the evening

    jussit cogere oves stabulis que referre
star coerced them to collect the sheep in the stables, and to count up

numerum, et processit olympo invito.
their number, and proceeded in the sky unwillingly *relinquishing the song.*

ECLOGUE VII.

MELIBÆUS.—CORYDON.—THYRSIS.

MELIBÆUS.

FORTE Daphnis consederat sub argutâ ilice; que
By chance Daphnis sat beneath a whispering oak; both

Corydon et Thyrsis compulerant greges in unum:
Corydon and Thyrsis had driven their flocks together:

Thyrsis oves, Corydon capellas, distentas lacte:
Thyrsis *his* sheep, Corydon *his* goats, swelled out with milk:

ambo florentes ætatibus, ambo Arcades: et pares
both in the prime of their age, both Arcadians: and equal

cantare, et parati respondere. Hic caper ipse, vir
to sing, and prepared to reply. Here the goat himself, the husband

gregis, deerraverat mihi, dum defendo teneras myrtos
of the flock, had wandered from me, while I defend the tender myrtles

à frigore; atque ego aspicio Daphnin: ubi ille videt
from the cold; and I see Daphnis: when he beholds

me contrà, inquit: O Melibæe, ades huc ocyus;
me opposite, he says: O Melibæus, do you come here quickly;

tibi caper salvus, et hœdi; et si potes cessare quid,
your goat is safe, and the kids; and if you can loiter at all,

10 requiesce sub umbrâ. Juvenci ipsi venient
rest beneath the shade. The bullocks themselves shall come

per prata huc potum. Hic Mincius prætexit virides
through the meadows here to drink. Here Mincius has lined its green

ripas tenerâ arundine, que examina resonant
banks with the tender reed, and swarms *of bees*, resound

è sacrâ quercu. Quid facerem? ego habeam neque
from the sacred oak. What could I do? I had neither

Alcippen, nec Phyllida, quæ clauderet domi agnos
Alcippe, nor Phyllis, who would shut up at home the lambs

depulsos à lacte; et erat magnum certamen, Corydon
weaned from milk; and there was a great contest, Corydon

cum Thyrside. Tamen posthabui mea seria
with Thyrsis. Yet I have postponed my serious *affairs*

illorum ludo. Igitur, ambo contendere alternis ver-
to their sport. Therefore, both *began* to contend in alternate ver-

sibus: Musæ volebant meminisse alternos
ses: The Muses wished *me* to have commemorated alternate

20 Corydon hos, Thyrsis referebat illos in
verses. Corydon *rehearsed* these, Thyrsis recited those in

ordine.
order.

CORYDON.

Libethrides nymphæ, noster amor, aut concedite carmen
Ye Libethrian nymphs, our love, either grant a song

mihi, quale meo Codro (ille facit
to me, such as you have granted to my Codrus: (he makes verses

proxima versibus Phœbi), aut, si omnes non pos-
next to the verses of Apollo), either if we all can-

sumus, hic arguta fistula pendebit sacrâ pinu.
not do it, here my tuneful pipe shall hang on the sacred pine.

THYRSIS.

Arcades pastores ornate crescentem poëtam hederâ,
Ye Arcadian shepherds adorn your rising poet with ivy,

ut ilia Codro rumpantur invidiâ. Aut si laudârit
that the sides of Codrus may be burst with envy. O if he should praise

ultra placitum, cingite frontem baccare, ne mala
me beyond my wish, bind your forehead with lady's glove, lest an evil

lingua noceat futuro vati.
tongue should hurt the future poet.

CORYDON.

Delia, parvus Mycon hoc caput setosi apri tibi,
Delia, little Mycon offers this head of a bristly boar to you,

et ramosa cornua vivacis cervi. Si hoc fuerit 30
and the branching horns of a lusty stag. If this may have been

proprium, stabis tota de levi marmore, evincta
appropriate, you shall stand out entire from smooth marble, binding

suras puniceo cothurno.
your legs with crimson buskin.

THYRSIS.

Priape, est sat te exspectare sinum lactis et
O Priapus, it is enough for you to expect a pail of milk and

hæc liba quotannis: es custos pauperis horti. Nunc
these cakes yearly: you are the keeper of a poor garden. Now

fecimus te marmoreum pro tempore: at esto tu aureus,
we have made thee of marble for the time: but be thou of gold,

si fetura suppleverit gregem.
if breeding shall supply the flock.

CORYDON.

Galatea, Nerine, dulcior mihi thymo Hyblæ,
O Galatea, daughter of Nereus, sweeter to me than the thyme of Hybla,

candidior cycnis, formosior albâ hederâ: cum primus
more white than swans, more fair than white ivy: when first

pasti tauri repetent præsepia, si qua cura tui Cory-
the full fed bulls shall seek the stalls, if any care of your Cory

donis habet te, venito. 40
don possesses you, come.

THYRSIS.

Imò, ego videar tibi amarior Sardois herbis, hor-
Nay, I may seem to you more bitter than Sardinian herbs, more

ridior rusco, vilior projectâ algâ, si hæc lux
rough than furze, meaner than rejected sea-weed, if this day

non est jam longior mihi toto anno. Pasti
is not now longer to me than a whole year. Ye full fed

juvenci, ite domum ; ite, si quis pudor.
bullocks, go home ; go, if there is any modesty.

CORYDON.

Muscosi fontes, et herba mollior somno, et viridis
Ye mossy fountains, and grass softer than sleep, and the green

arbutus, quæ tegit vos rarâ umbrâ, defendite solsti-
arbute, which covers you with its thin shade, keep off the sol

tium pecori : jam torrida æstas venit ; jam
stice from the flock : already the burning summer approaches ; now

gemmæ turgent in læto palmite.
the buds swell on the fruitful vine.

THYRSIS.

Hic focus, et pingues tædæ ; hic plurimus ignis
Here is a hearth, and rich torches ; here is much fire

50 semper, et postes nigri assiduâ fuligine. Hic
always, and the posts are black with continual soot. Here

curamus frigora Boreæ tantum, quantum aut lupus
we regard the cold of Boreas as much, as either the wolf

numerum, aut torrentia flumina
regards the number of the flock, or the headlong streams regard their

ripas.
banks.

CORYDON.

Et juniperi, et hirsutæ castaneæ stant ; poma
And the junipers, and the rough chestnuts remain ; apples

jacent strata passim, quæque sub suâ arbore ; nunc
lie strewn every where, each one beneath its own tree ; now

omnia rident ; at si formosus Alexis abeat his
all things laugh ; but if fair Alexis should be absent from these

montibus, videas et flumina sicca.
mountains, you would see even the rivers dry.

THYRSIS.

Ager aret ; herba sitit moriens vitio aëris ·
The field is dried up ; the grass thirsts dying by the impurity of the air

Liber invidit pampineas umbras collibus : omne
Bacchus has envied his vine shadows from the hills : every

nemus virebit adventu nostræ Phyllidis ; et pluri-
grove will be green by the coming of our Phyllis ; and abun-

60 mus Jupiter descendet læto imbri.
dant Jupiter descends in a joyful shower

CORYDON.

Populus gratissima Alcidæ, vitis Iaccho, myr-
The poplar is most acceptable to Hercules, the vine to Bacchus, the
tus formosæ Veneri, sua laurea Phœbo; Phyllis amat
myrtle to fair Venus, his own laurel to Apollo; Phyllis loves
corylos: dum Phyllis amabit illas, nec myrtus nec
hazels while Phyllis shall love these, neither the myrtle nor
laurea Phœbi vincet corylos.
the laurel of Phœbus shall excel the hazels.

THYRSIS.

Fraxinus pulcherrima in silvis, pinus in hortis
The ash is most beautiful in the woods, the pine in the gardens
populus in fluviis, abies in altis montibus; at si,
the poplar by the rivers, the fir in the lofty mountains; but if,
formose Lycida, revisas me sæpius, fraxinus in
beautiful Lycidas, you shall revisit me oftener, the ash in
silvis, pinus in hortis cedet tibi.
the woods, the pine in the gardens shall yield to thee.

MELIBÆUS.

Memini hæc, et Thyrsin victum, contendere
I remember these *things*, and that Thyrsis conquered, contended
frustra. Ex illo tempore, Corydon, Corydon est 70
in vain. From that time, Corydon, Corydon is
nobis.
for us.

ECLOGUE VIII.

PHARMACEUTRIA.—DAMON.—ALPHESIBŒUS.

MUSAM pastorum Damonis et Alphesibœi
Let *us sing* the muse of the shepherds Damon and Alphesibœus.
quos certantes juvenca, immemor herbarum, mirata est,
whom contending the heifer, unmindful of her grass, admired
quorum carmine lynces stupefactæ, et flumina mutata
by whose song the lynxes stood amazed, and the rivers changed
suos cursus, requiêrunt; dicemus musam Damonis et
in their courses, rested; let us sing the muse of Damon and
Alphesibœi. Tu mihi, seu jam superas saxa
Alphesibœus. Do you *assist* me, whether now you pass over the rocks
magni Timavi, sive legis oram Illyrici æquoris:
of great Timavus, or coast along the shore of the Illyrian sea

en, unquam ille dies erit, cum liceat mihi
lo, ever will that day be, when it will be allowed to me

dicere tua facta? en, erit, ut liceat mihi ferre
to sing your deeds? lo, will it be, that it may be allowed to me to extend

10 tua carmina, sola digna Sophocleo cothurno
your verses, alone worthy of Sophocles' buskin (i. e. *tragic style*)

per totum orbem? principium à te; desinet
through the whole globe? my commencement is from you; my muse shall end

tibi. Accipe carmina cœpta tuis jussis, atque sine
with you. Receive my songs begun by your orders, and allow

hanc hederam serpere inter victrices lauros circum tibi
this ivy to creep amidst the victorious laurels around your

tempora. Vix frigida umbra noctis decesserat
temples. Scarcely had the cold shadow of night departed

cœlo, cum ros gratissimus pecori, in tenerâ herbâ;
from the sky, when the dew is most grateful to the flock, on the tender grass

Damon, incumbens tereti olivæ, cœpit sic.
Damon leaning on his tapering olive, began thus.

DAMON.

Lucifer, nascere, que præveniens, age almum diem;
O Lucifer, arise, and going before, lead on the cheering day:

dum, deceptus indigno amore conjugis, Nisæ, queror;
while, deceived by the unworthy love of my bride, Nisa, I complain:

20 et moriens; tamen extremâ horâ, alloquor deos,
and dying, yet in my last hour, I address the gods,

quamquam profeci nil illis testibus. Mea
although it has profited me nothing that they were witnesses. My

tibia, incipe Mænalios versus mecum. Mænalus semper
pipe, begin Mænalian verses with me. Mænalus always

habet que argutum nemus, que loquentes pinos: ille
has both a tuneful grove, and singing pines: he

semper audit amores pastorum, que Panâ, qui primus
always listens to the loves of the shepherds, and Pan, who first

non passus calamos inertes. Mea tibia, incipe
did not suffer his reeds to lie slothful. My pipe, begin

Mænalios versus mecum. Nisa datur Mopso! quid
Mænalian verses with me. Nisa is yielded to Mopsus! what

amantes non speremus? Jam gryphes jungentur
may we lovers not expect? Now griffins shall be yoked

equis; que sequenti ævo, timidi damæ venient
with horses; and in the following age, cowardly fallow deer shall come

cum canibus ad pocula. Mopse, incide novas
with dogs to the cups. O Mopsus, cut your new nuptial

faces; uxor. ducitur tibi. Marite, sparge nuces; Hespe
torches; a wife is led out for you. O husband, scatter nuts; Hespe

30 rus deserit Œtam tibi. Mea tibia, incipe Mæna
rus deserts Œta for you. My pipe, begin Mæna

lios versus mecum. O conjuncta digno viro! dum des-
lian verses with me. O united to a worthy man! while you

picis omnes, que dum mea fistula est odio tibi, que dum
despise all men, and while my pipe is hateful to you, and while

capellæ, que hirsutum supercilium, que prolixa
my goats, and shaggy eye-brow, and long

barba, nec credis quemquam deûm curare
beard are hated by you, nor do you believe any one of the gods to care

mortalia. Mea tibia, incipe Mænalios versus mecum.
for mortal concerns. My pipe, begin Mænalian verses with me.

Vidi te parvam, legentem roscida mala cum matre
I beheld you a little girl, gathering dewy quinces with your mother

in nostris sepibus (ego eram vester dux). Jam tum alter
in our hedges (I was your guide). Then another

annus ab undecimo ceperat me: jam poteram contingere
year from the eleventh had overtaken me: now I could touch

fragiles ramos à terrà. Ut vidi, ut perii, 40
the brittle branches from the ground. How I gazed, how I wasted away,

ut malus error abstulit me! Mea tibia, incipe
how the destructive delusion stole me away! My pipe, begin

Mænalios versus mecum. Nunc scio quid amor sit:
Mænalian verses with me. Now I know what love is:

Ismarus, aut Rhodope, aut extremi Garamantes edunt
Ismarus, or Rhodophe, or the most distant Garamantes bore

illum in duris cotibus, puerum nec nostri generis, nec
him on the hard cliffs, a boy neither of our race, nor

sanguinis. Mea tibia, incipe Mænalios versus mecum.
blood. My pipe, begin Mænalian verses with me.

Sævus amor docuit matrem commaculare manus san-
Cruel love has taught a mother to stain her hands in the

guine natorum: tu, mater, crudelis quoque: mater
blood of her sons: you, O mother, were cruel likewise: was the mother

magis crudelis, an ille puer improbus? ille 50
more cruel, or was the boy more wicked? the

puer improbus, tu crudelis quoque, mater. Mea
boy was wicked, you were cruel also, O mother. My

tibia, incipe Mænalios versus mecum. Nunc et lupus
pipe, begin Mænalian verses with me. Now also the wolf

fugiat oves ultro; duræ quercus ferant aurea
flies from the sheep of his own accord: the hardy oaks bear golden

mala; alnus floreat narcisso; myricæ sudent pinguia
apples; the alder shall flower with narcissus; tamarisks perspire rich

electra corticibus; et ululæ certent cycnis: Tityrus
amber from their barks; and owls shall contend with swans: Let Tityrus

sit Orpheus; Orpheus in silvis, Arion inter delphinas.
be Orpheus; Orpheus in the woods, Arion among the dolphins.

Mea tibia, incipe Mænalios versus mecum. Omnia
My pipe, begin Mænalian verses with me. All things

fiant vel medium mare. Silvæ, vivite. De
may become even as in the midst of the sea. Ye woods, live. I shall

ferar præceps de speculâ aërii montis in undas:
be borne headlong from the height of an airy mountain to the waves:

60 habeto hoc extremum munus morientis. Tibia,
accept this the last favour of your dying *friend.* My pipe,

desine, jam desine Mænalios versus. Damon hæc:
cease, now cease Mænalian verses. Damon *uttered* these

Vos Pierides, dicite, quæ Alphesibœus responderit.
words: Ye Pierian Muses, say, what Alphesibœus replied

Omnes non possumus omnia.
All *men* cannot *do* all *things.*

ALPHESIBŒUS.

Effer aquam et cinge hæc altaria molli vitta;
Bring out water and bind these altars with a soft fillet;

que adole pingues verbenas, et mascula thura, ut
and burn rich vervain, and male frankincense, that

experiar avertere sanos sensus conjugis magicis sacris.
I may try to pervert the sound senses of my wife by magic sacrifices.

Nihil nisi carmina desunt hic. Mea carmina, ducite,
Nothing except charms are wanting here. My charms, lead,

ducite Daphnin ab urbe domum. Carmina vel possunt
lead Daphnis from the city home. Charms even can

70 deducere lunam cœlo: Circe mutavit socios
draw down the moon from heaven; Circe changed the companions

Ulyssei carminibus: frigidus anguis, in pratis, rumpi-
of Ulysses by charms: the cold snake, in the meadows, is

tur cantando. Mea carmina, ducite, ducite Daphnin ab
burst by charming. My charms, lead, lead Daphnis from

urbe domum. Primum circumdo tibi hæc tria licia
the city home. First I surround for thee these three threads

diversa triplici colore; que duco effigiem ter circum
variegated with a triple hue; and lead thy image thrice around

hæc altaria. Deus gaudet impare numero. Mea car-
these altars. The god rejoices in an unequal number. My

mina, ducite, ducite Daphnin ab urbe domum. Ama-
charms, lead, lead Daphnis from the city home. Ama-

rylli, necte ternos colores tribus nodis. Amarylli, necte
ryllis, bind three colours in three knots. O Amaryllis, bind

modo: et dic necto vincula Veneris. Mea carmina,
them now: and say I bind the chains of Venus. My charms

ducite, ducite Daphnin ab urbe domum. Ut hic limus
lead, lead Daphnis from the city home. As this clay

80 durescit, et ut hæe cera liquescit, uno que eodem
hardens, and as this wax melts, by one and the same

igni, sic Daphnis amore. Sparge molam, et incende
fire, thus Daphn s by *my* love. Scatter the cake, and burn

fragiles lauros bitumine. Malus Daphnis urit me; ego
brittle laurels with pitch. Cruel Daphnis burns me; I

hanc laurum in Daphnide. Mea carmina, ducite,
burn this laurel upon Daphnis. My charms, lead

ducite Daphnin ab urbe domum. Talis amor
lead Daphnis from the city home. May such love *possess*

Daphnin, qualis cum bucula fessa quærendo juvencum
Daphnis, as when a heifer wearied with seeking the bull

per nemora atque altos lucos, perdita procumbit in
through the groves and lofty forests, abandoned she lies down on

viridi herbâ propter rivum aquæ, nec meminit decedere
the green grass near a river of water, nor remembers to depart

seræ nocti; talis amor teneat; nec sit mihi
late at night; let such love possess *Daphnis;* nor let it be my

cura mederi. Mea carmina, ducite, ducite Daphnin ab
care to heal him. My charms, lead, lead Daphnis from

urbe domum. Ille perfidus olim reliquit has
the city home. The faithless *swain* formerly left these   90

exuvias mihi, cara pignora sui; quæ nunc ego
clothes to me, the dear pledges of himself; which now I

mando tibi, terra, in limine ipso: hæc pignora debent
commit to you, O earth, in the entrance itself: these pledges owe

Daphnin. Mea carmina, ducite, ducite Daphnin ab
Daphnis *to me.* My charms, lead, lead Daphnis from

urbe domum. Mœris ipse dedit mihi has herbas,
the city home. Mœris himself has given to me these herbs,

atque hæc venena lecta Ponto; plurima nascuntur
and these poisons gathered in Pontus; many *such* grow

Ponto. Ego vidi Mœrin sæpe fieri lupum his, et
in Pontus. I have seen Mœris often become a wolf by them, and

condere se silvis, sæpe excire animas imis sepulcris,
hide himself in the woods, often to call forth souls from the deep tombs

atque traducere satas messes alio. Mea carmina
and to lead off the growing harvests to another place. My charms

ducite, ducite Daphnin ab urbe domum. Ama-
lead, lead Daphnis from the city home. Ama-   100

rylli fer cineres foras: que jace trans caput
ryllis bring the ashes out: and cast *them* over *your* head *into*

fluenti rivo: ne respexeris. Ego aggrediar Daphnin
a flowing stream: do not look back. I will attack Daphnis

his: ille nihil curat deos, curat nil carmina.
with them: he nothing cares for the gods, he cares nothing for *my* charms

Mea carmina, ducite, ducite Daphnin ab urbe domum.
My charms, lead, lead Daphnis from the city home.

Aspice, cinis ipse corripuit altaria tremulis flammis
Behold, the ashes itself has seized the altars with tremulous flames

suâ sponte, dum moror ferre sit bonum. Certe,
spontaneously, while I delay to bear *them* off may it be for good. Truly,

est nescio quid; et Hylax latrat in limine.
there is *here* I know not what; and *the dog* Hylax barks in the entrance.

Credimus ? an qui amant, ipsi fingunt somnia
Do we believe *it?* or do *those* who love, themselves feign dreams

sibi ? Carmina, parcite, jam parcite, Daphnis venit
to themselves? My charms, cease now cease, Daphnis comes

ab urbe.
from the city

ECLOGUE IX.

Lycidas.—Mœris.

LYCIDAS.

Mœri, quo pedes te ? an in urbem quo
Mœris, where do your feet *bear* you? whether into the city where

via ducit ?
the way leads?

MŒRIS.

O Lycida, vivi pervenimus, ut advena possessor,
O Lycidas, living have we come *to this*, that a strange possessor,

nostri agelli, discret (quod nunquam sumus veriti);
of my little field, should say (which never had we feared),

Hæc sunt mea; veteres coloni, migrate, nunc victi,
These are mine; ye ancient husbandmen, remove, now conquered,

tristes, quoniam fors versat omnia, mittimus hos hœdos
sad, since chance upturns every thing, we send these kids

illi (quod nec vertat bene).
to him (which *I pray* may not turn out well).

LYCIDAS.

Certe, equidem, audieram vestrum Menalcan servasse
Truly, indeed, I had heard that your Menalcas had saved

10 omnia carminibus, qua colles incipiunt sub-
all *the tract* by *his* verses, where the hills begin to

ducere se, que demittere jugum molli clivo,
withdraw themselves, and to depress their height by a gentle declension,

usque ad aquam, et cacumina veteris fagi jam fracta.
even to the water, and the tops of the old beech now broken.

MŒRIS.

Audieras, et fama fuit: sed, Lycida, nostra
You had heard *it*, and the report was *so:* but, O Lycidas, our

carmina valent tantum inter martia tela, quantum dicunt
verses prevail as much amid martial weapons, as they say

Chaonias columbas aquilâ veniente ; quod nisi sinistra
Chaonian doves do. the eagle approaching; but unless the ill-omened

cornix monuisset me ante ab cavâ ilice, incidere
raven had admonished me before from the hollow oak, to lay aside

novas lites, quâcumque nec hic tuus Mœris, nec
new controversies, by any means neither this your Mœris, nor

Menalcas ipse, viveret.
Menalcas himself, had now been alive.

LYCIDAS.

Heu, tantum scelus cadit in quemquam ! Heu !
Alas ! can so great wickedness fall to any one ! Alas !

Menalca, tua solatia pene rapta nobis simul
Menalcas, your consolation was almost taken from us at the same time

tecum ! quis caneret nymphas ? quis spargeret
with yourself! who would have sung the nymphs ? who had strewn

humum florentibus herbis, aut induceret fontes
the ground with flowering herbs, or had overspread the fountains

viridi umbra ? vel carmina quæ tacitus sublegi 20
with a verdant shade ? or the songs which silently I stole

tibi nuper, cum ferres te ad Amaryllida, nostras
from you lately, when you withdrew yourself to Amaryllis, our

delicias ? Tityre, pasce capellas, dum redeo ; via
darling ? O Tityrus, feed my goats, until I return ; the way

est brevis ; et, Tityre, age pastas potum : et,
is short ; and, Tityrus, drive them when fed to drink : and,

inter agendum, caveto occursare capro : ille ferit
while driving, beware not to encounter the he-goat : he strikes

cornu.
with his horn.

MŒRIS.

Imo hæc quæ canebat Varo, necdum perfecta. Vare,
Rather these which he sang to Varus, nor yet are they finished. O Varus,

cantantes cycni ferent tuum nomen sublime ad sidera,
the singing swans shall bear your name on high to the stars,

modo Mantua superet nobis. Mantua, væ ! nimium
provided Mantua may remain to us. Mantua, alas ! too

vicina miseræ Cremonæ !
near the wretched Cremonæ !

LYCIDAS.

Sic tua examina fugiant Cyrneas taxos, sic 30
Thus may your swarms escape Cyrnean yew trees, thus

vaccæ pastæ cytiso, distentent ubera. Incipe,
may your heifers fed upon cytisus, swell out their udders. Begin,

si habes quid Et Pierides fecere me poetam :
if you have any thing. Likewise the Muses have made me a poet.

et sunt mihi carmina: pastores quoque dicunt me vatem:
and there are to me   verses: the shepherds   also   call   me   a poet.

sed ego   non credulus   illis: nam adhuc videor dicere
but   I do   not   confide   in them   for   as yet   I seem   to sing

digna neque Varo,   nec Cinnâ,   sed velut anser,
things worthy neither of Varus,   nor of Cinna,   but   as   a goose,

strepere inter argutos olores.
to hiss   among the tuneful   swans.

MŒRIS.

Quidem ago id, et Lycida, ipse tacitus voluto mecum,
Indeed   I do that, and, O Lycidas, do you in silence revolve it   with me.

si valeam meminisse: neque est   ignobile carmen.
if   I can   remember it: nor   is   it a degraded   song.

Ades huc, ô Galitea: quisnam ludus est   undis?
Come here, O Galitea.   what   sport   is there among the waves?

hic purpureum ver; hic humus fundit varios flores
here   is blooming   spring; here   the earth   pours forth various   flowers

40   circum flumina; hic candida populus imminet antro
around   the rivers; here the white   poplar   hangs over the cave

et lentæ vites texunt umbracula. Ades huc: sine
and the slender vines interweave   shades.   Come   here.   suffer

insani fluctus feriant litora.
the mad   waves that they strike the shore.

LYCIDAS.

Quid   quæ audieram te solum canentem   sub
What   is this which I had heard you alone   singing   beneath

purâ nocte? memini numeros, si tenerem verba.
the clear night?   I remember the numbers, if   I could retain the words

MŒRIS.

Daphni, quid   suspicis antiquos ortus   signorum?
O Daphnis, why do you look upon the ancient rising of the constellations?

Ecce astrum Dionæi Cæsaris processit; astrum quo
Behold   the star of Dionæan   Cæsar   has proceeded;   the star by which

segetes gauderent frugibus et quo   uva duceret
the corn fields   rejoice   in their fruits and by which the grape   derives

colorem in apricis collibus. Daphni, insere   pyros:
its colour   on the sunny   hills.   O Daphnis,   plant   your pear trees

50   nepotes carpent tua poma. Ætas fert om-
your offspring   shall pluck your   fruit.   Time bears off   a

nia: animum quoque. Ego memini me   puerum
things: the mind   even.   I   remember   myself when   a child

sæpe condere longos soles cantando. Nunc tot
often   to have spent   long   days   in singing.   Now   so many

carmina oblita mihi; jam vox ipsa quoque
songs   are forgotten   by me   now the voice itself   also

fugit   Mœrim: lupi   priores   videre Mœrım.   Sed
has escaped   Mœris: the wolves   first   beheld   Mœris.   But

tamen Mẹnalcas referet   ista   tibi sæpe satis.
yet   Menalcas   will relate these things to you often enough.

LYCIDAS.

Ducis   nostros amores in   longum   causando.
You draw out   my   loves   for   a long time in making excuses.

Et nunc aspice omne æquor stratum silet tibi, et
And now   behold   all   the sea spread out is still for you, and

omnes auræ ventosi murmuris ceciderunt. Adeo hinc est
all   the airs of windy murmuring have ceased.   Thus here   is

nobis   media   via : namque sepulcrum Bianoris incipit
for us   an intermediate way :   for   the tomb   of Bianor   begins

apparere. Hic ubi agricolæ stringunt densas 60
to appear.   Here where the farmers   strip   the thick

frondes, hic, Mœri, canamus : hic depone hœdos.
leaves,   here, O Mœris, let us sing :   here   place   your kids

Tamen veniemus in urbem. Aut si veremur ne nox
Yet   let us come to   the city.   Or if we dread lest night

colligat pluviam ante, licet eamus cantantes usque
should collect rain   first, although we should go   singing   thus

(via   minus lædet). Ut eamus cantantes, ego levabo
(the way will be less   tedious).   As we go   singing,   I will relieve

te hoc fasce.
you of this burden.

MŒRIS.

Puer, desine   plura, et agamus quod nunc instat.
O boy,   cease to speak more, and let us do what now   presses

Canemus carmina melius tum, cum ipse venerit.
us. We shall sing songs   better then, when he has come.

ECLOGUE X.

GALLUS.

ARETHUSA concede hunc extremum laborem mihı.
ARETHUSA   yield   this   last   labour   to me

Pauca carmina sunt dicenda meo Gallo, sed quæ Lycoris
A few   songs   are to be sung to my Gallus, but which   Lycoris

ipsa legat. Quis neget carmina Gallo ? Sic amara
herself may read.   Who will deny   verses   u Gallus? Thus may bitter

Doris non intermisceat suam undam tibi, cum labere
Doris not intermingle her wave with you, when you glide

subter Sicanos fluctus. Incipe; dicamus solicitos amores
eneath the Sicilian billows. Begin; let us sing the auxious loves

Galli, dum simæ capellæ attondent tenera virgulta.
of Gallus, while the flat-nosed goats crop the tender shrubbery.

Non canimus surdis; silvæ respondent omnia. Quæ
We sing not to the deaf; the woods respond to all. What

nemora, aut qui saltus habuere, vos puellæ Naiades,
groves, or what lawns detained you, ye maiden Naiads.

10 cum Gallus periret indigno amore? nam neque
when Gallus perished by unworthy love? for neither did

juga Parnassi, nam neque ulla Pindi, neque
he heights of Parnassus, for neither did any heights of Pindus, nor

Aonia Aganippe fecere moram vobis. Etiam lauri,
of Aonian Aganippe cause delay to you. Even the laurels,

etiam myricæ flevere illum. Etiam pinifer
even the tamarisks mourned him. Also the pine bearing

Mænalus, et saxa gelidi Lycæi, fleverunt illum
Mænalus, and the rocks of the cold Lycæus, mourned him

jacentem sub solâ rupe. Et oves stant circum, nec
lying beneath a lonely rock. And the sheep stand around. nor

pœnitet illas nostri; nec pœniteat te pecoris, ô divine
are they ashamed of us; nor be thou ashamed of thy flock, O divine

poeta: et formosus Adonis pavit oves ad flumina. Et
poet and fair Adonis fed sheep by the rivers. Aud

upilio venit; tardi bubulci venere; Menalcas uvidus
the shepherd came; the slow herdsmen came; Menalcas moist

de hibernâ glande venit. Omnes rogant, Unde est tibi
from the wintery mast came. All ask, Wheuce is to you

20 iste amor? Apollo venit: inquit, Galle, quid
this love? Apollo came: he said, O Gallus, why

insanis? Lycoris tua cura secuta est alium que per
are you mad? Lycoris your care has followed another both through

nives, que per horrida castra. Et Silvanus venit,
the snows, and through the dreadful camp. And Silvanus came.

agresti honore capitis, quassans florentes ferulas et
with the rustic honours of his head, shaking the flowering fennels and

grandia lilia. Pan Deus Arcadiæ venit, quem ipsi vidimus,
large lilies. Pan the God of Arcadia came, whom we have seen,

rubentem sanguineis baccis ebuli que minio. Et in-
blushing with the bloody berries of the elder, and vermilion. And he

quit, Quis erit modus? amor non curat
says, What will be the limit of our grief? love does not regard

talia. Nec crudelis amor lacrymis, nec gramina
such things. Neither is cruel love satisfied by tears, nor is grass

30 rivis, nec apes saturantur cytiso, nec capellæ
by rivers nor are bees satisfied with cytisus, nor goats

fronde. At ille tristis, inquit, Tamen, Arcades, canta-
with leaves. But he mournful, says, Nevertheless, ye Arcadians, ye shall

bitis hæc vestris montibus; Arcades soli periti cantare.
sing these things on your mountains; ye Arcadians aione skilled to sing.

O quam molliter tum mihi ossa quiescent si olim vestra
O how gently then will my bones rest if hereafter your

fistula dicat meos amores. Atque utinam fuissem
pipe will declare my loves. And I wish I had been

unus ex vobis, que aut custos vestri gregis, aut vinitor
one of you, and either a keeper of your flock, or a vintager

maturæ uvæ! Certe, sive esset mihi Phyllis sive
of the ripe grape! Truly, whether there should be to me Phyllis or

Amyntas, seu quicunque furor (quid tum, si Amyntas,
Amyntas, or any other flame (what then, if Amyntas

fuscus? et violæ nigræ, et vaccinia sunt nigra), ja-
is brown? and violets are black, and hyacinths are black), thus

cerent mecum inter salices sub lentâ 40
would have reclined with me among the willows beneath the slender

vite; Phyllis legeret serta mihi, Amyntas
vine; Phyllis would have gathered garlands with me, Amyntas

cantaret. Hic gelidi fontes, hic mollia prata,
would have sung. Here are cold fountains, here are soft meadows,

Lycori, hic nemus; hic consumerer tecum ævo
O Lycoris, here is a grove; here I might consume with you my life

ipso. Nunc insanus amor detinet me in armis duri
itself. Now maddening love confines me to the arms of direful

Martis, inter media tela, atque adversos hostes. Tu,
Mars, amidst darts, and hostile foes. Thou,

procul a patriâ (nec sit mihi credere), vides tantum
far off from thy country (let me not believe it), beholdest only

Alpinas nives et frigora Rheni. Ah, dura! sola
Alpine snow and the rigors of the Rhine. Ah, cruel maid! alone

sine me, ah, ne frigora lædant te! ah, ne aspera
without me, ah, let not the colds injure thee! ah, let not the rough

glacies secet teneras tibi plantas. Ibo, et modulabor
ice cut thy tender feet. I will go, and attune

carmina avenâ Siculi pastoris, quæ sunt condita 50
songs on the reed of the Sicilian shepherd, which are composed

mihi Chalcidico versu. Est certum, malle
by me Chalcidican (elegaic) verse. It is determined, that I had rather

pati in silvis, inter spelæa ferarum, que incidere meos
suffer in the woods, among the dens of wild beasts, and carve m

amores teneris arboribus: illæ crescent; amores,
oves on the tender trees: they shall grow; so my loves,

crescetis. Interea lustrabo Mænala nymphis
rou shall increase. In the meantime I will range Mænalus with nymphs

mistis, aut venabor acres apros. Non
mingled in my train, or I will hunt the savage boars. Not

frigora vetabunt me circumdare Parthenios saltus canibus.
colds   shall forbid me to encircle   Parthenian lawns with dogs.

Jam videor mihi   ire . per rupes, que sonantes lucos:
Now I seem to myself to go through rocks, and sounding groves:

libet   torquere Cydonia spicula   Partho   cornu;
it pleases me to hurl Cydonian darts from the Parthian bow;

60 tanquam hæc   sint medicina nostri   furoris,
   as if   these things may be a medicine of my maddening love,

aut ille Deus discat   mitescere   malis   hominum.
or that God can learn to become gentle by the misfortunes of men.

Jam rursus neque Hamadryades, nec carmina   ipsa
Now again neither the nymphs of the groves, nor songs themselves

placent nobis; rursus silvæ ipsæ concedite.
please   us;   again ye woods yourselves give place to my despair.

Nostri labores non possunt mutare illum; nec si que
Our   labours cannot   change   him; not if even

bibamus   Hebrum mediis frigoribus, que subeamus
we should drink the Hebrus in the midst of colds, and undergo

Sithonias nives aquosæ hiemis; nec si, cum moriens
the Sithonian snows of the stormy winter; nor if, when the dying

liber aret in altâ ulmo, versemus oves Æthio-
bark dries up on the lofty elm, we should tend the sheep of the Ethio-

pum sub sidere cancri. Amor vincit omnia:
pians beneath the constellation of the crab. Love conquers all things:

et nos cedamus amori. Divæ Pierides, erit   sat
and let us yield to love. Ye divine Muses, it shall be enough

70 vestrum poetam cecinisse hæc   dum sedet et
   for your   poet to have sung these songs while he sits and

texit   fiscellam gracili hibisco: vos facietis hæc
interweaves a basket with the slender bulrush: you shall make these

maxima   Gallo; Gallo, cujus amor crescit mihi tantum
very important to Gallus; to Gallus, whose love increases to me as much

in horas, quantum viridis alnus subjicit se novo
in an hour, as   the green alder raises itself in the early

vere. Surgamus: umbra solet esse gravis cantantibus:
spring. Let us rise: the shade is wont to be oppressive to singers:

umbra juniperi gravis: umbræ nocent et frugibus.
the shade of the juniper is oppressive: shades injure also the fruits.

Capellæ, saturæ, ite domum; ite, Hesperus venit.
Ve goats, well fed, go home; go, the evening star approaches.

THE GEORGICS

OF

PUBLIUS VIRGILIUS MARO.

BOOK I.

QUID faciat lætas segetes : quo sidere convenia
WHAT can make joyful corn-fields : by what constellation it may be proper

vertere terram, ô Mæcenas, que adjungere vites ulmis,
to turn up the earth, O Mæcenas, and to join the vines to the elms;

quæ cura boûm, qui cultus sit habendo pecori,
what is the care of oxen, what nursing shall be for preserving the flock,

atque quanta experientia parcis apibus ; hinc incipiam
and how great experience for the frugal bees; hence I will begin

canere. Vos ô clarissima lumina mundi; quæ   10
to sing. Ye brightest lights of the world; that

ducitis annum, labentem cœlo. Liber et alma Ceres,
lead out the year, gliding through the sky. Bacchus and cheering Ceres,

si vestro munere tellus mutavit Chaoniam glandem pingui
if by your favour the earth has changed Chaonian mast for the rich

aristà, que miscuit Acheloia pocula uvis inventis :
ears of corn, and intermingled Achelous cups with grapes discovered :

et vos, Fauni, præsentia numina agrestium ; que Fauni
and you, ye Fauns, ye present deities of rustics; both ye Fauns

que puellæ Dryades simul ferte pedem. Cano
and ye maiden Dryads at the same time advance your foot. I sing

vestra munera; que tu, ô Neptune, cui prima tellus,
your offerings; and thou, O Neptune, to whom first the earth.

percussa magno tridenti, fudit frementem equuum ;
struck with your great trident, sent forth the neighing horse;

et cultor nemorum, cui ter centum nivei
and thou inhabitant of the groves (*Aristæus*), for whom three hundred snowy

juvenci tondent pinguia dumeta Ceæ ; ipse Pan, custos
bullocks crop the rich shrubbery of Cææ; thou, Pan, keeper

ovium, linquens patrium nemus, que saltus Lycæi, si tua
of sheep, leaving your native grove, and lawns of Lyceus, if your

44

Mænala tibi curæ, Tegeæe,   adsis favens, que Miner
Mænalus is your care,   O Tegean *Pan*, be present favouring, and   Miner-

va inventrix oleæ,   que   puer monstrator   unci
va   inventress of the olive, and *thou* boy   discoverer of the crooked

20 aratri, et Silvane, ferens teneram cupressum ab
plough, and Silvanus, bearing a tender   cypress   from

radice, que omnes Dì que Deæ, quibus studium
the foot, and all ye Gods and Goddesses, whose   study   *it is*

tueri arva, omnes, que qui alitis novas fruges de nullo
to guard the fields, all,   both who cherish new   fruits from   no

semine ;   que   qui demittitis   satis   largum
seed   *sown ;* and   who send down on the corn-fields a copious

imbrem   cœlo,   que adeo tu, Cæsar, quem est incer-
shower   from heaven, and   thus   thou, Cæsar, whom it is   doubt-

tum quæ concilia Deorum sint habitura mox, velisne
ful   what councils of the Gods are about to be held soon, whether

invisere   urbes,   que curam terrarum : et maximus
you will visit the cities, and the care of the earth; and   the most

orbis accipiat   te   auctorem frugum, que poten-
extended globe shall receive thee the author of fruits, and   power-

tem tempestatum, cingens tempora   maternâ   myrto ;
ful   in tempests,   binding your temples with your maternal myrtle,

an   venias   Deus   immensi   maris,   ac
whether you shall come the God of the wide-spread   sea,   and

nautæ colant tua numina sola ; ultima Thule serviat
the sailors worship thy divinity alone; most remote Thule shall preserve

30 tibi, que Tethys   emat   te   generum
thee, and Tethys shall purchase thee   for a son-in-law

sibi   omnibus undis ; anne   addas   te novum
for herself with all her waves; whether thou wilt add thyself a new

sidus   tardis mensibus, quâ locus panditur inter
constellation to the slow months,   where a place lies open between

Erigonen que Ehelas   sequentes jam ardens
Erigone   and the claws (*of the scorpion*) pursuing   now the burning

Scorpius ipse contrahit brachia tibi, et relinquit plus
Scorpion himself   draws   in his arms for you, and   leaves   more

justâ   parte cœli.   Quidquid   eris (nam
than an equal part of heaven   Whatever *deity* you will be   (for

nec   Tartara sperent te   regem,   nec   tam
neither does Tartarus expect you for its king,   nor *permit* that so

dira   cupido regnandi veniat tibi ; quamvis Græcia
dreadful a desire of reigning should come to you ; although   Greece

miretur Elysios campos, nec Proserpina repetita,
admires *her* Elysian plains,   nor does Proserpine redemanded,

curet sequi matrem) da facilem cursum, atque annue
care   to follow *her* mother) grant an easy   course, and   yield

40 audacibus   cœptis : que miseratus agrestes
to *our* daring undertakings · and compassionating the rustics

45

ignaros viæ, mecum ingredere, et jam nunc assuesce
ignorant of the way, with me enter, and even now be accustomed

vocari votis. Novo vere, cum gelidus humor liquitur
to be invoked by vows. In the new spring, when cold moisture distils

canis montibus, et putris gleba resolvit se ze-
from the hoary mountains, and the rotten clod unbinds itself to the

phyro ; jam tum mihi taurus incipiat ingemere de-
west winds; even then let my bull begin to groan under the

presso aratro, et vomer attritus sulco
deep-pressed plough, and let the ploughshare worn in the furrow

splendescere. Illa seges demum respondet votis
shine. That corn-field at length answers to the wishes

avari agricolæ, quæ sensit bis solem;
of the avaricious farmer, which felt twice the summer sun;

bis frigora : immensæ messes ruperunt illius
twice the cold of winter: immense harvests have burst his

horrea. At priusquam scindimus ignotum æquor
store-houses. But before we cut up the unknown plain

ferro, sit cura prædiscere ventos, et 50
with the iron plough, let it be our care to foretell the winds, and

varium morem cœli, ac que patrios cultus que
the varied manner of the weather; and both our fathers' cultivation and

habitus locorum ; et quid quæque regio ferat,
the habits of the places; and what each region produces,

et quid quæque recuset. Hic segetes, illic uvæ
and what each one refuses. Here corn, there grapes

veniunt felicius : arborei fetus, atque gramina
increase more happily: the forest produce, and grasses

injussa virescunt alibi. Nonne vides ut Tmolus
spontaneous flourish elsewhere. Do not you see how Tmolus

croceos odores, India mittit ebur, molles
produces saffron odours, India sends forth ivory, the effeminate

Sabæi sua thura ? At nudi Chalybes send forth
Sabæans their own frankincense? But the naked Chalybes

ferrum, que Pontus virosa castorea, Epirus palmas
steel, and Pontus strong-scented castor, Epirus the choice

Eliadum equarum. Continuo natura imposuit has leges
Elian mares. At first nature established these laws

que æterna fœdera certis locis, quo tempore 60
and eternal rules on certain places, at which time

primum Deucalion jactavit lapides in vacuum orbem.
first Deucalion threw stones into the empty globe,

unde homines, durum genus, nati. Ergo age,
whence men, a hardy race, were produced. Therefore come on,

fortes tauri invertant pingue solum terræ extemplo
et the strong bulls turn over the fertile soil of the earth immediately

a primis mensibus anni ; que pulverulenta æstas
from the first months of the year; and let the dusty summer

coquat jacentes glebas maturis solibus. At si tellus
bake   the scattered   clods   with timely   suns.   But if the earth

non fuerit fecunda, erit sat suspendere tenui sulce
should not be   fertile,   it will be enough   to raise it up   by a light furrow

sub Arcturum ipsum : illic ne herbæ officiant lætis
beneath   Arcturus   itself: there lest   the grass   injure   the joyous

frugibus : hic ne exiguus humor deserat sterilem
fruits: here lest   the scanty   moisture   desert the unproductive

70   arenam. Tu idem patiere tonsas novales cessare
     sand.   Do you also   suffer   the mown   new fields   to rest

alternis, et segnem campum durescere situ.
in alternate years, and   the slothful   plain   to harden   with rust.

Aut ibi seres flava farra, sidere mutato, unde
Or   there you shall sow the yellow   corn,   the season being changed, whence

prius sustuleris lætum legumen quassante siliquâ,
before you have borne away the abundant   pulse   with shaking   pod

aut tenues fetus viciæ, que fragiles calamos tristis
or   the light   offspring of the vetch, and the brittle   stalks   of the coarse

lupini, que sonantem silvam. Enim seges lini urit
lupine,   and   the rattling   grove.   For   a crop   of flax burns

campum, avenæ urit, papavera perfusa Lethæo
the plain,   a crop   of oats   burns it,   poppies   tinctured with Lethean

somno urunt. Sed tamen labor facilis alternis,
sleep   burnt   it.   But   yet   your   labour is easy in alternate years,

tantum ne pudeat saturare arida sola pingui fimo ;
only   be not   ashamed   to fill   the dry   soil   with rich   manure;

80   neve jactare immundum cinerem per effetos
     nor   fail   to scatter   filthy   ashes   through the worn-out

agros. Sic quoque arva requiescunt, fetibus mutatis :
fields.   Thus   also   the fields   rest,   the produce being changed:

nec interea est nulla gratia inaratæ terræ.
nor   in the meantime is there   no   favour   to the unploughed   land.

Sæpe etiam profuit incendere steriles agros, atque
Often   also   it has profited   to burn   the barren   fields,   and

urere levem stipulam crepitantibus flammis ; sive inde
kindle the light   straw   in the rattling   flames;   whether from thence

terræ concipiunt occultas vires et pinguia pabula ; sive
the lands   receive   secret   powers and   rich   substance ;   or

per ignem omne vitium excoquitur illis, atque inutili
by   the fire   all   impurity   is dried up   from them,   and the useless

humor exsudat; seu ille calor relaxat plures vias, et
moisture   sweats off;   or   the   heat   lays open   more   ways, and

cæca spiramenta, qua succus veniat in novas
the dark   vents,   through which   sap   may come   into the young

90   herbas ; seu durat magis et astringit hiantes
     plants;   or   whether it hardens more   and   binds   the opening

venas, ne tenues pluviæ, ve acrior potentia rapidi
veins,   lest the light   showers,   or   more active   power   of the powerful,

solis, aut penetrabile frigus boreæ adurat. **Adeo**
sun, or the piercing cold the north wind may hurt it. Thus

multum juvat arva, qui frangit inertes glebas rastris,
he much assists the fields, who breaks the sluggish clods with harrows,

que trahit vimineas crates (que ne flava Ceres
and draws the osier hurdles (and neither does yellow Ceres

nequicquam spectat illum ab alto Olympo), et qui rursus
in vain behold him from lofty Heaven), and he who· again

perrumpit tellurem quæ suscitat terga, proscisso æquore,
breaks up the earth which raises the furrows, in the ploughed plain,

aratro verso in obliquum, que frequens exer-
the harrow being turned in an oblique direction, and frequently exer-

cet atque imperat arvis. Agricolæ, orate humida
cises and subdues the fields. Ye farmers, pray for moist

solstitia, atque serenas hiemes. Farra lœtissima, **100**
summers, and clear winters. Corn is most joyous

ager lætus hiberno pulvere. Mysia jactat se
and the field is glad in the wintery dust. Mysia boasts herself

tantum nullo cultu, et ipsa Gargara mirantur suas messes.
so much with no culture, and even Gargara admires his own harvests.

Quid dicam qui, semine jacto, cominus inse-
What shall I say of him who, the seed being cast, immediately pur-

quitur arva, que ruit cumulos male pinguis arenæ?
sues the fields, and piles up heaps of unfruitful sand?

deinde inducit fluvium, que sequentes rivos, satis?
then he leads the stream, and following rivulets, to the growing corn?

et cum exustus ager æstuat, herbis, morientibus, ecce!
and when the burnt field dries up, the herbs, dying, lo!

elicit undam supercilio clivosi tramitis: illa cadens
leads down the water to the brow of a rough tract: it falling

per lêvia saxa, ciet raucum murmur, que temperat
through the smooth rocks, excites a hoarse murmuring, and cools

arentia arva scatebris. Quid qui, ne **110**
the parched fields with rills. What shall I say of him who, lest

culmus procumbat gravidis aristis, depascit luxuriem
the stalk should fall with heavy ears of corn, feeds down the abundance

segetum in tenera herbâ cum primum sata æquant
of the corn-fields in the tender plant when first the corn equals

sulcos, que qui deducit collectum humorem paludis
the furrows, and who draws off the collected moisture of the meadow

bibulâ arenâ? præsertim si amnis abundans incertis
with the spongy sand? especially if a river abounding in the doubtful

mensibus exit, et tenet omnia late ob-
months goes forth, and covers all things far around with

ducto limo, unde cavæ lacunæ sudant tepido
spreading mud, whence the hollow ditches perspire with warm

humore. Nec tamen (cum labores que hominum que
moisture. Nor yet (when the labours both of men and

48

boum experti sint hæc versando terram;) improbus
of oxen have tried these things in cultivating the earth;) the mischievous

anser; que Strymoniæ grues, et intuba amaris fibris,
goose; and Strymonian cranes, and succory with bitter fibres.

120 officiunt nihil, aut umbra nocet.
injure nothing, or does the shade injure.

Pater ipse haud voluit viam colendi
The Father *of the Gods* himself does not will that the way of cultivating

esse facilem, que primus movit agros per artem,
should be easy, and first moves the fields by art.

acuens mortalia corda curis, nec passus sua
sharpening mortal feelings by cares, nor does he suffer his own

regna torpere gravi veterno. Ante Jovem, nulli
realms to become useless by heavy sloth. Before Jupiter, no

coloni subigebant arva; nec quidem erat fas signare,
husbandmen subdued the fields; nor indeed was it right to mark out,

aut partiri campum limite. Quærebant in
or to divide the plain by a boundary. They sought *every thing* in

medium, que tellus ipsa ferebat omnia, liberius,
common, and the earth itself produced all *things*, more freely.

nullo poscente. Ille addidit malum virus atris serpentibus,
no one demanding. He added pernicious poison to black serpents,

130 que jussit lupos prædari, que pontum moveri;
and commanded the wolves to plunder, and the sea to be moved,

que decussit mella foliis, que removit ignem, et
and shook off honey from leaves, and removed fire, and

repressit vina currentia passim rivis; ut meditando
restrained wine running every where in rivers; that by meditating

usus extunderet varias artes paulatim, et quæreret
experience might elaborate various arts by degrees, and seek for

herbam frumenti sulcis, et excuderet abstrusum ignem
the blade of corn in the furrows, and strike out the hidden fire

venis silicis. Tunc primum fluvii sensere cava-
from the veins of the flint. Then first the rivers experienced the hol-

tas alnos; tum navita fecit numeros et nomina stellis,
lowed alders; then the navigator gave numbers and names to the stars,

Pleiadas, Hyadas, que claram Arcton Lycaonis. Tum
the Pleiades, Hyades, and the shining Bear of Lycaon. Then

inventum captare feras laqueis, et fallere
it was found out *how* to catch wild beasts with snares, and to delude

140 visco, et circumdare magnos saltus canibus.
with birdlime, and to surround the extensive lawns with dogs.

Atque alius jam verberat latum amnem fundâ,
And one now beat the broad stream with a casting net

petens alta; que alius trahit humida lina pelago. Tum
seeking the deep; and another draws the moist lines in the sea. Then

rigor ferri, atque lamina argutæ serræ (nam primi
the rigour of iron and plates of the grating saw (for the first

scindebant   fissile   lignum   cuneis),   tum   variæ
men   cut   the divisible   wood   with wedges),   then   various

artes venere. Improbus labor vincit omnia,   et
arts   came.   Severe   labour   overcame   all *things*, and

egestas urgens in duris rebus.   Ceres prima
poverty   urgent   in   our severe   circumstances.   Ceres   first

instituit mortales vertere terram ferro; cum jam
taught   mortals   to turn up   the earth   with steel;   when   now

glandes atque arbuta sacræ silvæ deficerent, et Dodona
acorns   and   arbutes   of the sacred   wood   failed,   Dodona

negaret victum. Et mox labor additus frumentis;
denied   food.   And presently labour   being added   to the corn;

ut mala rubigo esset culmos, que segnis   150
that pernicious mildew should corrode the stalks, and the dull

carduus horreret in arvis.   Segetes intereunt;
thistle   should bristle up in   the fields.   The harvests   die;

aspera silva subit, que lappæ que tribuli, que inter
a rough   wood   comes up, and   burrs   and brambles,   and amidst

nitentia culta infelix lolium et steriles avenæ
the shining   cultivated *fields* the hapless darnel and   barren   oats

dominantur. Quod nisi insectabere terram assiduis
rule.   But   unless you persecute   the earth with continual

rastris, et terrebis aves sonitu, et premes umbras
harrows, and   frighten the birds with noise,   and   restrain the shadows

opaci ruris falce, que vocaveris imbrem votis;
of the dark field with the sickle, and   invoke   the shower by vows;

heu, frustra spectabis magnum acervum alterius, que
alas,   in vain shall you behold   the great   hoard   of another,   and

solabere famem concussa quercu in silvis.
console   your appetite *by acorns* from the shaken   oak   in the woods

Et dicendum, quæ arma sint duris agrestibus;   160
And it is to be sung, what tools are to the hardy   rustics;

sine queis messes potuere nec seri, nec surgere.
without which   harvests   can   neither be sown,   nor   spring up.

Primum vomis, et grave robur inflexi aratri,
First   the ploughshare, and the heavy wood of the unbending plough,

que tarda volventia plaustra Eleusinæ matris,   que
and   slow   rolling   wagon   of the Eleusinian. mother, *Ceres*,   and

tribula que traheæ, et rastri iniquo pondere; præterea
threshing drays and   drags,   and harrows of unequal weight;   besides

virgea que vilis supellex Celei, arbuteæ crates, et
the osier   and common   furniture   of Celeus,   arbute   hurdles, and

mystica vannus Iacchi; omnia quæ   provisa multo
the mystical fan   of Bacchus;   all   which *things* provided   long

ante memor repones, si digna gloria divini
before   mindful   do you lay by,   if   the worthy   honour of the divine

ruris manet te. Continuo in silvis flexa ulmus
country awaits thee.   Forthwith   in   the woods   the flexile   elm

domatur magnâ vi in burim, et accipit formam
is forced with great strength into a plough handle, and receives the shape

170 curvi aratri. Huic temo, protentus a
of the crooked plough. To this a pole, extended from

stirpe in octo pedes, binæ aures, dentalia duplici
the stock to eight feet, two earth boards, coulters with a double

dorso aptantur. Et ante levis tilia cæditur jugo,
back are fitted. And first the slender lime tree is cut down for the yoke,

que alta fagus, que stiva, quæ torqueat imos currus
and the high beech, and the ploughtail, which may turn the low carriage

a tergo; et fumus explorat robora suspensa focis.
from behind; and smoke seasons the wood hung over fires.

Possum referre tibi multa præcepta veterum, ni refugis,
I can describe to you many commands of the ancients, unless you reject

que piget cognoscere tenues curas. Cum
them, and it grieves you to know these light concerns. When

primis area æquanda ingenti cylindro, et ver-
the first floor is to be levelled with a great roller, and to be

tenda manu, et solidanda tenaci cretâ, ne
exercised by the hand, and to be rendered firm by adhesive chalk, lest

180 herbæ subeant, neu victa pulvere fatiscat.
the grass should come up, nor overcome by dust it should crack.

Tum variæ pestes illudunt; sæpe exiguus mus
Then various plagues delude our hopes; often the little mouse

que possuit domos sub terris, atque fecit horrea;
both has placed his nest beneath the earth, and made his store-houses;

aut talpæ, capti oculis, fodêre cubilia; que bufo
or moles, deprived of their eyes, had dug their beds; and the toad

inventus cavis, et plurima monstra, quæ terræ ferunt;
discovered in hollows, and many monsters, which the earth produces;

que curculio atque formica, metuens inopi senectæ,
and the weevil and the ant, dreading helpless old age,

populat ingentem acervum farris. Item contemplator,
lays waste a great hoard of corn. Also take notice,

cum silvis, plurima nux induet se
when in the woods, the full bearing nut tree (the almond) shall clothe itself

in florem, et curvabit olentes ramos: si fetus
in its flower, and shall bend its scented branches. if the fruit

superant, pariter frumenta sequentur.
in quantity shall exceed the leaves, in like manner corn shall follow,

que magna tritura veniet cum magno calore. At si
and a great threshing shall succeed with great heat. But if

190 umbra exuberat luxuria foliorum, nequicquam
the shade abounds by a profusion of leaves, in vain

area teret culmos pingues paleâ. Vidi
the threshing floor shall bruise the stalks rich in chaff only. I have seen

equidem multos serentes medicare semina, et prius per-
indeed many sowing to medicate the seed, and first to

ſundere nitro et nigra amurcâ, ut fetus esse.
wash *them* with nitre and black lees of oil, that the fruit may be

grandior fallacibus siliquis ; et, quamvis properata exiguo
larger in the delusive pods ; and, although hastened by a little

igni maderent, vidi diu lecta, et
fire they might become moist, I have seen *them* for a long time selected, and

spectata multo labore, degenerare tamen, nisi hu-
culled out with much labour, to degenerate nevertheless, unless hu-

mana vis quotannis legeret quæque maxima manu.
man power yearly had chosen whichever were largest by the hand.

Sic omnia ruere fatis in pejus, ac sub-
Thus all things rush by the fates to a worse condition, and falling

lapsa retro referri ; non aliter quam qui vix 200
away backward are borne ; not otherwise than *he* who hardly

subigit lembum remigiis adverso flumine, si forte
guides his boat by oars on the opposing stream, if by chance

remisit brachia, atque alveus rapit illum præceps in
he relaxed his arms, and the stream bears him headlong on

prono amni. Præterea tam sidera Arcturi, que dies
the declining river. Besides as the stars of Arcturus, and the days

hœdorum sunt servandi nobis, et lucidus anguis,
of the kids are to be observed by us, and the shining snake,

quam quibus, vectis per ventosa æquora, in
as by those *who*, being borne through the stormy seas, towards

patriam, pontus et fauces ostriferi Abydi tentantur.
their country, the sea and straits of oyster bearing Abydos are attempted.

Ubi Libra fecerit horas diei que
When the constellation of the Scales has rendered the hours of the day and

somni parés, et jam dividit medium orbem luci atque
of sleep equal, and now has divided the midst of the globe by light and

umbris ; viri, exercete tauros, serite hordea cam- 210
shades ; O men, exercise your bulls, sow barley in the

pis, usque sub extremum imbrem intractabilis brumæ
fields, even to near the last shower of the unmanageable winter.

Necnon tempus tegere et segetem lini et Cereale
Likewise it is the time to hide both a crop of flax and Ceres'

papaver humo, et jamdudum incumbere rastris dum
poppy in the ground, and at length to press on with harrows while

licet siccâ tellure, dum nubila pendent. Satio
it is allowed in the dry ground, while the clouds hang over. The sowing

fabis vere : tum putreš sulci accipiunt te quoque,
for beans is in the spring : then the rotten furrows receive you also,

Medica ; et annua cura venit milio, cum candidus
ɔ Medic *plant ;* and the yearly care comes to the millet, when the shining

Taurus aperit annum auratis cornibus, et Canis ceɑens
Bull opens the year with gilded horns, and the Dog retreating

averso astro occidit. At si excercebis humum
froɩn the retiring star sets. But if you cultivate the ground

in triticeam messem que robusta farra, que instabis
for the wheaten harvest and the strong corn, and you strive

220 aristis solis. Eoæ Atlantides,
for ears of corn alone. Let the morning daughters of Atlas

abscondantur tibi, que Gnosia stella ardentis
(the Pleiades,) be concealed to you, and the Gnosian star of the burning

coronæ, decedat ante quam committas debita
crown (of Ariadne), withdraw before that you shall intrust the destined

semina sulcis, que quam properes credere spem anni
seeds to the furrows, and that you hasten to yield the hope of the year

invitæ terræ. Multi cœpere ante occasum Maiæ, sed
to the unwilling earth. Many have begun before the setting of Maiæ, but

exspectata seges elusit illos vanis aristis. Vero s:
the expected crop deluded them with empty ears. But if

seres que viciam que vilem faselum, nec asperna-
you should sow both the vetch and the mean kidney bean, nor do you

bere curam Pelusiacæ lentis, cadens Bootes mittet
despise the care of the Egyptian lentil, setting Bootes will furnish

signa haud obscura tibi. Incipe, et extende sementem ad
signs not obscure to you. Begin, and prolong the sowing to

230 medias pruinas. Idcirco aureus sol regit
the midst of the hoarfrosts. Therefore the golden sun governs

orbem dimensum certis mensibus, per duodena
the globe measured by certain months, through the twelve

astra mundi. Quinque zonæ tenent cœlum ; quarum
constellations of the world. Five zones possess the sky; of which

una semper rubens corusco sole, et semper torrida ab
one ever blushing with the glittering sun, and ever burning from

igni ; circum quam extremæ trahuntur dextrâ que
the fire; around which the extremities are drawn on the right and

lævâ, concretæ cæruleâ glacie, atque atris imbribus.
on the left, hardened by the azure ice, and by black storms

Inter has que medium, duæ concessæ ægris mortalibus
Among these and in the midst, two granted to sickly mortals

munere Divûm ; et via secta per ambas, qua
by the favour of the Gods; and a way cut through both, where

obliquus ordo signorum verteret se. Ut mundus
the winding order of the constellations might turn itself. As the world

240 consurgit arduus ad Scythiam que Riphæas arces ;
rises high to Scythia and the Riphean towers

premitur devexus in austros Libyæ. Hic vertex
it sinks bending towards the south winds of Lybia. Here the pole is

nobis semper sublimis ; at atra Styx videt, que profundi
to us for ever high raised; but black Styx sees it, and the deep

manes illum sub pedibus. Hic maximus anguis
shades behold it beneath their feet. Here the great snake

elabitur circum sinuoso flexu, que in morem fluminis,
glides around by a winding bend, and in the manner of a river,

per duas Arctos; Arctos, metuentes tingi æquore
through the two Bears; the Bears, fearing to be dipped in the water

oceani. Illic, ut perhibent, aut intempesta nox semper
of the ocean. There, as they say, either the stormy night ever

silet, et tenebræ densantur nocte obtentâ; aut
is silent, and darkness thickens around in the night prolonged; or

aurora redit a nobis, que reducit diem: que ubi
the morning returns from us, and brings back the day: and when

primus oriens afflavit nos anhelis equis, 250
the first rising sun breathes upon us with panting horses,

illic rubens vesper accendit sera lumina. Hinc
there the blushing evening star kindles its late lights. Hence

possumus prædiscere tempestates dubio cœlo, hinc
we can foretell the storms in the doubtful sky, hence

que diem messis, que tempus serendi, et quando conveniat
both the day of harvest, and the time of sowing, and when it is proper

impellere infidum marmor remis; quando deducere
to drive through the faithless sea with oars; when to draw out

armatas classes, aut evertere tempestivam pinum silvis.
the armed ships, or to overthrow the seasonable pine in the woods.

Nec frustra speculamur obitus et ortus signorum,
Nor in vain do we watch the settings and risings of the constellations,

que annum parem quatuor diversis temporibus. Si
and the year equal by four different seasons. If

quando frigidus imber continet agricolam,
at any time the cold shower shall confine the farmer to his house,

datur maturare quæ mox forent properanda 260
it is allowed to accomplish what soon will be to be hastened

cœlo sereno. Arator procudit durum dentem obtusi
when the sky is clear. The ploughman sharpens the hard point of the blunted

vomeris, cavat lintres arbore; impressit aut
ploughshare, hollows out boats from the tree; imprints either

signum pecori, aut numeros acervos. Alii exacuunt
a mark on the flock, or the numbers on the heaps of corn. Others sharpen

vallos, que bicornes furcas, atque parant Amerina
the stakes, and two horned forks, and prepare Amerine willow

retinacula lentæ viti. Nunc facilis fiscina texatur
bands for the slender vine. Now let the flexile basket be woven

rubeâ virgâ: nunc torrete fruges igni, nunc
from the bramble twig: now roast your grain by the fire, now

frangite saxo. Quippe etiam fas et jura
grind it with the mill stone. For even right and the laws

sinunt exercere quædam festis diebus. Nulla religio
permit to execute certain labours on holy days. No religion

vetuit deducere rivos, prœtendere sepem segeti, 270
has forb'd to draw off streams, to extend a hedge to the corn,

moliri insidias avibus, incendere vepres, que mersare
to contrive snares for birds, to burn briars, and to plunge

gregem balantum salubri fluvio. Saepe agitator
a flock of bleating *sheep* in the healthful river. Often the driver

tardi aselli onerat costas oleo, aut vilibus pomis; que
of the lazy ass loads his ribs with oil, or cheap apples; and

revertens reportat incusum lapidem, aut massam
returning *some* brings back the indented *mill* stone, or a mass

atrae picis, urbe. Luna ipsa dedit alios dies felices
of black pitch, from the city. The moon herself has given other days happy

operum, alio ordine. Fuge quintam pallidus
for labours, by another order. Fly the fifth *upon this* pale

Orcus; que Eumenides satae. Tum nefando partu
Pluto, and the Furies were born Then by a dreadful birth

terra creat que Coeum que Iapetum que saevum
the earth produced both Coeus and Iapetus and cruel

Typhoea, et fratres conjuratos rescindere coelum.
Typhoeus, and the brothers having conspired to tear down heaven.

280 Scilicet ter conati sunt imponere Ossam Pelio,
For thrice did they attempt to place Ossa on Pelion,

atque involvere frondosum Olympum Ossae : ter pater
and to roll leafy Olympus on Ossa : thrice father

disjecit exstructos montes fulmine. Septima
Jupiter threw down upraised mountains with his thunder. The seventh

post decimam felix, et ponere vitem, et domitare
after the tenth is fortunate, both to plant the vine, and to tame

prensos boves, et addere licia telae ; nona melior
the restrained oxen, and to add the woof to the web; the ninth is better

fugae, contraria furtis. Adeo multa dedere se
for flight, opposed to theft. Thus many *things* have rendered themselves

melius gelidâ nocte ; aut cum Eous irrorat terras
better in the cold night; or when the East sprinkles the earth

novo sole. Nocte leves stipulae melius, · nocte
by the early sun. By night the light stubble is better, by night

arida prata tondentur : lentus humor non deficit noctes.
the dry meadows are mown : the gentle moisture does not fail in the night.

290 Et quidam pervigilat ad seros ignes hiberni
And some one watches by the late fires of the winter

luminis, que inspicat· faces acuto ferro. Interea,
light, and points matches with a sharp knife. In the meantime,

conjux, solata longum laborem, cantu
the wife, consoled in her long-continued toil, with the song *of her hus-*

percurrit telas arguto pectine ; aut deco-
band, runs over the webs with the shrill *sounding* shuttle; or boils

quit humorem dulcis musti vulcano, et despumat undam
down the liquor of sweet must by the fire, and skims the wave

trepidi aheni foliis. At rubicunda ceres succiditur
of the trembling caldron with leaves. But the blushing corn is cut up

medio aestu ; et area terit tostas fruges medio
in the mid-*day* heat; and the floor wears out the parched grain by mid-

æstu. Nudus ara, nudus sere: hiems ignava
day heat. Naked plough, naked sow: winter is a slothful season

colono. Agricolæ plerumque fruuntur
for the planter. Farmers for the most part enjoy what they have

parto frigoribus, que læti curant mutua 300
gained in the colds of winter, and joyful they provide mutual

convivia inter se; genialis hiems invitat
feasts among themselves; the festive winter invites them to pleasure

que resolvit curas. Ceu cum jam pressæ cârinæ
and relieves their cares. As when now the strained ships

tetigere portum, et læti nautæ imposuere coronas
have touched the harbour, and the glad sailors have placed their garlands

puppibus. Sed tamen tunc tempus stringere et
on the sterns. But nevertheless then it is time to strip both

q .ernas glandes, et baccas lauri, que oleam, que
the oaken mast, and the berries of laurel, and olive, and

cruenta myrta: tunc ponere pedicas gruibus, et
bloody myrtle berries: then to place foot traps for cranes, and

retia cervis, que sequi. auritos lepores; tum figere
nets for stags, and to follow the long eared hares; then to pierce

damas, torquentem stupea verbera Balearis fundæ,
the does, hurling hempen cords of the Balearian sling.

cum alta nix jacet, -cum flumina trudunt
when the deep snow lies on the ground, when the rivers push along

glaciem. Quid dicam tempestates et sidera 310
the ice. What shall I say of the tempests and constellations

autumni? atque quæ vigilanda viris, ubi jam
of autumn? and what things are to be avoided by men, when now

que dies brevior et æstas mollior? vel cum
both the day is shorter and the summer is milder? or when

imbriferum ver ruit; cum spicea messis jam
the shower-bearing spring pours down; when the spiky harvest now

inhorruit campis, et cum lactentia frumenta turgent
bristles up in the plains, and when the milky fruits swell

in viridi stipula. Sæpe ego, cum agricola induceret
on the green stalk. Often I, when the farmer has led

messorem flavis arvis, et jam stringeret hordea
the reaper into the yellow fields, and now has bound up the barley

fragili culmo, vidi omnia prœlia ventorum con-
with brittle straw, have seen all the conflicts of the winds com-

currere, quæ late eruerent gravidam segetem, ab
bine, which far around up-tore the heavy corn, from

imis radicibus, expulsam sublime: ita nigro tur-
their lowest roots, driven high: thus in the black whirl

bine hiems ferret que levem culmum, que 320
wind, a storm would bear both the light straw, and

volantes stipulas. Sæpe etiam immensum agmen aquarum
the flying stubble. Often also a great mass of waters

venît cœlo; et nubes collectæ ex alto glomerant
shall come to the sky; and the clouds collected from the deep gather

fœdam tempestatem atris imbribus: arduus æther
a foul storm with black showers: the lofty sky

ruit et ingenti pluviâ diluit læta sata, que
pours forth and with much rain washes the joyful cornfields, and

labores boum; fossæ implentur, et cava flumina
the labours of the oxen, the ditches are filled, and the deep streams

crescunt cum sonitu, que æquor fervet spirantibus
increase with a *great* sound, and the sea boils *with* foaming

fretis. Pater ipse molitur fulmina corusca dex-
shoals. Father *Jupiter* himself handles thunderbolts brandished with his

trâ in mediâ nocte nimborum; quo motu
right hand in the midst of a night of storms; by which commotion

maxima terra tremit; feræ fugêre, et humilis
the great earth trembles; the wild beasts have fled, and humbling

330 pavor stravit mortalia corda per gentes. Ille
fear has prostrated mortal hearts through the nations. He

dejicit aut Atho, aut Rhodopen, aut alta Ceraunia,
hurls down either *mount* Athos, or Rhodope, or high Ceraunia,

flagranti telo: austri et densissimus imber in-
with his flaming dart: the south winds also the thickening shower re-

geminant; nunc nemora, nunc litora plangunt ingenti
double: now the groves, now the shores resound with a great

vento. Metuens hoc, serva menses et sidera cœli;
wind. Fearing this, observe the months and constellations of the sky;

quo frigida stella Saturni receptet sese: in quos
where the cold star of Saturn withdraws itself; to what

orbes cœli Cyllenius ignis erret. In primis
orbs of heaven Mercury's fire wanders Among your first

venerare Deos; atque refer annua sacra magnæ
duties reverence the Gods; and bear annual sacrifices to great

Cereri; operatus in lætis herbis, sub casum extremæ
Ceres; offering on the joyful grass, about the end of extreme

340 hiemis, jam sereno vere. Tunc agni pin-
winter, now in the serene spring. Then the fields are

gues et tunc vina mollissima: tunc somni dulces, que
rich and then the wine is most mellow: then slumbers are sweet, and

umbræ densæ in montibus. Cuncta agrestis pubes
the shadows are thick on the mountains. All the rustic youth

tibi adoret Cererem, cui tu dilue favos lacte,
for you shall adore Ceres, for whom you bathe the honey-comb with milk.

æt miti baccho; que ter felix hostia eat circum
and mellow wine; and thrice let the joyous victim go around

novas fruges; quam omnis chorus, et ovantes socii co-
the new grain; whom all the band, and shouting companions ac

mitentur, et vocent Cererem clamore in tecta; que
company, and invoke Ceres with a shout to their houses and

ne   quisquam   supponat   falcem   maturis aristis, ante
let *not*   any one   apply   *his* sickle to the ripe corn, before

quam   redimitus   tempora   tortâ   quercu,
that   bound   *as to his* temples with a wreathed oak,

det   incompositos motus et dicat carmina 350
let him give unstudied motions and sing songs

Cereri. Atque ut possimus discere hæc certis
to Ceres. And that we may learn these things by certain

signis, quæ æstus que pluvias et ventos agentes frigora;
signs, both heats and rains and the winds driving on the cold;

pater   ipse   statuit   quid menstrua luna
father *Jupiter* himself has determined what the monthly moon

moneret; quo signo austri caderent, quid agricolæ
should foretell; by what sign the south winds shall fall, what the farmers

videntes sæpe tenerent armenta propius stabulis. Con-
seeing often shall keep their herds near to the stables. Im-

tinuo, ventis surgentibus, aut freta ponti agitata inci-
mediately the winds arising, or the shallows of the sea agitated be-

piunt tumescere; et aridus fragor audiri altis
gin to swell; and a dry rustling noise to be heard in the high

montibus; aut litora resonantia longe misceri, et
mountains; or the shores resounding afar off to be disturbed, and

murmur nemorum increbrescere. Jam tum unda male
the murmuring of the groves to increase. Now then the wave hardly

temperat sibi a curvis carinis, cum celeres 360
restrains itself from the crooked ships, when the swift

mergi revolant ex medio æquore, que ferunt clamorem
cormorants fly back from the midst of the sea, and bear their cry

ad litora, que cum marinæ fulicæ ludunt in sicco; ·que
to the shores, and when the sea coots sport on the dry *land*, and

ardea deserit notas paludes, atque volat supra altam
the heron deserts the known marshes, and flies above the high

nubem. Sæpe etiam, vento impendente, videbis stellas
cloud. Often also, the wind threatening, you shall see the stars

labi præcipites cœlo; que longos tractus flammarum
glide swift through the sky: and the long traces cf flames

albescere a tergo per umbram noctis; sæpe levem
to whiten up from behind through the shade of night; often the light

paleam et caducas frondes volitare; aut plumas nantes
straw and falling leaves fly about, or feathers swimming

in summâ aquâ colludere. At cum fulminat de
on the top of the water to sport together. But when it thunders from

parte trucis Boreæ, et cum domus que   Euri
a part of the stern north, and when the house both of the east wind 370

que Zephyri tonat; omnia rura natant plenis fossis,
and the west wind thunders. all the fields swim with full ditches.

atque omnis navita legit humida vela ponto. Imber
and every seaman gathers up his moist sails on the sea The shower

nunquam obfuit imprudentibus : aut æriæ grues fugêre
never injures the unadvised · either the airy cranes have escaped

illum surgentem imis vallibus ; aut bucula, suspiciens
it rising in the lowest vales; or the heifer, gazing

cœlum, captavit auras patulis naribus ; aut
on the sky has caught the air in her wide spread nostrils; or

arguta hirundo volitavit circum lacus, et ranæ
the shrill sounding swallow has flown around the lakes, and the frogs

cecinere veterem querelam in limo. Et sæpius
have sung forth their old complaint in the mud. And often

formica, terens angustum iter, extulit ova tectis
the ant, wearing a narrow path, has borne her eggs from her covered

380 penetralibus ; et ingens arcus bibit ; et exercitus
     retreats; and the great bow has drunk; and an army

corvorum, decedens e pastu magno agmine, incre-
of crows, departing from the pasture in a great band, sounded

puit densis alis. Jam videas varias volucres
with close pressed wings. Now you may see the various birds

pelagi, et quæ rimantur circum Asia prata in
of the sea, and those which search around the Asian meadows in

dulcibus stagnis Caystri, certatim infundere largos rores
the pleasant pools of Cayster, eagerly pour copious dews

humeris ; nunc objectare caput fretis, nunc currere
on their shoulders; now plunge their heads in the waters, now run

in undas, et gestire studio lavandi incassum. Tum
among the waves, and sport in the delight of washing in vain. Then

improba cornix vocat pluviam plenâ voce, et sola
the ill-boding crow invokes the rain with full voice, and alone

spatiatur secum in sicca árenâ. Nec quidem
stalks along by herself upon the dry sand. Nor indeed

390 puellæ, carpentœ nocturna pensa, nescivere
     were the maids, carding their nightly tasks, ignorant

hiemem ; cum viderent oleum scintillare ardente testa,
of the storm; when they saw the oil to sparkle in the burning lamp,

et putres fungos concrescere. Nec minus, ex imbri
and the rotten clots harden. Nevertheless, from the storm

poteris prospicere, et certis signis cognoscere, soles et
you may foresee, and by sure signs know, the suns and

aperta serena. Nam tum neque acies videtui
the open clear skies. For then neither does the edge seem

obtusa stellis, nec luna surgere obnoxia radiis
blunted to the stars, nor the moon to arise opposed to the rays

fratris ; nec tenuia vellera lanæ ferri per
of her brother; nor are the light fléeces of wool (fleecy clouds) borne through

cœlum. Alcyones, dilectæ Thetidi, non pandunt
the sky Halcyons, birds beloved by Thetis, do not open

pennas ad tepidum solem in litore ; immundi sues
heir wings to the warm sun upon the shore; filthy swine

non meminere jactare solutos manipulos 400
do not remember to scatter loose sheaves *of corn*

ore. At nebulæ magis petunt ima que
with their mouths. But mists rather seek low *places* and

recumbunt campo : et noctua, servans occasum solis
rest upon the plain : and the owl, observing the setting of the sun

de sumno culmine, nequicquam exercet seros cantus.
from the high roof, in vain repeats her evening songs.

Nisus apparet sublimis in liquido ære, et Scylla dat
Nisus appears high in the clear sky, and Scylla gives

pœnas pro purpureo capillo. Quacumque illa fugiens
punishment for the purple lock. Wherever she flying

secat levem æthera pennis, ecce, inimicus, atrox
cuts the light air with her wings, lo, the hostile, cruel

Nisus insequitur per auras magno stridore : qua
Nisus pursues *her* through the air with great noise : where

Nisus fert se ad auras, illa, fugiens raptim, secat
Nisus raises himself to the skies, she, flying swiftly, cuts

levem æthera pennis. Tum corvi ingeminant liquidas
the light air on wings. Then the ravens redouble their liquid

voces ter aut quater presso gutture ; 410
notes thrice or four times in their compressed throats ;

et sæpe altis cubilibus, læti nescio quâ dulcedine
and often in their high nests, joyful I know not by what delight

præter solitum, strepitant inter se foliis :
beyond their wonted *pleasure*, make a great noise together in the leaves :

imbribus actis, juvat revisere parvam progeniem,
the showers having passed, it delights *them* to revisit their little offspring,

que dulces nidos. Equidem, haud credo, quia ingenium
and pleasant nests. Indeed, I do not believe, that this capacity

sit illis divinitus, aut major
for enjoyment can be theirs from heaven, or *that there is to them* a greater

prudentia rerum fato : verum ubi tempestas et
foresight of things *bestowed* by fate : but when the weather and

mobilis humor cœli mutavere vias, et jupiter,
changeful moisture of the sky have altered their courses, and the air,

humidus Austris, densat quæ modo erant
damp with south winds, condenses *those things* which lately were

rara, et relaxat quæ densa : species animorum
rare, and rarifies *those* which *were* condensed : views of the mind

vertuntur, et pectora concipiunt nunc alios motus
are changed, and their breasts conceive now these emotions 420

alios, dum ventus agebat nubila. Hinc ille concentus
now others, while the wind drove on the clouds. Hence that concert

avium in agris, et pecudes lætæ, et corvi ovantes
of birds in the fields, and the flocks *were* joyful, and the ravens exulting

gutture. Si vero respicies ad rapidum solem,
with their throats. If indeed you will look to the rapid sun,

que lunas sequentes ordine ; crastina hora nunquam
and the moons following in succession , to-morrow's hour never

fallet te, neque capiere insidiis serenæ
shall delude you, nor shall you be cheated by the snares of a clear

noctis. Cum primum luna colligit revertentes
night. When first the moon has collected the returning

ignes, si comprenderit nigrum æra obscuro cornu ;
fires, if she has embraced the murky air with her obscure horn ;

maximus imber parabitur agricolis que pelago. At,
a very great storm will be prepared for the farmers and for the sea. But,

430 si suffuderit virgineum ruborem ore erit
if she shall diffuse a virgin blush over her face, there will be

ventus. Aurea Phœbe semper rubet vento. Sin
wind. The golden moon always blushes in the wind. But if

pura in quarto ortu (namque is certissimus auctor), nec
spotless in the fourth rising (for this is the surest authority), nor

ibit obtusis cornibus per cœlum ; et totus
she will proceed with blunted horns through the sky , and all

ille dies, et qui nascentur ab illo, ad exactum
that day, and those which proceed from it, to the completed

mensem, carebunt pluvià que ventis : nautæ servati
month, shall be deprived of rain and winds the sailors preserved

solvent vota in litore Glauco ; et Panopeæ, et
shall pay their vows upon the shore to Glaucus; and Panopea, and

Inoo Melicertæ. Sol quoque et exoriens,
Ino the mother of Malicerta. The sun also both rising,

et cum condet se in undas, dabit signa. Cer-
and when he hides himself in the waves, shall give signs. The

tissima signa sequuntur solem, et quæ refert
surest signs follow the sun, both those which he brings back

440 mane, et quæ, astris surgentibus.
in the morning, and those which he ushers in, the stars arising.

Ubi ille variaverit nascentem ortum maculis, conditus
When he shall variegate his rising beam with spots, concealed

in nubem, que refugerit medio orbe ; imbres
in a cloud, and shall escape the sight with half his orb; showers

sint suspecti tibi : namque Notus, sinister que
may be expected by you : for the south wind, injurious both

arboribus, que satis, que pecori, urget ab alto. Aut
to trees, and corn, and the flock, hurries from the deep. Or

ubi, sub lucem diversi radii rumpent sese inter
when, about the dawn diversified rays shall force themselves amidst

densa nubila ; aut ubi Aurora, linquens croceum cubile
the thick clouds; or when Aurora, leaving the saffron couch

Tithoni, surget pallida ; heu, tum pampinus male
of Tithonus, shall arise pale; alas, then the vine leaf hardly

defendet mites uvas ; tam multa horrida grando salit
shall defend the mild grapes ; so much direful hail leaps

crepitans in tectis.   Profuerit magis meminisse hoc
rattling   on the roofs.   It would profit   more to have remembered this

etiam, cum jam decedet Olympo   emenso;   450
also,   when now   he sets   heaven   being measured over;

nam sæpe videmus varios colores errare in ipsius
for   often   we behold various   colours   to wander over   his

vultu.   Cæruleus denuntiat pluviam : igneus   Euros.
face.   The azure *sky* menaces   rain :   the fiery   east winds.

Sin maculæ incipient immisceri rutilo igni ;
But if   the spots   should begin   to be mingled   with glittering   fire,

tunc videbis omnia fervere pariter vento   que
then   you will see   all   *things*   to rage   together   by the wind and

nimbis.   Non quisquam moneat me ire per altum
storms.   Let no one   admonish   me to go through the deep

illâ nocte, neque convellere funem a   terrâ.   At si
on that night,   neither   tear away   the cable from   the land.   But if

orbis erit lucidus, que cum referet diem, que
his orb shall be   clear,   both   when   he shall restore the day,   and

condet relatum ; frustra terrebere nimbis,
shall conceal it   ushered in ;   in vain   shall you be frightened   by clouds,

et cernes silvas moveri claro Aquilone. De-   460
and you shall see the woods   moved   by the fair   north wind.   Fi-

nique quid serus Vesper vehat, unde ventus agat
nally   what   the late   evening   shall bring, whence   the wind shall drive

serenas nubes, quid humidus Auster cogitet, sol dabit
the serene clouds,   what the moist   south wind   intends, the sun shall give

signa tibi.   Quis audeat dicere solem   falsum ? Ille
signs to you.   Who can dare   to say   the sun   *is*   false ?   He

etiam sæpe monet cæcos tumultus instare, que
also   often   admonishes   that blind   disturbances   threaten,   and

fraudem et operta bella tumescere.   Ille etiam miseratus
fraud   and secret   wars   swell around.   He   also   compassionating

Romam, Cæsare exstincto, cum texit nitidum caput
Rome,   Cæsar   being killed,   when he covered his shining   head

obscurâ ferrugine, que impia secula timuerunt æternam
with dark   purple,   and impious   ages   feared   eternal

noctem ; quanquam illo tempore tellus quoque et
night;   although   at that   time   the earth   also   and

æquora ponti, que obsœni canes, que importunæ   470
the waters of the sea, and   filthy   dogs, and   clamorous

volucres, dabant signa.   Quoties vidimus Ætnam,
birds,   gave   signs.   How often   have we seen   Ætna,

undantem fornacibus ruptis, effervere in agros Cy-
waving   from its furnaces   bursting,   to boil over upon the fields   of the

clopum, que volvere globos flammarum que liquefacta
Cyclops,   and   to roll   globes   of flames   and   melted

saxa !   Germania audiit sonitum armorum toto cœlo :
rocks !   Germany   hears the sound   of arms   through the whole sky;

Alpes tremuerunt insolitis motibus. Ingens vox
the Alps shook with unusual commotions. A great voice

quoque exaudita vulgo per silentes lucos, et
also was heard every where through the silent groves, and

simulacra, pallentia miris modis visa sub ob-
ghosts, pale in wonderful forms were seen beneath the

scurum noctis; que pecudes locutæ. Infandum! amnes
dark cloud of night; and the cattle spoke. O abominable! the rivers

sistunt, que terræ dehiscunt; et mœstum ebur illacrymat
stand still, and the earth opened wide; and the mournful ivory weeps

480 templis, que æra sudant. Eridanus, rex
in the temples, and brazen images sweat. Eridanus, the king

fluviorum, proluit silvas, contorquens insano vortice,
of rivers, overflows the woods, turning in maddening whirl,

que tulit armenta cum stabulis per omnes campos.
and bore along herds with their stables through all the plains.

Nec eodem tempore aut minaces fibræ·
Nor at the same time either did the threatening fibres fail

apparere tristibus extis, aut cruor cessavit manare
to appear in the dismal entrails, or did blood cease to flow

puteis; et urbes resonare alte per noctem, lupis
from wells; and the cities to resound far through the night, the wolves

ululantibus. Non plura fulgura alias ceciderunt
howling. Not more lightnings elsewhere fell

sereno cœlo; nec diri cometæ toties arsere.
from the clear heaven; nor did direful comets so often burn.

Ergo, Philippi videre Romanas acies concurrere iterum
Therefore, Philippi beheld the Roman armies rush together again

490 inter sese paribus telis: nec fuit indignum
among themselves with equal weapons: nor was it unworthy

Superis Emathiam et latos campos Hæmi pinguescere
the Gods that Emathia and the broad plains of Hæmus to become enriched

bis nostro sanguine. Scilicet et tempus veniet, cum,
twice by our blood. For also the time shall come, when,

illis finibus, agricola, molitus terram incurvo aratro,
in those boundaries, the farmer, tilling the earth with the crooked plough,

inveniet pila exesa scabra rubigine, aut pulsabit
shall find darts corroded by consuming rust, or shall strike

inanes galeas gravibus rastris, que mirabitur grandia ossa
empty helmets with heavy harrows, and shall admire the large bones

effossis sepulcris. Patrii Dî, Indigetes,
from the excavated tombs. O my country's Gods, ye native Deities,

et Romule, que mater Vesta, quæ servas Tuscum
and thou O Romulus, and mother Vesta, who preservest Tuscan

500 Tiberim et Romana palatia; saltem ne prohibete
Tiber and the Roman palaces; at least do not forbid

hunc juvenem succurrere everso sœclo. Jampridem
this youth to relieve this overturned age. Long since

luimus   perjuria   Loamedonteæ   Trojæ   nostro
we have suffered for the perjuries   of Laomedon's   Troy   by our

sanguine.   Jampridem, Cæsar, regia cœli invidet te
blood.   Long since,   O Cæsar, the palace of heaven envies you

nobis, atque queritur   curare triumphos hominum :
to us,   and   complains   that you   care for the triumphs   of men :

quippe ubi fas atque nefas versum,   tot bella   per
for   when right and   wrong are confounded, so many wars   through

orbem ; tam multæ facies scelerum ;   non ullus   dignus
the globe ; so   many   forms   of crimes ;   there is no   worthy

honos   aratro :   arva   squalent   colonis
honour   to the plough · the fields are overgrown with weeds, the husbandmen

abductis   et curvæ falces conflantur in rigidum enses.
being driven away and the crooked sickles are melted into   hard   swords.

Hinc   Euphrates, illinc Germania, movet bellum ;
On this side the Euphrates, on that   Germany,   excites   war ;

vicinæ urbes ferunt arma : inter   se   legibus
neighbouring cities bear hostile arms : among themselves treaties   510

ruptis :   impius Mars sævit   toto   orbe. Ut cum
being violated : merciless Mars   rages through the whole globe.   As   when

                 quadrigæ   effudere   sese   carceribus,
chariots drawn by four horses   loose   themselves from the goals,

addunt se in spatia, et auriga, frustra tendens retina-
hasten   to   the race, and the charioteer in vain   holding   the

cula,   fertur   equis,   neque   currus   audit
bridle, is borne away by the horses,   nor   does the chariot   regard

habenas.
the reins.

BOOK II.

HACTENUS   cultus arvorum, et   sidera
HITHERTO   I have sung the husbandry   of fields, and the constellations

cœli ; nunc   canam . te,   Bacche, necnon silvestria
of heaven ; now I will celebrate thee,   O Bacchus,   also   the wild

virgulta tecum, et prolem   tarde crescentis olivæ.
shrubs   with thee, and the offspring of the slowly growing   olive

Huc, ô pater Lenæe: omnia hic   plena tuis
Come   here, O father Bacchus :   all things here are   full   of thy

muneribus: ager floret tibi gravidus pampineo au-
favours.   the field thrives for thee   teeming   with the viny   au-

tumno, vindemia spumat plenis labris : veni huc, ô
tumn;   the vintage foams with full vats : come here, O

pater Lenææ, et mecum tinge nudata crura novo
father Bacchus, and with me imbrue your naked legs with new

musto, cothurnis direptis. Principio, natura est
wine, your buskins being torn off In the first place, nature is

10 varia creandis arboribus : namque aliæ veniunt
    various in producing trees : for some come up

ipsæ suâ sponte, nullis hominum cogentibus
themselves of their own accord, no *labours* of men forcing

que tenent campos late et curva flumina :
them, and spread over the fields far around and crooked streams :

ut molle siler, que lentæ genistæ, populus et canentia
as the soft osier, and the slender broom, the poplar and whitening

salicta glaucâ fronde. Autem pars surgunt de
willows with sea green leaf. But a part arise from

posito semine ; ut altæ castaneæ, que æsculus quæ
planted seed; as the high chestnuts, and the bay oak which

frondet Jovi, maxima nemorum, atque
puts forth leaves *in honour* to Jove, the greatest *tree* of the groves, and

quercus habitæ oracula Graiis. Densissima silva
oaks esteemed oracles by the Greeks. A very abundant forest

pullulat aliis ab radice, ut cerasis que
of young shoots springs to others from the root, as to cherries and

ulmis : etiam parva Parnassia laurus subjicit se sub
to elms : also the small Parnassian laurel raises itself beneath

ingenti umbrâ matris. Natura primum dedit hos
the great shade of its mother. Nature first has given these

20 modos : his omne genus silvarum que fruticum,
    means : by these every kind of wood and fruit trees,

que sacrorum nemorum, viret. Sunt alii quos
and of sacred groves, flourishes. There are others which

usus ipse reperit sibi viâ. Hic
experience itself has found out for itself by art.* This *man*

abscindens plantas de tenero corpore matrum,
cutting the shoots from the tender body of *their* mothers

deposuit sulcis : hic obruit arvo stirpes, que
has planted *them* in furrows : this has covered in the ground stocks, and

sudes quadrifidas, et vallos acuto robore, que
stakes divided in four parts, and poles with sharp pointed wood and

aliæ silvarum exspectant pressòs arcus propaginis, et viva
some of the trees expect the bent arches of a shoot, and living

plantaria suâ terrâ. Aliæ egent nil radicis : que
nurseries in their own land. Others want nothing of *any* root : and

putator haud dubitat mandare terræ summum cacumen,
the pruner does not hesitate to commit to the earth the highest top

referens Quin et, mirabile dictu, oleagina 30
restoring it to her But even, wonderful to be told, the wild olive

radix, candicibus sectis, truditur e sicco ligno. E
root, its trunk being cut up. shoots out from dry wood. And

sæpe videmus ramos alterius vertere impune
often have we seen the branches of one tree to change without injury

in alterius: que pyrum mutatam ferre insitis
into those of another: and the pear transformed to bear engrafted

mala et lapidosa corna rubescere prunis. Quare
apples, and stony wild cherries to redden on plum trees. Wherefore

agite, ó agricolæ, discite proprios cultus generatim, que
come on, O farmers, learn appropriate cultivation for each kind, and

mollite feros fructus colendo: neu segnes
soften the wild fruits by nutrition: ner permit that unfruitfu

terræ jaceant: juvat conserere Ismara baccho,
lands be idle: it delights to plant even Ismarus with the vine

atque vestire magnum Taburnum olea. Que tu
and to cover extensive Taburnus with the olive. And do you

ades, que decurre inceptum laborem una, ô
be present, and pursue this begun labour together with me O thou my

decus, ô. merito maxima pars nostræ famæ, Mæcenas,
glory, O deservedly the greatest part of my fame, Mæcenas,

que volans da vela patenti pelago. Ego non 40
and flying give sail on the opening sea. I do not

opto amplecti cuncta meis versibus; non, si sint mihi
wish to embrace all things in my verses; not, if there can be to me

centum linguæ, que centum ora ferrea vox: ades
a hundred tongues, and a hundred mouths an iron voice: come here

et lege oram primi litoris. Terræ in
and coast along the margin of the nearest shore. The lands are in ou

manibus: non tenebo te hic ficto carmine, atque
hands: nor will I detain you here with a feigned song, and

per ambages et longa exorsa. Quæ
lead you through windings and long introductions. Those plants which

tollunt se in oras luminis, suâ sponte,
raise themselves to the borders of light, of their own free will

surgunt infecunda quidem, sed læta et fortia; quippe
arise unproductive indeed, but healthful and strong; for

natura subest solo. Tamen si quis inserat hæc
nature is under the soil. Yet if any one shall engraft these

quoque aut mandet mutata subactis scrobibus, 50
also or commit them transplanted to prepared trenches,

exuerint silvestrem animum; que frequenti cul-
they will lay aside their wild disposition; and by frequent cul-

tu, haud tarda sequenter in quascunque artes
tivation, not slowly. will they follow into whatsoever arts

voces. Nec et non, quæ exit sterilis
vou may invite them to. Also, the shoot which comes barren

ab imis stirpibus. faciet hoc, si sit digesta
from the lowest roots, will accomplish this, if it be spread

per vacuos agros: nunc altæ frondes, et rami
through the empty fields: now the high leaves, and branches

matris opacant, que adimunt fetus crescenti,
of its mother overshade it, and take away fruit from it growing,

que urunt ferentem. Jam arbos, quæ sustulit
and consume it producing fruit. Now the tree, which raises

se jactis seminibus, venit tarda, factura
itself from planted seeds, comes up slow, about to make

ambram seris nepotibus: que poma degenerant
a shade for its late offspring: and the fruits degenerate

oblita priores succos: et uva fert turpes
having forgotten their former juices: and the grape vine produces base

60 racemos prædam avibus. Scilicet labour est impen-
clusters plunder for birds. For labour is to be

dendus omnibus, et omnes cogendæ in sulcum, ac
expended on all, and all are to be forced into the furrow, and

domandæ multâ mercede. Oleæ truncis, vites
subdued by much pains. Olives grew from truncheons, vines

propagine meliùs respondent, myrtus Paphiæ
from the shoot better answer our views, the myrtle of Paphian

de solido robore. Eduræ coryli nascuntur
Venus from the solid wood. Hardy hazels grow

plantis, et ingens fraxinus, umbrosa arbos Herculeæ
from shoots, and the great ash, and the shady poplar tree of Hercules'

coronæ, que glandes Chaonii patris: etiam ardua
crown, and the mast of the Chaonian father Jupiter: also the lofty

palma nascitur, et abies visura marinos casus
palm grows, and the fir about to visit maritime misfortunes

Vero horrida arbutus inseritur ex fetu nucis, et
Get the rough arbute is engrafted from the fruit of the walnut, and

70 steriles platani gessere valentes malos.
barren plane trees have borne strong apples.

Fagus incanuit castaneæ, que ornus
The beech has whitened with blossoms of the chestnut, and the mountain ash

albo flore pyri: que sues fregere glandem
with the white flower of the pear and swine have broken mast

sub ulmis. Nec est simplex modus inserere atque
beneath elms. Nor is it the same method to engraft and

imponere oculos. Nam qua gemmæ trudunt
to place buds (to inoculate). For where the buds push

se de medio cortice, et rumpunt tenues tunicas,
themselves from the middle of the bark, and break the tender coats

angustus sinus fit in nodo ipso: includunt germen
a narrow opening is made in the knot itself they enclose the bud

ex aliena arbore huc, que docent inolescere udo
from another tree here, and teach it to harden in the moist

libro. Alii rursum, enodes trunci resecantur, et via
bark. Or again, the knotless trunks are cut, and a way

finditur alte in solidum cuneis, deinde feraces
is cloven deeply in the solid wood with wedges, afterwards fruitful

plantæ immittuntur ; nec tempus longum, et ingens 80
suckers are introduced; nor is the time long, and a great

arbos exiit ad cœlum felicibus ramis, que miratur novæ
tree goes forth to heaven with happy branches, and admires new

frondes et poma non sua. Præterea haud unum
leaves and fruits not its own. Besides there is not one

genus ; nec fortibus ulmis, nec salici, que oto,
kind only; neither to the strong elms, nor the willow, and lote tree

nec Idæis cyparissis; nec pingues olivæ nascuntur in
nor the Idean cypresses; nor do fat olives grow in

unam faciem, orchites, et radii, et pausia, amara
one shape, the orchites, and the radii, and the pausia, with bitter

baccâ; que poma et silvæ Alcinoi ; nec idem
berry; and the apples and the orchards of Alcinous; nor is the same

surculus Crustumiis que Syriis pyris, que gravibus
shoot to the Crustumian and the Syrian pears, and to the heavy

volemis. Eadem vindemia non pendet nostris arboribus,
volemi. The same vintage does not hang from our trees,

quam Lesbos carpit de Methymnæo palmite. Sunt
which Lesbos plucks from the Methymnæan vine. There are

Thasiæ vites, sunt et albæ Mareotides; hæ habiles 90
Thasian vines, there are also white Mareotides; these adapted

pinguibus terris, illæ levioribus ; et Psythis
to fertile lands, those more congenial to lighter soils; and the Psythian

utilior passo, que tenuis lageos tentatura pedes
more useful when dried, and the light lageos about to try the feet

olim, que vinetura linguam ; purpureæ, que preciæ :
hereafter, and about to bind the teague; the purple, and precocious.

et quo carmine dicam te, Rhætica, nec
and in what verse shall sing thee, O Rhætian vine, nor

ideo contende Falernis ellis. Sunt etiam Amminæe
thus contend in Falernean cellars. There are also Amminear

vites, firmissima vina; quibus et Tmolus, 100
vines, producing very powerful wines; which even Tmolus,

st Phsnæus ipes rex, assurgit : que
and Phsnæus himself king of meuatais, rises to (i. e. honours): and

minor Argitis, cui non ulla certaverit aut fluere
the lesser Argitis, with which not any has contended either to flow

tantum, aut durare per totidem annos. Ego nos
so much, or to last for so many years. I will not

transierim te, Rhodia accepta Dis et secundis
pour thee, O Rhodian grape received by the gods and at second

moonsis. et bumaste, tumidis racemis. Sed
tables, and thee O bumastes. with swelling clusters. Bu

neque est numerus   quam multæ species nec quæ
neither is the number *recounted* how many kinds nor what

sint nomina; enim neque refert comprendere
may be the names; for neither does it concern *us* to comprehend

numero; quem, qui velit scire, idem velit discere
in number; which, whoever would know, the same would learn

quam multæ arenæ Libyci æquoris turbentur Zephyro;
how many sands of the Libyan sea are disturbed by the west wind

aut, ubi Eurus violentior incidit navigiis, nosse quot
or, when the east wind more violent falls upon the ships, to know how many

Ionii fluctus veniant ad litora. Nec vero possunt omnes
Ionian waves come to the shores. Nor indeed can all

terræ ferre omnia. Salices nascuntur flumini-
lands produce all *kinds of trees.* Willows grow by ri-

110   bus, que alni crassis paludibus; steriles orni
vers, and alders in thick marshes; barren wild ashes

saxosis montibus; litora lætissima myrtetis: denique
in rocky mountains; the shores *are* most gladdened by myrtles: finally

Bacchus amat apertos colles: taxi Aquilonem et
Bacchus loves the open hills· yew trees *love* the north wind and

frigora. Aspice et orbem domitum extremis
the colds. See also the globe subdued by the most distant

cultoribus, que Eoas domos Arabum, que pictos
cultivators, both the eastern dwellings ·of the Arabians, and the painted

Gelonos. Patriæ divisæ arboribus. India sola fert
Geloni. Countries are separated by trees. India alone produces

nigrum ebenum: thurea virga est Sabæis
the black ebony· the frankincense shrub is for the Sabeans

solis. Quid referam tibi balsama que sudantia
only. Why should I relate to you balsams also perspiring

odorato ligno, et baccas semper frondentis acanthi?
from the odorous wood, and the berries of the ever leafing acanthus?

120   quid nemora Æthiopum canentia
why *should I describe* the groves of the Æthiopians whitening

molli lana? utque Seres depectant tenuia vellera
with soft wool? and how the Seres comb down light fleeces

foliis? aut quos lucos India propior Oceano,
from leaves? or what forests India nearer to the Ocean,

extremi sinus orbis, gerit? ubi haud ullæ sagittæ
the fartherest borders of the globe, produces? where not any arrows

potuere vincere summum æra arboris jactu: et illa
can surpass the loftiest height of a tree in their flight and that

gens quidem non tarda sumtis pharetris. Media fert
nation indeed is not slow ·in using quivers. Media produces

tristes succos que tardum saporem felicis mali; quo
the bitter juices and lasting taste of the happy apple. than

non ullum præsentius auxilium venit, ac agit
which not any more ready aid comes, and drives away

atra **venena** membris, siquando sævæ novercæ
black poison from the limbs, if at any time merciless stepmothers

infecere pocula, que miscuerunt herbas, et non innoxia
have infected bowls, and mingled herbs, and not harmless

verba. Ipsa arbos ingens que simillima
words of enchantment. This tree is large and most like

lauro faciem; et, si non jactaret alium odorem
to the bay tree in form; and, if it had not cast another smell

late, fuerat laurus. Folia haud labentia ullis
far around, it had been a laurel. Its leaves do not fall by any

ventis; flos apprima tenax. Medi fovent
winds; the flower is very tenacious The Medes correct their

animas et olentia ora, et medicantur anhelis senibus
breaths and offensive mouths, and cure panting old men

illo. Sed neque silvæ Medorum, ditissima terra,
with it. But neither the groves of the Medes, that most fertile land,

nec pulcher Ganges, atque Hermus turbidus auro,
nor beautiful Ganges, and Hermus thickened with gold,

certent laudibus Italiæ : non Bactra, neque Indi,
can contend with the praises of Italy. not Bactra, nor the Indians,

que tota Panchaia pinguis thuriferis arenis ; non
and all Panchaia rich in incense bearing sands, nor

tauri, spirantes ignem naribus, invertêre hæc loca,
bulls breathing fire from their nostrils, have turned up these places,

dentibus immanis hydri satis : nec seges 140
the teeth of a huge hydra being sown : nor has a harvest

virûm horruit galeis que densis hastis : sed gravidæ
of men bristled up with helmets and thickening spears: but teeming

fruges, et Massicus humor Bacchi, implevere,
fruits, and the Massic juice of Bacchus, have filled the country,

que oleæ que læta armenta tenent. Hinc bellator equus,
and olives and joyful herds possess it. Hence the warrir horse,

arduus, infert sese campo; hinc albi greges, et
bold, bears himself to the plain; hence white flocks, and

taurus, maxima victima, sæpe perfusi tuo sacro flumine,
the bull, the greatest victim, often bathed in thy sacred stream,

Clitumne, duxere Romanos triumphos ad templa Deûm.
O Clitumnus, have led the Roman triumphs to the temples of the Gods.

Hic assiduum ver, atque æstas alienis mensibus :
Here is perpetual spring, and summer in unusual months:

pecudes bis gravidæ, et arbos bis utilis 150
the cattle are twice teeming, and the tree is twice useful

pomis. At rabidæ tigres, et sæva semina leonum,
for fruits. But maddening tigers, and the direful progeny of lions,

absunt ; nec aconita fallunt miseros legentes ; nec
are absent ; nor does wolfsbane deceive the wretched gatherers ; nor

squameus anguis rapit immensos orbes per humum, neque
does the scaly snake drag his huge folds along the ground, neither

colligit se in spiram ta to tractu. Adde
docs he collect himself in a spire with so large a train. Add

tot egregias urbes, que laborem operum ; tot
so many renowned cities, and the labour of works; so many

oppida congesta manu præruptis saxis ; que flumina
towns built up by the hand with broken rocks; and rivers

labentia subter antiquos muros. An memorem
gliding beneath ancient walls. Whether shall I commemorate

mare, quod supra, que quod alluit infra ? Anne
the sea, which *flows* above, and that which flowed beneath? Whether

tantos lacus ? te, maxime Lari ? que te,
sh..ll *I describe* its great lakes? thee, the largest O Larus? and thee,

160 Benace, assurgens fluctibus et marino fre-
O Benacus, rising with the waves and marine com

mitu ? an memorem portus, que claustra addita
motion? whether shall I describe harbours, and the enclosures added

Lucrino, atque æquor indignatum magnis stridoribus,
to the Lucrine *lake*, and the sea raging with great noises,

quâ Julia unda sonat, ponto longe refuso, que
where the Julian wave resounds, the sea far off being upturned, and

Tyrrhenus æstus immittitur Avernis fretis ? hæc eadem
the Tuscan tide is admitted to the Avernian straits? this same

ostendit rivos argenti, que metalla æris venis,
country exhibits rivers of silver, and mines of copper in its veins,

atque fluxit plurima auro. Hæc extulit acre
and flowed most abundant with gold. This land has raised a brave

genus virûm, Marsos, que Sabellam pubem, que Ligurem
race of men, the Marsii, and the Sabellan youth, and the Ligurian

assuetum malo, que Volscos verutos : hæc
accustomed to hardship, and the Volsci bearing spits: this *has*

Decios, Marios, que magnos Camillos, Scipiadas
brought up the Decii, the Marii, and the great Camilli, Scipios

duros bello, et te, maxime Cæsar, qui jam nunc
hardened by war, and thee, the greatest O Cæsar, who even now

170 victor in extremis oris Asiæ, avertis imbellem
victorious in the most remote coasts of Asia, you drive the peaceful

Indum Romanis arcibus. Salve, Saturnia tellus, magna
Indian from the Roman towers. Hail, Saturnian land, great

parens frugum, magna virûm : tibi ingredior res
parent of fruits, great *parent* of heroes. for thee I enter upon subjects

antiquæ laudis, et artis, ausus recludere sanctos fontes,
of ancient praise, and art, daring to lay open the holy fountains,

que cano Ascræum carmen per Romana oppida. Nunc
and I sing an Ascrean verse through Roman towns. Now

locus ingeniis arvorum ; quæ robora
is *the opportunity to describe* the dispositions of fields; what powers

cuique quis color, · et quæ natura sit
ar to each, what complexion, and to what its nature may be best suited

ferendis rebus. Primum, difficiles terræ, que maligni
for producing things. First, rugged lands, and unfruitful

colles, ubi tenuis argilla, et calculus dumo- 180
hills, where *there is* a light clay, and gravel in the

sis arvis, gaudent Palladiâ silvâ vivacis olivæ.
bushy fields, rejoice in Minerva's wood of the long-lived olive.

Plurimus oleaster, surgens eodem tractu, est
The abundant wild-olive, arising in the same region, is

indicio; et agri strati silvestribus baccis. At humus,
a proof: and the fields overspread with wild berries. But the ground,

quæ pinguis, que læta dulci uligine, que campus qui
which is rich, and joyful with sweet moisture, and the plain which

frequens herbis, et fertilis ubere, qualem sæpe sole-
abounding with grass, and fertile with richness, such as often we are

mus despicere cavâ convalle montis; amnes
accustomed to look down upon in the hollow vale of a mountain; rivers

liquuntur summis rupibus huc, que trahunt felicem
flow from the high rocks here, and draw along the rich

limum; que qui editus Austro, et pascit filicem
slime; and which is raised high to the south, and feeds the fern

invisam curvis aratris: hic olim sufficiet 190
hateful to the crooked ploughs: this hereafter will supply

tibi vites prævalidas, que fluentes multo Baccho; hic
to you vines very strong, and flowing with much wine; this

fertilis uvæ, h'c laticis, qualem libamus pateris
is rich in the grapes, th s in liquor, such as we pour from goblets

et au.o, cum pinguis Tyrrhenus inflavit ebur ad
and gold, when the fat Tuscan has blown his ivory *trumpet* at

aras, et reddimus fumantia exta pandis lancibus.
the altars, and we offer smoking entrails in bending dishes.

Sin magis studium tueri armenta que vitulos, aut
But if rather your study is to preserve herds and calves, or

fetus ovium, aut capellas urentes culta, petito
the offspring of sheep, or goats destroying the cultivated *fields*, seek

saltus, et longinqua saturi Tarenti, et campum qualem
the lawns, and distant fields of fruitful Tarentum, and the plain such as

infelix Mantua amisit, pascentem niveos cycnos
unhappy Mantua has lost, feeding snow-white swans

herboso flumine. Non liquidi fontes, non gramina,
by the grassy stream. Nor are liquid fountains, nor grass,

desunt gregibus: et quantum armenta carpent 200
wanting to the flocks: and as much as the herds crop

longis diebus, gelidus ros reponet tantum exiguâ
in the longer days, the cool dew replaces as much in the short

nocte. Terra fere nigra, et pinguis sub presso
night. Land almost black, and rich beneath the pressed

vomere, et cui putre solum (namque imitamur
ploughshare, and to which there is a rotten soil (for we imit t

hoc arando) optima frumentis. Non cernes plura
this in ploughing) is best for corn. You will not see more

plaustra tardis juvencis, decedere domum ex ullo
wagons with slow bullocks depart home from any

æquore. Aut unde iratus arator devexit silvam,
plain. Or from whence the angry ploughman has borne a wood,

et evertit nemora ignava per multos annos, que eruit
and upturned the groves slothful for many years, and has overturned

antiquas domos avium, cum imis stirpibus; illæ pe-
the ancient dwellings of the birds, with their lowest roots; they have

210 tiere altum nidis relictis; at campus
sought the lofty sky their nests being abandoned; but the plain

rudis enituit, vomere impulso. Nam
uncultivated looks bright, the ploughshare being driven through it. For

quidem jejuna glarea clivosi ruris vix ministrat humiles
indeed the hungry gravel of a hilly field hardly supplies low

casias que rorem apibus; et negant alios agros ferre
cassia and rosemary for the bees; and they deny that other fields produce

æque dulcem cibum, et præbere curvas latebras serpentibus,
equally sweet food, and furnish winding retreats for serpents,

scaber tophus et creta exesa nigris chelydris.
as do the rough rotten stone and chalk corroded by black water-snakes

Quæ exhalat tenuem nebulam, que volucres fumos,
The soil which sends forth light mist, and flying smoke

et bibit humorem, et ipsa remit it ex se cum
and drinks in moisture, and itself gives it ack from itself when

vult; que quæ semper vestit se suo viridi gramine,
it will; and which always clothes itself with its own green grass,

220 nec lædit ferrum scabie et salsâ rubigine;
nor injures the iron (plough) with scurf and salt rust;

illa intexet ulmos tibi lætis vitibus; illa est
that will intertwine the elms for you with joyful vines; that is

ferax oleæ; experiere colendo illam;
productive of the olive; try it by cultivating it; you will find it

et facilem pecori, et patientem unci vomeris.
both friendly to the flock, and enduring the crooked plough.

Dives Capua et ora vicina jugo Vesevo,
Rich Capua and the coast near to the mountain Vesuvius,

et Clanius non æquus vacuis Acerris, arat
and the Claunius not just to the ravaged Acerræ, ploughs

talem. Nunc dicam, quo modo possis
such a soil. Now I will declare, by what mode you can

cognoscere quamque requiras sit rara,
know each should you require that it may be thin,

an sit densa supra morem; quoniam altera favet
or that it may be dense above measure; since the one favours

frumentis, altera Baccho; densa magis cereri;
corn, the other wine; the dense is more fit for corn

que   quæ rarissima   Lyaeo ; ante,   capies   230
and *that* which is thinnest *is best* for wine; first, you shall mark

locum   oculis,   que jubebis puteum demitti alte in
a place with *your* eyes, and   order   a well   to be sunk   deep   in

solido,   que rursus   repones   omnem humum, et
the solid *ground,* and   again   you shall replace   all   the ground, and

æquabis summas arenas pedibus.   Si   deerunt   uber
level down the high   sands   with *your* feet.   If they are deficient the soil

erit   rarum, que aptius   pecori   et almis vitibus :   sin
will be   thin,   and   fitter   for the flock and cheering   vines :   but if

negabunt   posse   ire in   sua   loca,   et   terra
they deny   *themselves* to be able to go into   their own places,   and   earth

superabit, scrobibus repletis,   ager   spissus ;   exspecta
shall abound,   the ditches   being filled,   the soil   is dense ;   expect

cunctantes glebas, que crassa terga, et proscinde terram
delaying   clods,   and   thick   ridges, and   cut up   the earth

validis juvencis.   Autem salsa tellus, et quæ perhibetur
with strong bullocks.   But   the salt   land, and which   is esteemed

amara, infelix frugibus, (ea   nec   mansuescit   240
bitter,   unhappy   for fruits,   (it   neither   becomes soft

arando,   nec   servat   genus Baccho, aut sua nomina
by ploughing, nor does it preserve the kind to the wine, or their own   names

romis)   dabit   tale specimen.   Tu   deripe   qualos
the fruits) will give   such   an example.   Do you   tear down   baskets

spisso vimine, que cola prælorum   fumosis   tectis.
of the close twigs,   and strainers of vine presses from the smoking   roofs.

Ille   malus ager, que dulces undæ   a   fontibus calcentur
Let this impure soil,   and   sweet   waters   from the fountains   be trodden

huc ad plenum :   scilicet omnis aqua eluctabitur, et
here to   the full   *brim :*   for   all   the water   will escape,   and

grandes guttæ ibunt   per   vimina.   At manifestus sapor
large   drops   will pass through the vines.   But the evident   taste

faciet indicium ; et amaror torquebit tristia ora tentantium
will give   the proof ;   and bitterness will torture the sad   faces   of tasters

sensu.   Item discimus denique hoc pacto, quæ tellus
by the sensation.   Also   we learn   finally   by this method,   what   land

sit   pinguis : jactata manibus haud unquam fatiscit,
may be   rich :   tossed about by the hands it will not   ever   crumble,

sed lentescit ad digitos habendo in morem picis.   250
but   stick   to the fingers in handling   in the manner of pitch.

Humida   alit majores herbas, que ipsa   lætior
A moist   *soil* produces larger   herbs,   and   itself is more abundant

justo.   Ah, ne illa sit nimium fertilis mihi, neu
than is proper.   Ah,   let it not   be   too   rich   for me,   nor

ostendat se prævalidam primis aristis !   Quæ est
exhibit   itself   too strong   in its first   ears !   That which   is

gravis, prodit se tacitam pondere ipso ; que   quæ
heavy,   betrays itself   silently by its weight   itself ;   and *that* which

ævis.   **Est promptum prædiscere nigram oculis et**
is light.   It is   easy   to learn   the black by the eyes and

quis color   cuique.   At est difficile exquirere sceleratum
what colour is   to each.   But it is difficult   to distinguish   the accursed

frigus : tantum piceæ, que nocentes taxi interdum, aut
cold :   only   pitch trees,   and the hurtful yews sometimes,   or

aigræ hederæ pandunt vestigia.   His   animadversis
tho black   ivy   betray   their marks.   These things being observed

memento excoquere terram multo   ante,   et circumdare
remember   to dry   the soil   long   beforehand, and   to surround

magnos montas scrobibus, ostendere supinatas glebas
arge   mountains   with trenches,   to exhibit   the upturned   clods

260   **Aquiloni,   antequam infodias lætum   genus**
     to the north wind,   before   you plant   the fruitful   race

vitis.   Putri   solo optima   arva; venti,   que
of the vine.   In the crumbled soil   are the best   lands; the winds,   and

gelidæ pruinæ, et robustus fossor, movens labefacta jugera,
cold   frosts,   and strong   ditcher, stirring the loosened   acres,

curant   id.   At si haud ulla vigilantia fugit quos viros,
take care of that.   But if   not   any watchfulness escapes those   men,

ante exquirunt similem locum ubi prima seges paretur
first   let them seek   a like   place   where the first nursery is prepared

arboribus, et quo   mox   digesta   feratur ;   ne
for the trees,   and where   presently   arranged in order   it may grow; lest

somina   ignorent matrem subito mutatam.   Quin
the young plants be ignorant   of their mother suddenly   changed.   But

etiam   signant regionem cœli in cortice, ut resti-
also   let them mark   the region of the sky upon   the bark,   that they may

270   **tuant   modo quo   quæque steterit,**
     restore it   to the same situation in which   each   had stood,

parte   quâ quæque tulerit Austrinos calores, quâ
in the part where   each   had borne   the southern   heats,   where

obverterit terga   axi.   Est adeo multum consuescore
it had turned   its back to the pole.   It is   thus   much   to acquire a habit

in teneris.   Quære prius,   an   sit melius ponere
in tender   years.   Inquire first,   whether it may be   better   to place

vites collibus, an plano.   Si metabere agros pinguis
the vines on hills,   or on the plain.   If   you measure the fields   of a rich

campi, sere densas ; Bacchus non   segnior in
plain,   plant   thick ;   the vine   will not grow   more slothful in

denso   ubere ; sin solum acclive tumulis, que
a thick   planted   soil ;   but if   the soil   is sloping from the ascent,   and

supinos colles, indulge ordinibus ; nec secius omnis   via
declining   hills,   indulge   in rows ;   not otherwise all   the way

quadret   secto limite   arboribus positis in unguem.
may square with the cut   path,   the trees   being placed   in exact order

Ut sæpe ingenti bello, cum   longa   legio explicu;
As often   in a great   war,   when a long-extended legion has unfold

cohortes, et agmen stetit aperto campo, que 280
its bands, and the army stood on the open plain, and

acies directæ, ac omnis tellus fluctuat late
the battalions are arrayed, and all the land waves far around

renidenti ære, nec dum miscent horrida prœlia,
with shining brass, nor for a while do they mingle dreadful battle,

sed dubius Mars errat in mediis armis; omnia
but doubtful Mars wanders in the midst of arms let all the divisions

viarum sint dimensa paribus numeris, non modo uti
of your ways be measured with equal proportions, not only that

prospectus pascat inanem animum, sed quia non
the prospect may feed the hungry mind, but because not

aliter terra dabit æquas vires omnibus, neque
otherwise will the land give equal strength to all, neither

rami poterunt extendere se in vacuum.
the branches can extend themselves to the vacant air.

Forsitan et quæras quæ fastigia sint scrobibus.
Perhaps also you will ask what depth may be to the trenches.

Ausim committere vitem vel tenui sulco. Arbos
I would dare to commit the vine even to a light furrow. The tree

defigitur altius ac penitus terræ; in primis esculus, 290
is planted deeper and low in the earth; especially the esculus,

quæ quantum vertice ad æthereas auras, tantum
which as much rises with its head to etherial skies, so much

tendit radice in Tartara. Ergo, non hiemes non
it sinks with its root to Hell. Therefore, not winters nor

flabra, neque imbres convellunt illam; manet immota,
blasts, nor showers can overthrow it, it remains unmoved.

que per multos annos volvens multa secula virûm
and for many years revolving many ages of men

durando vincit. Tum late tendens fortes
by enduring outlasts them. Then far around extending its strong

ramos et brachia huc illuc, ipsa media sustinet
branches and arms this way and that, it in the midst sustains

ingentem umbram. Neve tibi vineta vergant ad caden-
a great shade Nor let your vineyards incline to the set-

tem solem, neve sere corylum inter vites; neve pete
ting sun, nor plant the hazel among the vines; nor seek

summa flagella, aut defringe summas plantas ex 300
the highest shoots, or break the topmost twigs from

suo arbore, (tantus amor terræ;) neu læde semina
their tree. (so great is their love of the earth;) nor hurt the shoots

retuso ferro; neve insere silvestres truncos
with the blunted steel nor plant among the wild trunks

oleæ. Nam sæpe ignis excidit incautis pastoribus,
of the olive. For often fire falls from the careless shepherds,

qui, primum tectus furtim sub pingui cortice,
which, first covered secretly beneath the rich bark.

comprendit robora, que elapsus in altas frondes,
seizes   the wood,   and   gliding   among   the high   leaves.

dedit   ingentem sonitum coelo: inde secutus victor,
gave forth   a great   sound   to heaven: then   following victorious

regnat per   ramos,   que   per   alta   cacumina, et
reigns through the branches,   and   through the lofty   tops,   and

involvit totum nemus flammis, et crassus piceâ cali-
involves the whole   grove   in flames, and   thick   with pitchy   dark

gine, ruit atram nubem ad coelum, præsertim si tempestas
ness, hurries a black   cloud   to heaven,   especially   if   a tempest

310   incubuit silvis   a   vertice, que ventus glomerat
      broods over the woods from   on high,   and the wind   gathers

incendia, ferens.   Ubi hoc   non valent
the flames, bearing them *high up*. When this takes place, they are not strong

a   stirpe ; que cæsæ, possunt reverti atque revirescere
from the root,   and   cut,   they can be returned   and   revive again

similes   imâ   terrâ : infelix oleaster, amaris
like *to what they were* in the deep earth: the hapless wild olive, with bitter

foliis,   superat. Nec quisquam tam prudens auctor
leaves, *alone* survives.   Nor   let any   so   wise   counsellor

persuadeat tibi movere   terram,   Boreâ   spirante.
persuade   you   to move   the earth,   the north wind   blowing.

Tum hiems claudit rura   gelu, nec, semine   jacto,
Then   winter   shuts up the fields with frost, nor,   the seed being thrown,

patitur concretam radicem affigere   terræ.   Satio est
permits   the frozen   root   to fasten in   the earth.   Planting   is

320   optima   vinetis,   cum,   rubenti vere,   candida
      best   for vineyards, when, in the blushing spring,   the white

avis,   invisa longis colubris, venit ; vel sub prima
bird (*the stork*), hated   by long water-snakes, comes,   or beneath the first

frigora autumni, cum rapidus sol nondum   contingit
colds   of autumn,   when   the swift   sun   not yet   has touched

hiemem   equis, jam æstas   præterit. Ver adeo
the winter with *his* horses, now the summer has passed. The spring thus

frondi   nemorum,   ver   utile   silvis ;
is best for the leaf   of the groves,   the spring is useful for the woods;

vere   terræ tument, et poscunt genitalia semina.
in the spring the lands   swell,   and demand the procreative   seeds

Tum omnipotens pater, Æther,   descendit in
Then   the almighty   father,   the sky, (i. e. Jupiter,) descends upon

gremium lætæ conjugis, fecundis imbribus, et magnus,
the bosom of his joyful wife,   with fertilizing showers, and   great,

commistus magno corpore, alit omnes fetus.
himself, mingling with her great   body,   cherishes   all   her offspring.

Tum avia virgulta resonant canoris avibus ; et armenta
Then the lonely shrubbery resounds with tuneful birds;   and the herds

repetunt venerem certis diebus. Almus ager parturit, que
renew *their* love   on certain days.   The fair field brings forth, and

arva laxant sinus tepentibus auris Zephyri; 330
the lands open their bosoms to the warm gales of the west wind.

tener humor superat omnibus; que gramina audent
the tender moisture abounds in all, and the plants dare

credere se in tuto novos soles; nec pampi-
to trust themselves in safe *confidence* to the new suns, nor does the

nus metuit surgentes Austros, aut imbrem actum
vine fear the rising south winds, or the shower driven

cœlo magnis Aquilonibus; sed trudit gemmas,
along the sky by powerful north winds; but puts forth their buds,

et explicat omnes frondes. Crediderim non alios
and spreads out all their leaves. I should have believed that not any other

dies illuxisse primâ origine crescentis mundi, ve
days had shone on the first origin of the rising world, or

habuisse alium tenorem; illud erat ver; magnus orbis
had any other direction; it was spring, the great globe

agebat ver, et Euri parcebant hibernis flatibus;
enjoyed the spring, and the east winds spared the wintry blasts;

cum primum pecudes hausere lucem, que ferrea 340
when first the flocks drew in the light, and the iron

progenies virûm extulit caput duris arvis, que
offspring of men raised *their* heads from the hard fields, and

feræ immissæ silvis, et sidera cœlo.
the wild beasts were let loose in the woods, and the stars in the sky.

Nec teneræ res possent ferre hunc laborem,
Nor the tender produce *of the earth* could endure this labour.

si tanta quies non iret inter que frigus que calorem,
if so great a rest did not pass between both the cold and the heat.

et indulgentia cœli exciperet terras. Quod superest,
and the indulgence of heaven had overtaken the earth. What remains,

quæcunque virgulta premes per agros, memor
whatsoever plants you press down through the fields, mindfu.

sparge pingui fimo, et occule multâ terrâ:
sprinkle *them* with rich manure, and cover *them* with abundant earth

aut infode bibulum lapidem, aut squalentes conchas
or bury around *them* spongy stone, or rough shells

inter; enim aquæ labentur, que tenuis halitus
among *them*; for the waters glide into, and a light vapour

subibit, atque sata tollent animos. Jamque 350
enters *them*, and the plants arouse their strength. And now

reperti, qui urgerent super saxo atque
they are found who would press them from above with a stone and

pondere ingentis testæ; hoc munimen ad effusos
the weight of a great potsherd; this is a protection to the out-pouring

imbres; hoc munimen ubi æstifer Canis findit
showers; this is a guard when the heat-bearing Dog-star cleaves

hiulca arva siti. Seminibus positis, superest
the gaping fields with thirst. The shoots being planted, it remains

deducere terram sæpiús ad capita, et jactare duros
to draw the earth often to their heads, and to throw the hard

bidentes ; aut exercere solum sub presso vomere, et
drags; or to till the soil beneath the pressed ploughshare, and

flectere luctantes juvencos, inter vineta ipsa ; tum
to guide the struggling bullocks among the vineyards themselves; then

aptare levês calamos, et hastilia rasæ virgæ : que
to prepare smooth reeds, and spears of the peeled rod; and

fraxineas sudes, que bicornes furcas ; viribus quarum
ashen stakes, and two horned forks, by the strength of which

360 assuescant eniti, et contemnere ventos, que
they may be accustomed to climb, and to despise the winds, and

sequi tabulata per summas ulmos. Ac est
to follow the scaffolding through the highest elms. And it is *our interest*

parcendum teneris dum prima ætas adolescit novis
to spare the tender *vines* while their first age sprouts with new

frondibus ; et, dum lætus palmes agit se ad auras,
leaves; and, while the joyful vine raises itself to the skies,

immissus per purum laxis habenis, acies ipsa
being sent through the clear sky with relaxed reins, the edge itself

falcis nondum tentanda ; sed frondes carpendæ, que
of the knife not yet *is* to be tried; but the leaves are to be plucked, and

interlegendæ uncis manibus. Inde ubi jam amplexæ
to be selected with bent hands. Then when now embracing

ulmos validis stirpibus exierint, tum stringe
the elms with their strong stalks they have gone forth, then strip

comas, tum tonde brachia, ante reformidant ferrum ; tum
their leaves, then trim their branches, before they dread the knife, then

370 denique exerce dura imperia, et compesce fluentes
finally exercise severe authority, and restrain the flowing

ramos. Etiam sepes texenda et omne pecus tenen-
branches. Also a hedge is to be woven and all the cattle are to be

dum, præcipue dum frons tenera que imprudens
restrained, especially while the branch is tender and unskilled

laborum, cui super indignas hiemes que potentem solem,
in labours, which besides the severe winters and powerful sun,

silvestres uri que sequaces capreæ assidue illudunt ;
the wild buffaloes and pursuing goats continually mock;

oves, que avidæ juvencæ, pascuntur. Nec frigora
the sheep, and greedy heifers, feed *upon* them. Nor *do* the colds

concreta canâ pruinâ aut gravis æstas incumbens
hardened by hoary frost or the oppressive heat resting on

arentibus scopulis, tantum nocuere quantum illi greges,
the dried rocks, so much injure *them* as the flocks

que venenum duri dentis, et cicatrix signata in admorso
and the poison of the hard tooth, and the scar marked upon the bitten

380 surpe. Ob non aliam culpam caper cæditur Baccho
stock For no other fault the goat is slain to Bacchus

omnibus aris, et veteres ludi ineunt proscenia: que
on every altar, and ancient plays enter on the stage: and

Theseidæ posuere præmia ingeniis circum pagos
the Athenians placed rewards to their wits around the villages

et compita: atque inter pocula læti saliere per
and cross roads: and amidst their bowls joyful they danced upon

unctos utres in mollibus pratis. Nec non Ausonii
smeared bottles in the soft meadows. Likewise the Ausonian

colon., gens missa Trojâ, ludunt incomptis versibus,
colonists, a race sent from Troy, sport in homely verses,

que soluto risu; que sumunt horrenda ora cavatis
and unrestrained laughter; and take up hideous faces from hollowed

corticibus; et vocant te, Bacche, per læta carmina,
barks of trees; and invoke thee, O Bacchus, by joyful songs,

que suspendunt mollia oscilla tibi ex altâ pinu. Hinc
and they hang soft images to thee from the lofty pine. Hence

omnis vinea pubescit largo fetu; que cavæ 390
every vineyard sprouts forth with copious fruit; and the hollow

valles, que profundi saltus complentur, et
vales, and the deep lawns are filled with various produce, and

quocumque Deus circumegit honestum caput. Ergo
wherever the God moved around his honest head. Therefore

rite dicemus suum honorem Baccho patriis carminibus,
in order let us sing his own honour to Bacchus in our patriotic songs,

que feremus lances et liba, et sacer hircus, ductus
and let us offer dishes and cakes, and the sacred goat, led

cornu, stabit ad aram; que torrebimus pinguia
by the horn, shall stand at the altar; and we will roast the fat

exta in colurnis verubus. Est etiam ille alter labor
entrails on hazel spits. There is also that other labour

curandis vitibus, cui nunquam est satis exhausti,
in providing for the vines, to which never is there enough of painstaking,

namque omne solum scindendum que ter, que quater
for every soil is to be cut up both thrice, and four times

quotannis, que gleba frangenda æternum versis 400
yearly, and the clod is to be broken for ever by inverted

bidentibus: omne nemus levandum fronde. Labor, actus
drags; every grove is to be stripped of its leaves. Labour, driven

in orbem, redit agricolis, atque annus volvitur in se
in a circle, returns to the farmers, and the year rolls round upon itself

per sua vestigia. Et jam cum olim vinea posuit
through its own footsteps. And now when at last the vineyard has laid

seras frondes, et frigidus Aquilo decussit honorem
aside its late leaves, and the cold north wind has shaken honour

silvis; jam tum acer rusticus extendit curas in
from the woods; even then the bold countryman prolongs his cares to

venientem annum, et persequitur vitem relictam, attondens
the approaching year, and pursues the vine abandoned, cutting off

curvo   dente Saturni, que fingit   putando
the roots. with the crooked hook   of Saturn,   and he forms *:* *by pruning*

Primus fodito humum, primus cremato sarmenta devecta,
First   dig   the ground, first   burn   the bushes borne away,

et primus referto vallos sub tecta ; postremus metito.
and first return the stakes beneath your roof,   last   reap

410 Bis umbra ingruit vitibus ; bis herbæ obducunt
     Twice the shade invades the vines ; twice the weeds overspread

segetem densis sentibus ; uterque labor durus. Laudato
the crop with frequent thorns,   each   toil is difficult.   Praise

ingentia rura ; colito exiguum.   Nec non etiam aspera
large   fields ; cultivate a small   *one.*   Also   the rough

vimina rusci   per   silvam, et fluvialis arundo
twigs of butcher's broom through the wood, and the river   reed

cæditur ripis ; que cura   inculti   salicti exercet.
is cut up on the banks ; and care of the uncultivated willow employs

    Jam vites vinctæ; jam arbusta reponunt   falcem ;
us. Now the vines are tied ; now the groves lay aside the pruning knife ;

jam effetus   vinitor canit extremos antes : tamen
and the toil-spent vine-dresser sings   his last   rows :   yet

tellus solicitanda, que pulvis movendus ; et jam Jupiter
the earth must be urged, and the dust must be moved ; and now the weather

420 metuendus maturis uvis.   Contra   non est
     is to be dreaded by the ripe grapes. On the other hand there is not

ulla cultura oleis ; neque illæ expectant procurvam
any cultivation to the olives ; nor do they expect   the crooked

falcem   que tenaces rastros, cum semel hæserunt
pruning knife and tenacious harrows,   when   once they are fastened

arvis,   que tulerunt auras. Tellus ipsa, cum reclu-
in the fields,   and have endured the air. The earth itself, when   it is

ditur unco   dente, sufficit humorem satis   et
opened by the crooked fork,   supplies moisture for the plants and

gravidas fruges,   cum vomere.   Hoc
heavy   fruits, *when it is opened* by   the ploughshare. With this

nutritor olivam, pinguem et placitam paci. Poma
nourish the olive,   rich   and propitious to peace. Fruit trees

quoque ut primum sensere valentes truncos, et habuere
also   as   first   they felt their strong trunks, and   obtain

suas   vires, nituntur ad sidera raptim propriâ vi,
their own strength, rise up to the stars swiftly by their own strength.

que haud indigna nostræ opis.   Nec minus   interea
and not unworthy of our assistance. Nevertheless in the mean time

omne nemus gravescit fetu, que inculta   aviaria
every   grove   is heavy with fruit, and the uncultivated retreats of birds

430 rubent sanguineis baccis : cytici   tondentur ;
     redden with bloody berries : the cytisus trees are cropped *by the*

alta silva ministrat tædas, nocturni ignes pascuntur,
flocks ; the lofty wood supplies   torches,   nightly   fires   are fed

et fundunt lumina. Et homines dubitant
and pour out their lights And do men hesitate

serere atque impendere curam? Quid sequar
to sow and to bestow their care? Why should I pursue

majora? salices, que humiles genistæ, illæ
greater subjects? willows, and the humble broom, these

sufficiunt aut frondem pecori, aut umbram pastoribus,
supply either leaves for the flock, or shade for shepherds,

que sepem satis, et pabula melli. Et juvat
and a hedge for cornfields, and food for honey. And it delights

spectare Cytorum undantem buxo, que lucos Nary-
to behold Cytorus waving with box-wood, and groves of Nary-

ciæ picis; juvat videre arva non obnoxia rastris, non
cian pine; it delights to see fields not subject to harrows, nor

ulli curæ hominum. In Caucaseo vertice, steriles 440
to any care of men On the Caucasian mount, barren

silvæ ipsæ, quas animosi Euri assidue que frangunt
trees themselves, which the angry east winds continually both break down

que ferunt; aliæ dant alios fetus; dant pinos,
and bear away, some of these produce other supplies; they produce pines,

lignum utile navigiis, que cedros que cupressos domibus.
a wood useful for ships, and cedars and cypresses for dwellings.

Hinc agricolæ trivere radios rotis, hinc tympa-
Hence the farmers have turned spokes for wheels, hence drum-shaped cover-

na plaustris, et posuere pandas carinas ratibus.
ings for wagons, and have placed bending keels for ships

Salices fecundæ viminibus, ulmi frondibus; at myrtus
Willows are fruitful in vines, elms in leaves; but the myrtle

validis hastilibus, et cornus bona bello; taxi torquentur
for strong spears, and the cornel is good for war, yew trees are bent

in Ityræos arcus. Necnon leves tiliæ aut buxum
into Ityrian bows. Also do the smooth lime trees or the box

rasile torno, accipiunt formam, que cavantur
polished by the turner, receive form, and they are hollowed out

acuto ferro. Necnonet levis alnus, missa 450
by the sharp steel. Also the light alder, sent *upon*

Pado, innatat torrentem undam; nec non et apes condunt
the Po, swims on the boiling wave also the bees conceal

examina cavis corticibus, que alveo vitiosæ
their swarms in hollow barks, and in the cavity of a rotten

ilicis. Quid æque memorandum Baccheïa dona tule-
oak. What equally to be commemorated *have* Bacchus's gifts pro-

runt? Bacchus et dedit causas ad culpam; ille domuit
duced? Bacchus also has given causes for blame; he has tamed

letho furentes Centauros, que Rhœtum que Pholum, et
by death the raging Centaurs, both Rhœtus and Pholus, and

Hylæum, minantem Lapithis magno cratere. O
Hylæus. threatening the Lapithæ with a great goblet. O

agricolas, nimium fortunatos, si nôrint sua bona!
farmers, too happy, if they could know their own good!

quibus, procul discordibus armis, justissima tellus
to whom far from discordant arms, the most righteous earth

460 ipsa fundit facilem victum humo. Si alta
herself pours forth the ready food from the ground. If the lofty

domus superbis foribus, non vomit ingentem undam
mansion with proud doors, does not pour out a great tide

salutantium mane totis ædibus; nec inhiant
of visiters in the morning from all its rooms; nor do they gaze on

postes varios pulchrâ testudine, que vestes illusas
pillars variegated with beautiful tortoise, and dresses wrought

auro, que Ephyreïa æra; nec alba lana fucatur
from gold, and Corinthian brass; nor is white wool stained

Assyrio veneno, nec usus liquidi olivi corrumpitur
with Assyrian poison, nor is the use of liquid oil corrupted

casiâ; at secura quies, et vita nescia fallere, dives
by cassia; but peaceful rest, and a life ignorant to deceive, rich

variarum opum; at otia, latis fundis, speluncæ, que
in varied wealth; but leisure, at their spacious farms, grottos, and

vivi lacus; at frigida Tempe, que mugitus boum, que
living lakes; but the cool vale, and the lowing of oxen, and

470 molles somni sub arbore, non absunt. Illic
soft slumbers beneath the tree, are not wanting. There

saltus, ac lustra ferarum; et juventus patiens operum
are lawns, and dens of wild beasts; and youth enduring toils

que assueta parvo; sacra deûm que patres
and accustomed to a little; the sacrifices of the gods and fathers

sancti. Justitia, excedens terris, fecit extrema
held in reverence. Justice, departing from the earth, placed her last

vestigia per illos. Vero dulces Musæ accipiant me
footsteps among them. But let the sweet Muses receive me

primum ante omnia, quarum sacra fero, perculsus
first before all things, whose sacred images I bear, struck

ingenti amore, que monstrent vias cœli, et
with great love, and point out to me the ways of heaven, and

sidera, varios defectus solis, que labores
constellations, the various eclipses of the sun, and labours

lunæ; unde tremor terris; quâ vi alta maria
of the moon; whence trembling to the earth; by what power the deep seas

tumescant, obicibus ruptis, que rursus residant
swell, their ramparts being broken, and again settle down

480 in se ipsa; quid hiberni soles tantum properent
upon themselves; why the wintry suns so much hasten

tingere se oceano, vel quæ mora obstet tardis
to dip themselves in the ocean, or what delay hinders the slow

noctibus. Sin frigidus sanguis circum præcordia obstiterit
nights. But if the cold blood around my heart prevent

ne possim accedere has partes naturæ, rura et rigui
hac [cannot approach these parts of nature, let the fields and flowing

amnes in vallibus placeant mihi, inglorius amem
streams in the vales please me, unhonoured let me love

flumina que silvas. O, ubi campi que Sperchius
the rivers and the woods. O, where are the plains and Sperchius

et Taygeta, bacchata Lacænis virginibus!
and Taygetus, rendered sacred to Bacchus by the Lacedemonian maids!

O, qui sistat me in gelidis vallibus Æmi, et protegat
O, who will place me in the cold valleys of Hæmus, and protect me

ngenti umbra ramorum? felix qui potuit 490
with a great shade of branches? happy is he who could

cognoscere causas rerum atque subjecit omnes metus et
know the causes of things and subdue all fears and

inexorabile fatum, que strepitum avari Acherontis
implacable fate, and the noise of greedy hell beneath his

pedibus! et ille fortunatus qui novit agrestes Deos, que
feet! and he is happy who knows the rustic gods, both

Pana, que senem Silvanum, que sorores Nymphas. Non
Pan, and the old Silvanus, and the sisters Nymphs. Not

fasces populi, non purpura regum, et discordia agitans
the rods of the people, nor the purple of kings, and discord pursuing

infidos fratres, aut Dacus descendens ab conjurato
faithless brothers, or the Dacian descending from conspiring

Istro, flexit illum; non Romanæ res, que regna
Danube, has influenced him; nor the Roman affairs, and the kingdoms

peritura; neque ille aut doluit miserans inopem,
about to perish; nor did he either grieve compassionating the destitute.

aut invidit habenti. Carpsit fructus quos 500
or did he envy him possessing. He plucked the fruits which

rami, quos volentia rura ipsa tulere suÆ
the branches, which the willing fields themselves produced of their own

sponte; nec vidit ferrea jura, que insanum forum, ant
accord; nor did he see the iron laws, and the mad court, or

tabularia populi. Alii solicitant cæca fretis
the public tribunals of the people. Some weary the blind sees

emis, que ruunt in ferrum, penetrant aulas et
with oars, and rush upon the sword, they advance to the halls and

limina regum. Hic petit urbem que miseros Pena
palaces of kings. This man seeks a city and its miserable house

tes excidiis, ut bibat gemmâ, et dormiat
hold gods with destruction, that he may drink from gems, and sleep

Sarrano ostro. Alius condit opes quo incubat
on Tyrian purple. Another conceals wealth and broods over

defosso auro. Hic stupet, attonitus
buried gold. This one becomes giddy, astonished by sleqvence

rostris; plausus que plebis que patrum per
at the rostra; applause both of the people and the fathers through

cuneos (enim geminatur) corripuit hunc hiantem.
the benches (for it is redoubled) has seized this *man* gaping:

510 gaudent, perfusi sanguine fratrum, que
they rejoice, sprinkled with the blood of their brothers, and

mutant domos et dulcia limina exilio, atque quærunt
exchange their homes and sweet dwellings for exile, and seek

patriam jacentem sub alio sole. Agricola dimovit
a country lying beneath another sun. The farmer has removed

terram incurvo aratro : hinc labor anni : hinc
the earth with his crooked plough : hence the labour of the year : hence

sustinet patriam, que parvos nepotes : hinc armenta boum,
he upholds his country, and his little offspring : hence his herds of oxen,

que meritos juvencos. Nec requies, quin annus
and deserving bullocks. Nor *is there* rest, but the year

exuberet aut pomis, aut fetu pecorum, aut mergite
abounds either in fruits, or the produce of cattle, or the bundles

Cerealis culmi ; que oneret sulcos proventu, atque
of Ceres' straw; and loads the furrows with provision, and

vincat horrea. Hiems venit ; Sicyonia bacca
overloads the barns. The winter comes; the Sicyonian berry

teritur trapetis, sues læti glande redeunt ;
is pounded in oil presses, swine rejoiced with mast return;

520 silvæ dant arbuta ; et autumnus ponit varios
the woods produce arbutes; and the autumn lays by its varied

fetus ; et mitis vindemia coquitur alte in apricis saxis.
fruits ; and the mild vintage is ripened high up on the sunny rocks.

Interea dulces nati pendent circum oscula,
In the mean time sweet children hang around the kisses *of their pa-*

casta domus servat pudicitiam ; vaccæ demittunt
rents, the chaste family preserves its modesty : heifers hang down

lactea ubera ; que pingues hœdi luctantur inter se
their milky udders ; and the fat kids struggle among themselves

adversis cornibus in læto gramine. Ipse agitat
with opposing horns upon the joyful grass. He passes

festos dies ; que fusus per herbam, ubi ignis in
his feast days; and stretched upon the grass, where a fire *was* in

medio, et socii coronant cratera ; libans vocat
the midst, and his companions crown the goblet; pouring forth he invokes

te, Lenææ ; que ponit magistris pecoris certamina
thee, O Bacchus; and places to the masters of the flock contests

530 velocis jaculi in ulmo ; que nudat prædura
of the swift dart on the elm; and lays bare his hardy

corpora agresti palæstrâ. Veteres Sabini olim co-
body for the rustic wrestling match. The ancient Sabines formerly cul-

luere hanc vitam, et Remus et frater hanc :
tivated this *joyous* life, and Remus and his brother *observed* this :

sic fortis Etruria crevit ; scilicet Roma est facta pulcher-
thus brave Etruria increased; for Rome is become the most

‹ıma rerum, que una circumdedit septem arces sibi
beautiful of things, and alone has surrounded seven towers to herself

muro. Etiam ante sceptrum Dictæi regis, et antequam
by a wall. Also before the sceptre of the Dictean king, and before

impia gens epulata est cæsis juvencis, aureus Saturnus
the impious race feasted on slain bullocks, golden Saturn

agebat hanc vitam in terris. Necdum etiam audierant
passed this life on the earth. Nor yet also had they heard

classica inflari; necdum enses impositos duris 540
that trumpets were blown; nor yet that swords placed on hard

incudibus crepitare. Sed nos confecimus immensum
anvils rattled. But we have completed this immeasurable

æquor spatiis, et jam tempus solvere fumantia
plain with its boundaries, and now it is time to free the smoking

colla equûm.
necks of our horses.

BOOK III.

CANEMUS te quoque, magna Pales, et te,
WE will sing thee also, O great Pales, and thee, *Apollo,*

pastor memorande ab Amphryso; vos silvæ, que
O shepherd to be commemorated by Amphrysus; ye woods, and

amnes Lycæi. Omnia cætera carmina, quæ tenuis-
streams of Lycæus. All other songs, which might have

sent vacuas mentes, jam vulgata. Quis nescit
occupied empty minds, now are rendered common. Who is ignorant of

aut durum Eurysthea, aut aras illaudati Busiridis?
either severe Eurystheus, or the altars of the unworthy Busiris?

Cui Hylas puer non dictus, et Latonia Delos,
By whom has Hylas the youth not been sung, and Latonian Delos,

que Hippodame, que Pelops insignis eburno humero,
and Hippodame, and Pelops remarkable for his ivory shoulder,

acer equis? via est tentanda quâ possim
bold *and victorious* with horses? the way is to be attempted by which I may

tollere me quoque humo, que victor,
raise myself also from the ground, and a conqueror *by fame*

volitare per ora virûm. Ego primus, rediens 10
fly through the mouths of men. I first, returning

Aonio vertice, deducam Musas mecum in patriam,
from the Aonian mount, will lead the Muses with me into *my* country

(modo vita supersit) primus referam Idumæas palmas
(if life remain) first I will restore the Idumean palms

tibi, Mantua, et in viridi campo, ponam templum de
to thee, O Mantua, and on the green plain, I will place a temple of

marmore propter aquam, ubi ingens Mincius errat tardis
marble near the water, where great Mincius wanders in slow

flexibus, et prætexit ripas tenerâ arundine. In
windings, and has lined its banks with the tender reed. In

medio erit mihi Cæsar, que tenebit templum. Illi
the midst shall be my Cæsar, and he shall hold the temple. To him

ego, victor, et conspectus in Tyrio ostro, agitabo
I, a conqueror, and conspicuous in Tyrian purple, will dive

centum quadrijugos currus ad flumina. Mihi cuncta
an hundred four horsed chariots by the rivers. For me all

Græcia, linquens Alpheum, que lucos Molorchi, decer-
Greece, leaving Alpheus, and the groves of Molorchus, shall con-

20 net cursibus et crudo cæstu. Ipse, ornatus
tend in race-courses and the raw gauntlet. I myself, having adorned

caput foliis tonsæ olivæ, feram dona. Jam nunc
my head with leaves of shorn olive, will bear gifts. Even now

juvat ducere solennes pompas ad delubra, que videre
it delights me to lead solemn pomps to the temples, and to see

cæsos juvencos ; vel ut scena discedat frontibus versis,
slain bullocks; or as the scene withdraws with fronts inverted,

que ut intexti Britanni tollant purpurea aulæa. In
and as the interwoven Britons raise the purple curtains. Upon

foribus, faciam, ex auro que solido elephanto, pugnam
the doors, I will form, from gold and solid ivory, the battle

Gangaridum, que arma victoris Quirini ; atque hic
of the Giants, and the arms of victorious Quirinus; and here

Nilum, undantem bello, que magnum fluentem, ac
the Nile, waving with war, and majestic flowing, and

columnas surgentes navali ære. Addam domitas urbes
the columns rising with naval brass. I will add the conquered cities

30 Asiæ, que pulsum Niphatem, que Parthum fidentem
of Asia, and beaten Niphates, and the Parthian trusting

fugâ que versis sagittis ; et duo tropæa, rapta
in flight and his inverted arrows; and two trophies, snatched

manu ex diverso hoste, que gentes bis triumphatas
by the hand from a different foe, and nations twice triumphed over

ab utroque litore. Et Parii lapides stabunt spirantia
from each shore. And Parian marbles shall stand as if breathing

signa, proles Assaraci, que nomina gentis demissæ ab
statues, the offspring of Assaracus, and the names of the nation descended from

Jove, que Tros parens, et Cynthius auctor
Jove, both Tros the parent of Rome, and Cynthian Apollo the founder

Trojæ. Infelix invidia metuet Furias, que severum
of Troy Wretched envy shall fear the Furies, and the cruel

amnem Cocyti, que tortos angues Ixionis, que
river of Cocytus, and the wreathed snakes of Ixion, and

immanem rotam et saxum non exsuperabile.
the dreadful wheel and the stone not to be surmounted.

Interea sequamur silvas Dryadum, que 40
In the mean time let us follow the woods of the Dryads, and

saltus intactos : tua haud mollia jussa, Mæcenas.
the lawns untouched thy not gentle commands, O Mæcenas.

Mens inchoat nil altum sine te : en, age,
My mind attempts nothing exalted without thee · lo, come on,

rumpe segnes moras ; Cithæron vocat ingenti clamore,
break through slothful delays ; Cithæron calls you with great cry,

que canes Taygeti, que Epidaurus domitrix equorum ;
and the dogs of Taygetus, and Epidaurus the subduer of horses,

et vox ingeminata assensu nemorum remugit.
and a voice redoubling by the assent of the groves re-echoes.

Tamen mox accingar dicere ardentes pugnas
Yet presently I shall be prepared to sing the glowing battles

Cæsaris, et ferre famâ nomen per tot annos,
of Cæsar, and to carry by fame his name through so many years,

quot Cæsar abest ab primâ origine Tithoni. Seu
as Cæsar is distant from the first origin of Tithonus. Whether

quis, miratus præmia Olympiacæ palmæ, pascit equos,
any one, admiring the rewards of the Olympic palm, feeds horses,

seu quis fortes juvencos ad aratra, 50
whether any one feeds strong bullocks for the plough,

legat præcipue corpora matrum. Forma bovis
let him choose especially the bodies of mothers. The form of the heifer

optima cui caput turpe, cui cervix plurima, et
is best whose head is rough, whose neck is large, and whose

palearia pendent à mento tenus crurum ; tum nullus
dewlaps hang from her chin down to her legs ; then there is no

modus longo lateri ; omnia magna ; pes etiam,
measure to her long side, all things are large ; her foot even,

et hirtæ aures sub camuris cornibus. Nec
and her rough ears beneath her crooked horns. Nor

vacca insignis maculis et albo, displiceat mihi,
let the heifer distinguished for spots and white, displease me,

aut detrectans juga, que interdum aspera cornu, et
or refusing the yoke, and sometimes rude with her horn, and

faciem propior tauro, que quæ tota ardua, et gra-
in her face nearer to a bull, and which is entirely high, and walk-

diens verrit vestigia imâ caudâ. Ætas 60
ing she sweeps her footsteps with the end of her tail The age

pati Lucinam que justos Hymenæos desinit ante
to endure Lucina and just marriage rites ends before

decem, incipit post quatuor annos ; cætera nec
ten, begins after four years, the other age is neither

habilis feturæ, nec fortis aratris. Interea dum
fit   for breeding, nor   strong for the ploughs. In the mean time while

læta juventus superat gregibus, solve mares; primus
joyful   youth   abounds in the flocks, let loose the males;   first

mitte pecuaria in Venerem, et suffice aliam prolem ex
send forth your cattle to   Love,   and supply   one   offspring from

alia generando. Quæque optima dies ævi prima fugit
another by breeding. Each   best   day of life first   flies

miseris mortalibus; morbi, que tristis senectus, et
from wretched mortals;   diseases, and   sad   old age,   and

labor, subeunt; et inclementia duræ mortis rapit.
labour, succeed; and the cruelty of hard death bears them off

Erunt semper quarum corpora malis mutari
There will be always *those* whose   bodies you may wish to be chang

70 enim semper refice, ac, ne post requiras
   therefore always repair *them*, and, lest afterwards you should seek

amissa anteveni, et sortire sobolem armento
them when lost anticipate, and choose out an offspring from the herd

quotannis. Necnon et idem delectus est equino pecori
yearly.   Likewise the same choice is to the horse flock.

Tu modo impende præcipuum laborem jam inde a
Do you now pay   especial attention even thence from

teneris quos statues submittere in spem
their tender *years* to those which you shall determine to bring up for the hope

gentis. Continuo pullus generosi pecoris ingreditur
of the race. Immediately the colt of a generous flock   walks

altius in arvis, et reponit mollia crura; primus audet
higher in the fields, and replaces his pliant legs; first he dares

et ire viam, et tentare minaces fluvios, et committere
also to go the way, and to attempt the threatening rivers, and   to trust

sese ignoto ponti; nec horret vanos strepitus.
himself to an unknown bridge; nor does he dread vain   noise.

Illi ardua cervix, que argutum caput, brevis alvus, que
To him *is* a lofty neck, and sharp head, short belly, and

80 obesa terga; que animosum pectus luxuriat toris.
   fat back; and *his* bold breast swells out with folds.

Spadices que glauci honesti; deterrimus color
The brown and dark grey are becoming; the worst colour *is*

albis, et gilvo. Tum si qua arma dedere sonum
to the white, and to the dun. Then if any arms have given a sound

procul, nescit stare loco, micat auribus,
afar off, he knows not to stand in his place, he moves quickly with his ears,

et tremit artus, que premens collectum ignem, volvit
and trembles in his joints, and restraining the collected fire, he rolls *it*

sub naribus. Juba densa, et jactata, recumbit in
under his nostrils. His mane is thick, and thrown about, rests upon

dextro armo. At duplex spina agitur per lumbos,
his right shoulder But a double spine runs along his loins,

que ungula cavat tellurem, et graviter sonat solido
and   his hoof hollows out the earth,   and   heavily   sounds   with solid

cornu. Talis fuit Cyllarus, domitus habenis Amy- 90
horn.   Such was Cyllarus,   subdued   by the reins of Amy-

clæi Pollucis, et bijuges equi Martis, quorum Graii
clæan Pollux,   and the yoked horses of Mars,   whom the Grecian

poëtæ meminere, et currus magni Achillis. Talis
poets commemorate, and the chariot *horses* of great Achilles.   Such

et pernix Saturnus ipse effudit jubam equinâ
also swift   Saturn   himself spread his mane   on his horse-*assumed*

cervice, adventu conjugis, et fugiens, implevit altum
neck,   at the coming   of his wife, and   flying,   filled   lofty

Pelion acuto hinnitu. Abde hunc domo, quoque
Pelion with sharp neighing.   Shut   him   in the stable,   also

ubi aut gravis morbo, aut jam segnior annis deficit,
when either heavy by sickness, or   now more slothful by years he fails,

ignosce senectæ nec turpi. Senior frigidus in Venerem,
pardon old age   not degraded. Being older *he is* cold   in   love,

que frustra trahit ingratum laborem; et, si quando
and   in vain he prolongs the thankless   toil;   and, if at any time

est ventum ad prœlia, ut quondam magnus ignis sine
he comes   to the contest, as   when   a great   fire without

viribus, in stipulis; furit incassum. Ergo
strength, *rages* in the stubble, *so he* rages   powerless.   Therefore

notabis animos que ævum præcipue; hinc 100
you will mark their courage and   age   especially;   afterward

alias artes, que prolem parentum, et quis dolor
other qualities, and the race of *their* parents,   and what sorrow *is*

cuique victo, quæ gloria palmæ. Nonne vides?
to each when conquered, what   glory   of victory   Do you not see?

cum, præcipiti certamine, currus corripuere campum, que
when, in swift   strife,   chariots have seized   the plain,   and

ruunt effusi carcere; cum spes juvenum arrectæ,
rush pouring forth from the goal; when the hopes of the youth   are raised,

que pulsans pavor haurit exsultantia corda; illi instant
and   panting   fear exhausts their exulting   hearts;   they   urge on

torto verbere, et proni, dant lora; axis
with the twisted lash,   and bending forward, they give the reins; the axle

fervidus vi volat; que jam humiles, que jam elati
glowing with violence   flies; and now   low,   and now raised

sublime, videntur ferri per vacuum aëra, atque
high,   they seem to be borne through the vacant   air,   and

assurgere in auras. Nec mora nec requies; 110
to rise   to the skies. Neither delay nor   rest *is granted them;*

at nimbus fulvæ arenæ tollitur; humescunt spumis que
but   a cloud of yellow sand   is raised; they are moist with foam and

flatu sequentûm; tantus amor laudum, victoria
the breathing of those following, so great *is* the love   of praise,   victory

est tantæ curæ. Erichthonius primus ausus jungere
is so great a care. Erichthonius first dared to join

currus et quatuor equos, que victor insistere rapidis
chariots and four horses, and victorious to rest on the rapid

rotis. Pelethronii Lapithæ, imposlti dorso,
wheels. The Pelethronian Lapithæ, placed upon the back of the horses,

dedere fræna que gyros, atque docuere
applied the reins and taught him his turnings, and instructea

equitem sub armis insultare solo, et glomerare
the horseman under arms to leap over the ground, and to gather up

superbos gressus. Uterque labor est æquus; magistri
his proud steps. Each labour is equal; the masters

120 æque exquirunt que juvenem, que calidum
equally seek out a horse both youthful, and warmed

animis, et acrem cursibus; quamvis ille
with courage, and swift in the course; not an old one, although he

sæpe egerit hostes versos fugâ, et referat Epirum
often has driven the foes turned in flight, and may boast Epirus

patriam, que fortes Mycenas, que deducat gentem
for his country, and brave Mycenas, and derive his race

origine Neptuni ipsâ. His animadversis, instant
from the origin of Neptune itself. These things being observed, they attend

sub tempus, et impendunt curas distendere
about the time of generation, and they direct their cares to swell him out

denso pingui, quem legêre ducem, et
with firm fat flesh, whom they have chosen a leader, and

dixere maritum pecori; que secant pubentes herbas,
have declared the husband to the herd; and they cut up young herbs,

que ministrant fluvios, que farra; ne nequeat superesse
and supply water, and provender; lest he cannot survive

blando labori, que invalidi nati referant jejunia
the pleasant toil, and the weak offspring should resemble the leanness

patrum. Autem volentes tenuant armenta ipsa
of their sires. But they who wish it make lean the breed mares themselves

130 macie. Atque, ubi jam nota voluptas
by abstinence. And, when now the known pleasure

solicitat primos concubitus, que negant frondes, et
invites the first connexion, both they deny to them leaves, and

arcent fontibus; sæpe etiam quatiunt cursu,
drive them from the fountains; often also they drive them in the race,

et fatigant sole, cum area gemit graviter
and weary them in the sun, when the barn-floor groans heavily

tunsis frugibus, et cum inanes paleæ jactantur ad
with beaten fruits, and when the empty straw is thrown about to

surgentem Zephyrum. Faciunt hoc, ne nimio luxu
the rising west wind. They do this, lest by too much luxury

sit obtusior usus genitali arvo, et oblimet
there may be a too weak use in the genital soil, and it make full

inertes sulcos ; sed sitiens rapiat Venerem, que recondat
the sluggish passages ; but eager may seize enjoyment, and store it

interius. Rursus, cura patrum cadere, et matrum
within. Again, the care of sires *begins* to fall off, and of mothers

succedere, cum errant gravidæ, mensibus exactis. Non
to succeed. when they wander teeming, the months being passed. Let not

quisquam passus sit illas ducere juga gravibus 140
any one suffer them to drag the yokes in heavy

plaustris, non superare viam saltu, et carpere prata
wagons. nor to pass over the way by leaping, and to run over the meadows

acri fugâ, que innare rapaces fluvios. Pascant in
in swift flight. and to swim over the rapid rivers. Let them feed in

vacuis saltibus, et secundum plena flumina, ubi muscus,
the vacant lawns, and near to the full rivers, where there is moss,

et ripa viridissima gramine, que speluncæ tegant
and a bank most green with grass, and caves may protect *them*

et umbra saxea procubet. Est, circa lucos Silari,
and the shade of a rock may lie over *them*. There is, about the groves of Silarus,

que Alburnum, virentem ilicibus, plurimus volitans,
and Alburnus, verdant with holm trees, a very abundant flying

cui asylo est Romanum nomen, Graii vocantes
insect, to which asylus is the Roman name, the Greeks naming

vertêre œstron, asper, sonans, acerba, quo
have translated *it* œstron. *a creature* rough, noisy, harsh, by which

tota armenta exterrita, diffugiunt silvis, æther con- 150
whole herds terrified, fly from the woods, the air

cussus mugitibus furit, que silvæ, et ripa sicci
shaken by their bellowing rages, and the woods. and the bank of the dry

Tanagri. Juno, meditata pestem Inachiæ juvencæ,
Tanagrus. Juno. meditating destruction to the Inachian heifer,

quondam exercuit horribiles iras hoc monstro. Arcebis
formerly executed direful anger on this monster You will drive

hunc quoque gravido pecori (nam acrior instat
this likewise from the teeming flock (for more fierce it threatens

mediis fervoribus), que pasces armenta, sole recens
in the midst of the heat), and you will feed the herds, the sun newly

orto, aut astris ducentibus noctem. Post partum,
having arisen, or the stars leading on the night. After the birth,

omnis cura traducitur in vitulos ; que continuo inurunt
all the care is transferred to the calves; and forthwith they brand

notas et nomina gentis ; et quos malint
on them the marks and names of the race ; and *those* which they may wish

aut submittere habendo pecori aut servare sacros
either to keep for breed for preserving the flock or to keep sacred

aris, aut scindere terram, et invertere campum 160
for the altars, or to cut up the earth, and to upturn the plain

horrentem fractis glebis ; cætera armenta pascuntur per
ough with broken clods; the other herds feed through

virides herbas. Jam hortare vitulos, quos tu formabis
the green grass. Now encourage the calves, which you will form

ad studium atque agrestem usum, que insiste viam domandi
for labour and rustic use, and enter on the way of taming

dum animi juvenum faciles, dum ætas
them while the dispositions of the young are tender, while their age

mobilis. Ac primum subnecte cervici laxos circulos de
is plastic. And first bind to their neck loose collars of

tenui vimine : dehinc ubi colla libera assuêrint
the tender vine: then when their necks before free shall have been used

servitio, junge pares juvencos aptos e torquibus
to servitude, unite in pairs your bullocks fitted from the chains

ipsis, et coge conferre gradum ; atque jam
hemselves, and compel them to lift together their step; and now

170 sæpe inanes rotæ ducantur illis per terram, et
often let empty wheels be drawn by them along the ground, and

signent vestigia summo pulvere. Post
let them stamp their footsteps on the surface of the sand. Afterwards

faginus axis, nitens sub valido pondere,
let the beechen axle, struggling beneath the powerful weight,

instrepat, et æreus temo trahat junctos orbes.
creak, and let the brazen beam drag the united wheels.

Interea carpes non gramina tantum indomitæ pubi,
In the mean time you will pluck not grass alone for the unbroken young

nec vescas frondes salicum, que palustrem ulvam,
bullock, nor the esculent leaves of willows, and the marshy sea grass,

sed sata frumenta, manu : nec fetæ vaccæ,
but springing corn, with your hand: nor will the teeming heifers,

more patrum, implebunt tibi nivea mulc-
in the manner of your fathers, fill for you the snowy milk-

tralia, sed consument tota ubera in dulces natos.
pails, but expend all their udders upon their fond offspring.

Sin studium magis ad bellum, que feroces turmas,
But if your desire is rather for war, and fierce troops,

180 aut prælabi Alphea flumina Pisæ rotis, et
or to glide by the Alphean streams of Pisa with wheels, and

agitare volantes currus in luco Jovis ; primus labor
to drive flying chariots in the grove of Jupiter; the first toil

equi est videre animos atque arma bellantûm, que
of the horse is to behold the animation and weapons of warriors, and

pati lituos, que ferre rotam gementem tractu,
to endure trumpets, and to sustain the wheel groaning in the space,

et audire sonantes frænos stabulo ; tum magis atque
and hear the sounding reins in the stable; then more and

magis gaudere blandis laudibus magistri, et amare
more to be pleased with the flattering praises of his master, and to delight

sonitum plausæ cervicis. Atque audiat hæc
in the sound of the patted neck. And let him hear these

jam   primo depulsus ab ubere   matris, que in vicem
now *when* first   weaned   from the udder of his mother, and in   turn

det   ora   mollibus capistris   invalidus, que etiam
let him yield his mouth to the pliant head-stalls *yet being* weak,   and   even

tremens, etiam inscius   ævi. At ubi
trembling,   also unconscious *from the inexperience* of his age. But when

quarta æstas accesserit, tribus   exactis,   mox   190
the fourth summer has advanced,   three being completed, presently

incipiat   carpere gyrum, que sonare compositis gradibus,
let him begin   to take the ring,   and to beat in measured   steps,

que sinuet alterna volumina crurum ; que sit similis
and let him bend the alternate joints   of his legs ;   and be·   like

laboranti.   Tum   provocet   auras cursibus ; ac volans
to one labouring. Then let him challenge the winds in swiftness; and   flying

per aperta æquora, ceu liber   habenis, vix   ponat
through the open plains,   as free   from the reins, hardly let him place

vestigia summâ   arenâ. Qualis cum densus   Aquilo
his footsteps on the surface of the sand. As   when the continual north wind

incubuit ab Hyperboreis oris, que differt hiemes
has come over from   the northern   coasts,   and scatters the storms

Scythiæ atque arida nubila ; tum altæ segetes, que
of Scythia and   the dry clouds ;   then the high corn-fields,   and

natantes campi, horrescunt lenibus flabris, que summæ
waving   plains,   shudder from gentle blasts,   and the tops of

silvæ   dant sonorem, que longi fluctus urgent   200
the woods give forth a sound,   and the extended waves   hasten

ad litora. Ille volat verrens   simul   arva,   si-
to the shores. He   flies   sweeping at the same time the fields, at the

mul   æquora fugâ.   Hic vel ad metas   et
same time   the seas   in his flight.   He   either   at the boundaries and

maxima   spatia Elei   campi   sudabit,   et
the most extended race-grounds of the Elean   plain   will sweat,   and

aget cruentas spumas   ore,   vel melius   feret
force bloody   foam   from his mouth,   or more kindly   will draw

Belgica esseda molli   collo. Tum   demum sinito
the Belgic chariot by his soft   neck.   Then   at length   permit

magnum corpus crescere   jam domitis,   crassa
a great   body   to grow *to them* now   tamed,   from thickening

farragine ; namque   ante   domandum,   tollent
provender ;   for *if fattened* before *they are* subdued,   they will exert

ingentes animos, que   prensi negabunt pati   lenta
too great   courage, and *when* reined   will refuse to endure the slender

verbera, et parere duris lupatis. Sed non ulla industria
lash,   and to obey the hard bits.   But not   any   attention

magis firmat   vires,   quam   avertere Venerem, et
more   establishes *their* strength,   than   to prevent   lust,   and

stimulos   cæci amoris, sive usus boum,   210
the provocatives of blinding   love,   whether the care of oxen,

sive equorum est gratior cui. Atque ideo rele-
or of horses is more grateful to any one. And thus they send

gant tauros procul, atque in sola pascua, post
away the bulls afar, even into the lonely pastures, behind

oppositum montem, et trans lata flumina, aut servant
an intervening mountain, and across broad rivers, or keep *them*

clausos intus ad satura præsepia : enim femina carpit
shut up within at the fattening stalls for the female consumes

vires paulatim, que. urit videndo, nec patitur
his strength by degrees, and burns him by seeing, nor does she permit him

meminisse nemorum nec herbæ. Illa quidem dulcibus
to remember the groves nor the grass She indeed by bland

illecebris et sæpe subigit superbos amantes decernere
allurements even often compels her proud lovers to fight

inter se cornibus. Formosa juvenca pascitur in
among themselves with their horns. A fair heifer is fed within

220 magnâ silvâ ; illi alternantes multâ vi,
     an extensive forest ; they, *i.e. the bulls*, alternately with great violence,

miscent prœlia crebris vulneribus : ater sanguis lavit
join battle with frequent wounds : blackening blood bathes

corpora ; que cornua versa, urgentur in ob-
their bodies ; and their horns being inclined, are driven against their

nixos cum vasto gemitu ; que silvæ et magnus
striving *foes* with great groaning ; and the woods and great

Olympus reboant. Nec mos stabulare bellantes
Olympus resound. Nor *is it* the custom to stable the warring *bulls*

una ; sed alter victus abit, que exsulat longe
together ; but the one conquered departs, and goes to exile far off

ignotis oris, multa gemens ignominiam, que plagas
to unknown coasts, much lamenting his degradation, and the blows

superbi victoris, tum amores quos inultus amisit ;
of his haughty conqueror, as *also* the loves which unavenged he has lost ;

et aspectans stabula, excessit avitis regnis.
and beholding the stables, he departs from his ancestral realms.

Ergo exercet vires omni curâ, et pernox jacet
Therefore he exerts his strength with all care, and by night he lies

230 instrato cubili inter dura saxa, pastus hirsutis
     on an unspread couch amidst hard rocks, having fed on rough

frondibus et acutâ carice ; et tentat sese, atque discit
leaves and prickly sedge ; and he tries himself, and learns

irasci in cornua, obnixus trunco arboris ; que
to be angry against his horns, striving against the trunk of a tree, and

lacessit ventos ictibus, et proludit ad pugnam sparsâ
assails the winds with blows, and flourishes to the fight with sprinkled

arenâ. Post, ubi robur collectum, que vires
sand. Afterwards, when his strength is collected, and his powers

receptæ, movet signa, que præceps fertur in
are recovered, he advances the standard, and headlong is borne upon

oblitum hostem; ut fluctus cum cœpit albescere in
his forgetful foe; as a wave when it has begun to whiten in

medio ponto, trahit sinum longius, que ex alto que ut
the midst of the sea, draws a train farther, and from the deep and as

volutus ad terras, sonat immane per saxa, nec minor
rolled to the land, sounds wonderfully through the rocks, nor less

monte ipso procumbit; at ima unda exæstuat
than a mountain itself falls; but the low wave boils

vorticibus, que subjectat nigram arenam alte. 240
in whirlpools, and raises the black sand on high.

Adeo omne genus in terris, que hominum que ferarum,
Thus every kind on the earth, both of men and of wild beasts,

et æquoreum genus, pecudes, que pictæ volucres, ruunt
and the watery race, the flocks, and painted birds, rush

in furias que ignem : idem amor omnibus. Non
into the madness and fire of love: the same love is to all. Not

alio tempore leæna, oblita catulorum, sævior
at any other time has the lioness, forgetful of her whelps, more savage

erravit in agris; nec informes ursi dedere vulgo
wandered in the fields; nor have deformed bears caused every where

tam multa funera que stragem per silvas : tum aper
so many deaths and such slaughter through the woods: then the boar

sævus, tum tigris pessima. Heu ! tum male
is fierce, then the tiger is most ravenous. Alas! then unsafely

erratur in solis agris Libyæ. Nonne vides, ut
men wander in the lonely fields of Libya. Do you not see, how

tremor pertentet tota corpora equorum, si 250
trembling thrills through all the bodies of the horses, if

tantum odor attulit notas auras ? Ac jam . neque
only smell has brought the well known air? And now neither

fræna virûm, neque sæva verbera, non scopuli que cavæ
the reins of men, nor cruel lashes, nor cliffs and hollow

rupes, atque objecta flumina, torquentia montes cor-
rocks, and intervening streams, twisting down mountains borne

reptos undâ retardant eos. Sabellicus sus ipse
away by the wave retard them. The Sabellian boar himself

ruit, que exacuit dentes, et prosubigit terram pede,
rushes out, and sharpens his teeth, and tears up the earth with his foot,

fricat costas arbore, atque durat humeros hinc atque
he rubs his ribs with a tree, and hardens his shoulders on this side and

illinc ad vulnera. Quid juvenis cui durus amor
on that to wounds. What does the youth on whom cruel love

versat magnum ignem in ossibus ? nempe serus cæcâ
exercises its powerful fire in his bones? why indeed late in the dark

nocte natat freta, turbata abruptis procellis, super
night he swims the straits, disturbed by bursting storms, over

quem ingens porta cœli tonat, et æquora 260
whom the great gate of heaven thunders, and the seas

illisa   scopulis reclamant :   nec possunt. miseri
dashed against rocks   resound·   nor can   his miserable

parentes revocare,   nec virgo moritura   super
parents recall   *him*, nor the maid about to die on account o.

crudeli funere. Quid   variæ lynces Bacchi, et acre
his cruel death. What *do* the spotted lynxes of Bacchus, and the fierce

genus luporum atque canum?   quid cervi, quæ prœlia
race of wolves and of dogs *do*? what the stags, what contests

imbelles   dant? Scilicet ante   omnes furor equarum
do they being weak give? Truly in comparison of all the madness of mares

est insignis : et Venus ipsa dedit   mentem,   quo
is distinguished : and Venus herself has given *this* disposition, at what

tempore Potniades quadrigæ absumpsere membra Glauci
time the Potnian mares   consumed the limbs of Glaucus

malis.   Amor ducit illas trans Gargara, que trans sonan-
with their jaws. Love leads them across Gargarus, and over the re-

270   tem Ascanium : superant montes, et tranant
    sounding Ascanius : they bound over the mountains, and swim over

flumina ; que continuo ubi flamma   subdita   avidis
the rivers; and immediately when the flame *is* conveyed to their greedy

medullis, magis vere   (quia calor redit   ossibus
marrow,   rather in the spring (because the heat returns to their bones

vere)   omnes illæ versæ in Zephyrum   ore,
in the spring) all they turning to the west wind with their mouth.

stant altis rupibus, que exceptant leves auras ; et
stand on the high rocks, and await the gentle gales ; and

sæpe sine ullis conjugiis   gravidæ   vento,
often without any cohabitation becoming pregnant by the wind,

mirabile dictu, diffugiunt per saxa et scopulos, et
wonderful to be told, they fly over rocks and cliffs, and

depressas convalles ; non tuos,   Eure, neque ad
sunken   valleys;   not to thy *domains*, O Eurus, nor to

ortus Solis, in Boream que Caurum, aut unde
the rising of the sun, to the north wind and west wind, or whence

nigerrimus Auster nascitur, et contristat cœlum pluvio
the darkest south wind arises, and saddens the sky with rainy

280   frigore. Hinc demum lentum virus, quod
    cold.   Hence at length a ductile poison, which

pastores dicunt hippomanes vero nomine, destillat ab
shepherds call hippomanes by its true name, distils from

inguine, hippomanes, quod sæpe malæ novercæ   legêre
their groin, hippomanes, which often wicked stepmothers have gathered.

que miscuerunt   herbas et non innoxia verba.
and mingled *among* herbs and not harmless words.

Sed interea   tempus fugit, fugit irreparabile, dum
But in the mean while time flies, it flies irrecoverably, while

capti amore vectamur circum singula.   Hoc
captivated by love we are borne around particular *subjects*. This

satis armentis. Altera pars curæ superat, agitare
is enough for herds. Another part of our care exceeds *it, namely*, to manage

lanigeros greges, que hirtas capellas. Hic labor:
the wool-bearing flocks, and rough goats. This *is* labour

fortes coloni sperate laudem hinc. Nec sum
O hardy husbandmen expect praise from hence. Nor am I

dubius animi, quam magnum sit vincere ea
doubtful in mind, how great *a task* it is to excel · these *themes*

verbis, et addere hunc honorem angustis rebus. 290
in words, and to add this ornament to mean subjects.

Sed dulcis amor raptat me per ardua deserta Parnassi;
But sweet love hurries me through the high deserts of Parnassus;

juvat ire jugis, qua nulla orbita priorum
it delights me to go through the heights, where no path of my predecessors

divertitur molli clivo Castaliam. Nunc Pales
turns by gentle declension to the Castalian *stream*. Now O Pales

veneranda, nunc sonandum magno ore. Incipiens,
to be revered, now to be sung in a great strain. Beginning

edico oves carpere herbam in mollibus stabulis, dum
I command the sheep to eat grass in soft stables, until

mox frondosa æstas reducitur; et sternere duram
presently the leafy summer is restored; and to spread the hard

humum multâ stipula, que manipulis filicum subter,
ground with much straw, and with bundles of fern under

ne frigida glacies lædat molle pecus, que ferat
them, lest the cold ice may injure the gentle flock, and produce

scabiem que turpes podagras. Post, digressus 300
the scab and filthy gouts. Afterwards, having departed

hinc, jubeo sufficere frondentia arbuta capris.
from *this* matter, I command to supply leafy arbutes to the goats,

et præbere recentes fluvios, et opponere stabula
and to furnish *to them* fresh streams, and to build their stables

a ventis, hiberno Soli conversa ad medium
safe from the winds, to the winter sun turned toward the mid-

diem; cum jam olim frigidus Aquarius cadit,
day (*i e* the south); when now at last the cold *sign* Aquarius sets,

qui irrorat extremo anno. Hæ quoque tuendæ
and bedews the extremity of the year. These also are to be guarded

non is non leviore curâ; nec erit usus minor;
by us with no lighter care *than the sheep;* nor will their use be less,

c amvis Milesia vellera, incocta Tyrios rubores, mutentur
enough Milesian fleeces, steeped in Tyrian red, should be sold

magno. Soboles hinc densior,
for a great *price.* The offspring (i. e. *from the goats*) from hence more numerous,

hinc copia largi lactis. Quammagis mulctra spuma-
hence a supply of abundant milk. The more the milk pail shall

verit exhausto ubere, læta flumina magis manabunt
foam from their exhausted udder, joyous streams the more shall flow

310 pressis   mammis.   Nec minus   interea
from their pressed   dugs.   Nevertheless   in the mean time

tondent barbas, que incana menta que comantes setas
they shear the beards, and hoary chins and flowing bristles

Cinyphii   hirci, in usum castrorum, et velamina
of the Cinyphian goat, for the use of camps, and coverings

miseris   nautis. Pascuntur vero silvas, et summa
for the wretched sailors. They are fed indeed in the woods, and lofty

Lycæi,   que horrentes rubos, et dumos amantes
heights of Lycæus, and on rough brambles, and bushes loving

ardua.   Atque ipsæ, memores, redeunt in   tecta,
high places.   And they, mindful, return to their shelters,

que ducunt suos,   et vix   superant limen   gra-
and lead out their young, and hardly do they pass the entrance with their

vido ubere. Ergo   avertes glaciem que nivales ventos
heavy udder. Therefore you will keep off the ice and snowy winds

omni   studio, quo minus est illis egestas mortalis
with every care, inasmuch as there is to them a want of human

320 curæ : ·que lætus   feres   victum, et virgea
attention : and gladly will you bring food, and osier

pabula, nec claudes   fœnilia   totâ   brumâ.
fodder, nor shut out from them hayracks through the whole winter.

At vero, cum læta æstas,   Zephyris vocantibus,
But indeed, when the joyful summer arrives, the west winds invoking,

mittes utrumque gregem in saltus atque in pascua ;
do you send each flock to the lawns and to the pastures ;

cum primo sidere Luciferi, carpamus frigida rura dum
with the first star of Lucifer, let us graze the cold fields while

mane   novum, dum gramina canent, et ros, gratissimus
the morning is fresh, while the grass is white, and the dew, most grateful

pecori,   est in tenerâ herbâ. Inde, ubi quarta hora
to the flock, is on the tender plant. Then, when the fourth hour

cœli   collegerit   sitim, et querulæ cica-
of the orb of heaven shall have brought on thirst, and the complaining grass-

dæ rumpent arbusta   cantu ; jubeto greges ad puteos,
hoppers shall burst the groves with their song; command the herds to the wells,

330 aut ad alta stagna, potare undam currentem ilignis
or to the deep pools, to drink water running in wooden

canalibus ; at mediis æstibus   exquirere umbrosam
troughs ; but in the meridian heats command to seek out a shady

vallem, sicubi magna quercus Jovis, antiquo robore,
vale,   wherever the great oak of Jupiter, of ancient firmness,

tendat ingentes ramos, aut sicubi nemus, nigrum crebris
extends its great branches, or wherever a grove, black with thick

ilicibus, accubet sacrâ umbrâ ; tum dare tenues aquas
holm oaks, hangs over with sacred shade ; then to give shallow waters

rursus, et pascere rursus ad occasum Solis, cum
again,   and to feed them again at the setting of the sun, when

frigidus Vesper temperat aëra, et jam roscida Luna reficit
the cold   evening   tempers   the air, and now the dewy moon refreshes

saltus,   que litora resonant halcyonem,   et   dumi
the lawns, and the shores resound   to   the halcyon   and the bushes

acanthida.   Quid prosequar   tibi versu,   pastores
to the nightingale.   Why   should I describe   to you   in song,   the shepherds

Libyæ,   quid   pascua,   et mapalia habitata   raris
of Libya,   why   the pastures, and   cottages   inhabited in scattered

tectis?   Sæpe   pecus pascitur diem que noctem,   340
dwellings?   Often their flock   is fed   day   and   night,

et   totum   mensem ex ordine, itque   in longa deserta
and the whole   month   in   order,   and goes into the long   deserts

sine ullis hospitiis;   tantum campi jacet.   Afer
without any places of shelter; so much of the plain lies around. The African

armentarius agit omnia secum,   que tectum que   La-
herdsman   bears all things with him,   both his house   and his house-

rem,   que arma que Amyclæum canem, que Cressam
hold god, and his arms and his Amyclian   dog,   and   his Cretan

pharetram;   non   secus ac acer Romanus, in patriis
quiver;   not otherwise than the bold   Roman,   in his native

armis, cum carpit viam sub   injusto fasce, et castris
arms,   when he takes his way beneath an unequal   load, and his camp

positis   ante exspectatum hosti, stat in agmine. At
being pitched before   he is expected by the foe, stands before his troop. But it is

non qua Scythiæ gentes que Mæotica unda, et Ister
not so where the Scythian nations are and the Mæotic   wave, and the Ister

turbidus, et torquens flaventes arenas;   que qua   350
troubled,   and turning   its yellow   sands;   and where

Rhodope porrecta sub medium axem redit: illic
Rhodope   stretching   beneath the middle   axis   returns: there

tenent armenta clausa stabulis;   neque   aut ullæ herbæ
they hold their herds   shut up in stables; neither does either any   grass

apparent campo, aut frondes   arbore;   sed terra jacet
appear   on the plain, or do leaves appear on the trees; but the earth   lies

late   informis niveis aggeribus, et alto gelu, que
far around deformed with snowy   mounds,   and deep   frost,   and

assurgit in septem ulnas. Semper hiems, semper   Cauri
rises   to seven   ells. It is always   winter, always the west winds

spirantes frigora. Tum Sol   haud unquam discutit
are breathing   cold.   Then the sun   does not   ever   scatter

pallentes umbras; nec cum invectus equis,   petit altum
the pale   shades; neither when   borne   by horses, he goes to the lofty

æthera;   nec cum lavit præcipitem currum rubro
sky;   nor when he bathes   his swift   chariot   in the red

æquore Oceani. Subitæ crustæ concrescunt in   currenti
surface of the ocean. Sudden crusts   harden   on   the running

flumine: jamque   unda sustinet ferratos orbes   360
stream: and now the wave   upholds   iron   wheels

iergo, illa hospita prius patulis puppibus, nunc
on its surface, that *wave* friendly before to broad ships, now

plaustris. Que æra dissiliunt vulgo, que vestes
to wagons. And brass vessels burst asunder everywhere, and dresses

indutæ rigescunt, que cædunt humida vina securibus,
put on grow stiff, and men cut up the *once* liquid wine with axes,

et totæ lacunæ vertêre in solidam glaciem, que horrida
and all the ditches have turned to solid ice, and the rough

stiria induruit impexis barbis. Interea ningit
icicle has grown hard on uncombed beards. In the mean time it snows

non secius toto aëre; pecudes intereunt; magna
not less through the whole sky; flocks die; great

corpora boum stant circumfusa pruinis; que cervi con-
bodies of cattle stand surrounded by frost; and stags in a

ferto agmine, torpent novà mole et vix exstant
crowded band, are benumbed *under* the new load and hardly stand out

370 summis cornibus. Non agitant hos canibus
with the tops of their horns. *Men* do not chase these with dogs

immissis, non ullis cassibus, ve pavidos formidine
let loose, nor with any nets, or frightened by dread

puniceæ pennæ: sed cominus obtruncant ferro
of the crimson feather: but forthwith they butcher *them* with the sword

frustra trudentes oppositum montem pectore;
in vain pushing on the opposing mountain *of snow* with their breast;

que cædunt rudentes graviter; et læti reportant
and they kill *them* braying grievously; and joyful they bear *them* off

magno clamore. Ipsi agunt secura otia in
with a great outcry. *The Scythians* themselves spend undisturbed leisure in

defossis specubus sub altâ terrâ, advolvêre que congesta
excavated caves beneath the deep earth, they have rolled both collected

robora que totas ulmos focis que dedere igni: hic
oaks and whole elms to the hearths, and committed *them* to the fire: here

ducunt noctem ludo; et læti imitantur pocula vitea
they spend the night in sport and joyful they imitate potions *of* wine

380 fermento atque acidis sorbis. Talis effrœna
with beer and sour service-berries. Such an ungoverned

gens virûm, subjecta Hyperboreo septemtrioni,
race of men, lying under the northern constellation of the bears,

tunditur Riphæo Euro, et corpora velantur ful-
is beaten by the Riphæan east wind, and their bodies are clothed with the

vis setis pecudum. Si lanicium tibi curæ, primum
tawny hair of cattle. If cloth manufacture *is* your care, first

aspera silva, que lappæ que tribuli absint; fuge
let the rough wood, and burs and thistles be far away; avoid

læta pabula; que continuo lege albos greges mollibus
rich fodder; and at first select white flocks with soft

villis. Autem quamvis aries ipse sit candidus, rejice
fleeces. But although the ram himself be white, reject

:llum, cui tantum nigra lingua subest udo palato, ne
him, to whom only a black tongue lies under his moist · palate, lest

infuscet vellera nascentûm pullis maculis, que
he should stain the fleeces of the young *lambs* with dark spots, and

circumspice alium pleno campo. Sic Pan 390
look about for another in the full field. Thus Pan

Deus Arcadiæ fefellit te, Luna, captam · niveo munere
the god of Arcadia deceived thee, O moon, captivated by the snowy offering

lanæ (si est dignum credere), vocans in alta nemora;
of wool (if it is worthy to believe), inviting *thee* to the deep groves;

nec tu aspernata vocantem. At ipse cui amor
nor didst thou despise *him* invoking *thee*. But let him to whom is the love

lactis, ferat cytisum que lotos frequentes, que salsas
of milk, bring cytisus and water-lilies in great plenty, and salted

herbas præsepibus. Hinc et amant fluvios magis,
herbs to the stalls. From this cause both they love the rivers more,

et magis tendunt ubera, et referunt occultum saporem
and more extend their udders, and bring back the secret taste

salis in lacte. Jam multi prohibent excretos hœdos a matri-
of salt in the milk. Now many keep away the grown kids from their

bus, que præfigunt prima ora capistris ferratis.
mothers, and they fasten the front of their mouths with muzzles armed with iron.

Quod mulsere die surgente que horis 400
That which they have milked the day arising and in the hours

diurnis premunt nocte: quod jam tenebris,
of day they coagulate at night. *that* which now *they milk* in the darkness,

et sole cadente, pastor exportans calathis sub
and the sun setting, the shepherd bearing it off in milk vessels about

lucem, adit oppida; aut contingunt parco sale,
daylight, goes to the towns; or they season *it* with a small portion of salt,

que reponunt hiemi. Nec cura canum fuerit postrema
and lay *it* up for winter. Nor let the care of dogs be last

tibi; sed una pasce veloces catulos Spartæ, que acrem
to you; but at once feed the swift whelps of Sparta, and the strong

Molossum pingui sero. Nunquam, illis custodibus,
Molossian *dog* with rich whey. Never, they being *your* guards,

horrebis nocturnum furem stabulis, que incursus
shall you dread the nightly thief in the stables, and the ravages

luporum; aut impacatos Iberos a tergo. Sæpe
of wolves; or restless Spaniards *attacking you* behind. Often

etiam agitabis timidos onagros cursu, et leporem
also you shall pursue the cowardly wild asses in the chase, and the hare

canibus, venabere damas canibus. Sæpe tur- 410
with dogs, you shall hunt the hinds with dogs. Often you

babis latratu apros pulsos silvestribus
shall disturb with the barking *of dogs* boars banished from their wild

volutabris, agens, que per altos montes premes
dens, driving *them*, and through the lofty mountains you shall pursue

ingentem cervum ad retia   clamore.   Disce et accen-
the huge   stag   to the toils with a shout.   Learn also   to

dere odoratam cedrum stabulis,   que agitare graves
burn   the odorous   cedar   in the stables,   and to drive off offensive

chelydros   nidore   Galbaneo.   Sæpe   sub
water-snakes with the scent of *gum* Galbanum.   Often   beneath

immotis   præsepibus, aut vipera, mala   tactu, deli-
the permanent   stalls,   either the viper, injurious by its touch, has

tuit,   que exterrita, fugit   cœlum;   aut coluber
lain hid, and frightened, fled *the light of* heaven;   or the snake

acerba pestis boum, assuetus succedere tecto et umbræ,
the cruel plague of cattle, accustomed to approach the house and shade,

que aspergere virus pecori,   fovit humum.   Pastor.
and scatter   poison in the flock, lies close to the ground. O shepherd,

420 cape saxa manu,   cape robora; que dejice
     take stones in your hand, seize   clubs;   and strike *him*

tollentem   minas, et tumentem sibila colla;
down raising *himself in* his anger, and swelling his hissing neck;

jamque fugâ abdidit timidum caput alte, cum   medii
and now in flight he has hid his fearful head deeply, when his intermediate

nexus que agmina extremæ caudæ solvuntur, que
joints and the windings of the extremity of his tail are uncoiled, and

ultimus sinus trahit tardos orbes. Est etiam ille malus
the farthest curvature drags his slow spires. There is also that pernicious

anguis in Calabris saltibus, convolvens squamea terga
snake in the Calabrian forests,   rolling   its scaly back

sublato pectore, atque maculosus longam alvum grandibus
with uplifted breast, and   spotted *as to* its long belly with large

notis; qui, dum ulli amnes rumpuntur   fontibus,
marks; which, while any brooks   burst   from their fountains,

et dum terræ madent   udo   vere ac pluvialibus
and while the lands are wet by the moist spring and   the rainy

Austris, colit stagna, que habitans ripis, hic improbus
south winds, dwells in the pools, and inhabiting the banks, he   greedy

430 explet atram ingluviem piscibus que loquacibus
     fills   his black maw   with fish and   noisy

ranis. Postquam palus exhausta que terræ dehiscunt
frogs.   After   the marsh *is* drained and the lands gape wide

ardore,   exsilit   in   siccum,   et torquens flam-
with drought, he darts out upon   the dry ground, and rolling   his

mantia lumina, sævit agris,   que asper siti, atque
fiery eyes,   rages through the fields, both mad with thirst, and

exterritus æstu. Tum   ne   libeat mihi carpere
frightened by the heat. Then   let it not please me   to enjoy

molles somnos sub   dio,   neu jacuisse   dorso
gentle slumbers beneath the open air, nor to lie   at the edge

nemoris per herbas, cum novus, exuviis   positis,
of a grove, on the grass, when he renewed, his skin   being laid aside

que nitidus juventâ, relinquens aut catulos aut ova
and shining in youth, leaving either young ones or eggs

tectis, volvitur arduus ad solem, et micat trisul-
in his den, * he rolls on rising to the sun, and brandishes his three-

cis linguis ore. Docebo te quoque 440
forked tongue in his mouth. I will instruct you also

causas et signa morborum. Turpis scabies tentat
in the causes and signs of diseases. The foul scab taints

oves, ubi frigidus imber persedit altius ad vivum, et
the sheep, when the cold shower has penetrated deeply to the quick, and

bruma horrida cano gelu; vel cum sudor illotus
the winter rough with hoary frost; or when the sweat unwashed

adhæsit tonsis, et hirsuti vepres secuerunt
cleaves to them being sheared, and the rude briars have lacerated

corpora. Idcirco, magistri perfundunt omne
their bodies. Therefore, the chief shepherds bathe the entire

pecus dulcibus fluviis, que aries udis villis mersatur
flock in the sweet rivers, and the ram with moist fleece is plunged

in gurgite, que missus defluit secundo amni; aut
in the pool, and being sent away floats down the favouring stream; or

contingunt tonsum corpus tristi amurcâ, et miscent
they smear the shorn body with bitter lees of oil, and intermingle

spumas argenti que viva sulphura, que Idæas pices, et
litharge and fresh sulphur, and Idean pitch, and

ceras pingues unguine, que scillam, que 450
wax rich in ointment, and the sea leak and

graves helleboros, que nigrum bitumen. Tamen non
offensive hellebore, and black bitumen. Yet neither

est ulla magis præsens fortuna laborum, quam si
is there any more ready relief of their sufferings, than if

quis potuit rescindere summum os ulceris ferro:
any one could cut off the outward opening of the ulcer with a knife:

vitium alitur que vivit tegendo, dum pastor
the disorder is nourished and grows by being concealed, while the shepherd

abnegat adhibere medicas manus ad vulnera, et sedet
refuses to apply his healing hands to the wounds, and sits down

poscens Deos omnia meliora. Quin etiam
asking of the Gods all better things. But even

cum dolor lapsus ad ima ossa balantum,
when the disease gliding to the inmost bones of the bleating sheep,

furit, atque arida febris depascitur artus, profuit
rages, and a burning fever feeds upon their limbs, it has availed

avertere incensos æstus, et ferire venam salientem san-
to drive out the kindling heat, also to strike a vein spouting with

guine inter ima pedis; quo more Bi- 460
blood between the lowest parts of the foot, by which method the

saltæ solent, que acer Gelonus, cum fugit in
Bisaltæ were accustomed to bleed, and the brave Gelonian, when he flees to

Rhodopen atque in deserta Getarum, et potat lac concretum
Rhodope and to the deserts of the Getæ, and drinks milk thickened

cum equino sanguine. Quam videris, aut
with horses' blood. Whatever *sheep* you should see, either

succedere sæpius molli umbræ aut carpentem summas
to withdraw oftener to the soft shade or cropping the tops

herbas ignavius, que extremam sequi, aut
of the grass more slothfully, and the last to follow *the flock*, or

pascentem procumbere medio campo, et solam
hen feeding to lie down in the midst of the plain, and alone

decedere seræ nocti, continuo compesce culpam
to depart late at night, forthwith restrain the fault (*mischief*)

ferro priusquam dira contagia serpant per in-
with the steel before the dread contagion creeps through the

470 cautum vulgus. Turbo, agens hiemem,
unguarded flock. A whirlwind, driving on a storm,

non ruit tam creber æquore, quam multæ pestes
does not rush so frequent from the sea, as *there are* many plagues

pecudum. Nec morbi corripiunt singula corpora, sed
of cattle. Nor do diseases seize upon single bodies *only*, but

tota æstiva repente, que spem que gregem simul
entire summer folds suddenly, and the hope (i.e. *the lambs*) and the flock at once

que cunctam gentem ab origine. Tum sciat
and all the race from the first breed. Then he may know *the truth of*

si quis nunc quoque, tanto post,
this if any one *even* now also, at so great a space of time since *the laying waste,*

videat aërias Alpes, et Norica castella in
should view the airy Alps, and the Noric (*Bavarian*) castles on

tumulis, et arva Iapidis Timavi, que deserta regna
the hills, and the fields of Iapidian Timavus, and the deserted kingdoms

pastorum, et saltus vacantes longe que late. Hic
of the shepherds, and the lawns made vacant far and wide. Here

quondam tempestas miseranda coorta est,
formerly a storm *in its effects* to be dreaded arose,

morbo cœli, que incanduit toto æstu
from the corruption of the air, and became inflamed through the whole heat

480 autumni; et dedit omne genus pecudum, omne
of autumn; and gave every kind of cattle, every *kind*

ferarum . neci, que corrupit lacus, infecit pabula
of wild beast to death, and corrupted the lakes, *and* tainted the fodder

tabo. Nec erat via mortis simplex; sed ubi
with poison. Nor was the way of death uncomplicated; but when

ignea sitis, acta omnibus venis, adduxerat mise-
the fiery thirst, driven through all their veins, had contracted their

ros artus, rursus fluidus liquor abundabat; que trahebat
wretched limbs, again a fluid moisture abounded; and reduced

omnia ossa collapsa morbo minutatim in se. Sæpe
all their bones fallen by disease piecemeal together. Often

in medio honore Deum, hostia stans ad aram
in the midst of the worship of the Gods, the victim standing at the altar

dum lanea infula circumdatur nivea vittâ,
while the woollen fillet is bound about *its temples* with a snowy head-band,

cecidit, moribunda inter cunctantes ministros. Aut
has fallen, ready to die between the delaying sacrificers. Or

si sacerdos mactaverat quam ante, inde
if the priest had slain any *victim* before *it had fallen*, then

neque altaria ardent, fibris impositis, 490
neither do the altars burn, its fibres being placed on them,

nec potest vates, consultus, reddere responsa; ac cultri
nor can the prophet, being consulted, utter replies; and the knives

suppositi, vix tinguntur sanguine, que summa arena
being laid aside, hardly are tinged with blood, and the top of the sand

infuscatur jejunâ sanguine. Hinc vituli vulgo
is stained with sickly blood. Hence the calves everywhere

moriuntur in lætis herbis, et reddunt dulces animas
die upon the abundant grass, and yield their sweet lives

ad plena præsepia. Hinc rabies venit blandis canibus,
at the full stalls. Hence madness comes to the kindly dogs,

et anhela tussis quatit ægros sues, ac angit
and a panting cough shakes the sickly swine, and tortures *them*

obesis faucibus. Equus, victor, labitur infelix,
with swelled throats. The horse, *once* a conqueror, falls unhappy

immemor studiorum atque herbæ; que avertitur
unmindful of his labours and of the grass; and he is averse from

fontes, et crebra ferit terram pede; aures
the fountains, and often strikes the earth with his foot; his ears

demissæ, incertus sudor ibidem, et ille 500
are let down, an intermitting sweat *is* there, and that

quidem frigidus morituris; pellis aret et dura
indeed *is* cold *on horses* about to die; his skin is parched and *being* hard

ad tactum, resistit tractanti. Dant hæc signa primis
to the touch, resists *one* feeling *it*. They offer these symptoms in the first

diebus ante exitium. Sin in processu morbus
days *of sickness* before death. But if in progress *of time* the disease

cœpit crudescere, tum vero oculi ardentes, atque
has begun to grow worse, then indeed their eyes *are* inflamed, and

spiritus, attractus ab alto, interdum gravis
their breath, being drawn from the depth *of their breast*, *is* sometimes loaded

gemitu, que ima ilia tendunt longo singultu,
with groaning, and their inmost entrails distend *themselves* with a long sob,

ater sanguis it naribus, et aspera lingua premit
black blood proceeds from their nostrils, and their rough tongue presses

obsessas fauces. Profuit infundere Lenæos
their straitened jaws. It profited *at first* to pour into *their mouth* Lenæan

latices inserto cornu, ea visa una salus 510
liquors *(wine)* by an inserted horn, this seemed the only safety

morientibus : mox hoc ipsum erat exitio ; que
to the dying : presently this *remedy* itself was their destruction ; and

refecti ardebant furiis, que ipsi, jam sub
being refreshed they burned with madness, and they, even now under

ægrâ morte, laniabant suos artus, discissos nudis
painful death, tore their limbs, rent with their naked

dentibus. Dî meliora piis, que illum
teeth. May the gods *grant* better *things* to the pious, and that

errorem hostibus ! Autem ecce, taurus fumans sub duro
misfortune to our foes ! But lo ! the ox smoking before the hard

vomere concidit, et vomit cruorem mistum spumis
ploughshare falls, and vomits blood mingled with foam

ore, que ciet extremos gemitus. Tristis arator
from his mouth, and utters his last groans. The sorrowful ploughman

it, abjungens juvencum mœrentem fraternâ morte, atque
goes, unyoking the bullock mourning his brother's death, and

relinquit defixa aratra in medio opere. Non umbræ
leaves his fastened plough in the midst of his labour. Not the shades

520 altorum nemorum, non mollia prata possunt
of lofty groves, not the soft meadows can

movere animum, non amnis, qui volutus per saxa
influence his feelings, not the river, which having rolled over rocks

purior electro, petit campum : at ima latera solvuntur,
clearer than amber, seeks the plain : but his inmost sides are relaxed,

atque stupor urget inertes oculos ; que cervix fluit ad
and dimness presses down his sluggish eyes ; and his neck falls to

terram devexo pondere. Quid labor, aut
the earth with its bending weight. What does the labour *of oxen avail them,* or

benefacta juvant ? quid invertisse graves terras
what do their good deeds avail *them ?* what to have turned up the heavy lands

vomere ? atqui non Massica munera Bacchi, non
with the plough ? but neither the Massic gifts of Bacchus, nor

epulæ repositæ nocuere illis. Pascuntur frondibus et
feasts laid up in store have injured them. They feed on leaves and

victu simplicis herbæ, pocula sunt liquidi fontes,
the produce of simple grass, their bowls are flowing fountains,

atque flumina exercita cursu ; nec cura abrumpit
and rivers exercised with running ; nor does care break

530 salubres somnos. Dicunt, boves quæstias non alio
their healthful sleep. They say, that oxen were sought at no other

tempore illis regionibus ad sacra Junonis, et cur-
time in those regions for the sacrifices of Juno, and that *her* cha-

rus ductos ad alta donaria imparibus uris. Ergo
riots were drawn to her lofty shrines by unmatched buffaloes. Therefore *the*

ægre rimantur terram rastris, et infodiunt
husbandmen with difficulty tear the earth with harrows, and plant

fruges unguibus ipsis ; que trahunt stridentia plaustra
the corn with their nails themselves ; and draw the creaking wagons

contentâ cervice per altos montes. Lupus non explo-
with outstretched neck through the high mountains. The wolf does not medi-

rat insidias circum ovilia, nec nocturnus obambulat
tate a lying in wait around the sheepfolds, nor does he nightly walk about

gregibus; acrior cura domat illum. Timidi damæ
the flocks; a more active care rules him. The cowardly fallow deer

que fugaces cervi nunc vagantur inter canes et circum tec-
and flying stags now wander among dogs and about the

ta. Jam fluctus proluit prolem immensi 540
dwellings. Now the wave washes over the offspring of the immense

maris, et omne genus natantum in extremo
sea, and every kind of swimming creatures upon the farthest part of the

litore, ceu naufraga corpora; phocæ, insolitæ, fugiunt in
shore, as shipwrecked bodies; seals, unused to it, fly to

flumina. Et vipera moritur, frustra defensa curvis latebris,
the rivers. And the viper dies, in vain defended by crooked retreats,

et hydri attoniti, squamis astantibus. Aër est non
and water-snakes are astonished, their scales standing out. The air is not

æquus avibus ipsis, et illæ, præcipites, relinquunt
wholesome to the birds themselves, and they falling, headlong, leave

vitam sub alta nube. Præterea, nec jam refert
their life beneath a high cloud. Besides, neither now is it expedient

pabula mutari, que artes quæsitæ nocent; ma-
that the fodder be changed, and the arts of healing sought for are hurtful; the

gistri Phillyrides, Chiron, que Amythaonius, Me-
masters of medicine the son of Phillyra, Chiron, and Amythaon's son, Me-

lampus, cessere. Et pallida Tisiphone, emissa 550
lampus, have withdrawn. And pale Tisiphone, sent out

Stygiis tenebris in lucem, sævit; agit morbos que me-
from Stygian darkness to the light, rages; she spreads sickness and

tum ante, que surgens in dies, effert avidum caput altius.
dread before her, and rising to the day, raises her greedy head higher.

Amnes que arentes ripæ, que supini colles, sonant
The rivers and the dry banks, and the inclining hills, resound

balatu pecorum, et crebris mugitibus; jamque dat
with the bleating of sheep, and frequent bellowings; and now she gives

stragem catervatim, atque in stabulis ipsis aggerat
destruction in droves, and in the stables themselves heaps up

cadavera dilapsa turpi tabo, donec discant tegere
dead bodies fallen away by the foul contagion, until they learn to bury them

humo, ac abscondere foveis. Nam neque erat
in the ground, and to hide them in ditches. For neither was there

usus coriis, nec quisquam potest aut obolere 560
profit from the skins, nor is any one able either to cleanse

viscera undis, aut vincere flammâ; nec quidem
the entrails with water, or purge them by flame; nor indeed

possunt tondere vellera peresa morbo que illuvie, nec
can they shear the fleeces corroded by disease and filth. nor

attingere putres telas, verum etiam si quis tentârat invisos
touch   the rotten webs,   but   even   if any one had tried the hateful

amictus, ardentes papulæ atque immundus sudor seque-
dresses,   burning   blotches   and   filthy   sweat   over-

batur olentia membra; deinde sacer ignis edebat
spread   his offensive   limbs;   then   the erysipelas consumed

contactos artus moranti nec longo tempore.
the infected members   of him delaying, and not for long   time,   *to lay*
them aside.

BOOK IV.

PROTINUS exsequar cœlestia dona aërii mellis.
FORTHWITH   I will sing of   the celestial   gifts   of aërial   honey-

Aspice, etiam, hanc partem,   Mæcenas.   Dicam
Regard,   also,   this   part   *of my labours*, O Mæcenas.   I will sing

spectacula levium rerum admiranda tibi ; que magnanimos
a representation of light concerns to be admired by you; both the high-minded

duces, que mores totius gentis, ordine, et studia,
leaders *of bees*, and the manners of all the race, in order, and *their* pursuits,

et populos, et prœlia. Labor in tenui ! at
and kinds, and conflicts.   Toil   *bestowed* on a trifling *subject !* but

gloria non tenuis, si læva numina sinunt quem
the renown *is* not trifling, if the unpropitious deities   allow   any one

que Apollo vocatus audit.   Principio,
to accomplish the task and Apollo invoked attends. In the first place,

sedes petenda, que statio apibus, quo neque
a seat is to be sought, and   a settlement for the bees, where   neither

sit aditus ventis (nam venti prohibent ferre
can there be access for the winds   (for   the winds forbid them to bear

10   *their* pabula domum), neque oves que petulci hœdi
     their food   home),   nor   sheep   and frisking   kids

insultent floribus, aut bucula, errans campo, decu-
can tread down the flowers, or the heifer, wandering on the plain, can shake

tiat rorem, et atterat surgentes herbas: Et lacerti,
off   the dew, and bruise   the rising   plants.   And let the lizards,

picti squalentia terga, absint a pinguibus stabulis, que
painted on their scaly backs, be far from   the rich   hives,   and

meropes que aliæ volucres, et Progne signata pectus
woodpeckers and other   birds,   and Progne   marked on her breast

cruentis manibus. Nam vastant omnia late, que
with bloody   hands.   For they waste   all   *things* far around, and

ferunt volantes ipsas ore, dulcem escam
bear off the flying bees themselves in their mouth, pleasant food

immitibus nidis. At liquidi fontes, et stagna viren-
for their pitiless young. But let the clear fountains, and pools made

tia musco, et tenuis rivus fugiens per gramina,
green by moss, and the shallow rivulet swift running through the grass,

adsint; que palma aut ingens oleaster obumbret 20
be at hand; and let the palm or the great wild olive overshadow

vestibulum; ut, cum novi reges ducent prima examina
the entrance, that, when the new kings lead forth the first swarms

suo vere, que juventus emissa favis ludet,
in their own spring, and the youth let loose from the honeycombs sport,

vicina ripa invitet decedere calori, que ob-
the neighbouring bank may invite them to withdraw from the heat, and the in-

via arbos teneat frondentibus hospitiis. Conjice
tervening tree may detain them by its leafy protection. Cast

salices transversas et grandia saxa in medium, seu
willows placed across and large rocks in the midst of the water, whether

humor stabit iners, seu profluet, ut possint consistere
the water shall stand inactive, or shall flow, that they may stand on

crebris pontibus, et pandere alas ad æstivum solem;
them as on many bridges, and open their wings to the summer sun;

si forte præceps Eurus sparserit morantes, aut
if by chance the violent east wind has scattered the loitering bees, or

immerserit Neptuno. Circum hæc virides 30
plunged them in the sea. Around these places let green

casiæ et serpylla olentia late et copia thymbræ spirantis
cassia and thyme scenting far around and plenty of savory smelling

graviter floreat; que violaria bibant irriguum fontem,
strongly blossom; and let violet beds drink the flowing fountains,

Autem alvearia ipsa, seu fuerint suta
But let the bee-hives themselves, whether they may have been fastened toge-

tibi cavatis corticibus, seu texta lento vimine,
ther by you from hollowed barks, or woven from the slender vine,

habeant angustos aditus; nam hiems cogit mella
have narrow entrances; for the winter hardens the honey

frigore, que calor remittit eadem liquefacta: utraque
by cold, and the heat relaxes the same dissolved: each

vis pariter metuenda apibus; neque illæ nequicquam
power equally is to be dreaded by the bees; neither do they in vain

certatim linunt tenuia spiramenta cerâ in tectis, que
earnestly anoint the narrow openings with wax in their hives, and

explent oras fuco et floribus; que servant 40
fill the borders with moss and flowers; and they keep

gluten, collectum ad hæc ipsa munera, lentius et
the glue, collected for these very purposes, more adhesive even

visco, et pice Phrygiæ Idæ. Sæpe etiam
than birdlime, and the pitch of Phrygian Ida. Often also

fodêre   larem   sub   terrâ, latebris effossis (si
they have dug a dwelling-place beneath the earth, retreats being excavated (if

fama   est vera), que penitus   repertæ   que cavis
the report is   true),   and deeply   have they been found   both in hollow

pumicibus, que antro exesæ arboris. Tamen tu et
pumice-stones, and the cavity of a rotten   tree.   Yet do you also

unge   rimosa   cubilia circum levi · limo,   fovens,
smear · their chinky hives   around with light mud,   cherishing them,

et superinjice   raras frondes ; neu sine   taxum
and throw over their hives scattered leaves ,   nor permit a yew tree to stand

propius tectis,   neve ure rubentes cancros   foco,
near   to their hives,   nor burn reddening   crabs   in the fire,

neu crede   altæ paludi, aut ubi odor cœni gravis,
nor trust a hive to the deep marsh, or where the stench of mud is offensive,

aut ubi concava saxa sonant pulsu, que imago   vocis
or where the hollow rocks resound at the striking, and the echo of the voice

50 offensa resultat.   Quod superest, ubi aureus
    obstructed reverberates.   What remains,   when the bright

sol   egit   hiemem pulsam sub terras, que reclusit
sun   has banished the winter driven beneath the earth, and laid open

cœlum æstivâ luce ; continuo illæ peragrant saltus que
the heaven with summer light; forthwith they pass over the lawns and

silvas, que metunt purpureos flores, et leves libant summa
woods, and suck   the purple flowers, and light they sip the surface

flumina.   Hinc   nescio quâ dulcedine lætæ,
of the streams.   From these sources I know not by what   delight   rejoiced,

fovent   progeniem que   nidos ;   hinc excudunt
they feed their offspring   and their hives , from these sources they form

recentes ceras arte, et fingunt tenacia mella. Hinc ubi
fresh   wax by art, and make   adhesive honey. Henceforth when

jam suspexeris agmen emissum caveis,   nare ad
now   you shall behold a swarm let loose from their hives, to fly to

sidera cœli   per liquidam æstatem, que obscuram
the stars of heaven through the clear atmosphere, and the dark

60 nubem   trahi vento, contemplator semper
    cloud of them to be wafted by the wind,   observe   how always

petunt dulces aquas et frondea tecta :   tu
they seek sweet waters and leafy retreats where they may settle : do you

asperge jussos sapores huc, trita melisphylla, et ignobile
scatter the prescribed juices here, pounded   balm,   and the mean

gramen . cerinthæ : que cie tinnitus, et quate cym-
plant of the honeywort . and excite rising sounds, and strike   the

bala   matris   circum. Ipsæ consident   medi
cymbals of the mother of the Gods around. They   will light   on the medi

catis sedibus ; ipsæ condent   sese in   intima
cated   seats ;   they will conceal themselves within the inmost parts

cunabula suo more. Autem sin   exierint ad
of the hive in their own manner.   But   if they should go out to

pugnam (nam sæpe discordia incessit duobus regibus
battle (for often discord has come upon two kings

magno motu), continuo licet præsciscere longe
with great commotion), immediately you may foreknow long beforehand

que animos vulgi, et corda trepidantia bello;
both the tempers of the crowd, and *their* hearts eager for war;

namque ille Martius canor rauci æris increpat 70
for that martial sound of the hoarse trumpet arouses

morantes, et vox, imitata fractos sonitus tubarum,
the delaying, even a buz, imitating broken sounds of trumpets,

auditur. Tum trepidæ coëunt inter se, que
is heard Then trembling they assemble among themselves, and

coruscant pennis, que exacuunt spicula rostris,
shake in their wings, and sharpen their stings with their beaks,

que aptant lacertos, et densæ miscentur circa regem,
and prepare their claws, and condensed they muster around *their* king,

atque ad prætoria ipsa, que vocant hostem
even at *his* pavilion itself, and they call the enemy

magnis clamoribus. Ergo, ubi nactæ sudum ver,
with great cries. Therefore, when they have gained the serene spring,

que patentes campos, erumpunt portis, concurritur,
and the open plains, they rush out from the gates, they run together;

sonitus fit in alto æthere; mistæ glomerantur in
a sound is made in the lofty sky; commingled they gather in

magnum orbem, que cadunt præcipites: non densior 80
a great cluster, and fall headlong not more thick

grando aëre, nec tantum glandis pluit de concussâ
does hail *fall* from the air, nor does so much mast rain from the shaken

ilice. Ipsi per medias acies, insignibus
oak *The kings,* themselves *flying* through the midst of troops, with remarkable

alis, versant ingentes animos in angusto pectore; usque
wings, stir up great courage in a narrow breast; even

adeo obnixi non cedere, dum gravis victor subegit
thus striving not to yield, while the fierce conqueror compels

aut hos aut hos dare terga versa fugâ. Hi motus
either these or those to give their backs turned in flight. These motions

animorum, atque hæc tanta certamina, compressa jactu
of their minds, and these great contests, constrained by the throwing

exigui pulveris, quiescent. Verum ubi revocaveris
of a little sand, will cease. But when you shall have called back

ambos ductores acie, dede eum qui visus deterior
both leaders from battle, give him who has seemed the weaker

neci, ne prodigus obsit; sine melior regnet 90
to death, lest prodigal ne do injury; permit *that* the better may reign

in aulâ vacuâ. Alter erit ardens maculis squa-
in the hall free *from a rival.* The one will be glowing with spots

lentibus auro (nam sunt duo genera); hic melior,
covered with gold (for there are two kinds); this *is* the more valuable,

et insignis ore, et clarus rutilis squamis: ille
both remarkable for his countenance, and bright with glowing scales the

alter horridus desidiâ, que inglorius trahens latam alvum.
other hairy for sloth, and disgracefully dragging a broad belly.

Ut facies regum binæ, ita corpora gentis. Namque
As the forms of the kings are two, so are the bodies of the people. For

aliæ horrent, turpes ceu cum aridus viator venit ab
some bees are ugly, being filthy as when the thirsty traveller comes from

alto pulvere, et spuit terram sicco ore; aliæ
the deep dust, and spits the dirt from his dry mouth, the others

elucent, et coruscant fulgore, ardentes auro, et
shine, and glitter with brightness, glowing with gold, and

100 corpora lita paribus guttis. Hæc soboles
their bodies are marked with equal spots. This breed

potior; hinc, premes dulcia mella certo tempore
is the better, hence, you may press the sweet honey at a certain time

cœli; nec tantum dulcia quantum et liquida, et domi-
of the season; nor so much sweet as also clear, and about

tura durum saporem Bacchi. At cum examina
to subdue the harsh taste of the wine But when the swarms

volant incerta, que ludunt cœlo, que contemnunt
fly irregularly, and sport along the sky, and disregard

favos, et relinquunt tecta frigida, prohibebis
their combs, and abandon their hives to the cold, you will constrain

instabiles animos inani ludo. Nec magnus
their wavering dispositions from the vain sport. Nor is it a great

labor prohibere, tu eripe alas regibus; non
task to constrain them, do you tear the wings from the kings; no

quisquam audebit ire altum iter illis cunctantibus,
any one will dare to go a long journey while they are delaying,

aut vellere signa castris. Horti halantes
or to tear up the standards from their camps. Let gardens smelling

croceis floribus invitent, et tutela Hellespontiaci
of saffron flowers invite them, and the guardianship of Hellespontic

110 Priapi, custos furum atque avium, cum salignâ
Priapus, the watchman of thieves and of birds, with his willow

falce, servet. Ipse cui talia curæ ferens
sickle, preserve those gardens. He to whom such things are a care bearing

thymum que pinos de altis montibus, serat late
thyme and pines from the lofty mountains, may plant them far

circum tecta Ipse terat manum duro labore,
around the hives. Let him wear his hand with the hard labour of planting

ipse figat feraces plantas humo, et irriget amicos
let him place the fruitful plants in the ground, and diffuse friendly

imbres. Atque equidem, ni jam sub extremo fine
showers around them. And indeed, unless now about the last end

laborum, traham vela, et festinem advertere proram
of my labours, I should take in my sails, and hasten to turn the plow

terris ; forsitan et canerem, quæ cura colendi orna-
to the land; perhaps also I might sing, what care of cultivating should

ret pingues hortos, que rosaria Pæsti, biferi ;
adorn the rich gardens, and the rose-beds of Pæstum, bearing twice a year;

que quo modo intyba, et ripæ virides apio, 120
and in what manner the endives, and banks green with parsley,

gauderent, rivis potis, que cucumis tortus per
should rejoice, the streams being drunk up, and the cucumber winding through

herbam, cresceret in ventrem, nec tacuis-
the grass, should grow into a ventriform shape, nor would I have passed in si-

sem Narcissum comantem sera, aut vimen flexi acanthi,
lence the daffodil flowering late, or the vine of the yielding acanthus,

que pallentes hederas, et myrtos amantes litora. Nam sub
and the pale ivies, and myrtles loving the shores. For beneath

altis turribus Œbaliæ, qua niger Galesus humectat
the high towers of Tarentum, where the dark *stream* Galesus moistens

flaventia culta, memini me vidisse Corycium se-
the yellow cultivated *fields*, I call to mind that I have seen a Corycian old

nem, cui erant pauca jugera relicti ruris : illa seges
man, to whom were a few acres of untilled land: that land

nec fertilis juvencis, nec opportuna pecori, nec
neither *was* fit for bullocks, nor proper for flocks, nor

commoda Baccho. Tamen hic, premens olus rarum in
convenient for wine. Yet here, planting salad far apart among

dumis, que alba lilia circum, que verbenas, que 130
the bushes, and white lilies around, and vervain, and

vescum papaver, æquabat opes regum animis ; que
the esculent poppy, he levelled the wealth of kings to his thoughts; and

revertens domum serà nocte, onerabat mensas inemptis
returning home late at night, he loaded his tables with unbought

dapibus ; primus carpere rosam vere, atque poma
food ; *he was* the first to pluck the rose in spring, and fruits

autumno, et cum tristis hiems etiam nunc rumperet
in autumn, and when saddening winter still bursted

saxa frigore, et frænaret cursus aquarum glacie, ille
the rocks with cold, and restrained the flowing of waters by ice, he

jam tum tondebat comam mollis acanthi, increpitans
even then plucked the foliage of the soft acanthus, blaming

seram æstatem que morantes Zephyros. Ergo, idem
the late summer and delaying west winds. Therefore, the same

primus abundare fetis apibus, atque multo 140
was the first to abound in teeming bees, and an abundant

examine, et cogere spumantia mella pressis favis : illi
swarm, and to gather foaming honey from the pressed combs : for him

tiliæ atque uberrima pinus ; que quot pomis ferti-
lime trees and the most productive pine; and with so many fruits as the

lis arbos induerat se in novo flore, tenebat totidem
productive had clothed itself in the new flower, it retained just so many

matura autumno. Ille etiam distulit seras ulmos
ripened in autumn. He also set out late growing elms

in versum, que eduram pyrum, et spinos jam ferentes
in exact order, and the hardy pear, and thorn trees now bearing

pruna, que platanum jam ministrantem umbras potantibus.
plums, and the plane tree now supplying shades to drinkers

Verum equidem ipse, exclusus iniquis spatiis, prætereo
But indeed I, excluded by unequal space, pass over

hæc, atque relinquo memoranda post me
these *subjects*, and leave *them* to be commemorated after me

aliis. Nunc age, expediam quas naturas Jupiter ipse
by others. Now come, I will unfold what dispositions Jupiter himself

150 addidit apibus; pro quâ mercede, secutæ canoros
has bestowed on bees; for which reward, *they* pursuing the tuneful

sonitus Curetum que crepitantia æra, pavere regem cœli
sounds of the Curetes and the rattling brass, fed the king of heaven

sub Dictæo antro. Solæ habent natos
beneath the Dictæan cave. *They* alone *of all animals* have children

communes, consortia tecta urbis, que agitant ævum
in common, common dwellings of a city, and pass their life

sub magnis legibus; et solæ novere patriam et
beneath important laws; and alone they have known their country and

certos penates; que memores hiemis venturæ, expe-
a certain habitation; and mindful of winter about to come, they

riuntur laborem æstate, et reponunt quæsita in
undergo labour in summer, and lay up *their* gains in

medium. Namque aliæ invigilant victu, et
a common stock. For some watch diligently for food, and

pacto fœdere exercentur agris; pars, intra
by a fixed agreement are occupied in the fields; a part, within

160 septa domorum, ponunt lacrymam Narcissi,
the enclosures of their dwellings, lay up the tear of the Narcissus,

et lentum gluten de cortice, prima fundamina
and the clammy glue from the bark, for the first foundations

favis, deinde suspendunt tenaces ceras; aliæ
for the honeycombs, then they hang around the adhesive wax; others

educunt adultos fetus, spem gentis; aliæ stipant pu-
lead out the grown young, the hope of the race; others compress the

rissima mella, et distendunt cellas liquido nectare.
clearest honey, and swell out the cells with liquid nectar.

Sunt quibus custodia ad portas cecidit sorti;
There are *others* to whom guardianship at the gates falls by lot,

inque vicem speculantur aquas et nubila cœli; aut
and in turn they watch the waters and clouds of the sky; or

accipiunt onera venientum, aut agmine facto.
receive the loads of those coming, or a band being formed,

arcent fucos, ignavum pecus, â præsepibus. Opus
they drive off the drones, a slothful race, from the hives. The work

fervet ; que fragrantia mella redolent thymo. Ac veluti.
glows: and the fragrant honey smells strongly of thyme. And as,

cum Cyclopes properant fulmina lentis massis, 170
when the Cyclops forge in haste thunderbolts from ductile masses,

alii accipiunt que reddunt auras taurinis follibus; alii
some receive and give back the air in bull skin bellows; others

tingunt stridentia æra lacu. Ætna gemit, incudibus
dip the hissing brass in the water. Ætna groans, their anvils

impositis ; illi, inter sese, tollunt brachia magnâ
being placed; they, among themselves, raise their arms with great

vi in numerum, que versant ferrum tenaci
strength in order, and turn the iron with the grasping

forcipe: non aliter, si licet componere parva
tongs: not otherwise, if it is allowed to compare small *things*

magnis, innatus amor habendi urget Cecropias apes,
with great, the inborn love of possessing encourages the Athenian bees,

quamque suo munere. Oppida curæ gran-
each one in his own office. The hives *are* a care to the

dævis, et munire favos, et fingere Dædala tecta.
aged, both to fortify the combs, and to form artificial apartments.

At minores fessæ referunt se multâ 180
But the younger fatigued return in the advanced

nocte, plenæ crura thymo ; pascuntur et arbuta
night, full as to their legs with thyme; they feed also on arbutes

passim, et glaucas salices, que casiam, que rubentem
every where, and green willows, and cassia, and the blushing

crocum, et pinguem tiliam, et ferrugineos hyacinthos.
crocus, and the rich lime tree, and dark red hyacinths.

Quies operum una omnibus, labor unus
Rest *from fatigue* of labours *is* the same to all, labour *is* the same

omnibus. Mane ruunt portis, nusquam
to all. In the morning they rush from their gates, *there is* nowhere

mora. Rursus, ubi Vesper admonuit easdem tandem
delay. Again, when evening has admonished the same at last

decedere campis e pastu, tum petunt tecta, tum
to depart from the fields from feeding, then they seek their hives, then

curant corpora; sonitus fit, quo mussant circum
they provide for their bodies; a noise is made, and they buzz around

oras et limina. Post ubi jam compo-
the borders and thresholds *of their hives*. Afterwards when now they have

suere se thalamis, siletur in noctem, 190
settled themselves in their apartments, there is silence for the night,

que suus sopor occupat fessos artus. Nec vero
and their own sleep occupies their wearied limbs. Nor indeed

pluviâ impendente, recedunt longius a stabulis
the rain threatening do they retreat far from their dwellings,

aut credunt cœlo, Euris adventantibus ; sed, tutæ
or trust to the sky, the east winds approaching; but safe

sub mœnibus urbis, aquantur circum, que tentant
beneath the ramparts of their city, they draw water around, and attempt

breves excursus : et sæpe tollunt lapillos, ut instabiles
short excursions : and often they take up little stones, as tottering

cymbæ saburram, fluctu jactante : librant sese
boats have ballast, the wave tossing : they poise themselves

his per inania nubila. Mirabere illum morem
with these through the empty clouds. You will wonder that that custom

placuisse apibus adeo, quod nec indulgent concubitu,
has pleased the bees so much, that neither do they indulge in marriage,

nec segnes solvunt corpora in Venerem, aut edunt
nor slothful do they relax their bodies in love, or produce

200 fetus nixibus. Verum ipsæ legunt natos e
their young by travail. But they gather their young from

foliis et suavibus herbis ore : ipsæ sufficiunt
leaves and sweet herbs with their mouth : they supply

regem que parvos Quirites ; que refingunt aulas et
a king and little citizens ; and rebuild *for them* halls and

cerea regna. Sæpe etiam attrivere alas errando
waxen kingdoms. Often also have they worn their wings in wandering

in duris cotibus, que ultro dedere animam sub fasce :
over hard cliffs, and voluntarily yielded their life under their burden :

tantus amor florum, et gloria generandi mellis. Ergo
so great is their love of flowers, and the glory of producing honey. Therefore

quamvis terminus angusti ævi excipiat ipsas (enim
although the boundary of a narrow life limit them (for

neque plus septima æstas ducitur), at genus manet
more *than* the seventh summer is passed over), yet the race remains

immortale, que fortuna domus stat per multos annos,
immortal, and the fortune of the house continues through many years,

et avi avorum numerantur. Præterea non
and grandfathers of grandfathers are numbered. Besides not

210 Ægyptus, et ingens Lydia, nec populi Parthorum,
Egypt, and great Lydia, nor the people of the Parthians,

aut Medius Hydaspes, sic observant regem. Rege
or Median Hydaspes, are so obedient to their king. Their king

incolumi, est una mens omnibus ; amisso, rupere
being safe, there is one disposition to all ; he being lost, they have broken

fidem ; que ipsæ diripuere constructa mella, et solvêre
their faith ; and they have torn down their fabricated honey, and loosened

crates favorum. Ille custos operum ; admiran-
the wattled texture of their combs. He *is* the keeper of their labours ; they ad-

tur illum ; et omnes circumstant denso fremitu, que
mire him ; and all stand around with frequent buzzing, and

frequentes stipant, et sæpe attollunt humeris,
in great numbers guard *him*, and often *they* raise *him* on their shoulders

et objectant corpora bello, que petur† pulchram
and expose their bodies *to death* in war. and seek a glorious

mortem   per   vulnera.   Quidem,   his   signis,
death   through   wounds.   Some,   *induced*   by these   signs,

atque   secuti   hæc exempla,   .   dixere,   partem
and   reflecting on these   examples *of prudence*, have declared, that a portion

divinæ   mentis, et æthereos   haustus,   esse api-   220
of the divine   mind,   and celestial   emanations, belong   to

bus ; namque   Deum   ire   per   omnes, que   terras, que
bees;   for   that God   passes through   all,   both the earth, and

tractus   maris,   que profundum cœlum.   Hinc   pecu
the regions of the sea,   and the exalted   sky.   That from him

des, armenta, viros, omne genus ferarum,   quemque
flocks,   herds,   men,   every   kind of wild beasts, *and* every individual

nascentem,   arcessere   tenues   vitas   sibi.   Sci-
coming into the world   attract   their delicate lives   to themselves.   Foras-

licet   deinde   omnia   reddi,   ac   resoluta
much as *they have said* that afterwards all things are restored, and being dissolved

referri   huc ;   nec esse   locum   morti ;   sed
are brought back   here ,   and that there is not   a state   of annihilation;   but

viva   volare   in numerum sideris, atque succedere alto
that alive they fly *each* into the order   of his star, and   lodge   in high

cœlo.   Si quando   relines   angustam sedem,
heaven.   If at any time you will break open the narrow   dwelling *of the bees*,

que   mella servata   thesauris,   prius fove   ore
and *plunder* the honey   stored   in their treasuries,   first   hold in your mouth

haustus aquarum,   sparsus,   que   prætende   230
draughts   of water,   sprinkling them,   and   carry before *you*

manu   fumos sequaces.   Bis   cogunt
with your hand   smoke   pursuing *them*.   Twice   they *who keep bees* collect

gravidos fetus :   duo tempora   messis ;   simul Tay-
their heavy produce   *there are* two   times   of honey-harvest ; as soon as   Tay-

gete, Pleias,   ostendit honestum os   terris,   et reppulit
gete,   the Pleiad,   has shown   her beautiful   face to the earth, and driven back

spretos   amnes Oceani   pede ;   aut ubi eadem, fugiens
the spurned   waters of the ocean with her foot ; or   when the same, yielding to

sidus   aquosi piscis, descendit   tristior   cœlo
the constellation of the watery   fish   descends   more sad   from the sky

in   hibernas undas.   Est   illis ira supra modum, que
into the wintery   waters.   There is to them rage above   measure,   and

læsæ   inspirant   venenum   morsibus,   .et,   affixæ
wounded   they dart in   poison   by stinging,   and,   fastened

venis,   relinquunt   cæca   spicula,   que   ponunt
to the veins,   they leave   their hidden   stings,   and   lay down

animas in vulnere.   Sin   metues   duram   hiemem,
their lives   in the wound   But if   you shall dread the pinching   winter,

que   parces   futuro,   que miserabere   contusos   240
and   will spare for the future,   and   will pity   their drooping

animos, et fractas   res,   at   quis   dubitet   suffire
courage,   and impaired   state,   yet   who   can hesitate   to perfume

thymo, et recídere inanes ceras? nam sæpe
them with thyme, and to cut off the empty wax? for often

ignotus stellio adedit favos, cubilia congesta
a skulking lizard consumes the honeycombs, and their cells *are* filled

blattis lucifugis; que fucus immunis sedens
with moths avoiding the light; and the drone free from *labour* sitting

ad aliena pabula, aut asper crabro imparibus armis
at another's honey, or the cruel hornet with unequal arms

immiscuit se, aut durum genus tineæ; aut aranea,
has joined himself in battle, or the direful race of the moth; or the spider,

invisa Minervæ, suspendit laxos casses in foribus. Quo
hateful to Minerva, hangs his loose nets on the doors. By how much

magis fuerint exhaustæ, hoc acrius omnes
the more they shall have been exhausted, by so much the more actively all

incumbent sarcire ruinas lapsi generis, que complebunt
will strive to supply the ruins of the fallen race, and they will fill

250 foros, et texent horrea floribus. Si vero
the cells, and will build combs from flowers. If indeed

(quoniam vita tulit nostros casus apibus
(since life has introduced our misfortunes to the bees

quoque) corpora languebunt tristi morbo, quod jam
also) their bodies shall faint with sad disease, this now

poteris cognoscere non dubiis signis: continuo est
you may know by undoubted signs. In the first place there is

ægris alius color; horrida macies deformat vultum;
to the sick another colour, dreadful leanness deforms their countenance;

tum exportant corpora carentum luce tectis, et
then they bear off the bodies of those deprived of life from the hives, and

ducunt tristia funera; aut illæ, connexæ pedibus, pendent
lead out sad funerals, or they, united by the feet, hang

ad limina, aut omnes cunctantur intus in clausis
at the doors, or all stay within in their closed

ædibus, que ignavæ fame, et pigræ frigore
dwellings, both slothful through hunger, and dull cold

260 contracto. Tum gravior sonus auditur, que
being caught. Then a deeper sound is heard, and

susurrant tractim, ut quondam frigidus Auster
they buzz continually, as when the cool south wind

immurmurat silvis; ut mare solicitum stridet, undis
rustles in the woods, as the sea agitated roars, the waves

refluentibus; ut rapidus ignis æstuat clausis
flowing back; as the rapidly spreading fire rages in the enclosed

fornacibus. Hic jam suadebo incendere galbaneos
furnaces. Here now I will advise *you* to burn galbanian

odores, que inferre mella arundineis canalibus, ultro
odours, and to bring honey *to them* in reedy troughs, voluntarily

hortantem, et vocantem fessas ad nota pabula. Et
encouraging, and calling *them* languid to the known food. And

proderit admiscere tunsum saporem gallæ, que arentes
it will profit to intermingle the expressed juice of a gall, and dried

rosas, aut defruta pinguia multo igni, vel passos
roses, or boiled wine made rich by much fire, or dried

racemos de Psythiâ vite, que Cecropium thymum,
clusters of grapes from the Psythian vine, and Cecropian thyme,

et grave olentia centaurea. Est etiam flos 270
and the strong scented centaury. There is also the flower

in pratis, cùi amello agricolæ fecere
star-wort in the meadows, to which star-wort the farmers have given

nomen; herba facilis quærentibus; namque tollit
its name, a plant plain to those seeking it; for it rears

ingentem silvam de uno cespite, ipse aureus;
a great number of stalks from one bushy root, itself of a golden colour;

sed in foliis, quæ plurima funduntur circum,
but in its leaves, which in great abundance are spread around,

purpura nigræ violæ sublucet. Sæpe aræ
the purple of the dark violet shines. Often the altars

Deùm ornatæ torquibus nexis. Sapor
of the Gods are ornamented with wreaths woven from it. The taste

asper in ore; pastores legunt illum in ton-
is bitter in the mouth; the shepherds gather it in the

sis vallibus, et prope curva flumina Mellæ.
new-mowed valleys, and near the winding streams of Mella.

Incoque radices hujus odorato Baccho, que ap-
Boil the roots of it with fragrant wine, and

pone, pabula, plenis canistris 280
place them, as nourishment for the bees, in full baskets

in foribus. Sed si omnis proles subito defecerit
before the doors. But if all the stock suddenly shall fail

quem, nec habebit unde genus novæ stirpis
any one, and he shall not have the means whence the race of a new stock

revocetur; tempus et pandere memoranda
may be restored; it will be time even to lay open the memorable

inventa Arcadii magistri, quoque modo jam
discoveries of the Arcadian master, and by what method now

insincerus cruor sæpe tulerit apes cæsis juvencis;
putrid blood often has bred bees from slain bullocks;

expediam omnem famam altius, repetens ab
I will trace the whole report at large, rehearsing it from

primâ origine. Nam qua fortunata gens Pellæi Cano-
its first original. For where the happy nation of Pellæan Cano-

pi accolit Nilum, stagnantem effuso
pus dwells near the Nile, laying under water the country with an overflowing

flumine, et vehitur circum sua rura pictis phaselis;
stream, and sails around its own fields in painted galleys

que qua vicinia pharetratæ Persidis urget, 290
and where the neighbourhood of quivered Persia is hard by

et fecundat viridem Ægyptum nigrâ arenâ, et
that nation, and enriches verdant Egypt with black mud, and

amnis, devexus usque a coloratis Indis, ruens, dis-
the river, poured down even from the tawny Indians, rushing, runs

currit in septem diversa ora; omnis regio jacit
out into seven different mouths, all the country places

certam salutem in hâc arte. Primum exiguus locus
sure relief in this art. First a small place

eligitur, atque contractus ad ipsos usus; premunt hunc
is selected, and procured for these purposes; they enclose this

locum imbrice, que angusti tecti, que arctis parietibus;
place with the tile, both of a narrow roof, and with closed walls;

et addunt quatuor fenestras obliquâ luce a quatuor
and they add four windows with transverse light from the four

ventis. Tum vitulus, jam curvans cornua fronte,
winds. Then a steer, now bending his horns in his forehead,

bimâ quæritur: geminæ nares, et
two years old is sought out both his nostrils *are closed,* and

300 spiritus oris obstruitur huic reluctanti multa,
the breath of his mouth is obstructed to him struggling much.

que vicera, tunsa per integram pellem, solvuntur
and his entrails, beaten through his unbroken skin, are burst *within*

perempto plagis. Linquunt positum sic in clauso,
him killed by blows. They leave *him* laid out thus in an enclosed

et subjiciunt costis ramea fragmenta, thymum,
place, and place beneath his ribs branchy fragments *of trees,* thyme,

que recentes casias. Hoc geritur Zephyris primum
and fresh cassia. This is done the west winds first

impellentibus undas, antequam prata rubeant novis
driving the waves, before . the meadows blush with new

coloribus, antequam garrula hirundo suspendat nidum
colours, before the chattering swallow hangs his nest

tignis. Interea tepefactus humor in teneris
from the rafters. In the mean time the warm moisture in his tender

ossibus æstuat; et animalia visenda miscentur miris
bones ferments; and animals to be wondered at are mustered in strange

310 modis, trunca pedum primo, et mox stridentia
ways, short in their feet at first, and soon after buzzing

pennis, magis que magis carpunt tenuem aëra; donec, ut
with wings, more and more they enjoy the light air; until, as

imber effusus æstivis nubibus, erupere; aut ut
a shower poured out from summer clouds, they have burst forth; or as

sagittæ pulsante nervo, si quando leves Parthi
arrows from the impelling string, if at any time the light Parthians

ineunt prima prælia. Musæ, quis, quis Deus extudit
enter on their first contests Ye Muses, what, what God invented

hanc artem nobis? unde nova experientia hominum
this art for us? whence *does* this new experience of men

cepit ingressus?   Pastor   Aristæus, fugiens Peneïa
take   its origin?   The shepherd Aristæus, flying from Peneian

Tempe, apibus amissis, que morbo que fame, ut
Tempe, his bees being lost, both by disease and by hunger, as

fama, astitit tristis ad sacrum caput extremi amnis,
the report is, stood mournful by the sacred fountain of the rising river,

querens multa: atque affatus parentem hâc
complaining much· and having accosted his mother with this 320

voce: Mater Cyrene, mater, quæ tenes ima
address: O mother Cyrene, O mother, who inhabitest the depths

hujus gurgitis, quid genuisti me, invisum fatis, præ-
of this pool, why did you bear me, hateful to the fates, from

clarâ stirpe Deorum, si modo Thymbræus Apollo,
the renowned race of the gods, if now Thymbræan Apollo,

quem perhibes, est pater? aut quo est amor nostri
whom you declare my father, is my father? or whither is the love of us

pulsus tibi? quid jubebas me sperare cœlum?
banished from you? why did you command me to hope for heaven?

En, te matre, relinquo hunc honorem ipsum mortalis
Lo, you being my mother, I yield this honour itself of mortal

vitæ, quem solers custodia frugum et pecudum vix
life, which the diligent care of fruits and cattle scarcely

extuderat tentanti omnia. Quin age, et
had struck out for me attempting all things. But come on, and

ipsa erue felices silvas manu; fer inimicum
do you tear up these happy groves with your hand; bear hostile

ignem stabulis, atque interfice messes; ure
to my ox-stalls, and destroy my ripe corn; burn 330

sata, et molire validam bipennem in vites:
my standing corn, and wield the strong axe against my vines,

si tanta tædia meæ laudis ceperunt te. At mater
if so great neglect of my praise has seized you. But his mother

sensit sonitum sub thalamo alti fluminis: circum
heard the sound beneath the chamber of the deep river. around

eam nymphæ carpebant Milesia vellera, fucata saturo
her the nymphs were carding Milesian fleeces, dyed with the rich

colore hyali: que Drymo, que Xantho, que Ligea, que
colour of sea-green: both Drymo, and Xantho, and Ligea, and

Phyllodoce, effusæ nitidam cæsariem per candida
Phyllodoce, disheveling their shining hair over their white

colla; Nesæe que Spio, que Thalia que Cymodoce, que
necks: Nesæe and Spio, and Thalia and Cymodoce, and

Cydippe, et flava Lycorïas; altera virgo, altera tum
Cydippe, and beautiful Lycorias, the one a maid, the other then

experta primos labores Lucinæ, que Clio,
having experienced the first labours of Lucina and Clio 340

et Beroë soror, ambæ Oceanitides, ambæ auro,
also Beroë her sister, both daughters of Oceanus both adorned with gold,

ambæ incinctæ pictis pellibus; atque Ephyre, atque
both girt with painted skins, and Ephyre, and

Opis, et Asia Deïopeia, et velox Arethusa, sagittis
Opis, and Asia Deiopeia, and swift Arethusa, her arrows

tandem positis: inter quas Clymene narrabat
at length being laid aside: among whom Clymene was relating

inanem curam Vulcani, que dolos Martis, et dulcia
the vain care of Vulcan, and the deceits of Mars, and his pleasant

furta, que numerabat densos amores Divùm
thefts, and was enumerating the many loves of the gods

Chao: dum captæ quo carmine devolvunt mollia
from Chaos. whilst delighted by this song they wind off their soft

pensa fusis, luctus Aristæi iterum impulit
tasks from *their* spindles, the complaint of Aristæus again struck

350 maternas aures, que omnes vitreis sedilibus
his mother's ears, and all in their glassy seats

obstupuere: sed ante alias sorores, Arethusa prospiciens,
were amazed but before the other sisters, Arethusa looking out,

extulit flavum caput summâ undâ; et procul,
raised her beautiful head from the surface of the water; and afar off,

O soror Cyrene, non frustra exterrita tanto gemitu,
said: O sister Cyrene, not in vain alarmed by so great mourning,

Aristæus ipse, tua maxima cura, tristis, stat lacrymans
Aristeus himself, thy greatest care, sad, stands weeping

tibi, ad undam genitoris Penei, et dicit te crudelem
to you, at the fountain head of your father Peneus, and calls you cruel

nomine. Mater, percussa mentem novâ formidine,
by name. The mother, struck in her mind by sudden fear,

ait huic: Age, duc, duc ad nos; fas illi tangere
said to her. Come, lead, lead him to us, it is allowed for him to reach

limina Divûm. Simul jubet alta flumina
the courts of the gods. At the same time she orders the deep rivers

360 discedere late, qua juvenis inferret gressus. At
to withdraw on either side, where the youth should direct his steps. But

unda, curvata in faciem montis, circumstetit illum, que
the water, being arched into the form of a mountain, surrounded him, and

accepit vasto sinu, que misit sub amnem.
received *him* in its vast bosom, and conveyed *him* beneath the river.

Jamque ibat mirans domum genetricis, et humida
And now he went admiring the palace of his mother, and the liquid

regna, que lacus clausos speluncis, que sonantes lucos,
realms, and the lakes enclosed in caverns, and the sounding groves,

et, stupefactus ingenti motu aquarum, spectabat
and, astonished at the great commotion of the waters, beheld

omnia flumina labentia sub magnâ terrâ, diversa
all the rivers gliding beneath the great earth, distinguished

locis; que Phasim que Lycum, et caput,
in their places both Phasis and Lycus, and the fountain

unde Enipeus primum erumpit se, unde pater
whence Enipeus first bursts itself, whence father

Tiberinus, et unde Aniena fluenta, que Hypanis
Tiber, and whence Anio's stream, and Hypanis

sonans saxosum, que Mysus Caïcus, et 375
roaring among the rocks, and Mysian Caïcus, and

Eridanus, taurino vultu, auratus gemina cornua,
Eridanus, with his bull-like countenance, gilded *as to* his two horns,

quo non alius amnis influit violentior per
than which not any river flows more violently through

pinguia culta in purpureum mare. Postquam
fruitful cultivated *fields* into the purple sea. After

perventum est in tecta thalami pendentia pu-
he had come to the roof of her grot hanging with pu-

mice, et Cyrene cognovit inanes fletus nati,
mice stones, and Cyrene had known the vain complaints of her son,

germanæ dant liquidos fontes manibus, ordine, que
her sisters pour pure waters on his hands, in order, and

ferunt mantilia tonsis villis. Pars onerant mensas
bring towels with soft nap. A part load the tables

epulis, et reponunt plena pocula. Aræ adolescunt
with feasts, and replace the full bowls. The altars blaze

Panchæis ignibus. Et mater ait; cape carchesia
with Panchæan fires. Also the mother says; take goblets

Mæonii Bacchi, libemus Oceano. Simul 380
of Mæonion wine, let us make a libation to Oceanus. At once

ipsa precatur que Oceanum, patrem rerum, que sorores
she prays both Oceanus, the parent of things, and the sister

nymphas, quæ centum silvas, quæ servant
nymphs, who *rule over* an hundred woods, who preside over

centum flumina. Ter perfudit ardentem Vestam
an hundred streams. Thrice she sprinkled glowing Vesta

liquido nectare; ter flamma subjecta ad summum
with pure nectar; thrice the flame being roused to the top

tecti reluxit: quo omine firmans animum, ipsa
of the roof shone forth: by which omen confirming her mind, she

sic incipit: In Carpathio gurgite Neptuni, est vates,
thus began; In the Carpathian gulf of Neptune, is a prophet,

cæruleus Proteus, qui metitur magnum æquor piscibus,
azure Proteus, who measures the great sea with fishes,

et juncto curru bipedum equorum. Hic nunc 390
and a yoked chariot of two-footed horses. He now

revisit portus Emathiæ, que patriam Pallenen: et
revisits the harbours of Emathia, and his country Pallene: and *we*

nymphæ, et grandævus Nereus ipse, veneramur hunc;
nymphs, and the aged Nereus himself, worship him;

namque vates novit omnia quæ sint, quæ fuerint,
for the prophet knows all *things* which are, which have been,

quæ   trahantur,   mox   ventura :   quippe   ita
which   are continued,   presently   about to come to pass :   for   thus

visum est   Neptuno, cujus immania armenta et turpes
it seemed good   to Neptune,   whose   huge   herds   and shapeless

phocas pascit sub gurgite. Nate, hic prius capiendus
seals   he feeds beneath the pool.   O son, he   first   is to be taken

tibi vinclis, ut expediat omnem causam morbi, que
by you in chains, that he may unfold   all   the cause of the disease, and

secundet eventus. Nam non dabit ulla præcepta sine
favour   the event.   For   he will not give   any   commands without

vi,   neque   flectes   illum   orando ;   tende   duram
violence, nor   can you influence   him   by entreaty ;   apply   severe

400   vim et vincula   capto :   doli   circum hæc
     force and   chains   to him taken : his frauds   about   these

inanes demum frangentur. Ego ipsa, cum   sol
becoming   vain   at last   will be destroyed.   I   myself, when the sun

accenderit medios æstus, cum herbæ sitiunt, et jam
has kindled   his meridian   heat,   when the grass   dries up, and now

umbra est gratior pecori, ducam te in   secreta
the shade   is   more grateful to the flock, will lead thee into the retirement

senis,   quo fessus recipit   se   ab   undis, ut
of the old man, whither wearied he withdraws himself from the waves, that

facile aggrediare jacentem somno. Verum ubi tene-
easily   you may attack him   reclining   in sleep.   But   when   you

bis   correptum   manibus, que vinclis, tum variæ
shall hold him seized   with your hands,   and   chains,   then   varied

species atque   ora   ferarum illudent. Enim subito
forms   and   countenances of wild beasts will deceive you.   For   suddenly

fiet   horridus sus, que atra tigris, que squamosus
he will become a rough   bear,   and black   tiger,   and   a scaly

draco, et leæna fulvâ cervice ; aut dabit acrem sonitum
dragon, and a lioness of yellow   neck ;   or   will give the violent   sound

410   flammæ, atque ita excidet vinclis ; aut dilapsus in
     of flame,   and thus will escape from chains ; or   gliding into

tenues aquas abibit. Sed quanto magis ille vertet
the light   waters he shall escape. But by how much the more he shall change

se   in omnes formas, tanto magis, nate, contende tena-
himself into   all   shapes, so much the more, O son,   stretch the grasp

cia vincla, donec erit talis, corpore mutato, qualem
ing chains,   until he shall be such, his body being changed,   as

videris   cum tegeret lumina, somno   incepto.
you may have seen him when he covered his eyes,   sleep   having begun

       Ait   hæc,   et   diffudit liquidum
to overpower him. She said   these things,   and poured around   the liquid

odorem ambrosiæ, quo   perduxit totum corpus
odour   of ambrosia, with which she anointed   the entire   body

nati ;   at dulcis aura spiravit illi crinibus compo-
of her son ; but the pleasant gale breathed on him from his locks disposed

sitis, atque habilis vigor venit membris. Est ingens
in order, and a vigorous strength came to his limbs. There is a great

specus in latere exesi montis, quo plurima
den in the side of an excavated mountain, where in great abundance

unda cogitur vento, que scindit sese in 420
the water is collected by the wind, and divides itself into

reductos sinus; olim tutissima statio nautis deprensis.
retired bays; formerly a very safe station for sailors caught in a storm.

Proteus tegit se objice vasti saxi. Hic
Proteus conceals himself by the projection of a great rock. Here

nympha collocat juvenem aversum a lumine, in late-
the nymph places the youth turned away from the light, in dark

bris, ipsa resistit procul obscura nebulis. Jam rapidus
ness, she stands back afar off darkened by mists. Now the rapid

Sirius, torrens sitientes Indos, ardebat cœlo, et igneus
dog-star, burning the thirsty Indians, glowed in the sky, and the fiery

sol hauserat medium orbem; herbæ arebant, et radii
sun had finished half his circuit; the grass dried up, and the rays

coquebant cava flumina tepefacta faucibus
of the sun boiled the hollow streams warmed in their channels

siccis ad limum; cum Proteus ibat e fluctibus petens
dried to clay; when Proteus went from the waves seeking

consueta antra. Humida gens vasti ponti, 430
his accustomed cave. The watery nation of the vast sea,

exsultans circum eum, dispergit amarum rorem. Phocæ
exulting around him, scattered the briny dew. Seals

sternunt se, diversæ in litore. Ipse, velut olim
stretch themselves, scattered along the shore. He, as when

custos stabuli in montibus, ubi vesper reducit
the keeper of a stall upon the mountains, when the evening brings back

vitulos e pastu ad tecta, que agni acuunt lupos,
the calves from pasture to shelter, and the lambs provoke the wolves,

balatibus auditis, considit medius scopulo, que
their bleatings being heard, sits in the midst on a rock, and

recenset numerum. Cujus, quoniam
counts up the number of his flock. Of confining whom, because

facultas oblata est Aristæo; vix passus senem
opportunity was offered to Aristæus; hardly did he suffer the old man

componere defessa membra, ruit cum magno
to rest his wearied limbs, he rushes on with a great

clamore, que occupat jacentem manicis. Contra, ille,
cry, and seizes him reclining in chains. On the other hand, he,

non immemor suæ artis, transformat sese 440
not unmindful of his art, converts himself into

omnia miracula rerum, que ignem que horribilem
all the wonders of strange things, both fire and a dreadful

feram, que liquentem fluvium. Verum ubi nulla fallacia
wild beast, and a flowing river. But when no deception

reperit fugam, victus, redit in sese, atque tan
provided escape, overcome, he returned to himself, and a

dem locutus ore hominis : Quisnam jussit te
ength spoke with the voice of a man : Who has commanded you

confidentissime juvenum, adire nostras domos ?
most confident of youth, to approach our dwellings ?

quidve petis hinc ? inquit. At ille ait : Proteu, scis,
or what do you seek here ? he said. But he said : Proteus, you know,

ipse scis, neque est cuiquam fallere te ; sed tu desine
you know, nor is it for any one to deceive you ; but do you cease

velle : secuti præcepta Deûm, venimus huc quæ-
to desire it : pursuing the commands of the gods, we have come hither to

450 situm oracula lapsis rebus. Effatus tantum,
question the oracles about our fallen affairs. Having said only

ad hæc denique vates intorsit oculos, ardentes
this, at these words finally the prophet turned his eyes, glowing

glauco lumine ; et frendens graviter, sic resolvit
with azure light ; and gnashing his teeth violently, thus he opened

ora fatis : Iræ non nullius numinis exercent
his mouth to the fates : The rage of no subordinate deity persecutes

te ; luis magna commissa : Orpheus, miserabilis,
you ; you suffer for great offences : Orpheus, wretched,

haudquaquam ob meritum, suscitat tibi has
by no means on account of his desert, excites against you these

pœnas, ni fata resistant ; et sævit graviter
punishments, unless the fates should oppose ; and rages fiercely

pro conjuge raptâ. Illa puella, quidem, moritura,
for his wife stolen from him. The maid, indeed, about to die,

dum præceps fugeret te per flumina, non vidit, ante
while headlong she fled thee along the rivers, did not see, before

pedes in altâ herbâ, immanem hydrum servantem
her feet among the high grass, a dreadful water-snake guarding

460 ripas. At chorus Dryadum, æqualis, implêrunt
the banks. But the band of Dryads, her associates, filled

supremos montes clamore : Rhodopeïæ arces fleruht,
the loftiest mountains with their cry : the Rhodopeïan rocks wept,

que alta Pangæa, et Mavortia tellus Rhesi, atque Getæ,
and lofty Pangæa, and the martial land of Rhesus, and the Getæ,

atque Hebrus, atque Actias Orythyia. Ipse solans ægrum
and Hebrus, and Attic Orythia. He assuaging his pining

amorem cavâ testudine, te dulcis conjux, secûm
love with his hollow shell, sang of thee O sweet wife, by himself

in solo litore, te die veniente, canebat te
on the lonely shore, he sang of thee the day approaching, he sang of thee

decedente. Ingressus Tænarias fauces, alta ostia
the day departing. Having entered the Tænarian straits, the high gates

Ditis, et lucum caligantem nigrâ formidine, adiit
of Pluto, and the grove dark with gloomy horror, he approached

que Manes, que tremendum regem, que corda nescia
both the manes, and the dreaded king, and hearts not known

mansuescere humanis precibus. At tenues umbræ, 470
to become softened by human prayers. But the light shades,

commotæ cantu, que simulacra carentum luce, ibant
being moved by his song, and the ghosts of those deprived of life, went

de imis sedibus Erebi ; quam multa millia avium
from the lowest mansions of Erebus ; as many thousands of birds

condunt se in silvis, ubi vesper aut hibernus
conceal themselves in the woods, when evening or a wintry

imber agit de montibus ; matres atque viri, que
rain drives them from the mountains; mothers and husbands, and

corpora magnanimûm heroum defuncta vitâ, pueri,
the bodies of high-minded heroes deprived of life, boys,

que innuptæ puellæ ; que juvenes impositi
and unmarried maids; and youth placed

rogis. ante ora parentum quos niger
on funeral piles before the faces of their parents whom the dark

limus, et deformis arundo Cocyti, que inamabilis palus,
clay, and mishapen reed of Cocytus, and the unlovely lake,

tardâ undâ, circum alligat, et Styx novies inter-
with slow moving wave, around hems in, and Styx nine times flowing

fusa coërcet. Quin domus ipsæ, atque 480
between restrains. But the mansions themselves, and

intima Tartara lethi, que Eumenides implexæ
the inmost Tartarean depths of death, and the Furies intertwining

cæruleos angues crinibus, obstupuere ; que Cerberus
azure snakes in their hair, were astounded; and Cerberus

inhians tenuit tria ora ; atque rota Ixionii
gaping wide restrained his three mouths; and the whirling of Ixion's

orbis constitit cantu. Jamque referens pedem,
wheel was stayed by his song. And now withdrawing his foot,

evaserat omnes casus ; que Eurydice reddita
he had escaped all casualties ; and Eurydice restored

veniebat ad superas auras, sequens pone ; namque
approached to the upper air, following behind ; for

Proserpina dederat hanc legem ; cum subita dementia
Proserpine had given this condition; when sudden madness

cepit incautum amantem, ignoscenda quidem, si
seized the inconsiderate lover, pardonable indeed, if

Manes scirent ignoscere. Restitit, que immemor,
he Shades knew how to pardon. He stopped, both thoughtless

neu ! que victus animi, respexit suam Ery- 490
alas! and overcome in mind, he looked back upon his Ery-

dicen jam sub luce ipsâ : ibi omnis labor effusus,
dice now on the verge of the light itself: there all his labour was lost,

atque fœdera immitis tyranni rupta, que fragor
and the conditions of the merciless tyrant were broken, and a noise

ter auditus Avernis stagnis. Illa inquit,
thrice was heard in the Avernian pools. She said, *Unhappy hus-*

Quis perdidit et me, miseram, et te, Orpheu:
band! who has ruined both. me, wretched, and yourself, O Orpheus!

quis tantus furor? En iterum crudelia Fata vocant
what great madness *is this?* Lo again the pitiless Fates call

me retro, que somnus condit natantia lumina Jamque
me back, and sleep closes my flowing eyes. And now

vale: feror circumdata ingenti nocte; que tendens
farewell - I am borne away surrounded by extensive night; and stretching

invalidas palmas tibi, heu! non tua. Dixit:
my powerless hands to you, alas! not your own. She said:

et subito fugit diversa ex oculis, ceu fumus
and suddenly fled a different way from his eyes, as smoke

500 commixtus in tenues auras; neque præterea vidit
commingled in the thin air; nor more did she see

illum, prensantem umbras nequicquam, et volentem
him, grasping the shades in vain, and wishing

dicere multa; nec portitor Orci passus
to say many things: nor did the ferryman of hell suffer *him*

amplius tansire objectam paludem. Quid faceret?
any more to pass over the intervening lake. What could he do?

quo ferret se, conjuge bis raptâ?
whither could he withdraw himself, his wife twice snatched away?

quo fletu Manes? quâ voce moveret
by what weeping *could he soothe* the Shades? by what language could he move

numina? Illa quidem, jam frigida, nabat Stygiâ
the gods? She indeed, already dead, sailed in the Stygian

cymbâ. Perhibent, illum flevisse septem totos menses ex
boat. They say, that he wept seven whole months in

ordine, sub aëriâ rupe, ad undam deserti Strymonis,
succession, beneath a high rock, by the wave of the Strymon,

et evolvisse hæc sub gelidis antris, mulcentem
and mused on these *griefs* beneath the cold caves, soothing

510 tigres, et agentem quercus carmine: qualis
the tigers, and leading the oaks with *his* song: as

Philomela, mœrens sub populeâ umbrâ, queritur
Philomela, mourning beneath the poplar shade, laments

amissos fetus, quos durus arator, observans implumes
her lost young, which the cruel ploughman finding unfeathered

nido, detraxit; at illa flet noctem, que
in the nest, took out; but she mourns *through* the night, and

sedens ramo, integrat miserabile carmen, et implet
sitting on a branch, renews her wretched song, and fills

loca late mœstis questibus. Nulla Venus,
the places far around with mournful complaints. No love,

que nulli Hymenæi, flexere animum. Solus lustrabat
and no nuptial rites, moved his mind. Alone he surveyed

Hyperboreas glacies, que nivalem Tanaïm, que arva
the northern ice, and the snowy Tanaïs, and the fields

nunquam viduata Riphæis pruinis, querens Eurydicen
never bereaved of Riphean frosts. lamenting that Eurydice

raptam, atque dona Ditis irrita; quo
had been taken, and that the rant of Pluto *was* unavailing, which

munere spreto, matres Ciconum, inter sa-   520
rite being despised, the dames of the Ciconians, at the sa-

cra Deùm que orgia Bacchi, nocturni, sparsere
cred rites of the gods and orgies of Bacchus, celebrated in the night, scattered

juvenem discerptum per latos agros. Tum
the youth torn *in pieces* through the broad fields. Then

quoque cum Oëagrius Hebrus, portans caput, revulsum
also when Oëagrian Hebrus, floating *his* head, torn

a marmoreâ cervice, medio gurgite, volveret,
from his beautiful neck, in the midst of its stream, rolled it along,

vox ipsa, et frigida lingua, vocabat Eurydicen, ah!
his voice itself, and cold tongue, called Eurydice, alas!

miseram Eurydicen, animâ fugiente; ripæ
unhappy Eurydice, while his soul was departing; the banks

referebant Eurydicen toto flumine. Proteus
re-echoed Eurydice through all the stream. Proteus *said*

hæc, et dedit se jactu in altum æquor;
these *words*, and plunged himself by a leap into the deep sea;

quaque dedit torsit spumantem undam sub
and where he cast himself he turned the foaming wave round

vertice. At Cyrene non: namque affa-   530
his head. But Cyrene *did* not: for she ac-

ta timentem ultro: Nate, licet depo-
costed her trembling *son* voluntarily: O son, it is allowed to you to lay

nere tristes curas animo. Hæc omnis causa mor
aside mournful cares from your mind. This *is* all the cause of your

bi; hinc nymphæ, cum quibus illa agitabat choros
grief; hence the nymphs, with whom she exercised dances

in altis lucis, misere miserabile exitium apibus.
in the deep groves, sent wretched desolation to the bees.

Tu supplex tende munera, petens pacem, et venerare
Do you humbly present offerings, sueing for peace, and venerate

faciles Napæas, namque dabunt veniam
the kindly wood nymphs: for they will grant pardon

votis, que remittent iras. Sed dicam prius
to your vows, and will relax their wrath. But I shall declare first

ordine, qui sit modus orandi. Delige quatuor
in order, what may be the method of entreating. Select four

eximios tauros præstanti corpore, qui nunc depascunt
choice bulls of a comely form, which now feed upon

summa viridis Lycæi, et totidem juvencas 540
the heights of green Lycæus, and as many heifers

cervice intactâ. Constitue quatuor aras his ad alta
with necks untouched. Place four altars by them at the lofty

delubra Dearum, et demitte sacrum cruorem
shrines of the goddesses, and let out the sacred blood

jugulis ; que desere ipsa corpora boum frondoso
from *their* throats; and leave the bodies of the cattle in the leafy

luco. Post, ubi nona Aurora ostenderit suos ortus,
grove. Afterwards, when the ninth morning has displayed her dawn,

mittes Letnæa papavera inferias Orphei,
you shall present Lethean poppies as funeral offerings to Orpheus,

venerabere placatam Eurydicen, vitulâ cæsâ, et
you shall venerate appeased Eurydice, a calf being slain, and

mactabis nigram ovem, que revises lucum.
shall sacrifice a black sheep, and shall revisit the grove.

Haud mora: continuo facessit præcepta matris;
There is no delay: forthwith he executes the orders of his mother;

venit ad delubra; excitat monstratas aras, ducit quatuor
comes to the shrines; erects the appointed altars, leads out four

550 eximios tauros præstanti corpore, et totidem
choice bulls of excellent body, and as many

juvencas cervice intactâ. Post, ubi nona
heifers with their necks untouched. Afterwards, when the ninth

Aurora induxerat suos ortus, mittit inferias Orphei,
morning had led up her dawn, he offers the sacrifices to Orpheus,

que revisit lucum. Hic vero aspiciunt subitum monstrum
and returns to the grove. Here indeed they behold a sudden prodigy

ac mirabile dictu; apes stridere toto utero per
and wonderful to be told; that bees are humming in all the carcass within

liquefacta viscera boum, et effervere ruptis costis,
the dissolved entrails of the cattle, and bursting through the broken sides,

que immensas nubes trahi ; jamque confluere sum-
and that immense clouds are drawn out; and that now they fly together to the

mâ arbore, et demittere uvam lentis ramis. Canebam
top of a tree, and hang down a cluster from the slender branches. I sung

hæc super cultu arvorum, que pecorum, et super
these *things* about the culture of fields; and of flocks, and about

560 arboribus, dum magnus Cæsar fulminat ad altum
trees, while great Cæsar thunders by the deep

Euphratem bello, que victor, dat jura per volentes
Euphrates in war, and a conqueror, gives laws through willing

populos, que affectat viam Olympo. Illo tempore dulcis
states, and attempts his way to heaven. At that time pleasant

Parthenope alebat me, Virgilium, florentem studiis
Naples cherished me, Virgil, flourishing in the pursuits

ignobilis   oti ;   qui   lusi   carmina pastorum
of unhonoured retirement ; who have composed   songs   of shepherds,

que audax juventâ cecini te, Tityre, sub tegmino
and   daring in youth have sung thee,   O Tityrus, beneath the shelter

patulæ   fagi.
of a spreading beech.

Pocket Literal
Translations of the Classics

Cloth Binding. Each, 75 Cents

These translations have been prepared with great care. They follow the original text literally, thus forming a valuable help to the student in his efforts to master the difficulties which beset him.   Pleasing sketches of the authors appear in the form of an introduction to each of the volumes.

The books are in a convenient form, being exceptionally handy for the pocket.   They are printed from clear type, and are attractively and durably bound.

Cæsar's Commentaries—Eight Books.

Cicero's Defence of Roscius.

Cicero on Old Age and Friendship.

Cicero on Oratory.

Cicero's Select Orations.

Cicero's Select Letters.

Cornelius Nepos, complete.

Horace, complete.

Juvenal's Satires, complete.

Livy.—Books 1 and 2.

Livy.—Books 21 and 22.

Ovid's Metamorphoses.—Books 1–7.

Ovid's Metamorphoses.—Books 8–15.

Plautus' Captivi and Mostellaria.

Sallust's Catiline and The Jugurthine War.

Tacitus' Annals.—The First Six Books.

Tacitus' Germany and Agricola.

Terence' Andria, Adelphi, and Phormio.

Virgil's Aeneid.—Six Books.

Virgil's Eclogues and Georgics.

Viri Romae.

Aeschylus' Prometheus Bound and Seven Against Thebes.

Aristophanes' Clouds, Birds, and Frogs.—In one Vol.

Demosthenes' On the Crown.

Demosthenes' Olynthiacs and Philippics.

Euripides' Alcestis and Electra.

Euripides' Medea.

Herodotus.—Books 6 and 7.

Homer's Iliad.—Nine Books.

Homer's Odyssey.—13 Books.

Lysias' Select Orations.

Plato's Apology, Crito and Phaedo.

Plato's Gorgias.

Sophocles' Oedipus Tyrannus, Electra, and Antigone.

Xenophon's Anabasis. — Five Books.

Xenophon's Memorabilia, complete.

Goethe's Egmont.

Goethe's Faust.

Goethe's Hermann and Dorothea.

Goethe's Iphigenia In Tauris.

Lessing's Minna von Barnhelm.

Lessing's Nathan the Wise.

Schiller's Maid of Orleans.

Schiller's Maria Stuart.

Schiller's William Tell.

All the above books may be obtained, post free, at prices named

DAVID McKAY COMPANY, Philadelphia